U.S.
CIVIL
AIRCRAFT
VOL. 7

This work is dedicated to the preservation and perpetuation of a fond memory for the men and the planes that made a future for our air industry. And, to help kindle a knowledge and awareness within us of our debt of gratitude we owe to the past. . . . .

LIBRARY OF CONGRESS CATALOG CARD NUMBER 67-15967
COPYRIGHT 1978 AERO PUBLISHERS, INC.
PRINTED IN THE UNITED STATES OF AMERICA

U.S. CIVIL AIRCRAFT

VOL. 7

(ATC 601 - ATC 700)

By

JOSEPH P. JUPTNER

ISBN 0-8168-9174-5

AERO PUBLISHERS, INC.
329 West Aviation Road, Fallbrook, CA 92028

ACKNOWLEDGEMENTS

Any historian soon learns that in the process of digging for obscure facts and information he must oftentimes rely on the help of numerous people, unselfish and generous people, many of whom were close to, or actually participated in, various incidents or events that make up the segment of history recorded here, and have been willing to give of their time and knowledge in behalf of this work. To these wonderful people I am greatly indebted, and I feel a heart-warming gratitude; it is only fitting then that I proclaim their identity.

My thanks to Gordon S. Williams and Peter M. Bowers of the Boeing Co.,; Gerald H. Balzer; Harvey H. Lippincott of United Technologies; Wm. T. Larkins; Everett J. Payette, commercial photographer; Kenneth D. Wilson; Wm. Wagner of Ryan Aeronautical Library; E. L. "Jack" Wright; Theron K. Rhinehart of the Fairchild Co.; Edward Peck; Ray Brandly of the National Waco Club; Joe Christy; Harry S. Gann of McDonnell-Douglas; Ken M. Molson; Bob Pickett of Cessna; Robt. F. Pauley; George E. Cull, former Stearman-Hammond engineer; Merle C. Olmsted; Warren D. Shipp, noted photographer; Ralph Nortell; Gil Perlroth of Eastern Airlines; Ruth M. Reinhold; Anne Vitaliano of American Airlines; Robert T. Smith; Ann Whyte of Pan Am; Mauno Salo; Dan McGrogan of TWA; Ted Businger; John W. Underwood, noted historian; Wm. H. Wright; John R. Wells, noted DC-3 historian; Walter M. Pentecost; Mitch Mayborn of Flying Enterprise; Emil Strasser; Edward D. Williams of United Airlines; and the many others who contributed their bits to this effort.

FOREWORD

Taking a quizzical look at this 1936-38 period one would be inclined to guess at first that it would have to be just a tuning-up period, a leveling off to enjoy the many great advancements that were introduced in the two-year period just previous. So much had happened in that time, and so much had been achieved, that one could not even criticize had the aviation industry decided to coast awhile and rest on its past laurels. But, that was not to be. This "game" that everyone called "the aviation industry" was an assemblage of special individuals; some were dedicated individuals, dedicated to aviation's future, some were restless individuals that couldn't leave well-enough alone, and some were individuals who soon brushed aside their latest accomplishments to go on to something else. This was the phenomenon within the industry, and it had always been like this. So, at this particular time the aircraft industry was not exactly percolating, but at least it was squirming within looking for new avenues to progress.

No Sir, the aviation industry was not resting on its past laurels. We thought the Douglas DC-2 "Airliner" was simply marvelous, but the new DC-3 was now even better. One could now fly from coast to coast in 15 hours for less than $150.00 while at sleep in the cradle of luxury. Airlines at last were making money with the DC-3, and it was fast becoming the standard equipment of every major airline in the world. Airplane factories, large and small, some new and some old, were humming with production all over the land. Production of civil aircraft in the first quarter of 1936 had increased nearly 35% over the same period in 1935, the first quarter of 1937 showed an increase of 25%, and production continued to increase again in 1938. The most noticeable increase, of course, was in the building of lightplanes; 100 were built in the first 3 months of 1936, and soon manufacturers were rolling out 75 and even 100 airplanes per month. There were so many new airplanes around to dazzle the airplane-buyer at this time that it is hard to understand how he could make a rational choice. Yessir, the aircraft industry was showing unmistakable signs of improved health and continued growth.

Everyone was enjoying the increased activity. Business was getting better for everybody and many, many businesses were now using airplanes as a matter of course. The airplanes for business had become more comfortable too, more practical, and even faster; we now had several 200 m.p.h. commercial airplanes. Flying schools once again were operating from dawn to dusk, and the weekend flier was flying every weekend and not just once in a great while. The "puddle-jumpers" like those of Taylor, Piper, and Aeronca were dotting the airports all over the country, and box-car loads were being shipped out almost every day. It was a great feeling to drop in on some little airport to see it lined with dozens of airplanes, and hear the drone of many engines overhead. Maybe this period of 1936-38 did not produce any major advances in aeronautical science, but we did pretty well at that, and we had a whole lot more of everything. As we hastened to our daily chores we tried not to notice as war-clouds were forming over Europe, this had nothing to do with us, but there was an excitement of sorts in the air, and yet it was fearful too.

Jos. P. Juptner

TERMS

To make for better understanding of the various information contained herein, we should clarify a few points that might be in question. At the heading of each new chapter, the bracketed numerals under the ATC number, denote the first date of certification; any amendments made are noted in the text. Unless otherwise noted, the title photo of each chapter is an example of the model that bears that particular certificate number; any variants from this particular model, such as prototypes and special modifications, are identified. Normally accepted abbreviations and symbols are used in the listing of specifications and performance data. Unless otherwise noted, all maximum speed, cruising speed, and landing speed figures are based on sea level tests; this method of performance testing was largely the custom during this early period. Rate of climb figures are for first minute at sea level, and the altitude ceiling given is the so-called service ceiling. Cruising range in miles or hours duration is based on the engine's cruising r.p.m., but even at that, the range given must be considered as an average because of pilot's various throttle habits.

At the ending of each chapter, we show a listing of registered aircraft of a similar type; most of the listings show the complete production run of a particular type and this information we feel will be valuable to historians, photographers, and collectors in making correct identification of a certain aircraft by its registration number.

In each volume there are separate discussions on 100 certificated airplanes and we refer to these discussions as chapters, though they are not labeled as such; at the end of each chapter there is reference made to see the chapter for an ATC number pertaining to the next development of a certain type. As each volume contains discussions on 100 aircraft, it should be rather easy to pin-point the volume number for a chapter of discussion that would be numbered as A.T.C. #93, or perhaps A.T.C. #176, as an example. The use of such terms as "prop," "prop spinner," and "type," are normally used among aviation people and should present no difficulty in interpreting the meaning.

TABLE OF CONTENTS

ATC # 601
(4-15-36)
ARROW "SPORT", MODEL F.

Design of "Arrow F" instigated by government's search for "poor man's airplane".

The Development Section of the (BAC) Bureau of Air Commerce completed 2 years of research and development in July of 1936 for the improvement of private-owner aircraft, and also a fruitless search for Gene Vidal's "ideal airplane." Of the various projects authorized and tested (some 14 in all) only the "Arrow F" and the "Hammond Y" showed any promise of being suitable. Most of the BAC-sponsored projects in search of "everyman's airplane" embodied radical features in airplane design, but the Arrow "Model F" was surprisingly conventional in both design and construction. Perhaps the only thing unusual about it at all was the powerplant—a Ford V-8 automobile engine. The engine was modified so very little that almost all parts could be purchased from the local "Ford" dealer. Ironically, the specifications for the "people's airplane" that Eugene Vidal first had in mind (a small low-winged monoplane to carry 2, and powered by a V-8 automobile engine) fitted the Arrow "Sport F" to a tee. Apparently he later had change of mind because development money was awarded to several other manufacturers and Arrow Aircraft was, more or less, left to fend for itself with its own meager capital. Original design of the "Sport F" was instigated by the government's search for a small inexpensive two-seated airplane, an airplane that would feature simplicity, and reasonable safety. Low maintenance and

operating costs were also stressed. Automobile engines were particularly favored as a power source because of their relative simplicity and low cost. The target was a $700 airplane, but of course, that was and continued to be a ridiculous dream! All manufacturers who joined the scheme went fairly radical in their versions of the "people's airplane," but being more practical, Arrow Aircraft chose a conventional configuration and then powered it with an excellent modification of a reliable automobile engine. After all the bally-hoo, and the rosy promises, the BAC ordered only one "Arrow F" mainly to test the feasibility of using automobile engines in private-owner aircraft. Received in 1936 the "Bureau" acknowledged delivery of the "Arrow," but enthusiasm for the whole idea of "everyman's airplane" had already cooled considerably. So what did "the people" think of the "Arrow F"—were they enthused, was it to be the answer to a long-time dream? Well, not exactly. Many were enthused, of course, and many bought the "Sport F" and were happy with it, but as for the man-in-the-street, it surely was not for him.

Arrow's first design of this airplane was planned to use the popular Kinner K5 engine of 100 h.p. and it was to cost $3495 at the factory. But then, this was nowhere near the projected goal of a $700 airplane. The prohibitive cost of an aircraft engine is what kept the price of air-

Engine in "Arrow F" basically same as used in 1937 Ford auto.

planes so high, so Arrow then decided to develop their own version of a low-cost aircraft powerplant. Under direction of chief engineer Louis Imm a standard Ford V-8 automobile engine was stripped of non-essentials and converted for use in aircraft. Trimmed of 150 lbs. of weight the modified engine was still rather heavy, but it was cheap and would be quite easy to maintain. And best of all, exchange price for a whole new remanufactured engine would cost only $57.00! Amateur adaptations of automobile and motorcycle engines for aircraft had long been common, but Arrow Aircraft was the first to receive full government approval for a converted automobile engine. With this modified auto engine the "Arrow Sport F" could now sell for $1500, based on a foreseeable production of 1000 airplanes. F. Pace Woods and pilot Jimmy Hurst flew the "Sport F" to Detroit for a demonstration; car-builder Henry Ford was pleased, but not particularly interested, although he did say he could build a 100 h.p. V-8 auto-type engine suitable for aircraft for $90, if it could be manufactured in lots of 10,000 units. One shudders to think of that many amateur-pilots flying around at any one time!

The Arrow "Sport F" was a strut-braced, low-winged, monoplane with side-by-side seating for 2 out in the open. There was plenty of room inside, but the wide and very deep seat was uncomfortable for smaller people; smaller people required stacks of pillows to see out properly. Much of the solicited comment leads one to suspect that this was an unfortunate little airplane. The control was heavy much like in a larger airplane, all-round performance was rather unimpressive, and some called it a one-speed airplane—it did just about everything at 70 m.p.h. The glide was unusually steep and the stiff-legged landing gear assured one of more

bum landings than good ones. To make matters worse, poor airflow down the fuselage caused uncertain control at low speeds; many of these problems were, of course, amplified at full gross load. When flown solo it was a pretty good airplane. The modified "Arrow" (Ford) V-8 engine was rated 82 h.p. at 3075 r.p.m.; a gear reduction of nearly 2 to 1 slowed the propeller r.p.m. down to a more efficient speed. In general, the engine was very reliable, but did suffer in extreme summer heat. People owned this airplane with varying degrees of enthusiasm—one owner reported 600 hours of care-free service and he actually liked the airplane. Others were not that happy. This approval issued 4-15-36 was for all airplanes manufactured prior to 3-9-37; approval expired as of that date. This affected some 14 or so airplanes, and all were later eligible to be modified to new specifications (see ATC # 613). The "Sport F" and its "Arrow V-8" engine were manufactured by the Arrow Airplane & Motor Corp. at Lincoln, Neb. Mark Woods was pres.; George Woods was Sr. V.P.; F. Pace Woods was V.P.; John Aldrich was sec-treas.; Nelson Storey was sales mgr.; L. E. Miller was gen. mgr., and later also sales mgr.; Louis Imm was chf. engr.; and Clark Beisemeier was factory superintendent.

Listed below are specifications and performance data for the Arrow "Sport F" as powered with 8 cyl. Arrow (Ford V-8) engine rated 82 h.p. at 3075 r.p.m.; length overall 21'4"; height overall 8'10"; wingspan 36'7"; wing chord 66"; total wing area 185 sq. ft.; airfoil NACA-2212; wt. empty (wet) 1172 lbs.; useful load 503 lbs.; payload with 20 gal. fuel 198 lbs.; bag. allow. 28 lbs.; gross wt. 1675 lbs.; max. speed 95; cruising speed (2900 r.p.m.) 86; landing speed (with flaps) 45; landing speed (no flaps) 48; climb 500 ft. first min. at sea level; ser. ceiling 12,000 ft.; gas cap. 20 gal.; oil cap. (in sump) 2 gal.; cruis-

"Arrow F" tested by BAC, showing drag flaps and wheel streamlines.

ing range at 5.5 gal. per hour was 3.5 hours or 300 miles; price $1500 at factory. Available also for $800 down and bal. of $700 in 12 mos. (Wt. empty is with water in radiator—6.5 gal. at 54 lbs.)

The fuselage framework was built up of welded chrome-moly (C/M) steel tubing faired to a rounded shape with spruce fairing strips, then fabric covered. The cavernous open cockpit seated 2 side-by-side with good protection offered by a large Pyralin windshield. A man-sized stepover showed the cockpit to be both wide and deep; for a smaller person this called for extra pillows to sit on just to see out. A baggage compartment aft of the seat, though quite large, was allowed only 28 lbs. A push-pull throttle control was in the center and dual control wheels were provided. The low-mounted wing, in 2 halves, was built up of solid spruce spar beams with spruce and plywood truss-type wing ribs; completed framework was covered in fabric. Vee-type struts of streamlined dural tubing braced the wing halves from the top fuselage longeron. Drag-brake panels, inset slightly from the trailing edge on underside of the wing, were manually operated to offer slightly lower landing speeds; drag-brakes not to be lowered above 90 m.p.h. Actually, the drag-brake area was of minimal proportion and had little effect. The narrow semi-cantilever landing gear of 2 streamlined vees was snubbed with shock-cord; 7.00x5 wheels mounted 4-ply tires and were fitted with Bendix mechanical brakes. The optional full-swivel tail wheel was fitted with 10x3 tire; a spring-leaf tail skid was standard. The fabric-covered tail group was built up of welded steel tubing; fore and aft trim was accomplished by adjusting tension of a bungee-cord mounted to the control column. The modified Ford V-8 engine was naturally water cooled, so a radiator was mounted below the engine compartment and

provided with adjustable shutters to maintain proper engine temperature. Carburetor air was warmed by an adjustable heat-box. An "Arrow" hand-operated cranking mechanism was provided to start engine from the cockpit. A Fahlin wooden prop, Willard battery, Autolite engine-driven generator, ammeter, engine-driven (AC) fuel pump, wobble (emergency) pump, float-type fuel gauge, air speed indicator, Pyrene fire extinguisher, tachometer, altimeter, oil press. & temp. gauges, water temp. gauge, and dual wheel-type controls were standard equipment. Wheel brakes, tail wheel, navigation lites, compass, and wheel pants were optional. For details of modified Arrow "Sport F" see chapter for ATC # 613.

Listed below are Arrow "Sport F" entries as gleaned from registration records:

-12581;	Arrow F	(# E-1)	Arrow 90	1934
NS-72;	”	(# 1)	Arrow 82	1936
NC-16470;	”	(# 2)	”	”
-16481;	”	(# 3)	”	”
-16482;	”	(# 4)	”	”
-16483;	”	(# 5)	”	1937
-16484;	”	(# 6)	”	”
-16485;	”	(# 7)	”	”
-17020;	”	(# 8)	”	”
-17021;	”	(# 9)	”	”
-17022;	”	(# 10)	”	”
-17023;	”	(# 11)	”	”
-17024;	”	(# 12)	”	”
-17093;	”	(# 13)	”	”
-17094;	”	(# 14)	”	”
-17095;	”	(# 15)	”	”
-17096;	”	(# 16)	”	”
-17097;	”	(# 17)	”	”

ATC # 601 eligible for all aircraft manufac-

California dealers for "Arrow F" show off Ford V-8 installation.

tured prior to 3-9-37; ATC # 601 expired as of that date; ser. #14 was delivered 3-8-37 and several nearly completed examples were on the assembly floor, so this certificate could actually apply to the first 17 airplanes; subsequent airplanes were manufactured on ATC # 613.

ATC # 602
(4-16-36)
BEECH, C-17-L (C-17-B).

Outstanding view of Beech model C-17-B.

Contemplating the year just past Walter Beech considered he certainly had darn good luck with the B-17 series of 1935, but he reflected too that the C-17 series proposed for 1936 could no doubt be improved. The extent of the improvements for the new line were not all that much, but a few items were of some significance. The landing gear was now shortened and angle of the horizontal stabilizer was rearranged to permit better flare-out for a 3-point landing. As it turned out this proved to be quite an improvement after all. The C-17 series for 1936 were still rather difficult to land properly when flying solo, but with a full load of people and baggage they landed almost as easily as any "Cub," or so they said. The first examples offered in the series for 1936 were the model C-17-L as powered with a 225 h.p. radial engine, and the C-17-B as powered with a 285 h.p. radial engine. The C-17-B had the most to offer and it was actually the better value, so it became the most popular of the two. There was fast-growing confidence in the claims made for "Beech" performance, so these 2 models attracted many more prospects and sold quite well. In the first quarter Beech Aircraft had sold twice as many airplanes as in the year before, and this ratio held up pretty well throughout most of the year.

The roster of owners included many big names in business, but the air-minded oil companies had the edge in numbers. Export business was beginning to pick up also; 3 of the C-17-L and 6 of the C-17-B were shipped to countries overseas. One example with a litter for one went to New Zealand as an air-ambulance to serve in the rugged interior. To add to their versatility the models C-17-L and C-17-B were also offered as seaplanes (SC-17-L and SC-17-B) on Edo pontoons. Late in 1936 a C-17-B was tested on amphibious float gear by Edo the float-maker; the airplane was fine off water, but strictly a sweat-producing ordeal for the pilot on land. After only a few flights the project was abandoned. The low-powered "Beech" was not a 200 m.p.h. airplane, but they were quite fast for an airplane of this type. At the Miami Air Races for 1936 a C-17-B nosed-out another "Beechcraft" to win an exciting free-for-all at 185 m.p.h.

The Beech C-17-L and C-17-B were speedy cabin biplanes with seating arranged for 4 or 5; the inverse stagger used by these two models was becoming the world-wide trademark of the unusual "Beechcraft," and both also had retracting landing gears. Nearly everyone recognized the Beech biplane by now, but it was still the most

Beech model C-17-B (Jacobs 285) was fastest airplane in its class.

novel commercial airplane of these times. Prospective customers when taken up for a demonstration were always thrilled with the performance available, but were often quite dubious of the new-fangled retracting landing gear and other advances in the design to which they were unaccustomed. More speed per horsepower was its forte' primarily, but quality and luxury were also built in, so it was still one of the best buys of the decade. The model C-17-L with its 225 h.p. Jacobs engine was the most economical of the series, but there were always those that wanted just a little more of everything, so the C-17-B was offered to them with 285 h.p. The increase in performance more than made up for the increase in price. The model C-17-L was powered with the popular Jacobs L-4 engine, and the C-17-B was powered with the Jacobs L-5 engine; both were available in either the "M" (magneto) or "MB" (magneto-battery) versions of the Jacobs engine. Both of these airplanes performed remarkably well, they stretched out more mileage out of every gallon of fuel, carried just about as much payload as any airplane in this class, and were not particularly fussy about where they operated from. At least one C-17-B was used for charter-flights because of its ability to get in and out of the small fields so prevalent at this time. The customers were happy with the speedy service, and for the pilot-operator it was a fairly "easy buck." Flight characteristics of these two airplanes were extremely pleasant, but an airplane of this type requires a certain amount of "learnin'." Both of these airplanes were a combination of uncommon beauty, practical luxury with pinch-penny economy, and the fastest transportation available in this type of airplane. The type certificate was issued 4-16-36

and some 45 examples were built in all; only 4 of these were the C-17-L. Manufactured by the Beech Aircraft Co. in Wichita, Kan.

Listed below are specifications and performance data for the Beech model C-17-L as powered with Jacobs L-4 engine rated 225 h.p. at 2000 r.p.m. at sea level; length overall 24'5"; height overall 8'2"; wingspan upper & lower 32'0"; wing chord upper & lower 60"; total wing area 273 sq. ft.; airfoil Clark CYH; wt. empty 1850 lbs.; useful load 1300 lbs.; payload with 46 gal. fuel 755 lbs. (4 pass. & 75 lb. bag.); gross wt. 3150 lbs.; max. speed 175 at sea level; cruising speed (.75 power) 155 at sea level, 162 at 5000 ft., 166 at 7200 ft.; landing speed with flaps 45; climb 850 ft. first min. at sea level; ser. ceiling 15,500 ft.; gas cap. 46 gal.; oil cap. 5 gal.; cruising range (.75 power) at 13.2 gal. per hour 560 miles; price $7495 at factory, later raised to $8550. Performance figures shown are with Curtiss-Reed (fixed-pitch) metal prop—figures slightly less with Hartzell wooden prop. Gross wt. later increased to 3165 lbs.

Model C-17-L also eligible as seaplane (SC-17-L) on Edo model 38-3430 twin-float gear, specifications & data same as above except as follows: wt. empty 2200 lbs.; useful load 1325 lbs.; payload with 46 gal. fuel 842 lbs. (4 pass. & 125 lb. bag., including 37 lb. mooring gear); gross wt. 3525 lbs.; max. speed 145 at sea level; cruising speed (.75 power) 133 at 5000 ft.; landing speed (with flaps) 55; climb 700 ft. first min. at sea level; take-off (full load) under 30 secs.; ser. ceiling 12,000 ft.; gas cap. 46 gal.; oil cap. 5 gal.; cruising range (.75 power) 500 miles; price approx. $12,000 at factory. The 285 h.p. model C-17-B also eligible as seaplane (SC-17-B) on Edo model 38-3430 twin-float gear with a

Beech model C-17-L (Jacobs 225) slated for charter service in New Zealand.

slightly higher performance—both models using Curtiss-Reed metal prop; Lycoming-Smith controllable prop was optional.

Listed below are specifications and performance data for the Beech model C-17-B as powered with Jacobs L-5 engine rated 285 h.p. at 2000 r.p.m. at sea level; all figures & dimensions same as for C-17-L except as follows: wt. empty 1850 lbs.; useful load 1300 lbs; payload with 46 gal. fuel 755 lbs. (4 pass. & 75 lb. bag.); payload with 74 gal. fuel 649 lbs. (3 pass. & 125 lb. bag.); gross wt. 3150 lbs.; max. speed 185 at sea level; cruising speed (.75 power) 165 at sea level, 173 at 5000 ft., 177 at 7200 ft.; landing speed (with flaps) 45; climb 1100 ft. first min. at sea level; ser. ceiling 18,000 ft.; gas cap. normal 46 gal.; gas cap. max. 74 gal.; oil cap. 5-6 gal.; cruising range (.75 power) at 17.5 gal. per hour 480-680 miles; price was $9250 at factory. C-17-B equipped with Curtiss-Reed metal prop—wooden prop not eligible. Gross wt. later raised to 3165 lbs.

The stubby fuselage framework was built up of welded C/M (4130) steel tubing, heavily faired to shape with wooden formers and fairing strips, then fabric covered. The cabin walls were insulated, sound-proofed, and windows were of safety glass; the large one-piece windshield was molded to shape of shatter-proof glass. Front seats were individual and the rear bench-type seat was wide enough to seat 3 across. The baggage compartment with allowance for up to 125 lbs. was down low behind rear seat; only 60 lbs. was allowed in this compartment when 3 occupied the rear seat. Anchor and mooring rope

for seaplane (25 lbs.) was part of the baggage allowance. Control wheels were either swing-over or T-column type; cabin heater and fresh-air vents were also provided. A large door on left side provided easy entry off the wing-walk; an extra door on right side was optional. The rugged wing framework was built up of solid spruce spar beams with spruce & plywood truss-type wing ribs spaced about 8 in. apart; the leading edges were covered with dural sheet and the completed framework was covered with fabric. Differential ailerons were in the lower wings, and decelerator flaps were mounted on underside of lower wings also. The so-called "drag flaps" were manually operated. The upper wing, in one piece, was fastened directly to top of fuselage; an unusual I-strut assembly connected upper and lower wings together, and streamlined steel wires completed the interplane bracing. A 23 gal. fuel tank flanked either side of the fuselage in the upper wing; a 28 gal. fuel tank in lower fuselage was optional for the C-17-L and standard for the C-17-B. Two welded steel tube (4130) trusses were fitted to underside of the fuselage structure for fastening of lower wings and mounting of the electrically-operated retractable landing gear; landing gear folded inward into fuselage belly, and 10x3 tail wheel retracted also. Autofan 7.50x10 wheels with (4 or 6 ply) low-pressure tires were fitted with mechanical brakes. General (24 in.) streamlined wheels and tires were optional. The fabric covered tail group was a composite structure of welded 4130 steel tubes, steel channels, and spruce ribs; elevators were fitted with adjustable trim tabs. A tool compartment near the tail-post (for 25 lb. tool roll) was used as ballast to achieve trim. A Hartzell wooden prop (C-17-L), Curtiss-Reed metal prop (C-17-B), electric engine starter, Bosch or Eclipse engine-driven generator, Exide battery, ammeter, swing-over control wheel, parking brake, compass, fuel gauges, fuel pump, wobble-pump, fire extinguisher, cabin vents & heater, bonding & shielding for radio, para-

C-17-B tested on EDO amphibious floats; tricky handling discouraged use.

flares, assist ropes, first-aid kit, and complete set of engine & flight instruments were standard equipment. A Curtiss-Reed metal prop (for C-17-L), Lycoming-Smith control prop (for C-17-B), oil-cooling radiator, navigation lights, landing lights, Heywood air-operated engine starter, radio gear, and extra fuel capacity were optional. The next Beech 'Staggerwing'' development was the model C-17-R as described here in the chapter for ATC # 604.

Listed below are C-17-L and C-17-B entries as gleaned from various records:

NC-15812;	C-17-B	(# 67)	Jacobs 285
-15813;	C-17-L	(# 83)	Jacobs 225
-15841;	C-17-B	(# 84)	Jacobs 285
-15842;	''	(# 85)	''
-15843;	''	(# 86)	''
-15844;	''	(# 87)	''
-15845;	''	(# 88)	''
-15846;	''	(# 89)	''
-15847;	''	(# 90)	''
-15848;	''	(# 91)	''
-15849;	''	(# 92)	''
-15840;	''	(# 93)	''
-16435;	''	(# 94)	''
-16436;	''	(# 95)	''
-16437;	''	(# 96)	''
-16438;	''	(# 97)	''
-16439;	''	(# 98)	''
-16440;	''	(# 99)	''
-16441;	''	(# 100)	''
-16442;	''	(# 101)	''
-16443;	''	(# 102)	''
-16444;	''	(# 103)	''
;	''	(# 104)	''
-16446;	''	(# 105)	''
-16447;	''	(# 106)	''
ZK-AEU;	C-17-L	(# 107)	Jacobs 225
VH-UXP;	C-17-B	(# 108)	Jacobs 285
-15836;	C-17-L	(# 109)	Jacobs 225
-15838;	C-17-B	(# 110)	Jacobs 285
-17060;	''	(# 111)	''
-17061;	''	(# 112)	''
NS-15839;	''	(# 121)	''
PP-TCQ;	''	(# 123)	''
ZS-BBC;	C-17-L	(# 124)	Jacobs 225
-17063;	C-17-B	(# 125)	Jacobs 285
-17065;	''	(# 126)	''
-17062;	''	(# 127)	''
NS-17064;	''	(# 128)	''
VH-UYI;	''	(# 129)	''
-17072;	''	(# 130)	''
-17073;	''	(# 131)	''
-17074;	''	(# 132)	''
-17078;	''	(# 133)	''
-17079;	''	(# 134)	''
-17080;	''	(# 135)	''

This approval for ser. # 67 and up; ser. # 83 later to France; ser. #88 used as photo-plane; ser. # 90 as seaplane in N.H.; ser. # 99 tested on Edo amphibious floats; ser. # 100 first as C-17-L; ser. # 104 to Argentina; ser. # 105 first as C-17-L; ser. # 107 to New Zealand; ser. # 108 to Australia; reg. no. for ser. # 109 first used on C-17-E that went to Japan; ser. # 121 to Maine Dept. of Forestry; ser. # 123 first as NC-16448; ser. # 124 to Johannesburg, So. Africa; ser. # 127 later to France; ser. # 128 to New Jersey Forest Fire Service; ser. # 129 to Colombia in 1939; this approval expired 9-30-39; 3 of C-17-L to USAAF as UC-43J; 10 of C-17-B to USAAF as UC-43G.

ATC # 603
(4-29-36)
FAIRCHILD, MODEL 45-A.

Fairchild model 45-A was a "perfect lady" in the air.

The Fairchild "Model 45" proudly described as "Sedan of the Air" was designed specifically as a small high-speed transport having the capacity, comfort, and convenience generally associated with an expensive automobile. Outstanding features in this airplane included a large, roomy cabin interior that was entered almost without effort through large doors on each side, and a luxurious interior that fairly invited one to settle down in comfort. All this too with an above-average performance that was meted out with almost miserly economy. In appearance, from whatever angle, the matronly-looking "Forty Five" was an appealing airplane that looked capable and invited confidence. The aerodynamic features were rather impressive to those who knew about such things, and they all had definite flight and performance functions; every part of the airplane had some good reason for being. Built with traditional Fairchild quality the structure as used in the Model 45 was somewhat complex and more costly, yet to have varied from this would have resulted in just another so-so airplane. The prototype airplane in the "Forty Five" series was designed for the 225 h.p. Jacobs engine, having first flown in May of 1935. As is often the case, before a sec-one airplane is built, there was comment by people in the project about "what a terrific airplane this would be if it had more power!!" This, of course, prompted further study and redesign. As a consequence, only the prototype was powered with the Jacobs engine; subsequent examples of the "45" were coming out powered with the 320 h.p. Wright engine. These were now

the Model 45-A, a more expensive airplane, but actually more to the liking of the corporate, and affluent people that would be buying this airplane. We sometimes pause to wonder—is not man's progress driven by his faculty of never being satisfied! So then, who did line up to buy the new 45-A? Well, there were several oil companies, a building contractor in California (his 3rd Fairchild, by the way), a mining company in Nevada, one went to the Diamond K Ranch in New Mexico, and others to sportsman-pilots on the eastern seaboard; two were delivered to the Argentine Navy, one to the U. S. Navy air-arm as a transport to haul VIP (Very Important People), and the last example was finally sold in March of 1939. This might appear to be a very unimpressive record for such a fine airplane, but we have to consider that as the nation's economy improved the wealthy got wealthier and were more able to buy newer, more expensive airplanes that began to appear shortly in prolific selection.

The gracefully rounded Fairchild 45-A was a cantilever-winged low wing cabin monoplane with seating arranged for five. The objective in creating the "Forty Five" was to give the owner, whether private or corporate, an economical five-place airplane which combined speed, luxury, and strength with flight characteristics and handling features that would permit operation from the smaller fields by non-professional pilots. In soft, uncrowded seating to tolerate the longer flights, there was quiet, ample visibility, and plenty of room for a pile of baggage. To obtain this combination of high speed, ample range

Model 45-A provided outstanding utility; ship shown slated for So. Africa.

and payload with reasonable horsepower, it was deemed necessary to take advantage of the useful aerodynamic features of low-wing design. Most airplanes of this particular type were demanding machines designed for professionals and flown by expert pilots. The "Forty Five," however, was a soft-hearted, gentle airplane that could be flown by most any pilot without much difficulty. Fairchild wanted this airplane to be the best available in an economical light transport, so it was loaded with thoughtful details, things that produced convenience for the pilot and care-free comfort for his passengers. As powered with the 7 cyl. Wright R-760-E2 engine rated 320 h.p. the "45-A" made every single horsepower count, and so delivered a performance well above average. Inherently kind to non-professional pilots the "Forty Five" was gentle to its very bones and those who knew it intimately loved it forever. The type certificate for the Model 45-A was issued 4-29-36 and some 16

examples of this model were manufactured by the Fairchild Aircraft Corp. at Hagerstown, Md.

Listed below are specifications and performance data for the Fairchild model 45-A as powered with the Wright R-760-E2 engine rated 320 h.p. at 2200 r.p.m. at sea level (350 h.p. at 2400 r.p.m. for take-off); length overall 30'1"; height overall 8'2"; wingspan 39'6"; wing chord at root 94"; wing chord at tip 47"; total wing area 248 sq. ft.; airfoil NACA-2218 at root tapering to NACA-2209 at tip; wt. empty 2512 lbs.; useful load 1488 lbs.; payload with 90 gal. fuel 733 lbs. (4 pass. & 53 lbs. bag.); gross wt. 4000 lbs.; max. speed 170 at sea level; cruising speed (1950 r.p.m.) 150 at sea level and 164 at 8000 ft.; landing speed (with flaps) 54; stall speed (no flaps) 62; climb 1000 ft. first min. at sea level; ser. ceiling 18,700 ft.; gas cap. normal 90 gal.; a 120 gal. or 150 gal. gas cap. optional; oil cap 6-7-8 gal.; cruising range (1950 r.p.m.) at

45-A as JK-1 transport in U.S. Navy.

"Sedan of the Air" appealed to sportsmen because of its good nature.

20.8 gal. per hour 650 miles with normal cap.; range could be extended to 1150 miles with 150 gal. fuel; price approx. $12,000 at factory.

The construction details and general arrangement of the Fairchild model 45-A were typical to that of the earlier "45" as described in the chapter for ATC # 588 of USCA/C, Vol. 6. The most significant difference in the new 45-A was installation of the 7 cyl. Wright engine and other minor modifications necessary to this combination. Overall, the 45-A had become longer, a little taller, heavier when empty, and gross wt. was increased by 400 lbs. The extra horsepower of the Wright engine handled this extra burden easily, and still paid off in a bonus performance. All the latest instrumentation and navigational aids were available in the 45-A, including complete radio gear. For pilot convenience on long flights both elevator and rudder trim tabs were adjustable in flight. A Hamilton-Standard metal fixed-pitch prop was standard equipment, but the Hamilton-Standard "controllable" prop was

optional, and usually installed at the factory to customer order. An electric engine starter, engine-driven generator, Exide battery, cabin heater and ventilator, navigation lights, cabin lights, 8.50x10 low-pressure tires on wheels fitted with brakes, 10.5 in. swiveling tail wheel, parking brake, fire extinguisher bottle, ash trays, assist ropes, 2 baggage compartments, and first-aid kit were standard equipment. Parachute-type seats, radio gear, pressure-type fire extinguishing system, landing lights, 30 gal. or 60 gal. extra fuel cap., entry door on left for pilot, custom interiors, and custom colors were optional. The next Fairchild development was the model A-942-B amphibious flying-boat as described here in the chapter for ATC # 605.

Listed below are Fairchild 45-A entries as gleaned from company records:

NC-15955;	45-A	(# 4001)	Wright 320
-16361;	"	(# 4002)	"
-16362;	"	(# 4003)	"
-16363;	"	(# 4004)	"
-16364;	"	(# 4005)	"
-16365;	"	(# 4006)	"
;	"	(# 4007)	"
;	"	(# 4008)	"
;	"	(# 4009)	"
-16864;	"	(# 4010)	"
-16865;	"	(# 4011)	"
-16876;	"	(# 4012)	"
-16877;	"	(# 4013)	"
-16878;	"	(# 4014)	"
-16879;	"	(# 4015)	"
-16880;	"	(# 4016)	"

Forward cabin of 45-A shows roomy layout.

This approval for ser. # 4001 and up; ser. # 4002 later as ZS-AML in So. Africa; ser. # 4006 to U.S. Navy Bureau; ser. # 4007-4008 to Argentine Navy; ser. # 4009 as Fairchild demonstrator; ser. # 4016 del. 3-39; this approval expired 2-27-42.

ATC # 604
(5-6-36)
BEECH, MODEL C-17-R.

Beech model C-17-R was fitted with "seven league boots".

After the exciting reputation built up by the model B-17-R, Walter Beech insisted that there just had to be another powerful (420 h.p.) Wright-engined model for the new sales year just ahead. This new ship was groomed as the C-17-R and before it was entirely completed Beech people honestly felt they had another winner. Women pilots were finally allowed to fly in the famous Bendix Trophy dash, beginning with this one in 1936, so Olive Ann Beech, with the intuition she became noted for, coaxed Louise Thaden and Blanche Noyes to fly the C-17-R in the grueling race. The girl-pilots felt they had less than a fair chance against the all-out racing planes that were entered, but decided to try for the $2500 that had been posted for the first woman to finish, regardless of her position in the race. They would have a fighting chance for that much money at least. As luck would have it, most all of the top competition was left by the wayside in the long race, because of one problem or another, and the two lady-pilots with the C-17-R wound up as winners!! They were flabbergasted, of course, but extremely happy when finally convinced they had won the race. Louise and Blanche had nursed the C-17-R across the country from New York to Los Angeles on 65% power (in 14 hrs. 55 min.) averaging 165.346 m.p.h. for the trip. By the time the Bendix dash was over this particular C-17-R had already been promised and sold to an anxious customer in Honduras. As a way out Walter Beech ordered another C-17-R completed (using the same NC number) so that Louise Thaden could demonstrate it around the nation, and cash-in on the helpful publicity. Not many knew that this was a different airplane (because it was labeled as the Bendix winner) but, it didn't seem to matter that much to anyone. Louise Thaden was later awarded the Harmon Trophy for 1936 as the "most outstanding woman flyer in America." In January of 1937 this airplane, with Louise Thaden attending, was exhibited at the National Aviation Show held in New York City; she used the airplane for about a year and then it was sold to her publisher. Walter Beech had promised the C-17-R a good reputation, and now it was fact. Five of the C-17-R were exported, about a dozen were sold here in the U.S.A., and in a surprise move the U. S. Navy acquired one as the JB-1, a personnel transport. Up to now Beech didn't think much of the military orders and didn't pursue the business, but war clouds over Europe in 1938-39 caused him to at least take a slight interest.

The model C-17-R was a typical Beech negative-stagger-wing cabin biplane with seating arranged for 4 or 5. This airplane was the top of the line for 1936, so the interior environment was rather plush, and usually embellished with scads of costly extras. The Beech 17, any Beech

C-17-R was Bendix Race winner; Louise Thaden in foreground.

17, and especially those with a big engine, was a little awkward looking when sitting on its wheels, but once in the air with its wheels tucked up neatly into the smooth belly, she was transformed into flashing beauty, graceful as a dragonfly. Many of the C-17-R were ordered with custom colors, and every single one of them was a spectacular showpiece; can you imagine the pride one must have in owning an airplane such as this. The Beech "Staggerwing" was not a racing airplane, but several pilots did race them; they were fast and they were steady. At the Mile-High Air Races for 1936 held in Denver, Beech-pilot "Bill" Ong captured the Phillips Trophy in a C-17-R; in the following year it was won again by another Beechcraft. As powered with the big 9 cyl. Wright R-975-E3 engine rated 420 h.p. the C-17-R had plenty of muscle for an unbelievable performance, and blessed too with an abundance of power reserve. Owners of the model C-17-R were scattered in varied parts of the country and there weren't many places, within reason, that they couldn't go. The C-17-R still had the lever-operated wheel brakes, so pilots claimed it required at least 3 hands to land it! Surely, the C-17-R, like others in the Beech big-power series, was not meant for the average pilot, but those that "learned the how of it" were rewarded with some exciting times. This type certificate was issued to the C-17-R on 5-6-36 (for ser. # 73 and up) and some 18 examples of this model were manufactured by the Beech Aircraft Co. at Wichita, Kan.

Listed below are specifications and performance data for the Beech model C-17-R as powered with the Wright R-975-E3 engine rated 420 h.p. at 2200 r.p.m. at 1400 ft. (450 h.p. at 2250 r.p.m. for takeoff); length overall 24'5"; height overall 8'2"; wingspan upper and lower 32'0"; wing chord upper and lower 60"; total wing area 273 sq. ft.; airfoil Clark CYH; wt. empty 2250 lbs.; useful load 1650 lbs.; payload with 98 gal. fuel 847 lbs. (4 pass., 125 lb. bag., 42 lb. extra equipment); gross wt. 3900 lbs.; max. speed 211 at sea level; cruising speed (.68 power using 285 h.p.) 185 at sea level, 195 at 5000 ft., 202 at 10,000 ft.; landing speed (with flaps) 59; climb 1400 ft. first min. at sea level; ser. ceiling 21,500 ft.; gas cap. 98 gal.; oil cap. 6 gal.; cruising range (.68 power) at 23.5 gal. per hour 800 miles; price $14,500 at factory. Eligible with fixed-pitch Curtiss-Reed, or Hamilton-Standard metal controllable-pitch props. Gross wt. allowance later increased to 3915 lbs.

The C-17-R was also eligible as a seaplane (SC-17-R) on Edo model 39-4000 Twin-float gear with Hamilton-Standard "controllable" prop; specifications and data same as above except as follows; wt. empty 2700 lbs.; useful load 1405 lbs.; payload with 98 gal. fuel 602 lbs. (3 pass. and 92 lb. bag.); payload with 70 gal. fuel 770 lbs. (4 pass. and 90 lb. bag.); gross wt. 4105 lbs.; max. speed 175 at sea level; cruising speed (.68 power) 130 at sea level, 150 at 9000 ft.; landing speed (with flaps) 62; climb 1100 ft. first min. at sea level; ser. ceiling 18,000 ft.; gas cap. 98 gal.; oil cap. 6 gal.; cruising range (.68 power) at 23.5 gal. per hour 550 miles; price approx. $18,500 at factory.

The construction details and general arrangement of the model C-17-R were typical to that of other Beech models in this period. The only significant difference was mounting of the supercharged Wright R-975-E3 engine and some

Model C-17-R was JB-1 in U.S. Navy.

slight modifications necessary for this combination. The interior of every C-17-R was rather plush, and fitted with cabin vents and a cabin heater. Typical of all models the forward right seat slid back on a track to provide room for entry to the front; parachute-type seats were optional. A large entry door was on the left side, but an extra door on the right was optional. The large baggage compartment behind the rear seat had allowance for 125 lbs., but only 75 lbs. was allowed when 3 occupied the rear seat. A special golf-bag compartment was also optional. Anchor and mooring rope (25 lbs.) was part of the baggage allowance for seaplane. A 23-gal. fuel tank was mounted in fuselage front, a 47 gal. tank in fuselage rear (both under floor), and a 23-gal. tank in one lower wing root for a normal total of 98 gal.; an extra 23 gal. tank in opposite lower wing root was optional. Oil supply could be increased to 7 or 9 gal. The electrically-operated landing gear used "Beech-made" oil-spring shock struts; 7.50x10 wheels were fitted with (6 ply) low-pressure tires and Autofan brakes. As a seaplane (SC-17-R) the ship was fitted with Edo 39-4000 pontoons and extra fin area; the float installation weighed approx. 527 lbs. When a Hamilton-Standard controllable prop was used a 25 lb. tool-roll (for ballast) was fitted in the tail cone to balance the extra weight. The metal controllable prop had to be used on the seaplane; it was only an option for the landplane. Drag flaps and balanced ailerons were on the lower wings; drag flaps not to be extended above 100 m.p.h. Rudder and elevator were both fitted with adjustable trim tabs. A Curtiss-Reed metal prop, electric engine starter, battery, Eclipse generator, ammeter, fuel gauges, engine-driven fuel pump, hand wobble pump, throw-over control wheel, compass, clock, complete set of engine and flight instruments, oil-cooling radiator, 10x4 swiveling

tail wheel, bonding and shielding for radio, wiring for navigation lights, ash trays, assist ropes, and first-aid kit were standard equipment. Navigation lights, landing lights, para-flares, radio gear, pressure-type fire extinguisher, 24 in. (General) streamlined wheels and tires, T-type control column, extra navigational aids, and camera installation were optional. The next Beech development was the model C-17-E as described here in the chapter for ATC # 615.

Listed below are C-17-R entries as gleaned from various records:

NC-15487;	C-17-R	(# 73)	Wright 420
-15833;	″	(# 74)	″
NC-282Y;	″	(# 75)	″
-15834;	″	(# 76)	″
-15835;	″	(# 77)	″
-15837;	″	(# 79)	″
NC-2;	″	(# 80)	″
-15835;	″	(# 81)	″
-16434;	″	(# 82)	″
CF-BBB;	″	(# 113)	″
G-AENY;	″	(# 114)	″
-0801;	″	(# 115)	″
NC-2000;	″	(# 116)	″
G-AESJ;	″	(# 118)	″
-17068;	″	(# 119)	″
CF-BIF;	″	(# 120)	″
-16445;	″	(# 122)	″

This approval for ser. # 73 and up; ser. # 73 also as model C-17-E; ser. # 77 was winner of 1936 Bendix Race; ser. # 80 to Dept. of Commerce; ser. # 81 as stand-in for winner of 1936 Bendix Race; ser. # 82 to Porto Rico; ser. # 113 to Canada; ser. # 114 to England; ser. # 115 to U.S. Navy as JB-1; ser. # 118 to England; ser. # 120 to Canada; 5 of C-17-R as UC-43E in USAAF; approval expired 9-30-39.

C-17-R on floats in "Canadian bush".

ATC # 605
(5-16-36)
FAIRCHILD, MODEL A-942-B

View shows lines that made Fairchild A-942-B once fastest "amphibian" in the world.

It really doesn't mean all that much to say that the Fairchild model A-942-B was a large, high-performance, single-engined amphibian, so it is better to point out that for years it was also known as the "Baby Clipper" or better yet as the "Jungle Clipper." In all accounts the Fairchild "Jungle Clipper" was always portrayed as high adventure along the steamy Amazon River, exploring the wilds of New Guinea, or shuttling merchants back and forth along the Yangtze River in China. This was true because the "Baby Clipper" (also in Fairchild records as the Model 91) was designed in cooperation with Pan American Airways engineers for service in coastal and sheltered waters of So. America and other parts of the world, areas where its adaptability to primitive conditions would be best suited. At first, in a flush of eagerness, Pan Am ordered 6 of these airplanes, but the traffic and revenue realized actually did not justify purchase of all 6 airplanes. The airline finally settled for 2 and later a third. As the others were now released for disposal elsewhere, one was shipped to Japan, and one was fitted as a very plush six-place "Air Yacht" for famous speed-boat king Gar Wood. The "Ninety One" that made the most headlines was the "Jungle Clipper" (NR-777) used by Richard Archbold of the N. Y. Museum of Natural History for his expedition into the wilds of New Guinea. Pan American Airways ordered all their "Model 91" with the big Pratt & Whitney "Hornet" engine as the A-942-A; the A-942-B under consideration here was, of course, identical to a tee, but it mounted the big Wright "Cyclone" engine instead. There was absolutely no difference in the performance

or general nature of the airplane with either engine, but if the customers have a choice they sometimes do choose. We have to concede here that the Fairchild "Baby Clipper" was indeed an unusual airplane, and in spite of its small number it did leave a lasting mark on the face of aviation history.

The Fairchild model A-942-B, like the earlier A-942-A, was a big single-engined cantilever high-winged monoplane of the flying boat type; seating was normally arranged for 8 passengers and a crew of 2. In one instance the passenger interior was specially arranged for boat-builder Gar Wood to seat 4 people in over-stuffed comfort rivaling that of any yacht. As we can see in any view, this unusual flying boat was carefully designed to eliminate the many drag-producing factors usually associated with a large airplane of this type. Elimination of drag made the "Model 91" a fast airplane; at one time it happened to be the fastest single-engined amphibian in the world! Most airplanes that operated from land and also water paid dearly in loss of performance to achieve this dual-purpose ability, but outside of the extra weight the "Baby Clipper" suffered very little loss. Graceful and roundish to its very tail-post, the "Ninety One" fairly bristled with advanced ideas, and fell heir to the formula for utility and efficiency as suggested by Pan Am engineers, and so ably developed by Fairchild. Tailor-made for the river routes in So. America, and in China, where it earned the name "Jungle Clipper," this big flying-boat proved its robust nature and its unwavering devotion to duty in many years of service. As now powered with the popular 9 cyl.

Unusual configuration was most advanced for "amphibian" design.

Wright "Cyclone" engine of 760 h.p. the model A-942-B got around to quite a respectable performance throughout its operating range, and too it was considerably faster than the average airplane of the amphibious type. The type certificate for the model A-942-B was issued 5-16-36 and it is likely that 5 examples of this version were either manufactured or converted by the Fairchild Aircraft Corp. at Hagerstown, Md., a division of the Fairchild Aviation Corp.

Listed below are specifications and performance data for the Fairchild model A-942-B as powered with Wright "Cyclone" SGR-1820-F52 engine rated 760 h.p. at 2100 r.p.m. at 5600 ft. (875 h.p. at 2200 r.p.m. for takeoff); length overall 46'8"; height overall (on wheels) 17'0"; wingspan 56'0"; wing chord at root 130"; wing chord at tip 65"; total wing area 483 sq. ft.; airfoil at root Clark Y-18; airfoil at tip Clark Y-1!;

wt. empty 6500 lbs.; useful load 3200 lbs.; payload with 180 gal. fuel and 2 pilots 1668 lbs. (8 pass. and 308 lbs. bag.); gross wt. 9700 lbs.; baggage allowance to 480 lbs.; max. speed 175 at 5800 ft.; cruising speed (.75 power) 155 at sea level; cruising speed (.66 power) 151 at 8000 ft.; landing speed (with flaps) 63; stall speed (no flaps) 70; takeoff from water 22 secs.; climb 975 ft. first min. at sea level; climb to 10,000 ft. in 13 mins.; ser. ceiling 17,900 ft.; climb to ser. ceiling in 40 mins.; gas cap. normal 180 gal.; gas cap. max. 354 gal.; oil cap. 15-25 gal.; cruising range (.75 power) at 44 gal. per hour 610 miles; cruising range (.66 power) at 37 gal. per hour 720 miles; price averaged $50,000 at factory, and up to $70,000 for custom orders. Gross wt. allowance later increased to 10,500 lbs. for amphibian type, and to 10,700 lbs. for the flying-boat without landing gear. With the extra

A-942-B used by Richard Archbold for expedition to New Guinea.

Chas. A. "Lindy" Lindbergh was pleased with ability of A-942-B.

modifications necessary for this combination. The following details applied to both models in general. Due to control arrangements and all it was necessary to do, it actually took 2 pilots to fly this airplane; this was later remedied and 1 pilot could do the job, after practice. Ser. # 9405 and up were so modified at the factory; earlier ships were also eligible for one pilot operation when modified to conform. Total baggage or freight allowance was 1000 lbs.; 650 lbs. forward of pilot, and 350 lbs. aft of cabin. Extra fuel cap. was available to a total of 354 gal.; the extra fuel was a 34 gal. and a 40 gal. tank in the engine nacelle, and a 100 gal. tank in forward fuselage. Flaps not to be extended above 100 m.p.h. The Model 91, in both versions, was eligible to operate as an amphibian, or without landing gear as a flying boat. All standard equipment and optional equipment was same as listed for A-942-A. The next Fairchild development was the Ranger-powered model 24-C8F as described here in the chapter for ATC # 610.

Listed below are Model 91 entries as gleaned from various records:

NC-14743;	A-942-A	(# 9401)	Hornet 750
-14744;	"	(# 9402)	"
-15952;	"	(# 9403)	"
-16359;	A-942-B	(# 9404)	Cyclone 760
-16690;	"	(# 9405)	"
-19130;	"	(# 9406)	"
NR-777;	"	(# 9407)	"

weight, performance deteriorated only slightly.

The construction details and general arrangement of the model A-942-B were typical to that of the earlier A-942-A as described fully in the chapter for ATC # 587. The most significant change in the A-942-B was installation of the Wright "Cyclone" engine and some

This approval for ser. # 9401 and up; ser. # 9403 later modified to A-942-B; ser. # 9403 reg. in Brazil as PP-PAT; ser. # 9404 later shipped to Japan; ser. # 9405 was custom-built and sold to Gar Wood for $62,200; ser. # 9406 was last airplane to be completed; this approval expired 12-14-40.

ATC # 606
(5-18-36)
PORTERFIELD, 35-V.

The rare Porterfield 35-V with 65 h.p. Velie M-5 engine.

Plane-builder Ed Porterfield did very well with the LeBlond-powered 35-70, in fact it was the mainstay of their business, but with introduction of the "Model 35-V" they had hoped to present an airplane of more outstanding value. As the nation's economy was getting healthier the price of everything was steadily inching up, and so was the price of airplanes; each year it was costing a little more to buy one. As the story goes, and it sounds credible, the Model 35-V was conceived because a good number of the old (brand-new) 'Velie M-5' engines were still available from a stock-pile, and at rock-bottom prices. This combination would then permit the selling of an airplane comparable to the average of this type, but for at least $300 to $400 less. What the buyer actually saved he could then spend on a speed-ring, wheel brakes, tail wheel, etc. Mind you, the Velie 65 was a very good engine, and had been for years, but it was now out of production. On top of all this Porterfield also had a deal—"You buy it and we'll teach you to fly it"—for free. And too, buying a Porterfield was made easier—1/3 down and balance payable in 12 months. By now, "Porterfield" airplanes were all over the world, operating in at least 14 different countries, and of course, all over the U.S.A. One of the 35-V operated in the Los Angeles area as a trainer, keeping very busy, and students liked it very much. Another one operated in the Bakersfield area as a cross-country trainer and it did very

well in the mountains. To sum it up quickly, the Model 35-V was a good airplane, an exceptional value, and a creditable addition to the "Porterfield" lineup. But after all, it didn't seem to fare very well in the market-place of 1936-37; but in general things were looking up. Aircraft production in the first quarter of 1936 increased by 1/3 over the same period in 1935, continuing the upward trend that began to show up in 1934. The most noticeable increase was in the manufacture of light airplanes; at least 100 were manufactured in the first 3 months of 1936.

The slim-waisted "Porterfield" model 35-V was a light cabin monoplane with seating arranged for 2 in tandem. It was hoped that the 35-V would be favored by economic circumstance because it was purposely planned to be relatively cheap; and too, it was well able to fill the role of pilot-trainer, a very economical business plane, or just for the varied pleasures of the sportsman-pilot on a budget. As powered with the rerated 65 h.p. Velie M-5 engine the Model 35-V mustered up a decent performance and it operated from just about anywhere. Pilot-owners were lavish in their praise for the "Porterfield" airplane, and it is quite likely they must have had a good word or two for the 35-V also. It was easy to buy and to own a "Porterfield" on the pay-as-you-fly plan, and lessons to fly the airplane were given free if you were not already a pilot. The formula for a good-selling airplane was built into the 35-V, but the appeal

Legend shows Porterfield "Flyabout" was available with different engines.

of an airplane to the private owner was taking on new aspects at this time, so perhaps the 35-V had become old-fashioned. There were so many new airplanes coming out at this time to dazzle the airplane-buyer that it is hard to understand how he could make a rational choice. The type certificate for the Model 35-V was issued 5-18-36 and some 11 or more examples of this model were manufactured by the Porterfield Aircraft Corp. at Kansas City, Mo. Ed E. Porterfield was pres. & gen. mgr.; Mrs. Porterfield was V.P.; Noel R. Hockaday was sec.; Edgar Smith was sales mgr.; and H. W. Barlow was now chf. engr.

Listed below are specifications and performance data for the Porterfield model 35-V (Flyabout) as powered with the Velie M-5 engine rated 65 h.p. at 2000 r.p.m. at sea level; length overall 20'4"; height overall 6'7"; wingspan 32'0"; wing chord 56"; total wing area (incl. fuselage section) 147 sq. ft.; airfoil Mod. Munk M-6; wt. empty 796 lbs.; useful load 514 lbs.; payload with 18 gal. fuel 217 lbs. (1 pass., 30 lb. bag., and 17 lb. for extras); baggage allowance 30 lbs.; gross wt. 1310 lbs.; max. speed (with speed-ring) 112; cruising speed (1850 r.p.m.) 103; landing speed 40; climb 750 ft. first min. at sea level; ser. ceiling 15,000 ft.; gas cap. 18 gal.; oil cap. 2.5 gal.; cruising range (1850 r.p.m.) at 4.5 gal. per hour 395 miles; price $1795 at factory.

The construction details and general arrangement of the Porterfield 35-V were typical to that of the earlier model 35-70 as described in the chapter for ATC # 567. The only difference of note in the Model 35-V was installation of the Velie M-5 engine and any modifications necessary for this combination. A large rectangular door on the right side provided easy entry to the tandem seating; a baggage compartment with allowance for up to 30 lbs. was behind the rear seat. The cabin was like a solarium—

there were windows everywhere you look. Engine and flight instruments were kept to bare necessities, and dual stick-type controls were provided. The 18 gal. fuel tank was mounted high in the fuselage just behind the firewall. The split-type landing gear of 69 in. tread was fitted with 18x8-3 Goodyear airwheels and no brakes; wheel brakes were optional. Custom-made metal wheel pants were also optional. A spring-leaf tail skid was the standard installation, but a tail wheel assembly was optional. A wooden prop, Pyrene fire extinguisher bottle, safety belts, and first-aid kit were standard equipment. A battery, navigation lights, wheel brakes, tail wheel, and speed-ring engine cowl were available in the "Deluxe" version, or optional on the "Standard" version. The next Porterfield development was the Warner-powered Model 35-W as described here in the chapter for ATC #611.

Listed below are Model 35-V entries as gleaned from registration records:

NC-15887;	35-V	(# 200)	Velie M-5
-16451;	"	(# 201)	"
-16462;	"	(# 202)	"
-17003;	"	(# 203)	"
;	"	(# 204)	"
-17034;	"	(# 205)	"
-17076;	"	(# 206)	"
-17077;	"	(# 207)	"
-17030;	"	(# 208)	"
-17009;	"	(# 209)	"
-18070;	"	(# 210)	"

This approval for ser. # 200 and up; ser. # 203 to Porto Rico; reg. no. for ser. # 204 unknown; ser. nos. 205-206-207-208-209 all reg. in Calif.; ser. # 209-210 mfg. in 1937, all others mfg. in 1936; this approval expired 5-5-41.

ATC # 607
(5-21-36)
DOUGLAS "SLEEPER," DST-G2.

Douglas (DST) "Skysleeper" revolutionized long-distance air travel.

In the summer of 1934 American Airlines (AA) became interested in buying a sleeper-version of the popular DC-2, but Don Douglas shied away from the offer saying it couldn't be done. But, when C. R. Smith, American Airlines president, said he would promise to buy 20 of the sleeper-planes Douglas half-heartedly approached his engineers to find out if it would be feasible, and practical. Wm. Littlewood, AA engineer, was enthusiastic about the idea, and had already roughed-out some sketches of how it could be done. Douglas engineers soon agreed that with some redesigning the basic DC-2 could be stretched, fattened up, and fitted with a bigger wing to do the job. Wind-tunnel tests helped iron out the details for a longer, wider, circular cross-sectioned fuselage, and these tests also dictated modifications to the wing which would be of greater span, and would use a slightly different airfoil section. Preliminary design work on the new "Sleeper" began in the Fall of 1934, and the basic structure began taking shape in Dec. of that year. First formal details of the new ship were published in the "Fortune" magazine for May of 1935. On Dec. 17 of 1935, on the 32nd anniversary of powered flight by the Wright Bros., the new Douglas Sleeper Transport (DST) was rolled out for flight; and thus began a saga of achievement and dedication that would surpass that of any other airplane ever built. Carl A. Cover flew the maiden voyage over Santa Monica as everyone watched, and they say he was pleased beyond words with its overall performance. She was comfortable, safe, sound, and beautiful—and she was timely. Vigorous shake-down tests were then run through Jan. of 1936 and she was prepared for certification. The plane was technically labeled the DST, but better known as the "Douglas Sleeper." Yes, just about the time the greatness of the DC-2 "Douglas Airliner" was becoming common, they at Douglas Aircraft again startled the industry with the new "Douglas Sleeper Transport." Of course, there were already other sleeper-planes in use, of which the Curtiss "Condor" was best known, but the DST was the first airplane designed specifically to provide spacious and luxurious sleeping accommodations for air-travel at night. The shiny DST was tall and a big airplane with its wing stretching out to 95 feet; when loaded it weighed over 12 tons. On the inside the DST was fitted with 14 to 16 comfortable berths affording complete privacy; upper berths that could be folded up into the ceiling and lower berths that were converted quickly into deeply upholstered chairs. The day-time capacity was then as much as 28 passengers. In the Spring of 1936 "Sleepers" were already coming off the line; the DST for its first public showing was put on display at the Pan-American Auditorium in downtown Los Angeles where thousands of people

DST prototype shown was basis for all DC-3 designs; was first plane to be designed specifically as a "sleeper transport."

had a chance to walk through and admire the new mode of transportation. The first of the "Sleeper Transport" was delivered to American Airlines on June 8 of 1936 and began service between Chicago and New York on June 25. On July 4 of 1936 AA began non-stop service from Los Angeles to Chicago, a 10-hour flight, and coast-to-coast service was inaugurated on Sept. 18. Passengers boarded the big "Sleeper" in New York at 5:10 p.m. and arrived in Los Angeles early the next morning; east-bound and west-bound trips were flown daily under the slogan "sleep cradled on the wings of luxury."

The model DST (Douglas Sleeper Transport) was a large twin-engined, low-winged, transport monoplane designed especially for cross-country night travel. The generous interior dimensions were fitted with up to 16 convertible berths offering sleep or rest in complete privacy; for the first time dressing rooms and lavatory facilities were available separately for men and women. When not used the upper berths were folded up into the ceiling; lower berths were convertible into comfortable lounge-chairs for day-time travel, and a well-stocked galley with steam-table offered rather tasty meals in flight. In general appearance the DST was quite similar to the earlier DC-2, but looking from the front head-on one could see that dimensions of the fuselage were rounded-out to very much larger proportion. The cabin interior was 6'6" high, 7'8" wide, and 27'8" long for a roominess never before offered. In loaded condition the DST weighed a good 2½ tons more than the DC-2, but it conducted itself with considerable verve for such a large airplane. Here was indeed a new mode of transportation, a way to travel swiftly, and sleep comfortably in the cradle of luxury. The Douglas DST prototype was rolled out mounting 2 of the new Wright "Cyclone G" engines that were supercharged more highly for operation at greater altitudes; the DST was actually available with 5 different "Cyclone G" engines

which differed only in the amount of supercharging applied. Each operator had their own reasons for picking particular "Cyclone" engines for their mode of service. According to record this approval applied to the models DST-G2, DST-G2E, DST-G5, DST-G102, DST-G102A, DST-G103, and DST-G202A; each model was powered with the big 9 cyl. Wright "Cyclone G" engines, and was more or less the same, but varied only in the model of engines installed and some slight changes to interior arrangement, decor, and equipment. At first the DST "Sleeper" was a big promotional advantage, but it was eventually overshadowed by the greater versatility of its sister-ship, the DC-3. The type certificate for the "Cyclone-powered" DST was issued 5-21-36 and some 21 examples of this version were manufactured by the Douglas Aircraft Co. at Santa Monica, Calif.

Listed below are specifications and performance data for the Douglas model DST-G2 as powered with 2 Wright "Cyclone" GR-1820-G2 engines rated 850 h.p. at 2100 r.p.m. at 5800 ft. (930 h.p. at 2200 r.p.m. for takeoff); length overall 64'6"; height overall 16'11"; wing span 95'0"; wing chord at root 170" tapered to tip; total wing area 987 sq. ft.; airfoil at root NACA-2215; airfoil at tip NACA-2206; wt. empty 15,-750 lbs.; useful load 8250 lbs.; payload with 650 gal. fuel 3475 lbs. (16 pass., 3 crew, 755 lbs. baggage-mail); gross wt. 24,000 lbs.; max. speed 212 at 6800 ft., 219 at 11,500 ft.; cruising speed (.75 power) 184 at 10,000 ft.; landing speed (with flaps) 65; climb 970 ft. first min. at sea level; ser. ceiling 23,300 ft.; gas cap. 650 gal.; oil cap. 50 gal.; cruising range (.75 power) at 93.6 gal. per hour 1250 miles. Model DST-G2 was 19 place airplane as sleeper (16 berths and crew of 3) or 31 place (28 pass. and crew of 3) as day-plane. DST also available with GR-1820-G5 engine rated 850 h.p. at 2100 r.p.m. at 4300 ft.; no noticeable change in specs or performance.

Specifications and performance data for

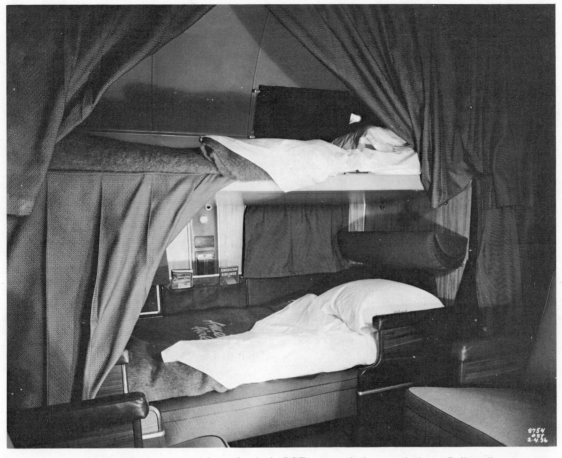

Interior shows upper and lower berths in DST; accomodations as plush as "Pullman" train.

model DST-G102 as powered with 2 Wright "Cyclone" GR-1820-G102 engines rated 900 h.p. at 2200 r.p.m. at 6000 ft. (1100 h.p. available for takeoff) same as above except as follows: wt. empty 16,300 lbs.; useful load 8100 lbs.; payload with 650 gal. fuel 3205 lbs. (16 pass., 3 crew, and 485 lbs. baggage-mail); gross wt. 24,400 lbs.; max. gross wt. of 24,800 lbs. later allowed; max. speed 216 at 7000 ft.; cruising speed (.75 power) 197 at 10,000 ft.; cruising speed (.66 power) 185 at 10,000 ft.; landing speed (with flaps) 67; stall speed (no flaps) 80; climb 980 ft. first min. at sea level; ser. ceiling 21,800 ft.; gas cap. normal 650 gal.; gas cap. max. 820 gal.; oil cap. max. 66.5 gal.; cruising range (.75 power) at 100 gal. per hour 1280 miles; cruising range was most often extended by using .70 power at 97 gal. per hour. The GR-1820-G102A engine was rated 900 h.p. at 2300 r.p.m. at 6700 ft. in the model DST-G102A. DST also available with GR-1820-G103 engines rated 860 h.p. at 2300 r.p.m. at 11,000 ft.; no noticeable change in performance.

Specifications and performance data for model DST-G202A as powered with 2 Wright "Cyclone" GR-1820-G202A engines rated 1000 h.p. at 2300 r.p.m. at 4500 ft. (1200 h.p. available for takeoff); same as previous listings except as follows: empty wt. 16,857 lbs.; useful load 7543 lbs.; payload with 650 gal. fuel 2733 lbs. (14 pass., 3 crew, 353 lbs. baggage-mail); gross wt. 24,400 lbs. (max. gross wt. of 24,800 lbs. later allowed); max. speed 219 at 7000 ft.; cruising speed (.75 power) 198 at 10,000 ft.; landing speed (with flaps) 67; climb 1065 ft. first min. at sea level; ser. ceiling 22,750 ft.; gas cap. max. 822 gal.; oil cap. max. 66.5 gal.; cruising range (.75 power) at 112 gal. per hour 1130 miles. The various "Cyclone G" engines differed only with respect to the compression ratio and to the amount of supercharging applied; on some the "blower ratio" was greatly increased for more power at higher altitudes, using fuels of higher octane rating.

The construction details and general arrangement of the DST "Sleeper" were typical to that of the earlier DC-2 except for a longer, wider fuselage, and the installation of sleeping accommodations. The main cabin was divided into four sections on each side of a center aisle. Each section contained 2 seats (36" wide) facing each other; these seats when folded together formed the lower berth. The upper berth pulled down from the ceiling; a small window above the regular cabin window (called "bunk window") provided the upper-berth occupants a look-see out. Each berth was equipped with a luggage rack, a clothes net, reading lamp, and a call button. For the first time on a sleeper-plane separate dressing rooms were provided for men and women; these rooms were complete with mirrors, linens, and running water. Toilet facilities were separately located adjacent to each dressing room. A commissary or galley, forward of the main cabin, was equipped to provide tasty hot or cold food and drink for a fairly elaborate meal. The luggage and mail bins were across the aisle from the galley, and another large (107 cu. ft.) baggage compartment was behind the cabin area. For those who desired a compartment of their own, the DST later offered an option called the "Sky Room", a fully enclosed stateroom. The "Sky Room" was forward on the right-hand side with sleeping accommodations for 2 or plush seating for four; a table could be set up between seats. This extra-fare compartment was secluded, and royally appointed for day or night travel. The next Douglas development was the DC3-G2 as described here in the chapter for ATC # 618.

Listed below are DST entries as gleaned from registration records:

NC-14988;	DST-G2	(# 1494)	2 Cyclone 850
-16001;	"	(# 1495)	"
-16002;	"	(# 1496)	"
-16003;	"	(# 1497)	"
-16004;	"	(# 1498)	"
-16005;	"	(# 1499)	"
-16006;	"	(# 1500)	"
-16007;	"	(# 1549)	"
-18144;	DST-G102	(# 1976)	2 Cyclone 900
-21769;	"	(# 2149)	"
-21752;	"	(# 2165)	"
-25685;	DST-G202A	(# 2216)	2 Cyclone 1000
-25686;	"	(# 2217)	"
-28345;	"	(# 2224)	"
-25650;	"	(# 2225)	"
-25651;	"	(# 2226)	"
-28325;	"	(# 2263)	"
-28350;	"	(# 2264)	"
-28394;	"	(# 3250)	"
-28393;	"	(# 3251)	"
-33643;	"	(# 4129)	"

This approval for ser. # 1494 and up; ser. # 1494 thru 1500 & # 1549 were DST-144; ser. # 1976 was DST-217; ser. # 2149, 2165 were DST-217A; ser. # 2216-17 were DST-217B; ser. # 2263-64 were DST-217C; ser. # 2224-25-26 were DST-318; ser. # 3250-51 were DST-318A; ser. # 4129 was DST-406; 9 of Cyclone-powered DST to USAAF as C-49F in 1942.

ATC # 608
(5-28-36)
STINSON, SR-8B.

Stinson "Reliant" SR-8C with 260 h.p. engine was a favorite in business.

A brand new (SR-7) "Reliant" had just been introduced a few months earlier, and behind-the-scenes excitement had not yet subsided, when already Stinson Aircraft was grooming yet another new "Reliant" series for the Fall season. These (SR-8) "Reliant" models were also the revolutionary mating of the standard "Reliant" fuselage with an adaptation of the unique sesqui-spar wing design. The wing with its double taper had worked beautifully on the Stinson "Tri-Motor"; it was calculated that the wing could do wonders for the "Reliant" also, and it surely did. Because of its double taper from the center, and the way it joined the fuselage the airplane soon became popularly known as the "Gull-Wing Stinson." The "Reliant's" wing didn't really "gull," it just looked that way. Everybody was naturally impressed with this airplane, some were even amazed, and everyone in aviation came to regard this combination very highly. Its staunch, business-like pose was tempered with more than a little grace, and the clincher was in the way the "Gull Wing Reliant" conducted itself. There is no doubt that some expected a little compromise here and there, a little trade-off, but there was none—the new series SR-8 was every inch a "Stinson Reliant," and a little bit better. To offer a good variety this new series was available with 3 different Lycoming engines of 225-245-260 h.p., and a long list of useful op-

tions. Because of inevitable price raises throughout the industry, the model SR-8 was also competing with higher-priced and expensively-built airplanes, so Stinson craftsmen were exercising extra patience in manufacture, along with their skills and years of experience. As each shiny-new "Reliant" was rolled out from final assembly it was a veritable show-piece, and often turned out to be the culmination of someone's long-time dream. The roster of owners was the usual mixture of commercial operators, the sportsman-pilots, and business-people; some were so anxious they were waiting in the doorway for delivery. Some had even brought along an older "Stinson" to trade; in some cases they were buying their 2nd or 3rd Stinson. A late 1936 "Reliant" (an SR-8B), one of 9 ordered by the Bureau of Air Commerce, was the 800th airplane Stinson Aircraft had built in the 10 years since its beginning in the second-story loft of a building in downtown Detroit. Another "Reliant" was flown off to Alaska to operate in "the bush" alongside other "Stinson" airplanes, some of which were going on 10 years old.

The robust Stinson "Reliant" model SR-8 was a high-winged cabin monoplane with seating arranged for 4 or 5. In general, the new SR-8 series was a normal "Reliant," even similar to those of years past, but it is surprising what the new wing was doing for its character. With its maximum thickness and double taper radiating from the struts station the wing looked absolutely massive. In fact, the whole airplane appeared practically indestructible, but the slender wingtips and the "knobby" engine cowl kept it from looking heavy and unwieldy. The wing taper at the roots presented far less cross-section in this area, so in effect, the visibility was greatly improved also. Span-wise distribution of the airflow from the center out split the intensity of gusts and air-loads as they radiated to the fuselage frame; this then had a tendency to divert the jolts and soften the ride. Pilots claimed the "Reliant" when loaded had the stability of an iron bridge, and plowed through rough air like an ocean-liner. As powered with the 9 cyl. Lycoming R-680-B6 engine rated 245 h.p. the model SR-8B (the most popular of the SR-8 series for 1936) had plenty of hustle, and impressed novice and expert alike in the way it conducted itself in any situation. As powered with the Lycoming R-680-B4 engine rated 225 h.p., it was noticeable that the SR-8A had less power, and as powered with the Lycoming R-680-B5 engine rated 260 h.p., it was also noticeable that the SR-8C had more power. As each season brought out new models the "Reliant" was steadily getting more handsome, bigger, and a little better; pilots who knew this airplane intimately were quick to brag on it. The type certificate for the models SR-8A, SR-8B, SR-8C was issued 5-28-36 and about 90 examples (varying amounts of each) were built in all. Manufactured by the Stinson Aircraft Corp. on its factory-field in Wayne, Mich.

Listed below are specifications and performance data for the "Reliant" model SR-8A as powered with Lycoming R-680-B4 engine rated 225 h.p. at 2100 r.p.m. at sea level; length overall 27'0"; height overall 8'6"; wing span 41'7"; max. wing chord 96"; wing chord at tip 38"; total wing area 256.5 sq. ft.; airfoil Mod. Clark Y; empty wt. 2262 lbs.; useful load 1113 lbs.; payload with 50 gal. fuel 610 lbs. (3 pass. and 100 lbs. bag.); gross wt. 3375 lbs.; max. speed 145; cruising speed (.75 power) 136 at 3000 ft.; landing speed (with flaps) 53; climb 725 ft. first min. at sea level; ser. ceiling 12,800 ft.; gas cap. 50 gal.; oil cap. 4.5 gal.; cruising range (.75 power) at 14 gal. per hour 475 miles; price approx. $6500 at factory. SR-8A was 4-place airplane, and not eligible as seaplane.

Specifications and data for model SR-8B as powered with Lycoming R-680-B6 engine (with controllable prop) rated 245 h.p. at 2300 r.p.m. at sea level, same as above except as follows: length overall 27'2"; height overall 8'5"; wt. empty 2347 lbs.; useful load 1403 lbs.; payload with 70 gal. fuel 780 lbs. (4 pass. and 100 lbs. bag.); gross wt. 3750 lbs.; max. speed 147 at sea level; cruising speed (.75 power) 138 at 3000 ft.; landing speed (with flaps) 57; climb 800 ft. first min. at sea level; ser. ceiling 13,800 ft.; gas cap. 70 gal.; oil cap. 4.5 gal.; cruising range (.75 power) at 14.5 gal. per hour 645 miles; price approx. $7500 at factory. Specifications and data for SR-8B as seaplane on Edo 39-4000 twin-float gear same as listings above except as follows: wt. empty 2680 lbs.; useful load 1320 lbs.; payload with 70 gal. fuel 697 lbs. (4 pass. and 17 lbs. bag.); anchor and mooring gear in-

An SR-8CM on floats in the "Canadian bush".

An SR-8BM used by Father Schultes in missionary work.

cluded in bag. allowance; gross wt. 4000 lbs.; max. speed 132; cruising speed (.75 power) 124 at sea level; landing speed (with flaps) 62; climb 675 ft. first min. at sea level; ser. ceiling 10,000 ft.; cruising range (.75 power) at 14.5 gal. per hour 580 miles; price approx. $10,000. Operators sometimes flew at fast-cruise using .88 power burning 17 gal. per hour. The R-680-D6 engine was also eligible.

Specifications and data for model SR-8C as powered with Lycoming R-680-B5 engine (with controllable prop) rated 260 h.p. at 2300 r.p.m. at sea level, same as above except as follows: wt. empty 2370 lbs.; useful load 1380 lbs.; payload with 70 gal. fuel 757 lbs. (4 pass. and 77 lbs. bag.); gross wt. 3750 lbs.; max. speed 148; cruising speed (.75 power) 140 at 3000 ft.; landing speed (with flaps) 57; climb 825 ft. first min. at sea level; ser. ceiling 14,500 ft.; gas cap. 70 gal.; oil cap. 4.5 gal.; cruising range (.75 power) at 15 gal. per hour 630 miles; price approx. $10,000 at factory. The SR-8C was also eligible as seaplane on Edo 39-4000 twin-float gear at 4000 lb. gross wt. Performance of the SR-8C as seaplane would be slightly improved over SR-8B as seaplane because of the extra power. Operators sometimes flew at fast-cruise using .85 power burning 17.5 gal. per hour. The R-680-D5 engine was also eligible. Stinson used to display prices of their "Reliant" proudly, but now that prices were so inflated, they only quoted prices on request.

The construction details and general arrange-

ment of the SR-8 type were typical to that of the earlier SR-7 as described in the chapter for ATC # 594, including the following. The 3 "Reliant" (SR-8) discussed here were all fitted with the improved B-version of the Lycoming engine; late models in this series also used the D-version. The SR-8B and SR-8C had slightly wider fuselage to allow more room for occupants in back; 3 could sit on the rear seat now without overlapping shoulders. The SR-8A was held to 4 places. Fuselage exterior was metal-clad forward of the doors, and all windows were of shatter-proof glass. Normally the cabin was upholstered in long-wearing leather, but a selection of fine fabrics was available. Fifty lbs. of luggage was allowed under rear seat, and 50 lbs. in compartment behind the rear seat; when only 2 occupied the rear seat luggage in rear compartment could be increased to 100 lbs. A 25 gal. fuel tank in the root of each wing was standard for the SR-8A, and a 35 gal. tank in each wing for the SR-8B and SR-8C; a 41 gal. fuel tank in each wing was optional. The semi-cantilever landing gear of 113 in. tread was fitted with "Aerol" (air-oil) shock struts that were buried in underside of the fuselage; 7.50x10 wheels were fitted with 8.50x-10 (4 ply) tires and hydraulic brakes. Wheel streamlines (pants) were optional. The multi-purpose version of the SR-8 were designated "M" (as SR-8BM, etc.); these had 2 doors on the right side for easier loading, and metal-lined cabin walls for protection against damage from cargo. Right front and rear seat could be remov-

An SR-8B dons skis in Canadian winter; SR-8 was a plane for all seasons.

ed quickly to haul bulky freight and large parcels. The M-version was also available as seaplane on Edo twin-float gear; the seaplanes were fitted with Lycoming-Smith controllable props, and this was optional also for the landplane-skiplane version. Wing flaps not to be extended above 122 m.p.h. An electric engine starter, battery, generator, cabin heater and ventilator, wiring for navigation lights, wheel brakes, dual control wheels, parking brake, 10.5 in. tail wheel, Pyrene fire extinguisher, assist ropes, ash trays, cabin lights, and first-aid kit were standard equipment. Extra instruments, extra fuel cap., parachute-type seats, radio gear, navigation lights, landing lights, para-flares, wheel streamlines, and skis were optional. The next "Reliant" development was the Wright-powered SR-8D and SR-8E as described here in the chapter for ATC # 609.

Listed below are SR-8A, SR-8B, SR-8C entries as gleaned from registration records:

NC-16138;	SR-8B	(# 9702)	Lyc. 245
-16133;	"	(# 9708)	"
-16142;	"	(# 9710)	"
-16143;	"	(# 9711)	"
-16132;	"	(# 9712)	"
-16144;	"	(# 9713)	"
-16145;	SR-8A	(# 9714)	Lyc. 225
-16146;	SR-8B	(# 9715)	Lyc. 245
-16147;	SR-8A	(# 9716)	Lyc. 225
-16121;	SR-8C	(# 9717)	Lyc. 260
-16148;	SR-8B	(# 9718)	Lyc. 245
-16150;	"	(# 9719)	"
-16152;	"	(# 9723)	"
-16156;	"	(# 9729)	"
-16157;	"	(# 9730)	"
-16158;	"	(# 9731)	"
-16159;	"	(# 9732)	"
CF-AZV;	SR-8CM	(# 9733)	Lyc. 260
-16161;	SR-8B	(# 9734)	Lyc. 245
-16162;	"	(# 9735)	"
-16160;	"	(# 9738)	"
-16166;	"	(# 9739)	"
-16165;	"	(# 9742)	"
-16168;	"	(# 9743)	"
-16169;	"	(# 9744)	"
-16171;	"	(# 9746)	"
-16172;	SR-8A	(# 9747)	Lyc. 225
-16173;	SR-8B	(# 9748)	Lyc. 245
-16176;	"	(# 9751)	"
-16174;	"	(# 9753)	"
-16180;	"	(# 9754)	"
-16182;	"	(# 9756)	"
-16178;	"	(# 9760)	"
-16179;	"	(# 9761)	"
NX-16184;	SR-8CM	(# 9764)	Lyc. 260
-16199;	SR-8BM	(# 9767)	Lyc. 245
-16186;	SR-8B	(# 9768)	"
NS-16188;	"	(# 9770)	"
-16189;	"	(# 9771)	"
-16190;	"	(# 9772)	"
-16191;	"	(# 9773)	"
-16192;	"	(# 9774)	"
-16193;	"	(# 9775)	"
-16194;	SR-8C	(# 9776)	Lyc. 260
-16195;	SR-8B	(# 9777)	Lyc. 245
PP-TBP;	"	(# 9778)	"
-16197;	"	(# 9779)	"
-17105;	"	(# 9782)	"
-17106;	"	(# 9784)	"
-17170;	"	(# 9790)	"

-17112;	"	(# 9791)	"
-17113;	SR-8C	(# 9792)	Lyc. 260
-17101;	SR-8B	(# 9794)	Lyc. 245
-17115;	"	(# 9798)	"
-17116;	SR-8C	(# 9801)	Lyc. 260
NS-74;	SR-8B	(# 9803)	Lyc. 245
NS-75;	"	(# 9805)	"
NS-76;	"	(# 9807)	"
NS-77;	"	(# 9809)	"
NS-78;	"	(# 9812)	"
NS-79;	"	(# 9813)	"
NS-81;	"	(# 9815)	"
NS-82;	"	(# 9816)	"
NC-17172;	SR-8C	(# 9817)	Lyc. 260
-17119;	SR-8B	(# 9819)	Lyc. 245
-17123;	"	(# 9821)	"

-17125;	"	(# 9822)	"
-17127;	SR-8CM	(# 9824)	Lyc. 260

This approval for ser. # 9702 and up; approx. 20 ser. nos. not shown—either unknown, or exported to foreign countries; ser. # 9710 later mod. to SR-8C; ser. # 9732 later to Alaska; ser. # 9733 to Canada on skis; ser. # 9764 del. to Lycoming Motors; ser. # 9760, 9761, 9772, 9773 to Gulf Oil Corp.; ser. # 9778 later to Brazil; ser. # 9803, 9805, 9807, 9809, 9812, 9813, 9814, 9816 del. to Bureau of Air Commerce; ser. # 9822 to Porto Rico; SR-8B in USAAF as UC-81 (5), and SR-8C in USAAF as UC-81L (2); this approval expired 9-30-39.

ATC # 609
(6-3-36)
STINSON, SR-8D

Stinson "Reliant" SR-8D warming up its 285 h.p. Wright engine.

Even through depression-years "Stinson" was dedicated to building the type of airplanes that most people wanted, at a price that most could still afford to pay. Having corporate ties with "Lycoming Motors" it is natural too they would "push" the "Junior" and "Reliant" models with these engines, but if customers wanted "Wright" engines it behooved Stinson to satisfy these people also. Because the Wright engines were more costly and the delivered price of an airplane was not so much a determining factor, these versions were generally equipped with most of the options, and finished usually in more deluxe fashion. In a word, the Wright-powered "Reliant" was generally a finer and better airplane. Offered as the SR-8D with 285 h.p. Wright engine, and as the SR-8E with the 320 h.p. Wright engine, Stinson quietly claimed that these particular "Reliant" possessed "balanced performance," a combination of reasonably high cruising speeds, with exceptional lifting capacity, and a high degree of maneuverability. The Wright-powered "Reliant" was not exactly snooty, but it did seem to stand a little taller among other airplanes; Stinson vowed it was more safe, more convenient, and more enjoyable. Whenever Stinson Aircraft brought out new models, and at times this was quite often, they bally-hooed loudly that they now had more speed, greater comfort, better vision, and were easier to fly

than ever; it's hard to believe that this was always possible, but most pilots claimed it was so. As we reflect back, the culmination of 10 years of achievement was mirrored in this "Reliant," an awesome depiction of Stinson's ten-year progress. As of 15 Oct. 1936 the company claimed there were 695 "Stinson" airplanes still in active operation, some working day in and day out, and a few of these were now nearly 10 years old. In late Jan. of 1937 four "Reliant" left the factory in snow-bound Michigan and headed for the west coast; 2 were the SR-8E, one was an SR-8D, and one was an SR-8B. The 3 Wright-powered versions were for the flying "Fuller Family" of San Francisco; they had plenty of money and they loved flying. Young and enthusiastic Dana Fuller shortly embarked on a flying vacation to Alaska and back.

The Stinson "Reliant" model SR-8D and SR-8E was a high-winged cabin monoplane with seating arranged for 5. A relatively large airplane, this "Reliant" had a man-sized cabin that offered room and comfort to spare in surroundings comparable to those in airplanes of much higher price. The SR-8 amazed one and all in all that it had to offer. Much of the operating paraphernalia had been continually improved, pilot aids were numerous, and features designed to assure passenger comfort and well-being were more practical and increasingly more efficient.

"Duke" Schiller, famous bush-pilot, prepares SR-8EM for delivery to Canada.

Even though it had appearance no one need be ashamed of, and would certainly look well on anyone's flight line, the SR-8D and SR-8E did not shirk from working and several of them did just that with uncommon skill and devotion to duty. These two "Reliant" (SR-8D, SR-8E) were more expensive airplanes, but it probably figures out that those who could afford an airplane of this type during these times could surely afford the little extra it would take to buy themselves more power and the extra performance. Because the Wright-powered "Reliant" was the better of the SR-8 series they attracted many of the big business-houses, and also beckoned to famous people; the roster of owners was a very impressive list. As powered with the 7 cyl. Wright R-760-E1 engine rated 285 h.p. the model SR-8D performed exceptionally well and did its utmost to bring out the good qualities credited to the "Reliant" design. As powered with the Wright R-760-E2 engine rated 320 h.p. the SR-8E, as top of the line, was slanted to appeal to a certain clientele, a clientele that could afford all the extras, and would stand to benefit most with an airplane of this type. In general, the new SR-8 was a very impressive airplane with very good performance, an above-average utility, it fostered an understandable pride of ownership, and was just about as reliable as an airplane can get; in particular, the SR-8D and SR-8E were all this and a little more. It is extremely difficult to make a good airplane better, but "Stinson" was doing it, a little at a time. The type certificate for the models SR-8D, SR-8E was issued 6-3-36 and some 34 examples in this series was manufactured by the Stinson Aircraft Corp. at Wayne, Mich.

Listed below are specifications and performance data for the Stinson "Reliant" model SR-8D as powered with Wright R-760-E1 engine rated 285 h.p. at 2100 r.p.m. (using controllable prop) at sea level; length overall 27'2"; height overall 8'6"; wingspan 41'7"; max. wing chord 96"; wing chord at tip 38"; total wing area 256.5 sq. ft.; airfoil Mod. Clark Y; wt. empty 2395 lbs.; useful load 1405 lbs.; payload with 82 gal. fuel 705 lbs. (3 pass. and 150 lbs. bag., or 4 pass. and 25 lbs. bag.); gross wt. 3800 lbs.; max. speed 150 at sea level; cruising speed (.75 power) 140 at sea level; landing speed (with flaps) 58; climb 980 ft. first min. at sea level; ser. ceiling 14,000 ft.; gas cap. 82 gal.; oil cap. 5 gal.; cruising range (.75 power) at 17 gal. per hour 645 miles; price approx. $10,500 at factory. SR-8D also eligible as seaplane on Edo 39-4000 twin-float gear at 4000 lb. gross wt. Performance of SR-8D (285 h.p.) as seaplane was slightly improved over SR-8C (260 h.p.) as seaplane (ATC # 608) due to extra power.

Specifications and data for model SR-8E as powered with Wright R-760-E2 engine rated 320 h.p. at 2200 r.p.m. at sea level (350 h.p. available for takeoff) same as above except as follows: wt. empty 2502 lbs.; useful load 1298 lbs.; payload with 82 gal. fuel 598 lbs. (3 pass. and 88 lbs. bag.); payload with 50 gal. fuel 790 lbs. (4 pass. and 100 lbs. bag.); gross wt. 3800 lbs.; max. speed 158 at sea level; cruising speed (.75 power) 148 at sea level; landing speed (with flaps) 58; climb 1050 ft. first min. at sea level; ser. ceiling 15,000 ft.; gas cap. 82 gal.; oil cap. 5 gal.; cruising range (.75 power) at 19 gal. per hour 610 miles; price approx. $12,000 at factory. The SR-8E was also eligible as a seaplane on Edo 39-4000 twin-float gear at 4000 lb. gross wt.; no performance figures available for this model as seaplane.

The construction details and general arrangement of SR-8D and SR-8E were just about the same as for "Reliant" described in chapters for ATC # 594 and ATC # 608, including the following. The most significant difference in the SR-8D, SR-8E, was installation of the Wright engines and any minor modifications necessary to this combination. The more-recent "Reliant" was of such basic design that it permitted frequent improvements without actually obsoleting the airframe. In this way the SR-8 series were a continuance in a well-known reputation for performance, comfort, and reliability that could hardly be challenged by anyone on an item for item basis. "You get more for your money at Stinson"—and this continued to be true. Fuselage of the SR-8 was widened so that rear seat was now 52 in. wide at the elbows; plenty of room for 3. The SR-8D and SR-8E were also available in the "M" (Multi-Purpose) version suitable for freight or ambulance operation; both models were also available as seaplanes. Normal fuel cap. was 82 gal. (a 41 gal. tank in each wing root); the SR-8D used 73 octane fuel, and SR-8E used 80 octane fuel. Fuel cap. to 130 gal. was available. Baggage allowance was 150 lbs. (50 lbs. under rear seat, and 100 lbs. in rear bag. compt.); this included anchor and mooring gear (25 lbs.) for seaplane. The airfoil on the SR-8 (a modified Clark Y) was flatter on the bottom and had a sharper leading edge; the right wing-tip had "wash-out" and the left tip had "wash-in" for better behavior in the "stall." A controllable prop, electric engine starter, generator, battery, cabin heater and ventilators, leather upholstery, wheel brakes, parking brake, Pyrene fire extinguisher, navigation lights, cabin lights, windshield and windows of safety-glass, assist ropes, ash trays, safety-belts, and first-aid

kit were standard equipment. A constant-speed prop, extra instruments, extra fuel cap., landing lights, paraflares, parachute-type seats, oil cooler, radio gear, wheel streamlines, Edo pontoons, skis, and custom finish were optional. The next "Reliant" development was the SR-9 series as described here in the chapter for ATC # 621.

Listed below are SR-8D and SR-8E entries as gleaned from registration records:

NC-16136;	SR-8E	(# 9701)	Wright 320
-16137;	"	(# 9703)	"
-16140;	SR-8D	(# 9704)	Wright 285
-16141;	"	(# 9705)	"
-16134;	"	(# 9709)	"
-16149;	"	(# 9721)	"
-16151;	"	(# 9722)	"
-16153;	"	(# 9724)	"
-16154;	"	(# 9726)	"
NC-59V;	"	(# 9727)	"
-16163;	"	(# 9736)	"
-16164;	"	(# 9737)	"
-16167;	"	(# 9740)	"
-16155;	SR-8E	(# 9741)	Wright 320
-16170;	SR-8D	(# 9745)	Wright 285
-16177;	SR-8E	(# 9752)	Wright 320
-16181;	SR-8D	(# 9755)	Wright 285
-16175;	"	(# 9758)	"
-16185;	SR-8DM	(# 9763)	"
-16129;	SR-8E	(# 9765)	Wright 320
-16187;	SR-8D	(# 9769)	Wright 285
-16198;	SR-8E	(# 9780)	Wright 320
-17100;	"	(# 9781)	"
-17111;	"	(# 9783)	"
-17103;	SR-8D	(# 9786)	Wright 285
-16183;	"	(# 9787)	"
-17108;	"	(# 9788)	"

"Reliant" SR-8E was powered with 320 h.p. Wright engine.

-16196;	SR-8E	(# 9789)	Wright 320
-18427;	SR-8D	(# 9796)	Wright 285
-17102;	SR-8E	(# 9797)	Wright 320
-17104;	"	(# 9799)	"
-17118;	"	(# 9804)	"
-17124;	SR-8D	(# 9806)	Wright 285
NC-2214;	SR-8E	(# 9818)	Wright 320
-17126;	"	· (# 9823)	"

This approval for ser. # 9701 and up; ser. # 9721 later mod. to SR-8E; ser. # 9765 to Curtiss-Wright Corp.; ser. # 9783 to Red Streak Airways of Mass.; ser. # 9789 to Chas. J. Correll, the "Andy" of the "Amos and Andy" team of radio fame; ser. # 9806 on floats in R.I.; one SR-8E as UC-81B in USAAF; this approval expired 9-30-39.

Profile shows robust lines of "Reliant" in SR-8 series.

ATC # 610
(6-2-36)
FAIRCHILD, 24-C8F.

Fairchild 24-C8F was handsome combination with inline "Ranger" engine.

Under almost continuous modification and improvement since 1932 the rather demure "Fairchild 24" was fast gaining a worldwide reputation as being an airplane that any pilot, regardless of age or experience, could fly well with ease and in perfect safety. In this new Ranger-powered model 24-C8F for 1936 Fairchild Aircraft now had a ship that was perhaps even a little easier to fly, noticeably smoother, a little roomier, somewhat sturdier, and costing even less for everyday operation and upkeep. Along with these important qualities was the built-in bonus of smartness, a refreshing amount of comfort, practical utility in everyday use, and a rather exquisite finish over pleasant contours. Honestly, an airplane that just about anyone could be proud of, even a millionaire. There was some hesitance, a sort of wait and see, when Fairchild introduced a Ranger-powered "Twenty Four" the year previous as the 24-C8D, but in due time the combination was accepted and a good future for it was being predicted. Most of the comment around where fliers gathered was that this new airplane (the 24-C8F) was just about as nice as an airplane can be. Sure, the 6 cyl. "Ranger" engine with its long crankshaft was perhaps not as snappy or gutsy as the more familiar and more popular Warner "Super Scarab" radial, and there were still some cooling problems with the "Ranger" at high altitudes in extreme summer heat, but otherwise the 24-C8F was a thoroughly enjoyable airplane; an airplane that was an ex-

cellent vehicle for those that took to flying as a sport, or occasionally as an added convenience in their daily life. From all the praises received by this airplane we can assume it was a happy creation for the private pilot.

The Fairchild model 24-C8F was a rather neat and pleasant-looking high-winged cabin monoplane with seating arranged for 2 or 3. The so-called "rumble seat" in back, normally occupied by a third person, could be folded back out of the way to make room for piles of luggage, an armful of sporting gear, or just about enough of anything for up to a week's vacation. If need be, the 24-C8F could even double as a handy freighter with about 400 lbs. or so strapped down in the cabin. As it stood there quite tall, it was easy to walk up to this airplane without hunching over, and a large door on each side offered convenient step-up into the widened cabin area. A rather handsome decor with soft cushions, fine upholstery, and decorative interior trim prompted one to fly more often, on visits here and there, dressed neatly or in one's finest. Generally, the 24-C8F was an owner-flown airplane, and treated with almost lavish respect; most owners felt obliged to take good care of it and the airplane was quick to return the affection. The 24-C8F was not a millionaire's airplane, but a millionaire sportsman from Texas was fascinated with this new model and bought it on the spot; he had been flying an older "Twenty Four" which he traded in. As powered with the 6 cyl. inverted inline "Ranger" 6-390-D engine

Fairchild 24-C8F was big favorite with week-end pilots.

rated 145 h.p. the 24-C8F nonchalantly demonstrated a seemingly effortless performance with a reserve of power that assured peace of mind. The sweet-running 6 cyl. "Ranger" engine with its inherent smoothness had some beautiful characteristics, and the 24-C8F seemed quite happy with the association. The long, slender nose produced a gracefully streamlined appearance that was quite pleasant to look at, and it added some steadiness to normal flight; flying the long-nosed 24-C8F was simple and a pleasing experience. This was now the second Fairchild 24 with "Ranger" power, and its behavior gave assurance that the Ranger-powered version would have a solid place in the "Twenty Four" lineup from now on. The type certificate for the model 24-C8F was issued 6-2-36 and some 41 examples of this model were manufactured by the Fairchild Aircraft Corp. at Hagerstown, Md.

Listed below are specifications and performance data for the Fairchild model 24-C8F as powered with Ranger 6-390-D3 engine rated 150 h.p. at 2350 r.p.m. at sea level; length overall 24'10"; height overall 7'4"; wingspan 36'4"; wing chord 66"; total wing area 173 sq. ft.; airfoil (NACA) N-22; wt. empty 1569 (1536) lbs.; useful load 831 (864) lbs.; payload with 40 gal. fuel 398 (431) lbs. (2 pass. and 58-91 lbs. bag.); figures in parentheses as later allowed; gross wt. 2400 lbs.; max. speed 130 at sea level; cruising speed (.80 power) 120 at sea level; cruising speed (2100 r.p.m.) 121 at 7200 ft.; landing speed (with flaps) 50; landing speed (no flaps) 57; takeoff run 460 ft.; climb 715 ft. first min. at sea level; ser. ceiling 14,100 ft.; gas cap. 40 gal.; oil cap. 3 gal.;

cruising range (.75 power) at 9.5 gal. per hour 460 miles; price $5540 at factory. Early examples of the 24-C8F used the 6-390-D engine rated 145 h.p. at 2250 r.p.m. at sea level; there was very little apparent difference in performance.

Specifications and data for 24-C8F as seaplane (24-C8FS) on Edo 44-2425 twin float gear same as above except as follows: length overall 29'0"; height overall (on water) 12'0"; wt. empty 1763 lbs.; useful load 787 lbs.; payload with 40 gal. fuel 355 lbs. (2 pass. and 15 lbs. bag.); gross wt. 2550 lbs.; max. speed 117 at sea level; cruising speed (.80 power) 110 at sea level; cruising speed (2100 r.p.m.) 108 at 5000 ft.; landing speed (with flaps) 52; landing speed (no flaps) 59; climb 510 ft. first min. at sea level; ser. ceiling 11,000 ft.; cruising range (.75 power) at 9.5 gal. per hour 420 miles; price approx. $7000 at factory. Seaplane allowed 27 lbs. baggage which included 15 lbs. for anchor and mooring gear.

The fuselage framework, now widened, was built up of welded 4130 steel tubing, heavily faired to a rounder contour with spruce formers and fairing strips, then fabric covered. The modish interior was arranged to seat 2 or 3; the 2 front seats were side by side, and a folding seat could be erected for a third person in back. The folding seat was placed in the middle and baggage was placed in the space on either side, or the seat could be folded up and the whole area back there used for luggage and packages. Various amounts of baggage were allowed according to payload available. The cabin walls were lined with Kapok, and upholstered in rich

On Edo floats the 24-C8F was excellent seaplane.

Bedford cord, or natural leather. The large dash-panel had ample space for radio gear and extra instruments, and was also fitted with a handy glove compartment. The windshield of shatter-proof glass was slanted back at a steeper angle, and all other windows were of heavy Pyralin. A large cabin door and assist ropes on each side provided easy step-up into the cabin; the pilot seat was adjustable, and visibility was adequate from any seat. The interior was pleasantly quiet, almost everything was handy, and all plane-engine controls were operated effortlessly on ball bearings; dual stick-type controls, and adjustable sun-shades were also provided. Cabin ventilators and a cabin heater were an optional extra. The sturdy wing, in 2 halves, was built up of solid spruce spars routed to an I-beam section with spruce and mahogany plywood truss-type wing ribs; the leading edges were covered with mahogany plywood sheet and the completed framework was covered in fabric. The Freise-type "slotted" ailerons were very effective at lower speeds; split-type trailing edge wing flaps, manually operated, allowed a steeper approach and lowered the landing speed. Flaps not to be lowered above 94 m.p.h. A 20 gal. fuel tank was mounted in the root end of each wing-half; an extra 20 gal. tank could be mounted in place of the rear seat. The wing-bracing struts were tied-in effectively into a very strong truss with the out-rigger type landing gear. The novel semi-cantilever landing gear of 110 in. tread, first introduced on the 24-C8E, was designed to create less drag, but it was a little spindly as compared to the standard sport-type gear. If desired, the sport-type gear with wheel pants was available as a replacement; wheel pants were also available for the semi-cantilever gear. Low-pressure 6.50x10 tires on Warner wheels were equipped with toe-operated mechanical brakes; Fairchild-made oleo-spring shock struts had a full 8 in. travel to soak up abnormal shock. Fittings were provided in the fuselage to mount Edo 44-2425 pontoon gear; skis for winter flying were also available. The tail group was a composite structure of cantilever design; horizontal stabilizer and vertical fin were made up with spruce spars and ribs covered with mahogany plywood sheet. Rudder and elevators were of welded steel tubes and formers covered with fabric; the right elevator was fitted with adjustable trim tab. A Hartzell wooden prop, electric engine starter, 12-volt battery, oil-cooling radiator, wheel brakes, 8 in. full-swivel tail wheel, parking brake, wiring for navigation lights, fire extinguisher, compass, safety-belts, assist ropes, ash trays, first-aid kit, and tool kit were standard equipment. A Curtiss-Reed metal prop, engine-driven or wind-driven generator, navigation lights, landing lights, paraflares, bonding and shielding, radio gear, clock, sport-type gear with wheel pants, Edo twin-float gear, skis, aux. fuel tank, and extra instruments were the options available. The next development in the Fairchild 24 was the model 24-H as described here in the chapter for ATC # 632.

Listed below are 24-C8F entries as gleaned from registration and factory records:

NC-15987;	24-C8F	(# 3100)	6-390-D
-16676;	”	(# 3101)	”
-16677;	”	(# 3102)	”
-16678;	”	(# 3103)	”
-16679;	”	(# 3104)	”

-16680;	"	(# 3105)	"
-16681;	"	(# 3106)	"
-16682;	"	(# 3107)	"
-16683;	"	(# 3108)	"
-16684;	"	(# 3109)	"
-16685;	"	(# 3110)	"
-16810;	"	(# 3111)	"
-16811;	"	(# 3112)	"
-16812;	"	(# 3113)	"
-16813;	"	(# 3114)	"
-16814;	"	(# 3115)	"
-16815;	"	(# 3116)	"
-16816;	"	(# 3117)	"
-16817;	"	(# 3118)	"
-16818;	"	(# 3119)	"
-16819;	"	(# 3120)	"
-16826;	"	(# 3121)	6-390-D3
-16827;	"	(# 3122)	"
-16828;	"	(# 3123)	"
-16829;	"	(# 3124)	"
-16830;	"	(# 3125)	"
-16831;	"	(# 3126)	"
-16832;	"	(# 3127)	"
-16833;	"	(# 3128)	"

-16834	"	(# 3129)	"
-16835;	"	(# 3130)	"
-16851;	"	(# 3131)	"
-16852;	"	(# 3132)	"
-16853;	"	(# 3133)	"
-16854;	"	(# 3134)	"
-16855;	"	(# 3135)	"
-16856;	"	(# 3136)	"
-16857;	"	(# 3137)	"
-16858;	"	(# 3138)	"
-16859;	"	(# 3139)	"
-16860;	"	(# 3140)	"

This approval for ser. # 3100 and up; ser. # 3106, 3126, 3128, 3130 not verified; ser. #3100 through # 3110 were equipped with semi-cantilever landing gear; ser. # 3111 and up were equipped with sport-type landing gear; ser. # 3107 on Edo floats; ser. # 3121 and up had (150 h.p.) 6-390-D3 engine; ser. # 3133 and 3137 to Porto Rico; one each 24-C8F to England and Argentina; 4 of 24-C8F to Coast Guard as J2K-1; one 24-C8F to USAAF as UC-61J; this approval expired 9-30-39.

24-C8F showing optional sport-type landing gear.

ATC # 611
(7-10-36)
PORTERFIELD, 35-W.

Porterfield 35-W was best of "Flyabout" series.

Miscellaneous flying by miscellaneous fliers was finally making a comeback, and airplanes such as the "Porterfield" were helping to make that possible. Among those numbered as miscellaneous fliers was a small group that passed as sportsman-pilots, pilots who didn't need an airplane necessarily to help them make a living. Also, they were pilots who could usually afford to spend a little more money for a somewhat better airplane. This then was the segment of the market that the "Model 35-W" was tailored for. As the "Deluxe Sport," or simply as the Model 90, the 35-W was powered with the 5 cyl. Warner "Scarab Jr." engine of 90 h.p., and came fully equipped for better enjoyment. To include those sportsman-pilots that weren't all that flush with money at one time, the "Deluxe Sport" was available for $965 down and balance payable in 12 months. "Buy it on time and pay as you fly." The first formal exhibit of the 35-W was at the New York City Air Show in January of 1937, and then at the Los Angeles Air Show in March where the show-plane was sold on the first day of the exhibit. One owner picked up his "Deluxe Sport" at the factory and flew it to Montana where he lived; the "Sport," he said, would enable him to visit friends and relatives that were scattered all over the state. In October of 1937 a Los Angeles couple slipped away from friends, and eloped to Las Vegas in a 35-W to get married; they decided they couldn't wait any longer to get married, and it did make for spectacular local news. A doctor in California was quite proud of his "Sport" and used it frequently for fun and relaxation from business pressures; sometimes he would just wash and polish it. It has been said that a flying-school operator had one on the flight-line, but he only used the 35-W for advanced phases of pilot instructions, not everyone got to fly it. It was generally felt that the 35-W "Deluxe Sport" was not just another "Porterfield" so it was perhaps treated with a little more respect. By late 1938 the Model 90 (35-W) known as the "Deluxe Sport" had run its course and a few left-over airframes were modified into a version called the Model 75-C. By this time the so-called "flat four" aircooled engine (horizontally opposed) had taken over the lightplane industry by storm, so Porterfield redesigned this airplane to mount the 4 cyl. Continental engine of 75 h.p. The "radial" aircooled engine was losing favor by now, and Porterfield was amazed to find that the "flat four" of 75 h.p. was delivering almost the same performance at less operating cost. The 75-C was basically the same airplane except for a redesigned tail-group

Warner-powered 35-W offered high performance on a budget.

and the front end which was fashioned into new lines to fit the new engine.

The Porterfield model 35-W was a perky-looking little cabin monoplane with seating arranged for 2 in tandem. Because it was designed more or less as a sport-plane it was more fully equipped and available in a broader choice of colors and schemes. And too, because it was a "Sport" it was more or less pampered, and not relegated to back-breaking duties that befell other "Porterfield" airplanes. As powered with the popular 5 cyl. Warner "Scarab Jr." engine of 90 h.p. it delivered a creditable performance, and was perhaps the top-dog in this type of airplane. Louise Thaden, popular aviatrix, who generally flew the "Travel Air" or "Beechcraft" types, set a closed-course record for lightplanes in the 35-W at 109.58 m.p.h. during a race meet. The 35-W was not considered fast, but it could move out when pushed a little. Porterfield Aircraft was still manufacturing the Model 35 in its various other versions, of which the 35-70 was the most popular, but a new day for the lightplane was looming on the horizon, and Porterfield was preparing for it. They had a front-line contender in the model CP-50, and the proven 35-W was later modified into the interesting Model 75-C. It was hard to realize how easy the "old 35" airframe could become a new airplane. The type certificate for the model 35-W was issued 7-10-36 and some 25 or more examples of this model were manufactured by the Porterfield Aircraft Corp. at Kansas City, Mo. Early in 1937 Porterfield Aircraft was forced to move to larger quarters and set up a schedule for the manufacture of 3 airplanes per day; they also had purchased the famous "Richards Field"

which was the very first airport to operate in the Kansas City area.

Listed below are specifications and performance data for the Porterfield 35-W (35-90) as powered with 5 cyl. Warner "Scarab Jr." (Series 40) engine rated 90 h.p. at 2025 r.p.m. at sea level; length overall 20'1"; height overall 6'9"; wingspan 32'0"; wing chord 56.25"; total wing area (incl. fuselage section) 147 sq. ft.; airfoil Mod. Munk M-6; wt. empty 825 lbs.; useful load 501 lbs.; payload with 18 gal. fuel 200 lbs. (1 pass. & 30 lbs. bag.); gross wt. 1326 lbs.; max. speed (with ring cowl & wheel pants) 133; cruising speed (.90 power) 120 at sea level; cruising speed (.75 power) 110; landing speed 42; takeoff run 230 ft.; climb 900 ft. first min. at sea level; ser. ceiling 16,500 ft.; gas cap. 18 gal.; oil cap. 3 gal.; cruising range (.75 power) at 5.9 gal. per hour 340 miles; price at factory first quoted as $2695, then quickly changed to $2895, by September of 1937 it was $2995, and finally (completely equipped) for $3145. First available for $698 down and 12 monthly pmts., finally raised to $998 down and 12 monthly pmts.

The model 75-C was built around the 35-W airframe and faired out in front to blend in with dimensions of the 75 h.p. Continental engine, which of course, was a "flat four." No details were available for the 75-C at this time, but apparently the 75-C was still very similar to the 35-W and performed just about as well. It was reported that less than 20 of the 75-C were built.

The construction details and general arrangement of the Porterfield 35-W were typical to that of the Model 35-70 except as follows. The main difference of note was installation of the 5 cyl. Warner 90 engine and some slight modifications

Porterfield 75-C was designed to use up left-over "Flyabout" parts.

necessary to this combination. Another difference of interest was the amount of optional equipment available for the 35-W "Deluxe Sport." Because it was in the sport-type category the 35-W was normally equipped with many features available only as options on other Porterfield models. The 35-W was clearly the best looking, best equipped, and best performing airplane in the "35" series. This airplane could be flown solo from either seat. The 5 cyl. Warner engine was cowled in nicely with a drag-reducing ring, and the exhaust manifold was fitted with carburetor heater. Normally a wooden prop was installed, but a ground-adjustable metal prop was optional. The baggage compartment with allowance for up to 40 lbs. was behind the rear seat; an outside door to this compartment was optional. The 18x8-3 Goodyear "airwheels" were equipped with disc-type brakes; 6.00x6 wheels and tires were also available. Streamlined metal wheel pants for either wheel size were optional. The spring-leaf tail skid was standard, but a 6x2 steerable tail wheel assembly was optional. A battery, wind-driven generator, navigation lights, landing lights, a parking brake, radio gear, and carpet for the floor were other options. The 75-C was identical in most respects except that it was powered with the Continental A-75-8 engine rated 75 h.p. at 2600 r.p.m. There seems to be no rhyme or reason as to why the 75-C was included on this same approval when very often a new ATC was required for much less, but unofficial hangar-talk tells it this way; there were a bunch of fuselage frames left over from 35-W

production, so it was decided to use up these left-overs in the 75-C design. The prototype 75-C (32312) first flew in the Fall of 1939. The next Porterfield development was the model CP-50 as described here in the chapter for ATC # 690.

Listed below are Model 35-W entries as gleaned from registration records:

NC-16401;	35-W	(# 301)	Warner 90
-17012;	"	(# 302)	"
-17013;	"	(# 303)	"
;	"	(# 304)	"
;	"	(# 305)	"
-17014;	"	(# 306)	"
-17047;	"	(# 307)	"
;	"	(# 308)	"
-17049;	"	(# 309)	"
-18520;	"	(# 310)	"
;	"	(# 311)	"
-18745;	"	(# 312)	"
-18746;	"	(# 313)	"
-18747;	"	(# 314)	"
-18744;	"	(# 319)	"
-20700;	"	(# 320)	"
-19448;	"	(# 321)	"
;	"	(# 322)	"
-20705;	"	(# 323)	"

This approval for 35-W ser. # 301 and up, also for 75-C ser. # 650, 1651 and up; no listing available for ser. # 304, 305, 308, 311, 314, 315, 316, 317, 318, 322, and up; approval expired 4-20-42.

Howard model DGA-8 was patterned after the famous "Mr. Mulligan".

Very few airplanes have the classic lineage that is enjoyed by the "Howard" DGA monoplanes. This heritage was hammered-out mostly by the enthusiasm and dedication of one man, one Ben O. Howard. After some 12 years of dreams, schemes, and back-breaking work the "formula" devised by Benny Howard was to exalt him in the hearts and minds of his fellow men. That particular year was 1935, a great year for air-racing, a year remembered by many as the "Benny Howard National Air Races." Airplanes designed and built by this unusual craftsman had taken all 3 of the main events— the celebrated Thompson, the Greve, and the Bendix Trophy races. The name on everyone's lips was "Mr. Mulligan," a long-legged, high-winged, cabin monoplane that certainly seemed out of place in a line-up of pure racing airplanes. The all-white "Mr. Mulligan" was not supposed to be a racing airplane—"what we wanted was a highly efficient four-place cabin airplane." The "we" in this case was Benny Howard and his friend the gifted Gordon Israel. Although quite normal in its basic configuration "Mr. Mulligan" was equipped with a special brand of design that the pair called "go-grease." The rousing success of this airplane (the DGA-6) laid the ground-work for a commercial series, and the first of these was simply called the DGA-7, although shortly after it was christened "Mr.

Flannigan." Even by November of 1935 rumors were already spreading that "Benny" was building a commercial version of "Mr. Mulligan," but only a few knew that it had been completed, tested, and delivered by early 1936. Four more airplanes were already on the floor in various stages of construction. The first model to be ear-marked for any volume production was the DGA-8, a 4-seater that also looked quite a lot like "Mr. Mulligan," but it was powered with the popular 7 cyl. Wright engine. This model was introduced to the private-owner and the business executive as a speedy conveyance to provide the utmost in performance, utility, and in reliability. Actually, performance of the DGA-8 was something special for its day. The model DGA-8 was formally announced in November of 1936 and one of the first examples was flown off to California on a leisurely shake-down cruise; with much showing-off along the way, it was then delivered to a waiting customer. The "Howard" was also a surprise appearance at the Pacific Aircraft & Boat Show (March 1937) where it created quite a stir among pilots who had waited long for a decent sight of it. The model DGA-8 was again the center of attraction when it appeared at the Chicago Air Show early in 1938; an example on floats was floating serenely in a pond of water. In May of 1938 Howard Aircraft received an order from the

DGA-8 of Cuban Navy commemorated discovery of "new world" with 22 nation tour; 20,000 mile flight was remarkable venture.

Bureau of Air Commerce (BAC) for 3 of the DGA-8 to be used for airline inspection service; the contract for $49,753 was a needed shot in the arm for the firm. Everyone knew by now that Benny Howard's colorful "DGA" designation stood for "Damn Good Airplane," and believe me, that statement was never disputed.

Benjamin Odell Howard got into aviation in 1922 when he took a job at the Curtiss warehouse in Houston, Texas, assembling war-surplus "Jennies" which were selling quite briskly. He soon acquired a war-surplus "Standard" J-1 of his own after a small down payment; with a few hours of practice he took up his first passenger, hoping to this way earn enough money to pay off what he owed on the plane. Ironically, the plane "stalled," then spun-in, killing the passenger and leaving Benny with a permanent limp from his injuries in the crash. After that he did some barnstorming around the country, but designing and building airplanes had become his passion. Soon he had completed his first home-built project, an open-seated biplane with a Curtiss OX-5 engine. Wanting a catchy designation for his airplanes he called them DGA-1, DGA-2, etc., the first of Howard's "Damn Good Airplanes." His model DGA-2 was a special job built for a rum-runner; it was a modified "Standard" with a "Hisso" engine so it could carry a good load of booze. For a short time Benny Howard was associated with the folks at Alexander Aircraft who built the popular "Eaglerock," and he also flew the mail runs for Robertson Air Lines and Universal Air Lines. In 1929 with his savings of some $2500 he began building the unbelievable little racing-plane called "Pete"—this was the DGA-3.

Powered with a 4 cyl. Wright-Gipsy engine this ship was a veritable phenomenon, and with it he won 5 "firsts" and 2 third places at the 1930 National Air Races. Here he earned the nickname "Pylon Polisher." Next came the twin racers (DGA-4 and DGA-5) called "Ike" and "Mike." This pair of speedsters was also successful and earned Benny Howard a small fortune. By now "Benny" was flying for United Air Lines and they frowned on his racing activities, so he was more or less grounded as a racing pilot. But, by special permission, he was allowed to participate in the 1935 Bendix Trophy Race, the race where he and Gordon Israel turned up winners in the "Mr. Mulligan" (DGA-6) by a very narrow margin. In 1936 the legendary "Mr. Mulligan" was back in the Bendix Race; with Benny Howard this time was his bride Maxine who was flying in her first race. After being ahead of the pack for most of the race a propeller blade tore itself loose over New Mexico, and the vibration just about tore the engine from its mounts. The emergency landing was a controlled crash; both Maxine and Benny had suffered grave injuries. Late that year Benny Howard was nearly healed and back to work with "United" as a research and test pilot. The Howard Aircraft Co. was formed early in 1936 and incorporated the following year; the plant used was the former "Mattie" Laird factory on West 65th Street near the Chicago Municipal Airport. Several of Laird's employees were hired on at Howard. The first few customers for the model DGA-8 paid full price in advance, so that Howard would have some money to work with; certainly a showing of faith and understanding.

As designed by Benny Howard and Gordon

"Mr. Flanigan" was prototype for Howard's commercial DGA series.

Israel the model DGA-8 was a 4-5 place high-winged cabin monoplane of near-normal lines, but of calculated proportion garnished with special treatment; this was the "go-grease" that Howard very often spoke of. The big, roomy cabin provided plenty of leg-room, sound-proofing muffled the engine noises, and a large baggage compartment kept the cabin area free of loose luggage. Of course, the big, round, cowled engine up front did hamper the view directly forward, but pilots learned ways to get around that. Because of the way it stood on its tall landing gear the DGA-8 looked bigger than it actually was, and it fairly struck an awe into those who saw it for the first time. Benny Howard was heard to say that the DGA-8 was so easy to handle even a novice pilot would have no problems, but that was not necessarily so! The proud DGA-8 was every inch a high-performance airplane and it had to be manipulated with tender but deliberate motion. As powered with the 7 cyl. Wright R-760-E2 engine rated 320 h.p. the DGA-8 was not the thundering monster that "Mr. Mulligan" was, but it was an exceptional airplane by any man's criteria. It even exceeded Benny Howard's optimistic expectations! This type certificate was issued 7-15-36 and some 12 or more examples of this model were manufactured by the Howard Aircraft Co. of Chicago, Illinois; the company was not yet incorporated at this time and wholly owned by Ben O. Howard and his associates. Gordon Israel was gen. mgr. & chf. engr.; Fred B. Novinger sales mgr.

Listed below are specifications and performance data for the Howard model DGA-8 as

powered with Wright R-760-E2 engine rated 320 h.p. at 2200 r.p.m. at sea level (350 h.p. at 2400 r.p.m. available for take-off); length overall 25'8"; height overall 8'9"; wing span 38'0"; wing chord at root 72"; total wing area 186 sq. ft.; airfoil NACA-2R12; wt. empty 2330 (2300) lbs.; useful load 1470 (1500) lbs.; payload with 48 gal. fuel 959 lbs.; figures in parentheses as later amended; gross wt. 3800 lbs.; max. speed 185 at sea level; cruising speed (1950 r.p.m.) 185 at 10,-000 ft.; cruising speed (.66 power) 186 at 8900 ft. and 191 at 12,000 ft.; landing speed (with flaps) 52; landing speed (no flaps) 63; climb 1800 ft. first min. at sea level; ser. ceiling 20,000 ft.; gas cap. 48-97 gal.; oil cap. 7-8 gal.; cruising range (2000 r.p.m. at 8900 ft.) at 17 gal. per hour 900 miles; price $14,850 at factory. Cap. to 127 gal. fuel and 11 gal. oil was optional.

Specifications and data for DGA-8 as seaplane on Edo 39-4000 twin-float gear same as above except as follows: wt. empty 2636 lbs.; useful load 1263 lbs.; payload with 97 gal. fuel 461 lbs. (2 pass. and 120 lbs. bag.); payload with 48 gal. fuel 755 lbs. (4 pass. and 75 lbs. bag.); gross wt. 3899 lbs.; gross wt. allowance for seaplane later raised to 4100 lbs.; performance with floats was less than landplane by about 5%. A lower dorsal fin, with larger vertical fin and rudder was required for off-water operation.

The fuselage framework was built up of welded 4130 steel tubing, heavily faired to shape with wooden formers and fairing strips, then fabric covered; the forward portion was covered with dural metal panels. Windows were of safety-glass and cabin walls were lined heavily with Seapak for sound-proofing and insulation. Ample cabin dimensions allowed comfortable

DGA-8 seaplane in Canadian service.

seating for 4, and just a little squeeze for 5. Baggage compartment behind the cabin had allowance for 120 lbs.; a hat shelf was provided behind the rear seat. Cabin door was normally on the right side, but an extra door on the left side was optional. Flight controls were dual wheels and rudder pedals. The robust wing framework was built up of solid spruce spar beams of heavy section with narrow-spaced spruce and plywood truss-type wing ribs. The entire wing framework was covered with plywood sheet and this in turn was covered with fabric; the Howard wing panels were exceptionally strong and stiff against torsion. Trailing edge type speed-reducing wing flaps, of 22 sq. ft. area, were manually operated; flaps not to be extended above 108 m.p.h. The semi-cantilever landing gear of 90 in. tread was of 2 streamlined legs connected to Howard-built internally-mounted shock struts; Goodyear wheels with hydraulic disc brakes were fitted with 7.50x10 (6 ply) tires and shrouded with metal wheel pants. A parking brake was also provided. The 10.5 in. streamlined, full-swivel tail wheel was provided with straight-ahead lock for takeoffs and landings. The fabric-covered tail group was built up of welded 4130 steel tube spars and sheet steel ribs; the elevators were fitted with aerodynamic "balance horns". For trim the horizontal stabilizer was adjustable in flight. A Hamilton-Standard controllable prop, an electric engine starter, generator, battery, complete set of flight and engine instruments, bonding and shielding for radio, navigation lights, and wheel pants were standard equipment. Cabin heater and ventilator, leather upholstery, fire extinguisher, landing lights, paraflares, radio gear, skis, and Edo pontoons were optional. The standard color schemes were White with Red or Black trim, or

two-toned with Stinson Green and Spartan Green; prototype was Metallic Blue and Bronze. The next Howard developments were the models DGA-9 and DGA-12 as described here in the chapter for ATC # 645.

Listed below are various early entries of Howard monoplanes, including the model DGA-8 as gleaned from registration records:

NR-2Y;	DGA-3	(# 67)	Wright-Gipsy
NR-55Y;	DGA-4	(# 68)	Menasco 160
NR-56Y;	DGA-5	(# 69)	Menasco 160
NR-273Y;	DGA-6	(# 70)	Wasp 550
X-14835;	DGA-7	(# 71)	Wright 420
NC-14871;	DGA-8	(# 72)	Wright 320
-14873;	"	(# 73)	"
-14872;	"	(# 74)	"
-14870;	"	(# 75)	"
-14874;	"	(# 76)	"
-14885;	"	(# 77)	"
;	"	(# 78)	"
-14887;	"	(# 79)	"
;	"	(# 80)	"
-18204;	"	(# 81)	"
-18209;	"	(# 84)	"

This approval for ser. # 71 and up; ser. # 67 ("Pete") first reg. as NR-601V; ser. # 71 briefly as DGA-7 with 420 h.p. Wright engine, modified to DGA-8; as 3 pl. the DGA-7 was first reg. to Ben O. Howard, then reg. as DGA-8 to Reggie Robbins; no listing for ser. # 78, 80, 82, 83; one of these could be CF-BET which was del. to Canada and operated on floats, one of these could be ship del. to Cuban Navy, and 2 of these could be airplanes del. to BAC; approval expired 11-12-40.

ATC # 613
(7-23-36)
ARROW, SPORT F.

Arrow "Sport F" with modified wing; shadow shows root-end cutouts.

A few of the "Arrow F" were hurriedly manufactured on ATC # 601 (issued 4-15-36). Then some 3 months later a new certificate was awarded for some modifications to the original design. It seems, from complaints, the original design had problems with airflow around the wing-root which sometimes caused poor control at lower speeds; also, the blanking-off of airflow sometimes "stalled" the whole tail group. This was very disconcerting, to say the least, and several accidents had been attributed to this condition. When the cause of the trouble was finally pin-pointed the wing-root was redesigned to improve the airflow down the fuselage, and a modification kit was distributed free to all owners of affected airplanes. Per instructions dated 6-28-37 the manufacturer sent out prints and necessary parts to make the so-called "gull wing" modification; this alleviated the airflow problem and restored proper control even at lower speeds. Most pilots conceded that it was now a better airplane, but performance was still relatively marginal and reports of behavior in the hands of a novice pilot discounted the possibility of the "Sport F" ever becoming the ideal airplane for the average man-in-the-street. Still, this pixie-like airplane did have an enthusiastic, though small, circle of admirers who enjoyed its novelty. When the "Sport F" finally arrived on the west coast, young Hilda Jarmuth became the first woman to fly it and she thought it was such a lovely airplane! About this time two of the new "Arrow Sport F" were ferried from the factory to a dealer in Seattle without incident, and across that part of the country, for that distance, this has to be a pretty fair endorsement of engine and airplane reliability.

Arrow Aircraft altogether had a life-span of some 14 years, and in that time they had built some wonderful little airplanes. Regards the new "Sport F," litigation in a battle for corporate control dragged on for months, and crippled the company's ability to build airplanes. There was always an extremely large backlog of orders, but insufficient capital for any sort of mass production. Production ended late in 1937 after some 100 airplanes were built and delivered; it is sad that each airplane was delivered at a substantial loss. In July of 1938 airplane ser. # 105 was

Arrow F was popular in plains of mid-west.

fitted with a 125 h.p. Menasco C-4 engine as the "Model M," in hopes of stimulating new business. However, rumors and strife were blighting the future of the Arrow Airplane & Motor Corp., so the hope of new business fell flat. In March of 1939, more as a last-ditch stand, the "Model M" was flown to Wright Field to participate in an Army training-airplane competition, but it lost out without even a chance of entering because of its side-by-side seating! The Army would only accept airplanes with tandem seating. Due to one disappointing circumstance after another, Arrow Aircraft was flat broke by now so the Menasco engine, taken on assignment, was removed from the airplane and shipped back. The mortgage holder promptly foreclosed on all assets, and by November of 1940 the company ceased to exist.

The Arrow Sport "Model F" on this approval was the same stub-nosed monoplane that seated 2, but it came blessed with a few modifications that made it a somewhat better airplane. Much of the distaste for this airplane centered around the bad airflow along the fuselage which could sometimes cause a steep sink-rate; it was this that scared the hell out of old-timers who were accustomed to more "float" in their approaches and landings. This problem "Arrow" rectified with a so-called "gull wing" modification at the wing roots. The gull-wing modification was quite simple and took place in the first 4 ribs from the end; a small notch was cut back in the leading edge and a sizable notch was cut in the trailing edge. This new geometry provided a better pattern of airflow to let the ship float longer and fall-off a little slower. Rudder and elevator control was also stronger and more predictable. The ship was actually quite stable now throughout the whole range of flight. Some

have said the "Arrow F" was actually a rather charming airplane; it made all the right noises, had all the tantalizing smells, and kept a pilot busy enough to be happy. Dual-time on the "Arrow" was averaging $5.50 per hour, and solo-time was going for about $4.50. The type certificate for this new version of the "Arrow F" was issued 7-23-36 and some 100 or more examples were built in all. Manufactured by the Arrow Aircraft Corp. at Lincoln, Neb. Company officers were same as listed previously except for the following changes: F. Pace Woods was gen. mgr.; Clark F. Biesemeier was now chf. engr., Dale M. Myers was sales mgr. & factory superintendent.

Listed below are specifications and performance data for the Arrow "Sport F" as powered with the 8 cyl. Arrow (Ford V-8) engine rated 82 h.p. at 3075 r.p.m. at sea level; length overall 21'4"; height overall 8'10"; wingspan 36'7"; wing chord 66"; total wing area 180 sq. ft.; airfoil NACA-2212; wt. empty (wet) 1172 lbs.; useful load 503 lbs.; payload with 20 gal. fuel 198 lbs.; bag. allow. 28 lbs.; gross wt. 1675 lbs.; max. speed (with coupe-top canopy) 100; cruising speed (2950 r.p.m.) 93; landing speed (with drag-flaps) 45; landing speed (no flaps) 48; climb 500 ft. first min. at sea level; ser. ceiling 12,000 ft.; gas cap. 20 gal.; oil cap. (in sump) 8 qts.; cruising range (2950 r.p.m.) at 6 gal. per hour 300 miles; price $1500 at factory, optional equipment was extra. Wt. empty is with water in radiator, 6.5 gal. at 54 lbs.

The construction details and general arrangement of the "Arrow F" as approved on this ATC were more or less identical to that as approved on ATC # 601 including the following. The most significant change made in this group of airplanes was the change in wing root design. For

Arrow F with winter enclosure.

those airplanes not so fitted, a kit with blueprints, instructions, and material was supplied by the manufacturer to do this job in the field. The kit was supplied free of charge. According to BAC record this modification only applied to airplanes ser. # 1 through # 53; airplanes ser. # 54 and up were apparently built to this new configuration at the factory. The modified "Arrow" (Ford V-8) automobile engine was approved 8-12-35 after stringent government testing. With single (battery) ignition the engine weighed 402 lbs. dry; 6.5 gal. of engine coolant (water) added 54 lbs. to engine weight. Max. r.p.m. of the engine was rather high, so the prop shaft was geared down 1.95 to 1; normal prop r.p.m. was then 1700 or less. The engine used 70 octane fuel and "cruise consumption" ranged from 5 to 6 gal. per hour. The generator and fuel pump were mounted on the engine, and battery was mounted in engine compartment. A new crankcase for the engine was cast in one piece, and this eliminated the excessive seepage experienced with the early welded-up sheet metal case. There was a novel pull-starter in the cockpit; a cable and ratchet claw were connected to engine crankshaft to turn over the engine for starting. Because of "gearing" in the engine the large propeller turned in the opposite direction. The 20 gal. fuel tank was mounted high in the fuselage ahead of the cockpit, and better filled from the right wingwalk because the filler-neck was on that side. The "Arrow F" was still available with the open cockpit, but a demountable coupe-top enclosure was optional. The "Arrow F" was slightly faster with the coupe-top mounted because it smoothed out the airflow over the fuselage; it was allowable to fly with the canopy partially open. A placard warned never to exceed 135 m.p.h. at

any time. Standard equipment was same as listed in previous "Arrow" chapter; compass, clock, engine starter, navigation lights, wheel brakes, and wheel streamlines were optional.

Listed below are "Arrow F" entries as gleaned from various records:

NC-18000;	Arrow F	(# 18)	Arrow 82
-18001;	"	(# 19)	"
-18002;	"	(# 20)	"
-18003;	"	(# 21)	"
-18004;	"	(# 22)	"
-18010;	"	(# 23)	"
-18011;	"	(# 24)	"
-18012;	"	(# 25)	"
-18013;	"	(# 26)	"
-18014;	"	(# 27)	"
-18015;	"	(# 28)	"
-18016;	"	(# 29)	"
-18017;	"	(# 30)	"
-18018;	"	(# 31)	"
-18019;	"	(# 32)	"
	(see below)		
-18752;	"	(# 93)	"
-18753;	"	(# 94)	"
-18754;	"	(# 95)	"
-18755;	"	(# 96)	"
-18756;	"	(# 97)	"
-18757;	"	(# 98)	"
-18758;	"	(# 99)	"
-18759;	"	(# 100)	"
-18760;	"	(# 101)	"
-18761;	"	(# 102)	"
-18762;	"	(# 103)	"
-18763;	"	(# 104)	"
-18764;	Mod. M	(# 105)	Menasco 125
-18765;	Arrow F	(# 106)	Arrow 82
-18766;	"	(# 107)	"

This approval for ser. # 54 and up; ser. # 1 thru # 53 also eligible when modified to conform; NC-18090 was ser. # 33 and both reg. nos. & ser. nos. ran consecutively to NC-18099 which was ser. # 42; NC-18500 was ser. # 43 and both nos. ran consecutively to NC-18519 which was ser. # 62; NC-18700 was ser. # 63 and both nos. ran consecutively to NC-18729 which was ser. # 92; ser. # 82 later as PP-ABB in Brazil; ser. # 101 thru # 107 completed in 1938; approval expired 11-22-40.

Cockpit view shows dual control wheels.

ATC # 614
(7-25-36)
AERONCA, MODEL LC.

Aeronca model LC was last of low-winged series.

As part of the "Aeronca L" series the Model LC was a similar dainty-looking low-winged cabin monoplane, an airplane that still seemed a rather unusual type coming from a factory that had built nothing but comical little flivver-planes. But, aeronautical engineers do have their dreams occasionally, and it is dreams such as these that spawned a vehicle well ahead of its time. Two versions of the "Model L" had already been in production for nearly a year, and they were going well, but "Aeronca" calculated that a third version with a little more power and added appointments would extend the life of this design a while longer. The roster showed that owners were pretty well strung out over the country, but the largest group seemed to be centered in California. Because of the terrain differences encountered in a day's flying, Californians tested the mettle of an airplane nearly every time they went up; because of its lasting popularity here we have to assume the LC did very well in California. There was no need to make excuses for the "Aeronca L" in any version, because it was a delightful airplane with a strong character, but actually there were not enough pilot-owners patient enough to put up with its somewhat sassy behavior at times. The "Model LC", as discussed here, was powered with the Warner "Scarab Jr." engine, and though higher-priced than either the LA or

LB, it was still easy enough to buy at 1/3 down and balance in 12 monthly payments. Even in 1936 the plant was still putting out quite a few of the lovable C-3, and already there were plans to replace this comical little "flivver" with the "Aeronca K," so the future of the "Aeronca L" and especially the LC was becoming doubtful. Then too, interest seemed to be falling off gradually, so the L-series was finally phased out altogether in 1937.

The "Aeronca" model LC was a dainty low-winged cabin monoplane with side-by-side seating for two. This coupe-type airplane was not all that unusual except for its sharply tapered cantilever wing, and its rakish cantilever landing gear. This landing gear was the more unusual because it was fully encased in large metal streamlined "boots." By its very visage and nature you would have to call the "LC" a sport-plane, because it was happier that way; its charm lay in its playful nature and not in its capacity for general work. The rugged airframe was laid out in good aerodynamic proportion and its any-angle beauty was always enough to turn heads wherever it went. Not everyone was impressed with this airplane in the same manner, but a few thought it was the most beautiful thing with wings! As powered with the reliable 5 cyl. Warner "Scarab Jr." engine of 90 h.p. the LC was a spritely machine with a habit-forming per-

LC was also available as seaplane.

sonality. Having the highest power of models in this series, the LC delivered above-average performance and its flight characteristics were described in varying degrees of delightful, down to nasty, but still fun to fly! "A quick and snappy airplane," one said, "but not as responsive as a Monocoupe." While performance was normally excellent, the "stall" characteristics were scary to some; it "spun" fast and clean with very little encouragement, but recovered quite easily. Some also said she behaved well, but watched you out of the corner of her eye, so to speak, to see if you were paying attention. We must admit that no hum-drum airplane would ever bring out comments such as these. Altogether the LC was a good ship, quite at home on the little airports, and good for many hours of fun. The type certificate for the Model LC was issued 7-25-36 and some 25 or more examples were manufactured by the Aeronautical Corp. of America on Lunken Airport in Cincinnati, O. The roster of company officials remained the same as for the previous year except that Walter J. Friedlander became Pres. early in 1937, and Roger E. Schlemmer was still Chf. Engr. About mid-1938 the manufacturing rights, design data, jigs, tools, dies, and all fixtures for the L-type were up for sale, but apparently no sale was reported.

Listed below are specifications and performance data for the "Aeronca" model LC as powered with 5 cyl. Warner "Scarab Jr." engine rated 90 h.p. at 2025 r.p.m. at sea level; length overall 22'4"; height overall 7'0"; wingspan 36'0"; mean aero. chord 58.8"; total wing area 150 sq. ft.; airfoil NACA-2218 at root and NACA-2209 at tip; wing chord at root 72"; wt.

empty 1034 lbs.; useful load 646 lbs.; payload with 28 gal. fuel 286 lbs.; gross wt. 1680 lbs.; max. speed 123; cruising speed (1900 r.p.m.) 108; landing speed (with drag-flap) 48; climb 650 ft. first min. at sea level; ser. ceiling 15,500 ft.; gas cap. 28 gal.; oil cap. 3 gal.; cruising range (1900 r.p.m.) at 5.6 gal. per hour 520 miles; price $3275 at factory.

Specifications and data for LC as seaplane (LCS) as mounted on Edo 47-1965 twin-float gear same as above except as follows: length overall 23'10"; height overall (on water) 9'0"; wt. empty 1193 lbs.; useful load 659 lbs.; payload with 28 gal. fuel 298 lbs.; gross wt. 1852 lbs.; max. speed 116 at sea level; cruising speed (1900 r.p.m.) 100; landing speed (with flap) 55; climb 500 ft. first min. at sea level; ser. ceiling 12,000 ft.; cruising range at 5.6 gal. per hour 475 miles; price $4325 at factory.

The construction details and general arrangement of the "Aeronca LC" was typical to that of the models LA and LB as described in the chapter for ATC # 596, including the following. The main difference in the model LC was installation of the "Scarab Jr." engine, and even that was hardly noticed with the speed-ring cowl shrouding the cylinders. 18x8-3 Goodyear air-wheels were standard, but Hayes wheels with brakes fitted with 7.00x5 tires were optional. Dual stick-type controls were provided, and trimming tab on elevator was adjustable in flight. Baggage allowance was 116 lbs. A Hartzell wooden prop, speed-ring engine cowl, a compass, navigation lights, full-swivel tail wheel, fuel gauge, fire extinguisher bottle, and first-aid kit were standard equipment. An electric engine

An Aeronca LC that migrated to Canada.

starter, battery, wind-driven generator, cabin heater, landing lights, paraflares, radio gear, and drag-flaps were optional. The seaplane was mounted on Edo 47-1965 pontoons and the electric engine starter was then standard equipment. The next Aeronca development was the Model K as described here in the chapter for ATC # 634.

Listed below are Aeronca model LC entries as gleaned from registration records:

NC-16274;	LC	(# 2021)	Warner 90
-16287;	"	(# 2028)	"
-16289;	"	(# 2029)	"
-16292;	"	(# 2030)	"
-16531;	"	(# 2037)	"
-16543;	"	(# 2044)	"
-16544;	"	(# 2045)	"
-16548;	"	(# 2046)	"
-16559;	"	(# 2047)	"
-16568;	"	(# 2049)	"
-16574;	"	(# 2050)	"
-17405;	"	(# 2051)	"
-17410;	"	(# 2052)	"
-17421;	"	(# 2053)	"
-17425;	"	(# 2054)	"
-17430;	"	(# 2055)	"
-17442;	"	(# 2056)	"
-17450;	"	(# 2057)	"
-17478;	"	(# 2058)	"
-17480;	"	(# 2059)	"
-17484;	"	(# 2060)	"
-17496;	"	(# 2061)	"
-17787;	"	(# 2062)	"
-18824;	"	(# 2063)	"
-18880;	"	(# 2064)	"

This approval for ser. # 2015, 2021, 2028, and up; ser. # 2015 first as model LA, eligible when modified to conform; ser. # 2029 as LCS on floats; this approval expired 9-30-39.

ATC # 615
(7- -36)
BEECH, C-17-E.

Most of the rare Beech C-17-E were shipped to Japan.

On occasion a customer would voice a preference for the 7 cyl. Wright R-760 engine, so Walter Beech felt more or less obliged to do them the favor, and it wasn't all that much trouble anyhow. Besides, he always favored the Wright radial engines and had a special liking for the 7 cyl. R-760. The Beech series 17-E, whether in the earlier B-17-E or in this new (1936) model C-17-E, was never much of a seller, but the company must have felt it was a worthwhile addition to the lineup. Since the days of the famous "Whirlwind" the Wright engines had a terrific reputation overseas, so when Japanese interests were contemplating a "Beech" purchase they apparently insisted on Wright power, and Beech just happened to already have a C-17-E handy. They purchased ser. # 78 and Virgil Adamson was "shipped with the airplane" to help set it up. Work on the airplane went very slow because assembling the complicated airplane was being done by Japanese workmen as a training exercise, workmen who would later build examples of the C-17-E right from scratch in a Japanese factory. It took nearly 4 months of patience to unpack and assemble the C-17-E that Virgil Adamson had brought over, and it was flight-tested by a Japanese crew; Adamson had planned to go

along, but the cabin was overflowing with eager Japanese, so he was left behind. Later when Adamson left the harbor for the boat-trip home the C-17-E they had put together was circling overhead, and diving down as a salute to the man who had helped them put together their first "Beechcraft." According to record the Japanese then built 14 examples of the C-17-E type in 1938, 5 were built in 1939, and one in 1940. The complete airplane was built and assembled in Japan, but the Wright engines were boxed and shipped out from the U.S.A. Twenty examples were finally built and apparently none had survived the rigors and ravages of WW2. The Beech C-17-E was barely known in the U.S.A., but it was a well-known plane in Japan.

The Beech model C-17-E was typical to other "Stagger-Wing" types described here, and it too was arranged to seat 4 or 5. The only difference of any significance in the C-17-E was that it was powered with the popular 7 cyl. Wright engine, and that it was the model selected by Japanese interests to be manufactured by them in their homeland under a licensing agreement. In retrospect, the licensing agreement was a rather dubious move, but aircraft companies were reaching out at this time for all the business they could get. No doubt we here in the U.S.A. felt far removed from any involvement in the bickerings abroad, so everybody here was selling to anyone that would buy; just about all of the aircraft companies were doing it. There is no service record available of the 20 or so C-17-E type that the Japanese had built, but it is almost certain that they were used only for various transport purposes. It is unusual that absolutely none had survived the war. So what of the C-17-E in this country? Of the 2 that were actually built here by Beech, both were shipped to Japan. The only other on record is ser. # 73 which first started out as a C-17-R with 420 h.p. Wright engine, and apparently was later modified to a C-17-E by a change of engines. As to what kind of an airplane the C-17-E was, it is safe to assume that this airplane would compare favorably with the C-17-B which also had a 285 h.p. engine. The amount of power installed is not always the measure of an airplane, so there might have been some subtle differences only noticeable to an expert pilot. The type certificate was issued in July of 1936 (no specific date given) and no more than 3 examples appear here under this approval. Manufactured by the Beech Aircraft Co. at Wichita, Kan. The inimitable Walter Beech was pres. & gen. mgr.; R. K. Beech was V.P.; Olive Ann Beech was sec-treas.; Wm. A. Ong was sales mgr.; and Ted Wells was chf. engr.

Listed below are specifications and performance data for the Beech model C-17-E as powered with Wright R-760-E1 engine rated 285 h.p. at 2100 r.p.m. at sea level; length overall 24'5"; height overall 8'2"; wingspan upper and lower 32'0"; wing chord upper and lower 60"; total wing area (incl. fuselage section) 273 sq. ft.; airfoil Clark CYH; wt. empty 2050 lbs.; useful load 1550 lbs.; payload with 98 gal. fuel 747 lbs. (4 pass. and 67 lbs. bag.); gross wt. 3600 lbs.; max. speed 185 at sea level; cruising speed (.75 power) 165 at sea level, 173 at 5000 ft., 177 at 7200 ft.; landing speed (with flaps) 48; climb 1200 ft. first min. at sea level; ser. ceiling 18,500 ft.; gas cap. 98 gal.; oil cap. 6 gal.; cruising range (.75 power) at 17.5 gal. per hour 865 miles; price not listed. Gross wt. later approved at 3615 lbs. Performance figures shown are with fixed-pitch Curtiss-Reed metal prop.

The construction details and general arrangement of the model C-17-E were typical to that of others in the 1936 "Stagger-Wing" series. The only significant difference was installation of the 7 cyl. Wright R-760-E1 engine, and some slight modifications necessary for this combination. Data listed in the chapters for ATC # 602 and # 604 will apply unless otherwise noted. The C-17-E was available with many options and because this model was more or less custom-made, many, or most, of the options were included before delivery. Extra range was offered by an assortment of tank installations that provided 98-121-144 or 167 gal. fuel capacity; oil supply was then increased to 9 gal. The baggage hold was available with an optional golf-bag compartment; normal baggage allowance was 125 lbs., but only 75 lbs. was allowed when 3 occupied the rear seat. An extra entry door was available on the right side, and a camera installation was optional too. A fixed-pitch Curtiss-Reed metal prop was normally provided, but a Hamilton-Standard ground-adjustable, or a "controllable" (two-position) prop was optional. An electric engine starter, Exide battery, Eclipse generator, ammeter, engine-driven fuel pump, fuel gauges, wobble pump, swing-over control wheel, wheel brakes, 7.50x10 wheels fitted with 6-ply low-pressure tires, 10x3 retracting tail wheel, oil-cooling radiator, navigation lights, landing lights, paraflares, bonding and shielding for radio, cabin heat and ventilation, safety-glass throughout, ash trays, assist ropes, and first-aid kit were generally included as standard equipment. Radio gear, parachute-type (Switlik) seats, T-type control column, 24 in. General wheels and tires, pressure-type fire extinguisher, extra fuel and oil cap., and seaplane gear were optional. The next Beech development was the twin-engined Model 18-A as described here in the chapter for ATC # 630; the next Model 17 development was the D-17-R as described here in the chapter for ATC # 638.

Listed below are C-17-E entries as gleaned from various records:

NC-15487;	C-17-E	(#73)	Wright 285
-15836;	"	(#78)	"
;	"	(#117)	"

This approval for ser. # 73 and up; ser. # 73 first reg. as a C-17-R; ser. # 78 later reg. as J-BAOI in Japan; ser. # 117 also shipped to Japan; this approval expired 9-30-39.

ATC # 616
(10-14-36)
LOCKHEED, MODEL 12-A.

Lockheed model 12-A shows its underside as it glides to landing.

Riding in on the coat-tails of the popular "Electra" (Model 10) the new Model 12 (Electra Jr.) was, upon its introduction to service, the fastest transport airplane in the world, being capable of over 230 m.p.h. The "Model 12" was similar to the "Electra" in many ways, but it was a good bit smaller and a whole lot sassier. Actually, the "Twelve" was designed to Bureau of Air Commerce (BAC) specifications called out for a small, fast airliner to serve the many feeder-lines that had not much choice in the selection of up-to-date equipment. Lockheed was rightfully proud of the new "Electra Jr." and billed it as an airliner specially designed for all the business of the smaller lines, and all the local business of the larger lines. The airlines that did equip with the Model 12 were very happy with it, but this airplane had quite an appeal to big-business also; the roster of owners was like a roll-call of the biggest names in this country. The BAC which laid down specs for this airplane in the first place, received one of the first examples off the line (Nov. of 1936), and it was equipped as a flying laboratory; it was crammed to the hilt with gadgets to test the newest aids to navigation, to study blind-flying methods, and operation in severe weather. Bennett Griffin was the pilot; he and "the Twelve" went where pilots normally fear to tread. After a turn or two at the wheel Milo Burcham was convinced the

"Twelve" was equipped with seven-league boots, so he flew one in the 1937 Bendix Trophy race and finished 5th; not a bad showing. Normally, the Model 12 carried 2 pilots and 6 passengers as an airliner, but on occasion 2 passengers were traded off for more fuel to extend the range. The custom-built "Club" version was more plush than the airliner and seating was arranged according to order; the more fancy arrangements were usually limited to 3 or 4 passengers. The airplane we are talking about here was the Model 12-A that was powered with two 9 cyl. Pratt & Whitney "Wasp Jr." SB engines of 400 h.p. each, and that's where it inherited all its verve; the earlier "Electra" (Model 10) had the same engines, but it was a lot larger and heavier, and not nearly so spritely. The speed and high performance of the "Twelve" was tailor-made for the smaller airlines and for big-business; it also had considerable appeal to the military services both here in the U.S.A. and abroad. Lockheed was known as the "merchant of speed" the world over, and the Model 12 was continuing to prove it so.

The Lockheed "Electra Jr." (Model 12) was a smallish, low-winged, twin-engined monoplane of all-metal construction; seating could be arranged in various patterns for up to 8 people. In general, it would be proper to say that the "Model 12" was but a scaled-down version of

Lockheed 12-A prototype prepares for maiden flight.

the earlier "Model 10," but there was more to it than that. The main reason for the "Electra Jr." being was high performance, and this was achieved by using the same amount of power in a much smaller airplane. This high power-to-weight ratio gave the "Twelve" its sassy nature, and its ability to out-fly, and out-climb any other "twin." It was not exactly a go-anywhere airplane, but it could use most of the smaller airports; this ability was especially attractive to the needs of businessmen who could then drop in to conduct business in the smaller towns. The abilities in this airplane were first tailored to the needs of the smaller lines that brought passengers in to the main cross-country routes, but corporations took quite a fancy to this "small twin," so the bulk of "Model 12" production was flying around displaying the various company banners. As powered with 2 "Wasp Jr." SB engines rated 400 h.p. each the "Electra Jr." had power to spare and this, of course, was bound to show up in its personality. It was always eager, but never unruly, and handled very nicely; pilots liked to fly it. At first Lockheed Aircraft wasn't too sure of what the future had in store for the "Model 12," but soon the airplane itself dispelled all doubts, and Lockheed pointed to it with pride. The type certificate for the Model 12 was issued 10-14-36 and some 95 or more examples of this model were manufactured by the Lockheed Aircraft Corp. at Burbank, Calif.

Listed below are specifications and performance data for the Lockheed Model 12-A as powered with 2 "Wasp Jr." SB engines rated 400 h.p. at 2200 r.p.m. at 5000 ft. (450 h.p. at 2300 r.p.m. for takeoff); length overall 36'4"; height overall 9'9"; wingspan 49'6"; wing chord at root 126"; wing chord at tip 42"; total wing area 352 sq. ft.; airfoil Clark Y-18 at root tapering to Clark Y-9 at tip; wt. empty 5765 (5960) lbs.; useful load 2635 (2690) lbs.; payload with 150 gal. fuel and 1 pilot 1320 (1375) lbs. (6 pass. and 300-355 lbs. bag.); gross wt. 8400 (8650) lbs.; figures in parentheses as later amended; max. speed 225 at 5000 ft.; cruising speed (.75 power) 213 at 9600 ft.; landing speed (with flaps) 64-65; climb 1400 (1360) ft. first min. at sea level; ser. ceiling 22,900 (22,300) ft.; gas cap. normal 150 gal.; gas cap. max. 200 gal.; oil cap. 10-14 gal.; cruising range (.75 power) at 42 gal. per hour 750-950 miles; price not listed. Suggested normal cruise was at .75 power, and max. cruise was at .65 power.

The construction details and general arrangement of the Model 12-A were typical to that of the "Electra" model 10-A as described in the chapter for ATC # 551, except as follows. The fuselage of the 12-A was much smaller with arrangement for 2 pilots and 6 passengers; the entry door was on the left side in back, and pilots walked through the cabin area to their compartment in front. Three passengers were seated each side of a center aisle in normal use, but other arrangements in the cabin were optional. Some of the business-plane arrangements had plush over-stuffed chairs, a desk and typewriter, and even a couch for napping; lavatory facilities were standard equipment in all versions. A baggage compartment was behind the cabin area with

Lockheed 12-A as C-40 transport in USAAF service.

outside door on right side, and another compartment was in the nose; the two compts. held 63 cu. ft. with allowance for up to 400 lbs. The tapered cantilever wing panels were bolted to the center-section (C/S) panel which supported the two engine nacelles, and the retractable landing gear; the C/S panel also contained 4 fuel tanks with cap. to 200 gals. The landing gear was of 2 cantilever assemblies fitted with "Aerol" shock struts which retracted into the engine nacelles; 30x13-6 Goodyear airwheels with hydraulic disc brakes were fitted with 6-ply tires. Tires by General (31 in.) were optional. Split-type trailing edge wing flaps of generous area were electrically operated; adjustable trim tabs were fitted to the elevator and one rudder. Hamilton-Standard controllable (two-position) props, electric engine starters, battery, generator, exhaust collector-rings, oil coolers, fuel gauges, navigation lights, retractable landing lights, cabin lights, paraflares, fire extinguishing system, wheel fenders, tail wheel, cabin heater and ventilators, 6 airline-type seats, lavatory, and dual controls were standard equipment. Custom in-

Model 12-A was popular in Canadian service.

Unusual version of C-40 was tested with tricycle gear.

terior with couch, cockpit partition with door, constant-speed props, automatic pilot, radio gear, dual set of brake pedals, extra instruments, abrasion boots for control surfaces, and extra fuel cap. were optional. The next Lockheed development was the Wright-powered model 12-B as described here in the chapter for ATC # 652.

Listed below are Model 12-A entries as gleaned from various records:

NC-16052;	12-A	(# 1201) Wasp Jr. 400	
-16076;	"	(# 1202)	"
-16077;	"	(# 1203)	"
NC-17;	"	(# 1204)	"
-16079;	"	(# 1205)	"
G-AEMZ;	"	(# 1206)	"
NC-58Y;	"	(# 1207)	"
NC-2072;	"	(# 1208)	"
-17309;	"	(# 1209)	"
-17310;	"	(# 1210)	"
-17311;	"	(# 1211)	"
G-AEOI;	"	(# 1212)	"
-16057;	"	(# 1213)	"
-16085;	"	(# 1214)	"
-17341;	"	(# 1215)	"
-17342;	"	(# 1216)	"
-17373;	"	(# 1217)	"
-17374;	"	(# 1218)	"
CF-CCT;	"	(# 1219)	"
-17376;	"	(# 1220)	"
-18127;	"	(# 1221)	"
-18125;	"	(# 1222)	"
-18126;	"	(# 1223)	"
-17379;	"	(# 1224)	"
NR-869E;	"	(# 1225)	"
-18130;	"	(# 1226)	"
-18137;	"	(# 1229)	"
VH-ABH;	"	(# 1236)	"
VT-AJN;	"	(# 1237)	"
G-AFCO;	"	(# 1238)	"
XB-ABW;	"	(# 1239)	"
-18946;	"	(# 1240)	"
-18947;	"	(# 1241)	"
-18948;	"	(# 1242)	"
-18955;	"	(# 1243)	"
-18956;	"	(# 1244)	"
-18957;	"	(# 1245)	"
-18958;	"	(# 1246)	"
-18965;	"	(# 1247)	"
-18970;	"	(# 1250)	"
-18976;	"	(# 1251)	"
-18996;	"	(# 1252)	"
G-AFKR;	"	(# 1267)	"
-17396;	"	(# 1268)	"
-17397;	"	(# 1269)	"
G-AFPF;	"	(# 1270)	"
-17399;	"	(# 1271)	"
NX-18964;	"	(# 1272)	"
-21770;	"	(# 1273)	"
G-AFXP;	"	(# 1274)	"
-18977;	"	(# 1275)	"
-18147;	"	(# 1276)	"
-18900;	"	(# 1277)	"
NC-4000;	"	(# 1280)	"
NC-2630;	"	(# 1281)	"
-19967;	"	(# 1282)	"
NC-2002;	"	(# 1284)	"
G-AGDT;	"	(# 1285)	"
-25624;	"	(# 1286)	"
-33615;	"	(# 1287)	"
NACA-99;	"	(# 1292)	"
-34965;	"	(# 1293)	"
-33650;	"	(# 1294)	"

This approval for ser. # 1201 and up; prototype first-flight on 6-27-36; ser. # 1204 to BAC, also as NC-1; ser. # 1221 later to Venezuela as YV-VOD; ser. # 1227 as JO-1 to U.S. Navy, used by Naval Attache' in Brazil; ser. # 1228 and 1249 as model 12-B (see ATC # 652); ser. # 1230-31-32-33 as JO-2 to U.S. Navy; ser. # 1234-35 to Minister of War (Brazil); ser. # 1248 to Venezuela; ser. # 1253 as XJO-3 to U.S. Navy; ser. # 1254 thru 1266 to USAAF as C-40 series; ser. # 1268 later as NACA-97; ser. # 1278-79 to Brazil; ser. # 1283 as JO-2 to U.S. Navy; ser. # 1288 thru 1291 to Brazil; ser. # 1293-94 were model 12-25, the last 2 civil 12-A manufactured; ser. # 1295 through 1314 were model 12-26 to Netherlands East Indies (del. 1941-42); 17 a/c were also built as model 212 and del. to Netherlands East Indies Air Force; 130 a/c were manufactured in all from 1936 thru 1942.

ATC # 617
(8-24-36)
KINNER "SPORTWING, B-2-R.

The Kinner "Sportwing" B-2-R later became the "Timm 160".

As of Jan. 1937 the "Kinner Airplanes" factory had not turned out any airplanes in over a year, and there was some talk about closing the doors. Prior to this "Kinner" had modified one of their late B-2 "Sportwing" models into what they called a B-2-R, using the 160 h.p. Kinner R5 engine; it definitely showed promise of strong appeal to the playboy type of sportsman-pilot. A few more were built on speculation and one was sold to a local California sportsman, who had traded in his older "Kinner" airplane on the new model. But, the anticipated demand for this sporting vehicle just did not develop. It was about then that Otto Timm, long-time airplane builder and pilot, became interested in the project and decided to try his hand with it. When the Kinner firm finally did go bankrupt, and were forced to close their doors for the time being, Otto Timm had acquired design rights and manufacturing rights to the "Sportster" and to the "Sportwing." The Kinner "Sportwing" B-2-R was then revived more or less on paper as the "Timm Model 160." Having something like this in mind all along, Timm tried to interest the Army Air Corps in this airplane as a primary trainer, but the Army wasn't interested at all because of the side by side seating. Eventually, the design was modified into a two-seated tandem layout, but the Army was more or less committed to other designs, so the Sportster-

Sportwing lost out again. Outside of this strong hope there seemed to be no other future for the "Timm 160," even though it was a natty airplane of unmistakable sporting nature, a plane that commanded admiration wherever it went. In mid-1937 the Timm Aircraft Co. had doubled its factory and shop space at the Grand Central Air Terminal in Glendale by taking over the space formerly used by the Kinner Airplane & Motor Co. Well versed and experienced in this type of work, the Timm shop converted several aircraft for record flights and special missions; various custom-built and experimental airplanes were on the shop floor in various stages of construction just about all the time. The aircraft repair and modification business became its mainstay once again, but Otto Timm still dreamed of building airplanes.

The Timm "Model 160" (nee Kinner B-2-R) was an open cockpit low-winged monoplane with side by side seating for two. Basically, it was a super-sport version of the standard "Sportwing," and the added power thumping through its frame gave it a personality all its own. As introduced in the first few examples the B-2-R (later Timm 160) projected a very saucy appearance with its taut, spraddle-legged stance, and its hefty lines. It had the look of performance and power, but it still managed to look rather neat and tidy. Designed especially for the playboy-type the B-2-R was not associated with normal chores, but it seemed ever-ready to go along with the whims of a sporting pilot; it was a true sport-plane and this seemed to be its undoing. As powered with the 5 cyl. Kinner R5 (Series 2) engine of 160 h.p. the B-2-R (Timm 160) was blessed with confidence and ability; a good pilot could make it all look so easy. This "Sportwing" design was very maneuverable and it was sure-footed in its every move; it was the type of airplane that made a pilot feel good. As the "Timm 160" its sport-type role was played down somewhat, and it was presented more or less as a trainer; it would have been a good trainer for advanced stages of piloting, but in this category it was bucking a lot of big names, and a lot of good airplanes. The "Sportwing," and especially the B-2-R, had not the occasion to touch upon the lives of many people, but those that had the occasion have not forgotten it. The type certificate for the Timm 160 (nee Kinner B-2-R) was issued 8-24-36 and some 4 or more examples of this model were modified from Kinner Airplanes production by the Timm Aircraft Co. at Glendale, Calif. There is no record of this model actually being in Timm production. Otto W. Timm was pres. & chf. engr., R. A. Powell was V.P. & gen. mgr.; Wally D. Timm was sec-treas. & sales mgr. By 1939 the Timm plant and its operation had been moved to Van Nuys, Calif.

Listed below are specifications and performance data for the Kinner "Sportwing" B-2-R (before it became Timm 160) as powered with 5 cyl. Kinner R5 engine rated 160 h.p. at 1850 r.p.m. at sea level; length overall 24'7"; height overall 7'3"; wing span 34'5"; wing chord 72"; total wing area (incl. fuselage section) 198 sq. ft.; airfoil Clark Y; wt. empty 1397 lbs.; useful load 803 lbs.; payload with 42 gal. fuel 358 lbs. (1 pass. & 188 lbs. for bag. & extras); gross wt. 2200 lbs.; max. speed 132 at sea level; cruising speed (1750 r.p.m.) 120 at sea level; landing (stall) speed 45; climb 1040 ft. first min. at sea level; ser. ceiling 17,800 ft.; gas cap. 42 gal.; oil cap. 3.2 gal.; cruising range (1750 r.p.m.) at 10 gal. per hour 460 miles; price not listed.

Listed below are specifications and performance data for the Timm 160 as powered with 5 cyl. Kinner R5 (Series 2) engine rated 160 h.p. at 1850 r.p.m. at sea level; length overall 24'7"; height overall 7'3"; wingspan 34'6"; wing chord (constant) 72"; total wing area (incl. fuselage section) 198 sq. ft.; airfoil Clark Y; wt. empty 1431 lbs.; useful load 739 lbs.; payload with 41 gal. fuel 300 lbs. (1 pass. and 130 lbs. for bag. and extras); gross wt. 2170 lbs.; max. speed 130; cruising speed (.90 power) 125; cruising speed (1675 r.p.m.) 110; landing (stall) speed 45; climb 1050 ft. first min. at sea level; ser. ceiling 17,950 ft.; gas cap. 41 gal.; oil cap. 3.25 gal; cruising range (1675 r.p.m.) at 9.7 gal. per hour 440 miles; cruising range (.90 power) at 10.5 gal. per hour 480 miles; price not listed.

The construction details and general arrangement of the Timm 160 (nee B-2-R) were typical to that of the Kinner "Sportwing" B-2 as described in the chapter for ATC # 522. The major difference in the B-2-R type was installation of the Kinner R5 engine and any

A "Timm 160" that evolved from a Kinner B-2-R.

modifications necessary for this combination. A special bull-nosed cowling was used for the R5 engine which directed airflow around base of the cyls. The wide, open cockpit, entered from either side, was well protected by a large windshield and free from drafts; a small cubby-hole with allowance for 11 lbs. of personal items was in bulkhead behind the seat. There was ample room for 50 lbs. of baggage in each wing-stub; if parachutes were carried, then 20 lbs. each was deducted from the baggage allowance. A fuel tank of 41 gal. cap. was high in the fuselage behind dash-panel providing gravity fuel flow. A wooden prop, exhaust collector-ring; air-operated Eclipse engine starter, battery, fuel gauge, 6.50x10 wheels and tires, mech. wheel brakes, wheel streamlines, 8 in. tail wheel, fire extinguishing bottle, bonding and shielding for radio, wiring for navigation lights, dual controls, and first-aid kit were standard equipment. Extra instruments, clock, compass, navigation lights, landing lights, paraflares, cockpit canopy enclosure, and radio gear were optional. The next Timm development was the model 2SA trainer as described in the chapter for ATC # 733.

Listed below are Kinner B-2-R (Timm 160) entries as gleaned from various records:

NC-14927;	B-2-R	(# 148)	Kinner R5
-14964;	"	(# 226)	"
-14965;	"	(# 230)	"
-16098;	"	(# 231)	"

This approval for ser. # 226 and up; ser. # 148, the experimental prototype, was first as model B-2; ser. # 230-31 later labeled as Timm 160; approval expired 2-16-39.

ATC # 618
(8-27-36)
DOUGLAS, DC3-G2.

American Airlines DC-3 "Flagship" with Wright "Cyclone" engines.

As soon as design and mock-up of the DST "Sleeper" began shaping up it was quite obvious that the generous internal dimensions of the fuselage would be ideal also for various arrangements in a day-plane. So, while work was progressing steadily on the DST, a DC-3 was also being designed. But, the DC-3 was certainly not an afterthought, it just happened to be the inevitable development of a versatile airframe. First it was planned as a 21 passenger "coach type" day-plane with a crew of 3, and then it evolved into a 14 passenger "Club Car" version in which the air-traveler would receive extra care for extra fare. A custom version of the basic "Club Car" model was also available for the business executive and his entourage. By mid-1936 the DC-3 was already flying and American Airlines (AA) had ordered 21 to be delivered as soon as possible; AA took delivery of their first DC-3 (a DC3-G2) on 18 Aug. 1936. AA was the first airline to take delivery of the DC-3 and as fast as they were delivered were put to service on transcontinental routes. Eastern Air Lines (EAL) soon ordered 8 of the DC-3 for their eastern seaboard network; in Jan. of 1937 they inaugurated a daily one-stop round trip service in the 14 passenger DC-3 "Club Car" between New York and Miami. The lone stop was at Charleston, S. C., a 20 min. stop-over for

fuel. Travelers were now able to leave the "winter of New York" and arrive to enjoy the "summer of Miami" in just a few hours. At this time EAL employed male "stewards" and they were schooled in personal attention for air-travelers. Twenty-two started their duties in Dec. of 1936 and they were expected to handle movement of passengers into and out of the aircraft, the handling of baggage, serving meals, relieving the pilot of some of his paperwork, and tending to passenger needs and queries as they came up. With the expansion of their service Pan American Airways (Pan Am) ordered 8 of the DC3-G103 (a high-altitude version) for routes through Mexico, Central America, and the Panama Canal Zone, serving 6 Central American republics along the way; the round trip required 2 days. The Chinese airline CNAC, partly controlled by Pan Am, ordered 3 of the DC-3 for flights that connected with Pan Am's trans-Pacific routes. Transcontinental & Western Air (TWA) also ordered 9 of the DC-3 "Sky Club" and before long every airline in this country, and many from abroad had their names on the waiting list. In 1927 the air fare for a 33 hour flight from New York to San Francisco was $400.; in 1937 the 15 hour flight in the comfort of a DC-3 was only $149.50! As it crisscrossed the nation the DC-3 soon proved that it

70

was the first transport airplane that could make money by just hauling passengers.

The Douglas DC-3, as America's largest landplane, was an all-metal, low-winged, transport monoplane with a selection of many interior arrangements. The standard day-coach layout was 21 passengers in 3 rows of seats, with 7 seats in each row. This version was the most popular and used by most of the airlines here and abroad. The so-called "Club" version seated 14 passengers, 7 on each side of a center aisle, in overstuffed swiveling arm-chairs that offered room and comfort never before available for a reasonable fare. The "Club" flights did charge a little extra fare, but the service became very popular, especially on runs from New York to Chicago and runs from New York to Miami. The crew for all flights was pilot, a co-pilot, and a stewardess. All of the major airlines were equipped with some DC-3 by 1937, and all airlines kept ordering more and more to keep pace with increases in air travel; air travel was gaining popularity by leaps and bounds. In May of 1937 the scheduled airlines of America carried 98,000 passengers, and the following summer months

were even better. Passengers who experienced the delight of traveling by DC-3 were the best advertisers, they told everyone; this kind of endorsement snow-balled into a million passengers, many of whom became regular commuters. As powered with 2 of the 9 cyl. Wright "Cyclone" GR-1820-G2 engines rated 850 h.p. each the DC3-G2 delivered premium performance with the greatest economy, a happy combination that made money for the airlines. As engine development forged forward performance of the DC-3 was also improving; consequently, the DC3-G102 as powered with 2 of the Wright "Cyclone" GR-1820-G102 engines rated 900 h.p. each was the one being ordered in 1937. The Wright "Cyclone" GR-1820-G103 engine was a highly supercharged (high altitude) version developed for Pan Am whose routes operated generally at very high altitudes in countries south of our border. By 1939 the big 9 cyl. Wright "Cyclone" was operating at 1000 h.p. (1200 h.p. for takeoff) and that was nearing the limit for a single-row "radial" engine; all engines of higher power soon became "two-row radials" of larger displacement. Many think of

This Eastern Airline DC-3 was former "war-bird" transport.

A DC-3 of TWA high over Kansas.

the DC-3 as just one kind of airplane, but it was available with so many different engines and outfitted for so many different jobs that it actually became many different airplanes; pilots claim they had to get reacquainted with each different version. The type certificate for the "Cyclone-powered" DC-3 was issued 8-27-36 and some 265 or more examples, including 81 for export, were manufactured by the Douglas Aircraft Co., Inc. on Clover Field in Santa Monica, Calif. A note of interest: the second DC-3 was delivered to AA in July of 1936, they sold it to Ozark Air Lines in 1950; it had worn out 50 sets of engines by then! For all we know, it may still be flying!

Listed below are specifications and performance data for the Douglas model DC3-G2 as powered with 2 Wright "Cyclone" GR-1820-G2 engines rated 850 h.p. at 2100 r.p.m. at 5800 ft. (930 h.p. for takeoff); length overall 64'6"; height overall (3 point) 16'11"; wingspan 95'0"; wing chord at root 170" tapered to tip; total wing area 987 sq. ft.; airfoil at root NACA-2215; airfoil at tip NACA-2206; wt. empty 15,-300 lbs.; useful load 8700 lbs.; payload with 650 gal. fuel 3890 lbs. (21 pass., 3 crew, & 320 lbs. baggage-mail); gross wt. 24,000 lbs.; max. speed 212 at 6800 ft.; cruising speed (.75 power) 188 at 5800 ft.; landing speed (with flaps) 65; climb 950 ft. first min. at SL; ser. ceiling 20,800 ft.; gas cap. 650 gal.; oil cap. 50 gal.; cruising range (.75 power) at 93 gal. per hour 1260 miles; price not listed. Also available as model DC3-G2E.

Specifications and data for model DC3-G102 as powered with 2 Wright GR-1820-G102 engines rated 900 h.p. at 2200 r.p.m. at 6000 ft. (up to 1100 h.p. for take-off) same as above except as follows: wt. empty 15,750 lbs.; useful load 8650 lbs.; payload with 650 gal. fuel 3840 lbs. (21 pass., 3 crew, 270 lbs. baggage-mail);

gross wt. 24,400 lbs. (provisional gross wt. of 24,800 lbs. was allowed); max. speed 216 at 7000 ft.; cruising speed (.75 power) 190 at 6000 ft.; landing speed (with flaps) 67; landing speed (no flaps) 80; climb 900 ft. first min. at SL; ser. ceiling 21,800 ft.; gas cap. normal 650 gal.; gas cap. max. 822 gal.; oil cap. max. 66.5 gal.; cruising range (.75 power) at 100 gal. per hour 1235 miles. The DC-3 was also available with GR-1820-G102A engines rated 900 h.p. at 2300 r.p.m. at 6700 ft., or GR-1820-G103A engines rated 860 h.p. at 2300 r.p.m. at 11,000 ft.; the performance differed only with respect to amount of supercharging applied to the engines.

Specifications and data for model DC3-G202A as powered with 2 Wright GR-1820-G202A engines rated 1000 h.p. at 2300 r.p.m. at 4500 ft. (1200 h.p. for takeoff) same as above except as follows: wt. empty 16,398 lbs.; useful load 8002 lbs.; payload with 600 gal. fuel 3570 lbs. (19 pass., 3 crew, 340 lbs. baggage-mail); gross wt. 24,400 lbs. (provisional gross wt. of 24,800 lbs. was allowed); max. speed 219 at 4500 ft.; cruising speed (.75 power) 196 at 4500 ft.; landing speed (with flaps) 67; climb 980 ft. first min. at SL; ser. ceiling 22,750 ft.; gas cap. max. 822 gal.; oil cap. max. 66.5 gal.; cruising range (.75 power) at 112 gal. per hour 1020 miles; price for the DC-3 averaged about $100,000 each; prices varied according to engines and equipment specified.

The construction details and general arrangement of the Douglas DC-3 was basically similar to the earlier DC-2 except for the enlarged fuselage, the bigger wing, and the greater choice of interior layouts. From the pilot's point of view the DC-3 was a much "busier airplane" because there was now so much more to do, but the co-pilot was a great help in the cockpit. Each airplane was fitted with the latest in radio gear, the most advanced navigational aids, there were all sorts of aerodynamic aids that helped to fly the airplane, including an automatic-pilot, the engines were constantly monitored by all sorts of instruments, propellers were now of the "constant speed" type which changed pitch according to demands from the engine, cabin comfort was monitored by a very efficient air-conditioning system, and the young and usually pretty stewardess saw to it that everyone was comfortable and happy. All this required much work by the crew, but the mastery of it was not all that hard, and crews were proud of their ability. The big landing gear of the DC-3 with 18'6" tread was greatly improved; the long-stroke "oleos" soaked up the shock and roly-poly 45x17-16 tires smoothed out all bumps to barely a ripple. Sound-proofing and insulation minimized noise, weather and vibration to very comfortable levels, and chairs were adjustable to a most comfortable position. The "Club Car" version was naturally less crowded, more plush, and everyone was treated like a dignitary; it's no wonder the service was popular. The DC3-G103 high altitude version as built for Pan Am was even fitted with oxygen equipment for the passengers, as they ascended over the high mountain peaks of Mexico, and South America. The DC-3 was equipped with just about every piece of equipment and instrumentation ever devised by man for an airplane and its engines, so we must assume that the DC-3 was outfitted to do its job well. The next Douglas development was the "Twin-Wasp" powered DC-3A as described here in the chapter for ATC # 619.

Listed below are Cyclone-powered DC-3 entries as gleaned from various records:

NC-16009;	DC3-G2	(# 1545)	2 Cyc. 850
-16030;	"	(# 1546)	"
-16011;	"	(# 1547)	"
-16012;	"	(# 1548)	"
-16013;	"	(# 1551)	"
-16014;	"	(# 1552)	"
-16015;	"	(# 1553)	"
-16016;	"	(# 1554)	"
-16017;	"	(# 1555)	"
-16018;	"	(# 1556)	"
-16019;	"	(# 1557)	"
-16008;	"	(# 1588)	"
-16094;	DC3-G102	(# 1915)	2 Cyc. 900
-16095;	"	(# 1916)	"
-17331;	DC3-G2	(# 1917)	2 Cyc. 850
-17332;	"	(# 1918)	"
-17333;	"	(# 1919)	"
-17334;	"	(# 1920)	"
-17335;	"	(# 1921)	"
-16081;	DC3-G102	(# 1948)	2 Cyc. 900
-16082;	"	(# 1949)	"
-17336;	"	(# 1961)	"
-17337;	"	(# 1962)	"
-17338;	"	(# 1963)	"
-17339;	"	(# 1964)	"
-17320;	"	(# 1966)	"
-17321;	"	(# 1967)	"
-17322;	"	(# 1968)	"
-17323;	"	(# 1969)	"
-17324;	"	(# 1970)	"
-16083;	"	(# 1971)	"
-18113;	DC3-G103	(# 1989)	2 Cyc. 860
-18114;	"	(# 1990)	"
-18115;	"	(# 1991)	"
-18116;	"	(# 1992)	"
-18117;	"	(# 1993)	"
-18118;	"	(# 1994)	"

DC3-G103 was high-altitude version used by Pan American Grace in South and Central America.

-18119;	"	(# 1995)	"
-18120;	DC3-G2	(# 1996)	2 Cyc. 850
-18121;	"	(# 1997)	"
-18122;	"	(# 1998)	"
-18123;	"	(# 1999)	"
-18124;	"	(# 2000)	"
-18936;	DC3-G103	(# 2011)	2 Cyc. 860
-18937;	"	(# 2012)	"
-18949;	DC3-G102	(# 2013)	2 Cyc. 900
-18950;	"	(# 2014)	"
-18951;	"	(# 2015)	"
-18952;	"	(# 2016)	"

This approval also for models DC3-G2E, DC3-G102A (in USAAF as C-49E, C-50A-B-C-D & C-51), the DC3-G103A, and DC3-G202A (in USAAF as C-49A-B-C-D-J-K); 3 of DC-3 del. to CNAC (China) for $300,000. in Jan. 1937; ser. # 1966-67-68-69-70 were "Sky Club" for TWA; ser. # 1989-90-91-92-93-94-95 & # 2011 were high-altitude version del. to Pan Am; of the 265 a/c mfgd., this is only a partial listing.

ATC # 619
(11-28-36)
DOUGLAS, DC3A-SB3G.

An intimate look at the DC3A-SB3G as used by "United."

When the fleet of "Boeing 247" transports used by United Air Lines (UAL) was more or less obsoleted for front-line work by performance of the Douglas DC-2, UAL began seriously to consider purchase of the new DC-3; they needed something like the DC-3 to get back into cross-country competition with other major airlines. W. A. "Pat" Patterson, president of "United," calculated to get an edge on the competition if he could, so he ordered 20 of the DC-3A version which would mount powerful Pratt & Whitney engines and the newly-developed Hamilton-Standard "constant speed" propellers. The engines he would use were the new 14 cyl. two-row "Twin-Wasp" SB3G normally rated at 900 h.p. each that would give UAL the advantage of higher cruising speeds and higher operating altitudes. Of the 20 airplanes in the initial order, 10 would be of the luxurious 14 passenger "Club Car" type, and 10 would be of the standard 21 passenger day-coach type; christened the "Skylounge," the plush 14 passenger planes with arm-chair comfort were offering extra care for extra fare. The first of the DC-3A fleet was delivered in Sept. of 1936 and

UAL soon announced the "Skylounge" service from New York to Chicago; the flight was non-stop on a schedule of 4 hours one way, and it cost only $50. The "Skylounge" service was later offered coast-to-coast on a run from New York to San Francisco, via Chicago. The 21 passenger day-coach version was used on these runs also, but was making many more stops enroute. "United" bally-hooed their "Skylounge" service because of the favorable comment from customers; for about $150 the flight from San Francisco to New York, with 3 stops enroute, took only 15 hours 20 mins. West-bound flights took about 2 hours longer because of the prevailing winds that blew steadily out of the west. The UAL fleet were called "Mainliner" and their service whether Skylounge, Day-Coach, or Sleeper, was becoming very popular again; the record for passengers carried in a month's time was being broken continuously as each month went by. By 1937 domestic airlines were employing 270 young women as "hostesses" on just about every flight in this country; some 42 men were also employed as "stewards," but these were mostly on lines to

DC-3A leaves on its journey west.

foreign countries. The airlines were finally getting a break, they were beginning to make money, and taking on the stature of big business.

The Douglas model DC3A-SB3G, like other versions in the DC-3 series, was an all-metal low-winged transport monoplane of a shape and arrangement that was an indelible forecast of the way things would go in the airline industry. Of very generous dimension and scientific aerodynamic proportion, the DC-3A as built for UAL had normal seating arranged for 21 passengers and a crew of 3; other interior arrangements were optional. This version, the DC-3A, because of more powerful engines and more efficient propulsion, now had more speed, more luxury, more reliability, and greater seat-mile economy than was ever assembled before in

any one airplane. The DC-3A was, of course, basically typical of the other DC-3 designs as built for other airlines, but it was a bit faster, and could operate at higher altitudes; all this because of the more powerful supercharged twin-row radial Pratt & Whitney engines. The 14 cyl. double-row "Twin Wasp" SB3G engines as installed in the DC3A-SB3G were normally rated 900 h.p. at 8000 ft.; they put out about 1100 h.p. for takeoff. "United" received their first DC-3A in Sept. of 1936 and 5 more were delivered in Dec. The "Skylounge" service was inaugurated in Dec. of 1936 between Los Angeles and San Francisco (also from New York to Chicago) and across the country schedules to New York were started early in 1937. With the silvery DC3A-SB3G

Loading cargo for cross-country shipment.

"Mainliner" it was now possible to span the nation in some 15 hours, and you had a choice of being one of 21 passengers in a coach at regular fare, or flying in absolute comfort on the 14 passenger "Skylounge" for extra fare, they say about 1¢ per mile more. Either way the cross-country journey was an impressive trip making air travel a pleasure never before experienced. Passengers traveled in confidence, saving time and saving money; happily, the airlines were making a profit too. UAL ordered more DC-3A periodically, and soon the fleet was so large they were passing each other as they criss-crossed the nation. Douglas had a terrific back-log of orders for various versions of the DST and DC-3; they were being grabbed up as soon as they rolled out of the plant door. When the U. S. Army and Navy finally realized that the makings of a world war lay ahead, they began drafting the DC-3 for military service right at the factory door; others were pulled out from airline service. The type certificate for the model DC3A-SB3G was issued 11-28-36 and some 115 or more examples, including 12 for export, were manufactured by the Douglas Aircraft Co., Inc. on Clover Field in Santa Monica, Calif.

Listed below are specifications and performance data for the Douglas DC3A-SB3G as powered with 2 "Twin Wasp" SB3G engines rated 900 h.p. at 2500 r.p.m. at 8000 ft. (1100 h.p. for takeoff); length overall 64'6"; height overall (3 point) 16'11"; wingspan 95'0"; wing chord at root 170" tapered to tip; total wing area 987 sq. ft.; airfoil NACA-2215 at root tapering to NACA-2206 at tip; wt. empty 15,830 lbs.; useful load 8570 lbs.; payload with 600 gal. fuel & 3 crew 4235 lbs. (21 pass. & 665 lbs. baggage-mail); gross wt. 24,400 lbs. (a provisional gross wt. of 24,800 lbs. was allowed); max. speed 215 at 8000 ft.; cruising speed (.75 power) 196 at 7000 ft.; landing speed (with flaps) 67; climb 920 ft. first min. at sea level; ser. ceiling 21,800 ft.; gas cap. normal 650 gal.; gas cap. max. 822 gal.; oil cap. normal 48 gal.; oil cap. max. 66.5 gal.; cruising range (.75 power) at 100 gal. per hour 1240 miles; price approx. $100,000 at factory. The 14 passenger "Club" version also carried up to 2800 lbs. of baggage-mail-cargo. The DC-3A was also available with 850 h.p. "Twin Wasp" SBG engines.

The DC3A-SB3G as built for United Air Lines was basically typical of other DC-3 types as built for other lines, except that it was powered with 2 of the Pratt & Whitney "Twin Wasp" engines; the engine nacelles and the cowlings were modified to suit dimensions of the engines, and the latest Hamilton-Standard "constant speed" (adjustable pitch) propellers were installed. The UAL "Mainliner" fleet of DC-3A consisted of the 14 passenger "Skylounge" that had swiveling overstuffed chairs in rich decor, and the 21 passenger day-coach version which was equally as comfortable, but passengers were hemmed in a little tighter; a

Preparation for a night-flight east in the "City of San Francisco."

DC-3A with normal 21-passenger layout.

high-density version later carried 28 passengers. The "Skylounge," being lightly loaded, also carried up to 2800 lbs. of baggage and cargo. The red-carpet treatment in the "Skylounge" was featuring steam-heating in the cabin, cool air ventilation, rich appointments, real silver service, fine china, and linens for hot meal service; there were game tables for playing cards, binoculars for observing the passing scenery, personal toilet kits for men and women, and specially selected stewardesses who were chosen for their good looks and pleasant personality. On a flight from New York to Chicago this super service cost about $2.00 or $3.00 more and it was well worth the cost. This service became so popular that it soon had to be offered on the coast-to-coast runs also. The pilots enjoyed making these "Skylounge" runs also, because the DC-3A were equipped with Sperry "automatic pilot." The next Douglas development was the DC-3B "Half-Sleeper" as described here in the chapter for ATC # 635.

Listed below are DC3A-SB3G entries as gleaned from registration records:

NC-16060;	DC3A-SB3G	(# 1900)	Twin-Wasp 900
-16061;	"	(# 1901)	"
-16062;	"	(# 1902)	"
-16063;	"	(# 1903)	"
-16064;	"	(# 1904)	"
-16065;	"	(# 1905)	"
-16066;	"	(# 1906)	"
-16067;	"	(# 1907)	"
-16068;	"	(# 1908)	"
-16069;	"	(# 1909)	"
-16070;	"	(# 1910)	"
-16071;	"	(# 1911)	"
-16072;	"	(# 1912)	"
-16086;	"	(# 1925)	"
-16087;	"	(# 1926)	"
-16088;	"	(# 1927)	"
-16089;	"	(# 1928)	"
-16090;	"	(# 1929)	"
-18111;	"	(# 1983)	"
-18112;	"	(# 1984)	"

ATC # 620
(12-23-36)
AIRCRAFT ASSOC. "CUB", J-2.

Aircraft Associates "Cub" J-2 was assembled in Long Beach; known unofficially as the "Western Cub."

Because of the catastrophic fire at the "Cub" plant in Bradford, Pa., production was drastically curtailed while they were digging out of the mess, and deciding what to do next. Fortunately, most of the jigs and dies could be saved. To assist in production while the Bradford plant was more or less out of commission, fuselage jigs and some other small tooling were sent to the so-called "western assembly plant" in Long Beach that was operated by Aircraft Associates, Inc. The "Western Cub," as it was called in company circles, had just won its approval some months earlier to be assembled in Long Beach from factory-made components sent from Bradford, so it was indeed fortunate that Taylor Aircraft had this to fall back on while recovering from the disastrous fire. The Bradford plant, or what was left of it, still manufactured wings, ribs, and other sundry items which were then shipped to Long Beach for assembly to fill orders in the western region. Fuselages and other items manufactured in Long Beach were then shipped

to Bradford for assembly there to fill orders in the east. This arrangement apparently lasted until Taylor Aircraft mopped up the mess in Bradford, and finally decided to move to Lock Haven, Pa., in June of 1937. The first "Cub" rolled out of the Lock Haven plant about mid-July. In Nov. of 1936 the price of a "Cub" was lowered to $1270, and in the projection for the coming year some 2500 airplanes were expected to come off the line in 1937. To show the confidence they had in this forecast, 1000 Continental A-40 engines were ordered for spring production. But, it was the fire that upset their rosy predictions. This period of "Cub" history (the Aircraft Associates deal) seems rather hush-hush and it was kept very quiet, but it did keep things going while the Taylor company worked its way out of a jam. Aircraft Associates sold 63 of the "Cub" in 1936 to become the largest distributor in the nation; it is easy to see why they were picked as an ally in time of crisis. It was said the "Western Cub" was one of the most popular exhibits at the Pacific Aircraft & Boat Show held in Los Angeles during mid-March of 1937.

The "Western Cub," as this version was called, was also a light cabin monoplane with seating arranged for 2 in tandem. It was not a new airplane model; it was the same as the ones that had been rolling out of the plant in Bradford for nearly a year. The model J-2, and this was also a J-2 version, was a neat little airplane, literally without complaint, and the people admired it. The 1000th "Cub" was rolled off the line in Dec. of 1936 and flown off to the Miami Air Races to celebrate the occasion. It was also during this time that the so-called "Western Cub" had won its ATC approval. The western assembly plant was organized mainly to help speed deliveries in the western region which accounted for a very big share of the total production coming out of Bradford, Pa. As powered with the 4 cyl. Continental A-40 engine rated from 37 to 40 h.p. the "Cub" J-2 was a deft little airplane that was pure fun to fly; every hop was a picnic. It was quite at home in the boon-docks and it expanded the joy of cow-pasture flying. Overall, the J-2 was terribly forgiving and it took a real dumbo to get himself in trouble with it. The "Cub" was never tricky, but she did enjoy a practical joke now and then, just so she wouldn't be taken entirely for granted. After all, a lady likes to be noticed now and then. The type certificate for the Aircraft Associates "Cub" J-2 was issued 12-23-36 and it was next to impossible to assess the amount of production that came out of this plant. A combination of production and assembly was carried out by Aircraft Associates, Inc. on the Long Beach Municipal Airport in Long Beach, Calif.

Listed below are specifications and performance data for the version called the "Western Cub" J-2 as powered with Continental A-40-3, -4, -5 engines rated 37-40 h.p.; this model same as Taylor "Cub" J-2 as approved on ATC # 595; length overall 22'5"; height overall 6'8"; wingspan 35'3"; wing chord 63"; total wing area 178.5 sq. ft.; airfoil USA-35B; wt. empty 563 lbs.; useful load 407 lbs.; payload with 9 gal. fuel 175 lbs.; gross wt. 970 lbs.; max. speed 87; cruising speed (2300 r.p.m.) 70; landing speed 30-35; climb 450 ft. first min. at sea level; ser. ceiling 12,000 ft.; gas cap. 9 gal.; oil cap. 4 qts.; cruising range (2300 r.p.m.) at 2.75 gal. per hour 210 miles; price $1270 at factory. Eligible as

landplane or seaplane; gross wt. later raised to 1000 lbs.

The construction details and general arrangement of the Aircraft Associates "Cub" J-2 were typical to that of the Taylor "Cub" J-2 as described in the chapter for ATC # 595. For the most part the Aircraft Associates "Western Cub" J-2 was a composite airplane assembled of parts that were manufactured in the plant at Long Beach, and shipped also from the plant in Bradford. These airplanes were rolled out unofficially as the "Western Cub" for delivery in the western region. It was also rumored, and it is quite likely, that several of the earlier "Cub" E-2 were run through the Long Beach plant for modification into the improved model J-2, but this could not be substantiated. By now the original "Silver Cub" had been dropped and the "Cub" J-2 was coming out in colors; the most popular colors seemed to be red or blue. The J-2 was rather bare, but adequate, and all gadgetry was simple and functional. A Sensenich wooden prop, dual stick-type controls, bobber-type fuel gauge, and first-aid kit were standard equipment. Navigation lights, a hot-shot battery, carburetor heater, cabin heater, and wheel streamlines were optional. The CAA Manual notes as pertains to ATC # 620; for this airplane specifications as noted in ATC # 595 will apply in their entirety. Major components must be manufactured in accordance with approved technical data for ATC # 595; parts mfgd. by Aircraft Associates, Inc. may be used provided such parts conform to approved technical data pertaining to ATC # 620. One can see that much more research is necessary to clarify the many points left hanging; additional information from those with knowledge of this operation would be greatly appreciated.

Listed below are some "Aircraft Associates" Cub J-2 entries as seen in registration records:

NC-17233;	Cub J-2	(# 899)	Cont. 40
-17234;	"	(# 900)	"
-17235;	"	(# 901)	"
-17236;	"	(# 902)	"

The block of registration numbers from NC-17810 thru -17827 were listed as Aircraft Associates "Cub" J-2 with ser. nos. running from # 1245 thru # 1262, and all were reg. in Calif.; this approval expired 9-30-39 and no aircraft of this model to be mfgd. after that date.

ATC # 621
(12-30-36)
STINSON "RELIANT", SR-9B.

A favorite of the series was SR-9C with 260 h.p Lycoming engine.

Introduced with a fanfare as the improved "Reliant" for the year 1937, the model SR-9 series were indeed a masterpiece of styling and elegance. A feature that quickly identified the new SR-9 was the big, molded, panoramic windshield which was curved to blend in nicely with the deeper engine cowl and forward fuselage lines; the plane also appeared to be much taller than it really was because the longer wing was outstretched at a greater angle. This made it seem to tower over other airplanes, even other "Reliants," in a near-regal loftiness. But, despite this apparent put-on, the SR-9 was friendly and not a haughty airplane as it seemed, an airplane that did its best to please and it took good care of its people. The SR-9 was also proving company claims that the "Reliant" could be steadily improved without making any great basic changes in the overall design; as a consequence, this new model offered the opportunity for more usable speed, the repetitive assurance of slower landings into tight places, better vision, a quieter, more comfortable cabin interior, and even improved accessibility for periodic inspection and maintenance. It's no wonder that owners of the older "Reliant" flew in by the score to trade up for an SR-9. This new "Reliant" for 1937 began rolling off the line the first week in Jan., and before long it was available with 3 different Lycoming engines; the model SR-9A (which no one actually wanted) had 225 h.p., the SR-9B had 245 h.p., and SR-9C had the 260 h.p. And, all 3 of these were also

available in "Standard" or "Deluxe" versions. As a no-frills working airplane to haul freight and other sundry articles, the SR-9 was available also as a "M" (multi-purpose) version; extra large doors and a metal-lined cabin interior were 2 of its more significant features. Several of the new models were exhibited at the Los Angeles Aircraft & Boat Show during March of 1937, and this showing prompted a caravan of SR-9 deliveries to the west coast. It was quite noticeable that costs were rising, and every one of the new "Reliant" were wearing higher price-tags, but airplane buyers were also more affluent so sales were quite brisk. Before the year was out almost 200 of the SR-9 were criss-crossing this nation, and serving too in several foreign countries.

The Stinson "Reliant" in the model SR-9 series was also a high-winged cabin monoplane with seating arranged for 5. From just about any angle it was a very handsome airplane and it loomed large on the apron where it could attract everyone's attention. Because the price of labor was going up, and prices of materials were steadily increasing, the "Reliant" was no longer a cheap airplane, but it was still one of the best bargains in the country. It was rather hard to categorize the SR-9 buyer because they ranged all the way from the weekend pilot to the millionaire, and they all seemed equally enthused about the SR-9. Outside of prancing around the countryside on errand or whim, the average SR-9 was not usually asked to do much every-

Head-on view shows unusual "Reliant" SR-9 configuration.

day work, but they certainly could do it if necessary. The multi-purpose version of the SR-9 (labled-M) could pitch in and work with the best of them over mountains and bush. As powered with 3 different Lycoming (225-245-260 h.p.) engines the SR-9 varied slightly in performance and temperament because of the varied power ratings, but it was a very good airplane in just about any combination. Performance was excellent throughout the whole flight range, and its abilities even exceeded the manufacturer's claims; and, to top it off, it had a most lovable disposition. It was actually the "Reliant's" amiable disposition that appealed to the sportsman-pilots more than its performance; for a long time pilots were bashful to admit that they loved the big "Reliant" because of the way it behaved. Stinson Aircraft surely must be commended on how they continued to make a real good airplane better and better. The type certificate for the models SR-9A, SR-9B, SR-9C was issued 12-30-36 and in all some 100 and more examples were manufactured by the Stinson Aircraft Co., Inc., in Wayne, Mich., a suburb out of Detroit.

Listed below are specifications and performance data for the "Reliant" model SR-9A as powered with Lycoming R-680-B4 engine rated

"Reliant" SR-9B was a favorite "working airplane."

225 h.p. at 2100 r.p.m. at sea level; length overall 27'11"; height overall 8'6"; wingspan 41'11"; max. wing chord 96"; wing chord at tip 38"; total wing area 258.5 sq. ft.; airfoil Mod. Clark Y; wt. empty 2450 lbs.; useful load 1250 lbs.; payload with 50 gal. fuel 742 lbs. (4 pass. & 62 lbs. bag.) gross wt. 3700 lbs.; max. speed 145 at sea level; cruising speed (.75 power) 135 at 3000 ft.; landing speed (with flaps) 55, climb 700 ft. first min. at sea level; ser. ceiling 12,000 ft.; gas cap. 50 gal.; oil cap. 5 gal.; cruising range (.75 power) at 14 gal. per hour 650 miles; price approx. $9000 at factory field.

Specifications and data for model SR-9B as powered with Lycoming R-680-B6 engine rated 245 h.p. at 2300 r.p.m. at sea level, same as above except as follows: wt. empty 2457 lbs.; useful load 1243 lbs.; payload with 70 gal. fuel 616 lbs. (3 pass. & 100 lbs. bag.); gross wt. 3700 lbs.; max. speed 147 at sea level; cruising speed (.75 power) 136 at 3000 ft.; landing speed (with flaps) 55; climb 800 ft. first min. at sea level; ser. ceiling 13,200 ft.; gas cap. 70 gal.; oil cap. 5 gal.; cruising range (.75 power) at 15 gal. per hour 610 miles; price listed as $9385 at factory field. Also available as SR-9BM, and available also with R-680-D6 engine.

Specifications and data for model SR-9C as powered with Lycoming R-680-B5 engine rated 260 h.p. at 2300 r.p.m.; same as above (all dims. same) except as follows: wt. empty 2515 lbs.; useful load 1235 lbs.; payload with 70 gal. fuel 608 lbs.; payload with 50 gal. fuel 727 lbs. (4 pass. & 47 lbs. bag.); gross wt. 3750 lbs.; max. speed 148 at 7000 ft.; cruising speed (.75 power) 140 at 7000 ft.; landing speed (with flaps) 57; climb 825 ft. first min. at sea level; ser. ceiling 14,500 ft.; gas cap. 70 gal.; oil cap. 5 gal.; cruising range (.70 power) at 14 gal. per hour 690 miles; price approx. $10,000 to $11,500 depending on equipment installed. Both SR-9B and SR-9C were eligible as a seaplane on Edo 39-4000 twin-float gear at 4000 lbs. gross wt. Also eligible with R-680-D5 engine.

Construction (material and methods) of the gull-winged "Reliant" had not changed for several years; the airframe was basically the same, but improvements had been incorporated all along. The fuselage was now wider, the doors were a little larger, the interiors were steadily improved, and exteriors glistened with extra coats of rubbed-down finish. Sometimes it was hard to improve, but eventually there was always a way found to make things a little better, or more convenient. On the SR-9 series the NACA-type engine cowling was now deeper, the engine was shielded for radio, and an oil-cooling radiator kept temperatures more consistent. The big, panoramic windshield, of molded safety-glass, was fashioned in a curve to offer a better view up front. Most of the hardware was redesigned, the interiors were colorful, and in good taste. Up to 150 lbs. of luggage could be carried; 50 lbs. was allowed under the rear seat, and 100 lbs. in the large compartment behind the seat. Rear compt. was allowed only 50 lbs. when 3 occupied the rear seat. Fuel tanks in the wing came in 25-35-39-41 gal. capacities, and tankage up to 130 gal. was optional. The multi-purpose (-M) model had 2 large doors on the right side for loading long or bulky items; it was also eligible as a ski-plane or a seaplane. The SR-9 was very

Interior of SR-9 shows off auto-like interior.

well equipped, and there were more than enough options available to suit anyone's needs. The next "Reliant" development was the Wright-powered SR-9D as described here in the chapter for ATC # 625.

Listed below are SR-9B, SR-9C entries as gleaned from registration records:

NC-17110;	SR-9B	(# 5100)	Lyc. 245
-17122;	"	(# 5101)	"
-17117;	"	(# 5102)	"
-17133;	"	(# 5103)	"
-17146;	"	(# 5104)	"
-17128;	"	(# 5105)	"
-17129;	"	(# 5106)	"
-17150;	SR-9C	(# 5107)	Lyc. 260
-17134;	SR-9B	(# 5108)	Lyc. 245
-17148;	"	(# 5109)	"
-17149;	"	(# 5110)	"
-17156;	SR-9BM	(# 5111)	"
-17151;	SR-9B	(# 5112)	"
-17152;	"	(# 5113)	"
-17153;	"	(# 5114)	"
-17154;	"	(# 5115)	"
-17163;	SR-9CM	(# 5116)	Lyc. 260
-17164;	"	(# 5117)	"
-17158;	SR-9B	(# 5118)	Lyc. 245
-17159;	SR-9C	(# 5119)	Lyc. 260
-17160;	SR-9B	(# 5120)	Lyc. 245
-17161;	SR-9C	(# 5121)	Lyc. 260
-17162;	"	(# 5122)	"
-17155;	SR-9B	(# 5123)	Lyc. 245
-17166;	"	(# 5151)	"
;	"	(# 5152)	"
-17169;	"	(# 5153)	"
-17171;	"	(# 5154)	"
-17174;	"	(# 5155)	"
;	"	(# 5156)	"
-18431;	SR-9CM	(# 5157)	Lyc. 260
-17167;	SR-9C	(# 5158)	"
;	"	(# 5159)	"
NC-2217;	"	(# 5160)	"
-17176;	SR-9B	(# 5161)	Lyc. 245
-17192;	SR-9BM	(# 5162)	"
-17175;	SR-9B	(# 5163)	"
-17181;	"	(# 5164)	"
-17177;	"	(# 5165)	"
-17178;	SR-9C	(# 5166)	Lyc. 260
-17179;	SR-9B	(# 5167)	Lyc. 245
-17180;	SR-9C	(# 5168)	Lyc. 260
-17187;	SR-9B	(# 5169)	Lyc. 245
-17184;	"	(# 5170)	"

-17182;	"	(# 5171)	"
-17189;	"	(# 5172)	"
-17190;	"	(# 5173)	"
-17195;	"	(# 5300)	"
-17196;	"	(# 5301)	"
-17197;	"	(# 5302)	"
-17185;	SR-9C	(# 5303)	Lyc. 260
-17183;	"	(# 5304)	"
-17199;	"	(# 5305)	"
-18401;	SR-9B	(# 5306)	Lyc. 245
;	"	(# 5307)	"
-18402;	"	(# 5308)	"
-18403;	SR-9C	(# 5309)	Lyc. 260
-18404;	"	(# 5310)	"
-18405;	SR-9CM	(# 5311)	"
-18406;	SR-9C	(# 5312)	"
-18407;	"	(# 5313)	"
-18409;	SR-9B	(# 5314)	Lyc. 245
-18408;	"	(# 5315)	"
-18415;	SR-9C	(# 5316)	Lyc. 260
-18413;	"	(# 5317)	"
-18416;	"	(# 5318)	"
-18417;	SR-9B	(# 5319)	Lyc. 245
-18418;	SR-9C	(# 5320)	Lyc. 260
-18423;	"	(# 5321)	"
-18424;	"	(# 5322)	"
-18432;	"	(# 5323)	"
-18419;	"	(# 5350)	"
-18438;	SR-9B	(# 5351)	Lyc. 245
-18434;	SR-9C	(# 5352)	Lyc. 260
NS-81Y;	"	(# 5353)	Lyc. 245
-18442;	SR-9C	(# 5354)	Lyc. 260
-18440;	"	(# 5356)	"
-18447;	"	(# 5357)	"
-18457;	"	(# 5358)	"
-18452;	SR-9B	(# 5359)	Lyc. 245
-18453;	SR-9C	(# 5362)	Lyc. 260
-18455;	"	(# 5363)	"
-21115;	"	(# 5365)	"
21114;	"	(# 5367)	"

This approval for ser. # 5100 and up; ser. # 5119 del. to Vultee; ser. # 5121 as Stinson demo; ser. # 5157 to Lycoming Motors; ser. # 5162 to Alaska; ser. # 5168 first as SR-9A later as SR-9E; ser. # 5304 on floats; ser. # 5316 manufactured July 1937 was 900th Stinson airplane powered with Lycoming engine; ser. # 5323 del. Errett L. Cord; ser. # 5362 del. to Eastern Air Lines; no listing available for # 5125-50, or # 5175-99, or # 5325-49; perhaps these gaps were intentional; expired 10-25-40.

Cessna C-37 "Airmaster" strikes a handsome pose.

They at Cessna Aircraft had designed the earlier model C-34 to such a good formula that there seemed to be no reason for change in the next few years, but by 1937 the requisites for private-owner airplanes had gone up considerably, so it was finally necessary to provide some change just to keep up with competition. The so-called improved "Cessna" for 1937 was introduced as the model C-37, and although it was hard to see where any changes had been made, the changes were some here and some there, and the C-37 was a better airplane for it. At a casual glance one could barely notice any change in external dimension, but the room inside was expanded, the cabin was now quieter, and a bit more comfortable. Most all the other changes and improvements were hidden in the recesses of structure, but the pilot and even the passengers could surely feel they were there. The "Cessna Cantilever Monoplane" had proven itself time and again as perhaps "the most efficient airplane in the world," so the model C-37 was hailed by A. K. Longren at the Los Angeles Air Show for 1937 as the newest member in this family. She, the C-37, would now be the reigning queen. Whereas the earlier C-34 failed to attract any big-names or famous personalities, the new C-37 did; although it is logical to consider that past accomplishments of the C-34 were most of the stimulus for this. The roster shows that Peter Dana, young playboy pilot, was a proud owner and flew coast-to-coast jaunts on several occasions; Noel Wien, noted "bush pilot," took a

C-37 back to Alaska with him because he had such good service with "Cessna" airplanes. Then, "Bob" Cummings, a famous Hollywood actor and enthusiastic aviator, picked up a new C-37 at the factory and flew it back to Hollywood by way of his hometown of Joplin, Mo. At stops along the way it is interesting to note that airport people were just about as interested in his role of airplane-owner as they were in the fact he was a famous movie actor. As an airplane the new "Cessna" for 1937 excited everyone, but despite claims for added room and all that, the C-37 had an interior arrangement that was still rather skimpy and it was an advantage to be on the slender side. But, such are the penalties one had to endure in a compact airplane that carried 4, and delivered all that brilliant performance on the miserly appetite of a 145 h.p. engine.

The Cessna model C-37 was a compact high-winged cabin monoplane with seating arranged for 4. Typical of previous "Cessna" designs, the C-37 was a cantilever (internally braced) monoplane that had eliminated all the drag-producing struts and braces as normally seen on other airplanes; because of this it was capable of uncanny speed and performance with an engine of modest horsepower output. Unencumbered by all these struts and braces, this "Cessna" poised gracefully with simple elegance, and its somewhat dainty appearance belied its actual strength. The C-37 was leveled more or less at the private-owner and the occasional sportsman-pilot, but its utility was also appealing to commercial operators who found it capable of many different jobs. As powered with the 7 cyl. Warner "Super Scarab" engine of 145 h.p., one can only heap praise on this airplane for the way it performed. It was a relatively fast airplane, quick and very responsive, it did very well at high altitudes, was very smooth in the air, and it was quiet. Some said it was "a hot airplane" and far too sensitive, but that's perhaps because it was so eager and so sensitive to power settings. It did very well on the short airstrips even at high elevations, and was a beautiful machine for cross-country flying, conducting itself with a nice even temper. Its flight characteristics can be best described as just lovely; it was fun to fly and it was fairly tolerant; it did take a little learning to become a good "Cessna pilot," but the rewards were of great personal satisfaction. Most of the C-37 led a long and useful life, and a few are flying even yet. The type certificate for the model C-37 was issued 2-8-37 and some 46 or more examples were manufactured by the Cessna Aircraft Co. at Wichita, Kan. Dwane L. Wallace was pres. & gen. mgr.; Albin K. Longren was V.P.; Dwight S. Wallace was sec-treas.; Cecil Lucas was sales mgr.; and Tom Salter was chf. engr. George Harte, long-time commercial operator, was contracted for all test-flying and promotion.

Listed below are specifications and performance data for the Cessna model C-37 as powered with Warner "Super Scarab" (Series 50) engine rated 145 h.p. at 2050 r.p.m. at sea level; length overall 24'8"; height overall 7'3"; wingspan 34'2"; wing chord at root 84"; wing chord at tip 58"; total wing area 182 sq. ft.; air-foil NACA-2412; wt. empty 1304 lbs.; useful load 946 lbs.; payload with 35 gal. fuel 540 lbs. (3 pass. & 30 lbs. bag.); gross wt. 2250 lbs.; max. speed (with metal prop & wheel pants) 162 at sea level; cruising speed (1925 r.p.m.) 143 at sea level; landing speed (with flaps) 48; landing speed (no flaps) 56; climb 800 ft. first min. at sea level; ser. ceiling 18,000 ft.; gas cap. 35 gal.; oil cap. 3.5 gal.; cruising range (1925 r.p.m.) at 9 gal. per hour 540 miles; price $5490 at factory; Deluxe version sold for $6000. Also eligible as seaplane on Edo 44-2425 twin-float gear & Curtiss-Reed metal prop; wt. empty was 1560 lbs.; useful load 940 lbs.; payload with 35 gal. fuel 534 lbs.; gross wt. 2500 lbs. Performance suffered proportionately due to extra drag and extra weight.

The construction details and general arrangement of the model C-37 were typical to that of the C-34 as described in the chapter for ATC # 573, except as follows. The cabin area was widened by 5 in. to offer more shoulder-room, the NACA engine cowl was improved by redesigning cyl. baffles, and the engine was fitted with an improved carburetor heat-box. The land gear shock-absorbing system was improved using 6.50x10 Warner wheels (of 7 ft. tread) with mechanical brakes; 22x10-4 Goodyear airwheels were optional. Normal fuel cap. was 2 tanks in the wing at 17.5 gal. each; an extra 10 gal. or 17.5 gal. tank was optional for greater range. The wing flaps were now electrically operated, but a manual flap handle was available instead; flaps not to be extended above 108 m.p.h. Baggage compartment behind the rear seat was limited to 48 lbs. A wind-driven generator was fitted into leading edge of the wing on the right

C-37 prototype tries its wings over wintry Kansas countryside.

Robt. Cummings, movie actor, stands proudly in front of "Spinach II," a Cessna C-37.

side to generate 4 amps at cruising speed; an engine-driven generator was optional. Inherent stability of the C-37 was such that it provided an excellent platform for aerial photography; several C-37 were converted to photo-planes. A Hartzell wooden prop, electric engine starter, battery, navigation lights, flap control, dual stick-type controls, dome light, 8 in. tail wheel, assist ropes, and first-aid kit were standard equipment. A Curtiss-Reed metal prop, cabin heater, landing lights, paraflares, wheel streamlines, radio gear, a camera or litter installation, Edo pontoons, and skis were optional. The next Cessna development was the model C-38 as described here in the chapter for ATC-# 668.

Listed below are C-37 entries as verified by company records:

X-17070;	C-37	(# 330)	Warner 145
NC-17059;	"	(# 342)	"
-17053;	"	(# 343)	"
-17056;	"	(# 344)	"
-17057;	"	(# 345)	"
-17086;	"	(# 346)	"
-17087;	"	(# 347)	"
-17088;	"	(# 348)	"
NPC-33;	"	(# 349)	"
-17090;	"	(# 350)	"
-17089;	"	(# 351)	"
-17058;	"	(# 352)	"
NPC-34;	"	(# 353)	"
CF-BFE;	"	(# 354)	"
-18030;	"	(# 355)	"
-18031;	"	(# 356)	"
VH-UZU;	"	(# 357)	"
-18032;	"	(# 358)	"
-18033;	"	(# 359)	"
-18034;	"	(# 360)	"
-18035;	"	(# 361)	"
-18036;	"	(# 362)	"
-18037;	"	(# 363)	"
-18045;	"	(# 364)	"
-18046;	"	(# 365)	"
-18047;	"	(# 366)	"
;	"	(# 367)	"
-18049;	"	(# 368)	"
-18550;	"	(# 369)	"
-18551;	"	(# 370)	"
-18552;	"	(# 371)	"
-18553;	"	(# 372)	"
-18554;	"	(# 373)	"
CF-BHB;	"	(# 374)	"
-18590;	"	(# 375)	"
-18591;	"	(# 376)	"
-18592;	"	(# 377)	"
-18593;	"	(# 378)	"
-18594;	"	(# 379)	"
-18595;	"	(# 380)	"
NR-18596;	"	(# 381)	"
-18597;	"	(# 382)	"
-18598;	"	(# 383)	"
-18599;	"	(# 384)	"
OH-VKF;	"	(# 385)	"
-18589;	"	(# 386)	"

This approval for ser. # 330, 342 and up; ser. # 349, 353 operated in Philippines; ser. # 354, 374 del. to Canada; ser. # 357 del. to Australia; ser. # 367 del. to Portuguese West Africa; ser. # 369 to movie actor Bob Cummings; ser. # 373 del. to "Steve" Wittman, noted racing pilot; ser. # 375 later to Norway as LN-FAK; ser. # 385 to Finland; ser. # 347, 381 as UC-77C in USAAF; ser. # 387 thru 399 not used; this approval expired 9-30-39.

ATC # 623
(1-22-37)
SIKORSKY, S-43-W.

Sikorsky S-43-W "amphibian" as used by Pan American Airways.

The big Sikorsky S-43 twin-engined amphibian certainly needs no introduction to the average airplane buff because it followed in a line of amphibious airplanes that were known practically the world over. As we see here it was patterned largely after the huge trans-Pacific "Clipper" (S-42), so the smaller S-43 type was an amphibious "parasol monoplane" also, but mounting only 2 engines in the wing. Totally suited for an air service that originated on land and terminated in the water, or vice versa, the hard-working S-43 inaugurated many new airline systems in both hemispheres. During its heyday the S-43 stood on the apron as the largest twin-engined "Amphibian" in the world. What has been said here to now mainly concerns the models S-43-A and S-43-B as described in some detail in the chapter for ATC # 593, but there was also a lesser-known version of this airplane listed as the S-43-W. Unless one had a trained eye for such things the difference in the S-43-W would be hard to detect because the difference was shrouded from view in the engine nacelles. All previous S-43 type were powered with Pratt & Whitney "Hornet" engines, but the S-43-W was unusual in that it was powered with 2 Wright engines, 2 big 9 cyl. "Cyclone" engines of 760 h.p. each. There were probably only 5 of these airplanes built, and the first 2 were ordered by Pan American Airways, for an affiliate line, for special service in China. Aviation people in China had a great respect for the "Wright" engine and they preferred it, so this order for 2 actually spawned the S-43-W version. Howard Hughes, the noted millionaire pilot and movie

producer, was preparing a special more powerful version of the S-43-W for a proposed around-the-world flight, but he finally chose to use another airplane. The last 2 airplanes in the S-43 series were both of the Cyclone-powered S-43-W type; they were manufactured for KNILM (an affiliate of KLM, the Royal Dutch Air Lines) in 1940 and 1941 for service to Java and other portions of the Dutch East Indies. These were troubled times in that portion of the world because the stage was being set for World War Two.

The Sikorsky model S-43-W "Amphibion" (a word coined by Sikorsky) was a large twin-engined amphibious "parasol monoplane" of the flying boat type. Seating was normally arranged for 16 passengers and a crew of 3, but a coach-style arrangement on short flights was able to squeeze in up to 25 people. Most airlines operated the S-43 as a "Duck" (amphibian), thereby being able to operate from land or water, but some lines operated the S-43 as a pure "flying boat" without the wheeled landing gear; removal of the undercarriage assembly added at least a half-ton to the payload. Of the 5 or so S-43-W that were built we know that one was a specially built airplane for Howard Hughes; the other 4 airplanes were typical of previous S-43 except for the engines used. As powered with 2 of the big 9 cyl. Wright "Cyclone" GR-1820-F52 engines rated 760 h.p. each, the S-43-W was exceptionally fast for such a large amphibious airplane, and its all-around performance was no less than outstanding. Its water characteristics were superb and it was equally deft on land or water; pilots loved the big S-43 and it stands to reason that the S-43-W was surely included. Some of these airplanes were delivered as flying boats (S-43-WB) and operated strictly in the water; on some routes this was more practical. The type certificate for the model S-43-W and S-43-WB was issued 1-22-37 and some 5 or more examples were manufactured by the Sikorsky Aircraft Div. at Bridgeport, Conn. The well-known Igor I. Sikorsky was V.P. in chrg. of engrg.; R. W. Clark was gen. mgr.; Michael Gluhareff was chf. engr. and Boris Sergievsky was chief pilot.

Listed below are specifications and performance data for the Sikorsky model S-43-W as powered with 2 Wright "Cyclone" GR-1820-F52 engines rated 760 h.p. at 2100 r.p.m. at 5800 ft. (875 h.p. at 2200 r.p.m. for takeoff); length overall 52'3"; height overall (on wheels) 17'8"; wingspan 86'0"; max. wing chord 11'6"; total wing area 781 sq. ft.; airfoil at root NACA-2218; airfoil at tip NACA-2209; wt. empty 13,-460 lbs.; useful load 6040 lbs.; payload with 400 gal. fuel, 3 crew 2970 lbs. (16 pass. & 250 lbs. bag.); gross wt. 19,500 (20,000) lbs; wt. in parentheses as later allowed; max. speed 186 at 5800 ft.; max. speed one engine 128 at 5800 ft.; cruising speed (.75 power) 177 at 5800 ft.; landing speed (with flaps) 65; climb 1100 ft. first min. at sea level; ser. ceiling 19,000 ft.; gas cap. 400 gal.; oil cap. 28-44 gal.; cruising range (.75 power) at 86 gal. per hour 775 miles; price not announced. The special S-43 for Howard Hughes, labeled S-43-H or S-43-WH, operated at 14,544 lbs. empty and 20,000 lbs. gross wt. with 2 Wright GR-1820-G102 engines rated 900 h.p. at 2300 r.p.m. at 6700 ft. using 87 octane fuel (1100 h.p. at 2350 r.p.m. for takeoff). This airplane sometimes operated with gross wt. to 25,000 lbs.

The construction details and general arrangement of the Sikorsky S-43-W were typical to that of the earlier S-43 as described in the chapter for ATC # 593. The only significant difference in the S-43-W was installation of the 2 Wright "Cyclone" engines and some modifications here and there that were necessary to this combination. The S-43-W was also eligible with Wright GR-1820-F62 engines. All S-43-W were equipped with Hamilton-Standard "constant speed" full-feathering hydramatic propellers. Normal gross wt. for the S-43-W was 19,500 lbs., but it was eligible for 20,000 lbs. gross wt. when a 20 in. (with 6-ply tire) tail wheel and revised fork were installed. Of the 53 (S-43 type) airplanes that were finally built, some 50 were operated as "amphibians," and 3 as pure "flying boats." Eclipse generators, Willard batteries, engine-driven fuel pumps, fuel gauges, dual control wheels, hydraulic wheel brakes, navigation lights, landing lights, paraflares, fire extinguishers, anchor & mooring gear, life jackets, Very pistol, canvas bailing buckets, fire-axe, tool kit, and first-aid kit were standard equipment. Complete radio gear, extra fuel cap., and inflatable life rafts were optional. The next Sikorsky development was the big 4-motored VS-44-A as described in the chapter for ATC # 752.

Listed below are Sikorsky S-43-W entries as gleaned from registration records:

NC-16929;	S-43-W	(# 4320)	2 Cyc. 760
-16930;	"	(# 4321)	"
NR-440;	S-43-H	(# 4327)	2 Cyc. 900
PK-AFT;	S-43-W	(# 4352)	2 Cyc. 760
PK-AFU;	"	(# 4353)	"

S-43-W (twin-tailed) as used by KNILM in Dutch East Indies.

This approval for ser. # 4320 and up; approved empty wt. for ser. # 4320 was 13,448 lbs.; approved empty wt. for ser. # 4321 was 13,468 lbs.; ser. # 4320-21 del. to China; ser. # 4327 del. to Howard Hughes, also as S-43-WH; approved empty wt. for ser. # 4327 was 14,544 lbs.; no approved empty wts. available for ser. # 4352-53; ser. # 4353 was last of the S-43 type to be built; approval expired 2-10-41.

Special S-43-W being readied by Howard Hughes for proposed world flight.

ATC # 624
(1-23-37)
REARWIN, MODEL 9000.

Rearwin "Sportster" 9000 was leveled at the sportsman.

They at Rearwin Airplanes introduced their Model 9000 (sometimes as 9000-W) to complement their "Sportster" line, a lineup which was already available with 3 different engines, but needed a boost to perk up interest in the series. This newest model had the 5 cyl. Warner 90 "Scarab Jr." engine, an engine which was taking on considerable popularity at this time among private-owners. As the top of the line the Model 9000 was being offered as a sport-type "Deluxe" airplane for those of moderate means; offered to pilots that would prefer an owner-flown airplane that was fitted with just about all the extras that one would care to have in an airplane of this type. For those who didn't have all that ready cash, the 9000-W was available for 1/3 down and balance in 12 monthly payments. First formal showing of the Warner-powered Model 9000 took place at the Pacific Aircraft & Boat Show held in Los Angeles during March 13-21 of 1937, and the interest shown was rather encouraging; at least 2 were sold during the show for use in California. Partnerships in owning an airplane have always been common, but in 1937 there were 15 St. Paul, Minn. businessmen who pooled together to buy a Rearwin "Sportster" for their weekend pleasure; now that is a rather unusual partnership. Popularity of the Rearwin

"Sportster" line was finally waning as the decade came to a close, but it was still holding up its popularity overseas, especially in Norway and Sweden; reports claim that 13 of the "Sportster" were manufactured in Sweden under license. The Rearwin "Sportster" had always been a good airplane, but requisites for private-owner airplanes were changing, and many airplanes of the "early thirties" had suddenly become old-fashioned.

The Rearwin "Sportster" Model 9000 (9000-W) was a light high-winged cabin monoplane with seating arranged for 2 in tandem. Most of the earlier "Rearwin" were low-cost utility-type airplanes, but this model blessed with the extra benefits that more power could produce, was aimed at those who didn't mind going into their pockets a little deeper for the available benefits. The Model 9000 as bedecked with bright colors, a speed-ring cowl, and wheel pants was a rather handsome airplane, and still tough enough to hold up well under amateur sport-type use. With "the slimness of an arrow" this "Sportster" poised a little slim-waisted for some, but it had more than enough leg-room and plenty of headroom. There was sufficient weight allowance too for up to 50 lbs. of baggage, and a long list of extra equipment. As powered with the 5 cyl.

Rearwin 9000 also popular at several flying schools.

Warner "Scarab Jr." engine rated 90 h.p. the Model 9000 was blessed with a particularly good performance, and it performed exceptionally well in the high country of the west. As an added feature the 9000-W was available as a seaplane on Edo pontoons; Juan Trippe, dynamic president of Pan American Airways, didn't fly very often because of the pressures of running a big airline, but he did enjoy taking out his float-equipped 9000 on an occasional jaunt over the waters of Long Island Sound. The Model 9000 was built up of good stuff, and it stood up well under hard service. After most owners had graduated to bigger and more expensive craft, this airplane most often took up a place at some flying-school where it was praised again by students and pilots alike. The type certificate for the Model 9000 (9000-W) was issued 1-23-37 and some 9 or more examples of this model were manufactured by Rearwin Airplanes on Fairfax Airport in Kansas City, Kan. The Model 9000 was first approved on a Group 2 certificate

The 9000 on floats as flown by Juan T. Trippe of Pan American Airways.

numbered 2-523 issued 9-3-36, but this was superseded by ATC # 624. Rae Rearwin was pres. & gen. mgr.; Kenneth Rearwin was sales mgr.; Royce Rearwin was service mgr.; and Robt. W. Rummel was chf. engr.

Listed below are specifications and performance data for the Rearwin "Sportster" Model 9000 (9000-W) as powered with Warner "Scarab Jr." (Series 50) engine rated 90 h.p. at 2025 r.p.m. at sea level; length overall 22'4"; height overall 6'9"; wingspan 35'0"; wing chord 62.5"; total wing area 166 sq. ft.; airfoil (NACA) Munk M-6; wt. empty 861 lbs.; useful load 599 lbs.; payload with 24 gal. fuel 270 lbs. (1 pass., 50 lbs. bag., & 50 lbs. for extra equipment); gross wt. 1460 lbs.; max. speed 120 at 1000 ft.; cruising speed (1825 r.p.m.) 110 at 1000 ft.; landing speed 42; takeoff run 320 ft.; climb 720 ft. first min. at sea level; ser. ceiling 15,000 ft.; gas cap. 24 gal.; oil cap. 2 gal.; cruising range (1825 r.p.m.) at 5.5 gal. per hour 420 miles; price approx. $3500 with "Deluxe" equipment at factory. Eligible as seaplane on Edo H-1525 or 46-1620 twin-float gear at 1615 lbs. gross wt.

The construction details and general arrangement of the Model 9000 (9000-W) were typical to that of models described in the chapters for ATC # 574 and # 591, except as follows. For 1937 the interior was sharpened up a bit, the control mechanism was fitted with ball-bearings, 30 lbs. of baggage was allowed in the cabin, and 20 lbs. of baggage was allowed aft of the cabin; the cushioned seat-backs were hinged to fold forward, and the airplane could be flown solo from either seat. The engine was fitted with a collector-ring, adjustable carburetor heat, and shrouded with a metal speed-ring (Townend-ring) cowl. The improved oleo-type landing gear was widened to 72 in., and fitted with 7.00x4 wheels and tires; mechanical brakes were optional. Goodyear 18x8-3 airwheels with multiple-disc brakes were also optional. The spring-leaf tail skid was fitted with a swiveling tail wheel assembly. A 12 gal. fuel tank was mounted in the root end of each wing-half; a sight-gauge was fitted to each (gravity-flow) tank. A wooden Flottorp prop, electric engine starter, a battery, wind-driven generator, navigation lights, dual stick-type controls, fire extinguisher bottle, safety-belts, and first-aid kit were standard as "Deluxe" equipment. A metal prop, engine-driven generator, dual set of brake pedals, cabin heater, cabin vents, parking brake, landing lights, Heywood air-operated engine starter, extra instruments, Edo pontoons, and skis were optional. The next Rearwin development was the "Speedster" model 6000 as described here in the chapter for ATC # 653.

Listed below are Rearwin Model 9000 entries as gleaned from registration records:

NC-16432;	9000	(# 490)	Warner 90
-16433;	"	(# 491)	"
-17042;	"	(# 532-D)	"
-18008;	"	(# 549-D)	"
-18073;	"	(# 559-D)	
-18547;	"	(# 569-D)	"
-18770;	"	(# 580-D)	"
-20713;	"	(#)	"
-21980;	"	(#)	"

This approval for ser. # 490 and up; ser. # 491 reg. to Juan T. Trippe on floats; letter -D designates "Deluxe"; no ser. nos. available for NC-20713 and NC-21980; approval expired 1-7-43.

ATC # 625
(2-2-37)
STINSON "RELIANT", SR-9D.

A Stinson "Reliant" SR-9E owned by Los Angeles newspaper.

Just like other models in the recently-introduced SR-9 series for 1937, the SR-9D and SR-9E were also a stylish and elegant machine, and generally more so, because they were powered with the more expensive Wright engine. If a customer dug up extra cash to pay for a Wright engine he would naturally want the rest of the airplane to complement his expensive purchase, so these 2 airplanes were most often dressed for show and loaded with all the optional extras. The roster of owners was like a Who's Who of those that had money. But, not only the well-to-do were captivated with these airplanes; it leaked out among the working pilots that this was also a good work-horse airplane, especially in the multi-purpose version, so several wound up working for their keep. Some wound up in Canada on floats for work "in the bush." Of course they were bound to get scarred up a bit and sometimes rather shabby looking, but the "Reliant" always kept up a pretty good appearance and she never let go of her dignity. The "deluxe version" of the SR-9D or SR-9E was actually a sight to behold, and it carried proudly the emblem or logo of many big corporations; there was the Hearst "Examiner," Texaco, Pure Oil, and N.Y.C. Police Dept. to name just a few. Even the Bureau of Air Commerce selected the special capabilities of the SR-9E for its work in the field, and bought 6. Wm. A. Mara, vice-president at Stinson, who was understandably proud of their new line, flew

an SR-9 out to the west coast for delivery in June of 1937; of course, he demonstrated the airplane at likely spots along the way. His slogan was "Enjoy flying - buy a Stinson." The tried and true Wright engine in a "Reliant" was always a good combination; early in 1937 the 100th "Reliant" with a Wright engine was pushed out for delivery to Cuba. Many more of the Wright-powered "Reliant" were yet to be built. You could almost tell when a Wright-powered "Reliant" was being readied in final assembly—the people acted a little special. The Stinson "Reliant" models SR-9D and SR-9E were high-winged cabin monoplanes with seating arranged for 4 or 5. The SR-9D and SR-9E were a handsome pair, and by now the tapered "Reliant" wing was as distinctive as a signature—it was this wing that made the "Reliant" a great airplane. The Wright-powered "Reliant" came through final assembly in much smaller number, because it was relatively expensive and it was sought by only a certain clientele. The bulk of the SR-9D and SR-9E were used in business, and some were flown off to service in primitive regions of Alaska and Canada, but a few were owned by the so-called sportsman-pilot and it was these that were the most pampered. The "Reliant" didn't mind working and even enjoyed it, but it literally glowed under pampering. As powered with the 285 h.p. Wright R-760-El engine the SR-9D performed very well throughout the flight range. Its behavior was a

"Reliant" SR-9EM (Multi-Purpose) operated by New York Police.

source of constant praise, and though its services were a little more expensive it was still considered a good investment for business or sport. Because of ever-increasing dimension and the inevitable gaining of weight, the newer "Reliant" series was no longer a go-anywhere airplane, as compared to the earlier Stinson monoplanes, but it still did a very impressive job of getting in and getting out when in good hands. Stinson pilots loved their airplanes and learned the very limits of their abilities. As powered with the 320 h.p. Wright R-760-E2 engine, the SR-9E did everything a little better than the SR-9D and its extra cost was money well spent. About half of the production in this Wright-powered series was SR-9E, and several were ordered as the multi-purpose version which spent most of their time hauling bundles, boxes, and other sundry freight. A "Reliant" could be everything to its owner, and it seemed quite happy in all that it did. The type certificate for the SR-9D and SR-9E was issued 2-2-37 and some 50 or more examples were manufactured by the Stinson Aircraft Co., Inc., at Wayne, Mich. Stinson had a very small strip alongside its plant that they called airport; it was small, but the "Reliant" roared out of there with room to spare.

Listed below are specifications and performance data for the "Reliant" model SR-9D as powered with Wright R-760-E1 engine rated 285 h.p. at 2100 r.p.m. at sea level; length overall 28'1"; height overall 8'6"; wingspan 41'11"; max. wing chord 96"; wing chord at tip 38"; total wing area 258.5 sq. ft.; airfoil Mod. Clark Y; empty wt. 2600 lbs.; useful load 1450 lbs.; payload with 78 gal. fuel 775 lbs. (4 pass. & 95 lbs. bag.); max. bag. allowed was 150 lbs.; gross wt. 4050 lbs.; max. speed 152 at sea level; cruising speed (.75 power) 140 at sea level; landing speed (with flaps) 60; climb 900 ft. first min. at sea level; ser. ceiling 14,500 ft.; gas cap. 78 gal.; oil cap. 5 gal.; cruising range (.75 power) at 17

gal. per hour 630 miles; price approx. $12,000 at factory field.

Specifications and data for model SR-9E (and SR-9ED or SR-9EM) as powered with Wright R-760-E2 engine rated 320 h.p. at 2200 r.p.m. at sea level (350 h.p. at 2300 r.p.m. for takeoff with control. prop) same as above except as follows: wt. empty 2640 lbs.; useful load 1410 lbs.; payload with 78 gal. fuel 735 lbs. (4 pass. & 55 lbs. bag.); gross wt. 4050 lbs.; max. speed 161 at 6500 ft.; cruising speed (.75 power) 150 at sea level; landing speed (with flaps) 60; climb 950 ft. first min. at sea level; ser. ceiling 17,500 ft.; gas cap. 78 gal.; oil cap. 5 gal.; cruising range (.75 power) at 19 gal. per hour 600 miles; price approx. $12,500 at factory field. Gross wt. allowance for both SR-9D and SR-9E later raised to 4100 lbs. Both models eligible as seaplanes on Edo WA-4665 twin-float gear at 4500 lbs. gross wt. The performance was reduced proportionately.

The construction details and general arrangement of the "Reliant" had been more or less the same for several years now, and the SR-9 series varied only in basic detail. Interiors progressively got bigger and a little finer, the entry doors were getting bigger and vision was being improved, extra fuel capacity was allowed for greater range and in-the-air or on-the-ground operation was enhanced by electrical or hydraulic aids, but outside of this the "Reliant" were pretty much alike. The most significant difference in the SR-9D and SR-9E, as compared to other models in the SR-9 series, was installation of the 7 cyl. Wright engine and any modifications required for this combination. Standard equipment installed left very little to be desired, but many useful options were still available at extra cost. The so-called multi-purpose type, designated "M," was specially prepared with extra large doors and a metal-lined interior; it could also be specially prepared

Six SR-9D being readied for delivery to Bureau of Air Commerce.

with an ambulance litter, or as a camera-plane. All models were also available as seaplanes on Edo WA-4665 twin-float gear. A Hamilton-Standard metal prop, electric engine starter, battery, generator, cabin heater & ventilator, leather upholstery, 8.50x10 (6 ply) tires, 10 in. tail wheel, Pyrene fire extinguisher, bonding & shielding for radio, oil cooler, dual control wheels, navigation lights, cabin lights, 2 baggage compartments, assist ropes, ash trays, seat belts, and first-aid kit were standard equipment. A Hamilton-Standard or Lycoming-Smith controllable prop, wheel streamlines, landing lights, paraflares, extra instruments, extra fuel cap., radio gear, and a special hand-rubbed finish were optional. The next Stinson development was the SR-9F as described here in the chapter for ATC # 640.

Listed below are SR-9D and SR-9E entries as gleaned from registration records:

NC-17121;	SR-9E	(# 5200) Wright 320
NC-50Y;	"	(# 5201) "
-17130;	SR-9D	(# 5202) Wright 285
-17131;	SR-9E	(# 5203) Wright 320
-17109;	SR-9D	(# 5204) Wright 285
-17136;	"	(# 5205) "
-17137;	SR-9E	(# 5206) Wright 320
-17147;	"	(# 5207) "
-17135;	"	(# 5208) "
-17138;	"	(# 5209) "
-17132;	SR-9D	(# 5210) Wright 285
-17140;	SR-9E	(# 5213) Wright 320
-17141;	SR-9D	(# 5214) Wright 285
-17143;	SR-9E	(# 5216) Wright 320
-17145;	SR-9D	(# 5218) Wright 285
-17107;	"	(# 5219) "
-17114;	"	(# 5220) "
-17157;	SR-9E	(# 5224) Wright 320
-17144;	SR-9D	(# 5254) Wright 285
-17168;	SR-9E	(# 5255) Wright 320

An SR-9D operating as seaplane in Canada.

96

-17186;	SR-9D	(# 5256) Wright 285
-17188;	SR-9E	(# 5257) Wright 320
-17193;	"	(# 5258) "
-17173;	"	(# 5259) "
-18444;	"	(# 5263) "
-18420;	SR-9D	(# 5264) Wright 285
-18430;	SR-9E	(# 5266) Wright 320
-17198;	"	(# 5267) "
PP-TCM;	"	(# 5268) "
NS-3640;	SR-9EM	(# 5269) "
-18428;	SR-9E	(# 5401) "
-18436;	SR-9EM	(# 5402) "
PP-TDI;	SR-9D	(# 5403) Wright 285
-18454;	SR-9E	(# 5404) Wright 320
NC-83;	"	(# 5405) "

NC-84;	"	(# 5406) "
NC-85;	"	(# 5408) "
NC-86;	"	(# 5451) "
-18437;	"	(# 5450) "
NC-87;	"	(# 5452) "
NC-88;	"	(# 5453) "

This approval for ser. # 5200 and up; ser. # 5268 to Brazil on floats; ser. # 5403 also to Brazil; ser. # 5405, 5406, 5408, 5451-52-53 del. to BAC; no listing for ser. # 5225 through 5250 and ser. # 5275 and up—these ser. nos. may not have been used; three SR-9D as UC-81G, ten SR-9E as UC-81J, and one SR-9EM as UC-81M in USAAF in 1942; approval expired 10-25-40.

ATC # 626
(2-5-37)
WACO, MODEL YKS-7.

Handsome Waco model YKS-7 for 1939 had wider landing gear and other improvements.

The "Waco" model YKS-7 and ZKS-7 cabin biplanes as offered for the year 1937 were just a slight revision from the year's previous model, but had enough "on the ball", so to speak, to be billed as the most efficient and most economical 5 place airplane on the market. Both of these models were of the so-called "Standard" (S) series; the YKS-7 had the 225 h.p. Jacobs L-4 engine and the ZKS-7 had the 285 h.p. Jacobs L-5 engine. The more economical (225 h.p.) YKS-7 was the most popular of the two by far, and it cost less than $6000.; that was a lot of good airplane for the price. More than 50 of these airplanes (YKS-7 and ZKS-7) were manufactured and delivered in 1937 alone, and no matter where you wished to go from Troy you could just hitch a ride on one of these Wacos being delivered, and it was bound to go somewheres near your destination, even if you lived in Alaska. Naturally there was some noticeable improvement in the 1937 model, and the models offered for 1938-39 were improved still more; these versions of the "Standard Cabin" were getting to be quite an airplane. True, the "Standard Cabin" such as the YKS-7 or the ZKS-7 was still rather plain as compared to the fancier and more colorful "Custom Cabin", but the utility offered at the considerably lower price was a strong point that sold these 2 models in large quantity. With the sign of war clouds forming in Europe there was increasing nervousness in this country also, and to some extent this had effect on sales of the YKS-7 and ZKS-7, so production had to be tapered off; the last of these was built in 1941. In 1942 two of the YKS-

7 served in the USAAF as the UC-72K and 2 of the ZKS-7 served as the UC-72M. With the cessation of hostilities in 1945 most of the YKS-7 and ZKS-7 that had been stored away during this period were dusted off and continued on in doing what they do best.

The "Waco" model YKS-7 and ZKS-7 were tidy cabin-type biplanes with seating arranged for 4 or 5. Good-looking appointments with good-wearing qualities offered comfort and pleasant styling yet allowed the airplane to work steadily without becoming shabby. Visibility was ample all around, and the ride was kept pleasant with cabin heat or ventilation; heavy insulation was used against noise and extremes in weather. These airplanes were known to be very stable; this offered a relaxed and pleasant ride to the passengers. It was a boon to the pilot also who often had to fly long hours in dubious weather fighting capricious air-currents. Like their forebears these were versatile airplanes readily adaptable to work, business, or play; to further increase their utility they could be converted to a cargo-hauling freighter, air-ambulance, an air-taxi for charter, or mounted on pontoons to operate as a seaplane. As powered with the 7 cyl. Jacobs L-5 engine of 285 h.p. the model ZKS-7 delivered very good performance, and demonstrated an exceptional ability in all types of work and uses. Perhaps the nicest comment about this airplane was that it had all the nice habits of earlier versions of the S-type and none of the little annoying ones. It now had a wider, more stable landing gear, good foot-pedal wheel brakes, the controls were lighter and smoother,

Waco model ZKS-7 was popular with business houses.

it was very comfortable inside, and the ship was very stable throughout the range of flight—in all, a very nice airplane. The model YKS-7 as powered with the 225 h.p. Jacobs L-4 engine was certainly all of this except for a slight drop in performance because of less power available. The Jacobs engine of this time was a fine powerplant, but a little touchy on mixture and carburetor heat; it just took a little learning. The type certificate for the models YKS-7 and ZKS-7 was issued 2-5-37 and some 86 or more examples were manufactured by the Waco Aircraft Co. at Troy, Ohio. Clayton J. Brukner was pres.; Lee N. Brutus was V.P. & gen. mgr.; Hugh R. Perry was sales mgr.; A. Francis Arcier was chf. engr.

Listed below are specifications and performance data for the Waco model YKS-7 as powered with Jacobs L-4 engine rated 225 h.p. at 2000 r.p.m. at sea level; length overall 25'3"; height overall 8'6"; wingspan upper 33'3"; wingspan lower 28'3"; wing chord upper & lower 57"; wing area upper 130 sq. ft.; wing area lower 110 sq. ft.; total wing area 240 sq. ft.; airfoil Clark Y; wt. empty 1882 lbs.; useful load 1368 lbs.; payload with 70 gal. fuel 740 lbs. (4 pass. & 60 lbs. bag.); gross wt. 3250 lbs.; max. speed (105%) with Hartzell wood prop 146; cruising speed (.75 power) with Hartzell wood prop 130 at sea level; max. speed (105% power) with Curtiss-Reed metal prop 150; cruising speed (2000 r.p.m.) with Curtiss-Reed metal prop 140 at 6000 ft.; landing speed (with flaps) 50; climb 800 ft. first min. at sea level; ser. ceiling 15,000 ft.; gas cap. 70 gal.; oil cap. 5 gal.; cruising range (2000 r.p.m.) at 6000 ft. at 15 gal. per hour 590 miles; price first quoted at $5395, later raised to $5695 at factory. Available with Jacobs L-4M or L-4MB engines. Available also

as seaplane on Edo 38-3430 twin-float gear at 3540 lbs. gross wt.

Specifications and data for model ZKS-7 as powered with Jacobs L-5 engine rated 285 h.p. at 2000 r.p.m. at sea level, same as above except as follows: wt. empty 1928 (2020) lbs.; useful load 1322 (1230) lbs.; payload with 70 gal. fuel 694 (602) lbs. (4 pass. & 14 lbs. bag. or 3 pass. & 92 lbs. bag.); gross wt. 3250 lbs.; figures in parentheses as later amended; max. speed (105% power) with Curtiss-Reed metal prop 153; cruising speed (.75 power) 136 at sea level; cruising speed (2000 r.p.m. at 6000 ft.) 145; landing speed (with flaps) 50; climb 900 ft. first min. at sea level; ser. ceiling 16,000 ft.; gas cap. 70 gal.; oil cap. 5 gal.; cruising range (2000 r.p.m. at 6000 ft.) at 16.5 gal. per hour 560 miles; price first quoted at $6135, later raised to $6435, all prices FAF at factory field. The ZKS-7 was normally equipped with a Curtiss-Reed metal prop. Available with Jacobs L-5M or L-5MB engines. Available also as seaplane on Edo 38-3430 twin-float gear at 3540 lbs. gross wt.

In general, the construction details and general arrangement of the YKS-7 and ZKS-7 were similar to those described in the chapters for ATC # 528 and # 533, except as follows. Waco introduced many little improvements for 1937; all these without any major design changes. The interiors were a little more comfortable, both models were now approved as 5-place airplanes, there was slightly more glass area, and later models had a redesigned windshield. Landing gear tread was 87 in. for the 1937 models with mechanical brakes, but 1938 models introduced the new landing gear with 108 in. tread using oleo-spring shock struts of 8 in. travel, and hydraulic wheel brakes; foot-operated brake pedals were standard on all models now, but the

Utility of ZKS-7 assured commercial operators of making money.

traditional hand-lever braking system was available to those that preferred it. The landing gear was moved forward by 4 in., and all joints were fitted with "Lord" rubber bushings; 7.50x-10 wheels with brakes were fitted with 8.50x10 tires. A 35 gal. fuel tank was mounted in the root end of each upper wing-half and 15 gal. tanks in the lower wing roots were optional; baggage allowance was 100 lbs. Both models were also eligible as seaplanes, or ski-planes; for seaplane the normal vertical surfaces were then replaced with seaplane-type surfaces of more area. The Jacobs L-4 and L-5 engines were available in either the M or MB versions; the M was magneto ignition, and the MB was magneto-battery ignition. A Hartzell wooden prop, electric engine starter, battery, generator, oil cooler, parking brake, wheel cuffs, throw-over control wheel, wheel brakes, tail wheel, adj. front seat, navigation lights, fire extinguisher bottle, dome light, ash trays, assist ropes, tool kit, and first-aid kit were standard equipment. A Hamilton-Standard or Curtiss-Reed metal prop, leather upholstery, cargo interior, ambulance litter, wheel streamlines, parachute-type seats, Y-type control column, landing lights, paraflares, radio gear, air brakes (flaps), extra door, wing-walk, cabin heater, steerable tail wheel, special paint schemes, Edo pontoons, and skis were optional. The next "Waco" development was the model ZGC-7 as described here in the chapter for ATC # 627.

Listed below are YKS-7 and ZKS-7 entries as verified by company records:

NC-17452;	YKS-7	(# 4551)	Jac. L-4
-17453;	"	(# 4554)	"
-17457;	"	(# 4600)	"
-17458;	"	(# 4601)	"
-17455;	"	(# 4602)	"
LN-EAO;	"	(# 4603)	"
-17462;	"	(# 4604)	"
-17464;	"	(# 4605)	"
-17465;	"	(# 4606)	"
-17463;	"	(# 4607)	"
-17468;	"	(# 4608)	"
-17466;	"	(# 4609)	"
-17467;	"	(# 4610)	"
-17473;	"	(# 4611)	"
-17472;	"	(# 4612)	"
-17474;	"	(# 4613)	"
-17471;	"	(# 4614)	"
-17475;	"	(# 4615)	"
-17461;	"	(# 4616)	"
-17701;	"	(# 4617)	"
-17702;	"	(# 4618)	"
-17714;	ZKS-7	(# 4619)	Jac. L-5
CF-BDY;	YKS-7	(# 4621)	Jac. L-4
-17705;	"	(# 4622)	"
-17716;	"	(# 4623)	"
;	"	(# 4624)	"
-17713;	"	(# 4625)	"
-17704;	ZKS-7	(# 4626)	Jac. L-5
-17718;	YKS-7	(# 4627)	Jac. L-4
-17717;	"	(# 4628)	"
;	"	(# 4629)	"
-17726;	"	(# 4630)	"
-17728;	"	(# 4631)	"
-17729;	"	(# 4633)	"
-17732;	"	(# 4634)	"
;	ZKS-7	(# 4635)	Jac. L-5
-17734;	YKS-7	(# 4636)	Jac. L-4
NC-2258;	ZKS-7	(# 4637)	Jac. L-5
;	YKS-7	(# 4638)	Jac. L-4
-17735;	"	(# 4639)	"
-17736;	"	(# 4665)	"
-17737;	"	(# 4666)	"
-17741;	ZKS-7	(# 4667)	Jac. L-5
-17744;	YKS-7	(# 4668)	Jac. L-4
-17743;	"	(# 4669)	"
-17739;	ZKS-7	(# 4670)	Jac. L-5
;	YKS-7	(# 4671)	Jac. L-4
-19359;	"	(# 4673)	"
;	"	(# 4674)	"
-19352;	"	(# 4680)	"
-19353;	"	(# 4681)	"
-17746;	"	(# 4682)	"
TF-ORN;	"	(# 4683)	"
-17745;	"	(# 4684)	"

100

YKS-7 and ZKS-7 were big favorites in Canadian "bush."

-19350;	"	(# 4690)	"
-19351;	"	(# 4691)	"
NC-49;	"	(# 4692)	"
NC-50;	"	(# 4693)	"
NC-52;	"	(# 4694)	"
-19358;	"	(# 5200)	"
;	"	(# 5201)	"
-19363;	"	(# 5202)	"
-19366;	ZKS-7	(# 5203)	Jac. L-5
-19373;	YKS-7	(# 5204)	Jac. L-4
-19381;	"	(# 5205)	"
;	"	(# 5206)	"
-19376;	"	(# 5208)	"
-19384;	ZKS-7	(# 5209)	Jac. L-5
-19379;	YKS-7	(# 5210)	Jac. L-4
-19371;	"	(# 5211)	"
-19386;	"	(# 5212)	"
-20903;	ZKS-7	(# 5213)	Jac. L-5
-20902;	"	(# 5214)	"
NC-2335;	"	(# 5215)	"
;	YKS-7	(# 5216)	Jac. L-4
-20954;	ZKS-7	(# 5221)	Jac. L-5
-20905;	YKS-7	(# 5222)	Jac. L-4
-29370;	"	(# 5228)	"
NC-2258;	ZKS-7	(# 5231)	Jac. L-5
-20959;	"	(# 5232)	"
NC-2628;	"	(# 5233)	"
NC-2629;	"	(# 5234)	"
-20963;	"	(# 5235)	"
NC-6002;	"	(# 5236)	"
TF-SGL;	"	(# 5237)	"
-29377;	"	(# 5242)	"

This approval for ser. # 4551 and up; ser. # 4603 del. to Norway; ser. # 4621 del. to Fleet Aircraft of Canada; ser. # 4624, 4638, 4671, 4674, 5201, 5216 del. to Argentina; ser. # 4629 del. to Paraguay; ser. # 4635, 5206 del. to Johannesburg, So. Africa; ser. # 4683, 5237 del. to Iceland; ser. # 4692-93-94 del. to Bureau of Air Commerce; ser. # 4551 through 4694 all had narrow landing gear and mech. brakes; ser. # 5200 and up all had wide landing gear and hydraulic brakes; NC-2258 first used for ser. # 4637 "washed out" in crash 7-19-39—NC-2258 then used for ser. # 5231 by same owner, Reading Battery Co.; 2 of YKS-7 in USAAF as UC-72K; 2 of ZKS-7 in USAAF as UC-72M; approval expired 4-13-43.

ATC # 627
(2-12-37)
WACO, MODEL ZGC-7

Waco model ZGC-7 with 285 h.p. Jacobs engine was a "Custom Cabin" favorite.

The model ZGC-7 (Custom Cabin) "Waco" for the year 1937 was perhaps not as curvy as the beautiful YOC or CUC of a year or two back; the line seemed to have lost nearly all the interesting curves and bulges of the earlier craft, but it was still a rather full-figured airplane and a real smoothie. The new custom ZGC-7 was more gently beautiful in a pleasant arrangement of form and dimension; its emphasis was also upon things more comfortable and more stylish. It too was more or less a pampered airplane and usually belonged to some sportsman, or an executive of some business-house. Of course, like any "Waco Cabin" the ZGC-7 had no particular aversion towards working; it could and did work alongside the best of them, but it was usually treated more like a limousine than a station wagon. Appointments and equipment varied in the ZGC-7 according to customer tastes and needs, but most of the airplanes were quite plush in leather or fancy mohair, and embellished with numerous extras; there was enough gadgetry available for this airplane to please anybody. The fully-equipped ZGC-7 was fairly expensive, but to some people at least, even in these times, the plain lower-priced airplane was not good enough and not necessarily the best bargain. What sold the ZGC-7 "Custom Cabin" to most people was the neat simplicity that reflected charm and a rather subtle elegance; it was a nice combination of fashion and function. Among the many airplanes that Waco Aircraft exported in 1937 was a ZGC-7 (Custom) to Alexandria, Egypt, and a ZGC-7 "Freighter" to Alaska.

This airplane was also available with the 225 h.p. Jacobs L-4 engine as the YGC-7. but this was not nearly enough power for this much airplane, so nobody ordered this combination. It is of interest to note that as the year of 1936 came to a close there were 1140 "Waco" airplanes in active operation, and some of them were as much as 10 years old, and older.

The Waco model ZGC-7 was a "Custom Cabin" version for the year 1937, a cabin biplane with seating arranged for 5. There were many little improvements in the "Custom Cabin" for 1937 and all without any major design changes. By looking carefully one could see thinner framing around the cabin area which provided more glass, interior appointments appeared to be a bit more lavish, there was better control of interior comfort, and the pilot's job was made easier by an improved control system. There were several other mechanical improvements too that allowed for frequent operation and better servicing. The ZGC-7 "Custom" was now a better airplane, but it was a good bit more expensive too; basic prices for the "Custom" had gone up by $600 and more. Although leveled primarily at the sportsman or men of business, the robust and easy-going ZGC-7 could put on an apron over its finery and put out a good day's work; it was not basically a working airplane, but any "Waco" will gladly work if you want it to. The ZGC-7 was not conspicuous nor an outstanding personality, but it was a good airplane and even better than people expected. As powered with the 7 cyl. Jacobs L-5

ZGC-7 could show handsome lines from any angle.

engine of 285 h.p., the model ZGC-7 was inherently endowed with a broad range of good performance, it had some power reserve to play with, and could get downright frisky at times. Of course, when loaded down to full capacity, as it often was, it lost some of its verve, but it still did an admirable job at a slower pace. Inherently stable by design, with the self-control of good manners, the ZGC-7 was a pleasure to fly and operate, and it seemed quite happy with itself. The type certificate for the model ZGC-7 was issued 2-12-37 and some 28 or more examples were manufactured by the Waco Aircraft Co. at Troy, Ohio.

Listed below are specifications and performance data for the Waco model ZGC-7 as powered with Jacobs L-5 engine rated 285 h.p. at 2000 r.p.m. at sea level; length overall 26'7"; height overall 8'8"; wingspan upper 35'0"; wingspan lower 24'6"; wing chord upper 72"; wing chord lower 48"; wing area upper 168 sq. ft.; wing area lower 78 sq. ft.; total wing area 246 sq. ft.; airfoil Clark Y; wt. empty 2200 lbs.; useful load 1450 lbs.; payload with 70 gal. fuel 822 lbs. (4 pass. & 142 lbs. for bag. & extras); payload with 95 gal. fuel 665 lbs. (3 pass. & 155 lbs. for bag. & extras); gross wt. 3650 lbs.; max. speed (105% power) with Curtiss-Reed metal prop 159; cruising speed (2000 r.p.m. at 6000 ft.) 149; landing speed (with flaps) 52; climb 800 ft. first min. at sea level; ser. ceiling 16,500 ft.; gas cap. normal 70 gal.; gas cap. max. 95 gal.; oil cap. 5-6 gal.; cruising range (2000 r.p.m. at 6000 ft.) at 16.5 gal. per hour 600 miles; price first quoted at $8435, later raised to $8935 with standard equipment at factory. Also available with Hamilton-Standard control prop for a slight increase in performance. Gross wt. allowance later increased to 3800 lbs. for ser. # 4560 and up.

The construction details and general arrangement of the model ZGC-7 were quite similar to that of the C-6 as described in the chapters for ATC # 597-98. Among the noticeable improvements was more glass area, better control of cabin heating and ventilation, a better toe-operated hydraulic braking system, the control system was redesigned for more smoothness, and it was perhaps just a little quieter and just a little more comfortable. The "Custom Cabin" now had trailing-edge wing flaps and the landing gear was widened to a 108 in. tread. A metal-lined cargo-type interior was available with an extra door and room for 800 lbs.; normally, the baggage allowance was 100 lbs. A 35 gal. fuel tank was mounted in the root end of each upper wing-half; an extra 25 gal. fuel tank under rear seat was optional. A throw-over control wheel was standard, but a Y-type control column was optional. Horizontal stabilizer was adjustable for trim in flight, and a ground-adjustable trim tab was fitted to the rudder. A Curtiss-Reed metal prop, electric engine starter, battery, generator, oil cooler, cabin heater & ventilator, navigation lights, cabin lights, landing lights, wheel cuffs, 10.5 in. tail wheel, 7.50x10 wheels with 8.50x10 tires, hydr. wheel brakes, parking brake, ash trays, assist ropes, and first-aid kit were standard equipment. Special leather upholstery, custom paint & finish, an extra door, wheel pants, paraflares, bonding & shielding, radio gear, pressure-type fire extinguisher, and skis were optional. The next "Waco" development was the rare one-only model VQC-6 as described here in the chapter for ATC # 631.

Listed below are model ZGC-7 entries as verified by company records:

NC-17454;	ZGC-7	(# 4550)	Jac. L-5
-17459;	"	(# 4553)	"
-17711;	"	(# 4555)	"
-17703;	"	(# 4556)	"
NC-2218;	"	(# 4557)	"
NC-2280;	"	(# 4560)	"
-17708;	"	(# 4563)	"
SU-AAV;	"	(# 4564)	"
-17712;	"	(# 4565)	"

-17707;	"	(# 4566)	"
-17720;	"	(# 4567)	"
-17709;	"	(# 4568)	"
NC-2245;	"	(# 4569)	"
-17723;	"	(# 4570)	"
-17722;	"	(# 4571)	"
NS-40Y;	"	(# 4572)	"
-17719;	"	(# 4574)	"
NC-2270;	"	(# 4576)	"
-17727;	"	(# 4577)	"
-17730;	"	(# 4578)	"
NC-2269;	"	(# 4579)	"
-17742;	"	(# 4580)	"
-17733;	"	(# 4581)	"
-17738;	"	(# 4582)	"
-17725;	"	(# 4584)	"

-17747;	"	(# 4585)	"
NC-2271;	"	(# 4586)	"
NC-17748;	"	(# 4587)	"

This approval for ser. # 4550 and up; ser. # 4550 was shown at New York Aircraft Show for 1937; ser. # 4560 del. to Jacobs Engine Co.; ser. # 4564 del. to Egypt; ser. # 4565 del. to Alaska; ser. # 4571 was Waco company demonstrator; reg. no. NS-40Y first used on YOC (# 4279) by State of Indiana who traded airplane in on ZGC-7 (# 4572) which then became NS-40Y and ser. # 4279 then became NC-17740; ser. # 4576 later modified to AGC-7; 2 of ZGC-7 in USAAF as UC-72E; this approval expired 9-30-39.

Speed, payload, and performance made ZGC-7 a most versatile airplane.

ATC # 628
(2-15-37)
SPARTAN "EXECUTIVE", 7-W.

Spartan "Executive" was one of the most advanced airplanes of its time.

The Spartan Aircraft Co. tried at first to introduce the gleaming "Executive" ever so casually because it was primarily leveled at people with money and impeccable taste, but can you imagine the raised eyebrows, the oohs and the aahs it actually generated. It was like trying to keep in the rays of a powerful light under a leaky bushel! The new "Spartan" monoplane was clearly an airplane like no other; it was one of the best-looking airplanes on the flight-line, and it had a quality about it that put many airplanes to shame. The softly rounded, low-winged model 7-W was a complete departure from anything that Spartan Aircraft had ever done before and considering the favorable, slightly jealous reaction by those in the industry, it was hard for them at Spartan Aircraft to keep a straight face. Caught up with the enthusiasm of others the company advertised extensively to extol the virtues of the 7-W "Executive" and named it for what it really was, a truly plush executive-transport. The "Executive," as it was aptly named, had been under design back in 1934, and was more or less in secret development since 1935. As a leisurely project it had been designed to embody features heretofore unheard of in any one airplane of this type. As the name of the airplane would imply the elegant "Executive" was specifically designed for the use of men in big business, and it bid well to furnish them the fastest and the finest in private air transportation. Its smooth-flowing outward appearance had the look and the promise of speed, its bulk and its stance showed promise of a tough character, and a peek into its cavernous interior was enough to delight even the most critical. Someone once said "it was an airplane

fit for a king," and so it was; a version with a custom interior arrangement and other princely trappings was delivered to the King of Iraq. The "Executive" was fast; it was a 200 m.p.h. airplane that proved itself occasionally in competition, but it was not really aggressive. It was a quiet, modest airplane that revelled in its high performance, but it was always proper and ladylike. So why was it so slow in selling, how come only 34 examples were built? Was it the depressed times, was it over-priced, or was the market limited? As it turned out the Spartan "Executive" was neither a success nor a failure—perhaps it just came out too soon.

The "Spartan 7" was an idea that began taking shape back in 1934 when there wasn't much else doing at Spartan Aircraft. The prototype of the "Model 7" was the 4-place Model 7-X (X-13984) and it was powered with a 285 h.p. Jacobs L-5 engine. Its maiden flight was in Jan. of 1936 and though the airplane was considered a success it needed a lot more power to offer the kind of performance that "Spartan" had in mind for this design. Hence, a redesign to mount the popular "Wasp Jr." SB (400 h.p.) engine, and this then became the 7-W. First flight of the redesigned airplane as the 7-W was on 9-14-36 or thereabouts. By Jan. of 1937 the 7-W was eased into production and certification was already under way. James B. Ford was chief engineer at Spartan Aircraft during all this time, and is generally credited with design of the "Model 7," but 'twas also said it evolved from the ideas of several other people. Ed W. Hudlow was V.P. & sales mgr., James B. Ford was chf. engr., and T. A. Campbell was plant mgr. Benevolent W. G. Skelly, noted Oklahoma oilman, was pres. &

Des Moines "Register-Tribune" was very proud of the "Executive."

chrmn. of the board. Ed Hudlow, with Spartan since 1930, left in Nov. of 1937 to take a post with the Bur. of Air Commerce. In a reshuffle, Jess D. Green became gen. mgr., Stanley Ehlinger became sales mgr., and Walter C. Hurty became chf. engr. Sometime later Earl Weining became chf. engr. and Fred Tolley became factory superintendent. J. Paul Getty became financially interested in Spartan Aircraft during 1937, but took no active part in management until 1942.

The Spartan "Executive" model 7-W was a low-winged cabin monoplane with seating arranged for 5. Altogether it was one of the most advanced airplanes of this particular day, and it was also one of the most complicated. It was a head-scratching mixture of old-fashioned steel tube trusses for bridge-like strength that were hidden from view by softly rounded contours and a smooth metal skin. Of very generous dimension the "Executive" offered room galore in a quiet cabin that fairly invited one to come in, settle down in comfort, and enjoy the view. To offer the utility necessary in a private air-transport it was also equipped with all the latest aids to flying and operation; it had all the conveniences too for a comfortable trip whether it be a long cross-country jaunt, or just a short hop. Its sleek, finely sculptured appearance was quickly noticed and the airplane was admired wherever it went; it was easy to be proud of it. To build an airplane such as this required the efforts of many operations with the use of many different materials; in effect this was slow and costly and it drove the price to a figure not easily handled by just anyone during these times. Therefore, the roster of owners reads like a cross-section of monied firms and wealthy individuals; it was definitely designed to cater to the limousine trade. As powered with the 9 cyl. Pratt & Whitney "Wasp Jr." SB engine rated 400 h.p., the "Executive" 7-W offered just about the ultimate in performance for day-to-day use

in any part of the country. With all that power on tap it was a spirited airplane, but easy to manage, and it had very good manners; it took good care of its people. Based on comment, it was an airplane that pilots learned to love and respect. Maxwell Balfour, a Spartan executive, related to us that he flew an "Executive" for the company for over 20 years, and he loved every minute of it! That is quite an endorsement. The type certificate for the Model 7-W was issued 2-15-37 and some 34 examples of this model were manufactured by the Spartan Aircraft Co. at Tulsa, Okla.

Listed below are the specifications and performance data for the Spartan "Executive" model 7-W as powered with "Wasp Jr." SB engine rated 400 h.p. at 2200 r.p.m. at 5000 ft. (450 h.p. at 2300 r.p.m. available for takeoff); length overall 26'10"; height overall 8'0"; wingspan 39'0"; wing chord at root 108"; wing chord at tip 54"; total wing area 250 sq. ft.; airfoil NACA-2418 at root tapering to a NACA-2406 at tip; wt. empty 2987 lbs.; useful load 1413 lbs.; payload with 112 gal. fuel 519 lbs. (4 pass. & 9 lbs. bag.); payload with 68 gal. fuel 783 lbs. (4 pass. & 103 lbs. bag.); gross wt. 4400 lbs.; max. speed 212 at 5000 ft.; cruising speed (.75 power) 208 at 9600 ft.; cruising speed (.65 power) 190 at 9600 ft.; stall speed (no flaps) 80; landing speed (with flaps) 63; takeoff run approx. 1200 ft.; climb 1430 ft. first min. at sea level; ser. ceiling 24,200 ft.; gas cap. 112 gal.; oil cap. 7 gal.; cruising range (.75 power) at 24 gal. per hour 850 miles; price at factory was $23,500 and up.

The fuselage framework was a welded X4130 steel tube truss to which were bolted a series of formed 24-ST "Alclad" bulkheads and channel-type dural stringers; the stressed-skin "Alclad" metal sheet was then riveted to this framework. This was an unusual method of fabricating a fuselage, but it was very strong. The cavernous cabin was entered through a huge door on the left, and one was quickly impressed with all the

Spartan 7-W flown by Arlene Davis was entry in 1937 National Air Races.

room. Cabin walls were lined thickly with "Seapak" for sound-proofing and insulation making normal conversation easy, and the interior was kept at a comfortable level with cabin heat or ventilation; the formed windshield was of shatter-proof glass. The deep rear seat was wide enough for 3 across, and the front bucket-type seats were adjustable; the entire cabin was upholstered in rich Laidlow cloth. Misc. controls were grouped in the center so as to be easily operated from either front seat; a throw-over control wheel was standard, but dual control wheels were available. A large baggage compartment with allowance for 100 lbs. was behind the rear seat; entry to this compt. was on the outside left. There was also a shelf behind the rear seat for hats, gloves, maps, and the like. The cantilever wing framework was built up around a welded X4130 steel tube triangular main spar beam, some integrated upper and lower chord members, and tied together with all-metal 24-ST truss-type wing ribs; the wing framework was then covered with stressed-skin "Alclad" 24-ST metal sheet. The center-section (C/S) panel was integral to the fuselage structure leaving short wing-stubs for outer panel attachment. Ailerons and wing flaps were all-metal structures covered with fabric. The flap system was in 3 sections; a flap on each wing and a belly-flap mounted to the C/S. The belly flap was simply a "drag flap" and not generally used. The 112 gal. fuel supply was stored in 5 tanks; 3 were in the fuselage section under the floor, and one in each wing-stub. A reserve tank of 15 gal. cap., usually filled with 87 octane fuel for takeoff, was mounted just behind the dash panel; a total fuel capacity of 148 gal. was optional. 80 Octane fuel was used for all normal operations. The cantilever-leg retractable landing gear of 124 in. tread used "Aerol" shock struts, Goodyear 7.50x10 wheels with hydraulic multiple-disc brakes, and fitted with 8.50x10 (6 ply) tires; the landing gear and

wing flaps were vacuum-operated with provisions for manual operation in emergency, but later this was changed to electrical operation. The swiveling tail wheel with 10.5 in. tire was fitted with a fore & aft lock for take-off and landings. The cantilever tail group was a multicellular structure; fixed surfaces were covered in "Alclad" metal sheet and movable surfaces were covered in fabric. Both rudder and elevators had aerodynamic "balance horns;" elevators were fitted with adjustable trim tabs. A Hamilton-Standard controllable prop, electric engine starter, 12-volt battery, a generator, cabin heater & vents, wheel brakes, parking brake, Lux fire extinguisher, carburetor heat-box, engine-driven fuel pump, emergency wobble-pump, fuel gauges, ammeter, oil-cooling radiator, navigation lights, cabin lights, head-rests, assist cords, ash trays, seat belts, and first-aid kit were standard equipment. Fixed dual control wheels, radio gear, bonding & shielding, extra fuel & oil cap., prop spinner, a heavy Plexiglass windshield, paraflares, landing lights, custom colors, and custom interior were optional. The next "Spartan" development was the rare model 7-WP as described here in the chapter for ATC # 646.

Listed below are 7-W entries as gleaned from various records:

X-13984;	7-X	(# 0)	Jac. 285
NC-13992;	7-W	(# 7W-1)	Wasp Jr. 400
-13993;	"	(# 7W-2)	"
-13994;	"	(# 7W-3)	"
-13995;	"	(# 7W-4)	"
-13998;	"	(# 7W-5)	"
-17601;	"	(# 7W-6)	"
-17602;	"	(# 7W-7)	"
-17603;	"	(# 7W-8)	"
-17604;	"	(# 7W-9)	"
-17605;	"	(# 7W-10)	"
-20220;	"	(# 7W-11)	"
-17613;	"	(# 7W-12)	"

-17614;	"	(# 7W-13)	"
-17615;	"	(# 7W-14)	"
-17616;	"	(# 7W-15)	"
-17617;	"	(# 7W-16)	"
-17630;	"	(# 7W-17)	"
-17631;	"	(# 7W-18)	"
YI-SOF:	"	(# 7W-19)	"
-17632;	"	(# 7W-20)	"

This approval for ser. # 2, 6 and up; ser. # 1, 3, 4, 5, 8 del. to Mexico; ser. # 7 to Alaska; ser. # 9 later to Britain; ser. # 10 in 1938 Bendix Trophy Race; ser. # 16 later to Britain; ser. # 19 was "Eagle of Iraq"; reportedly the Texas Co. owned 6 of the 7-W and Sohio owned 2; possibly 4 of the 7-W to Spain during the Spanish Civil War; 16 of the 7-W were in USAAF as UC-71;3 of 7-W to Canada during WW2; only 24 of the 7-W were sold in U.S.A.; approval expired 10-20-41.

"Executive" profile shows design for speed.

7-W was one of few 200 m.p.h. airplanes.

ATC # 629
(2-19-37)
CURTISS-WRIGHT, A-19-R.

Curtiss-Wright A-19-R designed for advanced military training.

The Curtiss-Wright "Design 19" of 1935 was mainly an exercise in adapting the various techniques used in building large all-metal airplanes; C-W was adapting these techniques into the practical fabrication of small all-metal private-owner airplanes. The venture was sponsored by the Bureau of Air Commerce for the development of private airplanes, and the Curtiss-Wright Model 19-L "Coupe" (ATC # 589) emerged from this project. If we check back we will see that the model 19-L was a terrific little airplane, but it was not the type of craft suitable to the average pilot; it was too "hot" for most, and it was too expensive even as powered with the 90 h.p. Lambert engine. This same airplane was reportedly then tested with the 145 h.p. Warner "Super Scarab" engine as the model 19-W, and it can be easily imagined what a phenomenal airplane this must have been. During these tests they at Curtiss-Wright quickly realized the vast potential of this basic design; the basic concept of construction and configuration was modified as need be, and eventually was used in several outstanding airplanes such as the 19-R, the CW-21, CW-22, CW-23 and others. All of these airplanes reflect the basic ideas that were first born in the little 19-L. The 19-R series that followed were fashioned as a tandem-seated advanced trainer that borrowed heavily from the original concept; it was actually groomed to be in a competition for a government "basic trainer" contract, but it failed. The model A-19-R that we are concerned with here was then offered as a high-performance sportplane, a tandem-seated

low-winger with a nice "greenhouse" canopy over the occupants, but unofficially the airplane was really designed as a utility-trainer for use by the military, especially abroad. The Curtiss-Wright model A-19-R was not favored with much success, but the continued evolution of this design concept produced some very interesting airplanes.

The sporty Curtiss-Wright model A-19-R was an all-metal low-winged cabin monoplane with seating arranged for 2 in tandem. The cabin in this case was actually a "greenhouse" canopy with sliding panels for exit or entry. Curtiss-Wright stated with tongue in cheek that this model was suitable for business or sport, but they didn't hide the fact either that it was particularly suitable as a "basic trainer" for the military. As a basic trainer for the advanced phases of military flying its war-load would include machine guns (both fixed and flexible) and light practice bombs. As a sportplane the A-19-R would not carry this war-load so the weight of these items was available as payload. There was actually no room in the sportplane version for all this payload potential, so it generally operated several hundred pounds below its gross weight limits; and this then translated into extra performance. As powered with the 9 cyl. Wright R-975-E3 engine of 420 h.p. the A-19-R simply had a breathtaking performance and it was capable of rather high speeds. Its most notable feature was its terrific rate of climb and its ability to reach its service ceiling (23,000 ft.) in less than 15 minutes! The airplane was eager and very sen-

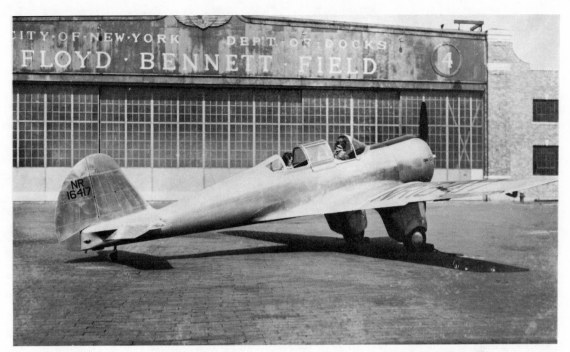

A-19-R was basis for several outstanding Curtiss-Wright designs.

sitive, so it required complete attention and a tender grip on the stick, but the rewards were well worth the necessary concentration. The 19-R and the A-19-R was rather scarce and it was apparently not an airplane of that much importance, but it did provide Curtiss-Wright with the incentive to pursue this basic concept, and develop other models that became outstanding airplanes. The type certificate for the model A-19-R was issued 2-19-37 and perhaps no more than 2 examples of this model were manufactured by the Curtiss-Wright Corp., St. Louis Airplane Div. at Robertson (St. Louis), Mo. C. W. France was gen. mgr. of the St. Louis plant; George A. Page was chf. engr.; and C. W. Scott was proj. engr.

Listed below are specifications and performance data for the Curtiss-Wright model A-19-R as powered with Wright R-975-E3 engine rated 420 h.p. at 2200 r.p.m. at 1400 ft. (450 h.p. available for takeoff); length overall 26'4"; height overall 7'6"; wingspan 35'0"; wing chord at root 84"; wing chord at tip 41"; total wing area 174 sq. ft.; airfoil CW-19 Spl.; wt. empty 1980 lbs.; useful load 1220 lbs.; payload with 96 gal. fuel 425 lbs.; gross wt. 3200 lbs.; max. speed 212 at 2000 ft.; cruising speed (.75 power) 190; cruising speed (.90 power) 202 at 2000 ft.; landing speed (with flaps) 56; stall speed (no flaps) 65; climb 2050 ft. first min. at sea level; ser. ceiling 22,900 ft.; gas cap. 96 gal.; oil cap. 6.5 gal.; cruising range (.75 power) at 23 gal. per hour 760 miles; fast cruise (.90 power) at 30 gal. per hour 600 miles; no price was announced.

The semi-monocoque fuselage framework was built up of 24ST "Alclad" bulkheads and stringers covered with 24ST "Alclad" metal sheet; the fuselage was of stressed-skin design, so the sheet metal covering carried a portion of the loads. Seating was in tandem and occupants were protected from wind and weather by a sliding canopy; the roomy cockpits were vented and heat was available. A full set of instruments and controls were provided in each cockpit; also, both cockpits were fitted with brackets and mounts for military hardware. The baggage compartment with allowance for 50 lbs. was a canvas zippered bag behind the rear seat. The tapering cantilever wing framework was of multi-cellular all-metal (24ST Alclad) construction using 5 spar beams and all-metal wing ribs placed at 20 in. intervals; the 24ST metal "stressed-skin" covering carried a big portion of the wing loads. The (C/S) center-section panel was fastened to underside of the fuselage and outer wing panels were then bolted to the butts of the C/S panel. A 35 gal. fuel tank was mounted in the C/S panel each side of the fuselage and fuel-level gauges were visible from either cockpit; the 48-gal. fuel tanks were optional. The split-type trailing-edge wing flaps were of all-metal structure and covered 55% of the span; flaps not to be lowered above 100 m.p.h. The cantilever landing gear of 83 in. tread was 2 separate units using oleo-spring shock struts of 8 in. travel; 7.50x10 wheels were fitted with 6.50x10 (6 ply) tires and hydraulic wheel brakes. Each landing gear unit was encased in a streamlined metal boot. The 8 in. tail wheel was steerable and fitted with a release for 360 deg. swivel. The cantilever tail group was of multi-cellular all-metal construction similar to the wing; elevators were fitted with adj. trim tabs. A Curtiss-Reed metal prop, electric engine starter, battery, generator, fuel pump, oil cooler, dual stick-type controls, navigation lights, cockpit lights, landing lights,

Model 19 fitted with retractable landing gear was labeled CW-22.

paraflares, fire extinguisher, bonding and shielding, tool kit, and a first-aid kit were standard equipment. A Hamilton-Standard controllable prop, and radio gear was optional. The next Curtiss-Wright development was the double-decked C-46 (CW-20) transport as described in the chapter for ATC # 772.

Listed below are 19-R and A-19-R entries as found in registration records:

NC-11781;	19-R	(#19R-1)	Wright 420
-16417;	A-19-R	(#19R-10)	"
-16421;	"	(#)	"

This approval for ser. # 19R-2 and up; approval expired 12-20-40.

ATC # 630
(3-4-37)
BEECH, MODEL 18-A

Beech 18-A used Wright engines; first airplane was sold to Ethyl Corp.

Nearly everyone was saying that the new twin-engined "Model 18" sure was a wide departure from what people would expect from Walter Beech, but conceded it was an interesting development in a type of airplane that was fast becoming popular at this time. So maybe it was similar to the Lockheed "Electra," and some pointed to a little bit of Douglas DC-2 in it, but no matter, this was a "Beech" no less and it was surely bound to elbow its way into the expanding market. By Nov. of 1935 the "Model 18" was already taking shape on the assembly floor, and a few select people were even allowed to see it. By June of 1936 Beech Aircraft was already hinting to potential customers that their new "Twin" would soon be available, and it would be able to operate from even the small pasture-type airports that dotted this country. The "Beech 18" finally made its long-awaited maiden flight on Jan. 15 of 1937 amid some local fanfare, and was approved for manufacture about 2 months later. Walter Beech, of course, proud of his new twin-engined airplane and boasted of hundreds of inquiries from business-houses, airlines, and government services from at least 10 different countries. But, the "Model 18" didn't acquire instant popularity. The first one was sold to the Ethyl Corp., an air-minded firm that a few years back had bought the very first "Stagger-Wing." A few were also delivered to Canada for "bush flying," but it was nearly 2 years before Beech could convince business people they needed this airplane. By then corporate executives learned they had to stay ahead of aggressive and progressive competition, and the "Beech 18" would help them do it. As a dream by Walter Beech, designed and fashioned by Ted Wells, the "Model 18" rolled out on the apron as a small, sturdy-looking airliner to seat 8; it was labeled simply as the 18-A and it was powered with two 7 cyl. Wright R-760-E2 engines rated 320 h.p. each. Shortly after its approval the "18" was dispatched with a crew from the factory on a demonstration tour that made a wide sweep around the country; they didn't sell many airplanes, but many people got to thinking and that was pleasant news to take back to the factory. Louise Thaden, an accomplished and famous aviatrix, also took her turn in demonstrating a new "Twin" and dropped it off in California. Prospects were still more or less unbelieving that this shiny all-metal "twin" was actually a "Beech," and it would take some more convincing. Who would guess at this time that this airplane, or variants of it, would eventually be built by the thousands.

The Beech model 18-A was an all-metal twin-engined low-winged monoplane with seating normally arranged for 6 passengers and a crew of 2. Because the airplane was designed for a multitude of services the interior could be arranged and fitted for just about any purpose; the ship was actually tailor-made at the factory to fit the job it would be doing. As we see, the airplane was an odd concept to be coming out of the Beech factory, but it was literally packed with innovations and special features that were not usually brought together in any one airplane. When they

An 18-A operating thru Canadian summer off water.

finally saw it, some were saying that Walter Beech "really stuck out his neck with this one"—insinuating that Beech had surely made a big mistake this time. But, the "Beech 18" proved them all wrong, as Walter Beech said it would. As powered with two 7 cyl. Wright R-760-E2 engines (a further proof that Beech had a special liking for the 7 cyl. Wright engine) of 320 h.p. each the 18-A was able to muster up an eye-opening performance with plenty of power in reserve. The power loading was relatively low so eagerness fairly surged through the frame, and it was always anxious to get going. The 18-A was a sight to see as it climbed out of the little airports not generally used by airplanes of this type, and it could maintain a safe single-engined ceiling of 8500 ft. Because it was designed to a purpose and not a price the Beech "Twin" was an expensive airplane, and it was some time before the ledger showed any sales to speak of. Beech realized he had to wait, and his patience paid off in the long run. The type certificate for the model 18-A was issued 3-4-37 and there was no accurate tally of how many were manufactured by the Beech Aircraft Corp. at Wichita, Kan. As assistant to Ted A. Wells, D. E. Burleigh was project engr. on Model 18 development.

Listed below are specifications and performance data for the Beech model 18-A as powered with 2 Wright R-760-E2 engines rated 320 h.p. at 2150 r.p.m. at sea level (350 h.p. available for takeoff); length overall 31'11"; height overall 9'5"; wingspan 47'8"; wing chord at root 126"; wing chord at tip 42"; total wing area 347 sq. ft.; airfoil NACA-230 series; wt. empty 4100 lbs.; useful load 2400 lbs.; payload with 160 gal. fuel & 2 crew 1172 lbs. (6 pass. & 152 lbs. bag.); payload with 210 gal. fuel & 2 crew 872 lbs. (4 pass. & 192 lbs. bag.); gross wt. 6500 lbs.; max. speed 202; cruising speed (.75 power) 167 at sea level; cruising speed (.66 power) 192 at 9600 ft.; landing speed (with flaps) 55; takeoff run approx. 500 ft.; climb 1250 ft. first min. at sea level; ser. ceiling 20,000 ft.; gas cap. normal 160 gal.; gas cap. max. 210 gal.; oil cap. 10-13 gal; cruising range (using 210 h.p. each engine) at 35 gal. per hour was slightly more than 4 hours; price $37,500 at factory. Eligible also as seaplane on Edo 55-7170 twin-float gear at 7000 lb. gross wt.

The semi-monocoque fuselage framework was built up of formed dural bulkheads, extruded dural stringers, and covered with a riveted 52SH metal skin. The "pilot's office" was very roomy and a large cabin window was at each passenger seat. The interior was heavily insulated and could be fitted with 6 seats, 4 overstuffed chairs, 2 overstuffed chairs and a couch, or cleared entirely with no obstructions for hauling bulky cargo. Entry was on the left side. The center-section (C/S) panel was a dural metal structure built around a huge steel tube monospar which carried all stresses imposed by the engines, landing gear, and wings. An 80 gal. fuel tank was cradled in the C/S on each side of the fuselage; extra fuel to 210 gal. was optional. Each retractable landing gear unit, fastened to the C/S panel, was a forked cantilever leg with air-oil shock struts of 8 in. travel fitted with 29x13-5 Goodyear airwheels with hydraulic brakes. The landing gear retraction was electrically operated, with manual controls for emergency. The wing framework, in 2 halves, was of dural ribs and stringers fastened to and around a short steel tube monospar with a dural girder extension out to the tip; the completed framework was covered with riveted 52SH metal skin. The wing-tips were rigged with a built-in 3.5 deg. "wash-out" to improve "stall" characteristics of the tapered wing. The ailerons were an all-metal structure with fabric cover; an adj. trim tab was on left aileron. Split-type trailing edge wing flaps were electrically operated; a manual control was provided for emergency. The semi-monocoque

18-A was designed for business and small airlines.

tail group (fixed) was built up of dural spars and ribs with a riveted 52SH sheet metal cover; the twin rudders and the elevators were built up of welded steel tubing and fabric covered. Trim tabs were fitted to the elevators and one rudder. Hamilton-Standard controllable props, electric engine starters, generators, 2 batteries, fuel pumps, a wobble-pump, oil coolers, dual control wheels, toilet equipment, fire extinguisher bottles, bonding & shielding, navigation lights, 12x5-3 tail wheel, assist ropes, ash trays, and first-aid kit were standard equipment. Curtiss-Reed metal (fixed-pitch) props, landing lights, paraflares, cabin heaters & vents, radio gear, pressure-type fire extinguisher, executive-type in-teriors, cargo interiors, Edo pontoons, and skis were optional. The next "Twin Beech" development was the model 18-B as described here in the chapter for ATC # 656.

Listed below are Model 18-A entries as gleaned from registration records:

NC-15810: 18A (# 62) 2 Wright 320

This approval for ser. # 62 and up; serial numbering of the Model 18 series ran concurrently along with numbering of the Model 17 series, so serial numbering for the 18 will appear in blocks of 5 or 10 airplanes; the next production run of the 18 was 10 airplanes with ser. # 169 thru # 178.

18-A seaplane (S-18-A) was an impressive sight on its beaching gear.

ATC # 631
(3-12-37)
WACO, MODEL VQC-6.

Waco model VQC-6 was one-only airplane used to test new line of Continental W-670 engines.

Waco Aircraft was such a prolific dispenser of new models that every once in a while they came up with a really rare one, usually a one-of-a-kind. This had been happening now for several years, and it happened again in the little-known VQC-6. Basically, the VQC-6 was the same type of airplane as those described previously on ATC # 597 and 598, a "Custom Cabin" type that the Continental Motors Corp. had been playing with to test a new line of engines. This particular airplane (X-16243) was first labeled a UQC-6 and was fitted with a 240 h.p "Continental" engine for test, but was relabeled a VQC-6 when a W-670-M1 high-compression engine of 250 h.p. was installed. The airplane was a test-bed for this engine also, and when developed to satisfaction this engine was then available to other "Waco" airplanes, models such as the VPF-7 and the VKS-7F. The VPF-7 was an open-cockpit trainer and the VKS-7F was a cabin-type navigational trainer; both airplanes were offered for the government's CPTP program. In a way the often-overworked VQC-6 played an important role in the developing of a new engine, but there was no other future planned for it, so it remained rather obscure and its exact identity was soon forgotten. Just in passing, we remember a comment made just about this time that we feel deserves retelling. "The Waco Aircraft plant is undoubtedly one of the most picturesque factory sites in America; the cluster of neat buildings is set in a natural garden of green, and the turf landing field resembles a country club bordered by clumps of trees and other green foliage—half the fun of picking up a new "Waco" airplane was the visit to this plant."

The Waco model VQC-6 was a typical "Custom Cabin" biplane with seating arranged for 4 or 5. At this time the VQC-6 was not exactly a has-been, but it was a little behind the other C-6 models because it had been busy testing various engines as an experimental airplane. The Continental Motors Corp. had been using it as a flying test-bed for developing a series of new engines. Now that was taken care of, so it was hinted that Waco Aircraft had the VQC-6 approved "to make a decent woman out of her;" the engines that the VQC-6 tested, especially the W-670-M series, were available for up-coming models in the 1937-38-39 period. As powered here in this instance with the 7 cyl. Continental W-670-M1 engine of 250 h.p. the VQC-6 might be easily compared to similar "Waco" models such as the DQC-6 and the ZQC-6. We can then assume correctly that its performance was comparable and very satisfactory; its inherent flight characteristics with the help of 250 h.p. should have been spirited and very pleasant. Waco Aircraft exhibited 3 airplanes at the Pacific Aircraft & Boat Show held in Los Angeles during mid-March of 1937 because they really liked "Waco" airplanes out on the west coast. Waco Aircraft also exhibited at least 2 airplanes on the floor of the New York Air Show because "Waco" airplanes were popular just about everywhere, and that's a fact. The type certificate for the model VQC-6 was issued 3-12-37 and only one example of this model was manufactured by the Waco Aircraft Co. at Troy, Ohio.

Listed below are specifications and performance data for the Waco model VQC-6 as powered with the Continental W-670-M1 engine rated 250 h.p. at 2200 r.p.m. at sea level; length overall 26'8"; height overall 8'7"; wingspan upper 35'0"; wingspan lower 24'6"; wing chord upper 72"; wing chord lower 48"; wing area upper 168 sq. ft.; wing area lower 76 sq. ft.; total wing area 244 sq. ft.; airfoil Clark Y; wt. empty 2030 lbs.; useful load 1470 lbs.; payload with 70 gal. fuel 842 lbs. (4 pass. & 162 lbs. bag. & extras); gross wt. 3500 lbs.; max. speed (105% power) with Curtiss-Reed metal prop 160; cruising speed (2000 r.p.m.) 150; landing speed (with flaps) 55; climb 800 ft. first min. at sea level; ser. ceiling 16,500 ft.; gas cap. normal 70 gal.; gas cap. max. 95 gal.; oil cap. 5-6 gal.; cruising range (2000 r.p.m.) at 15.2 gal. per hour 600 miles; price not announced.

The construction details and general arrangement of the model VQC-6 was typical to that of previous C-6 models as described in the chapters for ATC # 597-598, except as follows. The most significant difference in the VQC-6 was installation of the new Continental W-670-M1 engine, and some slight modifications necessary to this combination. This engine was "fuel injected" using high-compression cylinder heads and operated on a minimum of 80 octane fuel; a "Marvel" fuel-injector was used in place of a carburetor. It also had automatic lubrication of the overhead valve-gear. The fuel-injected engine was usually more economical, and less gals. per hour at cruise translated into more range, or more miles per gallon. This engine was available with either magneto or battery ignition; it was "dual ignition" in either case. The W-670-M1 engine weighed 460 lbs. dry without prop hub or starter, and cost $3100 at the factory; crating and shipping were extra. A metal Curtiss-Reed prop, electric engine starter, generator, Exide battery, NACA-type engine cowl, oil cooler, throw-over control wheel, cabin lights, navigation lights, wheel brakes, parking brakes, drag flaps, fire extinguisher bottle, fuel gauges, assist ropes, tool kit, first-aid kit, and log books were standard equipment. The next "Waco" development was the Wright-powered model DGC-7 as described here in the chapter for ATC # 639.

NC-16243; VQC-6 (# 4447) W-670-M1; this is the only example of the VQC-6; it was first registered as a UQC-6.

ATC # 632
(4-10-37)
FAIRCHILD, 24-H.

Fairchild model 24-H was improved Ranger-powered version for 1937.

Following the automobile industry's lead, as each new model year rolled around, the aircraft manufacturers were obliged also to hustle out their latest offerings for the public to see; offerings which invariably were described as bigger, faster, and better than the model built previous. All the nice things they had said about last year's model were then almost belittled and the new model was now touted as queen of the airwaves. Just about all of the aircraft manufacturers were now caught up in this cycle, and Fairchild was certainly no exception. So, for the year 1937, Fairchild Aircraft came out with a Ranger-powered "Twenty Four" they labeled the "Deluxe 24-H," and proceeded to tell everyone that it was now the finest airplane that years of know-how was able to produce. But, was it? For years Fairchild was noted far and wide for its honest method of doing business; they gave assurance, and you could bet on it, you would be getting a truly fine product. This manner of business was reflected in the many satisfied customers that Fairchild could boast of. So, when Fairchild boasted that the model 24-H for 1937 was a truly "deluxe airplane," an airplane that was now faster, more comfortable, climbed higher, flew longer, and had exclusive Raymond Loewy styling that would mark you as a person of good taste, well, you almost had to believe it. The fact that it was equipped in this manner with

deluxe appointments and expensive equipment, it was bound to show up on the bottom line; this airplane was going to cost about $600 more. This was to narrow somewhat the sphere of its potential customers; if you wished all those fancy trappings it was going to cost. As one of two models introduced for 1937, Fairchild was stressing quality in this airplane, and not utility. You could see a lot of quality in the 24-H that was obvious, but a good bit of the quality was hidden; you couldn't see it, but you could feel it was there. By some owners it was called "the gentle thoroughbred." The roster of owners was a short but impressive list that centered around the New England states where most of the money was during these times; however, 3 did get out to the west coast.

The Fairchild model 24-H was a neat high-winged cabin monoplane with seating arranged for 3. It was designed primarily to catch the eye of those with money to spend on airplanes. Raymond Loewy, prominent industrial designer, when he wasn't designing Studebaker automobiles, Sears-Roebuck refrigerators, or streamlined locomotives, was engaged to design dazzling features that Fairchild could dangle in front of customers to urge them to buy. Thus, the model 24-H turned out to be a very attractive airplane right from its glistening paint scheme and roll-down windows, to its harmonious interior

The Fairchild 24, and especially the 24-H, was a very practical family airplane.

and its electric gas gauges. It was not exactly a utility airplane, but then it wasn't meant to be; this was Fairchild's top-of-the-line for 1937 and it was strictly a deluxe machine. As powered with the 6 cyl. inverted inline aircooled "Ranger" 6-390-D3 engine rated 150 h.p. the 24-H was a rather lively airplane that was a definite improvement over any "Twenty Four" that was built to now. Much was new on this airplane such as styling and equipment available, but it did retain all of the good characteristics the "Fairchild 24" was noted for; it was gentle and had very good manners. Because it was leveled at a certain clientele it was mainly of interest to the weatlthier class and the market was not all that big. The type certificate for the model 24-H was issued 4-10-37 and some 25 examples of this model were manufactured by the Fairchild Engine & Airplane Corp. at Hagerstown, Md.; the "Ranger" engines were manufactured at Farmingdale, Long Island, N.y. Early in 1937 James S. Ogsbury, formerly of IBM, was engaged as pres. & gen. mgr. to streamline the ponderous Fairchild organization. He was also responsible for the new styling in the "24" for 1937. The reshuffle made for a smoother-working organization, but it actually did very little to sell more airplanes.

Listed below are specifications and performance data for the model 24-H as powered with 6 cyl. Ranger 6-390-D3 engine rated 150 h.p. at 2350 r.p.m. at sea level; length overall 24'10"; height overall 7'4"; wingspan 36'4"; wing chord 66"; total wing area 173 sq. ft.; airfoil (NACA) N-22; wt. empty 1550 lbs.; useful load 850 lbs.; payload with 40 gal. fuel 417 lbs. (2 pass. & 77 lb. bag.); gross wt. 2400 lbs.; max. speed 133 at sea level; cruising speed (.75 power) 122 at 7200 ft.; landing speed (with flaps) 50; stall speed (no flaps) 58; takeoff run 430 ft.; climb 715 ft. first min at sea level; ser. ceiling 14,100 ft.; gas cap.

40 gal.; oil cap. 3 gal.; cruising range (.75 power) at 9.5 gal. per hour 470 miles; price $6190 at factory.

Specifications and data for 24-H as seaplane (24-HS) on Edo 44-2425 twin-float gear, same as above except as follows; length overall 29'0"; height overall (on water) 12'0"; wt. empty 1777 lbs.; useful load 773 lbs.; payload with 40 gal. fuel 340 lbs. (2 pass. & no bag.); gross wt. 2550 lbs.; max. speed 118 at sea level; cruising speed (.75 power) 112 at 5000 ft.; landing speed (with flaps) 52; stall speed (no flaps) 60; climb 510 ft. first min. at sea level; ser. ceiling 11,000 ft., cruising range (.75 power) at 9.5 gal. per hour 425 miles; price not announced.

The construction details and general arrangement for the model 24-H was typical to that of the earlier 24-C8F as described here in the chapter for ATC # 610 except as follows. The model 24-H was strictly a deluxe airplane with custom finish and a rich, harmonious interior designed by Raymond Loewy; the mirror-like 16-coat hand-rubbed finish was offered in 6 color combinations. It had roll-down windows, cabin vents, and cabin heat. The pilot's seat was adjustable, there were chrome-plated dual stick-type controls, adjustable sun-shades, just about everything necessary for carefree flight and operation, and several kinds of radio gear were available. For extended cross-country flying a 20 gal. fuel tank was available in place of the 3rd seat; this making it a two-seater with over 6 hours range with still more extra allowance for baggage. The "Ranger" engine was completely mounted in rubber and its maintenance requirements were minimal; the close-fitting engine cowling could be completely removed in less than 4 minutes. A wooden prop was normally fitted, but a metal custom-fitted Curtiss-Reed "cruise prop" was available. The 24-H was also available as a (24-HS) seaplane on Edo 44-2425 twin-float

"Ranger" inline engine promoted a very neat configuration.

gear. An electric engine starter, engine-driven generator, battery, oil cooler, exhaust silencer, 6.50x10 wheels with brakes, wheel pants, parking brake, 8 in. tail wheel, wing flaps with manual control, dual stick-type controls, fire extinguisher bottle, cabin vents, cabin heater, compass, navigation lights, safety-glass windows, assist ropes, ash trays, glove compt., and first-aid kit were standard equipment. Special wheel fair-

ings, retractable landing lights, paraflares, extra instruments & radio gear were optional. The next "Twenty Four" development was the model 24-G as described here in the chapter for ATC # 633.

Listed below are Fairchild 24-H entries as gleaned from registration records:

NC-16871;	24-H	(# 3200)	6-390-D3
-16872;	"	(# 3201)	"
-16873;	"	(# 3202)	"
-16874;	"	(# 3203)	"
-16875;	"	(# 3204)	"
-16891;	"	(# 3205)	"
-16892;	"	(# 3206)	"
-16893;	"	(# 3207)	"
-16894;	"	(# 3208)	"
-16895;	"	(# 3209)	"
-16901;	"	(# 3210)	"
-16902;	"	(# 3211)	;;
-16903;	"	(# 3212)	"
-16904;	"	(# 3213)	"
-16905;	"	(# 3214)	"
-16906;	"	(# 3215)	"
-16907;	"	(# 3216)	"
-16908;	"	(# 3217)	"
-16909;	"	(# 3218)	"
-16922;	"	(# 3219)	"
-19125;	"	(# 3220)	"
-19126;	"	(# 3221)	"
-19127;	"	(# 3222)	"
-19128;	"	(# 3223)	"
-19129;	"	(# 3224)	"

This approval for ser. # 3200 and up; ser. # 3206, 3207, unverified; ser. # 3222 later to Switzerland as HB-EIL; approval expired 9-30-39.

A 24-H that found its way into Canada.

ATC # 633
(4-19-37)
FAIRCHILD, MODEL 24-G.

Fairchild 24-G "Deluxe" with Warner "Super Scarab" engine.

Fairchild Aircraft had quite a lineup for 1937. The long-nosed Ranger-powered 24-H described here just previously was the "custom model" aimed at those with money to spend, but the new 24-G was the one that Fairchild was all excited about. Powered with the famous and very popular 7 cyl. Warner "Super Scarab" engine the model 24-G was a new airplane offered in 2 different versions. There was first the "deluxe" 24-G version that was groomed to take its place alongside the custom 24-H; it was a handsome 3-place airplane that gleamed in its custom finish and stylish interior. It too was equipped with all the extras, and so it too was quite expensive. But, the queen of the ball, so to speak, was the "standard" version of the 24-G which was a no-frills airplane that turned out to be the cheapest 4-place airplane in the country. This was to be also the first "Fairchild 24" that could carry four people. In order to do this much of the usual niceties had to be eliminated, such as the wheel pants, wing flaps, roll-down windows, and the 16-coat hand-rubbed finish was traded for less coats of a cheaper paint; this for gain of 60 lbs. in weight for payload and for a price-tag that was over $600 less. We have to point out that the basic airframe was not cheapened in any way; it still possessed "Fairchild quality" and only the "gingerbread" was missing. By design the 24-G was a happy creation that offered just about everything that the average private pilot, or operator, could ask for and buyers were practically standing in line to get one. The best single customer for the 24-G was the (BAC) Bureau of Air Commerce; they ordered 23 and they wanted them completed for delivery in 90 days! Twelve were of the standard model with complete radio sending and receiving equipment, and 11 were of the standard model fitted with extra fuel tanks for over 6 hours of cruising range. The 12 radio-equipped airplanes were fitted with brand-new Warner engines and netted Fairchild some $66,528; strangely enough, the 11 long-range airplanes were sold without engines for $38,489. This was the largest order ever placed by the BAC, and they now had 68 airplanes in service around the country. Other 24-G were delivered as fast as they could be made up, and they took off to all parts of the country. At least 7 were operated as seaplanes, and one was flown off to Alaska to operate in "the bush."

The Fairchild model 24-G was a high-winged cabin monoplane with seating arranged for 3 and 4. The 24-G "Deluxe" was the 3-seater that had Raymond Loewy styling and many other nice things, things that would appeal more to the sportsman-pilot with more money to spend. It was a handsome airplane that pleased all and was no stranger to praise and affection. The 24-G "Standard" was the 4-seater that was designed primarily for utility; it promised to be more attractive to the operator who would use it for charter, pilot-training, and all the other chores that a good operator could muster up. It would

24-G as seaplane on Edo floats.

also be attractive to the private pilot who was now able to graduate to this type of airplane at a much lower price. Its beauty (the Standard) was more subdued, but it was no stranger to praise either. Even though the Ranger-powered 24-H with its inline engine promoted cleaner, more graceful lines, the stubbier 24-G with its "round" (radial) Warner engine was the clear favorite. As powered with the 7 cyl. Warner "Super Scarab" engine of 145 h.p. the 24-G, in either version, was a lively machine that did well in summer heat of the southwest, or winter's cold in the northeast; it did well too anywhere in between. By careful design the 24-G was endowed with everything that was good in a "Twenty Four," plus some added capabilities and traits that made it the most popular airplane that Fairchild had built to now. Of course, the Deluxe was a little faster than the Standard, landed slower, and had more conveniences, but the "Standard" gave up very little in performance and it was certainly a whole lot cheaper. The BAC picked the 24-G for its inspectors because of its low cost, its economy of operation, its relative comfort, the ample payload, and its ease of flying; and, so did a lot of other people. The type certificate for the model 24-G (both Standard & Deluxe) was issued 4-19-37 and 100 of these airplanes were manufactured by the Fairchild Engine & Airplane Corp. at Hagerstown, Md.

Listed below are specifications and performance data for the Fairchild model 24-G as powered with Warner "Super Scarab" (Series 50) engine rated 145 h.p. at 2050 r.p.m. at sea level; length overall 23'10"; height overall 7'4"; wingspan 36'4"; wing chord 66"; total wing area 173.16 sq. ft.; airfoil (NACA) N-22; wt. empty 1475 lbs.; useful load 925 lbs.; payload with 40 gal. fuel 492 lbs. (2 pass. & 152 lbs. bag. & extras); payload with 30 gal. fuel 552 lbs. (3 pass. &

42 lbs. bag.); gross wt. 2400 lbs.; max. speed 130 at sea level; cruising speed (.75 power) 118 at sea level; landing speed (with flaps) 48; landing speed (no flaps) 56; takeoff run 450 ft.; climb 675 ft. first min. at sea level; ser. ceiling 16,500 ft.; gas cap. normal 40 gal.; oil cap. 3 gal.; cruising range (.75 power) at 9 gal. per hour 475 miles; price at factory was $5290 for standard model, and $5890 for deluxe model; deluxe version was 60 lbs. heavier when empty; both models eligible as seaplanes on Edo 44-2425 twin-float gear at 2550 lbs. gross wt.

The construction details and general arrangement for the Fairchild model 24-G were more or less typical to that of the "Twenty Four" described here in the chapters for ATC # 610 and # 632, except for the following. The 24-G was powered with a "radial" engine, so its appearance was more blunt and the engine was tightly encased in a NACA-type low-drag cowling; the cowling panels were swung open for servicing. To enhance the utility of this particular airplane it was available as a "Deluxe" (3 pl.) version, and as a "Standard" (4 pl.) version. The 24-G Deluxe was, of course, equipped with aids, convenience, and styling were suited to private owners who flew only for the sport of it; the 24-G Standard was without many of these extras and was more suited to the flying-service operator who could willingly do without these extras in exchange for another passenger's seating. Among the niceties not included in the cheaper "Standard" version were wing flaps, wheel streamlines, Raymond Loewy styling, plush mohair upholstery, roll-down windows, electric fuel gauges, extra instruments, and costly paints in a hand-rubbed finish; all these omissions came to the tune of 60 lbs. saving in empty wt. and $600 less in delivered cost. So, the buyer had a choice of a 3-place airplane festooned with

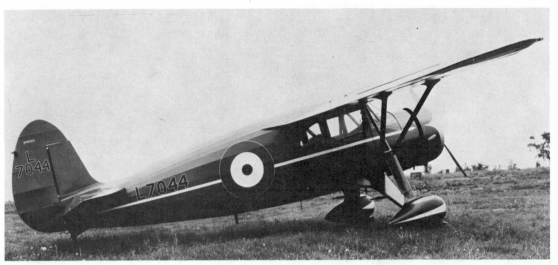

24-G combined strength, utility, and beauty.

gingerbread, or a plainer airplane that could carry 4 and performed just about as well. A wooden prop, electric engine starter, battery, generator, wheel brakes, wheel streamlines, 8 in. tail wheel, cabin heater, cabin vents, cabin lights, adj. sun-shades, glove compt., navigation lights, fire extinguisher, assist ropes, seat belts, first-aid kit, and a 16-coat hand-rubbed finish were standard equipment on the 24-G "Deluxe." A Curtiss-Reed metal prop, parachute-type front seats, extra 20 gal. fuel tank, landing lights, paraflares, oil cooler, radio gear, and Edo pontoons were optional. The next Fairchild development was the model 24-J as described here in the chapter for ATC # 663.

Listed below are Fairchild 24-G entries as gleaned from registration records:

NC-16866;	24-G	(# 2900)	Warner 145
-16867;	"	(# 2901)	"
-16868;	"	(# 2902)	"
-16869;	"	(# 2903)	"
-16870;	"	(# 2904)	"
-16881;	"	(# 2905)	"
-16882;	"	(# 2906)	"
-16883;	"	(# 2907)	"
-16884;	"	(# 2908)	"
-16885;	"	(# 2909)	"
-19100;	"	(# 2910)	"
-19101;	"	(# 2911)	"
-19102;	"	(# 2912)	"
-19103;	"	(# 2913)	"
-19104;	"	(# 2914)	"
-19115;	"	(# 2915)	"
-19116;	"	(# 2916)	"
-19117;	"	(# 2917)	"
-19118;	"	(# 2918)	"
-19119;	"	(# 2919)	"
-19132;	"	(# 2920)	"
-19133;	"	(# 2921)	"
NC-19;	"	(# 2922)	"
NC-20;	"	(# 2923)	"
NC-21;	"	(# 2924)	"

24-G seaplane demonstrating takeoff from snow covered runway.

Lineup of 24-G "Standard" for use by CAA.

NC-22;	"	(# 2925)	"
NC-23;	"	(# 2926)	"
NC-24;	"	(# 2927)	"
NC-25;	"	(# 2928)	"
NC-27;	"	(# 2929)	"
NC-28;	"	(# 2930)	"
NC-29;	"	(# 2931)	"
NC-30;	"	(# 2932)	"
NC-32;	"	(# 2933)	"
NC-36;	"	(# 2934)	"
NC-38;	"	(# 2935)	"
NC-39;	"	(# 2936)	"
NC-41;	"	(# 2937)	"
NC-42;	"	(# 2938)	"
NC-43;	"	(# 2939)	"
NC-44;	"	(# 2940)	"
NC-45;	"	(# 2941)	"
NC-47;	"	(# 2942)	"
NC-48;	"	(# 2943)	"
NC-46;	"	(# 2944)	"
-19170;	"	(# 2955)	"
-19171;	"	(# 2956)	"

-19172;	"	(# 2957)	"
-19173;	"	(# 2958)	"
-19174;	"	(# 2959)	"
-16886;	"	(# 2960)	"
-16887;	"	(# 2961)	"
-16888;	"	(# 2962)	"
-16889;	"	(# 2963)	"
-16890;	"	(# 2964)	"
-16896;	"	(# 2965)	"
-16897;	"	(# 2966)	"
-16898;	"	(# 2967)	"
-16899;	"	(# 2968)	"
-16900;	"	(# 2969)	"
-19105;	"	(# 2970)	"
-19106;	"	(# 2971)	"
-19107;	"	(# 2972)	"
-19108;	"	(# 2973)	"
-19109;	"	(# 2974)	"
-19110;	"	(# 2975)	"
-19111;	"	(# 2976)	"
-19112;	"	(# 2977)	"
-19113;	"	(# 2978)	"
-19114;	"	(# 2979)	"
-19120;	"	(# 2980)	"
-19121;	"	(# 2981)	"
-19122;	"	(# 2982)	"
-19123;	"	(# 2983)	"
-19124;	"	(# 2984)	"
-19137;	"	(# 2985)	"
-19138;	"	(# 2986)	"
-19139;	"	(# 2987)	"
-19140;	"	(# 2988)	"
-19141;	"	(# 2989)	"
-19142;	"	(# 2990)	"
-19143;	"	(# 2991)	"
-19144;	"	(# 2992)	"
-19145;	"	(# 2993)	"
-19146;	"	(# 2994)	"
-19162;	"	(# 2995)	"
-19163;	"	(# 2996)	"
-19164;	"	(# 2997)	"
-19165;	"	(# 2998)	"
-19166;	"	(# 2999)	"

This approval for ser. # 2900 and up; ser. # 2901, 2919, 2963, 2975, 2984, 2989, 2992 reg. on floats as 3 pl. seaplane; ser. # 2912, 2961, 2965, 2969, 2989 unverified; ser. # 2913 used in aerial surveys, ser. # 2920 as PP-TDQ in Brazil; ser. # 2922-44 del. to BAC; no listing for ser. # 2945-54; one 24-G in USAAF as UC-61H; approval expired 1-24-41.

ATC # 634
(4-30-37)
AERONCA, MODEL K.

The perky "Aeronca K" with 2 cyl. "Aeronca" engine.

By now it had been several years since "Aeronca" first astounded the fun-loving flying public and led it into the notion that people really could be coaxed to ride and even learn to fly in a "flivver airplane," an airplane that weighed less than 1000 lbs. fully loaded. This was accomplished by the early C-3, and it went on to be one of the all-time favorites in the lightplane field. By the time 1937 came around the venerable C-3 had just about run its course and orders for it were dwindling away little by little; production of the C-3 was then slowly phased out. In the meantime things were planned against the day this would happen, and the quietly-groomed "Model K" was rolled out for the public to see. It was different to say the least; it had only the 2 cyl. "Aeronca" engine to remind one that this was a relative of the famous C-3. The high-mounted wing was now braced with lift-struts instead of wires, it had a real honest-to-goodness undercarriage, and dual control wheels; and by gosh, it looked just like a real airplane. Aeronca wanted all to know too that the "K" was also the biggest of the current crop of lightplanes, and also the biggest value. The "Model K" soon proved itself as a rugged little rascal, and many of the flying schools that were using the old C-3 were now swapping for "the new K." Most student pilots liked the Model K and repeatedly soloed in it in 5 hours or less. This new design by Aeronca was far less distinctive than the old (C-3) bath-tub flivver, but it was a very nice little airplane and it had a lot going for

it; the future looked good. The brand-new "Aeronca K" made its formal debut at the New York Aircraft Show held during Jan. of 1937, and then treated the western folks to their first look when exhibited at the Los Angeles Air Show in March. They were happy to say the Model K was an immediate hit and dealers all over the country were clamoring for deliveries; by Nov. of 1937 Aeronca was building 3 of the Model K per day. The very first carload shipment of Model K airplanes went to the state of Washington; 6 complete airplanes could be crammed into a box-car, and it was quite a ceremony getting them out. The Model K was also available as (KS) seaplane on Edo twin-float gear; a tug-boat operator in the Seattle area used his Model K seaplane to direct his tug-boats during the day. In the evening, after work was done, he would just fly around over the bay to relax and watch the sun go down.

The new Aeronca model K was a light strut-braced, high-winged cabin monoplane with side by side seating for 2. The long slender wing and the tail group was pretty much the same, but it had little else to remind one of the old "Aeronca." The Model K was an early hit, but people didn't approach it with the comical attitude they did with the old C-3 because the "new K" didn't seem to evoke that kind of response. It just didn't look like a flivver airplane. Right away everyone was curious about it and many wanted to know for sure if the Model K had the makings of a good light airplane, so naturally it

The Aeronca K was popular in Canada also.

was much talked-about. It seems there was nothing but a good word for the new "K" and its popularity at first flush was gaining by leaps and bounds; it was soon on the flight-line of many flying schools, and it was an ideal airplane for the flying club. As a cheap, economical, owner-flown airplane it had much to offer the private pilot too whether he used it every day, or only on Sunday. As powered with the 2 cyl. Aeronca E-113-CB engine of 42 h.p. the Model K had better performance than most "Aeronca" pilots were used to, and it had an altogether different feel. Stability was just enough uneasy to keep pilots on their toes, and response was excellent; it "stalled and spun" clean, and recovery was fast. The Model K was soon proving itself to be an excellent trainer, student pilots could more easily make the transition to larger aircraft. Normally the little "K"

was a rather proper young lady, but look out, she did have a mischievous twinkle in her eye occasionally. Frame-wise the Model K was a rugged little rascal able to absorb a good deal of punishment, but the pilot had to absorb some of the punishment too; a hard, rough landing on the stiff-legged landing gear would almost jar your teeth out and this was certain to promote better landings. The cabin interior was noisy despite the enclosure, and a little bit of vibration was always present, but owning and flying the Model K was a happy experience that usually lasted for many years. The Model K was improved for 1938 and made available with other engines; for 1938 the "K" had wheel brakes, tail wheel, navigation lights, better upholstery, a lighted panel, and a softer, improved landing gear. The price had also gone up to $1745. The type certificate for the

The Aeronca K as seaplane on Edo floats.

In the winter the "K" was shod with skis.

Model K was issued 4-30-37 and some 350 or more examples of this model were manufactured by the Aeronautical Corp. of America on Lunken Airport in Cincinnati, Ohio. Walter J. Friedlander was pres.; H. V. Fetick was V.P. & treas.; C. S. McKenzie was gen. mgr.; J. C. Welsch was sales mgr.; and Roger E. Schlemmer was chf. engr. Roger Schlemmer left Aeronca sometime in early 1937 and James A. Weagle was appointed chf. engr.

Listed below are specifications and performance data for the "Aeronca" model K "Scout" as powered with 2 cyl. Aeronca E-113-CB engine rated 42 h.p. at 2500 r.p.m. at sea level; length overall 20'7"; height overall 6'7"; wingspan 36'0"; wing chord 50"; total wing area 146.35 sq. ft.; airfoil Clark Y; wt. empty 590 lbs.; useful load 450 lbs.; payload with 10 gal. fuel 215 lbs. (1 pass. & 45 lbs. for bag. & extras); gross wt. 1040 lbs.; max. speed 93 at sea level; cruising speed (.85 power) 85; landing (stall) speed 38; climb 450 ft. first min. at sea level; ser. ceiling 12,000 ft.; gas cap. 10 gal.; oil cap. 3 qts.; cruising range (.85 power) at 3 gal. per hour 255 miles; price was first $1745, lowered to $1480 in Nov. of 1937, and raised back to $1745 for 1938, all prices at the factory. Also available with Aeronca E-113-CD and E-113-CDB engines rated 45 h.p. Available also as (KS) "Sea Scout" seaplane on Edo D-1070 twin-float gear at 677 lbs. empty and 1125 lbs. gross wt.; seaplane had entry door on each side. The Aeronca E-113-CB engine cost $675 at the factory; crating and delivery were extra.

The fuselage framework was built up of welded 4130 and 1025 steel tubing, faired to shape with wooden formers and fairing strips, then fabric covered. A large entry door was on the right side; the seaplane had entry door on the left also, and this door was optional for landplane. The bench-type seat seated 2 across,

and a baggage shelf with allowance for 20 lbs. was behind the seat. The cabin was completely enclosed with Pyralin windows, and upholstered with serviceable fabrics; throttle was in the center and dual control wheels were provided. The wing framework, in 2 sections, was built up of solid spruce spar beams with spruce and plywood truss-type wing ribs; the leading edges were covered with dural metal sheet and the completed framework was covered in fabric. The slender wing was braced to each side of the fuselage at lower longeron by vee-type streamlined lift-struts. The 10 gal. fuel tank was mounted high in the fuselage just behind the firewall; a bobber-type fuel gauge was provided. The stiff-legged, semi-cantilever landing gear used oil-spring shock struts and was fitted with 16x7-3 Goodyear airwheels; wheel brakes and a steerable tail wheel were optional. The fabric-covered tail group was built up of welded 1025 steel tubing; left elevator was fitted with adjustable trim tab. A Flottorp wooden prop, fire extinguisher bottle, 2 flight instruments, 3 engine instruments, seat belts, first-aid kit, and log books were standard equipment. A cabin heater, carburetor heat-box, wheel brakes, carpet, pontoons, skis, tail wheel, and prop spinner cap were optional. The next Aeronca K development was the Model KC as described here in the chapter for ATC # 655.

Listed below are Aeronca K entries as gleaned from registration records:

X-17440;	Model K	(# K-1)	Aeronca Twin
NC-17481;	"	(# K-2)	"
-17483;	"	(# K-3)	"
-17482;	"	(# K-4)	"
-17486;	"	(# K-5)	"
-17491;	"	(# K-6)	"
-17485;	"	(# K-7)	"
-17489;	"	(# K-8)	"

-17488;	"	(# K-9)	"	-17793;	"	(# K-58)	"
-17494;	"	(# K-10)	"	-17788;	"	(# K-59)	"
;	"	(# K-11)	"	-17792;	"	(# K-60)	"
-17493;	"	(# K-12)	"	-17794;	"	(# K-61)	"
-17495;	"	(# K-13)	"	-17795;	"	(# K-62)	"
-17490;	"	(# K-14)	"	-17796;	"	(# K-63)	"
-17497;	"	(# K-15)	"	-17798;	"	(# K-64)	"
-17750;	"	(# K-16)	"	-17797;	"	(# K-65)	"
-17498;	"	(# K-17)	"	-17799;	"	(# K-66)	"
-17499;	"	(# K-18)	"	-18800;	"	(# K-67)	"
-17753;	"	(# K-19)	"	-18805;	"	(# K-68)	"
-17751;	"	(# K-20)	"	-18801;	"	(# K-69)	"
-17754;	"	(# K-21)	"	;	"	(# K-70)	"
-17755;	"	(# K-22)	"	-18803;	"	(# K-71)	"
-17492;	"	(# K-23)	"	-18804;	"	(# K-72)	"
-17756;	"	(# K-24)	"	-18806;	"	(# K-73)	"
-17757;	"	(# K-25)	"	-18807;	"	(# K-74)	"
-17758;	"	(# K-26)	"	;	"	(# K-75)	"
-17759;	"	(# K-27)	"	-18809;	"	(# K-76)	"
-17760;	"	(# K-28)	"	-18810;	"	(# K-77)	"
;	"	(# K-29)	"	-18811;	"	(# K-78)	"
-17752;	"	(# K-30)	"	-18814;	"	(# K-79)	"
-17763;	"	(# K-31)	"	-18812;	"	(# K-80)	"
-17764;	"	(# K-32)	"	-18813;	"	(# K-81)	"
-17765;	"	(# K-33)	"	-18815;	"	(# K-82)	"
-17766;	"	(# K-34)	"	-18816;	"	(# K-83)	"
-17767;	"	(# K-35)	"	-18817;	"	(# K-84)	"
-17768;	"	(# K-36)	"	-18818;	"	(# K-85)	"
-17769;	"	(# K-37)	"	-18819;	"	(# K-86)	"
-17770;	"	(# K-38)	"	-18820;	"	(# K-87)	"
-17773;	"	(# K-39)	"	-18821;	"	(# K-88)	"
-17771;	"	(# K-40)	"	-18822;	"	(# K-89)	"
-17772;	"	(# K-41)	"	-18823;	"	(# K-90)	"
-17774;	"	(# K-42)	"	-18825;	"	(# K-91)	"
-17775;	"	(# K-43)	"	-18826;	"	(# K-92)	"
-17776;	"	(# K-44)	"	-18829;	"	(# K-93)	"
-17762;	"	(# K-45)	"	-18827;	"	(# K-94)	"
-17778;	"	(# K-46)	"	-18828;	"	(# K-95)	"
-17780;	"	(# K-47)	"	-18830;	"	(# K-96)	"
-17779;	"	(# K-48)	"	-18831;	"	(# K-97)	"
-17781;	"	(# K-49)	"	-18832;	"	(# K-98)	"
-17782;	"	(# K-50)	"	-18833;	"	(# K-99)	"
-17783;	"	(# K-51)	"	-18834;	"	(# K-100)	"
-17784;	"	(# K-52)	"				
-17785;	"	(# K-53)	"				
-17790;	"	(# K-54)	"				
;	"	(# K-55)	"				
-17789;	"	(# K-56)	"				
-17791;	"	(# K-57)	"				

This approval for ser. # K-2 and up; ser. # K-45 reg. as (KS) seaplane; no listing available for ser. # K-11, K-29, K-55, K-70, K-75; because there were over 350 of the Model K built, this is only a partial listing; approval expired 12-12-40.

ATC # 635
(5-3-37)
DOUGLAS, DC3B-G102.

Douglas DC-3B was the unique "Half-Sleeper" used by TWA.

Douglas Aircraft was already delivering their newest transport airplanes to several major airlines, so it is only natural that Transcontinental & Western Air (TWA) would be in line to order some of the new transports also. After all, hadn't they precipitated the "revolution in airliners" by literally forcing design of the Douglas DC-1, and the subsequent DC-2? Innovation was always an underlying policy of TWA, so before they ordered any new Douglas equipment they weighed what was available against what they would be likely to need, and came up with an interior configuration that was a minor revolution in airliner design. At this time Douglas was busy building the DST "Sleeper" for night flights across the nation, and the new DC-3 with a coach-type arrangement was being built for daytime use. The airplane that TWA first ordered from Douglas was a double-duty "Half-Sleeper," the 18-place model DC-3B, which had sleeping berths for 8 up in the forward section and over-stuffed reclining chairs for 7 in the rear section. Thus, the DC-3B could be used on the TWA network either for night flights carrying 15 passengers, with both premium and economy fares on the same flight, or it could be converted to daytime seating for up to 23 passengers. This convertible arrangement was highly versatile and it allowed TWA dispatchers to arrange the interior quickly to suit the needs as each flight schedule came up. Formal designation of the "Sky-Sleeper" as built for TWA was the DC3B-G102 and it was powered with 2 of the

supercharged Wright "Cyclone" GR-1820-G102 engines developing 1100 h.p. each for takeoff. Later on TWA also ordered some of the standard DC-3 type for daytime flights on various parts of their network; some of these were fashioned into the plush 14-passenger "Sky Club" that offered commodious comfort for about a penny per mile extra. The "Sky-Sleeper" service and the "Sky Club" service became very popular with business people who were pleased with the extra attention that passengers received on these flights. TWA introduced their "sleeper flights" in May of 1937 using the so-called "SDT" (DC-3B) and launched regular service between California and New York in July; they were soon offering three 3-stop round trips daily. A Phoenix to San Francisco run was inaugurated in Nov. of 1938 and other routes were steadily radiating from the main network. TWA was popularly known as the "Lindbergh Line," but the legend was abolished in 1939, about the time that millionaire Howard Hughes became the principal stockholder. When America began its preparation for war in 1942 the big DC-3 fleet of TWA was reduced to 25 airplanes, and soon even these would be on war-duty.

The Douglas transport model DC3B-G102 as built primarily for TWA was typical of other DC-3 types, but it was an interesting variation on the standard arrangement. While the out-and-out (DST) "Sleeper" planes were scrounging around for paying passengers to fill the 14 to 16 berths on each flight, and the 21-passenger day-

DC-3B interior was convertible also to day-flights.

coach versions were minus any sleeping provisions whatever, the versatile (DC-3B) "Half-Sleeper" was providing sleeping quarters if requested by some and at least provided snoozing facilities for others. Fares were commensurate with accommodations provided and TWA was running flights fully loaded more often than not. In the dead of winter, when coast-to-coast revenue began to fall off, TWA instituted price cuts on all fares to stimulate travel; one could then travel just about as cheap by air as it would cost to travel by rail in Pullman accommodations. This move by TWA caused a little grumble among other major airlines that elected to hold the line on fares, even though passenger loads were falling off considerably. The major airlines fought bitterly on certain routes, the competition was terrific, but it all leveled out and the air-travelers benefitted in the long run. The airlines were actually wooing passengers, and that's as it should be. As traffic began to increase, all airlines were already thinking of larger, faster, and more comfortable airplanes to handle the inevitable popularity in air travel. In April of 1937, even while DC-3 production was humming at top speed to fill the enormous back-log of orders, the big 4-motored Douglas DC-4 was already taking shape on the assembly floor. In 1937-38-39 the airline industry was expanding by leaps and bounds; its mettle was soon to be tested for performance and stamina by the coming of a man-made holocaust known as World War Two. Meanwhile, TWA was building up its far-flung empire, and earning a reputation for innovation that often had startling effects on the industry. The type certificate for the model DC3B-G102 was issued 5-3-37 and at least 10 or more examples were manufactured by the Douglas Aircraft Co., Inc. on Clover Field in Santa Monica, Calif.

Listed below are specifications and performance data for the Douglas model DC3B-G102

as powered with 2 Wright "Cyclone" GR-1820-G102 engines rated 900 h.p. at 2200 r.p.m. at 6000 ft. (1100 h.p. available for takeoff); length overall 64'6"; height overall (3 point) 16'11"; wingspan 95'0"; wing chord at root 172" tapering to tip; total wing area 987 sq. ft.; airfoil NACA-2215 at root tapering to NACA-2206 at tip; wt. empty 15,750 lbs.; useful load 8650 lbs.; payload with 600 gal. fuel 4230 lbs. (21 pass., 3 crew, & 660 lbs. baggage-mail); gross wt. 24,400 lbs. (a provisional gross wt. of 24,800 lbs. for airline use was allowed); max. speed 215 at 7000 ft.; cruising speed (.75 power) 195 at 6000 ft.; cruising speed (.65 power) 180 at 8000 ft.; landing speed (with flaps) 67; stall speed (no flaps) 80; climb 920 ft. first min. at sea level; ser. ceiling 21,300 ft.; gas cap. normal 650 gal.; gas cap. max. 822 gal.; oil cap. max. 66.5 gal.; cruising range (.75 power) at 100 gal. per hour 1220 miles; max. cruising range (.65 power) with 822 gal. fuel 1650 miles; price was approx. $100,000.

Specifications and data for model DC3B-G202A as powered with 2 Wright "Cyclone" GR-1820-G202A engines rated 1000 h.p. at 2300 r.p.m. at 5000 ft. (1200 h.p. for takeoff) same as above except as follows: wt. empty 16,400 lbs.; useful load 8000 (8400) lbs.; max. payload with 600 gal. fuel 3970 lbs. (21 pass., 3 crew, & 400 lbs. baggage-mail); normal gross wt. 24,400 lbs.; max. gross wt. of 24,800 lbs. was allowed; max. speed 219 at 5000 ft.; cruising speed (.75 power) 198 at 5000 ft.; landing speed (with flaps) at 24,800 lbs. gross wt. was 70; climb 980 ft. first min. at sea level; ser. ceiling 22,750 ft.; gas cap. normal 650 gal.; gas cap. max. 822 gal.; oil cap. max. 66.5 gal.; cruising range (.75 power) at 112 gal. per hour 1050 miles; prices varied according to engines and equipment specified. The DC3B-G202A were the 10 original DC-3B that were modified to mount the more powerful engines in March of 1941.

A DC-3B "Skysleeper" getting some routine maintenance.

The model DC-3B was easily recognized by its 2 small "bunk windows" up forward just above the regular cabin windows; this was the sleeper section. Normally, this forward "sleeper section" was extended to 8 berths (4 upper & 4 lower), but on the "Deluxe Sleeper" flights (for extra fare) the upper berths were not used, giving passengers the advantage of more room. The rear section of the cabin was fitted with 7 reclining arm-chairs (for snoozing) and this was later increased to 9 seats. A steam-table was in the galley for serving hot meals. Thus, the DC-3B carried 11, 15, or 17 passengers as a sleeper-plane at night, and 23 passengers as a day-plane; all flights carried a crew of 3. As powered with 2 of the Wright "Cyclone" engines rated 900 h.p. each the DC-3B had a comfortable reserve of power and consequently did very well with "one engine out." The rate of climb on one engine was approx. 375 ft. the first minute and 128 m.p.h. could be easily maintained at 8500 ft. The DC-3B was also available with the Wright GR-1820-G103 high-altitude engines. Like all the other DC-3 type used by TWA the DC-3B "Half-Sleeper" was equipped with every navigational device known to man, plus de-icing equipment on propellers, wings, and empennage. It was also the first airplane to use the Sperry "automatic

pilot" as standard equipment. The pleasant atmosphere in the cabin of a DC-3 was informal, relaxed, and conducive to friendly chats among the passengers, many of which were flying for the first time. The pretty "stewardess" was also an important part of air travel; the stewardess was always a gracious lady and she made everyone feel like a dignitary. The next Douglas development was the DST-A "Sleeper" as described here in the chapter for ATC # 647.

Listed below are Douglas DC-3B entries as gleaned from registration records:

NC-17312;	DC3B-G102	(# 1922) Cyclone 900
-17313;	"	(# 1923) "
-17314;	"	(# 1924) "
-17315;	"	(# 1930) "
-17316;	"	(# 1931) "
-17317;	"	(# 1932) "
-17318;	"	(# 1933) "
-17319;	"	(# 1934) "
-18953;	"	(# 2027) "
-18954;	"	(# 2028) "

This approval for ser. # 1922 and up; this approval for models DC3B-G102, DC3B-G103, and DC3B-G202A; all 10 of the DC3B-G102 were later modified to DC3B-G202A.

TWA "stewardesses" were helpful, cheerful, and very pretty.

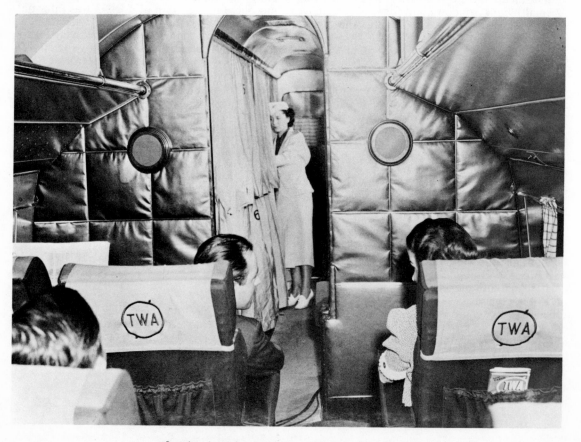

Interior shows berths in front and reclining seats in back.

The Welch OW-6M with 36 h.p. Aeronca engine was a cheap way to fly.

The little ground-hugging "Welch" monoplane may look a bit old-fashioned for this day and age (1937), but only because it was a long time in coming; it was a long time in developing, and it was a long time in getting approved for manufacture. The first "Welch" monoplane actually came out shortly after the well-known "Aeronca" made its bid, and we can see that the "Aeronca" had considerable influence on the "Welch" design, but there was enough of "Orin Welch" in the bones of it to keep it from being easily mistaken. From the beginning the Welch operation was strictly low-budget, so there was actually more enthusiasm than money, and this had a tendency to stifle progress in the project. Luckily, it was a family affair and the Orin Welch School of Aviation at Anderson, Ind. was able to nurture this project for the many years it took to develop the airplane and to get it government approved for manufacture. Very little bally-hoo had gone out on this little ship, there were not many who knew of it, but it was well known locally around Anderson where Orin Welch extolled its virtues and gave it plenty of exposure. Every airplane designer has his own idea about things, and the OW-6M described here reflected the ideas of Orin Welch. Orin Welch, pilot-mechanic-designer, was no stranger to the designing and building of airplanes, he already had several to his credit, so the model OW-6M was his creation to provide a light but rugged airplane that was cheap, very economical to own and operate, and easy to fly. The OW-6M was all this and more, but its builder had trouble convincing the populace. True, the "Welch" was scarce and it was never

produced in great number, but it did find a place in the overall scene and there are those who remember it fondly.

Orin Welch was a pioneer aviator in the state of Indiana. He was especially known around the city of Anderson, and like many of his cohorts used to mess around with (WWI) war-surplus "Jennies" and "Standards." In several examples during the "twenties" he modified them to fly faster, easier, carry more payload, and with the redesigning they became "Welch" biplanes. This was quite a thing among pilots of the early "twenties" and they used to vie with one another to see who could come up with the best modification. Many aircraft companies got started this way. Shortly after, during the light-airplane movement of the early "thirties," Orin Welch toyed with the idea of designing a flivver-plane, and produced an example in 1931. Like many another he must have been greatly influenced by the revolutionary "Aeronca" because his airplane bore an obvious resemblance. In the next few years several examples of the "Welch" monoplane were built with various powerplants, but except for the area around Anderson, Ind. they were hardly known elsewhere. For some five years Orin Welch struggled with financing and the complexities of "government approval;" in 1937 he finally made the grade, but almost too late. The first of the "Welch" monoplanes to be approved was the model OW-6M being described here.

The stubby-nosed "Welch" model OW-6M was a light strut-braced monoplane with side by side seating for 2. Basically, the OW-6M was a no-frills lightplane designed to sell at low cost,

The "Welch" was very much at home in rural areas of the midwest.

and was operated very cheaply. Being born and reared in a farm community it was therefore designed for use in such areas, mostly by private pilots who flew from pasture-type airports on weekends. Its cruising range was not much, but it did allow visits in the radius of a hundred miles or so. The Orin Welch School of Aviation had some of these OW-6M on its flight-line it was said, and it was described as a pretty good trainer. Had the "Welch" monoplane been available about 5 years sooner it is almost certain it would have had a good following. As powered with the 2 cyl. Aeronca E-113-B engine of 37 h.p. the OW-6M was certainly no great charger, but it did have an adequate performance and it was pleasant to fly. It was completely at home on the pasture-type airports, and as one pilot put it, it was a lovely sight-seeing platform. The type certificate for the model OW-6M was issued 5-10-37; it is not known how many examples of this model were manufactured by the Welch Aircraft Industries at Anderson and South Bend, Ind. Orin Welch was pres., gen. mgr., and chf. engr.; Gomer Welch was V.P.; John Welch was sales mgr.; and it was said that Lena Welch had charge of the books. This operation was pretty much a family affair.

Listed below are specifications and performance data for the Welch model OW-6M as powered with Aeronca E-113-B engine rated 37 h.p. at 2400 r.p.m. at sea level; length overall 20'8"; height overall 6'1"; wingspan 34'5"; wing chord 54"; total wing area 138 sq. ft.; airfoil Clark Y; wt. empty 519 lbs.; useful load 435 lbs.; payload with 9 gal. fuel 203 lbs. (1 pass. & 33 lbs. for bag. & extras); gross wt. 954 lbs.; max. speed 89; cruising speed (.75 power) 78; landing (stall) speed 35; climb 400 ft. first min. at sea level; ser. ceiling 11,000 ft.; gas cap. 9 gal.; oil cap. 4 qts.; cruising range (.75 power) at 2.7 gal. per hour 240 miles; price $995 at factory, later raised to $1195; also available for $398 down & balance in 12 monthly pmts. This airplane also available with Szekely SR-3-40, Salmson AD-9, and Welch 0-2-45 engines.

The fuselage framework was built up of welded 4130 and 1025 steel tubing, faired to shape with wooden formers and fairing strips, then fabric covered. A bench-type seat accommodated 2 across with access via a large entry door on the right side; a baggage shelf behind the seat had allowance for 9 lbs. The wing spar beams were built up of two-ply spruce webs into an I-beam topped with a spruce cap-strip; the truss-type wing ribs were of bass-wood. The leading edges were covered with dural metal sheet and the completed framework was covered in fabric. A 4.5 gal. fuel tank was in the leading edge of each wing-half straddling the fuselage. The fixed-type tripod landing gear of 57 in. tread used 16x7 Welch "cushioned wheels" and no brakes. The fabric-covered tail group was built up of welded 4130 and 1025 steel tubing; the horizontal stabilizer was ground-adjustable for trim. A wooden Flottorp prop, leaf-spring tail skid, and wiring for navigation lights were standard equipment. A tail wheel assembly, fire extinguisher bottle, navigation lights, and first-aid kit were optional. The next "Welch" development was the model OW-5M as described here in the chapter for ATC # 637.

Listed below are early "Welch" entries as gleaned from registration records:

-2476; Standard J-1, OX-5, Mod. by Orin Welch
-3506; Orin Welch Hi-Lift, OX-5, 1927-28
-5105; Welch OW-1 (# 101) Hisso
-378; Welch OW-3 (# 10) OX-5, 4POLB, 1928
-817; Welch OW-1 (# 103) OX-5, 1928
-415; Welch OW-3M (# 105) OX-5
X-952W; Welch OWX (# 1) Hisso, or Dayton-Bear
-11142; Orin Welch (# 106) Hisso
-13521; Welch OW-6M (# 109) Aeronca 37
X-14521; Welch OW-6S (# 110) Szekely 45
NC-14528; Welch OW-6M (# 112) Aeronca 37, 1935

This approval for ser. # 112 and up; approval expired 8-1-41.

ATC # 637
(5-17-37)
WELCH, OW-5M.

Welch OW-5M with 40 h.p. Continental engine.

In the course of its rather long development the little "Welch" monoplane was tried with many different engines; the choice was usually dictated by availability at a good price. Among the installations that were listed was the 3 cyl. Szekely engine which was no longer approved for "licensed" airplanes, the gem-like 9 cyl. Salmson AD-9 "radial" of some 40-50 h.p. which was a beautiful thing to tinker with, an experimental Rathel engine of 40 h.p., the 2 cyl. Aeronca E-113 engine, the flat-four Continental A-40 engine, the 2 cyl. Orin Welch-designed Welch O-2 engine of 45 h.p., and later the 4 cyl. Franklin 4AC-150 engine of 40 h.p. An old 6 cyl. Anzani engine of some 69 h.p., more or less, was even tried out for a time. Most all of these were experimental versions of the OW-M, of course. We are concerned here with the model OW-5M which was powered with the popular 4 cyl. Continental A-40-4 engine which cranked out an honest 40 horse. The Continental A-40 was a very popular engine at a good price, so it was used more often in the "Welch;" it performed just a wee bit better than the Aeronca-powered OW-6M, so the OW-5M was built in larger quantity. But then, a statement like this can be misleading when talking about only 5 or 6 airplanes. The OW-5M, when rolled out of final assembly, was strictly a low-cost airplane devoid of frills; at $995 it was just about the cheapest two-seated airplane that one could buy at this time. It was also offered for about $350 down with the balance payable in 12 months time. But, there were no lines forming at the Welch factory door; as we've hinted the "Welch" had been a long

time in coming and it missed the boat. It couldn't overcome the competition which was getting stronger all the time.

It is of interest to note that pilot-mechanic-designer Orin Welch also designed and built his own aircraft engine, the Welch O-2; an air-cooled 2 cyl. opposed engine that was quite similar to the Aeronca engine, and was supposed to be of high performance and good quality. This engine was also developed in the early "thirties" and for a time was available to home-builders of aircraft in a knock-down kit form to be assembled at home. All machining was already done and it was just a matter of assembly according to prints and detailed instructions. Whether the engine sold in any volume we cannot say. The Welch O-2 engine was rated 45 h.p. at 2500 r.p.m. using 72 octane fuel; it was available in the Welch monoplane model OW-7M. The displacement of the 2 cyl. O-2 engine was 135 cu. in. and bare wt. was 115 lbs.; it was manufactured in Anderson, Ind.

The Welch model OW-5M was a flivver-type strut-braced monoplane with side by side seating for 2. Basically, the OW-5M was a no-frills light airplane designed to sell at a very low cost, and to operate very cheaply. Being born and reared in a farm community it was therefore designed for use in such typical areas mostly by private pilots, owner-pilots who flew from pasture-type airports mostly on weekends. With 9 gals. of fuel aboard its cruising range was not much, but it did allow visits of a hundred miles or so. Orin Welch had a few of these OW-5M on the flight-line of his flying school, and it was described as a pretty good

Welch OW-5M was very popular with small flying clubs.

trainer. Had the "Welch" monoplane been available nationwide about 5 years sooner it is almost certain it would have had a good following among pilots who flew only for the fun of it, and wanted to do it cheaply. As powered with the 4 cyl. Continental A-40-4 engine of 40 h.p. the OW-5M was certainly no great charger either, but it did have an adequate performance for the low-time pilot, and it was pleasant to fly. It was completely at home on all the little unimproved airports, and as one pilot put it, it too was a lovely sight-seeing platform. The type certificate for the model OW-5M was issued 5-17-37 and some 6 or more examples were manufactured by the Welch Aircraft Industries at South Bend, Ind. At one time the Welch operation was a partnership between F. W. Bower and Orin Welch; Bower was sales mgr., and Orin Welch was pres. and chf. engr.

Listed below are specifications and performance data for the Welch model OW-5M as powered with Continental A-40-4 engine rated 40 h.p. at 2575 r.p.m. at sea level; length overall 20'6"; height overall 6'1"; wingspan 34'5"; wing chord 54"; total wing area 138 sq. ft.; airfoil Clark Y; wt. empty 540 lbs.; useful load 410 lbs.; payload with 10 gal. fuel 172 lbs.; gross wt. 950 lbs.; max. speed 90; cruising speed (.90 power) 85; cruising speed (.75 power) 80; landing (stall) speed 35; climb 450 ft. first min. at sea level; ser. ceiling 11,500 ft.; gas cap. 10 gal.; oil cap. (in sump) 4 qts.; cruising range (.75 power) at 2.9 gal. per hour 260 miles; price $995 at factory. In March of 1940 the OW-5M was offered for $899, or $299 down and balance in 12 monthly payments. It was also offered with the 40 h.p.

Franklin engine as the OW-8M for $1099 at factory.

The construction details and general arrangement of the Welch OW-5M was similar to that of the OW-6M as described here previously. The following applies to both models unless otherwise noted. Early models of the "Welch" monoplane were available also as open cockpit airplanes, without cabin sides, but all the later approved models were of the cabin type. The Welch used a peculiar control system wherein the throw-over control wheel was suspended from the roof to give occupants clear floor space; to some this was disconcerting and it took a little getting used to. A 5 gal. fuel tank (for OW-5M) was mounted in the leading edge of each wing half straddling the fuselage for gravity fuel flow. The simple tripod landing gear was a stiff-legged truss, and Welch-designed "cushioned" wheels absorbed the shock. The horizontal stabilizer was adjusted for trim on the ground only; a plate with several holes in it was mounted to front of stabilizer to allow negative or positive adjustment. A wooden Flottorp prop, leaf-spring tail skid, wiring for navigation lights, dual controls, and seat belts were standard equipment. A tail wheel assembly, 2 control wheels, fire extinguisher bottle, navigation lights, seat belts, and first-aid kit were optional.

Listed below are additional "Welch" entries as gleaned from registration records:

-13511;	OW-5M	(#99)	Rathel 40
-11382;	"	(#107)	Anzani 60
-13500;	"	(#108)	Cont. 40
-14527;	OW-7M	(#111)	Welch 45
-15778;	"	(#113)	"

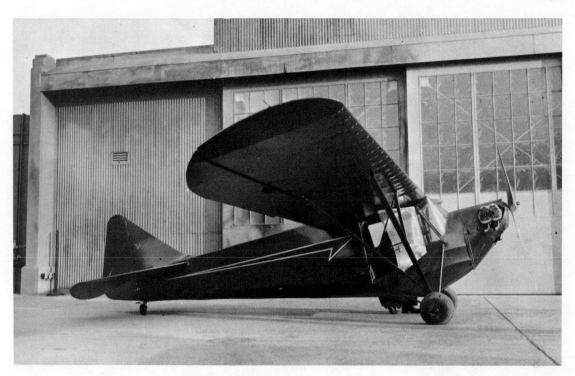

Welch design had strong "Aeronca C-3" flavor.

-18392;	"	(# 114)	"		-18379;	"	(# 124)	"
NC-18396;	OW-5M	(# 115)	Cont. 40		-20488;	"	(# 125)	"
-18394;	"	(# 116)	"		-20403;	"	(# 135)	"
-18395;	OW-7M	(# 117)	Welch 45		-20404;	"	(#)	"
-18397;	"	(# 118)	"					
-18393;	"	(# 119)	"					
-18348;	OW-5M	(# 120)	Cont. 40					
;		(# 121)						
-18381;	OW-5M	(# 122)	Cont. 40					
-18378;	"	(# 123)	"					

This approval for ser. # 115 and up; ser. # 99 later had Szekely 45 engine; ser. # 107 later had Salmson AD-9 engine; no listing for ser. # 121; no listing for ser. # 125 thru # 134; no listing for NC-20404; approval transferred to Hartmann Aircraft Corp. of Jordan, N.Y.

Beech model D-17-R with 420 h.p. Wright engine.

The Beech "Negative -Stagger-Wing" biplane, as it was called, continued to enjoy its strong magnetic appeal, especially in those models with the "big" engines. Beside the prestige enjoyed in owning one of these, they were an awful quick means of getting around the country by air. The Beech models powered with the 420 h.p. Wright R-975 engine, starting with the prototype 17-R of 1934, had always captured the admiration of individuals who wouldn't settle for second-best. The subsequent B-17-R had since made its indelible mark across the face of history, the C-17-R certainly had done likewise, and now in mid-1937 the D-17-R was confidently offered by Walter Beech and his people to do the same. As one of the top-of-the-line models in the 17-series the D-17-R was powered with the latest 9 cyl. Wright R-975-E3 engine rated 420 h.p. Then too, the D-17-R incorporated all of the improvements devised for this design in the past 2 years, including some innovations of its own; its performance was just about the best that any designer could muster with this amount of power. This was an often-heard comment: "The world gets pretty small when you fly a Beech." By this point in time, Walter Beech had purchased their factory buildings (the former "Travel Air" plant) in Wichita, it was fully equipped for all types of aircraft manufacture, nearly all the former employees were back to work again, and things were really looking up. Civil aircraft production in the first quarter of 1937 showed a 25% in-

crease over the same period in 1936, and the first quarter of 1936 had shown a 33% increase over the same period in 1935; so, the aircraft industry too was showing signs of improved health and continued growth.

The first example in the thundering D-17 series was the D-17-W, a brute of an airplane powered with a special geared "Wasp Jr." (R-985-SCG) engine, an engine that was supercharged and revved to deliver up to 600 h.p. To better handle this power the fuselage was lengthened by 13 in., the wing-flaps were moved to the lower wings, and the ailerons were moved to the top. The shorter landing gear and the longer fuselage arm helped considerably in getting the tail down for a 3-point in landing. This was a chronic complaint in the earlier "Stagger-Wing" series. The second of the D-17-W was built for aviatrix "Jackie" Cochran who used it for air-racing and several record attempts. In the Bendix Trophy Race of 1937, Miss Cochran placed 3rd in the D-17-W at 194.74 m.p.h., and Max Constant flying the same airplane placed 4th in the 1938 Bendix at 199.330 m.p.h. The D-17-W was a fast airplane, but it was a rather impractical experiment and Beech didn't care to pursue it, so both examples were later modified to the D-17-R. Entry of 5 people into the cabin was a prescribed ritual. The pilot got in first, he then slid the right front seat back so the co-pilot could get in, this seat was slid forward and the 3 passengers could then get in. This was not common only to the D-17-R;

D-17-R shows its unusual grace.

many other 4-5 seated cabin airplanes, including other models of the Beech, were forced to this sort of ritual also.

The Beech model D-17-R was one of the more outstanding examples of the famous "Stagger-Wing," and its appeal reached clear around the world. The plush cabin, usually upholstered in beautiful "Velmo" mohair, was arranged to seat 4 or 5, and extra fuel capacity was optional for those long cross-country trips. The space, power, and luxury in this airplane was overwhelming. The D-17-R was not an airplane that just anyone would go out and buy, so sales were not all that brisk, but the model remained in the lineup for several years and was still manufactured into 1940. A good portion of the production went overseas to China; the Republic of China ordered 2 of the D-17-R in 1937, 4 more were shipped in 1938, and another 4 were shipped in 1939. One of the D-17-R went to the Philippines, and another to Porto Rico. Of the D-17-R sold here in the U.S.A most were delivered to prominent men of business and a few to well-heeled sportsmen. As powered with the Wright R-975-E3 engine rated 420 h.p. the D-17-R was not a brute of an airplane, but its muscle was felt conspicuously as it slanted up; at 10,000 ft. it was a 200 m.p.h. airplane. The "Stagger-Wing" was rarely seen "polishing the pylons" at an air race, but on occasion they did. In 1937 a D-17-R flew in and won the Phillips Trophy Race at an average of 192.4 m.p.h.; speed was only one item in its bag of tricks and the "Beech" was good at it. Because of the benevolent "staggered wing" feature the D-17-R (and of course other models in the 17 series) had stability and flight characteristics that couldn't be matched by very many airplanes. This was a feature they all enjoyed and it made every owner a booster. The type certificate for the D-17-R was issued 5-20-37 and some 28 or more examples of this model were manufactured by the Beech Aircraft Corp. at Wichita, Kan.

Listed below are specifications and perfor-mance data for the Beech model D-17-R as powered with Wright R-975-E3 engine rated 420 h.p. at 2200 r.p.m. at 1400 ft. (450 h.p. at 2250 r.p.m. available for takeoff); length overall 25'11"; height overall 8'2"; wingspan upper & lower 32'0"; wing chord upper & lower 60"; wing area upper 148.2 sq. ft.; wing area lower (including fuselage area) 148.2 sq. ft.; total wing area 296.4 sq. ft.; airfoil NACA-23012; wt. empty 2515 lbs.; useful load 1685 lbs.; payload with 101 gal. fuel 860 lbs. (4 pass. & 180 lbs. for bag. & extras); gross wt. 4200 lbs.; max. speed 211 at sea level; cruising speed (.68 power using 285 h.p.) 202 at 9600 ft.; landing speed (with flaps) 60; landing roll (using brakes) 750 ft.; takeoff run 610 ft.; climb 1300 ft. first min. at sea level; service ceiling 20,000 ft.; gas cap. normal 101 gals.; oil cap. 6.5 gals.; cruising range (.68 power) at 23.5 gal. per hour 825 miles; price $18,870 at factory. Airplane also available for $12,900 less engine and propeller.

ment of the D-17-R were typical to that of other Model 17 described in this volume, including the following. The major difference of any significance was the big 9 cyl. Wright engine, and modifications necessary to this installation. The fuselage arm was lengthened by some 13 ins. to better handle the extra power, balanced ailerons were fitted to the upper wings, and full-length wing flaps were now on the lower wings for better ground effect. The D-models also had plywood covered wing tips for stiffness to alleviate any chance of displacement of form that would cause flutter. Dual control wheels were provided and toe-brakes were now on the rudder pedals for better handling. The wing flaps were electrically operated and could be stopped in any intermediate position; manual operation was possible in emergency. The landing gear of 86 in. tread was electrically operated for retraction and extension; it had manual crank for emergency. The side windows could be rolled down, and an extra entry door for right side was optional. The full-swivel tail wheel had fore-and-aft lock for takeoffs and landings. The new cantilever tail group was of heavier and stiffer construction; an adjustable "trim tab" was on the elevator and rudder. A fixed-pitch Curtiss-Reed metal prop, electric engine starter, generator, battery, fuel pump, swing-over or T-type control column, oil cooler, 7.50x10 wheels with 6-ply tires, wheel brakes, a parking brake, navigation lights, full set of engine & flight instruments, assist ropes, ash trays, and first-aid kit were standard equipment. A Hamilton-Standard ground-adjustable or "controllable" prop, landing lights, paraflares, radio gear, bonding & shielding, pressure-type fire extinguisher, parachute-type chairs by Irvin or Switlik, camera install., extra fuel cap., and Edo seaplane gear were optional. The next Beech development was the model E-17-L and the E-17-B as described here in the chapter for ATC # 641.

Listed below are D-17-R entries as gleaned from various records:

NC-17081;	D-17-R	(# 136)	Wright 420
-17082;	"	(# 137)	"
-18029;	"	(# 148)	"
-18562;	"	(# 164)	"
NC-400;	"	(# 166)	"
-18565;	"	(# 167)	"
-18576;	"	(# 180)	"
;	"	(# 181)	"
;	"	(# 182)	"
-18580;	"	(# 184)	"
-18584;	"	(# 188)	"
-18789;	"	(# 214)	"
-18790;	"	(# 215)	"
;	"	(# 217)	"
-18793;	"	(# 218)	"
;	"	(# 235)	"
;	"	(# 236)	"
;	"	(# 237)	"
;	"	(# 253)	"
-20792;	"	(# 278)	"
-20752;	"	(# 289)	"
-20776;	"	(# 313)	"
;	"	(# 325)	"
;	"	(# 326)	"
;	"	(# 328)	"
;	"	(# 329)	"
-20795;	"	(# 397)	"
-21919;	"	(# 405)	"

This approval for ser. # 136 and up; ser. # 136 first as D-17-W, later as D-17-R and D-17-S; ser. # 164 first as D-17-W, later as D-17-R; ser. # 166 del. to Bureau of Air Commerce; ser. # 181-82, 217, 235-36-37, 325-26, 328-29 to Republic of China; ser. # 218 del. to Puerto Rico; ser. # 253 del. to Philippines; ser. # 136 thru 188 mfgd. 1937; ser. # 214 thru 253 mfgd. 1938; ser. # 278 thru 329 mfgd. 1939; ser. # 397, 405 mfgd. 1940; 13 of D-17-R as UC-43A in USAAF; one D-17-W in USAAF as UC-43K.

A D-17-R in camouflage colors.

ATC # 639
(5-20-37)
WACO, MODEL EGC-7.

The Waco EGC-7 was popular in government services.

For each new series of models introduced Waco Aircraft would proudly say, "here, truly, is the last word in luxurious, practical, and economical air transportation." And, as sure as day became night, this always seemed to be so. It must be very difficult to keep making a good airplane better and better, but so far Waco Aircraft was doing it every year. The elegant "Custom Cabin" biplane by design was a natural partner for the popular 7 cyl. Wright engine, so for the year 1937 the Waco company introduced a model known as the DGC-7 with the 285 h.p. powerplant, and as the model EGC-7 with the 320 h.p. powerplant. We have to mention that the world-famous "Wright" engines were generally more expensive than other-make engines in a near-comparable power range, so this engine-airplane combination (DGC-7 and EGC-7) was rather expensive, and leveled particularly at a more wealthy clientele. As a consequence, only 7 of these Wright-powered versions were sold here in this country, but an order for 30 airplanes was received late in 1938 (through Interbraz) from the Brazilian Army for the 320 h.p. model EGC-7. These 30 airplanes were manufactured and delivered between 12-28-38 and 5-4-39. According to company record these Brazilian model EGC-7 were manufactured for export under this ATC number by a special waiver; a year or so later the Brazilian govern-

ment negotiated with Waco Aircraft and purchased the manufacturing rights of ATC # 639. We can guess they must have been very impressed with this airplane, but it is not known if any EGC-7 were actually built in Brazil. In 1937 the handsome EGC-7 was billed as "the finest Waco ever built" — yes, at that time we could very well believe it.

The Waco models DGC-7 and EGC-7 were offered for the year 1937-38 as "Custom Cabin" biplanes with ample seating for 5 people. This was the 3rd year now for the handsome "Custom" line, and each year they came out smartly improved, and perhaps each year just a little bit better. We have to imagine that the EGC-7 especially must have been quite an airplane because Waco Aircraft named it unflinchingly as "the finest Cabin Waco we have ever built." And, they meant this without reservation. Of course, everyone had their favorite "Waco," we all did, and if you wanted to know why — "just ask a pilot." As powered with the 7 cyl. Wright R-760-E2 engine of 320 h.p. this airplane (EGC-7) was surprisingly deft in getting around, and its high performance was a mild surprise to say the least; it did everything without much effort, and there seemed to be no end to what it could do. As powered with the 285 h.p. Wright R-760-E1 engine this airplane (DGC-7) was a good match for any airplane of like power, and it delivered

An EGC-7 shown in 1956 and still going strong.

only a shade less than its more powerful sister-ship, the EGC-7. They who took care of such things for the Brazilian Army must have been duly impressed also, because an order for 30 airplanes has got to be a good solid endorsement. The type certificate for the models DGC-7 and EGC-7 was issued 5-20-37 and some 38 or more examples of these models together were mfgd. by the Waco Aircraft Co. at Troy, Ohio. Johnnie Livingston, a competitive pilot long identified with "Waco" airplanes, left the company's employ as engineering test-pilot in May of 1937 to take full charge of his fixed-base operation in Waterloo, Iowa; he would sell "Waco" airplanes, of course.

Listed below are specifications and performance data for the Waco model DGC-7 as powered with Wright R-760-E1 engine rated 285 h.p. at 2100 r.p.m. at sea level (300 h.p. at 2250 r.p.m. available for takeoff); length overall 26'3"; height overall 8'8"; wingspan upper 34'9"; wingspan lower 24'6"; wing chord upper 72"; wing chord lower 48"; wing area upper 168 sq. ft.; wing area lower 76 sq. ft.; total wing area 244 sq. ft.; airfoil Clark Y; wt. empty 2230 lbs.; useful load 1570 lbs.; payload with 70 gal. fuel 942 lbs. (4 pass. & 262 lbs. for bag. & extras); payload with 95 gal. fuel 785 lbs. (4 pass. & 105 lbs. bag.); gross wt. 3800 lbs.; max. speed (105% power) 160 at sea level; cruising speed (.75 power) 150 at optimum altitude; landing speed (with flaps) 54; climb 800 ft. first min. at sea level; ser. ceiling 17,300 ft.; gas cap. normal 70 gal.; gas cap. max. 95 gal.; oil cap. 5-6 gal.; cruising range (.75 power) at 17 gal. per hour 600 miles at best altitude; basic price $10,390 at fac-

tory. Performance figures shown are with use of Curtiss-Reed (fixed-pitch) metal prop; in some instances the performance was improved with a Hamilton-Standard controllable prop.

Specifications and data for model EGC-7 as powered with Wright R-760-E2 engine rated 320 h.p. at 2200 r.p.m. at sea level (350 h.p. at 2400 r.p.m. for takeoff) same as above except as follows: wt. empty 2280 lbs.; useful load 1520 lbs.; payload with 70 gal. fuel 892 lbs. (4 pass. & 212 lbs. for bag. & extras); payload with 95 gal. fuel 735 lbs. (4 pass. & 55 lbs. bag.); gross wt. 3800 lbs.; max. speed (105% power) 168 at sea level; cruising speed (.75 power) 158 at optimum altitude; landing speed (with flaps) 54; climb 900 ft. first min. at sea level; ser. ceiling 18,500 ft.; gas cap. normal 70 gal.; gas cap. max. 95 gal.; oil cap. 5-6 gal.; cruising range (.75 power) at 18 gal. per hour 560 miles at best altitude; basic price $11,125 at factory. Performance figures shown are with use of Curtiss-Reed (fixed-pitch) metal prop; in some instances the performance was improved with a Hamilton-Standard controllable prop.

The construction details and general arrangement of the models DGC-7 and EGC-7 were typical to that of the ZGC-7 as described here in the chapter for ATC # 627. Waco Aircraft had used the same type of construction for these 2 models as it had been using for their "Custom" series in the past several years; improvements each time were numerous, of course, but not too easy to detect on just a casual walk-around. The most significant difference in these 2 models (DGC-7 and EGC-7) was the Wright engine installation and some small modifications necessary for this combination. Upholstery in the latest "Custom" was usually "Velmo" mohair, but leather or mohair with leather trim was optional. A throw-over control wheel was standard, but a Y-type column with 2 wheels was optional. The cabin was fitted with heat and ventilation, ash trays, map pockets, and assist ropes; a baggage compt. behind the rear seat was allowed 100 lbs. Entry door was on the left side; an extra door on the right was optional. Leading edges of the wing panels were normally covered with dural metal sheet, but plywood covering was optional; this to prevent dents in the leading edges from scattered debris. The new landing gear with 108 in. tread was fitted with toe-operated hydraulic wheel brakes, and 7.50x10 wheels were fitted with 8.50x10 tires; the tail wheel could be fitted with a "lock" to track straight ahead on takeoffs and landings. A 35 gal. fuel tank was mounted in the root end of each upper wing-half; 47.5 gal. tanks were optional. For longer range a 25 gal. tank could be fitted under the rear seat. Trailing edge wing flaps (of the plain aileron type) were fitted to the upper wings; flaps not to be extended above 100 m.p.h. The 30 airplanes (EGC-7) built for the Brazilian Army were fitted with EGC-8 wings, engine cowl, and landing gear; the fuselage and vertical tail surfaces were silver, the wings and horizontal surfaces were orange. A Curtiss-Reed metal prop, electric engine starter, battery, generator, oil cooler, cabin heater and ventilator, navigation lights, cabin lights, landing lights, wheel cuffs, fire extinguisher, first-aid kit, tool kit, and log books were standard equipment. A Hamilton-Standard controllable prop, 95 gal. or 120 gal. fuel cap., wheel pants, paraflares, radio gear, special interior, special paint schemes, and parachute-type seats were optional. The next Waco development was the famous UPF-7 as described here in the chapter for ATC # 642.

Listed below are DGC-7 and EGC-7 entries as gleaned from company records:

NC-2209;	EGC-7	(# 4558) Wright 320
-2241;	"	(# 4559) "
NC-17706;	DGC-7	(# 4561) Wright 285
-2239;	"	(# 4562) "
-1312;	EGC-7	(# 4573) Wright 320
-17724;	"	(# 4575) "
PK-DDV;	"	(# 4583) "
-17749;	"	(# 4588) "

This approval for ser. # 4550 and up; ser. # 4583 to Royal Netherlands Airways in Java; PK-DDV may have been PK-DDL; ser. # 4550 thru 4559 eligible only at 3500 lbs. gross wt.; ser. # 4560 and up eligible at 3800 lbs. gross wt.; ser. # 5245 thru 5274 del. to Brazilian Army; approval expired 2-28-41.

ATC # 640
(5-26-37)
STINSON "RELIANT", SR-9F.

The Stinson "Reliant" SR-9F was used by several oil companies.

This fabulous "Reliant", the thundering SR-9F, more or less had to be developed because of insistent demands by buyers of national prominence. Then too, it was 1931 since the last Pratt & Whitney powered Stinson (a "Junior" model W) had been built. With times getting better and better some of the monied customers were getting anxious to enjoy the extras their money could buy in a more powerful Stinson. As introduced early in 1937 the "Reliant" SR-9F was a shade smaller than the old "Model W", but it was over 600 lbs. heavier when empty, some 850 lbs. heavier at loaded gross weight, about 50 m.p.h. faster (with 100 h.p. more, of course), and cost exactly twice as much! This perhaps pictures the kind of progress that had taken place at Stinson Aircraft in the 6 years since. Stinson was rightfully proud of the new SR-9F, saying "this is the greatest airplane we have ever built," and you almost have to agree with that. It was indeed a superb airplane with "class" written all over it, an airplane surely designed for the executive and gentleman-pilot. But, was it only that? The husky SR-9F was actually an airplane with a many-faceted personality. When dressed up and polished to a fine shine it could "put on the dog" with the best of them, but it didn't mind getting its face dirty

either and would pitch in to get the job done no matter what. Actually the SR-9F was at ease on most any job, and it seemed to be happy doing it. Some have said it seemed to radiate with a kind of eagerness and a happy hum, they also said this radiance was contagious upon frequent exposure to it. The roster of owners read like a Who's Who of wealth and big business, but that's understandable—the SR-9F "Reliant" was a special kind of airplane, and it wasn't cheap.

The Stinson "Reliant" model SR-9F was a hefty high-winged cabin monoplane with seating arranged for 5. In the optional "Deluxe" version it was elegant, very plush, and usually adorned with all the extras that one could possibly buy for an airplane. Most often used in the pursuit of business matters as an executive-transport, the talented SR-9F offered speed and utility with an intimate type of comfort; this "Reliant" was an impressive airplane and had the habit of making its presence felt, and this was good for business. The massive-looking wing on the "Reliant" created plenty of lift which translated into short-field performance and a sizable payload. It is logical that the SR-9F with all its power would also be offered as a multi-purpose plane (SR-9FM) for freight or charter. The "M" (Multi-Purpose) version was usually fitted with a metal-

SR-9F slated for delivery to Australia.

clad interior and extra doors to allow the loading of kegs, boxes, and stuff; it was also available as a seaplane on Edo twin-float gear, or on skis. The Bureau of Air Commerce (BAC) needed an airplane such as this in Alaska, so they outfitted their hard-working SR-9F as the seasons permitted with wheels, skis, pontoons, and a two-way radio for inspection and regulatory service "in the bush." As powered with the 9 cyl. Pratt & Whitney "Wasp Jr." SB engine rated 400 h.p. plus, the SR-9F "Reliant" was a lively brute that revelled noisily in its high performance. Pilots practically worshiped its ability to get off quick, they loved its terrific climb-out, and when leveled off "on the step" they knew they were hard to catch. With all of this power surging through its bones the SR-9F was inclined to be a bit of a brute at times, but it was inherently amiable and responded well to firm handling. The type certificate for the "Reliant" model SR-9F was issued 5-26-37 and some 25 or more examples were manufactured by the Stinson Aircraft Corp. at Wayne, Mich. Cy Younglove was Stinson's roving sales mgr. at this time, and he had no trouble selling the "Reliant;" in fact, he had a waiting list.

Listed below are specifications and performance data for the "Reliant" model SR-9F as powered with "Wasp Jr." SB engine rated 400 h.p. at 2200 r.p.m. at 5000 ft. (450 h.p. at 2300 r.p.m. for takeoff)—(TB engine also available); length overall 27'11"; height overall 8'6"; wingspan 41'11"; max. wing chord 96"; wing chord at tip 38"; total wing area 258.5 sq. ft.; airfoil Mod. Clark Y; wt. empty 2990 lbs.; useful load 1510 lbs.; payload with 102 gal. fuel 668 lbs. (3 pass. & 150 lbs. bag.); payload with 78 gal. fuel 698 lbs. (4 pass. & 18 lbs. bag.); gross wt. 4500 lbs.; max. speed 173; cruising speed (.75 power) 165 at 7000 ft.; landing speed (with flaps)

63; climb 1510 ft. first min. at sea level; ser. ceiling 21,000 ft.; gas cap. 102 gal.; oil cap. 8 gal.; cruising range (.75 power) at 24 gal. per hour 500 miles; price $18,000 at factory field. Model SR-9FM was utility version with extra doors and interior fitted for freight and charter; takeoff run (loaded) was normally 545 ft. and landing run (using brakes) was normally 375 ft.

The fuselage framework, beefed-up considerably to handle 450 h.p., was built up of welded 4130 plate and steel tubing, faired to shape with wooden formers and fairing strips, then fabric covered. A large door on each side provided an easy step-up into the large cabin. The big, formed windshield offered a clear, panoramic view and all windows were of shatterproof glass. The adjustable front seats were individual, and the rear seat was wide enough to seat 3 across. The cabin area was insulated, sound-proofed, and upholstered in a variety of rich fabrics; cabin trim in real leather was optional. The main baggage compartment with outside door and an allowance for 100 lbs. was behind the rear seat; 50 lbs. of baggage was also allowed under the rear seat. The unusual tapered wing was built up around an alloy steel main spar beam, a formed dural rear spar, and built-up dural wing ribs; completed framework was covered in fabric. Three tanks (of 39-39-24 gal.) in the wing stored the 102 gal. fuel supply; an extra 24 gal. tank in the wing was optional. The cantilever landing gear of 9'8" tread was fitted with internally-housed spring-oil shock struts; 7.50x10 wheels were fitted with 8.50x10 tires and hydraulic brakes. Streamlined metal wheel pants were optional. The SR-9F was also eligible as a seaplane on Edo WB-5030 twin-float gear at 5030 lbs. gross wt.; the seaplane was about 478 lbs. heavier than the landplane version. The large fabric-covered tail group was built up of welded

4130 steel sheet and tubing; the horizontal stabilizer was adjustable for trim. A metal trim tab on the rudder was adjustable on the ground only. All movable control surfaces had aerodynamic balance. The swiveling tail wheel was fitted with a 10.5 in. streamlined tire. A Hamilton-Standard controllable prop, Eclipse electric engine starter, a generator, Exide battery, navigation lights, cabin lights, cabin heater, carburetor heater, cabin vents, dual control wheels, fire extinguisher, roll-down windows, plated hardware, map pockets, ash trays, assist ropes, seat belts, and first-aid kit were standard equipment. Bonding & shielding, radio gear, landing lights, paraflares, oil cooler, multi-purpose cargo interior, extra 19-24-50 gal. fuel tanks, and skis were optional. The next "Reliant" development was the model SR-10 series as described here in the chapter for ATC # 678.

Listed below are SR-9F entries as gleaned from registration records:

NC-2215;	SR-9FD	(# 5700)	Wasp Jr. 400
-;	SR-9F	(# 5701)	"
;	"	(# 5702)	"
;	"	(# 5703)	"
;	"	(# 5704)	"
;	"	(# 5705)	"
-17191;	"	(# 5706)	"
-17194;	"	(# 5707)	"
-18426;	"	(# 5708)	"
-18400;	"	(# 5709)	"
-18411;	"	(# 5710)	"
-18412;	"	(# 5711)	"
-18414;	"	(# 5712)	"
;	"	(# 5713)	"
-18422;	"	(# 5714)	"
-18425;	"	(# 5715)	"
-2085;	"	(# 5716)	"
-18429;	"	(# 5717)	"
;	"	(# 5718)	"
-18450;	"	(# 5719)	"
-18446;	"	(# 5720)	"
-18448;	"	(# 5721)	"
-18483;	"	(# 5722)	"
NC-89;	SR-9FM	(# 5723)	"
;	"	(# 5724)	"
;	"	(# 5725)	"
-18451;	SR-9FM	(# 5726)	"

This approval for ser. # 5700 and up; no listing available thru 1938 records for ser. # 5701-05, 5713-14, 5716, 5718, 5720, 5722, 5724-25; some SR-9F were exported, number not known; 4 of SR-9F in USAAF as UC-81E; approval expired 10-25-40.

SR-9F works through the Canadian winter on skis.

ATC # 641
(5-22-37)
BEECH, MODEL E-17-B.

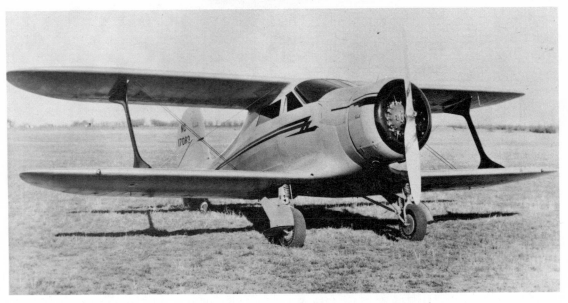

Beech model E-17-B with 285 h.p. Jacobs L-5 engine.

Beech Aircraft had done very well with the C-17 series in 1936, and the models were actually carried over into the sales year of 1937, but for 1938 it was high time to update these Jacobs-powered versions again. Yearly changes were a sales gimmick developed by the auto industry, and it seemed to work, so the aircraft industry started to do likewise. About mid-1937 two new models were introduced in the low-power group as the E-17-L and the E-17-B. The E-17-L was powered with the improved Jacobs L-4 engine, and the E-17-B was powered with the improved Jacobs L-5 engine. Both of these new models had incorporated in them all the improvements devised for the Model 17 up to then, which included the longer fuselage, ailerons in the upper wings, wing flaps in the lower wings, and toe-operated wheel brakes. The average "Beech" pilot considered the toe-operated wheel brakes the best improvement of all. The first bunch of these new airplanes quickly migrated to California and Texas where the Beechcraft was so popular, and then little by little to other states in the Union, and to foreign countries. Two were flown off to Canada where they operated on skis and floats, 5 were shipped off to India, and one even wound up in the wilds of Borneo. An E-17-B, here it was flown as a seaplane over primitive and treacherous jungle, flown by an avid missionary who endeavored to ease the plight of the "wild men of Borneo." Because pilots of Indian National Airways needed a fast airplane that could operate economically on small unimproved fields they picked the E-17-B as the best airplane for the job. The E-17-L and the E-17-B were listed as the models for 1938, but they were still available into 1940.

The models E-17-L and E-17-B were both cabin biplanes with seating arranged for 4 or 5. As both inherited all improvements to the design up to now they came up as somewhat heavier airplanes, but this seemed to be no detriment in any way. In fact, the E-17 series were considered as the best "Stagger-Wing" of all in the low-power group. The E-17-B was an especially good airplane "on floats" (SE-17-B), and was one of the few seaplanes that could make the operator some money. The 225 h.p. E-17-L was offered as the economy model with the improved Jacobs L-4 engine, but only 4 were built in this version; the bulk of the production was the model E-17-B as powered with the Jacobs L-5 engine rated 285 h.p. Here in the U.S.A. the roster of owners contained a few "famous names," but on the whole the E-17-B was delivered to owner-pilots and commercial operators across the land that depended on the airplane to earn them a living; and, this it could do very well. When cleaned, polished, and pampered the E-17-B could muster up the air and dignity of a shiny limousine, but it seemed to be just as happy when working. As powered with the 285 h.p. Jacobs L-5 engine the E-17-B had an enviable performance with this amount of power, and was one of the best airplanes in this class. The E-17-L with somewhat less power was still a very good airplane, but its

E-17-B shows its trim figure which promoted speed.

appeal to prospects who had a choice was far less. The type certificate for the E-17-L and E-17-B was issued 5-22-37 and some 55 examples in all were manufactured by the Beech Aircraft Co. at Wichita, Kan. Walter H. Beech was pres. & gen. mgr.; Ted A. Wells was now V.P. & chf. engr.; Olive Ann Beech was sec-treas.; R. K. Beech as purch. agent; J. B. Wasall as asst. engr.; and C. W. Drake in chg. of production.

Listed below are specifications and performance data for the Beech model E-17-B as powered with Jacobs L-5 engine rated 285 h.p. at 2000 r.p.m. at sea level; length overall 25'11"; height overall 8'2"; wingspan upper & lower 32'0"; wing chord upper & lower 60"; total wing area (incl. fuselage section) 296.4 sq. ft.; airfoil NACA-23012; wt. empty 2080 lbs.; useful load 1270 lbs.; payload with 77 gal. fuel 600 lbs. (3 pass. & 90 lbs. bag); payload with 63 gal. fuel 685 lbs. (4 pass. & no bag.); gross wt. 3350 lbs.; max. speed 185 at sea level; cruising speed (.75 power) 177 at 7200 ft.; landing speed (with flaps) 49; climb 1000 ft. first min. at sea level; ser. ceiling 18,000 ft.; gas cap. normal 77 gal.; gas cap. max. 125 gal.; oil cap. 5 gal.; cruising range (.75 power) at 17.5 gal. per hour 700 miles; price was $10,490 for 1937-38 ($9190 less engine & prop), and raised to $12,380 in 1939 at the factory. The E-17-B was also available as a seaplane on Edo twin-float gear at 3740 lbs. gross wt., or as a ski-plane. This airplane also available as an E-17-L when powered with 225 h.p. Jacobs L-4 engine; performance was proportionately less than that of E-17-B.

The construction details and general arrangement of the E-17-B were typical to that of other Beech models described here previously, including the following. The E-17-B had incorporated into it the longer fuselage arm, balanced ailerons in the upper wings, full-span wing flaps in the lower wings, and the toe-operated braking system. As a result it came up 230 lbs. heavier when empty (as compared to C-17-B), was allowed 30 lbs. less in payload, and was heavier by 200 lbs. at gross wt., but this seemed to have no effect on its overall performance. In fact, pilots have said that even 100 lbs. over gross seemed to have no effect at all. The E-models had plywood-covered wing tips for more stiffness, and balanced ailerons to ward off the possibility of flutter, but still retained the strut-braced tail group. The E-17-B was richly appointed and well equipped, but many more options were available at extra cost. All-leather upholstery was available for $60 extra, parachute-type seats were about $300 extra, and the seaplane version cost about $4000 more. Extra fuel cap. to 125 gal. was also available. A fixed-pitch Curtiss-Reed metal prop, Eclipse electric engine starter, Eclipse engine-driven generator, Exide battery, all necessary flight & engine instruments, wheel brakes, locking-type tail wheel, navigation lights, wobble-pump, seat belts, assist ropes, and first-aid kit were standard equipment. Pressure-type fire extinguisher, oil cooler, bonding & shielding, radio gear, landing lights, paraflares, and custom colors were optional. The next Beech development was the famous model D-17-S as described here in the chapter for ATC # 649.

Listed below are E-17-B and E-17-L entries as gleaned from various records:

NC-17083;	E-17-B	(# 138)	Jacobs L-5
-17084;	"	(# 139)	"
-17085;	"	(# 140)	"
-16449;	"	(# 141)	"
-17091;	"	(# 142)	"
-17092;	"	(# 143)	"
-18025;	"	(# 144)	"

E-17-B was one of the most efficient airplanes in the world.

-18026;	"	(# 145)	"
-18038;	"	(# 149)	"
-18039;	"	(# 150)	"
-18040;	"	(# 151)	"
-18041;	"	(# 152)	"
-18042;	"	(# 153)	"
-17066;	"	(# 154)	"
-17069;	"	(# 155)	"
-17071;	"	(# 156)	"
-18555;	"	(# 157)	"
-18556;	"	(# 158)	"
-18557;	"	(# 159)	"
CF-BHA;	"	(# 160)	"
;	E-17-L	(#161)	Jacobs L-4
-18560;	E-17-B	(# 162)	Jacobs L-5
NC-2388;	"	(# 163)	"
-18585;	"	(# 189)	"
-18043;	"	(# 190)	"
-18044;	"	(# 191)	"
-18558;	"	(# 192)	"
-18559;	"	(# 193)	"
-18564;	"	(# 194)	"
-18577;	"	(# 195)	"
-18587;	"	(# 196)	"
-18588;	"	(# 197)	"
-18775;	"	(# 198)	"
-18781;	"	(# 204)	"
NC-903;	"	(# 205)	"
NC-284Y;	"	(# 206)	"

-18784;	"	(# 207)	"
-18785;	"	(# 208)	"
NC-40Y;	"	(# 209)	"
-18561;	"	(# 210)	"
-18787;	"	(# 212)	"
-18788;	"	(# 213)	"
NC-91;	"	(# 219)	"
CF-BKQ;	"	(# 227)	"
-18570;	"	(# 228)	"
-19467;	"	(# 231)	"
VT-AKJ;	"	(# 232)	"
VT-AKK;	"	(# 233)	"
VT-AKL;	"	(# 234)	"
-19479;	"	(# 251)	"
VT-ALA;	"	(# 274)	"
-18778;	"	(# 280)	"
VT-ALV;	"	(# 336)	"
NC-293Y;	"	(# 388)	"
NC-114;	"	(# 411)	"

This approval for ser. # 138 and up; ser. # 156, 160, 208 later modified to E-17-L; ser. # 160, 227 del. to Canada; ser. # 161 del. to Argentina; ser. # 163 del. to Conn. Dept. of Aero.; ser. # 196 later modified with Jacobs L-6; ser. # 232-34, 274, 336 del. to Indian National Airways; ser. # 280 operated in Borneo on floats as PK-SAM; ser. # 388, 411 mfgd. 1940; 31 of E-17-B as UC-43D in USAAF.

ATC # 642
(6-5-37)
WACO, MODEL UPF-7.

The Waco UPF-7 strikes a handsome pose.

We know that literally thousands have learned to fly in "Waco" airplanes; some of our best pilots spent their first hours in the sky learning to manage and master this biplane. In the "twenties" fledgling pilots were cutting their teeth on the old beloved "Nine," and then the "Ten"; in the "thirties" future pilots were learning to master the art of flight in the various F-models that abounded, but none of these "Waco" were actually training airplanes as such. They were very excellent utility airplanes that happened to be suitable for training pilots. Except for the quasi-military "Model D," the only "Waco" airplane actually intended for pilot-training specifically in this country was the now-famous Continental-powered UPF-7 biplane. Designed with more or less singular purpose the model UPF-7 borrowed heavily from the successful sporting-type UMF and YMF designs of a year or two previous; in it was translated the otherwise sporting nature into capabilities of demonstrating and teaching the more advanced techniques of flight. By nature the UPF-7 was an all-around airplane capable of nursing a student pilot tenderly through the primary phases, and then going right into the advanced stages of flight whenever he was ready; because of this knack the UPF-7 was so popular among the schools participating in the government's CPTP program. The CPTP program, enacted on June 27 of 1939, was

designed to train thousands upon thousands of civilian pilots as a back-log in case of war; the training was dispensed through various educational institutions around the country. The CPTP act authorized nearly six million dollars for fiscal years 1939 and 1940; the act finally expired in 1944. The USAAF acquired a few of these "Waco" trainers as the XPT-14 and the YPT-14, but the bulk of popularity for the UPF-7 lay with the civilian schools; the schools were quite happy with it and most student pilots learned to love it dearly. When the hard-working UPF-7 was cavorting around in the sky during the late "thirties" and early "forties" it is doubtful if it ever dreamed that someday, as much as 35 years later, it would become just about the most popular sport-type airplane in America!

The "Waco" model UPF-7 was basically an open cockpit biplane with seating for 2 in tandem. At first the UPF-7 was also offered as a 3-place sportplane on this same approval, and 6 were manufactured as the VPF-7 for the Army Air Corps of Guatemala, but it was perhaps just a strategem to tide the design over while it was being promoted here more properly as a trainer. The graceful UPF-7 was a delicate yet masterful-looking machine, a combination of rounded elegance with a hint of brawn, that certainly would have appealed to a sporting pilot of this day, but the days of the open cockpit sport-biplane were just about over and Waco Aircraft

The UPF-7 as a YPT-14 in Army Air Corps.

knew it. As war clouds formed in Europe and the obvious threat to us drew nearer, the potential of the UPF-7 as a pilot-trainer became quite clear and Waco began their promotion of it in earnest; the airplane also did a very good job in selling itself. Unit production was very light going into 1938-39, but in the period of 1940-42 the entire production run of some 600 airplanes was absorbed into the accelerated CPTP program. The U. S. Army Air Corps, in search of a suitable primary trainer, had acquired 14 of the UPF-7 type as the XPT-14 and the YPT-14, but apparently the YPT-14 didn't have the downright beefy and brawny nature that the Air Corps was seeking. On the other hand, the CAA (Civil Aeronautics Authority) ordered 31 of the UPF-7 (with NACA-type engine cowl, painted black with orange wings) for their new private-flying section; a government inspector, who was also a pilot, was assigned with one of these airplanes to various districts to monitor civilian operations in that district. With ancestry of all the previous "Waco" biplanes coursing through its bones it is not surprising that the UPF-7 was never hesitant to take on whatever came up, and always did it well. As powered with the 7 cyl. Continental W670K engine of 220 h.p. the UPF-7 was able to take on many varied assignments and perform them all with confidence; this was a particularly good engine-airplane combination. The UPF-7 was maneuverable, predictable, and very capable; its flight characteristics were excellent

UPF-7 was popular in CPTP program.

UPF-7 on line at Boeing School of Aeronautics.

with good control, it was nimble enough for most aerobatics, and like all "Waco" biplanes it was a pleasure to fly. Perhaps many will say that the UPF-7 was no match for the earlier F-type sportplanes such as the UMF and YMF, but that's not necessarily so; the UPF-7 was a heavier, more gentle airplane and it only seemed less exciting. The type certificate for the model UPF-7 was issued 6-5-37 and this approval also included the VPF-7. More than 600 of these trainers were manufactured by the Waco Aircraft Co. at Troy, Ohio.

Listed below are specifications and performance data for the Waco model UPF-7 as powered with 7 cyl. Continental W670K or W670-6A engines rated 220 h.p. at 2150 r.p.m. at sea level; length overall 23'6"; height overall 8'6"; wingspan upper 30'0"; wingspan lower 26'10"; wing chord upper & lower 57"; wing area upper 135.8 sq. ft.; wing area lower 107.8 sq. ft.; total wing area 243.6 sq. ft.; airfoil Clark Y; wt. empty 1870 lbs.; useful load 780 lbs.; payload with 50 gal. fuel 280 lbs.; gross wt. 2650 lbs.; max. speed 130 at sea level; cruising speed (.75 power) 115 at optimum altitude; landing speed 50; landing run (over 50 ft. barrier) 980 ft. to complete stop; takeoff run (over 50 ft. barrier) 950 ft.; climb 900 ft. first min. at sea level; climb to 9000 ft. in 15 mins.; ser. ceiling 14,800 ft.; gas cap. 50 gal.; oil cap. 4 gal.; cruising range (.75 power) at 14 gal. per hour 400 miles; price $9500 at factory. In general, the proposed sport-type version of the UPF-7 was lighter, faster, and cheaper; the sport-type was designed to use NACA-type engine cowl and streamlined metal wheel pants. It was eligible as 3-place.

Specifications and data for the model VPF-7 as powered with Continental W670M engine rated 240 h.p. at 2175 r.p.m. at sea level, same as above except as follows: wt. empty 1880 lbs.; useful load 770 lbs.; payload with 50 gal. fuel 270 lbs.; gross wt. 2650 lbs.; max. speed 133 at sea level; cruising speed (.75 power) 117; landing speed 50; landing run (over 50 ft. barrier) 980 ft. to complete stop; takeoff run (over 50 ft. barrier) 920 ft.; climb 930 ft. first min. at sea level; climb to 9500 ft. in 15 mins.; ser. ceiling 15,000 ft.; cruising range (.75 power) at 15 gal. per hour 375 miles; price approx. $9500 at factory. In general, the proposed sport-type version of the VPF-7 was lighter, faster, and cheaper; the sport-type was designed to use the NACA-type engine cowl and streamlined metal wheel pants. It was eligible as 3-place.

The fuselage framework was built up of welded 4130 steel tubing, heavily faired to a well-rounded shape, then fabric covered. The fuselage was softly rounded, and of full figure, but it certainly wasn't frail. Each of the large open cockpits had a large built-up windshield before it, adjustable bucket-type seats with cushion, with full controls and instrumentation for both occupants. Front cockpit had entry door on left side, and rear cockpit entry was just an easy step-over from the fuselage step. Shock-proof instrument panels were fitted with one-inch thick crash pads, speaking tubes connected the 2 cockpits, and all other specified paraphernalia for Army-type pilot-training was included. On some early versions of the UPF-7 the Continental engine was encased in a deep NACA-type engine cowl, but generally it was left uncovered for quicker inspection and faster maintenance. The robust wing framework, in 4 panels, was built up of solid spruce spar beams with spruce truss-type wing ribs reinforced with mahogany plywood gussets; the leading edges were covered with dural metal sheet and the completed framework was covered with fabric. Metal-framed ailerons, one on each wing panel, were connected together in pairs with a streamlined push-pull strut. The center-section panel was mounted above the fuselage on splayed-out N-type struts; 2 fuel tanks of 25 gal. cap. each were mounted in this panel. The VPF-7 had 73.5 gal. fuel capacity. The robust landing gear of 75" and 101" tread was a strong tripod affair fitted with long-travel oleo-spring shock struts; 6.50x10 wheels with brakes were fitted with 7.50x10 4-ply tires. 7.50x10 wheels fitted with 8.50x10 tires were optional. The fabric-covered tail group was a composite structure of wood and welded steel; both rudder and elevators had aerodynamic balance. The horizontal stabilizer was adjustable for trim. A fixed-pitch Curtiss-Reed metal prop, nose-cowling, electric engine starter, 15 amp. generator, Exide battery, Fyr-Fyter fire extinguisher, dual stick-type controls, 2 complete sets of instruments, locking-type tail wheel, parking brake, rear-view mirror, seat belts, speaking tube, engine cover, cockpit cover, flight-report holder, and first-aid kit were standard equipment. The next Waco development was the model UKS-7 cabin biplane as described here in the chapter for ATC # 648.

Listed below are UPF-7 and VPF-7 entries as verified by company records:

VPF-7		(# 4651)	Cont. 240
;	"	(# 4652)	"
;	"	(# 4653)	"
;	"	(# 4654)	"
;	"	(# 4655)	"
;	"	(# 4656)	"
NC-20901;	UPF-7	(# 4659)	Cont. 225
40-14;	YPT-14	(# 5300)	"
40-15;	"	(# 5301)	"
40-16;	"	(# 5302)	"
40-17;	"	(# 5303)	"
40-18;	"	(# 5304)	"
40-19;	"	(# 5305)	"
40-20;	"	(# 5306)	"
40-21;	"	(# 5307)	"
40-22;	"	(# 5308)	"
40-23;	"	(# 5309)	"
40-24;	"	(# 5310)	"
40-25;	"	(# 5311)	"
40-26;	"	(# 5312)	"
;	"	(# 5313)	"
;	"	(# 5314)	"
;	"	(# 5315)	"

Ser. # 4651-56 rolled out 6-37 and del. to Guatemala; all 6 of these VPF-7 were returned to U.S.A. in 1959; ser. # 4659 (NC-20901) del. to U.S. Army Air Corps as XPT-14 (39-702) for test; ser. # 5300-12 del. to U.S. Army Air Corps as YPT-14; Air Corps kept 2 of the YPT-14 and 11 were turned over to CAA for CPTP program; ser. # 5313-15 rolled out 3-40 and del. to Venezuela; ser. # 5313-15 equipped with instruments in Spanish and metric system; all above airplanes had cowled engines, 99 in. Curtiss-Reed props, narrow landing gear, & modified to two-place.

Typical example of restored UPF-7 that are still flying.

NC-20970;	UPF-7	(# 5316)	Cont. 225
-20971;	"	(# 5317)	"
-20972;	"	(# 5318)	"
-20973;	"	(# 5319)	"
-20907;	"	(# 5320)	"
-20974;	"	(# 5321)	"
-20975;	"	(# 5322)	"
-20976;	"	(# 5323)	"
-20977;	"	(# 5324)	"
-20978;	"	(# 5325)	"
-20979;	"	(# 5326)	"

NC-29300 was ser. # 5327 and numbers ran consecutively to NC-29369 which was ser. # 5396; ser. # 5316 thru 5396 had W670-6A engines without NACA cowl & using 102 in. Curtiss-Reed prop; all were two-place.

-29900;	"	(# 5397)	"
-29901;	"	(# 5398)	"
-29902;	"	(# 5399)	"
-29903;	"	(# 5400)	"

NC-29904 was ser. # 5401 and numbers ran consecutively to NC-29999 which was ser. # 5496; engine was not cowled, and airplanes were two-place.

-30100;	"	(# 5497)	"
-30101;	"	(# 5498)	"
-30102;	"	(# 5499)	"
-30103;	"	(# 5500)	"

NC-30104 was ser. # 5501 and numbers ran consecutively to NC-30174 which was ser. # 5571; this block of airplanes had 96 in. Curtiss-Reed prop; NC-153 was ser. # 5572 and numbers ran consecutively to NC-185 which was ser. # 5604; ser. # 5572 thru 5604 assigned to Private Flying Section of CAA—were hand-rubbed finished in black fuselage, fin and rudder, the wings, stabilizer and elevators were Galatea Orange; ser. # 5530 was NC-152, ser. # 5530 should have been NC-30133 so this no. was assigned to ser. # 5605.

-30133;	"	(# 5605)	"
-30175;	"	(# 5606)	"
-30176;	"	(# 5607)	"
-30177;	"	(# 5608)	"
-30178;	"	(# 5609)	"
-30179;	"	(# 5610)	"
-30180;	"	(# 5611)	"
-30181;	"	(# 5612)	"

NC-30182 was ser. # 5613 and numbers ran consecutively to NC-30199 which was ser. # 5630; all had uncowled engines and were two-place.

-32000;	"	(# 5631)	"
-32001;	"	(# 5632)	"
-32002;	"	(# 5633)	"
-32003;	"	(# 5634)	"

NC-32004 was ser. # 5635 and numbers ran consecutively to NC-32199 which was ser. # 5831; this block was mfgd. 1941.

-39700;	"	(# 5832)	"
-39701;	"	(# 5833)	"
-39702;	"	(# 5834)	"
-39703;	"	(# 5835)	"
-39704;	"	(# 5836)	"
-39705;	"	(# 5837)	"
-39706;	"	(# 5838)	"
-39707;	"	(# 5839)	"
;	"	(# 5840)	"

Ser. # 5840 del. to Nicaragua; NC-39708 was ser. # 5841 and numbers ran consecutively to NC-39759 which was ser. # 5892; this listing represents over 600 airplanes; the last 60 airplanes were mfgd. in 1942.

ATC # 643
(6-11-37)
TAYLOR-YOUNG, MODEL A.

Taylor-Young "Model A" with 40 h.p. Continental engine was one of the finest lightplanes of this period.

As airplane-designer C. Gilbert Taylor often said — "let it be known that the Taylorcraft is not a second-generation Cub, it was designed especially to outdo the Cub." And, many will agree that it did outdo the "Cub." As a past master in light-plane design C. G. Taylor had his little drawer of secrets, secrets which he used to build airplanes that performed remarkably well on a ridiculous amount of power. When Taylor discovered that a wider side by side seated airplane, if properly designed and proportioned, would go as fast or faster than a narrow tandem-seated airplane he had the formula he wanted for the new "Taylorcraft" and put it hastily on paper. It took less than 3 months to build the first "Taylorcraft" and it was easy to see even then that it was going to be a big hit. A Group 2 approval was awarded the airplane in Dec. of 1936; Taylor laid out the building of a few more airplanes and began shopping around for some financing. An offer was eventually made by the city of Alliance, Ohio; they would furnish the former Alliance (Hess) "Argo" plant rent-free if Taylor would move his operation there, so he moved to Alliance. The 60x300 ft. plant, which had been idle for some years, began to hum again and soon Taylor had orders for more than 250 airplanes. A dealer organization was slowly forming and many dealers ordered airplanes without actually seeing what the airplane was really like — they believed Taylor when he said it

was about the best light airplane ever built. The "Taylorcraft" Model A was shown first at the New York Air Show for 1937, and then at the Los Angeles Air Show a few months later; the clamor for airplanes was unbelievable. One dealer said "selling Taylorcraft airplanes is like selling life-preservers at a shipwreck!!" Another dealer sold more than a dozen of these airplanes even before he had a demonstrator! The factory had turned out 17 airplanes in April and 40 of the "Model A" were put together in May; soon they were putting out 50 airplanes per month and yet they were way behind. The 200th airplane was delivered in mid-August of 1937 and the production schedule was boosted to 75 airplanes per month; the goal for 1938 was 450 airplanes. Now as the Taylor-Young "Model A" this airplane was powered with the flat-four 40 h.p. Continental A-40 engine and it was selling for $1495; it was also available for $495 down and balance in 12 monthly payments. The "Model A" won its approval as a seaplane in Dec. of 1937 and it was shown in Feb. at the Chicago Air Show for 1938; the "Taylorcraft" were selling like hot cakes and being delivered by the carload. Was the "Taylorcraft A" all that good? Well, sir, it was a novel little airplane and it pleased a lot of people, as C. G. Taylor said it would.

For C. Gilbert Taylor this airplane was another new adventure; his relation with the familiar "Cub" airplane and with Wm. T. Piper

C. G. Taylor congratulates purchaser of first production Model A.

had finally ended. Taylor and Piper, both in-dividualists, had never really been good friends, but they put up with each other for the sake of keeping the "Cub" operation going. Finally, the relation deteriorated to such a low level that C. G. decided he just had to buy up or move out; it was Piper that had bought him out. Leaving early in 1935 Taylor moved to Butler, Pa. and began building the first "Taylorcraft" in March; it was built in less than 3 months by a half-dozen people. Anxiously, "C. G." test-hopped the first airplane and Kenny Tibbets did balance of the test-flying for a government approval. Only a few had been built at Butler, Pa. when the move to Alliance, O. came up and there the "Model A" had received its ATC approval; just prior to approval the Taylor-Young Airplane Co. was formed. The rent-free factory was a great help,

but the terrific business that Taylor was doing (356 airplanes were built in 1937) called for more and more expansion and that would cost money; money for expansion became Taylor's continuous problem.

The Taylor-Young "Model A" was a light high-winged cabin monoplane with side by side seating for 2; a novel airplane that introduced several innovations to the light-plane market. Proving again that C. G. Taylor had a knack for designing light, inexpensive airplanes that looked and flew like a bigger airplane even though they were in the so-called flivver-plane category. The "Model A," as it was simply called, was a big-value airplane and it became an instant hit; by year's end they were being shipped in all directions by the box-car load. The most unusual thing about this new "Taylorcraft" was the fact

"Taylorcraft" delivered a lot of performance on 40 h.p.

that people were buying it almost sight unseen; they took it for granted that it would be a good airplane because C. G. Taylor said so. Realizing how the airplane was likely to be used Taylor built it to take punishment from student-pilots in summer or winter, in fair weather or foul, and at all levels of terrain; the training of new pilots was to be its strongest virtue. But, Taylor had a problem; the plant was humming along at full capacity and they just couldn't keep up with all the orders. What a nice problem. As powered with the popular "flat-four" Continental A-40-4 engine of 40 h.p. the Taylor-Young "Model A," as it was called starting in May of 1937, was a remarkable little airplane of big value and comparatively high performance. To prove that it had speed also in its repertoire it promptly won the Lightplane Derby, an event run during the National Air Races for 1937; the Derby was won by E. H. Spiller, another Taylor-Young A came in second, and an "Aeronca K" was third. On a lucky day, with a good strong wind on his tail, Wally Schanz flew a "Model A" from Pittsburgh to Basking Ridge, N.J., a distance of 315 miles, in less than 2 hours 15 mins.; flying at 7000 ft. he was averaging more than 130 m.p.h.! The "40 horse Taylorcraft" wasn't always this fast, but it was apparently the top-dog among popular lightplanes. Complementing all this aptitude was energetic maneuverability and a nice smooth feel; seasoned pilots loved it, and student-pilots became proud as peacocks when they learned to master it properly. The type certificate for the Taylor-Young "Model A" was issued 6-11-37 and some 600 or more examples were manufactured by the Taylor-Young Airplane Co. at Alliance, O. C. Gilbert Taylor was pres. & chf. engr.; Wm. C. Young was V.P. & gen. mgr.; Frank L. Sullivan was sec-treas.; and Stanley Vaughn was factory manager.

Listed below are specifications and performance data for the Taylor-Young "Model A" as powered with Continental A-40-4 engine rated 40 h.p. at 2575 r.p.m. at sea level; length overall 22'0"; height overall 6'8"; wingspan 36'0"; wing chord 63"; total wing area (incl. fuselage section) 168 sq. ft.; airfoil NACA-23012; wt. empty 586 lbs.; useful load 464 lbs.; payload with 10 gal. fuel 226 lbs. (1 pass. & 56 lbs. for bag. & extras); gross wt. 1050 lbs.; max. speed 91 at sea level; cruising speed (2200 r.p.m.) 82; landing speed 38; takeoff run 425 ft.; climb 425 ft. first min. at sea level; ser. ceiling 14,000 ft.; gas cap. 10 gal.; oil cap. 4 qts.; cruising range (2200 r.p.m.) at 3.5 gal. per hour 240 miles; price was $1495 at factory, raised to $1565 in May of 1938. Model A was also eligible as seaplane on Edo D-1070 or 54-1140 twin-float gear at 1130 lbs. gross wt.

The fuselage framework was built up of welded 4130 and 1025 steel tubing, faired to shape with wooden formers and fairing strips, then fabric covered. Entry door was on the right, and all windows and the windshield were of Du-Pont Plasticele; side windows opened out for ventilation. The 39 in. wide seat was padded with rubberized horse-hair, and cabin interior was upholstered completely with durable cloth. The firewall was insulated against heat, fumes, and noise. A novelty were the dual control wheels which protruded out from the panel; a baggage hamper was behind the seat-back. The strut-braced wing, in 2 panels, was built up of solid spruce spar beams and "Nicral" metal wing ribs; the leading edges were covered with dural metal sheet and the completed framework was covered in fabric. Metal-framed ailerons were aerodynamically balanced. A 10-gal. fuel tank was mounted high in the fuselage just ahead of the windshield; a bobber-type fuel gauge protruded from the tank cap. The split-axle landing gear of 72 in. tread was fitted with 6.00x6 wheels and tires; shock absorbing units were rubber compression-rings buried in the fuselage to eliminate drag. A spring-leaf tail skid was stan-

The "Model A" in Canada on skis; note one-bladed Everel prop.

dard, but a tail wheel attachment was optional. The fabric-covered tail group was built up of welded 1025 steel tubing. A Sensenich wooden prop, basic engine & flight instrument group, dual control wheels, seat belts, and first-aid kit were standard equipment. A left-hand entry door, wheel brakes, wheel pants, tail wheel assembly, hot-shot battery, cabin vents, cabin heater, carburetor heat-box, navigation lights, compass, leather upholstery, fancy control wheels, radio gear, custom paint, Edo pontoons, and skis were optional. The next Taylor development was the Model BC as described here in the chapter for ATC # 696.

Listed below are Taylorcraft entries as gleaned from registration records:

X-16393;	Model A	(# 25)	Cont. A-40
NC-15776;	''	(# 26)	''
-15757;	''	(# 27)	''
-15758;	''	(# 28)	''
-15759;	''	(# 29)	''
-15762;	''	(# 30)	''
;	''	(# 31)	''
-18301;	''	(# 32)	''
-18302;	''	(# 33)	''
-18303;	''	(# 34)	''
-18304;	''	(# 35)	''
-18305;	''	(# 36)	''
-15760;	''	(# 37)	''
-15761;	''	(# 38)	''
-18306;	''	(# 39)	''
-18307;	''	(# 40)	''
-18308;	''	(# 41)	''
-18309'	''	(# 42)	''

This approval for ser. # 26 and up; the prototype (ser. # 25) was mfgd. by the Taylor Aviation Co. at Butler, Pa.; subsequent airplanes were mfgd. by the Taylor-Young Airplane Co. at Alliance, O.; first approval issued was Group 2-529 issued 12-17-36 and superseded by ATC #643 issued 6-11-37; NC-18310 was ser. #43 and nos. ran consecutively to NC-18347 which was ser. #80; NC-18349 was ser. #81 and nos. ran consecutively to NC-18373 which was ser. #105; ser. #31, 75, 91 not verified; NC-19000 was ser. #106 and nos. ran consecutively to NC-19085 which was ser. #191; ser. #112, 123-24, 129, 132, 144, 147 not verified; no listing for ser. #192; NC-19087 was ser. #193 and nos. ran consecutively to NC-19099 which was ser. #205; from the info given here a listing could be made up for the first 180 airplanes; approval expired 4-3-41.

A pair of early "Model A" rolled out for fly-away delivery.

ATC # 644
(6-24-37)
STEARMAN-HAMMOND, Y-1-S.

Stearman-Hammond Y-1-S with a pusher-type Menasco engine; the installation had many advantages.

When seen in a flock of "regular" airplanes the unusual Stearman-Hammond stuck out like a sore thumb; everything about it seemed backwards or wrong. The two occupants sat way out in front, the engine was in back, the tail-group was perched on a couple of booms, the wing was there as a foundation, and everything was fastened to it; from all of this then hung a three-wheeled undercarriage. It is plain to see they had reached way back in history for some of these features, features that were common even in 1915. From the engineers' point of view this combination would provide utmost safety and flight characteristics that would coddle the amateur flier, and lessen his chances of making grave mistakes. After 3 years of development in a government-fostered program the Stearman-Hammond did not become "the poor man's airplane," but it certainly was an interesting approach; surely, it was a vehicle somewhat better suited to the man-in-the-street than the average airplane. Lloyd Stearman, who was naturally enthused with the S-H, claimed that anyone could "solo" this airplane after only 1 hour of instructions; this may seem far-fetched, but it was really possible. A 50-year-old businessman, with no previous experience with aircraft, soloed in a Y-1-S after 3.5 hours of dual instruction. To prove his proficiency he landed several

"bullseyes" in a marked circle. A young lady, the first time she had ever been in an airplane, taxied to the runway, took off, spend 20 minutes in the air making turns, landed, and taxied back to the hangar ramp with only vocal instructions offered by the pilot-instructor alongside her! The Gilmore Oil Co. bought the first model Y-1-S in So. California and used it extensively in promotion of their products. This airplane visited nearly every airport on the Pacific coast, and several people from each community were invited to fly it — people who had never flown before. The reaction was amazing and every one was flabbergasted because it was all so simple. Lloyd Stearman knew about airplanes and he was sure the Stearman-Hammond Y-1-S would help make flying a practical as well as an amusing sport or occupation. Ironically, the Stearman-Hammond wasn't selling, but it was one of the most talked-about airplanes in this country.

A gala open-house on Nov. 22 of 1936 marked the formal opening of the new Stearman-Hammond plant in So. San Francisco. Deliveries were scheduled for March of 1937, but for various reasons the schedule had to be amended several times. S-H started production of 8 airplanes in Jan. of 1937, and sub-assemblies were started for 17 more airplanes, with deliveries promised for as soon as possible. The first of the

Y-1-S shows its unusual configuration.

1937 model Y-1-S was ready for delivery on March 21, but it had to wait for approval. One example of the new Y-1-S was exhibited at the so-called Los Angeles Air Show during March and it was well received, especially among the general public who have no opinions formed about airplanes. About this time a dealer chain was being formed, and among the big-names interested in selling the Stearman-Hammond was the famous Roscoe Turner; one Y-1-S was shipped to KLM Airlines of Holland who planned to be the European distributor. Enthused with the people's reaction to the airplane, Tom Fowler and Samuel Metzger made a national demonstration tour with the Y-1-S hoping to form a nationwide "fly it yourself" chain, but the plan never did materialize. The Stearman-Hammond was a wonderful little airplane, and it seemed to be made to order for the average amateur flier; the question arises, why didn't it sell in the great quantities predicted? Well, it seemed that the company was always hard up for money, and that could have been their greatest stumbling-block. The airplane that practically anybody could fly, and almost anybody could afford to own, is still a dream.

The Stearman-Hammond model Y-1-S was a low-winged "pusher type" cabin monoplane with side by side seating for two. The highly unusual arrangement was calculated to provide easy entry right from the ground, a comfortable seating position away from noise and fumes, a very broad range of visibility, the dangerous whirling propeller was fenced-off by the twin tail-booms, and the tricycle landing gear eliminated many of the operating pitfalls experienced by amateur pilots. With the 3-wheeled undercarriage, and the way it was laid out, it was possible to taxi at 45 m.p.h. or higher, cross-wind landings and gusty winds were hardly a problem, and the airplane could actually be dropped-in from as much as 20 ft. without serious damage. As we have already pointed out the Stearman-Hammond was so simple to fly that the average person right off the street could fly it alone after 3 or 4 hours of instruction. To expert pilots with years of experience in the so-called regular airplane, "it just didn't seem real"! There was no mistaking the S-H because there was no other quite like it; to California residents who saw it frequently it was known as "The Bug," and through the grapevine it became the most talked-about airplane in America. As powered with the 4 cyl. inverted aircooled inline Menasco C4S-150 engine rated 150 h.p. the model Y-1-S was a better airplane than the earlier Y-125, but it was still a little sluggish when compared to the average airplane with similar power. This, however, seemed to be an acceptable trade-off in view of its other capabilities. There were those, of

A 68-year-old woman mastered this Y-1-S, then later received her private license.

course, that thought it was merely a weird contraption, but others took to it with an open mind and learned to enjoy it. As a highly advanced design, perhaps too many years ahead of its time, the S-H Y-1-S was doing its best to make it in a rather hostile environment. Try as it might, it finally gave up the battle in 1938, and soon fell by the wayside as another interesting memory. The type certificate for the model Y-1-S was issued 6-24-37 and no reliable records remain as to the actual number built. The Hammond Aircraft Co. was first founded in Ypsilanti, Mich., by Dean Hammond in 1932. In a reorganization as the Stearman-Hammond Aircraft Corp. at So. San Francisco, Calif., the well-known Lloyd Stearman became pres. & gen. mgr.; Dean B. Hammond was V.P.; Samuel Metzger was sales mgr.; and M. Carl Haddon was chf. engr.

Listed below are specifications and performance data for the Stearman-Hammond model Y-1-S as powered with a Menasco C4S engine rated 150 h.p. at 2260 r.p.m. at 3000 ft. (159 h.p. available for take-off); length overall 26'11"; height overall 7'11"; wingspan 40'0"; wing chord at root 83"; wing chord at tip 29.3"; total wing area 210 sq. ft.; airfoil Clark Y; wt. empty 1425 (1482) lbs.; useful load 750 (768) lbs.; payload with 40 gal. fuel 310 lbs. (1 pass. & 140 lbs. bag. & extras); gross wt. 2175 (2250) lbs.; figures in parentheses as later amended; max. speed 130 at 3000 ft.; cruising speed (.75 power) 121; cruising speed (.90 power at 5000 ft.) 129; landing speed (with flaps) 42; landing (stall) speed (no flaps) 52; climb 700 ft. first min. at sea level; ser. ceiling 17,000 ft.; gas cap. 43 gal.; oil cap. 4 gal.; cruising range (.75 power) at 9 gal. per hour 480 miles; price not announced.

The fuselage, or cabin pod, was an all-metal semi-monocoque structure of riveted 24ST members covered with smooth "Alclad" sheet metal. A large door on each side provided easy step-up entry right from the ground. The wide, padded seat sat two across and an 11 cu. ft. baggage compartment down low in behind was allowed 100 lbs. A shelf behind the seat was provided for hats, gloves, and other incidentals. The cabin was vented with cool air and a cabin heater was available. There was considerable window area in the cabin and visibility was excellent over the short nose. A throw-over control wheel allowed either occupant to fly the airplane; pedals on the floor were not for the rudders — pedal on the right was for the wheel brakes, and pedal on the left was a wing-flap control. The control wheel which operated the ailerons also steered the nose-wheel for maneuvering on the ground. The "pusher" (backwards) engine was mounted in rubber on a steel tube frame and it was completely cowled in; an improved air-scoop tunnel brought in cool air to the engine under ram pressure from the front. Engine cyls. were baffled to create forced-air cooling; oil temperature was controlled with an oil-cooling radiator. The engine thrust-line was mounted high enough so that propeller was above and ahead of wing's trailing edge; this to provide protection against kicked-up gravel and other runway debris. Numerous removable plates and zippered openings allowed complete inspection of fuselage and engine compartment. The all-metal (24ST Alclad) cantilever wing framework, in 3 sections, was built up around a single tapered box-type spar beam with truss-type wing ribs of square (51ST) alloy tubing; the leading edges were covered with dural metal sheet and the completed framework was covered in fabric. The wing's center-section (122 in. wide) was bolted to the cabin pod and outer wing panels were bolted to the stub-end. Two fuel tanks of 21.5 gal. capacity each formed the leading edge of the C/S panel; top side of this panel was covered with metal sheet. Split-type trailing edge wing flaps (25.5 sq. ft.), in 3 sections, covered more than half the span; flap control was manual (lever & pedal) through a range of 40 or 60 degs. Flaps not to be lowered above 80 m.p.h. Caution: airplane sinks rapidly on release of flaps. The ailerons were differential (35 deg. up & 15 deg. down) for establishing turns without rudder. Numerous plates and zippered openings allowed complete inspection of the wing and its mechanisms. The 3-wheeled landing gear of 109 in. tread was cast alloy forks attached to oil-spring shock struts of 18 in. stroke; main wheels were under the wing behind the C.G.; and a steerable wheel was in the nose. The nose-wheel was steerable through 43 degs. each side for ground stability and easier handling. Goodyear 18x8-3 airwheels were fitted with hydraulic disc brakes; wheel streamlines were optional. The all-metal (24ST) horizontal stabilizer and elevator were fastened between 2 all-metal (24ST) monocoque tail booms. Each tail boom was fitted with a fixed fin — no movable rudders were used. Elevator travel (restricted) was adjusted to 10 deg. up and 22 deg. down at the factory, and must not be altered; elevator had adj. trim tab. A wooden prop, electric engine starter, 12-volt battery, engine-driven generator, engine-driven fuel pump, wobble pump, fuel gauges, fuel press. warning light, dome light, ammeter, compass, navigation lights, engine & flight instruments, seat belts and first-aid kit were standard equip-

ment. General "streamined" wheels and tires (21 in. rear & 18 in. front), landing lights, fire extinguisher, wind-driven generator, and radio gear were optional. Henry Kaiser, famous industrialist, tried to revive the Stearman-Hammond after WW2, but had no luck either.

Listed below are Stearman-Hammond Y-1-S entries as gleaned from registration records:

NC-15521;	Y-1-S	(# 306)	Menasco C4S
-15522;	"	(# 307)	"
-15523;	"	(# 308)	"
-15524;	"	(# 309)	"
-15525;	"	(# 310)	"
:	"	(# 311)	"
-15526:	"	(# 312)	"
-15527;	"	(# 313)	"
-15528;	"	(# 314)	"
-15529;	"	(# 315)	"
-15530;	"	(# 316)	"
-15531;	"	(# 317)	"
-15532;	"	(# 318)	"
-15533;	"	(# 319)	"

This approval for ser. # 304 and up; no listing for ser. # 304, 305, 311; ser. # 308 del. to Gilmore Oil Co.; at least 8 of these aircraft reg. in Calif.; ser. # 316 not verified; ser. # 318 del. to Borrah Minnevitch, the famous harmonica virtuoso; two JH-1 target drones mfgd. for U.S. Navy.

The Y-1-S was designed as a "foolproof" airplane.

The trim DGA-9 with Jacobs L-5 engine.

The first commercial replica of Benny Howard's famous "Mr. Mulligan" was first reported as being powered with a 9 cyl. Wright engine of 420 h.p. and labeled the model DGA-7; this big engine was very shortly replaced with a 7 cyl. Wright engine of 320 h.p. and labeled the model DGA-8. Sometime later inquiries began coming in from interested parties and prospective buyers to see if they could get one of the "DGA" monoplanes with a Jacobs engine in it. Supposedly, not everyone relished the prospect of handling the "hot" Howard with a big engine in it. So, perhaps as a favor, Benny Howard and Gordon Israel designed the model DGA-9 for the 7 cyl. Jacobs L-5 engine of 285 h.p. to satisfy these inquiries; manufacturers often did this to sell a few more airplanes. This design was then later modified to mount the more powerful Jacobs L-6 engine of 300-330 h.p. as the model DGA-12; this was to please those that preferred the Jacobs engine. The actual performance loss was not so great because of the lowered available power, but it did make for a somewhat milder airplane. In essence, only a few could really notice the loss, and the DGA-9 or the DGA-12 still had that high level of sophistication so prevalent in a "Howard" monoplane. As of May in 1937, Benny Howard was flight-research engineer for United Air Lines, so he had very little time for the factory, and no time at all for air-racing, but he took advantage of all opportunities to exploit and promote sales of the various "DGA" monoplanes. In Aug. of 1937 a shiny-new DGA-9 was flown off to California as a demonstrator where it sparked considerable interest. Then in Oct. of 1937 a Jacobs-powered "Howard" (most likely a DGA-9) was flown to Point Barrow in the upper reaches of Alaska. One would hardly think of the sleek, sophisticated "Howard" monoplane as a bush-plane hauling furs and trappers, but they did leave their mark up there over the years.

The Howard models DGA-9 and DGA-12 were both fairly conventional strut-braced, high-winged cabin monoplanes (if you can call a "Howard" conventional) with seating arranged for 4 or 5. The interiors were tastefully upholstered and appointed more like that of a fine, expensive automobile, and noise levels in the cabin were low enough so that conversation could be held in normal tones. Best of all, the DGA-9 and the DGA-12 also had that air of sophistication that created a glowing pride in ownership, and attracted admiration wherever they went; this was half the fun in owning a Howard. The model DGA-9 was powered with

162

Howard DGA-9 owners beamed with pride, understandably.

the popular Jacobs L-5 engine rated 285 h.p., and the model DGA-12 was powered with the new Jacobs L-6 engine rated 300 h.p. We can hardly describe these as "economy models," but they were the cheapest of the DGA line and offered only a shade less in overall performance. The roster of owners showed no famous names, but every one of them was a satisfied customer. Both of the Jacobs-powered "Howard" monoplanes were a pleasure to own and to fly, and their rugged make-up assured years of good service. Both the DGA-9 and the DGA-12 were available also as "Deluxe" models with a controllable prop, extra fuel capacity, and an unbeatable custom finish. This approval was issued 6-25-37 and it covered both the DGA-9 and DGA-12; some 10 or more in all were manufactured by the Howard Aircraft Corp. at Chicago, Ill. Ben O. Howard was pres.; B. D. deWeese (formerly with Stinson) was V.P. & gen. mgr.; C. Freitag was sales mgr.; and W. Brownell was chf. engr. Incidentally, to explain the gap between models DGA-9 and DGA-12; the model DGA-10 was a proposed twin-engined monoplane that died on the drawing board, and the model DGA-11 is described here in the chapter for ATC # 672.

Listed below are specifications and performance data for the Howard model DGA-9 as powered with Jacobs L-5 engine rated 285 h.p. at 2000 r.p.m. at sea level; length overall 25'8"; height overall 8'5"; wingspan 38'0"; max. wing chord 72"; total wing area (incl. fuselage section) 186 sq. ft.; airfoil NACA-2R12; wt. empty 2150 lbs.; useful load 1450 lbs.; payload with 60 gal. fuel 868 lbs. (4 pass. & 120 lbs. baggage); gross wt. 3600 lbs.; gross wt. may be increased to 3800 lbs. with a controllable prop; max. speed 175 at sea level; cruising speed (.75 power) 166 at optimum altitude; landing speed (with flaps) 50; climb 1000 ft. first min. at sea level; ser. ceiling 18,000 ft.; gas cap. 60 gal.; oil cap. 7 gal.; cruising range (.75 power) at 17 gal. per hour 540 miles; price $9800 at factory. Model DGA-9 also eligible as seaplane on Edo twin-float gear using Hamilton-Standard controllable prop at 4100 lbs. gross weight.

Specifications and data for model DGA-12 as powered with Jacobs L-6 engine rated 300 h.p at 2100 r.p.m. at 3700 ft. (330 h.p. at 2200 r.p.m. for takeoff) same as above except as follows: wt. empty 2300 lbs.; useful load 1500 lbs.; payload with 97 gal. fuel 688 lbs.; payload with 60 gal. fuel 910 lbs.; gross wt. 3800 lbs.; max. speed (with controllable prop) 190; cruising speed 187 at 3700 ft.; landing speed (with flaps) 52; climb 1500 ft. first min. at sea level; ser. ceiling 19,000 ft.; gas cap. max. 97 gal.; oil cap. 8 gal.; cruising range at 18 gal. per hour 930 miles; price $12,800 at factory. Model DGA-12 also eligible as seaplane on Edo twin-float gear with Hamilton-Standard controllable prop at 4100 lbs. gross weight.

The construction details and general arrangement of the DGA-9 and DGA-12 were typical to that of the DGA-8 as described here in the chapter for ATC # 612. The following applies to all models in the DGA-8 to DGA-12 series. A shelf was added behind the rear seat for hats, jackets, gloves, and the like. Entry door was on the right side and a large fixed step was offered as an aid to easy entry or exit; a larger cabin door was offered as option. Parachute-type seats by Irvin or Switlik were available as an option for front and rear; custom interiors were available also. Any "Howard" could be "gassed" readily from ground level because fuel tanks were mounted in the fuselage belly. Normal capacity was a 60 gal. tank in front, and a 37 gal. tank in behind, but various other combinations up to 127 gals. were available. Fuel was fed by an engine-driven fuel pump, or a hand-operated wobble pump. The unique wing flaps on the "Howard" were arranged so that in a "go-around" (with full flaps down) when full throttle is applied they automatically and slowly returned to flight position as the forward speed and air pressure increased. This eliminated that sickening loss of altitude when flaps would normally be "dumped" for a go-around. The full-swiveling tail wheel was locked for takeoffs and landings to prevent wavering off course. Normally the DGA-9 was allowed a 60 gal. fuel capacity, and the DGA-12 was allowed 97 gals. Gross wt. of the DGA-9 could be increased to 3800 lbs. with the use of a controllable prop. Note: flaps must be extended for takeoff with DGA-9 when gross wt.

exceeds 3600 lbs.; flaps not to be extended above 108 m.p.h. when in flight. A Curtiss-Reed fixed-pitch metal prop, an electric engine starter, battery, generator, Pesco fuel pump, NACA-type engine cowl, 7.50x10 wheels with 6-ply tires, wheel brakes, parking brake, 10 in. tail wheel, bonding & shielding, navigation lights, cabin lights, seat belts, and first-aid kit were standard equipment. A Hamilton-Standard controllable prop, a choice of L-5M or L-5MB and L-6M or L-6MB engines, wheel pants, cabin heater & ventilator, landing lights, paraflares, pressure-type fire extinguisher, and extra instruments were optional. The next Howard development was the model DGA-11 as described here in the chapter for ATC # 672.

Listed below are DGA-9 and DGA-12 entries as gleaned from registration records:

NC-14886;	DGA-9	(# 200)	Jacobs L-5
-14889;	"	(# 201)	"
-18202;	"	(# 202)	"
-18203;	"	(# 203)	"
-18205;	"	(# 204)	"
-18206;	"	(# 205)	"
-18207;	"	(# 206)	"
-20400;	DGA-12	(# 400)	Jacobs L-6
-20401;	"	(# 401)	"
NC-55;	"	(#)	"

This approval for ser. # 200 and up (DGA-9) & for ser. # 400 and up (DGA-12); ser. # 200 owned & operated by Kathryn Hartigan, a lady-

The "Howard" lines that spelled high performance.

pilot; ser. # 203 may have been modified to DGA-8; ser. # 206 may have been modified to DGA-11; it is believed that NC-55 was a DGA-12, ser. no. unknown; no data available as to expiration date of this approval; these models were still available in 1940.

DGA-12 was fitted with more powerful Jacobs L-6 engine.

ATC # 646
(6-28-37)
SPARTAN, MODEL 7-WP.

The unusual "Spartan" 7-F, a proposed fighter-bomber; modified from the "Executive."

Frankly, no one to our knowledge has ever heard of the "Spartan" model 7-WP! The meager technical description published by CAA says only that it was a 3-place cabin monoplane powered with a Pratt & Whitney "Wasp Jr." SB engine rated 400 h.p. at 2200 r.p.m. at 5000 ft. Being listed as a model 7-WP we can assume at least that it must have been typical of the model 7-W that normally had room for 5; we then can assume also that the 3-place model 7-WP would probably be used for special purposes requiring a crew of 3 with room enough for equipment to perform a particular mission. We know that a 7-W was modified into a fighter-bomber (the 7-F) for possible export as an "armed reconnaissance airplane," but this version was soon aborted and the airplane brought back to civilian (7-W) specifications; it is doubtful this experimental version (the 7-F) was ever submitted for approval. We have also heard, but it cannot be confirmed, that one 7-W was converted to mount special cameras for high-altitude photographic purposes. Hence, the designation 7-WP could mean 7-W(Photographic), and this sounds the most logical. Because no facts or information was available for the 7-WP, either in company files or government publications, we have made the assumptions above; it is possible that somewhere along the line in researching we can unearth some definite facts about this particular airplane.

The "Spartan" model 7-WP was no doubt also a low-winged cabin monoplane similar to the 7-W, but listed as being held to 3 occupants. Because that is all we know of the so-called 7-WP we will include here some features of the 7-W not included in the chapter for ATC # 628. Besides being very roomy the cabin was very quiet; the engine noise was little more than a low rumble, and there was practically no vibration. It was easy to relax inside and conversation was easy. The 7-W was primarily designed as a fast personal-type transport for people who couldn't afford to be tied to an airline schedule, or had to go where the airlines didn't. Beside that, the "Executive" had speed enough to run and hide from most other airplanes. The 7-W was certainly not designed for the amateur, but it was pleasant to fly, and its stability was uncanny; it would stay exactly where you put it. The model 7-F we mentioned before was to be a fighter-bomber for export; it had a 30 caliber machine gun in the nose, an opening in the roof for a gun turret, and bomb-racks in the wings. This idea was aborted, but they later turned out a few fighter-bombers called "Zeus." The "Zeus" (8-W) was a two-place tandem-seated airplane, with a greenhouse canopy over the crew, that looked something like the "Executive" in a way; 4 were being delivered to a foreign country, but the ship was sunk and the airplanes were lost. The custom-built "Executive" delivered to the King of Iraq (YI-SOF) was literally an airplane fit for a king; the special interior was upholstered in red antique Velour trimmed in gold, and the King's crest was emblazoned on the tail and the wing tips. Complete with radio gear the special 7-W cost the King more than $30,000. During World War 2 a 7-W was impressed into USAAF service as the UC-71; this particular airplane was assigned to Secretary Wilson of the Dept. of Defense. Fifteen others were also used for various military service. With many countries already at war, and with America uncertain as to its role in the fracas, production of the "Executive" was suspended in 1940. After WW2, when markets for aircraft began to open up again, Spartan tried to revive the "Executive" in a tricycle-geared version as the Model 12, but they could see no future for it.

Listed below are additional details on the 7-W not covered previously. The large baggage compartment had outside door on the left, or could be reached from inside by lifting up the hat shelf. The big engine was mounted on a welded X4130 steel tube frame and fastened to "Lord" rubber mounts. The fuselage was fitted with inspection and access doors to check on various components, and removable center-section panels provided access to fuel tanks and other mechanisms. The retractable landing gear and the wing flaps were not to be extended above 120 m.p.h. The huge windshield was normally of formed shatter-proof glass, but could be replaced with ¼-in. thick "Plexiglass." The cabin was equipped with map-pockets on the sidewalls, there were gadget-pockets on the front seatbacks, there were armrests, headrests, ash trays, assist cords, and a cabin dome light. Anything that was not included could easily be ordered as an option. The Spartan "Executive" was a lovely airplane and has weathered the test of time and progress; about 8 or 9 of them are still flying!

ATC # 647
(6-30-37)
DOUGLAS, DSTA-SB3G.

DST-A for "United" had Pratt & Whitney engines.

After American Airlines had gambled millions of dollars on "sleeper-planes," and proved that it would be a popular service, and proved also that the service would eventually make the airline millions of dollars in profit, United Air Lines (UAL) decided to get into the "Sleeper" game also. The initial order from Douglas in late 1936 was for 8 of the huge "Sleeper Transport," and like the DC-3A already in use by UAL, they were to be powered with the new 14 cyl. supercharged Pratt & Whitney engines. As the model DSTA-SB3G these big "Sleepers" were powered with 2 "Twin-Wasp" (double-row radial) SB3G engines rated 900 h.p. each with up to 1150 h.p. available for one minute during takeoff. Scheduled cross-country "sleeper" service by UAL began on 20 July 1937 and by mid-August they were running 3 flights nightly; they were transporting passengers from Broadway to Hollywood, so to speak, in less than 17 hours. The regular coast-to-coast run was routed from San Francisco to New York on a schedule of 15 hrs. 20 mins. eastbound — the westbound flights took about 2 hours longer. By Nov. of 1937 the United Air Lines had completed its 20,000th coast-to-coast trip. In a move that was to benefit both airlines, Western Air Express (WAE) ordered 2 of the DSTA-SB3G for their Los Angeles to Salt Lake City run which tied into the UAL transcontinental system; the Salt Lake City run was routed through Las Vegas. Air-travelers on all routes were enjoying the "sleeper" service and found it a particular treat to arrive at their destination all fresh and all rested up. Another novel plan instituted by Western Air Express was the Fly-Ur-Car rental service whereby passengers could reserve an automobile for their use at destination. Rental of a late model sedan cost only $4.75 per day (no

deposit necessary) with the first 50 miles allowed free — additional mileage would cost 9¢ per mile. Only 10 years ago, air-travelers were riding along with the mail bags; now they were sleeping comfortably in a private berth!

The model DSTA-SB3G was a standard "Douglas Sleeper" in most every respect, except that it was powered with newly-developed Pratt & Whitney engines, and it was built to the specifications of United Air Lines; it was to be the queen of the "Mainliner" fleet. Majestically, it plied various segments of the cross-country route from New York to San Francisco, and also an overnight through coast-to-coast service. At first largely as a promotional deal, the DST nurtured a band of commuters who were to become crusaders for air travel. As we reflect back on the DST, and its sister-ship the DC-3, we have to agree that it was the most important airplane ever built in America; primarily, it had a terrific effect on the travel habits of modern civilization. It was the DST and then the DC-3 that proved what could be done with a good airplane, taking air travel more or less out of the experimental stage, and making it safe, dependable, and profitable. We have to concede that the vast networks of today are but extensions of the ideas first set forth by the DST and the DC-3. The model DSTA-SB3G as powered with 2 of the 14 cyl. double-row "Twin-Wasp" SB3G engines (normally rated at 900 h.p. each) was the finest transport airplane of its time; every day they were flying faster, higher, and more frequent than anything ever built before. From the pilot's point of view the DST (and DC-3) were very "busy" airplanes because there was so much to do, and so many things to watch, but it taught pilots to fly to a time-table in all kinds of weather and over all sorts of terrain; it also taught airline

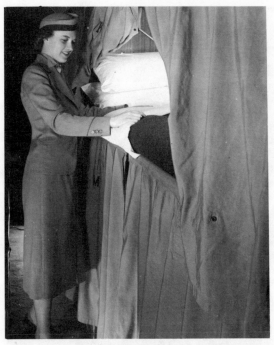

"United" hostess prepares upper berth in one of the DST-A.

Early morning risers could watch the sunrise.

management how to make money. The type certificate for the model DSTA-SB3G was issued 6-30-37 and some 10 or more examples were manufactured by the Douglas Aircraft Co., Inc., on Clover Field in Santa Monica, Calif.

Listed below are specifications and performance data for the Douglas DSTA-SB3G as powered with 2 "Twin-Wasp" SB3G engines rated 900 h.p. at 2500 r.p.m. at 8000 ft. (1100 h.p. available for takeoff); length overall 64'6"; height overall (3 point) 16'11"; wingspan 95'0"; wing chord at root 172" tapered to tip; total wing area 987 sq. ft.; airfoil NACA-2215 at root tapering to NACA-2206 at tip; wt. empty 16,100 lbs.; useful load 8700 lbs.; payload with 600 gal. fuel 4245 lbs. (14 pass., 3 crew, & 1865 lbs. bag-mail-cargo); gross wt. (for airline use) 24,800 lbs. max. speed 215 at 8000 ft.; cruising speed (.75 power) 195 at 7000 ft.; landing speed (with flaps) 67; takeoff run (fully loaded) 980 ft.; climb 920 ft. first min. at sea level; ser. ceiling 21,800 ft.; gas cap. normal 650 gal.; gas cap. max. 822 gal.; oil cap. normal 48 gal.; oil cap. max. 66.5 gal.; cruising range (.75 power) at 100 gal. per hour 1240 miles; basic price was over $100,000. The DST-A was also available with other variations of the "Twin-Wasp" SBG engine.

The construction details and general arrangement of the DSTA-SB3G were basically the same as described in the chapter for ATC # 540, except for various modifications to dimension and structure, and to customer's decision of interior arrangements. As a transcontinental The front sleeping compartment was often converted into a private "Sky Room" with isolation for 2, complete with private lavatory. On daytime flights this compartment was often con-

sleeper-plane the DSTA-SB3G was fitted with up to 14 berths (7 upper and 7 lower) in a cabin area that was 19'6" long x 7'8" wide x 6'4" high. verted into a smoking lounge for 4 people. Other facilities for passenger comfort were a Men's toilet, a separate Ladies' toilet, Men's dressing room, a Ladies' Lounge and dressing room, a galley with steam-table for hot meals, fold-away game tables, reading lamps, ash trays, magazine racks, individual vents, an air-conditioned cabin that held temperatures to 70 deg. even when it was 30 deg. below outside, and a call-button for the stewardess. A 110 cu. ft. lined cargo compartment with outside loading door was to the very rear; up forward, just behind the pilot station was a 35 cu. compartment for baggage and 2 bins for mail sacks. When all upper berths were folded up into the ceiling, and lower berths converted into divan-type seats for daytime travel the capacity was up to 28 passengers. All baggage, to the front and rear, was available during flight; small pieces of luggage could be stored under each seat. Each berth had an observation window, even the upper berth which had a small slit-window for a look out. The entire cabin area was soundproofed and well insulated so that people could converse easily in a comfortable environment. Improvements to the sturdy landing gear afforded such a degree of shock absorption that on a fairly good landing the sleeping passengers were not even aware that they had landed. Another nicety for the air-traveler was a portable air-conditioning unit that was hooked up to the cabin, prior to takeoff, and it brought the cabin to comfortable temperatures in summer or winter. For more reliable performance the DSTA-SB3G was later equipped with

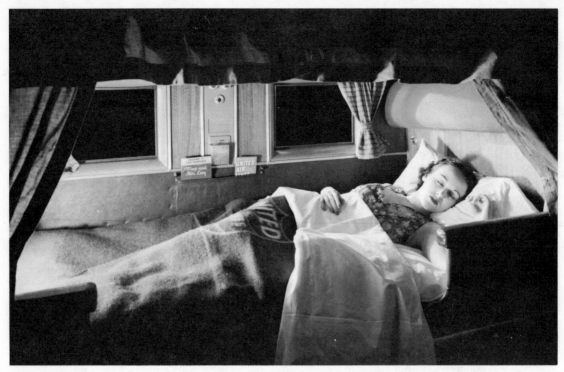

Lower berth rivaled "Pullman" comfort.

The cockpit of the DST-A was sometimes a busy place.

A "United" DST-A flies off into the setting sun.

constant-speed variable-pitch props, a complete de-icing system, a pressure-type fire extinguishing system, complete radio gear, and even a Sperry "automatic pilot." The silvery DST loomed large on the apron, it seemed to instill confidence into everyone, and it was probably one of the prettiest transports ever built. The next Douglas development was another version of the DC-3 as described here in the chapter for ATC # 669.

Listed below are DSTA-SB3G entries as gleaned from registration records:

NC-18103; DSTA-SB3G (# 1951) 2 Twin-Wasp 900

-18104;	"	(# 1952)	"
-18105;	"	(# 1953)	"
-18106;	"	(# 1954)	"
-18107;	"	(# 1955)	"
-18108;	"	(# 1956)	"
-18109;	"	(# 1957)	"
-18110;	"	(# 1958)	"
-18101;	"	(# 1959)	"
-18102;	"	(# 1960)	"

Ser. # 1951 thru 1958 were del. to United Air Lines; ser. # 1959-60 were del. to Western Air Express.

ATC # 648
(6-8-37)
WACO, MODEL VKS-7.

The Waco VKS-7F with 240 h.p. Continental W-670 engine.

The various seasonal changes wrought into the Continental-powered "Standard Cabin" models since 1931 were by now fairly obvious, but still pointed strongly to the airplane's continued role as one of the best utility airplanes in this country. The design had advanced steadily, but not recklessly, so better and better "Waco" airplanes were accepted easily and previous airplanes were not thrown into obsolescence. As part of the big lineup for the 1937-38 season Waco Aircraft introduced the VKS-7 to uphold their lead in utility airplanes. Versatility describes the new VKS-7 better than any one word, and versatility is why it was actually more than just one airplane. There was so much it could do, and it could go just about anywhere, so it was used for so many different jobs without question. The model VKS-7 was powered with the new Continental W670M engine of 240 h.p. and a companion model as the UKS-7 was offered too with the new Continental W670K engine of 225 h.p. As is most always the case, the higher-powered model was asked about the most and enjoyed the better acceptance. The model VKS-7 was being delivered from mid-1937 through the 1941 season, and it was doing rather well in export; 8 were delivered to Argentina and one to Canada. In 1942 the Civilian Pilot Training Program (CPTP), a program that was training civilian pilots as back-up in national emergency, was going strong; the Waco UPF-7

had already been enlisted as one of the airplanes to be used in earlier stages of pilot-training, and now the specially-designed VKS-7F was to be used for training duty also. Twenty of the specially-fitted VKS-7F were delivered as navigational trainers to be used in various phases of all-weather cross-country flying. This advanced training also included blind-flying under the hood. When civilian flying was curtailed due to the outbreak of war, at least 2 civilian versions of the VKS-7 were mustered into USAAF service as the UC-72D. After the war, most of the VKS-7 and VKS-7F were dusted off and continued in doing what they did best.

The Waco model VKS-7 was a tidy-looking cabin biplane with seating normally arranged for 4 or 5. Good-looking appointments with good-wearing qualities offered comfort and pleasant styling, yet allowed the airplane to work at most anything without becoming shabby. Visibility through a redesigned enclosure was ample all around, and the ride was kept pleasant with provisions for ventilation and cabin heat; heavy insulation was used against noise and temperature extremes. The VKS-7 was no limousine, but it was quite scrumptious for a working airplane. These "Waco Cabin" airplanes were known to be very stable; this offered a pleasant ride to first-time passengers, and it was a boon to pilots who had to spend many

VKS-7F was largely used as cross country trainer.

hours at the wheel. Like all the "Standard Cabin" before it, the VKS-7 was a versatile airplane readily adaptable to most kinds of work, to the needs of business, and it was also a very good family-airplane; to further increase its utility it could be converted as a cargo-hauling freighter, an air-borne ambulance, an air-taxi for charter, or mounted on pontoons as a seaplane. A later version called the VKS-7F was even converted for special duty as a navigational trainer, this because it was an excellent platform to teach the intricacies of through-the-weather blind flying. As powered with the Continental W670M engine of 240 h.p. the VKS-7 delivered very good performance over a broad range, and demonstrated repeatedly its exceptional ability in just about all it was asked to do. Perhaps the nicest comment about the S-7 type in general, and the VKS-7 in particular, was that it had all the nice habits of the earlier models, but none of the little annoying ones. The VKS-7 now had a wider, more stable landing gear, good foot-pedal wheel brakes, the controls were smoother, it was nice and comfortable inside, and the ship was stable even in rough air — in all matters a very nice airplane. The model UKS-7 as powered with the Continental W670K engine of 225 h.p. was certainly as good as all this too, except for a little drop in performance. The Continental W670 was an excellent engine of great reliability and good performance; the W670K was equipped with a carburetor, and the W670M was equipped with fuel injection. The type certificate for the models UKS-7 and VKS-7 was issued 6-8-37 and some 42 or more examples were manufactured by the Waco Aircraft Co. at Troy, Ohio.

Listed below are specifications and performance data for the Waco model UKS-7 as powered with Continental W670K engine rated

225 h.p. at 2100 r.p.m.; length overall 25'3"; height overall 8'6"; wingspan upper 33'3"; wingspan lower 28'3"; wing chord upper & lower 57"; wing area upper 130 sq. ft.; wing area lower 110 sq. ft.; total wing area 240 sq. ft.; airfoil Clark Y; wt. empty 1907 lbs.; useful load 1343 lbs.; payload with 70 gal. fuel 715 lbs.; gross wt. 3250 lbs.; max. speed (105% power) 147 at sea level; cruising speed (.75 power) 130; landing speed 50; climb 800 ft. first min. at sea level; ser. ceiling 15,000 ft.; gas cap. 70 gal.; oil cap. 5 gal.; cruising range (.75 power) at 15 gal. per hour 500 miles; price $5890 at factory. Performance figures shown are with Curtiss-Reed metal prop; landing gear tread was 87 ins.

Specifications and data for (1937) model VKS-7 with Continental W670M engine rated 240 h.p. at 2200 r.p.m. at sea level same as above except as follows: wt. empty 1917 lbs.; useful load 1333 lbs.; payload with 70 gal. fuel 705 lbs.; gross wt. 3250 lbs.; max. speed (105% power) 149; cruising speed (.75 power) 133; landing speed 50; climb 850 ft. first min. at sea level; ser. ceiling 15,500 ft.; gas cap. 70 gal.; oil cap. 5 gal; cruising range (.75 power) at 16 gal. per hour 500 miles; price $5890 at factory. Model VKS-7 of 1937 had Curtiss-Reed metal prop, narrow landing gear and mechanical wheel brakes.

Specifications and data for (1938-39) model VKS-7 with Continental W670M engine rated 240 h.p. at 2200 r.p.m. at sea level same as above except as follows: wt. empty 1960 lbs.; useful load 1290 lbs.; payload with 70 gal. fuel 662 lbs.; gross wt. 3250 lbs.; max. speed 145 at sea level; cruising speed (.75 power) 136 at 6000 ft.; landing speed 50; climb 850 ft. first min. at sea level; ser. ceiling 13,000 ft.; gas cap. 70 gal.; oil cap. 5 gal.; cruising range (.75 power) at 16 gal. per hour 490 miles; price $7770 at factory.

172

The UKS-7 and VKS-7 became popular private owner airplanes after WW2.

Model VKS-7 of 1938-39-40-41 had Curtiss-Reed metal prop, wide landing gear, and hydraulic wheel brakes; baggage allowance was 100 lbs.

Specifications and data for (1942) VKS-7F, a special cross-country trainer with Continental W670M engine same as above except as follows: wt. empty 2256 lbs.; useful load 994 lbs.; payload with 70 gal. fuel 366 lbs.; gross wt. 3250 lbs.; max. speed 145 at sea level; cruising speed 127 at sea level; cruising speed (.75 power) 136 at 6000 ft.; landing speed (with flaps) 48; climb 850 ft. first min. at sea level; ser. ceiling 13,000 ft.; gas cap. 70 gal.; oil cap. 5 gal.; cruising range (.75 power) at 16.5 gal. per hour 492 miles (leaving 15% fuel as reserve); price $12,500 at factory when outfitted as navigational trainer. The VKS-7F had two-position controllable props, wide landing gear, and mid-chord wing flaps.

In general, the contruction details and general arrangement of the VKS-7 (UKS-7) were similar to that of earlier S-type cabin biplanes by Waco, except for the updating that took place every year or so. Again, Waco introduced many little improvements for 1937-39; all these without any major design changes. The interiors were a little bigger, and a little more comfortable, all were now five-place airplanes, there was slightly more glass area, and the later models had a redesigned windshield of better form and better visibility. The landing gear tread was 87 ins. for the few 1937 models with mechanical brakes but 1938 models introduced the new, wide landing gear with 108 in. tread using long-travel oleo-spring shock struts and hydraulic wheel brakes; the foot-operated brake pedals were standard now, but the traditional hand-lever braking system was still available for those who would prefer it. The landing gear was moved forward by 4 ins.

and all joints were fitted with "Lord" rubber bushings; 7.50x10 wheels were fitted with 8.50x-10 tires. A 35 gal. fuel tank was mounted in the root end of each upper wing-half and extra 15 gal. fuel tanks in the lower wing roots were optional. Baggage compartment was behind the rear seat with allowance for 100 lbs. The special VKS-7F trainer was also fitted with mid-chord drag flaps and all the paraphernalia necessary for all-weather cross-country training. The VKS-7 was also eligible as a seaplane on Edo twin-float gear; the seaplane was required to use the redesigned fin and rudder area. A Curtiss-Reed metal prop, electric engine starter, battery, generator, oil cooler, throw-over control wheel, hydraulic wheel brakes, streamlined wheel cuffs, parking brake, adj. front seats, tail wheel, navigation lights, fire extinguisher, cabin lights, ash trays, roll-down windows, assist ropes and first-aid kit were standard equipment. A two-position controllable prop, cargo interior, leather upholstery, ambulance litter, extra door & wing-walk, landing lights, paraflares, parachute-type seats by Irvin or Switlik, Y-type control column, wheel pants, cabin heater, radio gear, steerable tail wheel with lock, air brakes, and special paint schemes were optional. The next Waco development was the models ZGC-8 and AGC-8 as described here in the chapter for ATC # 664.

Listed below are UKS-7, VKS-7, and VKS-7F entries as verified by company records:

NC-17700;	VKS-7	(# 4620) Cont. 240
-17721;	UKS-7	(# 4632) Cont. 225
CF-BDN;	VKS-7	(# 4672) Cont. 240
;	UKS-7	(# 5207) Cont. 225
LV-JAC;	VKS-7	(# 5217) Cont. 240
-20900;	"	(# 5218) "

LV-KAC;	"	(# 5219)	"
LV-LAC;	"	(# 5220)	"
-20955;	"	(# 5223)	"
LV-MAC;	"	(# 5224)	"
NC-2307;	"	(# 5225)	"
-20966;	"	(# 5226)	"
NC-1239;	"	(# 5227)	"
-29371;	"	(# 5229)	"
-29372;	"	(# 5230)	"
-29373;	"	(# 5238)	"
NC-2309;	"	(# 5239)	"
-29378;	"	(# 5241)	"
-31651;	"	(# 5275)	"
-;	"	(# 5276)	"
-31653;	VKS-7F	(# 5277)	"
-31656;	VKS-7	(# 5278)	"
-31660;	VKS-7F	(# 6101)	"
-31661;	"	(# 6102)	"
-31662;	"	(# 6103)	"
-31663;	"	(# 6104)	"
-31664;	"	(# 6105)	"
-31665;	"	(# 6106)	"
-31666;	"	(# 6107)	"
-31667;	"	(# 6108)	"
-31668;	"	(# 6109)	"
-31669;	"	(# 6110)	"
-31670;	"	(# 6111)	"
-31671;	"	(# 6112)	"
-31672;	"	(# 6113)	"
-31673;	"	(# 6114)	"
-31674;	"	(# 6115)	"
-31675;	"	(# 6116)	"
-31676;	"	(# 6117)	"
-31677;	"	(# 6118)	"
-31678;	"	(# 6119)	"
-31679;	"	(# 6120)	"

This approval for ser. # 4620 and up; ser. # 4620, 4632, 4672 had narrow landing gear and mech. wheel brakes; ser. # 5207 and up had wide landing gear and hydraulic wheel brakes; ser. # 4672 del. to Canada; ser. # 5207, 5217, 5219-20, 5224, 5276 del. to Argentina; ser. # 5218 to Continental Engine Co.; ser. # 5229-30, 5238 del. to Boeing School of Aeronautics; ser. # 5277 was factory demonstrator; ser. # 6101 thru 6120 were engaged in CPTP program; ser. # 6101 thru 6120 had the wide landing gear, hydraulic wheel brakes, mid-chord drag flaps, and Hamilton-Standard two-position controllable prop; VKS-7F also eligible with 250 h.p. W670M-1 engine; ser. # 6120 may have been the last "Cabin Waco" built.

ATC # 649
(7-16-37)
BEECH, MODEL D-17-S.

Beech D-17-S was as colorful as this paint job.

Except for 2 examples of the experimental D-17-W, the high-powered models of the Beech 17 series had always been powered with the big Wright engines. Walter Beech favored the Wright engines, of course, but he came to believe that the popular "Wasp Junior" (R-985) engine built by Pratt & Whitney might have great possibilities in the Model 17 airframe also. Early tests proved that indeed this was to be a great combination, and it was labeled the D-17-S. Several operators who owned earlier versions of the "Seventeen" indeed liked what they saw in the D-17-S, and bargained for a swap. Several were soon exported to Canada, one was delivered to Brazil, and in 1939 three of the D-17-S were delivered to the Army Air Corps as the YC-43. The D-17-S also appealed to the U. S. Navy air-arm and they procured 7 in 1939 as the GB-1; 3 more were delivered in 1940. In 1937-38 the cabin biplane as a small transport was leaving the scene fast; in fact there was only one other cabin biplane to choose from. But, the D-17-S didn't act like a biplane, it acted like it didn't even know it was a biplane, and it eventually was considered the standard of comparison the world over. One would hardly think that an airplane such as the D-17-S would be especially adept in primitive country using pitifully small airstrips at a high altitude, but as several operators would

tell you, it certainly was—"there are only a few airplanes that will out-perform the Stagger-Wing with a big engine, in a circumstance such as this." Many people looked upon such exploits still as daredevil stunts, but to a good Beech 17 pilot it was more or less in a day's work. Because of its nature the D-17-S acquired quite a reputation even before it was impressed into war-work, but its service during World War 2 must be acknowledged also. Beech Aircraft went into military production of the model D-17-S starting in 1941 and continued well into 1944. Of the 300 or so that were built, sandwiched in along with production of various versions of the "Twin Beech" (Model 18) during the hectic war years, many were shipped lend-lease to allied countries. But, so many of the recipients took such a liking to the "Beech" biplane that they were reluctant to give the airplanes back! Of the total that survived the fracas many were held over in our government's service, and eventually all were sold off as war-surplus. Some 250 or more of the Beech 17 were registered in the U.S.A. in 1966 (that's better than 10 years later), and well over 100 are still flying some 10 years after that. Those still flying today, and admired even more perhaps than when they were first built, are usually the model D-17-S because it was the most prolific and perhaps even the most popular model built.

The determined-looking model D-17-S was a typical "Stagger-Wing" biplane of the high-power group, and it too was arranged to seat 4 or 5. It would be hard to say that one Model 17 was better than another, or more handsome than another, but the design had come quite a long way since the prototype, so even the passage of time favored the D-17-S in many respects. Beech had a policy of rectifying most annoyances as soon as they came up, and owner's suggestions and even their whims, were always respected; it is only logical then that the Model 17 was becoming a better airplane as time went on. It stands to reason too that all this was inherited by the D-17-S and it showed up quite obviously in its daily posture and its everyday deeds. Many will think of the D-17-S as a war-time airplane, but we must remember that it had a very useful career in commercial or civil aviation long before it was called to war-time duties. When the call to

military duty did come, 11 of the civilian D-17-S were engaged in WW2 service for the U. S. Navy as the GB-1 and 13 were engaged by the USAAF as the UC-43B. As powered with the popular Pratt & Whitney (R-985) "Wasp Jr." SB engine rated 400-450 h.p. the model D-17-S seemed to be very happy in this combination, and performed in a manner that brought it constant praise. Owners were extremely proud of it, pilots respected and adored it, the casual passenger on his first ride couldn't believe it, and those at the airport always came up to admire it. Not many airplanes, even those modern-day machines built 30 years later, could generate all these sentiments. It has been written perhaps a hundred times that even by modern standards the high-powered "Stagger-Wing" remains as one of the most remarkable of airplanes. The type certificate for the model D-17-S was issued 7-16-37 and some 66 civil examples of this model were manufactured before Beech converted its efforts

A D-17-S in Air Corps colors as YC-43.

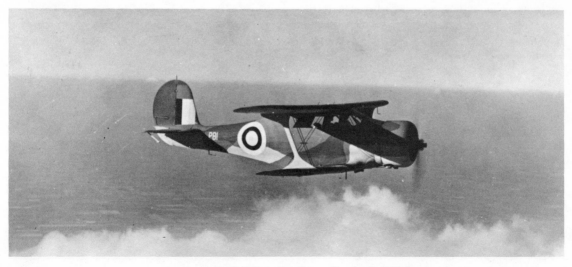

A D-17-S flown by Prince Bernhard of Holland.

176

to war-time production. Manufactured by the Beech Aircraft Corp. at Wichita, Kan.

Listed below are specifications and performance data for the Beech model D-17-S as powered with the "Wasp Jr." SB engine rated 400 h.p. at 2200 r.p.m. at 5000 ft. (450 h.p. at 2300 r.p.m. available for take-off); length overall 25'11"; height overall 8'0"; wingspan upper & lower 32'0"; wing chord upper & lower 60"; wing area upper 148.2 sq. ft.; wing area lower 148.2 sq. ft.; total wing area (incl. fuselage section) 296.4 sq. ft.; airfoil NACA-23012; wt. empty 2540 (2570) lbs.; useful load 1660 (1680) lbs.; payload with 100 gal. fuel 841 (861) lbs. (4 pass. & 161-181 lbs. for baggage & extras); gross wt. 4200 (4250) lbs.; max. speed 212; cruising speed 202 at 9700 ft.; landing speed (with flaps) 55; landing roll (with brakes) 750 ft.; takeoff run 610 ft.; climb 1250 ft. first min. at sea level; ser. ceiling 20,000 ft.; gas cap. 100 gal.; oil cap. 6.5 gal.; cruising range (.75 power) at 24 gal. per hour 800 miles; price $18,870 at factory. The D-17-S was also eligible as a seaplane on Edo twin-float gear at 4650 lbs. gross wt., and cost about $4000 more.

The construction details and general arrangement of the model D-17-S was typical to that of Beech models described here earlier, including the following. The huge, curved windshield of formed glass offered a panoramic view to occupants in front, and the whole cabin area was enclosed in shatter-proof glass; front side-windows could be rolled down as an extra convenience. The spacious interior offered that soft, luxurious feeling of sitting in a costly limousine. Custom interior trim and custom exterior finish was availabe on order at extra cost. The control column had a swing-over wheel, but a T-type column with 2 wheels was also available. Toe-operated hydraulic wheel brakes were Goodyear multiple-disc type; they were very effective, but required a soft touch. Wheels were 7.50x10 with 6-ply tires; 24 in. streamlined wheels and tires (General) with puncture-proof inner tubes were optional. The landing gear was, of course, retrac-

table and so was the tail wheel assembly. Normal fuel capacity was 100 gals., but in view of the tankage available (front fuselage 29 gal., rear fuselage 47 gal., one tank in each of the 4 wing roots at 23 gal. each) it was possible to store 168 gal. of fuel, or any combination of these for the range desired. Of course, all extra fuel had to be swapped for diminished payload. For extra strength and to preserve the airfoil form across the span the wing ribs were spaced 6.5 in. apart, and rib-stitched at 1 in. intervals; all 4 wing tips were reinforced with plywood sheet for extra stiffness. Fixed surfaces of the cantilever tail group were of spruce construction, and movable surfaces were a framework of steel tubes and sheet steel ribs. Elevators and the rudder were fitted with adjustable trim tabs. The D-17-S was also available as a seaplane on Edo WA-4665 twin-float gear. A fixed-pitch metal prop, electric engine starter, generator, battery, full set of engine & flight instruments, 100 gal. fuel cap., fuel pump, fuel gauges, oil cooler, navigation lights, assist ropes and first-aid kit were standard equipment. A Hamilton-Standard controllable prop, parachute-type seats by Irvin or Switlik, landing lights, paraflares, radio gear, and extra fuel cap. were other options available. The next Beech development was the model F-17-D as described here in the chapter for ATC # 689.

Listed below are D-17-S entries as gleaned from various records:

NC-18027;	D-17-S	(# 146)	Wasp Jr. 400
-18028;	"	(# 147)	"
-18563;	"	(# 165)	"
-18566;	"	(# 168)	"
-18575;	"	(# 179)	"
-18579;	"	(# 183)	"
-18581;	"	(# 185)	"
-18582;	"	(# 186)	"
NC-1324;	"	(# 187)	"
-18776;	"	(# 199)	"
-18777;	"	(# 200)	"
CF-BJD;	"	(# 201)	"
-18779;	"	(# 202)	"

An Army C-43 shows its trim profile.

In U.S. Navy the D-17-S was a GB-1.

CF-CCA;	''	(# 203)	''	VT-ALY;	''	(# 399)	''	
-18791;	''	(# 216)	''	-20755;	''	(# 400)	''	
CF-BLU;	''	(# 238)	''	-21917;	''	(# 401)	''	
:	''	(# 239)	''	-21918;	''	(# 402)	''	
-19482;	''	(# 254)	''	CF-DTE;	''	(# 403)	''	
-19493;	''	(# 263)	''	CF-DTF;	''	(# 404)	''	
-19494;	''	(# 264)	''	NC-240Y;	''	(# 406)	''	
-20793;	''	(# 279)	''	NX-21920;	''	(# 407)	''	
-19468;	''	(# 284)	''	:	''	(# 408)	''	
-19470;	''	(# 285)	''	NC-1030;	''	(# 409)	''	
-20799;	''	(# 286)	''	NC-133;	''	(# 415)	''	
-20750;	''	(# 287)	''	:	''	(# 416)	''	
:	''	(# 288)	''	:	''	(# 417)	''	
39-139;	''	(# 295)	''	-21926;	''	(# 418)	''	
39-140;	''	(# 296)	''	-21930;	''	(# 419)	''	
39-141;	''	(# 297)	''	-21933;	''	(# 421)	''	
1589;	''	(# 298)	''	NC-213;	''	(# 423)	''	
1590;	''	(# 299)	''	NC-21934;	''	(# 424)	''	
1591;	''	(# 300)	''					
1592;	''	(# 301)	''					
1593;	''	(# 302)	''					
1594;	''	(# 303)	''					
1595;	''	(# 304)	''					
-20768;	''	(# 306)	''					
-20777;	''	(# 314)	''					
-21904;	''	(# 327)	''					
PP-TGE;	''	(# 354)	''					
NC-239Y;	''	(# 355)	''					
NC-900;	''	(# 362)	''					
1898;	''	(# 385)	''					
1899;	''	(# 386)	''					
1900;	''	(# 387)	''					
-20753;	''	(# 395)	''					
NC-129M;	''	(# 396)	''					
-20779;	''	(# 398)	''					

This approval for ser. # 146 and up; ser. # 146 later with CAA as NC-71; ser. # 185 operated in Central America; ser. # 200 flown in Bendix Race by Jackie Cochran; ser. # 201, 203, 238, 403, 404 del. to Canada; ser. # 239 never assembled — used as spare parts; ser. # 279, 404 operated on floats; ser. # 285 later with CAA as NC-42; no listing available for ser. # 288, 408, 416-17; ser. # 295-96-97 del. in 1939 to Army Air Corps as YC-43; ser. # 298 thru 304 del. in 1939 to U.S. Navy as GB-1; ser. # 306 was in 1939 Bendix Race; ser. # 354 del. to Brazil; ser. # 385-86-87 del. to U.S. Navy as GB-1 in 1940; ser. # 399 del. to India; ser. # 424 remained as factory demonstrator, later used as prototype for G-17-S series.

ATC # 650
(8-24-37)
ARGONAUT "PIRATE", H-24

The versatile "Pirate" was designed for the sportsman.

Among the many daydreams that pilots had was the hankering to own a small amphibious airplane; an airplane that could fly them from the local airport to some hidden gem of a lake to do some leisurely fishing right off the bow. Or, perhaps to fly to some big lake-front town and partake of sights, sounds, and pleasures of the big city. Just imagine how easy this would be for an "amphibian," an airplane that operates off land or water, and can take you to wherever the action is. The little Argonaut "Pirate" was designed to be such an airplane. As we can see here the "Pirate" was a monoplane of the flying-boat type constructed just as simple as possible, and it did operate successfully from either land or water. The designer of an amphibious airplane doesn't have too many alternatives, so the "Pirate" was laid out somewhat in a manner reminiscent of other successful "amphibian" airplanes. As a personal-type airplane the little "Pirate" only had room for the pilot and a friend or two, but it did offer comfort and convenience at a very fair price; it was planned to sell for less than $5,000 and this was a lot of airplane for that amount of money. This dollar figure was, of course, based on the manufacture of hundreds of airplanes, but the "Pirate" was never to have that experience. The Argonaut "Pirate" was a belated venture into a field that had flourished for a while a little earlier, but despite all that the amphibious airplane had to offer it was still confronted with skepticism and firm resistance.

Argonaut had hoped to soften this resistance with what they had to offer, and it really could have in time, but perhaps the timing wasn't right. To be a success as an "amphibian" the airplane must operate well from land or water, and it must fly well from either. The "Pirate" did a fairly good job of being an "amphibian," but by its very nature the "amphibian" therefore must be a compromise; it can never be the best boat, nor can it be the best airplane. If one can accept that and live with it then the enjoyment available will almost have no bounds. Many pilots will still agree that for real sport-flying the best hours in your log-book will be those you spent in an "amphibian." It's a special treat to be able to fly off land, and water too.

The tidy Argonaut "Pirate" was a light cabin monoplane of the flying-boat type with seating arranged for 2 or 3. As a flying-boat with retracting landing gear the "Pirate" was able to operate as well off land or water. Designed especially for sport-flying this little craft was also a versatile method of transportation; it could land wherever it happened to be more convenient. The cabin was actually wide enough for 3 people, but to carry 3 at a time some fuel or baggage had to be left behind. Normally it would have to be considered a two-place airplane. As powered with the 4 cyl. inverted inline aircooled Menasco C4-125 engine rated 125 h.p. the "Pirate" was not blessed with high performance, but it did do an adequate job with the power available. Because

"Pirate" follows the classic amphibian configuration.

of the added utility and the paraphernalia it takes to make it, it takes a lot more power to do the job in an amphibian. For those who were in no big hurry to get there, but did want to enjoy the versatility of the amphibian, the "Pirate" was a suitable machine. The type certificate for the "Pirate" model H-24 was issued (after nearly 2 years of development) on 8-24-37, but apparently there were no examples built beyond the prototype and one other airplane. Manufactured by the Argonaut Aircraft, Inc. at No. Tonawanda, N.Y. with manufacturing facilities just out of Buffalo on "Consolidated" airport. J. Leroy Sutton was pres. and Howard J. Heindell was the V.P., gen. mgr., and chf. engr. In a reorganization during March of 1937, Howard Heindell had become pres., gen. mgr., sales mgr., and chf. engr. Later in 1937 the company began to fold under so Donald G. White took over and engaged George Gay to redesign the airplane for a bigger Menasco engine of 160 h.p.; this to offer better performance with 3 people at 2500 lbs. gross weight. Deliveries of the new plane were scheduled for 1938, but record beyond that was unavailable.

Listed below are specifications and performance data for the "Pirate" model H-24 as powered with Menasco C4 engine rated 125 h.p. at 2175 r.p.m. at 1000 ft.; length overall 27'1"; height overall (on wheels) 10'3"; wingspan 42'0"; wing chord 66"; total wing area 224.75 sq. ft.; airfoil Clark Y; wt. empty 1600 lbs.; useful load 650 lbs.; payload with 40 gal. fuel 218 lbs. (1 pass. & 48 lbs. bag.); payload with 20 gal. fuel 338 lbs. (2 pass. & no bag.); gross wt. 2250 lbs.; max. speed 104 at 1000 ft.; cruising speed (2050 r.p.m.) 89 at 1000 ft.; landing speed (with drag flaps) 48; climb 550 ft. first min. at sea level; ser. ceiling 10,500 ft.; gas cap. max. 40 gal.; oil cap. 3 gal.; cruising range (2050 r.p.m.) at 9 gal. per hour 180-350 miles; price $5450 at factory. This production model of the "Pirate" was larger, heavier, and lacked the get-up-and-go of the experimental prototype.

Just for reference we are including specifications and performance data of the prototype "Pirate" H-20 as powered with 125 h.p. Menasco C4 engine; length overall 26'0"; height overall 8'2"; wingspan 35'4"; wing chord 66"; total wing area 185 sq. ft.; airfoil Clark Y; wt. empty 1100 lbs.; useful load 870 lbs.; payload with 40 gal. fuel 437 lbs. (2 pass. & 97 lbs. bag.); gross wt. 1970 lbs.; max. speed 110; cruising speed (.75 power) 100; landing speed (with drag flaps) 42; climb 700 ft. first min. at sea level; ser. ceiling 12,000 ft.; gas cap. max. 40 gal.; oil cap. 3 gal.; cruising range (.75 power) at 8.5 gal. per hour 490 miles; price advertised as $4,975 at the factory.

The semi-monocoque single-step hull was an all-wood structure of 7-ply bulkheads connected together in bays with heavy spruce stringers, and boxed-in with plywood planking; the completed hull was then covered with doped fabric. The cabin in front (with 54 in. beam) was wide enough to seat 3 across; the center seat could be slid back for extra shoulder room if the 3 people were large. The cabin enclosure was of DuPont "Plasticelle"; for added comfort the cabin was heated and ventilated. A baggage compartment with allowance for up to 100 lbs. was behind the seats; anchor and mooring gear was stowed in the bow. Dual control wheels were provided; the right-hand set was quickly removable. The wing framework, in 2 sections, was built up of solid spruce spar beams with spruce and plywood truss-type wing ribs; the leading edges were covered with plywood sheet and the completed framework was covered in fabric. Drag flaps were mounted inboard of the ailerons on trailing edge of each wing; flaps were manually operated. The tip floats were a wood structure same as the hull, and were mounted on steel tube struts. The fully-cowled "pusher" engine was mounted above the wing on a steel tube frame; heavy steel streamlined wires formed the wing-bracing truss. The landing gear legs used Rusco rubber shock-rings and 19x9-3 Goodyear airwheels with pedal operated mechanical wheel brakes; the landing gear was retracted or extended by a hand-wheel in the cockpit. A full-swivel tail wheel was also provided. The fabric covered tail group was built up of welded steel tubing; one elevator was fitted with an adjustable trim tab. A Flottorp wooden prop, electric engine starter, a battery, cabin heater and vents, dual control wheels, anchor and mooring gear, Pyrene fire extinguisher, engine-driven fuel pump, wobble-pump, fuel gauge, fuel press. gauge, 8 instruments, compass, wheel brakes, navigation lights, and first-aid kit were standard equipment.

Listed below are the only known examples of the Argonaut "Pirate":

X-14760;   Pirate H-20   (# H20-100)Menasco 125
NC-15682;   Pirate H-24   (# H24-500)   "

ATC # 651
(9-15-37)
RYAN, MODEL SC-150.

SC-150 with inline Menasco engine.

High-performance sport trainers were the mainstay of Claude Ryan's business, but early on he felt he needed a private-owner "Coupe" of some sort to sell, so after several proposals and 2 years of development the gleaming "SC" (Sport Coupe) was rolled out (Aug. 1937) as a surprise for all to admire. Till now Ryan had been selling the open-cockpit "ST" to wealthy sportsmen, and to some of the better operators whose students liked to fly something with a little snap to it. Ryan knew where aviation's money was being spent, so the new "SC" was leveled in that direction also. Like the "ST" sport the "SC" coupe was almost entirely of metal fabrication, and actually the first successful 3-seater of this type. There was nothing really hot about the airplane, but its racy lines and its crouching stance gave off the feeling of high performance, and an energetic personality. We must admit here that Claude Ryan was a showman and a good airplane salesman; he allowed little bits of information about the "SC" to leak out as it was being built, so it was received with great interest and it completely satisfied the anticipation. The Ryan (SC) "Sport Coupe" was first designed around an aircooled inline Menasco engine because this combination had worked so well in the (ST) "Sport Trainer." But, the installation apparently was not entirely a rousing success in the SC, so tests were also run with a "radial" engine in a search for improvement; for whatever reasons, not disclosed, the Menasco-powered "SC" lost out in the decision, so it was built only in the one example for test. The predicted rosy future for the Ryan SC-150 was rather short-lived but it did set a trend as the first successful private-owner airplane to pioneer the low-winged, closed-cabin, all-metal concept for light civilian airplanes. The model SC-150 was actually listed as available into 1940, but Ryan Aero. didn't push it.

The Ryan model SC-150 was a low-winged, coupe-type monoplane with seating arranged for 2 or 3. The cabin area was completely enclosed with a sliding hatch to provide the comfort and convenience of a cabin-type airplane; the hatch could be slid open in flight, by varying amounts, for those who still enjoyed a little bit of draft or the wind in their face. The slender cowling that wrapped tightly around the inverted inline engine provided excellent visibility around the sides, and even a good view over the nose while taxiing; the view overhead was, of course, terrific. The unusual (patented) wing was sharply tapered, and the long fuselage-arm provided a balanced stability that guided the ship smoothly, even through rough air. The seat in the rear for the 3rd passenger was actually wide enough for two, but if the 3rd passenger was not carried this area could then be stuffed with well over 200 lbs. of assorted baggage; this could be quite handy for a couple of hunters, or fishermen. As powered with the 4 cyl. aircooled inverted inline Menasco C4S engine of 150 h.p. the model SC-150 was blessed with a good range of high performance, and offered the kind of snap that would appeal to a high-time sporting pilot. The SC-150 was capable, energetic, and eager to answer the slightest whim, but still a complete lady of nice manners when not prodded.Who's to say—there may have been valid reasons for discontinuance of this particular model, but initial enthusiasm at least seemed to indicate this was a pretty good

182

combination. The Ryan Aero. plant was expanding at this time to triple their production capacity, and the 100 or more employees under the direction of Fred Rohr were looking forward to building at least 100 airplanes. The type certificate for the model SC-150 was issued 9-15-37 and only a prototype was manufactured by the Ryan Aeronautical Co. on Lindbergh Field in San Diego, Calif. T. Claude Ryan was pres. & gen. mgr.; Earl D. Prudden was V.P. in chrg. of sales; E. A. Smith was sec.-treas.; Sam C. Breder was sales mgr.; & Millard C. Boyd was chf. engr.

Listed below are specifications and performance data for the Ryan model SC-150 as powered with Menasco C4S engine rated 150 h.p. at 2260 r.p.m. at 3000 ft. (159 h.p. at 2300 r.p.m. for take-off); length overall 26'7"; height overall 7'0"; winspan 37'6"; wing chord at root 99"; wing chord at tip 26"; total wing area 202 sq.ft.; airfoil NACA-2412; wt. empty 1335 lbs.; useful load 815 lbs.; payload with 37 gal. fuel 400 lbs. (2 pass. & 60 lbs. bag.); gross wt. 2150 lbs.; max. speed 150 at 3000 ft.; cruising speed (.75 power) 135 at 8000 ft.; landing speed (with flap) 45; run at take-off 525 ft.; climb 900 ft. first min. at sea level; ser. ceiling 18,000 ft.; gas cap. 37 gal.; oil cap. 3 gal.; cruising range (2050 r.p.m. at 8000 ft.) at 9.0 gal. per hour 470 miles; price was not announced.

The all-metal monocoque fuselage framework was built up of formed 24ST "Alclad" bulkheads, and covered with heavy-gauge 24ST "Alclad" formed metal sheet; this type of construction limits the number of parts to be fabricated, and makes possible an economical production of unit assemblies. The hatch-covered cabin was spacious, sound-proofed with "Seapak", well upholstered in genuine leather, and offered excellent visibility; windshield and hatch windows were of DuPont "Plasticele." The

length inside was 75 in., cabin height was 51 in., front seat was 43 in. wide, and rear seat was 40 in. wide. Baggage normally allowed was 60 lbs. in a compartment behind the rear seat; when a 3rd person was not carried the rear seat area became a handy baggage compartment for up to 230 lbs. The sliding hatch could be slid open to full-open position even in flight; also to any intermediate position. The dash-panel contained all necessary flight and engine gauges, and dual stick-type controls were provided. A 37 gal. fuel tank was mounted high in the fuselage just behind the firewall. The sharply tapered cantilever wing was a type of monospar wing wherein the single hollow spar beam formed the first third of the wing's front edge as a monocoque all-metal box; the wing ribs cantilevered from the spar's rear face to the trailing edge. The forward third of the wing was covered with "Alclad" (24ST) metal sheet, and rear 2/3 portion was covered in fabric. Differential ailerons were aerodynamically balanced, and also in static balance. The belly-flap (lever-operated) was a perforated "drag brake" of some 5 sq. ft. area that reduced the landing speed; the perforations allowed some air to flow through to prevent interference of the normal tail group air flow. The cantilever landing gear of 97 in. tread was of 2 streamlined assemblies employing "Aerol" (air-oil) shock struts of 6 in. stroke; the 18x8-3 Goodyear wheels with mechanical brakes were encased in metal wheel pants. A swiveling tail wheel was also provided. Fixed surfaces of the all-metal tail group were covered with 24ST "Alclad" metal sheet, and the movable surfaces were covered with fabric; the elevator was fitted with an adjustable "trim tab." A Hartzell wooden prop, electric engine starter, compass, wheel brakes, dual controls, oil cooler, fuel gauge, tail wheel, air brake, wheel pants, navigation lights, safety belts, and first-aid kit were

Inline engine emphasizes slimness of Ryan SC design.

SC was gentle because of long "control arm."

standard equipment. A metal propeller, wind-driven generator, battery, fire extinguisher, landing lights, paraflares, bonding & shielding, and radio gear were optional. The next Ryan development was the model SCW-145 as described here in the chapter for ATC # 658. NC-17372; SC-150 (# 201) Menasco C4S-150 This airplane later modified to model SCW-145 for test.

ATC # 652
(9-10-37)
LOCKHEED, MODEL 12-B.

Lockheed 12-B was "Electra Jr." with Wright engines.

For a period of time at least, most of the Latin-American countries seemed to have a distinct preference for the "Wright" aircooled radial engines. We can suppose that the many outstanding flights of the "turbulent twenties," and the exciting good-will tour by Chas. A. Lindbergh through Latin America left favorable impressions with the people; this no doubt created a high regard for the "Wright" engines. This trust in performance and service actually prevailed nearly all over the world, and especially so in Europe and the Orient. When ordering airplanes from American manufacturers during this particular period nearly all of the Latin-American countries emphasized a preference for installation of the Wright engines; this was quite true of exports from Stinson, Howard, Waco, and others. In some cases, if a manufacturer didn't have a standard model using the Wright engine, an appropriate modification was quickly designed. This was the position taken by Lockheed who experienced such demands before. The rare Model 12-B by Lockheed, more or less a sister-ship to the by-now-popular and exciting "Electra Jr.", was basically a similar airplane to all those Model 12-A that were already flying, except that it was powered with two of the latest Wright engines as specified by order. Powered with 2 of the latest 9 cyl. Wright R-975-E3 engines rated 420 h.p. each the model 12-B were procured for use by the Argentine Army. Two airplanes of the Model 12-B type were delivered to the Minister of War, and it is most likely they were used as utility-transports; in Latin-American countries, which learned to depend heavily on the airplane, this could mean an endless list of duties. There is no question that

the Lockheed model 12-B was up to it. Because only 2 of the Model 12-B were built they were little known, and extremely rare examples in the popular "Model 12" lineup.

As we can see here, you could actually walk around this airplane without suspecting that it was a Model 12-B; unless you were sharp enough to notice the two Wright engines, engines almost hidden from view by the tight-fitting NACA engine cowlings. By comparison the Lockheed "Electra Jr." model 12-B was also a twin-engined, all-metal, low-winged transport monoplane of a configuration introduced first by Lockheed's famous "Electra". Seating in the exported 12-B was no doubt normally arranged for 6 passengers and a crew of 2, but a custom interior could be quickly modified to suit a specific purpose. It is not known what arrangement was normally used by the Argentine Army, but most likely it was arranged and used as a utility-transport; it is suspected that there wasn't much the 12-B wouldn't be asked to do. In general, the smaller Model 12 was a scaled-down version of the popular Model 10, but with the same amount of power coursing through its innards, the smaller ship had performance characteristics not attainable by its larger sister-ship. One can then easily imagine that the 12-B would be well-suited as a high-performance military transport that could be adapted to many functions in a small air force. Lockheed sought military sales of the Model 12 right from the start; in fact, the prototype was being evaluated by the U.S. Army Air Corps only a few weeks after its maiden flight. Argentina had bought 2 of the Model 12-B and Brazil ordered a few of the Model 12-A. The U. S. Navy was operating the

The 12-B as delivered to Argentina.

12-A as the JO-1, JO-2, XJO-3, and the Army Air Corps was operating the 12-A as the C-40, C-40A, and C-40B. The government of Netherlands East Indies ordered 20 of the model 12-26 as military trainers, and then ordered 17 of the bomber-type Model 212. Records show the Model 12 served well in military service and paved the way for the fabulous Model 14 which became the "Hudson" bomber, one of the most famous airplanes of all time. The type certificate for the Model 12-B was issued 9-10-37 and only 2 examples of this model were manufactured by the Lockheed Aircraft Corp. at Burbank, Calif. At this particular time Currey Sanders was handling test-pilot chores at the plant while Marshall Headle was in Europe training pilots to fly the recently-bought "Electra" (Model 10) airplanes.

Listed below are specifications and performance data for the Lockheed model 12-B as powered with 2 Wright R-975-E3 engines rated 420 h.p. at 2200 r.p.m. at 1400 ft. (450 h.p. available for take-off); length overall 36'4"; height overall 9'9"; wingspan 49'6"; wing chord at root 126"; wing chord at tip 42"; total wing area 352 sq. ft.; airfoil Clark Y-18 at root tapering to Clark Y-9 at tip; wt. empty 6040 lbs.; useful load 2610 lbs.; payload with 150 gal. fuel 1265 lbs. (6 pass. & 245 lbs. bag.) gross wt. 8650 lbs.; max. speed 220 at 1400 ft.; cruising speed (.75 power) 207 at 5500 ft.; landing speed (with flaps) 65; climb 1360 ft. first min. at sea level; service ceiling 21,350 ft.; gas cap. normal 150 gal.; gas cap. max. 200 gal.; oil cap. 10-14 gal.; cruising range (.75 power) at 42 gal. per hour 700 miles; price not announced. Normal cruise was at .75 power, and max. cruise was at .65 power.

The construction details and general arrangement of the Model 12-B were typical to that of the Model 12-A as described here in the chapter for ATC # 616, and to some extent as described in the chapters for ATC # 551, 559, 584, and 590 A more direct comparison would be to say that the Model 12-B was more or less the same as the

Model 12-A except for installation of the 2 Wright engines; engine mounts and the engine cowlings were the only basic modifications necessary. Other details requiring change would be engine control hook-up and the rerouting of some plumbing. It is not known how the 12-B were arranged inside, but most likely they were fitted with passenger seats that could be easily removed when need for clear floor space would arise. Two baggage compartments of 63 ce. ft. cap. were allowed a combined total of 400 lbs. Being operated in Argentina, and quite often from unimproved airstrips, it is also likely the 12-B were equipped with heavy-duty (6-ply) tires, rubber "abrasion strips" on leading edges of wings and tail group, a supply of drinking water, flashlights, fire extinguisher bottles, tool kit, and first-aid kit. Metal propellers, electric engine starters, generator, battery, exhaust collector-rings, oil coolers, navigation lights, cabin lights, wheel brakes, parking brake, wheel fenders, tail wheel, fire extinguishers, cabin vents, and dual control wheels were standard equipment. Ham.-Std. controllable props, night-flying equipment, cabin heaters, custom interiors, radio gear, and auto-pilot were optional. The next Lockheed development was the "Super Electra" (14-H) as described here in the chapter for ATC # 657.

Ser. # 1228 and # 1249 are the only known examples of the Model 12-B.

As a wrap-up of the Model 12 series it might be of interest to note that 131 examples were built in all; of these 2 were the model 12-B and 129 were the model 12-A. Some 63 of the 12-A were in commercial service, 7 were operated by the U. S. Navy, 14 were operated by the U. S. Army Air Corps, 8 went to Brazil, 20 to the Netherlands East Indies as the Model 12-26, and 17 as the Model 212 light-bomber. Of the commercial versions at least one was operated in Canada, and 7 were operated in Great Britain; others went to Australia, India, Mexico, and Venezuela. During WW2 several were impressed into service with the RCAF.

ATC # 653
(9-28-37)
REARWIN, MODEL 6000.

Rearwin 6000 with Cirrus "Hi-Drive" engine.

Because of the "great depression" Rearwin's aircraft production had been suspended in 1932, but there was still development of new designs and the updating of older models. One of the first of these to fly was a racy-looking monoplane powered with a 4 cyl. inverted A.C.E. "Cirrus" engine. This flashy two-seater called the "Speedster" was a design by Noel Hockaday and Doug Webber; its maiden flight around the patch took place on 7-11-34. J. B. "Jack" LeClaire took it up for its first hop and came down very enthusiastic about its performance; but, ironically enough, during tests for ATC approval the "Speedster" could not meet government regulations for "spin recovery." The regulations at that time called for recovery from a "six-turn spin" in 1½ turns, and this the new "Speedster" model 6000 would not do. Once, on one of his many test-hops, LeClaire purposely spun the ship for 21 turns and recovered almost immediately with opposite control, but this method of recovery was not acceptable to government inspectors. They (Dept. of Commerce) wanted no less than "hands off" recovery! Surely, because of this, the Rearwin "Speedster" was not a dangerous airplane; very frisky perhaps, and it certainly kept a pilot on his toes, but the performance you could get was well worth the extra effort. Anxious to get this airplane "approved" Rearwin added modification after modification, and it took three long years to secure its ATC. So then, the

Cirrus-powered "Speedster" (Model 6000) finally received its certificate of approval in the late summer of 1937; test-pilot Bill Miller, who handled much of the test-flying now, flatly stated that the original design was a much better airplane than the final doctored-up version. The new approved version with its oversized fin, very small rudder, and its restricted up-elevator travel now met the government's spin recovery requirements hands-off, but its performance and maneuverability had become quite inferior to the spritely prototype set-up. During the course of this airplane's development, a period of some 3 years, many changes had taken place in the industry; by now the A.C.E. "Cirrus" engine was already out of production, so it was necessary to adapt the "Speedster" to the well-known Menasco engine, an engine which was also a 4 cyl. aircooled inverted inline powerplant that would fit the airplane's slender frame perfectly.

The Rearwin "Speedster" model 6000 was a light high-winged monoplane of dashing appearance with chummy seating arranged for two in tandem. Its slender lines of low frontal area made it a little tight inside for anyone of broad shoulders, but this enhanced the intimacy that pilots felt for this airplane. Because of its rather special nature this airplane was perhaps restricted in its normal use, and would have appeal only to the so-called sportsman-pilot. Had the "Speedster" been offered to the market back in 1934 it would surely have experienced a much better acceptance among the people that flew for the fun of it; but, the market had changed considerably by 1937, so the "6000" was almost an outmoded airplane. As powered with the 4 cyl. aircooled inverted inline A.C.E. Cirrus "Hi-Drive" engine the Rearwin "Speedster", with the slimness of an arrow, was taking advantage of low frontal area, and its relative swiftness on low power was quite astonishing. Although not quite as frisky as first designed in 1934, the 1937 modified "Speedster" was still pretty much of a show-off, and still instigated big grins of enthusiasm in all who flew her. It has been said that flying the "Speedster" to the limits of its capabilities was a stimulating experience guaranteed to bring a healthy glow to the cheeks. In all this time while the "6000" was being developed into an acceptable airplane, manufacture of the "Cirrus" engine had folded up in the interim, so subsequent designs of the "Speedster" were based on using the 4 cyl. Menasco engines. The type certificate for the Model 6000 was issued 9-28-37 and no more than two examples of this model were manufactured by Rearwin Airplanes, Inc. on Fairfax Field in Kansas City, Kan. Rae Rearwin was pres. & gen. mgr.; Albert R. Jones was V.P.; Geo. M. Prescott was sales mgr.; Wm. Henry Weeks was chf. engr.; & Wm. Miller was chf. pilot.

Listed below are specifications and performance data for the Rearwin model 6000 as powered with inverted A.C.E. "Cirrus Hi-Drive" (Mark 3) engine rated 95 h.p. at 2100 r.p.m. at sea level; length overall 22'2" (21'6"); height overall 6'10" (6'6"); wingspan 32'2"; wing chord 60"; total wing area 145 sq. ft.; airfoil NACA-2412; wt. empty 1067 (1052) lbs.; useful load 633 (613) lbs.; payload with 34 gal. fuel 240 (220) lbs.; baggage allowance 50 lbs.; gross wt. 1700 (1665) lbs.; max. speed 144 at 800 ft.; cruising speed (1870 r.p.m.) 122 at 800 ft.; landing speed 47 (45); climb 750 (760) ft. first min. at sea level; ser. ceiling 15,500 (16,000) ft.; figures in parentheses are for prototype airplane; gas cap. 34 gal.; oil cap. 2.5 gal.; cruising range (1870 r.p.m.) at 6.5 gal. per hour 600 miles; price approx. $3295 at factory field. This airplane was also to be available with 4 cyl. Menasco B-4 engine rated 95 h.p. at 2000 r.p.m. on special order.

The fuselage framework was built up of welded 4130 steel tubing, faired to shape with wooden formers and fairing strips, then fabric covered. The interior was chummy in overall width, but the tandem seating provided plenty of leg-room. The cabin area was surrounded with Pyralin windows, upholstered in serviceable fabrics, and a large entry door was on the right side; the front seat was adjustable. The baggage compt. with allowance for 50 lbs. was behind the rear seat; this compt. later restricted to 10 lbs. with 40 lbs. moved up under the rear seat. Solo flying from the front seat only. The wing framework, in 2 halves, was built up of two laminated spruce spar beams with spruce and plywood girder-type wing ribs; the leading edges were covered with dural metal sheet and the completed framework was covered in fabric. The wing halves were braced to lower fuselage longeron by vee-type steel tube (streamlined) struts. A 17 gal. fuel tank was mounted in the root end of each wing-half; the wing roots were "gulled" slightly for better visibility in this area. The streamlined cantilever landing gear of 70 in. tread was of 2 leg assemblies fitted with "Rusco" rubber shock rings; Goodyear 7.00x5 wheels and tires with mechanical brakes were encased in streamlined metal wheel pants. The 8 in. tail wheel was steerable. The fabric-covered tail group was built up of welded steel tubing; the horizontal stabilizer was adjustable for trim in

"Speedster" was fast, but it was ruined by "spin" qualifications.

flight. A Flottorp wooden prop, a hot-shot battery, fuel gauges, wheel brakes, navigation lights, wheel pants, dual stick-type controls, compass, engine & flight instruments, safety belts, & first-aid kit were standard equipment. A metal prop, storage battery electric engine starter, landing lights, Pyrene fire extinguisher, dual brake pedals, bonding & shielding, and radio gear were optional. The next Rearwin "Speedster" development was the improved model 6000-M as described here in the chapter for ATC # 661.

Listed below are the only known Model 6000 examples as gleaned from various records:

X-12588;   Model 6000   (# 301) Hi-Drive 95
NC-15865;   "   (# 302)   "

This approval for ser. # 302 and up; this approval expired 2-3-43.

ATC # 654
(9-29-37)
GRUMMAN "GOOSE", G-21-A.

First G-21-A was delivered to financier on Wall St.

The portly (G-21) "Goose" was the first commercial-type airplane designed by Grumman Aircraft. And, it is not so odd that the first civil airplane should be an "amphibian" because Leroy R. Grumman had a long-standing love affair with the amphibious airplane; ever since his association with Grover Loening back in the early "twenties." Grumman had been quite active in the design and the development of the famous "Loening Amphibian," and was occasionally credited with design of the retractable landing gear that folded up neatly into the unusual slipper-type hull. Grumman since then was achieving some success with his various military airplanes, but his old love of "amphibians" could not be denied, so his day-dreams and his tinkering finally came to being as the (G-21) "Goose". We might say that the Grumman "Goose" was actually born in Farmingdale, but it was adopted and reared by Wall St. By Sept. of 1937 Grumman had orders for 10 airplanes, and the roster was indeed very impressive: Earl Harriman was one of the first to order; also Wilton Lloyd Smith, a financier; there was Lord Beaverbrook of England; C. W. Deeds of United Aircraft; Gar Wood, the famous speed-boat king; there was Powell Crosley, Jr.; Henry S. Morgan, also of Wall St.; and strangely enough, Boris Sergievsky, the test pilot from Sikorsky Aircraft; and so on. Whether the "Goose" was "born with a silver spoon in its mouth" we cannot rightly say, but it surely wasn't ever pampered, or sheltered from harm. It was immediately evident that the twin-engined "Goose" was one tough airplane with an aggressive personality to match; the roughest, toughest chores or conditions were all in a day's work. Whether by design or coincidence the military took an early interest in the Grumman "Goose"; no doubt because of stories heard about its exceptional performance under most any conditions. It is fact that its rugged frame was built beyond the most extreme requirements. In 1938 the U. S. Army Air Corps ordered 31 of the G-21-A as the OA-9, the U. S. Navy ordered a batch as the JRF-1, 3 were delivered to the U. S. Coast Guard as JRF-2, and several civilian ships were custom-built to order. By early 1939 the "Goose" was being used by all of the U. S. Services, and varying amounts were exported to the Bahamas, Bolivia, Canada, New Guinea, Dutch East Indies, Peru, Portugal, and Venezuela. The Grumman "Goose" was indeed an early favorite, and we dare say that it remained a favorite throughout all these years; we say this because there are still quite a few working every day, and it looks like they have no intention of quitting.

The Grumman "Goose" model G-21-A was a twin-engined cabin monoplane of the flying-boat type with seating arranged for 4 to 6 passengers and a crew of two. As an "amphibian" this large craft was capable of operating successfully off

G-21-A gently breaking water on takeoff.

land or water, and did an admirable job in either case. All early examples of the "Goose" were fitted as plush "air yachts" for the pursuit of business or pleasure, but it was noted early that this utilitarian vehicle had special characteristics quite useful to a multitude of uses. As a consequence, many were soon fitted for air-sea rescue, military liaison, off-shore patrol, exploration, and air-ferry service. The "Goose" was a specialized airplane, but it never did ask for special treatment; it would surely go where most others feared to tread. As powered with 2 Pratt & Whitney "Wasp Jr." SB (R-985) engines rated 400-450 h.p. each the twin-engined G-21-A was blessed with very decent performance, and an un-wavering will to perform its duties in the best possible manner. Equipped with ample power reserve the "Goose" performed very well without being pushed, and always had that little bit left for the extra effort. The G-21-A was a whole lot of airplane, and it practically took two to fly her, but she responded well and convinced pilots that there were just rewards in a job well done. The big "Goose" was a trifle wobbly on land, but it was a literal swan in the water. Some have said that the portly "Goose" was surely built like a bridge with everything far stronger than it need be, but that was the secret of her willingness to take on any job, and to keep on doing it in the years to come. People board the "Goose", even

G-21-A in British (RAF) service.

G-21-A as JRF-2 in Coast Guard.

today, unmindful of the fact that she may be approaching 30 to 40 years of age! The type certificate for the model G-21-A was issued 9-29-37 and it is difficult to estimate the actual number built by the Grumman Aircraft Engrg. Corp. at Bethpage, Long Island, New York. Leroy R. Grumman was pres.; Leon A. Swirbul was V. P. & gen. mgr.; Jos. A. Stamm was sec.; Edmund W. Poor was treas.; and Wm. T. Schwendler was chf. engr. Albert Loening, brother of Grover Loening, was on board of directors. The Grumman Engrg. Corp. had been incorporated since 6 Dec. 1929.

Listed below are specifications and performance data for the Grumman "Goose" model G-21-A as powered with 2 "Wasp Jr." SB engine rated 400 h.p. at 2200 r.p.m. at 5000 ft. (450 h.p. available for take-off); length overall 38'4"; height overall (on wheels) 12'2"; wingspan 49'0"; total wing area 375 sq. ft.; airfoil NACA-23015 at root tapering to NACA-23009 at tip; wt. empty 5450 lbs.; useful load 2550 lbs.; payload with 220 gal. fuel & 2 pilots was 778 lbs. (4 pass. & 98 lbs. bag.); gross wt. 8000 lbs.; max. speed 201 at 5000 ft.; cruising speed (.75 power) 190 at 9600 ft.; landing speed (with flaps) 62; take-off run (on wheels) 800 ft. in approx. 11 sec.; take-off time (calm water) was approx. 18 sec.; climb 1300 ft. first min. at sea level; climb to 5000 ft. in 5 min.; climb to 9600 ft. in 10 min.; ser. ceiling 22,000 ft.; ceiling on one engine (full load) was 10,000 ft.; gas cap. 220 gal.; oil cap. 15 gal.; cruising range (using 600 h.p.) at 52 gal. per hour 750 miles; cruising range (using 500 h.p.) at 44 gal. per hour 900 miles; price varied from $68,000 at the factory. Prices varied because each airplane was custom-built to order.

The two-step, semi-monocoque, all-metal hull was built up of 24ST framing and covered with smooth 24ST "Alclad" metal sheet; the hull was divided into 6 watertight compartments. The nose compartment with entry thru a top-side hatch had stowage for anchor & mooring gear, for the radio gear, and space for excess baggage.

The pilot's compartment seated 2 side by side with dual wheel controls; the cockpit was enclosed with shatter-proof glass and visibility was quite adequate. Access to the huge main cabin was thru a large hatch on the left side just behind the wing; an emergency hatch was on the right side. The plush & roomy main cabin was normally arranged to seat 4 in large reclining chairs; other custom arrangements were optional. The cabin was well insulated, upholstered in fine fabrics, and vented with fresh air; a heater system kept the cabin comfortable. In space aft of the cabin was a pantry, lavatory, and a large compartment for baggage. The robust cantilever wing, in three sections, was built up with a deep all-metal (24ST) box-type spar beam and all-metal (24ST) cantilever wing ribs; forward portion was covered with smooth (24ST) metal sheet and rear portion was covered in fabric. The split-type, trailing-edge (two-position) wing flaps (of 36 sq. ft.) were vacuum-operated. A wire-braced, all-metal tip-float was anchored to each wing to prevent "heeling" in the water. Fuel tanks were built into the box-type wing beam. The retractable undercarriage of 90 in. tread folded up into inset wheel wells in the fuselage; on early models it was manually operated by worm & gear. The landing gear used "Aerol" (air-oil) shock struts with 32x8 Bendix wheels fitted with hydraulic brakes; the tail wheel was steerable and also retracted. The tail group was an all-metal (24ST) structure; fixed surfaces were covered with smooth (24ST) "Alclad" metal sheet and movable surfaces were covered with fabric. Both rudder and elevators had adjustable trim tabs. The commercial version was normally fitted with passenger seats and custom interior; the "service version" was fitted with equipment for general utility work such as photographic, ambulance, rescue, or patrol. Hamilton-Standard controllable propellers, electric engine starters, battery, generator, dual controls, navigation lights, bonding & shielding, cabin heater, pantry, lavatory, fire extinguishers, first-aid kit, and

"Goose" as XJ3F-1 in U.S. Navy service.

mooring gear were standard equipment. Hamilton-Standard "constant speed" props, landing lights, paraflares, radio gear, survival equipment, custom interiors, and custom finish were optional. The next Grumman (amphibian) development was the "Widgeon" model G-44 as described in the chapter for ATC # 734.

Listed below are Grumman G-21-A entries as gleaned from registration records:

NC-16910;	G-21-A	(# 1001)	2 R-985.
-16911;	"	(# 1002)	"
-16912;	"	(# 1003)	"
-16913;	"	(# 1004)	"
-16914;	"	(# 1005)	"
-16915;	"	(# 1006)	"
-16916;	"	(# 1007)	"
;	"	(#1008)	"
;	"	(#1009)	"
;	"	(#1010)	"
NC-1294;		(# 1011)	"
;	"	(# 1012)	"
;	"	(# 1013)	"
-20620;	"	(# 1014)	"
;	"	(# 1015)	"
;	"	(# 1016)	"
-20643;	"	(# 1017)	"
-20648;	"	(# 1018)	"
NC-2385;	"	(# 1019)	"
-20650;	"	(# 1020)	"
NC-3055;	"	(# 1054)	"
-3022;	"	(# 1055)	"
-3021;	"	(# 1058)	"
-2788;	"	(# 1059)	"

This approval for ser. # 1001 and up; in 1938 the U. S. Army Air Corps ordered 31 of the G-21-A as the OA-9 (similar to Navy JRF-1); in 1942 the USAAF ordered 3 as the OA-13A and 2 as the OA-13B; most of the listings beyond what is shown here were for service-type airplanes and those for export; no listing for ser. # 1008, 1009, 1010, 1012, 1013, 1015, 1016, 1021-1053, 1056-57, and up.

A veteran "Goose" as still used by Catalina Airlines — photo dated 1974!

ATC # 655
(10-2-37)
AERONCA "SCOUT", MODEL KC (CF).

Aeronca model KC with 40 h.p. Continental engine.

Unlike the old "Aeronca" C-3 the new "Model K" airframe was compatible to the adaptation of other airplane powerplants; this then produced an installation that blended well into the overall design without looking like it was stuck on as an afterthought. The new Model K was first offered with the 2 cyl. "Aeronca" engine, of course, and it sold very well in this combination, but in time the company learned via the grapevine that many out there would have preferred the 4 cyl. Continental A-40 engine. It was no big matter to redesign the basic Model K for this popular flat-four engine, so it was rolled out in no time as the Model KC. Except for the different engine the "KC" was basically similar, but it was noted too that some improvement to the basic design was in order, so these modifications were added as the new design developed. The most noticeable change now was the cowling that was wrought around the 4 cyl. engine, and the new split-axle landing gear that dispensed with the former stiff-legged appearance. Aeronca Airplanes had always been quite popular in California, so a brand-new "KC" was put on display at the May Co. department store in downtown Los Angeles; for many shoppers it was their first look up close of a light owner-operated airplane. The Model KC, being more austere than the Model K, was touted as the economy light-plane of the year, and they began selling briskly. Statistically, 1937 was a good year for Aeronca; they had built and sold more airplanes in 1937 than in any year since its beginning, two new airplanes were introduced to the lightplane market, the former "Flamingo"

factory on Lunken Airport was purchased, and all kinds of plans for expansion were under way. When Franklin Motors, a firm who had been building the "Franklin" (aircooled) automobile for many years, introduced their 4 cyl. "flat-four" airplane engine of 40 h.p., an engine quite similar to the Continental A-40, Aeronca bolted one of these onto the improved airframe and it became the Model CF. This was a follow-up model to the KC discussed here, and was quite similar in most respects. The "Aeronca" was a popular airplane, and those interested in buying an "Aeronca" of some kind were soon confronted with brow-furrowing selection.

The Aeronca KC (CF) "Scout" was a light, strut-braced, high-winged cabin monoplane with side by side seating for two. The new KC and the CF were pretty much the same and had very little to remind one of "the old Aeronca flivvers"; they looked just like real airplanes now and were treated with a whole new attitude. Anyone close to the workings of aviation could tell that great things were shaping up for the lightplane industry, and Aeronca, of course, was planning to be ready. They now had an airplane that was more versatile, and more adaptable to change as developments in engines and accessories progressed. Everyone was excited about development of the "flat-four" (horizontally opposed) engine, an engine which was promising unlimited possibilities in power range and in operating economy. The Model KC was then actually the first in a whole new generation of "Aeronca" airplanes. As powered with the 4 cyl. "opposed" aircooled Continental A-40 engine of 40 h.p. the model "KC" was more or less on a par with the "Model K," but it was some smoother and promised to be a better airplane in the long run. If you paid that much attention to your flying you would perhaps notice that performance was about the same, and the new softer landing gear was about the only difference. Flight characteristics were comparable they say, and on the whole the KC was a well-liked airplane; some grumbled that it was underpowered, but "Aeronca" was already planning to alleviate that short-coming as soon as possible. The "Franklin 4AC" was a newcomer to the ranks of lightplane engines, but it was not long before it elbowed its way into popularity. As installed in the Aeronca CF the "Franklin" was de-tuned to deliver only 40 h.p., so the model CF (only a few were built) was almost identical to the KC, and proved only that the "Aeronca" was now compatible with other aircraft engines. The type certificate for the model KC (CF) was issued first on 10-2-37 and some 40 or more examples were manufactured by the Aeronautical Corp. of America on Lunken Airport in Cincinnati, Ohio.

Listed below are specifications and performance data for the Aeronca model KC as powered with Continental A-40-4 engine rated 40 h.p. at 2575 r.p.m. at sea level; length overall 20'7"; height overall 6'6"; wingspan 36'0"; wing chord 50"; total wing area 146 sq. ft.; airfoil Clark Y; wt. empty 608 lbs.; useful load 452 lbs.; payload with 10 gal. fuel 214 lbs.; (1 pass. & 44 lbs. for bag. & extras); gross wt. 1060 lbs.; max. speed 93; cruising speed (.90 power) 85; landing (stall) speed 35; climb 450 ft. first min. at sea level; ser. ceiling 12,000 ft.; gas cap. 10 gal.; oil cap. 4 qts.; cruising range at 3 gal. per hour 225 miles; price was first $1590 at the factory, reduced to $1290 in 1939. Available first for $530 down & 12 mos. to pay. The KC was also eligible with Continental A-40-5 engine having dual ignition.

Listed below are specifications and performance data for the Aeronca model CF as powered with 4 cyl. Franklin 4AC-150 (Series 40) engine rated 40 h.p. at 1875 r.p.m. at sea level; length overall 20'7"; height overall 6'7"; wingspan 36'0"; wing chord 50"; total wing area 146 sq. ft.; airfoil Clark Y; wt. empty 628 lbs.; useful load 452 lbs.; payload with 10 gal. fuel 214 lbs.; gross wt. 1080 lbs. max. speed 90; cruising speed (.90 power) 85; landing (stall) speed 38; climb 440 ft. first min. at sea level; ser. ceiling 11,890 ft.; gas cap. 10 gal.; oil cap. 4 qts.; cruising range at 3 gal. per hour 250 miles; price not announced. The "Series 40" engine had single ignition and was highly de-tuned to qualify for 40 h.p.

The construction details and general arrangement of the model KC (CF) was typical to that of the Model K as described here in the chapter for ATC # 634, including the following. The finished fuselage was more or less the same with a bench-type seat for two across, and a small baggage shelf behind the seat; baggage allowance was 20 lbs. Entry door was on the right, but a door on the left was optional; the "Sea Scout" (seaplane) had 2 doors. Split side windows could be slid open, and dual control wheels were provided. Instruments were the bare minimum, and throttle was mounted in the center. This was the economy model, being several hundred dollars cheaper, so there were no frills to speak of. The most significant change in the Model KC (CF) was the split-axle landing gear which was simple tripod type using soft "oleo" shock struts; 16x7-3 Goodyear airwheels had no brakes. A spring-leaf tail skid was standard, but a steerable tail-wheel assembly was available. The fabric covered tail group was built up of welded steel tubing; an adjustable "trim tab" was fitted to the left elevator. The model CF with Franklin 4AC engine was heavier when empty, and had 4 lbs. of ballast on the tail-post for C.G. balance; otherwise all else

A "KC" in Canada.

KC was a modified K-type airframe.

was the same. A Sensenich wooden prop, dual control wheels, wiring for navigation lights, and a first-aid kit were standard equipment. Wheel brakes, 18x8-3 Goodyear airwheels cabin, heater, carpet on floor, fire extinguisher bottle, battery, navigation lights, extra door, tail wheel, custom upholstery, wheel pants, twin-ignition engine (KC only), extra 5 gal. fuel cap., Edo pontoons, and skis were optional. The next "Aeronca" development was the model KCA (50-C) as described here in the chapter for ATC # 675.

Listed below are Aeronca KC (CF) entries as gleaned from registration records:

NC-19747;	KC	(# KC-1)	Cont. A-40
-19764;	"	(# KC-2)	"
-19765;	"	(# KC-3)	"
-19766;	"	(# KC-4)	"
-19767;	"	(# KC-5)	"
-19768;	"	(# KC-6)	"
-19769;	"	(# KC-7)	"
-19770;	"	(# KC-8)	"
-19773;	"	(# KC-9)	"
-19772;	"	(# KC-10)	"
-19771;	"	(# KC-11)	"
-19782;	"	(# KC-12)	"
-19775;	"	(# KC-13)	"
-19776;	"	(# KC-14)	"
;	"	(# KC-15)	"
-19778;	"	(# KC-16)	"
-19779;	"	(# KC-17)	"
-19720;	"	(# KC-18)	"
-19786;	"	(# KC-19)	"
-19777;	"	(# KC-20)	"
;	"	(# KC-21)	"
;	"	(# KC-22)	"
;	"	(# KC-23)	"
;	"	(# KC-24)	"
-21097;	"	(# KC-25)	"
-19774;	"	(# KC-26)	"
-21099;	"	(# KC-27)	"
-19790;	"	(# KC-28)	"
;	"	(# KC-29)	"
-19789;	"	(# KC-30)	"
-22125;	"	(# KC-31)	"
-19799;	"	(# KC-32)	"
-22143;	"	(# KC-33)	"
-22158;	"	(# KC-34)	"
-22487;	"	(# KC-35)	"
NX-21355;	CF	(# CF-1)	Franklin 40
-22157;	"	(# CF-2)	"
NC-22196;	"	(# CF-3)	"
-22304;	"	(# CF-4)	"
-22391;	"	(# CF-5)	"
-23528;	"	(# CF-6)	"

This approval for ser. # KC-1 and up, and ser. # CF-1 and up; approval for both models expired 12-12-40.

ATC # 656
(10-29-37)
BEECH, MODEL 18-B.

As economy-twin 18-B had 285 h.p. Jacobs engines.

The lovely "Beechcraft" biplanes were selling steadily and in good number, so this had a comforting effect on Walter Beech, but the twin-engined "Model 18" was not selling yet, so typical in his aggressive policy when he thought he was right, Beech introduced yet another version of his twin-engined transport for the market to consider. This new version as the Model 18-B was comparable to the earlier 18-A except for the change in engines. The Wright engines in the 18-A carried a rather high price tag and maintenance was generally costing a pretty penny, so in the consideration of a more economical transport the choice of other engines was imperative. Beech already had experience with the Jacobs L-5 engine knowing that it was gaining steadily in popularity, and it was considerably cheaper to buy and to maintain. Two of these engines were mated with the "Beech Twin" and all went well. It was with this combination that Beech had hoped to create enough stir in the industry to flush out a few orders; the reaction was not immediate, but it was favorable and helped to get the ball rolling. This new Model 18-B was powered with 2 of the 7 cyl. Jacobs L-5 engines rated 285 h.p. and its downright usefulness was aimed at business, small feeder-lines, or it could be an ambulance, a freighter "in the bush," or even perform exploration in primitive countries. As a bonus in versatility it could operate on wheels, skis, or floats. Inquiries came in soon after the 18-B was announced, mostly from foreign countries, but it was some time before firm orders began showing up on the books. Ironically, prospects were still more or less unbelieving that this shiny, all-metal "Twin" was a genuine Beech product, and it was going to take still more convincing. Who could guess at this time, not even Walter Beech 'tis sure, that this airplane or some just like it, would eventually be built in the thousands. When Walter Beech was right he could be very demanding, demanding of himself and of other people too. To this end, towards the end of 1937, Walter Beech issued a request that required all engineers and company officials to be licensed pilots! If they were going to make decisions in structure, aerodynamics, policy, or whatever, he thought they had better know what an airplane is all about.

The Beech model 18-B was an all-metal, twin-engined, low-winged cabin monoplane with seating normally arranged for 6 passengers and a crew of two. Because the airplane was designed for a multitude of services the interior could be arranged and fitted for just about any purpose; the ship would be actually tailor-made at the factory to fit the job it would be doing, and it was tested to the customer's satisfaction before delivery. Truly, Beech was not delivering very many of the "Model 18" yet, but those already delivered were certainly being operated by satisfied customers. When trying to introduce a completely new model the manufacturer frequently is at a loss to know exactly what engine combinations will be the most popular, so he goes to low power for economy and higher power for performance; this gives the buyer a choice. The model 18-B as pictured here was on the low-power scale and specially designed to offer the

18-B rolled out on factory ramp.

best economy possible in this type of airplane. There were always those that were willing to trade off a little performance for better economy. As powered with 2 Jacobs L-5 engines of 285 h.p. each the model 18-B could be operated very economically, but it still delivered a respectable performance. It was still able to operate from the smaller airports, and was versatile enough to operate also on skis or floats. The thrifty 18-B had to be coaxed a little more to bring out its best, but it was willing and pilots seemed to be comfortable with it. Not many of this particular model were sold, so Beech was perhaps convinced that more powerful combinations, though more expensive, would eventually create the most interest. The type certificate for the model 18-B was issued 10-29-37 and perhaps no more than 3 or 4 examples of this model were manufactured by the Beech Aircraft Corp. at Wichita, Kan.

Listed below are specifications and performance data for the Beech model 18-B as powered with 2 Jacobs L-5 engines rated 285 h.p. at 2000 r.p.m. at sea level; length overall 31'11"; height overall 9'5"; wingspan 47'8"; wing chord at root 126"; wing chord at tip 42"; total wing area 347.5 sq. ft.; airfoil (tapered) NACA-230 series; wt. empty 4120 lbs.; useful load 2580 lbs.; payload with 160 gal. fuel & crew was 1110 lbs. (6 pass. & 170 lbs. bag.); gross wt. 6700 lbs.; max. speed 190 at 1500 ft.; cruising speed (.75 power) 180 at 8000 ft.; landing speed (with flaps) 56; take-off run 650 ft.; climb 1000 ft. first min. at sea level; ser. ceiling 17,000 ft.; gas cap. normal 160 gal.; gas cap. max. 210 gal.; oil cap. 10-16 gal.; cruising range (.75 power) at 32 gal. per hour 900 miles; price approx. $33,500 at factory. Model 18-B also eligible for 9 passengers & 2 pilots with reduced fuel load & no baggage. Single engine ceiling was 3500 ft.

The construction details and general arrangement of the Beech model 18-B was typical to that of the model 18-A as described here in the chapter for ATC # 630, including the following. The only significant difference in the 18-B was installation of the 7 cyl. Jacobs L-5 engines, and any modifications necessary to this new combination. The Jacobs L-5, L-5M, or L-5MB engines were eligible; a battery and a generator were required with each engine when operated on battery ignition only. The cabin interior could be fitted for as many as 9 passengers, or custom arrangements with couch and plush reclining chairs were also available; cleared of all seating the interior could be fitted for cargo. The 18-B landing gear of 12'11" tread used 29x13-5 Goodyear airwheels with hydraulic disc brakes; the 12x5-3 tail wheel was fitted with heavy-duty tire. The retractable landing gear and the wing flaps were operated by electric motors; manual operation was possible in emergency. Flaps not to be fully extended (60 deg.) above 117 m.p.h. An extra 50 gal. fuel tank could be mounted in forward baggage compartment for extra range; normal fuel cap. was 160 gals. in the wing. The 18-B was eligible as a sea plane; skis were also eligible. A full complement of night-flying equipment, extra instruments, and radio gear were also available. Hamilton-Standard controllable props, electric engine starters, batteries, generator, oil coolers, dual control wheels, fuel pumps, wobble pump, cabin heater, cabin lights, wheel brakes, parking brake, bonding & shielding, navigation lights, lavatory, & first-aid kit were standard equipment. Pressure-type fire extinguisher, dual brake pedals, wheel fenders, extra fuel cap. custom interiors, pontoons, skis, and radio gear optional. The next "Twin-Beech" development was the model 18-D as described here in the chapter for ATC # 684.

Listed below are 18-B entries as gleaned from registration records:

NC-15810;   18-B   (# 62)   2 Jacobs L-5
    -18583;   "   (# 170)   "
    -18567;   "   (# 171)   "
    -18569;   "   (# 173)   "

This approval for ser. # 62 and up; ser # 62 was modified from 18-A; ser. # 170 was fitted as 9 pl.; ser. # 171 was fitted as 8 pl.; ser. # 173 as seaplane to Puerto Rico; this approval expired 1-24-41.

18-B seaplane operated in Puerto Rico.

This 18-B promoted merits of "Twin Beech" on country-wide tour.

ATC # 657
(11-15-37)
LOCKHEED, MODEL 14-H (14-H2)

First delivery of 14-H were to Northwest Airlines.

Lockheed's new Model 14 was hailed as the "Super Electra" and it was "super" in every way; it was taller, bigger, better, faster and it was loaded with all sorts of innovative details. The "Super Electra" was an extremely capable airplane, and it was just about the only competition that came close to matching the Douglas DC-3. The first of this new series was the model 14-H, and as was the custom at Lockheed, the whole plant turned outdoors for a barbecue lunch and to watch the first 14-H take to the air. On this beautiful day in July 29 of 1937, test-pilot Marshall Headle roared off on the maiden flight amid a volley of clapping and cheers; this launched a memorable career for one of the finest airplanes that Lockheed Aircraft had built to now. Northwest Airlines was the first airline to place an order for the "14," and orders soon came in from all directions; in fact, most of the orders that poured in were from overseas, and from our neighbors to the north and south. A month after the prototype first flew, Lockheed already had orders for 24 airplanes, and inquiries just kept pouring in. The Polish airline known as LOT was so anxious for delivery of their "Fourteen" that they sent a crew of 5 to Burbank in May of 1938 to fly the airplane home; the fellows flew it back to Poland across the So. Atlantic Ocean as the first trans-oceanic delivery of a commercial airplane in history. "LOT" was so happy with the airplane that they quickly ordered 5 more; a year later they ordered 4 more to offer expanded services. Northwest Airlines had by now ordered nearly a dozen, about 15 of the

"Model 14" were delivered to lines in Canada, and others went to Algiers, Australia, East Africa, Venezuela, and Mexico. The first of the Model 14 were powered with 2 Pratt & Whitney "Hornet" engines of 750 h.p. each and were labeled the 14-H; the version with 2 of the improved 800 h.p. P & W engines was the 14-H2. The "Super Electra" was a stunning and beautiful airplane; before the year was out it was hailed as the "World's Fastest Airliner." The Lockheed 14 fairly bristled with innovative ideas; the most conspicuous was the unusual "Fowler Flap" that was destined to become one of the greatest aerodynamic developments of this time.

The Lockheed model 14-H (14-H2) was a robust-looking twin-engined, low-winged, twin-tailed transport monoplane with seating normally arranged for 10 passengers, 2 pilots, and a stewardess. Interior accommodations for airline work were quite comfortable, the hostess usually served meals from a galley, tended to passenger comforts, and handy compartments in the ship's belly were available for up to a ton of cargo. Capacity of the "Fourteen" was just about right for the smaller lines that had shorter routes and usually carried mixed loads; that is why the "14" garnered such popularity overseas where high performance on shorter hops was of more importance. Basically, the "Super Electra" was designed as a passenger transport that could mix in a little cargo and air express shipments on each flight, but the interior was also adaptable to various custom layouts. There was the plush "Club" version for the businessman, the special

14-H2 as operated by LOT in Poland.

all-cargo version, and a military utility version was also available. In any version the Model 14 offered twin-engined safety with maximum performance. As powered with 2 of the big 9 cyl. P & W "Hornet" S1E2-G engines rated 800 h.p. each the improved model 14-H2 had a terrific performance throughout the entire range of flight, and it was the fastest airplane of its kind in the world. Blessed with a hefty power reserve too, the 14 offered peace of mind in the tough places; it could climb out on one engine to 12,-000 ft. even when fully loaded. The ambitious 14 was a working airplane, and the pilots had to work at it to fly it, but it was good duty and most of the pilots enjoyed it. The robust "Super Electra" had muscle, stamina, and ambition, but she was always a lady. Usually asked to work among natural hazards that tore the heart out of an ordinary airplane, the "Fourteen" had fantastic ability to adapt, and it never seemed to get peeved or riled. The type certificate for the models 14-H and 14-H2 were issued 11-15-37 and some 52 or more examples were manufactured by the Lockheed Aircraft Corp. at Burbank, Calif.

Listed below are specifications and performance data for the Lockheed model 14-H as powered with 2 "Hornet" S1E-G engines rated 750 h.p. at 2250 r.p.m. at 7000 ft. (850 h.p. available for takeoff); length overall 44'4"; height overall 11'5"; wingspan 65'6"; wing chord at root 153"; wing chord at tip 48"; total wing area 551 sq. ft.; airfoil NACA-23000 series; wt. empty 10,300 lbs.; useful load 7200 lbs.; payload with 644 gal. fuel, 2 pilots, & stewardess was 2546 lbs. (10 pass. & 846 lbs. baggage-cargo); gross wt. 17,500 lbs.; max. speed 247 at 7000 ft.; cruising speed (.75 power) 227 at 7000 ft.; cruising speed (.65 power) 215 at 7000 ft.; landing speed (with flaps) 65; climb 1490 ft. first min. at sea level; service ceiling 24,300 ft.; gas cap. max. 644 gals.; oil cap. 44 gal.; cruising range (.75 power) at 84 gal. per hour 1500 miles; price approx. $85,000.

Specifications and data for model 14-H2 as powered with 2 "Hornet" S1E2-G engines rated 800 h.p. at 2300 r.p.m. at 5500 ft. (875 h.p. for take-off), same as above except as follows: wt. empty 10,700 lbs.; useful load 6800 lbs.; payload with 330 gal. fuel, 2 pilots, & stewardess was 4060 lbs. (11 pass. & 2190 lbs. baggage-cargo); gross wt. 17,500 lbs.; gross wt. are provisional wts. allowed for airline use; max. cap. was 11 pass., 2 pilots, stewardess, plus baggage & cargo; max. speed 250 at 5500 ft.; cruising speed (.75 power) 230 at 5500 ft.; cruising speed (.65 power) 218 at 5500 ft.; landing speed (with flaps) 65; climb 1500 ft. first min. at sea level; ser. ceiling 24,500 ft.; gas cap. normal 330 gal.; gas cap. max. 644 gal.; oil cap. max. 44 gal.; cruising range (.75 power) at 85 gal. per hour (330 gal.) 870 miles; price approx. $85,000.

The semi-monocoque fuselage framework was an all-metal oval structure using 3 main bulkheads, several intermediate frames, and longitudinal stringers of 24ST that were covered with riveted 24ST "Alclad" metal sheet. The standard interior was fitted with 11 passenger seats, and a fold-up seat for the stewardess; pilot's compartment was up front. Entry door was on left side. The cabin was soundproofed, insulated, and upholstered in fine Laidlow fabrics; there were 7 windows lining the left side and 8 windows lining the right side. The nose compartment had a volume capacity of 82 cu. ft. and 3 belly compartments had volume capacity of 42-26-40 cu. ft.; total capacity was up to 1900 lbs. in the belly and up to 1500 lbs. in the nose. The sharply tapered cantilever wing, in 3 sections, was an all-metal 24ST structure built up around a single main spar beam of a web-type truss, and truss-type all-metal wing ribs spaced 18 in. apart; the rib structure was supported by corrugated 24ST metal sheet on the top-side and numerous J-section stringers on the bottom side. The completed framework was covered with 24ST "Alclad" metal sheet. The large center-section (C-S) unit supported the fuselage, the engine

14-H2 in service over Canada.

nacelles, and the retracting landing gear; outer wing panels were bolted to butt-ends of the C-S panel. The "Fowler Flaps" were a novel variable-area device that actually created more wing area and extra lift; this slowed landing speeds by a good margin and reduced the take-off run by as much as 30 percent. The retractable landing gear of 15'6" tread was of 2 cantilever assemblies (one in each nacelle) which used "Aerol" shock struts of 10 in. travel; 15.00x16 wheels were fitted with 8-ply tires and hydraulic brakes. The engines were mounted in rubber and shrouded with NACA-type deep-chord ring cowlings; collector-rings were fitted with carburetor heat. Four fuel tanks (150 gal. front tank & 172 gal. rear tank on each side) were mounted in the C-S panel for a total of 644 gal.; a 22 gal. oil tank was in each engine nacelle. The twin-tailed empennage was a 24ST all-metal structure similar to the wing; both elevators and the rudders had adjustable trimming tabs. The balanced Freise-type ailerons were also fitted with an adjustable trim tab. Ham.-Std. controllable propellers, electric engine starters, generator, battery, fuel pumps, hydraulic pumps, oil coolers, carburetor heaters, hand-type & pressure-type fire extinguishers, cabin vents, cabin heater, cabin lights, up to 11 passenger seats, navigation lights, landing lights, paraflares, fold-up stewardess chair, lavatory, galley, drinking water tank, cabin carpet, complete set of engine & flight instruments, dual controls, 18 in. tail wheel, and first-aid kit were standard equipment. "Constant-speed" propellers, bonding & shielding, radio gear (Bendix), extra battery, extra generator, de-icer equipment, abrasion boots, leather upholstery and custom interiors were optional. The next Model 14 development was the Cyclone-powered model 14-F62 as described here in the chapter for ATC # 666.

Listed below are 14-H and 14-H2 entries as gleaned from various records:

Reg.	Model	Ser. No.	Engines
NC-17382;	14-H	(# 1401)	two S1E-G.
-17383;	"	(# 1402)	"
-17384;	"	(# 1403)	"
-17385;	"	(# 1404)	"
-17386;	"	(# 1405)	"
-17387;	"	(# 1406)	"
-17388;	"	(# 1407)	"
-17389;	"	(# 1408)	"
;	"	(# 1409)	"
VH-ABI;	"	(# 1418)	"
SP-BNE;	"	(# 1420)	"
SP-BNF;	"	(# 1421)	"
SP-BNG;	"	(# 1422)	"
SP-BNH;	"	(# 1423)	"
SP-BNJ;	"	(# 1424)	"
SP-BNK;	"	(# 1425)	"
CF-TCD;	14-H2	(# 1429)	two S1E2-G.
CF-TCE;	"	(# 1430)	"
-17392;	"	(# 1431)	"
XH-TEE;	"	(# 1432)	"
XH-TEF;	"	(# 1439)	"
CF-TCF;	"	(# 1450)	"
CF-TCG;	"	(# 1451)	"
CF-TCH;	"	(# 1471)	"
CF-TCI;	"	(# 1472)	"
CF-TCJ;	"	(# 1473)	"
CF-TCK;	"	(# 1474)	"
CF-TCL;	"	(# 1475)	"
CF-TCM;	"	(# 1476)	"
USN-1441;	"	(# 1482)	"
-18993;	"	(# 1483)	"
-17395;	"	(# 1486)	"
F-ARIU;	"	(# 1487)	"
F-ARIV;	"	(# 1488)	"
F-ARIY;	"	(# 1489)	"
SP-BPK;	14-H	(# 1492)	two S1E-G.
SP-BPL;	"	(# 1493)	"
SP-BPM;	"	(# 1494)	"
SP-BPN;	"	(# 1495)	"
CF-TCN;	14-H2	(# 1499)	two S1E2-G.
CF-TCO;	"	(# 1500)	"
CF-TCP;	"	(# 1501)	"
CF-TCQ;	"	(# 1502)	"
CF-TCR;	"	(# 1503)	"
CF-TCS;	"	(# 1504)	"
F-ARRE;	"	(# 1505)	"

F-ARRF;	''	(# 1506)	''
CR-AAV;	''	(# 1507)	''
CR-AAX;	''	(# 1508)	''
YV-ADI;	''	(# 1509)	''
YV-ADO;	''	(# 1510)	''
CR-AAZ;	''	(# 1511)	''

This approval for ser. # 1401 and up; ser. # 1402-09, 1431, 1432, 1439, to NWA; ser. # 1418 to Australia; ser. # 1420-25, 1492-95 to LOT; ser. # 1429-30, 1450-51, 1471-76, 1499-1502 to Trans-Canada A.L.; ser. # 1482 to U. S. Navy; ser. # 1483 to Santa Maria A.L.; ser. # 1486 to Max Fleischmann; ser. # 1487-89, 1505-06, to Algiers; ser. # 1503-04 to Canadian-Pacific A.L.; ser. # 1507-08, 1511 to East Africa; ser. # 1509-10 to Venezuela; this approval expired 1-24-41.

14-H2 shows muscle of its "Hornet" engines.

Lockheed 14 had oodles of room for cargo.

ATC # 658
(10-31-37)
RYAN, SCW-145.

Ryan SC-W145 was three-seater of high performance.

This Warner-powered Ryan SC was actually a follow-up model to the original inline powered coupe-type airplane introduced in Aug. of 1937, but it came out as almost an entirely different airplane. The 7 cyl. Warner "radial" engine, because of its shape, forced a redesign of the whole front end, so the former slim nose was traded off for a round, blunt nose encased in a big, low-drag NACA-type cowl. This installation most likely induced a slight penalty to aerodynamic cleanness, but it was a neat installation, looked very nice on the new "Sport Coupe" and it seemed to have more appeal to the aviation people in general. The long-time popular "Scarab-series" engine also had a far better reputation than the previous engine used, so its selection for the new model SCW-145 was a compromise leveled more to the pulse of the market. From just about any angle the SCW-145 was a good looking airplane combining more advanced features in its makeup than any other airplane of this type; this instigated both praise and interest wherever it was shown. Plane-builder T. Claude Ryan was especially proud of the SCW-145 and he dressed in his finest whenever he took it out on business. Versatility was actually designed into this airplane, so it could be different things to different people; the flying business man could point to its comfort and convenience, the week-end flier could point to its reliability, and the sportsman-pilot pointed to its

beauty and its captivating performance. But, this airplane did lack promotion. The Ryan Aero. plant was actually stressing more the manufacture and sale of the open-cockpit "ST" trainer, both here and abroad, so the SCW-145 "Coupe" was not pushed nor promoted all that much. All those SCW-145 in service had satisfied owners, according to the word around, and several of these airplanes are flying even yet.

The Ryan model SCW-145 was a low-winged, coupe-type cabin monoplane with seating arranged for 2 or three. The spacious cabin area was completely enclosed with a sliding canopy to provide the comfort and convenience of a true cabin-type airplane, but the hatch could be slid open in flight, by varying amounts, for those who still enjoyed a little breeze in the face. The large circular cowling that encased the "round" engine hampered forward visibility to some degree, but pilots soon learned how to get around that; the view overhead was, of course, just terrific. The unusual cantilever wing was sharply tapered, of generous area, and the long fuselage arm provided a balanced stability that guided the airplane comfortably even through very rough air. The rear seat that was meant for a 3rd passenger was actually wide enough for two, and it is quite likely the SCW did carry 4 on occasion. When the third occupant was not carried this area could then be stuffed and piled with well over 200 lbs. of assorted gear and luggage; this must have been

Claude Ryan beams while boarding an SC-W145.

quite handy for hunters or fisherman. As powered with the 7 cyl. Warner "Super Scarab" engine of 145 h.p. the model SCW-145 was blessed with a good range of high performance, and offered the kind of "snap" a sportsman-pilot would appreciate. To some the SCW might have looked "hot & racy," but its ample wing area was well disguised, and its proportion was designed for good behavior; good landings, they say, were almost like the touch-down of a feather. The SCW-145 was extremely capable, it was always energetic, and even over-eager when spurred into action, but basically a complete lady with a good disposition and very nice manners. Owner-pilots have claimed that handling of the Warner-powered SCW, both in the air and on the ground, was almost perfect. It would be hard to base an argument against that. The type certificate for the model SCW-145 was issued 10-31-37 and only a dozen or so were manufactured by the Ryan Aeronautical Co. on Lindbergh Field in San Diego, Calif.

SC-W145 shows off unusual wing planform.

Listed below are specifications and performance data for the Ryan model SCW-145 as powered with the Warner "Super Scarab" (Series 50) engine rated 145 h.p. at 2050 r.p.m. at sea level; length overall 25'5"; height overall 7'0"; wingspan 37'6"; wing chord at root 99"; wing chord at tip 26"; total wing area 202 sq. ft.; airfoil NACA-2412; wt. empty 1345 lbs.; useful load 805 lbs.; payload with 37 gal. fuel 390 lbs. (2 pass. & 50 lbs. bag.); gross wt. 2150 lbs.; max. speed 150 at 3000 ft.; cruising speed (1900 r.p.m.) 140 at 5000 ft. or 130 at 8500 ft.; landing speed (with air brake) 45; take-off run 500 ft.; climb 890 ft. first min. at sea level; ser. ceiling 17,200 ft.; gas cap. 37 gal.; oil cap. 3 gal.; cruising range (1900 r.p.m. at 8500 ft.) at 9.5 gal. per hour 450 miles; price not announced.

The construction details and general arrangement of the Ryan SCW-145 were typical to that of the original SC-150 as described here in the chapter for ATC # 651, including the following. The only significant difference in the model SCW-145 was installation of the Warner "Super Scarab" engine of 145 h.p. The 7 cyl. Warner engine was a "radial" so it altered the appearance of the airplane entirely, and brought out entirely new characteristics of operation and behavior. Well streamlined, the engine was completely shrouded with a deep-chord NACA-type cowl, but the cowling was split in two to open on either side for quick inspection and easy maintenance. Under normal conditions the Warner installation was perhaps quieter and more reliable. The hatch (canopy) slid back and forth on ball bearings, so it was easy to operate by hand, and it could be left open in various intermediate positions even while in flight; this was nice for those who wanted some of the feel of an open cockpit, but still preferred the protection of a cabin. The wide-stance landing gear of 97 in. tread was very stable and rather soft; it ironed out the roughness of uneven ground. Area of the belly-flap (air brake) was now increased to 10 sq. ft. so it had more drag effect; flap not to be extended above 108 m.p.h. A Hartzell wooden prop, electric engine starter, battery, mech. wheel brakes, wheel pants, compass, dual stick-type controls, fuel gauge, normal set of engine & flight instruments, shock-mounted dash panel, air brake, tail wheel, navigation lights, seat belts, and first-aid kit were standard equipment. A fixed-pitch metal prop, generator, oil cooler, fire extinguisher, landing lights, paraflares, bonding & shielding, and radio gear were optional. The next Ryan development was the supercharged "STA Special" as described here in the chapter for ATC # 681.

View shows effective "drag brake."

Listed below are SCW-145 entries as gleaned from registration records:

NC-17372;	SCW-145	(# 201)	Warner 145.
-18908;	"	(# 202)	"
-18909;	"	(# 203)	"
-18910;	"	(# 204)	"
-18911;	"	(# 205)	"
-18912;	"	(# 206)	"
-18913;	"	(# 207)	"
-18914;	"	(# 208)	"
PP-TEC;	"	(# 209)	"
-18915;	"	(# 210)	"
-18916;	"	(# 211)	"
-18917;	"	(# 212)	"

This approval for ser. # 201 and up; ser. # 201 first as model SC-150, later del. to Mexico as XA-CUT; ser. # 206 del. to Warner Motors; ser. # 208 del. to Firestone Tire & Rubber Co.; ser. # 209 del. to Brazil; one SCW-145 was operated as L-10 in USAAF.

ATC # 659
(8-26-38)
HARLOW, PJC-1 (PJC-2)

Harlow model PJC-1 shows highly advanced design.

Good natured and soft-spoken Max B. Harlow had spent a lot of time designing and engineering airplanes for other people; he finally got around to designing one for himself, an airplane such as you would come to expect from a man of his talents. The airplane was quite unusual in itself, but the unusual circumstance was that it was drawn up, laid out, and built by aeronautical engineering students at Pasadena Junior College. Being student-built as a class-room project it may suggest that this airplane was perhaps of doubtful integrity, but Max Harlow laid all doubts to rest because he personally supervised its development and construction. As the model PJC-1 this airplane was test-flown by Jack Kelley on 14 Sept. 1937 and showed promise of being the fastest little airplane in its class. A group of local investors were interested in the manufacture of this design, so they covered the expenses for its construction and the conducting of tests for its government approval. As the last part of its certification tests the PJC-1 was loaded with 400 lbs. of "lead shot" for the critical "spin test"; crossed-controls during this maneuver had promoted an unrecoverable "flat spin," so the pilot parachuted out and the airplane was destroyed. But, the PJC-1 had already proven itself admirably in all other tests, so the second airplane (PJC-2) was completed with limits in place to eliminate crossed-controls; it thus came through with its government approval in Aug. of 1938. The Harlow Aircraft Co. was incorporated in 1939 with some money from

Howard Hughes, and the plant was set up in a hangar on the Alhambra Airport. The first order was for 3 specially equipped airplanes to be operated by the CAA, a government agency that had taken over from the Bureau of Air Commerce. The first batch was delivered in April of 1940. While the PJC-2 order was being built, Max Harlow had designed a trainer-type called the PC-5, but it was of no interest to the U. S. government, so manufacturing rights were sold. War clouds in Europe and defense build-up in this country must have had a disconcerting effect on Harlow and his associates because there seemed to be no definite direction to this company's future. In late 1940 the Harlow Co. underwent a corporate shuffle and other interests had taken over. Max Harlow always did have a distaste for management chores, so he happily retreated to his teaching duties. Eventually, Max Harlow fell heir to all tooling and what was left of the PJC-2 project; there seemed to be no future for this airplane in the post-war scheme, so it remained in dead storage.

First and foremost an educator, Max Harlow was one of the first graduates from Stanford University in aeronautical engineering; he started out with "Thaden" in 1927 who had built the first all-metal airplane on the west coast. In 1928, under coaxing from Waldo Waterman, Harlow became chief engineer for "Bach" who was building an interesting tri-motored transport. Harlow later served as engineer on design projects by both Waldo Waterman (the "Rubber

PJC-2 as operated by CAA inspecters.

Duck") and Allan Lockheed's unusual "Uni-Twin." In the only non-aeronautical endeavor in his professional career, Harlow was employed by the Ruckstell Corp. to develop a powered surfboard. When "Bert" Kinner was fiddling with his famous folding-wing "Sportster" he let Harlow handle the engineering to get the airplane certificated; among other "Kinner" designs, Harlow also developed the lovely "Sportwing." When Harlow departed in 1934 he was loaded with "Kinner" stock as part payment for his services, but the stock was nearly worthless. A short stint with Northrop followed, and then with Douglas on the DC-2 project as stress analyst. Harlow's tenure at Pasadena Junior College began early in 1935 when he joined as a professor in charge of aeronautics. Some months later he contributed some design ideas to the famous "Hughes

Racer" flown by Howard Hughes. By then he had convinced administrators at the college of having aeronautical students produce an all-metal airplane as a class project; this would be the PJC-1. Construction of the PJC-1 started in Nov. of 1936 and 10 months later it was flying. It was unfortunate that the prototype crashed from a "flat spin," but the design was later vindicated in the PJC-2. Max Harlow retained his full-time teaching position, but on the side he was also project engineer and general manager of the Harlow Aircraft Co. which was building the PJC-2. At the same time he was also listed as chief engineer for Waldo Waterman, and for Security Aircraft. But, Max B. Harlow was a teacher, the "quiet professor," and he derived perhaps more satisfaction in developing technical talent in aeronautical engineers of the future.

Harlow offered transport features to private-owner.

The curvaceous Harlow model PJC-1 (PJC-2) was a light all-metal, low-winged, cabin monoplane with seating arranged for 2, 3, or 4. With only 2 occupants it could carry a big mound of baggage, with 3 occupants it could carry a fair amount of baggage, and with 4 occupants the baggage was limited to 25 lbs. unless the fuel load was shortened to allow for more baggage. The "Harlow" was a lovely little airplane of very advanced design, and it somehow looked and acted bigger than it really was. The first large order came from the Bureau of Air Commerce which stationed the airplanes in districts scattered around the country for use by government inspectors. Even tho' the prototype (PJC-1) had crashed in an unfair "spin test," the Bureau felt somewhat obligated for the mishap and gave the subsequent examples a clean bill of health, as it were. The government inspector-pilots enjoyed the little "Harlow," and were more than happy to use it in their work. As powered with the 7 cyl. Warner "Super Scarab" engine of 145 h.p., the trim PJC-2 squeezed a lot of performance from this amount of power, and set a standard of performance that lasted nearly 30 years. This pudgy, close-coupled airplane was eager and maneuverable, but easily manageable, and pilots enjoyed working with it very much. It's a pity that this remarkable airplane wasn't steered to more lasting success, it could have been, but the turmoil of uncertain times perhaps discouraged further development, and the investment of more capital. The type certificate for the Harlow model PJC-2 (PJC-1) was issued 8-26-38 (it was pending since 10-37) and some 9 or more examples of this model were manufactured by the Harlow Aircraft Co. on Alhambra Airport in Alhambra, Calif. J. B. Alexander was pres.; Max B. Harlow was V. P. & gen. mgr.; John C. (Jack) Kelley was sales mgr.; Dave C. Mendenhall was proj. engr.; and Francis Hoffman was plant mgr. In a reorganization, E. M. Allison became pres.; Frank der Yuen was V. P. & gen mgr.; Dave Mendenhall remained as chf. engr.; and Jack O'Meara was chief pilot.

Listed below are specifications and performance data for the Harlow (2 pl.) model PJC-1 as powered with Warner "Super Scarab" (Series 50) engine rated 145 h.p. at 2050 r.p.m. at sea level; length overall 23'4"; height overall 7'3"; wingspan 35'10"; wing chord at root 90"; wing chord at tip 42"; total wing area 185 sq. ft.; airfoil NACA-23012; wt. empty 1607 lbs.; useful load 687 lbs.; payload with 34 gal. fuel 283 lbs. (1 pass. & 113 lbs. bag.); gross wt. 2294 lbs.; max speed 165; cruising speed (.75 power) 145; landing speed (with flaps) 48; climb 850 ft. first min. at sea level; ser. ceiling 16,500 ft.; **gas cap.** 34 gal.; oil cap. 4 gal.; cruising range (.75 power) at 9 gal. per hour 500 miles; price not announced.

Specifications and data for model PJC-2 as powered with Warner "Super Scarab" (Series 50) engine rated 145 h.p., same as above except as follows; wt. empty 1661 lbs.; useful load 939 lbs.; payload with 34 gal. fuel 535 lbs. (3 pass. & 25 lbs. bag.); baggage to 80 lbs. was allowed with 25 gal. fuel; gross wt. 2600 lbs.; max. speed 160; cruising speed (.75 power) 140; landing speed (with flaps) 52; climb 750 ft. first min. at sea level; ser. ceiling 15,500 ft.; gas cap. max. 34 gal.; oil cap. max. 4 gal.; cruising range (.75 power) at 9 gal. per hour 490 miles; price $6985. This airplane was also eligible at 2486 lbs. gross wt. for 2 passengers & 130 lbs. baggage with 26 gal. fuel.

The oval semi-monocoque fuselage framework was built up of 24ST dural metal rings and 24ST dural extrusions to which was riveted a smooth 24ST "Alclad" metal skin. A large door was on the right with entry off the wing-walk. The cabin was well insulated, tastefully upholstered, and

"Harlow" was cleanest design in lightplane field.

had provisions normally for 2 seats and a huge (130 lb.) baggage compartment; or, it could be fitted with 4 seats and a smaller baggage compartment with allowance for up to 80 lbs. The baggage was accessible from inside or out. The curved windshield and the formed windows were of Pyralin. The cantilever wing, in one piece, was a semi-monocoque structure of 24ST dural ribs and heavy dural stringers covered with heavy-gauge 24ST "Alclad" metal sheet. The split-type trailing edge wing flaps were perforated and used for drag only—not to be used for takeoff. Flaps were electrically operated to 45 deg. deflection; not to be extended above 105 m.p.h. The 34 gal. fuel tank was mounted in the C-S panel under cabin floor; fuel pressure was provided by electric pump, or hand-operated wobble pump. The retractable landing gear of 90 in. tread used "Aerol" (air-oil) shock struts; the 2 cantilever assemblies were retracted electrically into wheel wells on underside of wing. Hayes wheels were fitted with 21 in. tires and hydraulic brakes. The tail wheel, with fore-and-aft lock, was full swivel; a steerable tail wheel was optional. The cantilever tail group was an all-metal (24ST), semi-monocoque structure; fixed surfaces were covered with "Alclad" metal sheet, and movable surfaces were covered in fabric. The elevators were fitted with adjustable trim tabs. A Hartzell wooden prop, electric engine starter, battery,

generator, dual controls, navigation lights, wing flaps, retractable landing gear, hydraulic wheel brakes, fuel gauge, fuel pumps, compass, carburetor air heater, first-aid kit, and seating for two were standard equipment. A Curtiss-Reed metal prop, cabin heater, cabin lights, radio gear, landing lights, paraflares, and seating for 3 or 4 were optional. The next Harlow development was the PC-5 trainer as described in the chapter for ATC # 735.

Listed below are Harlow entries as gleaned from various records:

NX-18136;	PJC-1	(# 1)	Warner 145.
NC-18978;	PJC-2	(# 1)	Warner 145.
NC-102;	"	(# 2)	"
NC-54;	"	(# 3)	"
;	"	(# 4)	"
;	"	(# 5)	"
NC-15;	"	(# 6)	"
;	"	(# 7)	"
NC-82;	"	(# 8)	"
NC-19983;	"	(# 9)	"
;	"	(# 10)	"

This approval for ser. # 1 and up; NX-18136 crashed during govt. tests; ser. # 2-3-4 and # 6-7-8 del. to CAA in 1940; ser. # 10 probably not completed; this approval expired 7-26-40.

ATC # 660
(10-31-37)
PIPER "CUB TRAINER", J-3.

The model J-3 was Piper's "40-horse Cub."

Shown here we have a very familiar airplane under a new name—now it will be known as the Piper "Cub"; it had a nice sound to it. Actually, it was several circumstances that lined up to make this happen. As nearly everyone knows, this airplane was known earlier world-wide as the Taylor "Cub" designed by C. G. Taylor. In March of 1937 the plant in Bradford, Pa. had burned down, under strained relationship Taylor finally decided to leave, and the company was looking anxiously for rebuilding or relocation. Relocating in Lock Haven, Pa. the company still operated as Taylor Aircraft for a while, but this became confusing because C. G. Taylor already had another business going; it was high time to make some changes. In Dec. of 1937 it was formally announced to the trade that the former Taylor "Cub" would from now on be the Piper "Cub," and we were reminded too that the "Cub," as a model J-3 had been redesigned extensively to become practically a new airplane. There were some useful changes in the new J-3, but to many it was still "the dear old Cub," and it would continue to be for many, many years. As the Piper "Cub" this airplane continued to soar in popularity; somehow it got around that it was now a better airplane. It was no trouble really to sell the new (J-3) "Cub," and dealers were buying the new line by the box-car load. One dealer from Oregon had a trailer hitched to his big Buick and he hauled a (knock-down) "Cub" at a time from the factory in almost a continuous shuttle. With better times flying schools were popping up all over, and a lot of them were buying the new Piper "Cub Trainer," a school in Texas guaranteed to solo a student for $56.50 cash. There was also talk of a young fellow in Texas who soloed a Piper "Cub" in the same day after only 2 hrs. 55 mins. of dual instruction. Then too there was the lad in Minnesota who soloed a "Cub" after only 2 hrs. 35 mins. of instruction; this has got to be some kind of record! Light-plane sales in this country were skyrocketing, and the "Cub" was being sold like never before; exports were also increasing. One of the largest orders overseas was 27 of the new "Cub" J-3 to Denmark. Happy with the business that was coming their way, Piper offered 3 models for early 1938; these were the "Cub Trainer," the "Cub Sport," and the "Cub Seaplane." They were all easy to buy; at $1270, you could get the "Trainer" for $425 down, the "Sport" was tagged at $1395 and it was available for $465 down. The "Cub Seaplane" was a terrific buy at $1895 and it was available for $635 down. Prices were lowered again in 1939 (Trainer was now $1249), and if you were not a pilot the dealer would teach you to fly your own "Cub" free! Otherwise, most operators were getting $5.00 per hour for dual time in a "Cub," and $4.00 per hour, or less, for solo time. Nobody was making a great deal of money, but it was a fun-way of life. The J-3 was the first of the "Piper" line, a line of airplanes that almost became a household word.

The new Piper "Cub" model J-3 was a light high-winged cabin monoplane with seating arranged for two in tandem. There is something inherently beautiful about a "Cub" in the way she conducts herself with charm and poise, calm and unafraid, and with a style all her own. With very definite feminine traits the "Cub" was always "she," or "her," to those who flew it, and to own a "Cub" was like a love affair. What could be more carefree fun than to fly around lazily in a "Cub," low and slow, while rubber-necking at the beautiful countryside; a flight that usually started and ended on some small grass-carpeted airport. You didn't bother much to look at gauges, because there were not all that many, and if you really did have to drop in somewhere any 500 foot level spot became your airport. It was no trouble getting out either. This new (J-3) "Cub" was still pretty much the same as the earlier J-2, but there were many little modifications that made it a somewhat better airplane. As powered with the popular 4 cyl. Continental A-40 series engine, rated now at a full 40 h.p., the model J-3 had some distinct improvements in performance, and it even handled a little better. The gains were not all that great, of course, but to a light-plane pilot who had to be a lot closer to his airplane, the gains were very noticeable and appreciated. There were some inconveniences in flying a "Forty Horse Cub" to be sure, but it was an honest airplane, easy to understand, and none but a real dodo could ever get hurt in it. For simple, inexpensive, and carefree flying it was one of the best. The type certificate for the "Cub" model J-3 (J3C-40) was issued 10-31-37 and literally hundreds were manufactured by the newly-organized Piper Aircraft Corp. at Lock Haven, Pa. At this point Wm. T. Piper was pres., treas., & gen. mgr.; Ted V. Weld was V. P., & Walter C. Jamouneau was chf. engr.

Listed below are specifications and performance data for the Piper "Cub" model J-3 as powered with Continental A-40-4 engine rated 40 h.p. at 2575 r.p.m. at sea level; length overall 22'3"; height overall 6'6"; wingspan 35'3"; wing chord 63"; total wing area 178.5 sq. ft.; airfoil USA-35B; wt. empty 578 lbs.; useful load 422 lbs.; payload with 9 gal. fuel 190 lbs. (1 pass. & 20 lbs. bag.); gross wt. 1000 lbs.; max. speed 87; cruising speed (2350 r.p.m.) 72; landing (stall) speed 32; climb 425 ft. first min. at sea level; ser. ceiling 10,000 ft,; gas cap. 9 gal.; oil cap. (in sump) 4 qts.; cruising range (2350 r.p.m.) at 3 gal. per hour 210 miles; price $1270 at factory in 1938, lowered to $1249, then $1098 in 1939, finally to $995 in 1940. Model J-3 was also eligible with Continental A-40-5 (twin ignition) engine as J3C-40, or with detuned Franklin 4AC-150 (Series 40) engine rated 40 h.p. at 1875 r.p.m. as J3F-40. Also as seaplane on Edo D-1070 twin-float gear at 1070 lbs. gross wt.; Edo 54-1140 pontoons were optional.

J-3 fitted with single-bladed "Everel" propeller.

The fuselage framework was built up of welded 4130 and 1025 steel tubing, lightly faired to shape, then fabric covered. Deeper seats of 26 in. width were mounted in tandem, and a large let down door provided entry from the right side with the aid of a step. The interior, now some 7 in. longer, was upholstered in whipcord, and dual stick-type controls were provided; the interior was still rather bare, but adequate, and all gadgetry was simple and quite functional. The new J-3 was now a true cabin airplane, but could be flown with the doors open. The slanted windshield and the cabin windows were of Pyralin; left side window could be slid back for ventilation. A small baggage shelf with allowance for 20 lbs. was behind the rear seat. A 9 gal. fuel tank (12 gal. optional) was mounted high in the fuselage just behind firewall; a simple bobber type fuel level gauge projected up through the tank filler cap. All fuel lines were now of flexible tubing. The engine cowling was slightly improved with emphasis on better cooling. The wing framework, in 2 halves, was built up with solid spruce spar beams and "Nicral" metal wing ribs; the leading edges were covered with dural metal sheet and the completed framework was covered in fabric. The wing was braced to lower fuselage with vee-type struts of a much heavier gauge. The simple tripod landing gear assembly of 72 in. tread was fitted with Rusco rubber shock rings; 7.00x4 wheels were fitted with low-pressure tires, and no brakes were provided. The spring-leaf tail skid was available with a steerable tail wheel assembly. The J-3 was available also on skis, and Edo D-1070 twin-float gear. The fabric covered tail group was built up of welded steel tubing; the horizontal stabilizer was adjustable in flight. The vertical fin was now larger and the rudder was fitted with aerodynamic balance horn. All movable controls were operated by cable. The standard "Piper" finish was now "Cub Yellow" with Black trim. A Sensenich wooden prop, dual controls, wiring for navigation lights, safety belts, and a first aid kit were standard equipment. A battery, navigation lights, carburetor heater, cabin heater, 18x8-3 Goodyear airwheels with brakes, a 12'gal. fuel tank, wheel pants, prop spinner, tail wheel assy., Edo D-1070 or 54-1140 twin float gear, and skis were optional. The next "Cub" development by Piper was the 50 h.p. model J3C-50 as described here in the chapter for ATC # 691.

Listed below are Piper "Cub" model J-3 entries as gleaned from registration records:

NC-20000;	J-3	(# 2000)	Cont. A-40
-20201;	"	(# 2001)	"
-20202;	"	(# 2002)	"
-20203;	"	(# 2003)	"
-20204;	"	(# 2004)	"
-20205;	"	(# 2005)	"
-20206;	"	(# 2006)	"
-20207;	"	(# 2007)	"
-20208;	"	(# 2008)	"
-20209;	"	(# 2009)	"
-20210;	"	(# 2010)	"

NC-20211 was ser. # 2011 and nos. ran consecutively to NC-20250 which was ser. # 2050; NC-20251 was ser. # 2051 and nos. ran consecutively to NC-20299 which was ser. # 2099; NC-20269 was a model J3F-40 as ser. # 2069; NC-20800 was ser. # 2100 and nos. ran consecutively to NC-20841 which was ser. # 2141; no listing for ser. # 2142; NC-20843 was ser. # 2143 and nos. ran consecutively to NC-20847 which was ser. # 2147; NC-20842 was ser. # 2148 and after that no sequence was intended.

-20849;	"	(# 2149)	"
-20851;	"	(# 2150)	"
-20852;	"	(# 2151)	"
-20848;	"	(# 2152)	"
-20853;	"	(# 2153)	"
-20855;	"	(# 2154)	"
-20860;	"	(# 2155)	"
-20856;	"	(# 2156)	"
-20863;	"	(# 2157)	"
-20858;	"	(# 2158)	"
-20862;	"	(# 2159)	"
-20866;	"	(# 2160)	"
-20857;	"	(# 2161)	"
-20861;	"	(# 2162)	"
-20870;	"	(# 2163)	"
-20868;	"	(# 2164)	"
-20865;	"	(# 2165)	"
-20867;	"	(# 2166)	"
-20875;	"	(# 2167)	"
-20876;	"	(# 2168)	"
-20864;	"	(# 2170)	"
-20879;	"	(# 2171)	"
-20869;	"	(# 2172)	"
-20871;	"	(# 2173)	"
-20850;	"	(# 2174)	"
-20872;	"	(# 2175)	"
-20873;	"	(# 2176)	"
-20887;	"	(# 2177)	"
-20881;	"	(# 2179)	"
-20882;	"	(# 2181)	"
-20884;	"	(# 2182)	"
-20885;	"	(# 2183)	"
-20883;	"	(# 2184)	"
-20890;	"	(# 2185)	"
-20889;	"	(# 2187)	"
-20891;	"	(# 2188)	"
-20892;	"	(# 2189)	"
-20893;	"	(# 2190)	"
-20894;	"	(# 2191)	"
-20896;	"	(# 2192)	"
-20898;	"	(# 2193)	"
-20899;	"	(# 2194)	"
-20886;	"	(# 2195)	"
-20897;	"	(# 2196)	"
-20895;	"	(# 2197)	"
-20145;	"	(# 2198)	"
-20147;	"	(# 2199)	"
-20146;	"	(# 2200)	"

This approval for ser. # 1100 thru 1200, # 1999 and up; no listing for ser. # 2169, 2178, 2180, and 2186; ser. # 2080 tested as J3P with Lenape engine; the J3C-40 was manufactured into 1939 and approx. 300 were built; this approval expired 10-15-39.

ATC # 661
(10-31-37)
REARWIN, "SPEEDSTER", 6000-M

Rearwin 6000-M was designed for the sportsman.

Getting the feisty "Speedster" approved for manufacture had been quite a frustrating experience for Rearwin Airplanes, but they finally made the grade after about 2 years of testing and development; it was an unnecessarily grueling ordeal and nearly threatened the life of a beautiful airplane. By the time the "Speedster" was approved the A.C.E. "Cirrus" Hi-Drive engine, as used in the first Model 6000, was no longer available so Rearwin had to look elsewhere for a similar engine. The search was not very difficult because Al Menasco had an engine that would easily fill the bill. The 4 cyl. "Menasco" inverted inline engine was being built in fair number; it had piled up a good record for reliability, and it was riding high in popularity because of its terrific success in racing airplanes. The 125 h.p. Menasco C-4 engine was practically tailor-made for the Rearwin "Speedster" and there was much promise for the combination. Rearwin redesigned the original airplane slightly, and offered it as the Model 6000-M; they offered it with the confidence that this was one of the finest airplanes in its class. All early tests of the 6000-M proved that it was agile and swift, so it was off to the Miami Air Races where it would show off its ability, and drum up some enthusiasm; reaction was good right from the start. In a 30-mile free-for-all for light airplanes the "Speedster" (6000-M) captured the pace and

averaged 149.7 m.p.h. around the pylons; not a bad performance on 125 h.p. Early interest in the flashy "Speedster" was gratifying to Rearwin, but it didn't last long, so Ray Beebe set out in May of 1938 on an extended national tour, demonstrating the new "Speedster" to Rearwin dealers; his demonstration was a big social success because the "Speedster" really was a colorful and interesting airplane, but orders still failed to come in as anticipated. A few of the "Speedster" were exported to foreign countries, but response over here was very light; its a pity that such a lovely airplane remained practically unwanted.

Manufacture of the famous "Cirrus" engines practically ceased in 1935, and the engines on hand did not last very long, but there were still hundreds out in service that would soon need parts and major maintenance. Sensing the need, Al Menasco bought up all remaining parts to offer parts and service to the "Cirrus" engines still in use. He also bought up all remaining "Wright-Gipsy" engines and parts so that he could offer "parts & service" to all the "Gipsy" engines still in service. This became a rather large part of Menasco's business, and kept these two fine engines in service for many years longer. Meanwhile, in Jan. of 1938, Rae Rearwin announced the purchase of all assets in the LeBlond Engine Corp. which had supplied engines to

6000-M was noted for its speed.

Rearwin and others for many years; all machinery, tools, jigs, and fixtures were later shipped to Kansas City. A caravan of some 20 railroad box-cars was used to make the move from Cincinnati. The engines were then manufactured and assembled by Rearwin, and called the "Ken-Royce" line. By late 1938, Rearwin Airplanes was employing about 60 assorted craftsmen to build their airplanes and engines; about 20% of Rearwin production was going overseas.

The Rearwin "Speedster" model 6000-M was a light high-winged cabin monoplane of a dashing appearance with chummy seating arranged for 2 in tandem. Its slender lines of low frontal area made it a little tight inside for anyone of broad shoulders, but this enhanced the intimacy that pilots felt for this airplane. Because of its rather special nature this airplane was restricted in its everyday use, and would more or less appeal only to the so-called sportsman-pilot. Had the "Speedster" been offered to the sportsman-pilot some 4 years earlier it would surely have captured a much better acceptance among the people that flew only for the fun of it. But, the market had changed considerably by 1938, and the Model 6000-M was darned near an outmoded airplane. As powered with the 4 cyl. aircooled inverted inline Menasco C-4 engine of 125 h.p. the Rearwin "Speedster," with the slimness of an arrow, was taking advantage of low frontal area and its relative swiftness on modest power was quite astonishing. Although

not quite as frisky as first designed in 1934, the redesigned model 6000-M was still pretty much of a show-off, and also instilled big grins of enthusiasm in all who flew her. It has been said, and there is no reason to disbelieve it, that flying the "Speedster" to its very limits was a stimulating experience; an experience guaranteed to bring a healthy glow up to the cheeks. It was that kind of airplane. The type certificate for the model 6000-M was issued retroactive to 10-31-37 and some 12 or more examples were manufactured by Rearwin Airplanes, Inc. on Fairfax Field in Kansas City, Kan. Robert W. Rummell was now chf. engr.; and Wm. Miller did most of the test-flying during this period.

Listed below are specifications and performance data for the "Speedster" model 6000-M as powered with Menasco C-4 engine rated 125 h.p. at 2175 r.p.m. at 800 ft.; length overall 22'10"; height overall 6'10"; wingspan 32'3"; wing chord 60"; total wing area (with "gulled" wing roots) 143.2 sq. ft.; airfoil NACA-2412; wt. empty 1067 lbs.; useful load 633 lbs.; payload with 34 gal. fuel 236 lbs. (1 pass. & 66 lbs. for bag. & extras); gross wt. 1700 lbs.; max. speed 150 at 800 ft.; cruising speed (1975 r.p.m.) 135 at 800 ft.; landing (stall) speed 48; climb 1200 ft. first min. at sea level; climb to 5000 ft. in 5 mins.; ser. ceiling 17,000 ft.; gas cap. 34 gal.; oil cap. 3 gal.; cruising range (1975 r.p.m.) at 8 gal. per hour 540 miles; price $4390 at factory field. Also available with 150 h.p. Menasco C4S engine as model 6000-MS; performance was proportionately better.

The construction details and general arrangement of the model 6000-M were more or less typical to that of the Model 6000 as described here in the chapter for ATC # 653, including the following. Leg room was ample at either seat; the front seat was adjustable. Standard upholstery was in serviceable fabrics, but real leather and custom fabrics were available. All airplanes had hand rubbed exterior finish. Because of C. G. limits, solo flying was permitted from front seat only. Baggage was stored in 2 compartments; 30 lbs. was allowed under rear seat, and 20 lbs. was allowed behind the rear seat. The windshield, side windows, and skylight were all of Pyralin. The wing roots were "gulled" slightly for better visibility in this area. Spar beams of the wing were reinforced with plywood gussets at all points of attachment and stress. A 17 gal. fuel tank was mounted in the root end of each wing-half; each tank was fitted with a fuel level gauge. The streamlined landing gear of 72 in. tread was of 2 cantilever assemblies fitted with Rusco rubber shock-rings; Goodyear 7.00x5 wheels and tires with mechanical brakes were encased in streamlined metal wheel pants. The 8 in. tail wheel was steerable. The horizontal stabilizer was adjustable for trim in flight. A Flottorp wooden prop, dual stick type controls, wheel brakes, fuel gauges, compass, normal set of engine & flight instruments, wiring for navigation lights, seat belts, and first-aid kit were standard equipment. Curtiss-Reed metal prop, storage battery, electric engine starter, wind-driven generator, Goodyear 18x8-3 airwheels with brakes, navigation lights, landing lights, paraflares, Pyrene fire extinguisher, carburetor heat-box, cabin heater, dual brake pedals, 6.00x6 wheels & tires, bonding & shielding, and radio gear were optional. The next Rearwin development was the "Cloudster" series as described in the chapter for ATC # 711.

Listed below are 6000-M entries as gleaned from registration records:

NC-	6000-M	(# 303)	Menasco C-4.
-19402;	"	(# 304)	"
-19410;	"	(#)	"
-19412;	"	(# 308)	"
-19415;	"	(# 309)	"
-20741;	"	(# 311)	"

This approval for ser. # 303 and up; 2 were exported to So. Africa, 1 to Peru, and 4 or more to undetermined countries; it has been estimated that up to 20 examples were built in all; this approval expired 1-7-43.

6000-M shows off tightly cowled engine and cantilever landing gear.

ATC # 662
(10-30-37)
BARKLEY-GROW, T8P-1

Barkley-Grow T8P-1 puts in a bid as light transport.

The concept for the twin-engined Barkley-Grow transport was molded around the patented Barkley "multi-spar" all-metal wing, a novel method of construction that provided exceptional bending and torsional strength. Barkley and Grow joined together early in 1936 at Detroit to incorporate this new structural design into a light transport airplane which seemed the most logical use for this idea. The first Barkley-Grow transport was rolled out in April of 1937 as the T8P-1, and it was flown on its maiden hop by Frank Cordova; Lee Gehlbach, famous racing-pilot, did much of the subsequent testing. Enthused over its ability, the T8P-1 was launched on a tour of the U.S.A. by the proud handfull of men that made up the company, but the airplane was often mistaken for a "Lockheed 10" or a "Beech 18" which it closely resembled. Turning then to the north and south of our borders, they finally picked up a few orders in Canada, and some in So. America. Alex Papana, the famous Roumanian pilot who became well-known in this country, used the second airplane for a proposed flight from New York to Roumania; after 2 unsuccessful attempts the flight was aborted and the airplane was sold to the Peruvian Air Force. Flown by Peruvian pilots this airplane finally did make a record flight from New York to Peru in Oct. of 1939; the record-breaker was later used to haul cargo throughout the jungles of Peru. Another T8P-1 saw service with Adm. Richard E. Byrd on his

Third Antarctic Expedition of 1939-41; it was used for South Pole exploration and served the expedition in other ways as well. Upon its return to the U.S.A. the T8P-1 was found to be extensively damaged by salt-water corrosion, so it was dismantled for inspection and finally destroyed. Several more of the T8P-1 were built, in fact about 11 in all, and they too served in Canada and in So. America; it seems that only one example was active in this country. Despite the enthusiastic acceptance of the T8P-1 at first, it soon became very hard to sell because of rising competition, and the company became deeply in debt with no way out. In June of 1940 the Barkley-Grow Corp. was sold to the Aviation Manufacturing Corp. (which also owned Stinson and Lycoming), and the company lost its identity. The Barkley-Grow transport (T8P-1) never did "make it" in a big way, but it did find a conspicuous niche in the halls of aviation history. It is possible that a few are out there flying yet.

Interest in aviation by Archibald Barkley went back to the Wright Bros. when he helped build some of their early gliders. After a stint with the Wright Co., with the Curtiss Aeroplane Co., and a tour of duty overseas with the Army in WWI, he came back to work for such aircraft builders as Stout, Ford, Verville, and others. An inventive person, Barkley introduced several innovations in airplane structure. Upon developing his patented all-metal wing, Barkley built a small cabin monoplane in 1931, the neat Barkley-

T8P-1 shows normal lines, but had innovations in its construction.

Warwick, that proved the integrity of his design. Comdr. Harold B. Grow, a naval officer, served with the Navy in France during WWI. In 1924 as a member of the U. S. Naval Mission, he helped organize the Peruvian Air Force, and remained there until 1930. On return to America he formed Grow, Joy & Co. in Detroit (aviation brokers), and he evetually joined forces with Barkley to form the Barkley-Grow Aircraft Corp. on the City Airport in Detroit, Mich. The plant was set up in the former Schlee-Brock hangar. The eventual sale of Barkley-Grow to AVCO scattered personnel to the up-coming war effort in Detroit auto plants, and the company's history remains as only a few notes in "Convair" records.

The Barkley-Grow model T8P-1 was a twin-engined, all-metal, low-winged, transport monoplane with seating normally arranged for 6 passengers and a crew of two. The versatile interior could also be arranged for hauling cargo, a high-density seating arrangement for 8 passengers, a custom "Club" (4 place) interior for the executive, or as an air ambulance. It was also offered as a light utility-bomber in various So. American countries. The T8P-1 made its way to several different parts of the world, but its finest hour was in the Yukon Territory where it helped change "bush flying" from a haphazard operation to a regularly scheduled airline system. The fixed landing gear on the T8P-1 was considered archaic and a detriment to some, but they loved

T8P-1 as operated in Canada.

218

it in Canada because they could make quick changes from wheels, to skis, to floats with very little bother. As powered with 2 Pratt & Whitney "Wasp Jr." SB engines rated 400 h.p. each the T8P-1 was endowed with very good performance throughout the whole range of flight. It was forever being compared with the Lockheed "Electra," but choosing one airplane over the other would only be a matter of choice; there was not that much difference. Flight characteristics and handling was more or less typical for an airplane of this type, and its best feature was its relative strength. It was built to take it, easily absorbing extremely hard work and punishment without flinching. Only a few of the T8P-1 are left, and most of these are in Canada hauling fish and mining supplies, but that's honest work for an honest airplane. The type certificate for the model T8P-1 was issued 10-30-37 and it seems that only 11 examples were manufactured by the Barkley-Grow Aircraft Corp. on the City Airport in Detroit, Mich. Harold B. Grow was pres. & gen. mgr.; Archibald S. Barkley was V.P. in chrg. of engrg.; and Dwight C. Maier was proj. engr. As a company officer the name of A. S. Barkley appears only in 1937, and the name of H. B. Grow was not included in 1939, so there was frequent juggling of company personnel, or so it seems.

Listed below are specifications and performance data for the Barkley-Grow model T8P-1 as powered with 2 "Wasp Jr." SB engines rated 400 h.p. at 2200 r.p.m. at 5000 ft. (450 h.p. each for takeoff); length overall 36'2"; height overall 9'8"; wingspan 50'9"; wing chord at root 126"; wing chord at tip 42"; total wing area 354 sq. ft.; airfoil NACA-23012; wt. empty 5448 lbs.; useful load 2802 lbs.; payload with 160 gal. fuel & 2 crew was 1397 lbs. (6 pass. & 377 lbs. bag.); gross wt. 8250 lbs.; max. speed 224 at 5000 ft.; cruising speed (.75 power) 204 at 9600 ft.; landing speed (with flaps) 65; climb 1420 ft. first min. at sea level; ser. ceiling 20,000 ft.; gas cap. normal 160 gal.; gas cap. max. 220 gal.; oil cap. 14-16 gal.; cruising range (.75 power) at 42 gal. per hour (160 gal.) was 750 miles; basic price was $37,500 at the factory. The prototype airplane as first tested was a lot lighter and peppier; in most cases this was usually normal. Serial # 1 and 2 were eligible only at 8250 lbs. gross wt.; ser. # 3 and up were eligible with gross wt. of up to 8750 lbs. The T8P-1 was also eligible as seaplane on Edo 65-9225A twin-float gear at 9200 lbs. gross wt.

The semi-monocoque fuselage framework was an all-metal (17ST) structure using formed rings and stringers covered with smooth "Alclad" metal sheet. Entry door was on the right side, and the cabin was normally arranged with 6 to 8 passenger seats. Various other custom arrangements were available. The cabin area was soundproofed, insulated, and then upholstered in various fabrics. The pilot's area up front was partitioned off from the cabin area, having an escape hatch in the roof; dual control wheels and a full complement of airline equipment was provided. The main cabin was fitted with cool air vents, cabin heaters, and a lavatory in back. A baggage compt. in the nose was allowed 250 lbs., and the compartment behind cabin area was allowed 180 lbs. The patented "Barkley" wing was of multi-spar construction having no wing ribs; the wing spars were a series of X-type span-wise beams riveted together and covered with smooth "Alclad" metal sheet. The engine nacelles were

T8P-1 in Canada on floats.

mounted into the wing's leading edge, and engines were mounted on steel tube frames with "Lord" rubber bushings. The fixed landing gear was of 2 cantilever assemblies mounted into the engine nacelles; each "leg" used an Aerol shock strut and was fitted with 30x13-6 Goodyear airwheels using multiple-disc hydraulic brakes. The landing gear legs were streamlined with formed metal cuffs and wheels were encased in metal wheel pants. The normal fuel supply was 2 tanks in each wing-half; an extra 30 gal. tank in each nacelle was optional. Ailerons and wing-flaps were of the Freise (offset-hinge) type; flaps had area of 48 sq. ft. and not to be lowered above 117 m.p.h. The cantilever tail group, with twin rudders, was an all-metal (17ST) multi-spar structure covered with smooth Alclad metal sheet; the elevator was fitted with adjustable trim tab. A fixed metal tab on the rudders was "trimmed" on the ground only. Hamilton-Standard controllable (constant-speed) propellers, electric engine starters, generator, battery, dual wheel-type controls, navigation lights, wheel brakes, parking brake, wheel pants, complete equipment for airline service, cabin vents, cabin heaters, carburetor heaters, oil coolers, fuel pumps, fuel gauges, fire extinguisher, lavatory and first-aid kit were standard equipment. Landing lights, paraflares, pressure-type fire extinguishers, bonding & shielding, radio gear, auto-pilot, extra fuel cap., custom interiors, skis, and pontoons were optional.

Listed below are T8P-1 entries as gleaned from various records:

NX-18388;	T8P-1	(# 1)	2 SB-400
YR-AHA;	"	(# 2)	"
CF-BLV;	"	(# 3)	"
CF-BMG;	"	(# 4)	"
CF-BMV;	"	(# 5)	"
CF-BMW;	"	(# 6)	"
NC-18470;	"	(# 7)	"
CF-BQM;	"	(# 8)	"
;	"	(# 9)	"
;	"	(# 10)	"
NC-26496;	"	(# 11)	"

This approval for ser. # 1 and up; ser. # 1 later to Canada as CF-BVE; ser. # 2 as OB-GGK in Peru; ser. # 3, 4, 6 to Yukon Southern Air Transport; ser. # 5 later as # 758 in RCAF; ser. # 7 used by Byrd in Antarctica during 1939-41; ser. # 8 to Canada—still flying regularly in 1968; ser. # 9-10 unknown; ser. # 11 actually to Canada as CF-BTX; this approval expired 10-25-40.

ATC # 663
(10-31-37)
FAIRCHILD, MODEL 24-J

24-J in "standard" version was a four-seater bargain.

Caught up in the aviation industry's frustration to introduce new and improved models for every new year, Fairchild naturally saw fit to participate, but somehow reluctantly. After all, how far can you go with improving an airplane without making drastic changes in the basic design? It is then commendable that Fairchild designers and engineers did solve the problem of making significant improvements without resorting to drastic change. The "Twenty Four" was already the finest airplane of its type, so Fairchild resorted to some ingenious redesigning that would offer improvement with the least disruption of basic design; all detail changes looked good and actually imparted a flavor of vast improvement. By better use of space an increase in cabin area length, width and height gave occupants substantially more room; the baggage compartment was now bigger and a convenient hat shelf was provided behind the rear seat. Getting in and out was also made easier. Even the windows were redesigned for convenience and better visibility. There were some aerodynamic changes too that gave the new "24" even better handling characteristics; the airplane now had a new "feel." To accomplish this the wing was mounted further back for a better C. G. (center of gravity) position, the fuselage shape was recontoured to more flowing lines, fin and rudder area was increased, and the landing gear was "cleaned up" a little. These were not drastic changes, and hardly noticeable, but they did create better responsiveness and an improvement in all-around stability. The "Twenty Four" had always been easy to fly, but now it was that much

easier. Pilots who were familiar with characteristics of earlier models were asked to fly and to evaluate this new "24" for 1938, and to a man they agreed it was now an even better airplane. Knowing that this airplane would be used by commercial pilots for profit, and private owners for fun and convenience, it was offered in a "Standard" version and a "Deluxe" version. In reflection, even Fairchild was surprised at what engineers can really do when asked to offer marketable improvement without resorting to drastic change. The "Twenty Four" design was now about 7 years old, but yearly design changes were often so subtle in all this time that it seemed the airplane had hardly changed at all.

The Fairchild model 24-J for 1938 was a light, high-winged cabin monoplane with seating arranged for four. It still looked very much like earlier models, but it was surprisingly different. Without gaining much more bulk the 24-J now had ample room for 4 people, room for piles of luggage, room for many more items that added to comfort, and all this with only a slight gain in total weight. This airplane was certainly a good example of brilliant engineering. Knowing that as many commercial pilots as private owner pilots would be interested in this airplane for different reasons, Fairchild offered the 24-J in both a "Standard" working version, and a plush and fancy "Deluxe" version. Owners of the "Standard" version had to do without wing flaps, wheel pants, plush interiors, and hand-rubbed paint jobs, but the saving was more than $600. As the specifications were laid out there were many objectives to be met when

24-J in "deluxe" version was ideal for family or business.

engineers were designing the "Twenty Four" for 1938, and Fairchild was later proud to boast that every one of these objectives were met, plus a few thrown in for good measure. As powered with the 7 cyl. Warner "Super Scarab" engine of 145 h.p. the model 24-J was quite an airplane. Looking at the figures we can see no appreciable performance gain to speak of, but the bonus was in the extra room, the extra payload, and extra equipment that was piled into this ship without penalizing its overall performance. The amiable "24" was always a nice flying airplane, but many were saying that the 24-J had a very nice feel to it, flying perhaps easier and even better. Stability was improved with a change in the C. G. and a larger tail-group, but responsiveness was not at all affected. The 24-J would "spin" they say, if deliberately aggravated into it, but recovery often required less than a full turn; that's downright decent. They tell too that this airplane was designed primarily for inexperienced or low-time pilots, but even the high-time pilots were enjoying it. The type certificate for the model 24-J was issued retroactive to 10-31-37 and some 40 examples of this model were manufactured by the Fairchild Aircraft Corp. at Hagerstown, Md.

Listed below are specifications and performance data for the Fairchild model 24-J as powered with Warner "Super Scarab" (Series 50 or 50A) engine rated 145 h.p. at 2050 r.p.m. at sea level; length overall 23'9"; height overall 7'3"; wingspan 36'4"; wing chord 66"; total wing area 174.3 sq. ft.; airfoil (NACA) N-22; wt. empty 1415 lbs.; useful load 1135 lbs.; payload with 40 gal. fuel 702 lbs. (3 pass., 170 lbs. bag., & 22 lbs. extras); gross wt. 2550 lbs.; max. speed 132 at sea level; cruising speed (.75 power) 120 at 8500 ft.; landing speed (with flaps) 48; take-off run approx. 550 ft.; climb 700 ft. first min. at sea level; service ceiling 15,000 ft.; gas cap. 40 gal.;

oil cap. 3 gal.; cruising range (.75 power) at 9 gal. per hour 500 miles; price $6190 at the factory. The model 24-J also eligible as seaplane on Edo 45-2880 twin-float gear at 2750 lbs. gross wt. The "Deluxe" version was 66 lbs. heavier when empty than the "Standard" version; gross wt. same for both.

The fuselage framework was built up of welded 4130 steel tubing, faired liberally to a shape with hardwood formers and fairing strips, then fabric covered. The entire fuselage was recontoured to allow insulation, wiring, and controls to be fitted to outside of the fuselage frame; thus a better use of space gave substantially more room inside. A relocated step and wider doors offered easier entry; the rear seat was now 42 in. wide for more comfort. Pilot's seat was adjustable and all seats were contoured for comfort; extra pieces of luggage could be stored under the rear seat, and radio gear could be mounted under front seats. The windshield was now molded into a curve for better airflow, and side windows could be cranked down if desired. Dual stick-type controls were provided, and dual brake pedals were optional. Alteration of ceiling lines added 3 in. to head room, and length of cabin was increased by 15 in. to provide for a 7 cu. ft. baggage compartment behind the rear seat. The robust wing framework, in 2 panels, was built up of solid spruce spars routed to an I-beam section with spruce and plywood truss-type wing ribs; the leading edges were covered with dural metal sheet and the completed framework was covered in fabric. The split-type wing flaps of 12 sq. ft. area were manually operated and were quite effective; ball-bearing mounted ailerons were of the (offset hinge) Freise type. In fact, all engine and plane controls were mounted in ball bearings, and were smooth as silk. A 20 gal. fuel tank was mounted in root end of each wing-half; 30 gal. tanks were optional. The hefty outrigger landing gear of 111 in. tread was cleaned up considerably, and tied in geometrically with the wing bracing struts for a very strong truss; 6.50x10 Warner wheels were fitted with brakes. The landing gear used Fairchild long-stroke, oil-spring shock struts; streamlined metal wheel pants were optional. A swiveling tail wheel was standard, but a steerable assembly was optional. The cantilever tail-group of increased area was a composite structure; the fixed horizontal stabilizer and the vertical fin were a spruce and plywood framework covered with plywood sheet. The rudder and elevators were of welded steel tubing, and covered with fabric; an adjustable "trim tab" was mounted on one elevator. A Flottorp wooden prop, electric engine starter, battery, dual controls, wiring for navigation lights, wheel brakes, hub fairings, and first-aid kit were furnished on "Standard" version; the "Deluxe" version was equipped with all this, plus a generator, wing flaps, navigation lights, cabin lights, cabin heater & fresh-air vents, deluxe upholstery, custom interior trim, wheel pants, steerable tail wheel, bonding & shielding, 7.50x10 wheels & tires, fire extinguisher, and hand-rubbed finish. A Curtiss-Reed metal prop, dual brake pedals, oil cooler, landing lights, paraflares, radio gear, and Edo pontoons were optional The next Fairchild development was the Ranger-powered model 24-K as described here in the chapter for ATC # 667.

Listed below are model 24-J entries as gleaned from registration records:

NC-19179;	24-J	(# 3400)	Warner 145
-20601;	"	(# 3401)	"
-20600;	"	(# 3402)	"
-20602;	"	(# 3403)	"
-20603;	"	(# 3404)	"
-20604;	"	(# 3405)	"
NC-303;	"	(# 3406)	"
-20615;	"	(# 3407)	"
-20616;	"	(# 3408)	"
-20617;	"	(# 3409)	"
-20618;	"	(# 3410)	"
;	"	(# 3411)	"
;	"	(# 3412)	"
;	"	(# 3413)	"
;	"	(# 3414)	"
;	"	(# 3415)	"
;	"	(# 3416)	"
;	"	(# 3417)	"
-18670;	"	(# 3418)	"
-19149;	"	(# 3500)	"
-19177;	"	(# 3501)	"
-19178;	"	(# 3502)	"
-19180;	"	(# 3503)	"
-19181;	"	(# 3504)	"
-19182;	"	(# 3505)	"
-19183;	"	(# 3506)	"
-19184;	"	(# 3507)	"
-19185;	"	(# 3508)	"
-20607;	"	(# 3509)	"
-20608;	"	(# 3510)	"
-20609;	"	(# 3511)	"
-20622;	"	(# 3512)	"
-20623;	"	(# 3513)	"
-20624;	"	(# 3514)	"
-20625;	"	(# 3515)	"
-18672;	"	(# 3516)	"
-18673;	"	(# 3517)	"
-18674;	"	(# 3518)	"
-18675;	"	(# 3519)	"
NC-1307;	"	(# 3520)	"
-18677;	"	(# 3521)	"
-18678;	"	(# 3522)	"
-18679;	"	(# 3523)	"
NC-19176;	"	(#)	"

This approval for ser. # 3440 and up ser. # 3406 also registered as NC-3033; ser. # 3409 to Alaska; ser. # 3410 and # 3521 to Puerto Rico; ser. # 3411-3416 to Aerial Transport Co. of Siam; ser. # 3506 to Alaska; ser. # 3509 on floats; ser. no. for NC-19176 is unknown; one 24-J served in USAAF as UC-61B; this approval expired 4-27-43.

24-J "deluxe" shows its Raymond Loewy styling.

ATC # 664
(10-30-37)
WACO, MODEL AGC-8

AGC-8 was a favorite in the "Custom Cabin" line.

The Waco models AGC-8 and ZGC-8 were part of the "Custom Cabin" line offered for 1938. Traditionally, Waco Aircraft leveled this line of airplanes at aviation-minded sportsmen and men of big business because this line of custom airplanes had the most appeal to this type of user. A versatile airplane such as this was very useful in the pursuit of business because contacts more often had to be made in towns where airlines never came; the "Waco" could go just about anywhere. Companies found this airplane an efficient tool that expedited business matters quickly, and it always made favorable impressions on those that were visited. Government services also found this "Custom" line an ideal vehicle for their various purposes, an airplane which assured more success in the carrying out of their particular function. The Dept. of Commerce in years past had been an enthusiastic user of "Waco" airplanes, the Bureau of Air Commerce also had many "Waco" airplanes in its fleet, and now the newly organized Civil Aeronautics Authority (CAA) had just placed an order for 8 of the Jacobs-powered model AGC-8. These custom-fitted airplanes (AGC-8) were placed in strategic points around the country for use by government inspectors. Other airplanes of this model went to the Forestry Div. in Oregon, to the TWA airline at its base in Kansas City, to the New York Dai-

ly News, and so on; there were several air-minded sportsmen on the list also. The model ZGC-8 was a similar airplane with slightly less power that appealed to the more economy-minded user; one of these was shipped off to the Provincial Police in Argentina, and one was shipped off to Bombay, India. Others went to fixed-base operators here in this country who could use their "Waco" for just about anything. It is appropriate to note here too that every one of these airplanes was originally built to order, and hand-crafted exactly to the customer's needs or tastes; some were very, very elegant, but all were designed for a certain use or purpose, and designed to please that certain customer.

The Waco models AGC-8 and ZGC-8 were "Custom Cabin" biplanes with seating normally arranged for 4 or 5. For the most part these were elegant airplanes; they were plush, comfortable airplanes with the ability to go almost anywhere, and pride enough to mix with any company. The "Custom Cabin" biplanes for the 1938 season, being built to order, had that subtle tailored look that reflected mechanical simplicity but with that certain glow of elegance; most certainly a nice combination of fashion and function. As a personal-type conveyance the 1938 "Custom Cabin" line was leveled primarily at the fly-for-fun sportsman, and at men of business, but any one of these airplanes could

AGC-8 as "work horse" with Forestry Div.

put on an apron over its finery and work alongside the best of them. By design and the builder's promise the C-8 series was not basically a working airplane, but a twelve-year heritage of pioneer spirit could still come to the surface when needed. Versatility was the plus built into every "Waco" airplane. The new AGC-8 and ZGC-8, both powered by "Jacobs" engines, were primarily small transports and they did their job well; quite a few of them were gaily finished and lavishly equipped, reflecting the owner's taste and the size of his wallet. As powered with the Jacobs L-6 engine of 300-330 h.p. the model AGC-8 had ample "horses" to play with so performance was relatively high, and it could get downright frisky at times. This airplane (AGC-8) was capable, and it was clearly the favorite of the two offered here. As powered with the Jacobs L-5 engine of 285 h.p. the ZGC-8 gave up only very little in performance because of less power, and it was perhaps every bit as capable, if not as aggressive. Inherently stable, with the self-control of good manners, both of these airplanes were a distinct pleasure to fly, fun to operate, and quite easy to own. A fully-equipped C-8 bedecked with tasteful colors and matching trim was a joy to behold, you can be assured, and it always turned heads wherever it went. The type certificate for the models AGC-8 and ZGC-8 was issued 10-30-37 and 21 of these were manufactured altogether by the Waco Aircraft Co. at Troy, Ohio.

Listed below are specifications and performance data for the Waco model ZGC-8 as powered with Jacobs L-5C engine rated 285 h.p. at 2000 r.p.m. at sea level (300 h.p. was available for takeoff); length overall 27'7"; height overall 8'7"; wingspan upper 34'9"; winspan lower 24'6"; wing chord upper 72"; wing chord lower 48"; wing area upper 168 sq. ft.; wing area lower 78 sq. ft.; total wing area 246 sq. ft.; airfoil Clark Y; wt. empty 2328 lbs.; useful load 1472 lbs.; payload with 70 gal. fuel 844 lbs. (4 pass. & 164 lbs. for bag. & extras); gross wt. 3800 lbs.; max. speed 164 at sea level; cruising speed (1900 r.p.m.) 145 at sea level; cruising speed (.75 power) 155 at 6000 ft.; landing speed (with flaps) 55; climb 800 ft. first min. at sea level; service ceiling 14,000 ft.; gas cap. normal 70 gal.; gas cap. max. 95 gal.; oil cap. 5-6 gal.; cruising range (best altitude) at 17 gal. per hour 600 miles; price $9895 at factory.

Specifications and other data for Waco model AGC-8 as powered with Jacobs L-6 engine rated 300 h.p. at 2100 r.p.m. at 3700 ft. (330 h.p. available for takeoff) same as above except as follows; wt. empty 2363 lbs.; useful load 1437 lbs.; payload with 70 gal. fuel 809 lbs. (4 pass. & 129 lbs. for bag. & extras); gross wt. 3800 lbs.; max. speed 170 at sea level; cruising speed (.75 power) 149 at sea level; cruising speed (.75 power) 161 at 6000 ft.; landing speed (with flaps) 55; climb 900 ft. first min. at sea level; ser. ceiling 15,500 ft.; gas cap. 70-95 gal.; oil cap. 5-6 gal.; cruising range (best altitude) at 18 gal. per hour 600 miles; price $10,495 at factory. The AGC-8 was eligible with Hamilton-Standard controllable propeller for an overall increase in performance.

The construction details and general arrangement of Waco models AGC-8 and ZGC-8 were typical to that of other models in the "Custom Cabin" line, including the following. The spacious interior was heavily lined with insulating material, and upholstered in fine broadcloth fabrics; mohairs, leather, or leather trim were optional. The entry door was on the left side, but a door on the right side was available also. A throw-over control wheel was standard but a Y-type column with 2 control wheels was optional. The front seats were adjustable, and all seats were filled with coil springs and were well padded. A large baggage compartment with allowance for 100 lbs. was behind the rear seat with access from inside or out; the top of the compartment was arranged as a hat-and-coat shelf. Cabin vents and a cabin heater kept the interior at a comfortable level. A 35 gal. fuel tank was mounted in each upper wing-root; 47.5 gal. tanks were optional. An extra 25 gal. tank could be mounted under rear seat, but this then held the airplane to 4 occupants. Wing flaps (vacuum-operated) were mounted in trailing edge of upper wing; flaps not to be lowered above 100 m.p.h. The robust landing gear of 108 in. tread used oil-spring shock struts; 7.50X10 wheels with pedal-operated hydraulic brakes were fitted with 8.50x10 low-pressure tires. Wheels were normally faired with hub fairings and metal cuffs, but streamlined wheel pants were optional. The swiveling tail wheel was fitted with a 10.5 in. streamlined tire; a tail wheel (fore & aft) lock was available. The tail group of composite structure had aerodynamic balance on rudder and elevators; one elevator was fitted with adjustable trim tab. Trim tab on rudder was fixed, but could be adjusted on the ground. A Curtiss-Reed metal prop, electric engine starter, battery, generator, oil cooler, hydraulic wheel brakes, wheel cuffs, cabin vents, cabin heater, fire extingusher, throw-over control wheel, swiveling tail wheel, navigation lights, wing flaps, cabin lights, assist ropes, parking brake, ash trays, and first-aid kit were standard equipment. A Hamilton-Standard controllable prop, wheel pants, tail wheel lock, landing lights, paraflares, bonding & shielding for radio, radio gear, extra fuel cap. to 120 gal., extra door (right side) & wingwalk, cargo-type interior, leather upholstery, extra instruments, and custom colors were optional. The next Waco

development was the Wright-powered model EGC-8 as described here in the chapter for ATC # 665.

Listed below are AGC-8 and ZGC-8 entries as gleaned from company records:

NC-2272;	AGC-8	(# 5001) Jacobs L-6
NC-19355;	ZGC-8	(# 5050) Jacobs L-5
;	ZGC-8	(# 5053) "
NC-19383;	AGC-8	(# 5054) Jacobs L-6
-19360;	ZGC-8	(# 5056) Jacobs L-5
-19364;	AGC-8	(# 5057) Jacobs L-6
VT-AKD;	ZGC-8	(# 5060) Jacobs L-5
NC-2284;	AGC-8	(# 5061) Jacobs L-6
NC-2312;	"	(# 5063) "
NC-2334;	"	(# 5065) "
-20909;	"	(# 5066) "
-20908;	"	(# 5067) "
-20905;	"	(# 5068) "
NC-53E;	"	(# 5069) "
NC-59;	"	(# 5070) "
NC-60;	"	(# 5071) "
NC-61;	"	(# 5072) "
NC-62;	"	(# 5073) "
NC-104;	"	(# 5074) "
NC-103;	"	(# 5077) "
NC-8;	"	(# 5078) "

This approval for ser. # 5001 and up; ser. # 5001 first tested as ZGC-8; ser. # 5043 del. to Provincial Police of Argentina; ser. # 5057 later modified to EGC-8; ser. # 5060 del. to Bombay, India; ser. # 5061 del. to New York Daily News; ser. # 5063 del. to TWA at Kansas City; ser. # 5065 later as EGC-8; ser. # 5068 del. to Forestry Div. of Oregon; ser. # 5069-70-71-72-73-74 and 5077-78 del. to CAA for use in Santa Monica, Chicago, Long Island, Fort Worth, and Washington, D.C.; 2 of AGC-8 del. to USAAF in 1942 as UC-72P; this approval expired 2-28-41.

ATC # 665
(10-30-37)
WACO, MODEL EGC-8

EGC-8 leveled at those who preferred Wright engines.

Waco Aircraft had a conservative policy—advance steadily, but never recklessly. Of course, we can see here that the Waco "Custom Cabin" biplane for 1938-39 was as elegant as ever if not even more so; this airplane was especially and only built to customer order, so the examples that rolled off the line as limited editions were really something to see. Each glistening airplane reflected the tastes of an individual, and also the amount of money he was willing to spend on his particular airplane. Needless to say, some of the "Custom Waco" were among the finest airplanes to be seen anywhere. There were many personal requirements that went in to make up a "Custom Cabin" airplane and one of the most important items was the engine. Pilots, owners, and operators each had very definite opinions about airplane engines, and in most cases would specify a certain model engine and settle for no other. That is why the "Waco Custom" biplane was offered with such a variety of engines, just to provide a satisfactory choice. Those that preferred the ever popular 7 cyl. Wright engine were offered the model EGC-8, the unobtrusively elegant "Custom Cabin" that was powered with the Wright R-760-E2 engine rated 320 h.p.; overall, this was a particularly good combination. The Waco model EGC-8 was not represented in very large number, and this is understandable because it was a special, custom-

crafted, and expensive airplane built to order; not all that many people deemed it necessary to have this particular combination. However, the EGC-8 was specifically picked for its engine, for its reliability, its high performance, and its almost uncanny ability to frequent hard-to-reach places. Sportsmen, and even businessmen, invariably picked some of the darndest places to go with an airplane, and they no doubt felt assured the capable EGC-8 would get them there, and back. The "Custom" line for 1938-39 was attracting some impressive clientele, and every airplane built was a showcase of tribute to the "Waco" tradition.

The Waco model EGC-8 was a "Custom Cabin" biplane with seating arranged for 4 or 5. As the top of the line for the 1938-39 season the EGC-8 was bulkier and heavier by comparison with past examples, but ability remained just as good in most cases, and even better in some cases. The subtle changes were barely noticeable, but the change of a curve here, an angle there, or perhaps a dimension was the secret that allowed progressively bigger loads to be piled into the "Custom Cabin" without detriment to its temperament, or ability. On the inside the new EGC-8 was no less than elegant, and on the outside the airframe was a nice balance of form and bulk; a shape that was quite distinctive yet very pleasant. In proper cir-

A former EGC-8 shown here in test with 6 cyl. Menasco engine.

cumstance the EGC-8 was a rather snooty airplane, especially if fitted like a limousine for the carriage trade, but it also could become all things to its owner; it was an amiable airplane and it aimed to please. It is of particular interest to note that for some owners this airplane was their second or third "Waco"—certainly it must take a good airplane to command such devotion. As powered with the 7 cyl. Wright R-760-E2 engine of 320 h.p., the model EGC-8 was capable of very high performance, a performance somewhat deceiving; it actually was doing better than one would expect, because it looked so easy. It also had the knack of slipping into hard-to-reach places, and worked its way out in a fashion that was amazing. It required a certain amount of skill to get the best out of this airplane, but its willingness to respond created an affectionate bond between this airplane and its pilot. Waco Aircraft was proud of their "Custom Cabin" line, and pointed to the EGC-8 as perhaps the finest one they had ever built; not many of the EGC-8 were built, but every one of them was a credit to its builder. "It makes good sense to own a Waco." The type certificate for the model EGC-8 was issued 10-30-37 and some 7 examples of this model were manufactured by the Waco Aircraft Co. at Troy, Ohio. Clayton J. Brukner was pres. & gen. mgr.; Lee N. Brutus was V.P. & treas.; L. E. St. John was sec.; Hugh R. Perry was sales mgr.; A. Francis Arcier was chf. engr.; and R. A. Pearson was factory superintendent.

Listed below are specifications and performance data for the Waco model EGC-8 as powered with Wright R-760-E2 engine rated 320 h.p. at 2200 r.p.m. at sea level (350 h.p. available for takeoff); length overall 27'4"; height overall 8'7"; wingspan upper 34'9"; wingspan lower 24'6"; wing chord upper 72"; wing chord lower 48"; wing area upper 168 sq. ft.; wing area lower 78 sq. ft.; total wing area 246 sq. ft.; airfoil Clark Y; wt. empty 2432 lbs.; useful load 1368 lbs.; payload with 95 gal. fuel 583 lbs. (3 pass. & 73 lbs. bag.); payload with 60 gal. fuel 793 lbs. (4 pass. & 113 lbs. bag.); gross wt. 3800 lbs.; max. speed 171 at sea level; cruising speed (1900 r.p.m.) 147 at sea level; cruising speed (.75 power) 159 at best altitude; landing speed (with flaps) 55; climb 980 ft. first min. at sea level; service ceiling 15,500 ft.; gas cap. max. 95 gal.; oil cap. 6 gal.; cruising range (.75 power) at 17.5 gal. per hour with 60 gal. was 510 miles—with 95 gal. was 780 miles; price $12,860 at factory. The model EGC-8 was eligible with Hamilton-Standard controllable propeller.

The construction details and general arrangement of the model EGC-8 were typical to that of the AGC-8 as described here in the previous chapter. The only significant difference in the EGC-8 was installation of the Wright engine and any modifications necessary to this combination. The "Custom" (C-8) line were more or less alike, and the engine installed decided the airplane's final designation. In fact, according to registry, a ZGC-8 and 2 of the AGC-8 were later modified to EGC-8 with installation of the Wright engine. Beautifully set up for cross-country commuting, the EGC-8 carried 95 gal. of fuel; a 47.5 gal. tank in each upper wing root. An extra 25 gal. tank could be mounted under rear seat, but this then held the airplane to 4 occupants only. Most of the EGC-8 were plush personal-type airplanes, but a cargo-type version with extra door and wing-walk on the right side was available. The standard exterior finish for the C-8 series was Gunmetal Gray, but custom colors were usually ordered. A Curtiss-Reed metal prop, electric engine starter, battery, generator, oil cooler, cabin vents, cabin heater, cabin lights, hydraulic wheel brakes, parking brake, wheel cuffs, swiveling tail wheel, throw-over control wheel, fire extinguisher, wing flaps, landing lights, ash trays, assist ropes, safety belts, and first-aid kit were standard equipment. A Hamilton-Standard controllable prop, wheel pants, tail wheel lock, bonding & sheilding for radio, radio gear, paraflares, pressure-type fire extinguisher, extra fuel cap. to 120 gal., extra door & wingwalk, cargo-type interior, Y-type control column, extra instruments, leather upholstery, and custom colors were optional. The next Waco development was the export-type model JHD as described here in the chapter for ATC # 670.

Listed below are EGC-8 entries as gleaned from company records:

| NC-19354; | EGC-8 | (# 5002) | Wright 320 |
| ; | " | (# 5051) | " |

-19365;	"	(# 5055)	"
-19382;	"	(# 5058)	"
-19375;	"	(# 5059)	"
NC-2329;	"	(# 5062)	"
NC-2279;	"	(# 5064)	"

This approval for ser. # 5051 and up; ser. # 5051 del. to Adastra Airways, Ltd., Australia; ser. # 5055 del. to State of Ohio; ser. # 5058 del. to Western Air Express in Burbank; ser. # 5064 del. to Henry King of Hollywood; ser. # 5002 was eligible when modified to conform; 4 of the EGC-8 were mustered into USAAF service as UC-72B during WW2.

A scuffed-up EGC-8 that once belonged to Western Air Express.

Lockheed 14-F62 as operated by Royal Dutch Airlines.

One of the outstanding things about Lockheed's model 14-F62 was the fact that of the 21 airplanes that were built in this model every one was boxed and shipped overseas. The largest order came from KLM (Royal Dutch Air Lines) who had placed an order for 11 airplanes; the first was delivered in Feb. of 1938. As they were delivered, 3 of the 14-F62 were put into service on the continent of Europe, 3 were to be used in the Dutch West Indies, and 5 of the 14-F62 were flown to Batavia in the Dutch East Indies. Here they were to be used by KNILM, the division of KLM that served the Orient. The British Overseas Airways ordered 8 of the 14-F62 and it was one of these that carried Neville Chamberlain to that historic visit with Adolph Hitler. The last 2 of the 14-F62, built in 1939, were delivered to Italy. In comparison the Lockheed model 14-F62 was not any different from the earlier 14-H and 14-H2 except for installation of Wright engines instead of Pratt & Whitney engines. The model 14-F62 (sometimes labeled 14-WF62) was powered with 2 of the big 9 cyl. geared and supercharged Wright "Cyclone" SGR-1820-F62 engines that were rated 760 h.p. at an altitude of 5800 ft.; a whopping 900 h.p. was available for takeoff. The routes of KLM and KNILM were over some of the most dismal terrain and through some of the most treacherous weather in the world, so it is commendable they chose the "Lockheed 14" to uphold their outstanding reputation for service. There was such a desperate need for airplanes in Europe at this time because their own factories

could not turn out enough to meet the critical demands. Therefore, they turned to the U.S.A. for whatever they could buy, but they bought only those airplanes they couldn't build for themselves. American transports undoubtedly were the best and the most advanced in the world, so this is what they were buying.

The Lockheed model 14-F62 was a robust, all-metal, twin-engined monoplane with seating arranged for 11 passengers and a crew of three; on some routes the crew was increased to 4 and payload was cut to 10 passengers, plus an allowable weight for baggage and cargo. The Model 14 was generally considered a low-winged monoplane, but its high mounting in the fuselage was such to expose belly compartments that were meant for cargo; this deep belly made it come very close to the mid-wing configuration. It was also rumored early that the "14" was especially designed to be converted quickly into a bomber if need be, so the belly would be a logical place for the bomb bay. Nonetheless, the interior accommodations for airline service were quite spacious, very comfortable, and rather quiet. The Royal Dutch Air Lines (KLM) had particularly good luck with Wright engines on its far-flung routes, so there is reasoning why they picked the model 14-F62 with its supercharged "Cyclone" engines; the 14-F62 provided Europe with the fastest air transportation available, this on the KLM routes radiating from Amsterdam in Holland. The KLM also used some of its 14-F62 in the Dutch West Indies linking with LAV in Venezuela; LAV was operating the Lockheed 14-

14-F62 of British Airways carried Neville Chamberlain to visit with Hitler.

H2 as was TACA that served Central America. The Royal Netherlands Indies Airways (KNILM) a division of KLM serving the Orient, flew the 14-F62 out of Batavia on routes in the Dutch East Indies until wartime harassment forced them to flee. The British Overseas Airways also flew the 14-F62 as they radiated outward on routes from England. As powered with 2 of the supercharged Wright "Cyclone" engines the model 14-F62 had a terrific performance that was well adapted to short hops and frequent stops; such flights were taxing on the airplane, and reliable high-performance was of great importance. Designed for a low power-loading, the 14-F62 was blessed with a hefty power reserve that instilled confidence and peace of mind over long stretches of water, or over high, jagged peaks. The Cyclone-powered 14-F62, like any "Fourteen," was a working airplane and pilots had to work at it to fly it well, but they always enjoyed it. The robust "Super Electra" (Model 14) had hidden muscle, abundance of stamina, and constant reliability in situations where it counted, but she was first and always a gracious lady; that is what they say. The type certificate for the model 14-F62 was issued 10-30-37 and 21 examples were manufactured by the Lockheed Aircraft Corp. at Burbank, Calif. Lockheed Aircraft now had about 2000 employees. There were no examples of the 14-F62 delivered here in the U.S.A.

Listed below are specifications and performance data for the Lockheed model 14-F62 as powered with 2 Wright "Cyclone" SGR-1820-F62 engines rated 760 h.p. at 2100 r.p.m. at 5800 ft. (900 h.p. at 2350 r.p.m. available for takeoff); length overall 44'4"; height overall 11'5"; wingspan 65'6"; wing chord at root 153"; wing chord at tip 48"; total wing area (including fuselage section) 551 sq. ft.; airfoil NACA-23000 series; wt. empty 10,750 lbs.; useful load 6750 lbs.; payload with 330 gal. fuel 4010 lbs. (11 pass. & 2140 lbs. bag.-cargo); payload with 644 gal. fuel 2146 lbs. (10 pass. & 446 lbs. bag.-cargo); gross wt. (provisional for airline use) 17,500 lbs.; max. speed 250 at 5800 ft.; cruising speed (.75 power) 228 at 13,000 ft.; cruising speed (.65 power) 215 at 5800 ft.; landing speed (with flaps) 65; climb 1520 ft. first min. at sea level; ser. ceiling 24,500 ft.; gas cap. max. 644 gal.; oil cap. max. 44 gal.; cruising range (.75 power) at 88 gal. per hour (with 330 gal.) 850 miles; no price was announced. The SGR-1820-F62 engine was later rerated to deliver 810 h.p. at 2350 r.p.m. at 6000 ft.; some improvement in performance would be noted.

The construction details and general arrangement of the Lockeed model 14-F62 were similar to the model 14-H as described here in the chapter for ATC # 657, including the following. The most significant difference in the 14-F62 was installation of the big supercharged Wright "Cyclone" engines, and any modifications necessary to this combination. The engines were fastened to "Lord" rubber mounts, and fitted with Hamilton-Standard "constant-speed" propellers; instrument panels were also fastened to "Lord" rubber mounts to lessen vibration to the various gauges. The 14-F62 were also fitted with a galley for serving hot meals, and complete lavatory for passenger comfort. Cold drinking water was also available. Fire extinguisher bottles and flashlights were accessible to the pilots and to the stewardess. The "14" was now available with a de-icing system for the propellers, and the wings; abrasion strips were also fitted to protect leading edges of the tail group. The 14-F62 was allowed a provisional gross wt. of 17,500 lbs. for airline use (standard gross wt. was 15,650 lbs.), but was not allowed to land at this greater weight; more than 2000 lbs. of fuel would have to be dumped. A pantry, extra water tank, plush carpeting, custom Laidlow upholstery, a radio operator's station, and emergency exits were now also available for the Model 14. It is fitting to mention that Harlan D. Fowler was inventor of the "Fowler Flap," a variable-area wing flap that revolutionized the use of "wing flaps" on transport airplanes. The elevators, rudders, and left aileron were fitted with adjustable "trim tabs." Hamilton-Standard props, electric engine starters, a generator, battery, full set of airline-type equipment, fuel pumps, hydraulic pumps, oil coolers, carburetor heaters, dual controls, pressure-type fire extinguisher, cabin ventilators, cabin heaters, cabin lights, emergency exits, navigation lights, landing lights, paraflares, a galley, lavatory, cabin carpet, and first-aid kit were standard equipment. Bonding & shielding, radio gear, de-icing equipment, extra battery, extra generator, fuel dump valves, and automatic-pilot were optional. The next Lockheed 14 development was the model 14-G3B as described here in the chapter for ATC # 673.

PJ-AIP;   14-F62   (# 1410) Wright 760

PK-AFM;	"	(# 1411)	"
PJ-AIT;	"	(# 1412)	"
PH-APE;	"	(# 1413)	"
PK-AFN;	"	(# 1414)	"
PK-AFO;	"	(# 1415)	"
PJ-AIK;	"	(# 1440)	"
PJ-AIM;	"	(# 1441)	"
PK-AFP;	"	(# 1442)	"
PK-AFQ;	"	(# 1443)	"
PH-ASL;	"	(# 1444)	"
G-AFGN;	"	(# 1467)	"
G-AFGO;	"	(# 1468)	"
G-AFGP;	"	(# 1469)	"
G-AFGR;	"	(# 1470)	"
G-AFKD;	"	(# 1484)	"
G-AFKE;	"	(# 1485)	"
G-AFMD;	"	(# 1490)	"
G-AFMR;	"	(# 1491)	"
EI-ABV;	"	(# 1497)	"
EI-ABW;	"	(# 1498)	"

This approval for ser. # 1410 and up; ser. # 1410, 1412-13, 1440-41, 1444 del. to KLM; ser. # 1411, 1414-15, 1442-43 del. to KNILM; ser. # 1467-70, 1484-85, 1490-91 del. to BOA; ser. # 1497-98 del. to Italy; this approval expired 1-24-41.

14-F62 shows off its "Cyclone" engines and 3-bladed props.

24-K in "standard" version was a great value.

Introduced as a companion model to the 24-J, the Ranger-powered model 24-K was offered at about the same time, and in the "Deluxe" version at least, was undoubtedly the "Grand Dame" of the Fairchild lineup for 1938. Heretofore, the radial-powered "Twenty Four" had always been the clear favorite, but the inline-powered version was steadily gaining in popularity, and already many looked to it as a better choice. The long-nosed, Ranger-powered model 24-K was truly a handsome airplane, truly handsome in every way, and it was drawing glances from people that could well afford the more expensive, or even the very best. It is not surprising then that the roster of owners contained names of sportsmen, millionaires, and some of the best known names in business. The "Twenty Four" for 1938 was a beautifully engineered airplane, and it is commendable that so much more room, comfort, and utility were built into the airplane without the gain of much bulk, and a whole lot of weight. With very little reservation we have to agree with company statements that it was the best airplane of its type, and comparable to some airplanes that cost nearly twice as much. The smooth-running (6 cyl.) "Ranger" engine was steadily improved and it too was becoming a very fine powerplant; for 1938 it was introduced as the 6-410-B which featured a modest increase in (cu. in.) displacement and several mechanical improvements.. The 6-410-B engine was capable of delivering up to 165 h.p. with surprising

economy, and very little maintenance. Many manufacturers were now trying to reach the private owner who flew his own light airplane, so the shared business in the market for 3 or 4 place airplanes was not all that much to each builder, but Fairchild always did have an inside track to this business, and usually got a large part of the share. The model 24-K was also offered in a "Standard" version that lacked some of the finery and gadgetry, but it had all that was needed to do a good job in whatever the operator decided to do. The fussed-with "Deluxe" version was, of course, loaded with finery and all kinds of gadgetry; it was truly an airplane that anyone would be proud to own.

The Fairchild model 24-K for 1938 was a light, high-winged cabin monoplane with seating arranged for four. It still looked very much like earlier models, but it was surprisingly different. In a walk up to it one got the feeling of poise and strength; it did seem rather massive, braced this way and that with oversized members for strength and reliability. Without gaining all that much bulk the 24-K now had ample room for 4 people, room for literally piles of baggage, so many more items to assure comfort, and all this with only a slight gain in total weight. True, she was more buxom now and did put on a little bit of weight, but she got around quite well and looked better than ever. This airplane was certainly a good example of brilliant engineering. Knowing that as many commercial pilots as

24-K in "deluxe" version spared no expense for convenience and comfort.

private owner pilots would be interested in this airplane for different reasons, Fairchild offered the 24-K in both a "Standard" working version and a plush, fancied-up "Deluxe" version. Owners of the "Standard" version had to get by without wing flaps, wheel pants, plush interior and hand-rubbed paint jobs, but the saving was more than $600 and 65 lbs. was added to the payload. The good looking "Deluxe" version was, of course, very plush and fitted with gadgetry to the heart's content; then too, if it wasn't included it was at least available as an option. Fairchild Aircraft was mighty proud of the 24-K and they had a right to be; even "the boss" (Sherman Fairchild) asked to have one of these at his disposal. As powered with the 6 cyl. aircooled inverted inline "Ranger" 6-410-B engine of 150-165 h.p., the 24-K had power enough for a very good all around performance, and could even become real sassy at times. Normally, this ship was very stable, somewhat easier to fly, and she was a perfect lady at all times; you couldn't help but like her immediately. She was reluctant to "spin," but if you worked at it she would do it, and most often recover in less than a turn. She was kind to the inexperienced, but showed her devilish side in the hands of a good pilot. A lot of care and concern went into the manufacture of the "24" for 1938 and these efforts were very evident. The type certificate for the model 24-K was issued 2-14-38 and some 34 examples of this model were manufactured by the Fairchild Aircraft Corp. at Hagerstown, Md. The team of Fairchild designers and engineers was led by A. J. Thieblot.

Listed below are specifications and performance data for the Fairchild model 24-K as powered with Ranger 6-410-B1 engine rated 150

h.p. at 2350 r.p.m. at sea level (165 h.p. at 2450 r.p.m. for takeoff); length overall 24'10"; height overall 7'3"; wingspan 36'4"; wing chord 66"; total wing area 174.3 sq. ft.; airfoil (NACA) N-22; wt. empty 1496 lbs.; useful load 1054 lbs.; payload with 40 gal. fuel 621 lbs. (3 pass. & 111 lbs. bag.); gross wt. 2550 lbs.; max. speed 138 at sea level; cruising speed (.75 power) 124 at sea level; landing speed (with flaps) 48; takeoff run 500 ft.; climb 760 ft. first min. at sea level; ser. ceiling 16,000 ft.; gas cap. 40 gal.; oil cap. 3 gal.; cruising range (.75 power) at 9.5 gal. per hour 500 miles; price $6530 at factory. The model 24-K was also eligible as seaplane on Edo 45-2880 twin-float gear at 2750 lbs. gross wt. Figures above shown for "Standard" version; the "Deluxe" version was 65 lbs. heavier when empty, gross wt. was same for both.

The construction details and general arrangement of the model 24-K was typical to that of the new 24-J as described here in the chapter for ATC # 663. The only significant difference was installation of the 6 cyl. aircooled inverted inline "Ranger" engine, an installation that changed the whole front end of the airplane. The "Ranger" was encased in a tight-fitting removable cowl and provided with baffles to promote even cooling to all of the cylinders. Getting into this airplane was real easy, and the amount of room inside was quite surprising. The seats were soft and contoured for comfort, there was ample elbow-room for everybody, and there was also plenty of under-seat room for small luggage and radio equipment. The baggage compt. (7 cu. ft.) behind the rear seat was allowed 140 lbs., and the lid to it was used also as a shelf for hats, coats, and the like; a small compartment under rear seat was allowed 30 lbs. There was a

Seaplane (24-K) as personal plane of Juan Trippe, Pan Am prexy.

glove compartment in the dash-panel, map pockets on the side-walls, and gadget pockets on doors, and front seat-backs. Cabin vents and a cabin heater kept it cozy and comfortable inside, and large windows provided pretty good visibility. Crank-down windows and adjustable sun shades were provided for extra convenience. Dual stick-type controls were provided, and all controls (plane & engine) were mounted on ball bearings for smooth and almost effortless manipulation. Interior appointments boasted of rich fabrics with wood trim and nickeled hardware; the exterior boasted of a 16-coat, hand-rubbed finish, and several color combinations were optional. A Flottorp wooden prop, electric engine starter, battery, generator, oil cooler, carburetor heater, 6.50x10 wheels with brakes, hub fairings, 8 in. tail wheel, dual controls, wiring for navigation lights, cabin lights, cabin vents, and first-aid kit were standard equipment. A Curtiss-Reed metal prop, cabin heater, wing flaps, wheel pants, navigation lights, landing lights, paraflares, bonding & shielding for radio, steerable tail wheel, dual brake pedals, and hand-rubbed finish were listed as "Deluxe" equipment. Radio gear, skis, and Edo pontoons were optional for both versions. The next Fairchild development was the model 24-R9 as described in the chapter for ATC # 706.

Listed below are 24-K entries as gleaned from registration records:

NC-19176;	24-K	(# 3300)	6-410-B
-19186;	"	(# 3301)	"
-19187;	"	(# 3302)	"
-19188;	"	(# 3303)	"
-19189;	"	(# 3304)	"
-19190;	"	(# 3305)	"
-8495;	"	(# 3306)	"
-20614;	"	(# 3307)	"
-20626;	"	(# 3308)	"
-20627;	"	(# 3309)	"
-1328;	"	(# 3310)	"
-20629;	"	(# 3311)	"
:	"	(# 3312)	"
-20636;	"	(# 3313)	"
:	"	(# 3314)	"
-2639;	"	(# 3315)	"
:	"	(# 3316)	"
-20640;	"	(# 3317)	"
-20641;	"	(# 3318)	"
-20635;	"	(# 3319)	"
-20637;	"	(# 3320)	"
-18671;	"	(# 3321)	"
-18676;	"	(# 3322)	"
-18680;	"	(# 3323)	"
-18681;	"	(# 3324)	"
:	"	(# 3325)	"
-18689;	"	(#)	"

Ser. # 3327 thru # 3349 apparently not used.

-20605;	"	(# 3350)	"
-20606;	"	(# 3351)	"
-20610;	"	(# 3352)	"
-20611;	"	(# 3353)	"
-20612;	"	(# 3354)	"
-20630;	"	(# 3355)	"
-20613;	"	(# 3356)	"

;   "   (# 3357)   "
-20631;   "   (# 3358)   "

This approval for ser. # 3300 and up; ser. # 3305 del. to Juan Trippe of Pan Am on floats; ser. # 3310 del. to Wm. K. Vanderbilt; ser. # 3315 del. to Standard Oil Dev. Corp.; ser. 3317 was at disposal of Sherman Fairchild; ser. # 3320 del.

to Reader's Digest Assoc.; ser. # 3324 del. to South Bend Tool & Die; ser. # 3350 del. to Diamond K Ranch in N.M.; ser. # 3356 del. to Lear Dev. Corp.; no listing for ser. # 3312,3314,3316,-3357; ser. # 3325 was probably exported; 3 of 24-K in USAAF as UC-61E; this approval expired 4-27-43.

"Deluxe" 24-K shows its Raymond Loewy styling.

This lovely C-38, shown here in 1938, is still flying!

There was not very much you could do with improving "the world's most efficient airplane," but Cessna Aircraft made a stab at it anyway. Everyone in the business was preparing their "new so-and-so for 1938" so Cessna was obliged to follow suit. The basic design had to stand pat, so all attention was concentrated to improving the innards to make a better airplane. Large friction-free ball- bearings throughout the systems provided a nice easy feel to everything, more of the optional equipment was provided now as standard, oil-draulic shock absorbing struts allowed it to tippy-toe over rough ground, and the landing gear legs were bowed out to provide more track. A huge belly-flap was introduced as a "drag brake" to slow the airplane down for landing, and a locking tail wheel was provided to induce a straight run down the landing path. The cabin interior was chummy as ever, but customers were offered a better choice of trim and appointments. So, the model C-38 was rolled out in Oct. of 1937 as the first "Airmaster" and Cessna was acknowledging that this was now the finest airplane they had built in their 27 year history! In reflecting back on some of the goodies that were built by Cessna Aircraft in that length of time, this statement speaks well indeed for the model C-38 for 1938. Although the C-38 didn't look all that different from earlier airplanes of the same design, it was an improved airplane, and still hard to match for its grace, strength and relatively high performance; many would quickly tell you that no airplane in the world could match it. Its uncanny ability to fly rock-steady and straight as an arrow introduced it to the intricate job of photo-mapping; six of the C-38 were employed in this type of work. The crews and the operators had naught but praise for this airplane. Noted "bush pilot" Noel Wien who learned to appreciate a strong, reliable airplane, was operating a C-38 (and other Cessna models) on his Wien Alaska Air Lines, and he would praise it on the least provocation. Not many of the C-38 were built, and this is a pity, but their presence was noted with all kinds of interest wherever they went.

The new Cessna model C-38 was also a compact high-winged, cabin monoplane, with seating arranged for four. Typical of many proven "Cessna" designs, the C-38 was a neat cantilever (internally braced) monoplane that dispensed with all the drag-producing struts, braces and wires as normally seen on other airplanes; because of this it slipped through the air at uncanny speeds, and delivered a rather high performance with modest horsepower. Shed of all the encumbering struts and braces the C-38 poised relaxed and gracefully on a wider undercarriage with confidence and elegance; but, its somewhat dainty, girlish appearance belied its actual strength. The four-place C-38 was leveled at the private owner, more or less, and at the occasional sportsman, but its boundless utility was also appealing to commercial operators who found it capable of so many different jobs. As powered with the gutsy 7 cyl. Warner "Super Scarab"

C-38 shows cantilever form pioneered by Clyde V. Cessna.

engine of 145 h.p. one can only heap praise on this airplane for the way it performed. It was a relatively fast airplane, quick with good response, enjoyed itself at the higher altitudes, it was rock-steady and smooth, and it was fairly quiet. Some have said of these "Airmaster" type that they were "hot" airplanes and very sensitive, but that's perhaps because the craft were so eager and so sensitive to power changes. This airplane was quite comfortable with the smaller airstrips, even at high alititudes, and conducted itself with a nice even temper on even the most arduous of cross-country flights. It did take a little learning to become a good Cessna pilot, but the rewards were paid off in pride and personal satisfaction. Here's an example of what a good C-38 pilot would have to say; it responded nicely, was nimble in execution, and literally fun to fly, but still it was fairly tolerant of error or abuse. It performed well up in the thin air, was sensitive to power settings, and didn't fuss much about "icing" conditons. The low-slung belly-flap made a swooshy noise in tall grass and crosswind handling was no problem. Even the short, rough airstrips were taken in stride. When most were asked about the single foremost characteristic of the "Airmaster" type, it was simply "they take good care of their people." That's about the best endorsement one could expect. The type certificate for the model C-38 was issued 6-25-38 but CAA made it retroactive to 10-30-37. Only 16 of the C-38 were manufactured by the Cessna Aircraft Co. at Wichita, Kan.

Listed below are specifications and performance data for the Cessna model C-38 as powered with the Warner "Super Scarab" (Series 50) engine rated 145 h.p. at 2050 r.p.m. at sea level; length overall 24'8"; height overall 7'0"; wingspan 34'2"; wing chord at root 84"; wing chord at tip 58"; total wing area 181 sq. ft.; airfoil NACA-2412; wt. empty 1370 lbs.; useful load 980 lbs.; payload with 35 gal. fuel 572 lbs. (3 pass. & 62 lbs. bag.); gross wt. 2350 lbs.; max. speed 162 at sea level; cruising speed (.75 power) 143 at sea level; cruising speed (.75 power) 150 at

8200 ft.; landing speed (with drag-flap) 49; take-off run 1000 ft.; climb 800 ft. first min. at sea level; ser. ceiling 18,000 ft.; gas cap. 35 gal.; oil cap. 3.5 gal.; cruising range (.75 power) at 9.5 gal. per hour 550 miles; price $6490 at factory. The C-38 was also eligible as seaplane on Edo 44-2425 twin-float gear at 2500 lbs. gross wt.; empty wt. was 1626 lbs.; useful load was 874 lbs., and payload with 35 gal. fuel was 466 lbs. Price with Edo pontoons was nearly $3,000 more. Seaplane must use Curtiss-Reed metal prop.

The construction details and general arrangement of the model C-38 were typical to that of the earlier C-34 and C-37, or as otherwise noted. The Warner engine was mounted in "Lord" rubber bushings to dampen vibration, and fitted with good carburetor heat; cruising speeds at 15 miles per gallon were not unusual. Two 17.5 gal. fuel tanks were mounted in the wing; 45 gal. and 52 gal. fuel capacity was also available. The unique "belly flap" could be deflected to 90 deg. for maximum drag, but not to be deflected beyond 70 deg. above 108 m.p.h.; this belly-flap was strictly a drag-brake to reduce forward speed without changing the ship's gliding attitude. The new cantilever landing gear legs were bowed out to increase the tread by 10.5 in. for more stability on the ground; the legs were fitted with oil-draulic shock struts with 6 in. travel. The 6.50x10 wheels were fitted with brakes; the brakes were very good, but needed frequent adjustment. The tail wheel swiveled in 360 deg. but it was provided with a fore-and-aft lock for takeoffs and landings. A wind-driven generator was normally used, but an engine-driven generator was optional. Painstaking care during production of this airplane created such surprising uniformity there was practically no variation in characteristics between one ship or another; then too, it was said, the wing and fuselage were built to last a life-time. A wooden prop, electric engine starter, wind-driven generator, battery, carburetor heat-box, exhaust collector ring, NACA-type engine cowl, wheel brakes, 8-in. tail wheel, navigation lights, dual stick-type controls, Plexiglass windshield & windows instead of Pyralin, panel lights, dome light, assist ropes, safety belts, and first-aid kit were standard equipment. A Curtiss-Reed metal prop, engine-driven generator, cabin heater, compass, extra fuel cap., landing lights, paraflares, bonding & shielding, radio gear, camera or litter installation, wheel pants, 22x10-4 Goodyear airwheels, pilot escape hatch, Edo pontoons, skis, and custom colors were optional. The next Cessna development was the model C-39 (C-145) as described in the chapter for ATC # 701.

Listed below are C-38 entries as gleaned from various records;

X-18048;	C-38	(# 400)	Warner 145.
NC-18794;	"	(# 401)	"
-18795;	"	(# 402)	"
-18796;	"	(# 403)	"
-19460;	"	(# 404)	"
-18797;	"	(# 405)	"
-18798;	"	(# 406)	"
-18799;	"	(# 407)	"
-19455;	"	(# 408)	"
-19456;	"	(# 409)	"
-19457;	"	(# 410)	"
-19458;	"	(# 411)	"
-19459;	"	(# 412)	"
-19461;	"	(# 413)	"
-19462;	"	(# 414)	"
-19463;	"	(# 415)	"

This approval for ser. # 401 and up; ser. # 400 eligible when modified to conform; ser. # 403 and # 414 later modified with installation of C-145 wing; ser. # 415 del. to Noel Wien in Alaska; this approval cancelled by Cessna on 8-27-42

C-38 prototype shows uncluttered form that allowed high performance with modest power.

Douglas (DC3A-S1CG) as operated by Pan Am.

This approval was apparently issued to update all previously built, Pratt & Whitney powered DC-3A models, and to allow installation of latest engine developments in those airplanes built from this date forward. United Air Lines (UAL) was the largest civilian procurer of the "Twin Wasp" powered versions, and in the course of service many interesting highlights were recorded. 'Twas said that UAL, in a year's time, had served more than 375,000 meals, hot and tasty meals. Dining in an airplane had finally come from a sandwich and an apple to well-balanced, tasty, full course meals. Of course, it was the pretty "stewardess" that made this possible. By 1940, UAL had some 150 stewardesses on their various runs; they were pretty and very efficient girls. In less than a year's time some 27 had resigned to get married; most likely there were plenty of eligible young bachelors roving the airways. To offset this problem, all new applicants had to solemnly promise not to marry for at least a year; still, the average turn-over in stewardesses was about 30% per year. The big DC-3 had certainly changed the scheme of things in airline operation; every major airline in the U.S.A. was equipped with these airplanes, and all had orders in for more. The affection of the airlines for the DC-3 was akin to the heroine's love for the guy that paid off the mortgage on the old homestead, and saved her from the clutches of the sneering, mustachioed villain. Within a few years after the first DC-3 was put into service all other airplanes were obsolete as far as the air-

lines were concerned. From 1937 into 1945, the year the four-engined transports were making their debut, the DC-3 enjoyed a virtual monopoly the world over; at least 90% of the world's airline business was hauled in the DC-3. With a great war on the horizon the DC-3 of the country's airlines, and those coming down the assembly line, were forced to don olive-drab colors and thus began an era for the DC-3 that is a completely fascinating story. Many books have been written on "The Grand Old Lady," and the stories told are almost unbelievable. So excellent was the basic design of the DC-3 that in some 10 years it was never changed; modified to do a certain job, yes, but not really changed. Over 10,000 of the DC-3 type were built before the last one rolled off the line in May of 1946; outside of some improvements here and there, it was basically the same as one rolled off the line in 1937. The DC-3 had made its mark with the airlines, but it was in World War 2 that most people got to know it best. It was at least once commended as one of the most valuable weapons of the war. Many of the war-weary DC-3, when retired from service, were converted into refurbished DC-3C and DC-3D versions to fly again as if there had been no war at all. Anyone who knows airplanes must salute the old DC-3, and concede she was certainly one of the best airplanes ever built!! The DC-3 output could be divided into two different series; there were those that favored the DC-3 with the various single-row Wright "Cyclone" engines, and there were those that favored the

Plush interior of DC-3A type.

DC-3A type with the various double-row "Twin Wasp" engines by Pratt & Whitney. We are concerned here with the DC-3A-S1CG which was the first of a new line that employed the latest "Twin Wasp" developments as they were periodically released. The P & W-powered DC-3 was a particularly good combination, and before long it became the most popular, both with the airlines and with the military services. UAL standardized in the DC-3A version and these were operating either as the 14 passenger "Club Car" transport, or as the more popular 21 passenger version which more people came to know. The DC-3A was a big, impressive airplane that appealed to the air-traveler, and its performance without seeming strain was a trait that created confidence. A good many people that were introduced to air travel via the DC-3, even a decade later, passed up flights on the more modern equipment because they preferred the "feel" of the DC-3; it was a more intimate and friendly way of traveling. The DC-3 was very good to pilots; it taught them to rely on her ability, and her willingness to do a job, no matter what. Pilots came to know and to accept that control response was slow, but very definite, and when trimmed out properly the DC-3 could fly "hands off" for hours, that is, if everyone remained seated! The DC-3 was also very strong, and as later proved, they would hardly wear out. Under stress the DC-3 didn't hardly realize what an overload was, consenting to carry just whatever was put in it, and there are fantastic

stories to prove it. It is almost embarrassing to relate the life and times of such a wonderful airplane in the space alloted here; may we suggest that there are many good books that do the subject more justice. The type certificate for the DC3A-S1CG and its variants was issued retroactive to 10-30-37 and amendments were attached on 5-1-39, 2-9-40, and 2-18-42. Amendments were added 7-10-44 for the DC-3C version and on 1-15-46 for the DC-3D version. There was no accurate tally available as to how many of these particular airplanes were manufactured by the Douglas Aircraft Corp. of Santa Monica, Calif.

Listed below are specifications and performance data for the Douglas model DC3A-S1CG as powered with 2 "Twin Wasp" GR-1830-S1CG engines rated 1050 h.p. each at 2550 r.p.m. at 7500 ft. (1200 h.p. available for takeoff); length overall 64'6"; height overall (3 point) 16'11"; wingspan 95'0"; wing chord 172" at root tapering to wing tip; total wing area 987 sq. ft.; airfoil NACA-2215 at root tapering to NACA-2206 at tip; wt. empty 16,653 (16,865) lbs.; useful load 8147 (8335) lbs.; payload with 600 gal. fuel 3727 (3915) lbs. (21 pass. & 345 lbs. baggage-cargo): gross wt. 24,800 (25,200) lbs. as provisional allowance for airline use; figures in parentheses as later allowed; max. speed 230 at 8500 ft.; cruising speed (.75 power) 205 at 7500 ft.; cruising speed (.70 power) 209 at 15,000 ft.; landing speed (with flaps) 67; takeoff run fully loaded approx. 1000 ft.; climb 1080 ft. first min. at sea level; service ceiling 23,500 ft.; gas cap.

normal 650 gal.; gas cap. max. 822 gal.; oil cap. 48-66 gal.; cruising range (.75 power) with 600 gal. at 105 gal. per hour 1050 miles; basic price was over $100,000. The DC3A-S1CG and subsequent variants were equipped with three-bladed Hamilton-Standard hydramatic "constant speed" controllable props—later fitted with "full feathering" device.

Listed below are early examples of the DC3A-S1CG as gleaned from various records:

NC-18938;	DC3A-S1CG	(# 2004)	GR-1830-S1CG.
-18939;	"	(# 2005)	"
-18940;	"	(# 2006)	"
-18941;	"	(# 2007)	"
-18942;	"	(# 2008)	;;
;	"	(# 2009)	"
-18943;	"	(# 2010)	"
-18944;	"	(# 2017)	"
-18945;	"	(# 2018)	"
-21711;	"	(# 2123)	"
-21712;	"	(# 2124)	"
-21713;	"	(# 2125)	"
-21714;	"	(# 2129)	"
-21715;	"	(# 2130)	"
-21716;	"	(# 2131)	"
-21730;	"	(# 2146)	"

Ser. # 1900 and up (as listed in the chapter for ATC # 619) also eligible when modified to conform; DC3A-SCG, DC3A-SC3G, DC3A-S1C3G, and DC3A-S4C4G also eligible on this approval; 21 of DC-3C and 28 of DC-3D (post-war conversions) were also eligible on this approval; the next Douglas development was the improved DSTA-S1CG "Sleeper" as described here in the chapter for ATC # 671.

A DC-3A of "United" dons military dress.

Post-war DC-3 as operated by Braniff Airways.

DC-3A cargoliner often transported unusual cargo.

DC-3A prepares for night-flight from Seattle.

Waco JHD designed for the air forces of small countries.

The military aspirations of Latin-American countries was beginning to build up because of unsettling world events. But, being held to a more modest budget than larger, more powerful countries, they had to be satisfied with the purchase of airplanes far less costly, and just barely adequate as front-line military machines. Waco Aircraft had already supplied many countries with quasi-military versions of some of their commercial and sport designs, but in the "Model D" they had a high-performance, two-seated biplane that was designed especially for varied military uses; it could be fitted with selected hardware to become a very useful military machine. The model JHD was the least expensive and the most economical vehicle in the "Model D" lineup; it was very suitable for an air force that had to operate on a very modest budget. As an armed military machine the "JHD" was designed for a rather wide variety of equipment to perform diverse duties. The versatile JHD was primarily a military basic trainer, but it could forcefully substitute as a two-seated fighter type airplane, a light dive-bomber, a low level attack airplane, an observation and photo ship, artillery spotter, liaison, or even marshalled to haul mail and cargo. As an "armed" airplane ready to participate in quelling any uprisings the JHD could mount one fixed .30 caliber machine gun in a lower wing, and one flexible mounted .30 caliber machine gun in the rear cockpit for the observer to operate. There were also provisions for one bomb rack; as thus fitted the JHD could provide useful armed support for infantry troops, and plenty of harrassment to opposing forces. In the true sense the "JHD" was not really a sophisticated war machine, but as a thrifty weapon to repel insurgence it promised to be quite effective. Undoubtedly fashioned to appeal to the romanticism of Latin-American people, the handsome JHD was also contoured beautifully with a flair, and its jaunty behavior went hand-in-hand with show of strength and military pomp.

The Waco model JHD was a military-type, convertible biplane with seating arranged in tandem for a crew of two. As an attraction to smaller, undeveloped nations that had less money to spend for military airplanes the model JHD offered utility and quite unusual versatility for a modest outlay of money. Wrapped up here in one practical machine was the ability to do "fighter" work, both as a single-seater and a two-seater, attack the enemy's critical positions as a "bomber," or engage in troop "strafing" and harrassment. For duties of less aggressive nature the JHD was adaptable to "observation" and "artillery spotting" via radio, photo-reconnoiter, or the evacuation of wounded if need be. Because of its lineage, flying over hazardous terrain and operating from ridiculously small airstrips was "a piece of cake" for the JHD. In less than one hour's time the

244

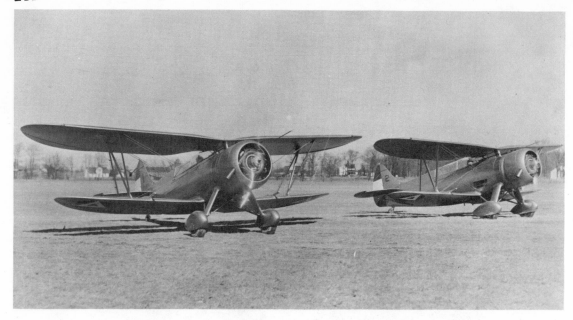

JHD prepared to leave factory for Uruguay.

JHD could be converted from one duty to another. For a high-performance airplane that cost about $20,000 this was indeed a bargain in a jack-of-all-trades military machine. In its primary role as a basic trainer the pilot's station was up front, but the rear cockpit also had controls and some instrumentation in case of any emergency; the back seat could be adjusted to rearward-facing or forward-facing positions. Both occupants were protected with a canopy enclosure with sliding panels; the gunner observer was partially enclosed at all times if he so desired it. Excellent visibility was assured by the large amount of wing stagger, the generous wing-root cutouts, and the position of occupants relative to the upper wing; such visibility in a biplane was exceptional. As powered with the 9 cyl. Wright R-975-E1 engine rated 330-365 h.p. the model JHD had the spirit of a sportplane with the performance necessary to be an efficient war-time machine. Quick response and excellent maneuverability was backed up by a beefy airframe that was designed to soak up tremendous airloads, or pilot inflicted punishment. As holstered down with firearms and other implements of war the JHD was similar to other versions of the custom built "Model D," but its lower power was some detriment to all its inherent performance; but, no excuses are in order because the JHD was the best specialized airplane available for the money. It is not known if the JHD was ever called into actual combat duty, but the capability was there, had it been needed. The type certificate for the model JHD was issued retroactive to 10-30-37 and some 6 examples of this model were manufactured by the Waco Aircraft Co. at Troy, Ohio. Records show that all JHD were sold completely armed and flown from the factory by government pilots sent up from Uraguay.

Listed below are specifications and performance data for the Waco model JHD as powered with Wright R-975-E1 engine rated 365 h.p. at 2100 r.p.m. at sea level; length overall 25'7"; height overall 8'11"; wingspan upper 32'9"; wingspan lower 27'0"; wing chord upper 66"; wing chord lower 57"; wing area upper 156.2 sq. ft.; wing area lower 100.1 sq. ft.; total wing area 256.3 sq. ft.; airfoil Clark Y; wt. empty 2435 (2543) lbs.; useful load 1001 (1182) lbs.; crew wt. 340 lbs.; gross wt. 3436 (3725) lbs.; wts. as listed are for basic trainer & two-seated armed fighter respectively; max. speed (105% power) 175; cruising speed (.70 power) 153 up to 6500 ft.; landing speed 55-60; climb 1350-1200 ft. first min. at sea level; ser. ceiling 15,500 ft.; gas cap. 89 gal.; oil cap. 6-8 gal.; cruising range (.70 power) at 22 gal. per hour 590 miles; price variable—approx. $20,000 or more if armed at the factory. Performance figures listed above are for airplanes without armament; decrease performance figures by 6% for airplanes with full armament. The JHD also eligible as seaplane on Edo twin-float gear at 3800 lb. gross wt. The JHD was also eligible as a sportplane when stripped of all armament and mountings thereof.

The construction details and general arrangement of the model JHD were typical to that of other "Waco D" models as described in the chapters for ATC # 543 and 581, including the following. As a two-place fighter-type airplane the JHD had one lower wing-mounted .30 caliber machine gun with remote controls and gun-sight in front cockpit. Magazines provided up to 500 rounds of ammo in boxes. An Air Corps type A-3 bomb-rack was in the belly; bombs totaling to 250 lbs. could be released by either of the crew. An upper fuselage tank of 56 gal. cap., and a lower fuselage tank of 33 gal. cap. allowed the total of 89 gal. of fuel; an extra

JHD "fighter" shows off its "arms."

10 gal. fuel tank in each upper wing root was optional. By reducing fuel load, or some of the armament, a two-way radio and a Fairchild camera could be installed for "recco" work. A compartment behind the rear seat was available for up to 150 lbs. of baggage-mail-cargo. A ground adjustable metal prop, electric engine starter, battery, generator, dual controls, instruments in both cockpits, navigation lights, landing lights, paraflares, bonding & shielding, wing-root fairings, wheel pants, 7.50x10 wheels with 8.50x10 tires, wheel brakes, cockpit enclosure, 10.5 in. tail wheel, fire extinguisher bottle, tool kit, and first-aid kit were classed as normal equipment. A Hamilton-Standard controllable prop, two-way radio, Fairchild camera, armament, and Edo pontoons were optional.

The next Waco development was the tricycle-geared model AVN-8 as described here in the chapter for ATC # 677.

Listed below are JHD entries as gleaned from company records:

JHD	(# 4710)	R-975-E1.
"	(# 4711)	"
"	(# 4712)	"
"	(# 4713)	"
"	(# 4714)	"
"	(# 4715)	"

This approval for ser. # 4710 and up; these 6 airplanes sold to government of Uraguay through Jorge Luro of Argentina; all 6 airplanes rolled out of assembly from 1-9-38 through 1-17-38.

Lineup of JHD awaiting delivery.

ATC # 671
(10-30-37)
DOUGLAS, DSTA-S1CG

DSTA-S1CG was "queen" of Mainliner fleet.

During this time the Douglas (DST) "Sleeper" was justly rated the queen of the skies, and mentioned frequently as the sister ship of the hard working DC-3. The DST "Sleeper" was a glamorous airplane; much attention was lavished on her appearance and the circumstance of her presence before the flying public. Therefore, she was constantly being fitted with latest improvements, more of better equipment, and the very latest available in powerplants. Pratt & Whitney was constantly improving and upgrading the mighty "Twin Wasp"; the latest version to be tested and approved early in 1938 was the 1200 h.p. SGR-1830-S1CG. With earlier "Twin Wasp" (SB3G) engines now nearing the overhaul stage, United Air Lines refurbished their earlier DST-A with these new engines on this approval, and the new DST examples, just coming off the line, were naturally being powered with the very latest in Pratt & Whitney engine development. We single out this approval for the DSTA-S1CG, but actually the DSTA-SCG, DSTA-SC3G, DSTA-S1C3G, and DSTA-S4C4G were also eligible. Perhaps all this tricky nomenclature is confusing, but it just involves the DST-A with variations of the "Twin Wasp" engine, engines which operated with varying "blower ratios" and rated horsepower ratings. Most airline pilots of the "Sleeper" preferred these new P & W engines because they were marvelously smooth in normal operation, and this treated the sleeping passengers to a feather bed ride. In a well handled DST-A the

passengers were "flying in the cradle of comfort." It is fact too that every passenger was treated like a very important person; they all loved it and told others. By 1939-40 most of the "DST" were operating with full-feathering "constant speed" propellers, many had prop de-icers, wing de-icers, tail group de-icers, and automatic pilots. The (DST) "Sleeper" was a Douglas masterpiece; it was loved and respected by all who flew her, and all who flew in her. Not many airplanes inspired such unswerving confidence. The majestic "Sleeper" was also known as the C-48B and C-49F when used in military service during World War 2; here the DST was stripped of its shiny glamor and doused with olive drab paint, but undaunted it continued to do a good job. Historians have marked Dec. 17 of 1903 as the point in time when man finally solved the riddle of heavier-than-air flight, but historians should also record another Dec. 17th, some 32 years later, as a date of almost equal importance. It was on this date in 1935 that the "Douglas Sleeper Transport" (DST) first took to the air and began a saga of accomplishment, inherent courage, and dedication that was to surpass that of any other airplane type ever built!

The Douglas (DST) "Sleeper" was a beautifuly proportioned transport airplane that was big enough to inspire confidence, yet proportioned to assure the highest performance possible in an airplane of this type. The uncanny ability to fly for hours if necessary on any one of its engines, in order to reach a haven of safety, was

"Sleeper" (DSTA-S1CG) demonstrates ability to fly safely on one engine.

another reason that airlines were practically standardizing on "Douglas" equipment the world over. Yet another reason was its proven strength; the DST, and the DC-3 which was practically the same airplane, were hard to break up and almost impossible to wear out. The Douglas "Sleeper" as generally operated had berths for 14 people; their comfort and safety was assured by a crew of three. Ironically, the nicety and novelty of being able to sleep on the way to your destination was not always convenient, nor even necessary, so the popularity of the "Sleeper" service finally began to wane. To offset this loss, the "Sleeper" was simply arranged as a day plane with coach-type seats; in some arrangements of high density seating it carried as many as 28 passengers. As powered with 2 "Twin Wasp" engines rated 1050 h.p. each the

Private berths in Douglas "Sleeper."

DSTA-S1CG had remarkable performance that allowed airlines to offer attractive scheduling, and a brand of service that was increasing air travel by leaps and bounds. The big DST was a "busy airplane" because the crew had so much more to do, but the airplane was patient, obedient, and quite easy to handle, so crews were never in over their heads, even having occasional moments to relax and reflect on the importance of their work. It goes without saying that the line's best pilots were chosen to fly the "Sleeper," and the most efficient stewardess was chosen also; such a combination was bound to produce happy air travelers. Because of its specialized nature the DST "Sleeper," was not built in such large numbers, as compared to the DC-3, but the DST must receive its proper meaure of credit because it was one of the finest airplanes in the world for what it was doing. The type certificate for the model DSTA-S1CG and its approved variants was issued early in 1938, but made retroactive to 10-30-37. It is estimated that 19 or more of the P & W-powered DST were manufactured by the Douglas Aircraft Co., Inc. on Clover Field in Santa Monica, Calif. This approval first issued 3-26-38 with subsequent amendments on 5-1-39, 2-9-40, and 2-18-42.

Listed below are specifications and performance data for the Douglas model DSTA-S1CG as powered with 2 "Twin Wasp" GR-1830-S1CG engines rated 1050 h.p. at 2550 r.p.m. at 7500 ft. (1200 h.p. available for takeoff); length overall 64'6"; height overall (3 point) 16'11"; wingspan 95'0"; wing chord 172" at root tapering to wing tip; total wing area 987 sq. ft.; airfoil NACA-2215 at root tapering to NACA-2206 at tip; wt. empty 16,430 (16,865) lbs.; useful load 8370 (8335) lbs.; payload with 600 gal. fuel 3950 (3915) lbs. (14 pass., 3 crew, & 1570 lbs. baggage-mail-cargo); provisional gross wt. for airline use was 24,800 (25,200) lbs.; wts. in parentheses as later amended; max. speed 229 at 8500 ft.; cruising speed (.75 power) 204 at 7500 ft.; cruising speed (.75 power) 207 at 15,000 ft.; landing speed (with flaps) 67; takeoff run (fully loaded) 1000 ft.; climb 1080 ft. first min. at sea level; ser. ceiling 23,500 ft.; gas cap. normal 650 gal.; gas cap. max. 822 gal.; oil cap. 48-66 gal.; cruising range (.75 power) with 600 gal. fuel at 105 gal. per hour was 1050 miles; basic price was over $100,000. DSTA-S1CG and variants were equipped with three-bladed Hamilton-Standard hydramatic "constant speed" controllable props—later fitted with "full feathering" device.

In general the DST-A was basically similar to the DC-3A in all respects except for arrangement of the interior. The main cabin was divided into 7 compartments; 3 were on either side of the aisle, and a private enclosed compartment on the right up forward called the "Sky-Room." Each compartment was converted into an upper berth and a lower berth; lower berths were 6'6" long and 36" wide, with upper berths only 30" wide.

United "Sleeper" prepares for night-flight across country.

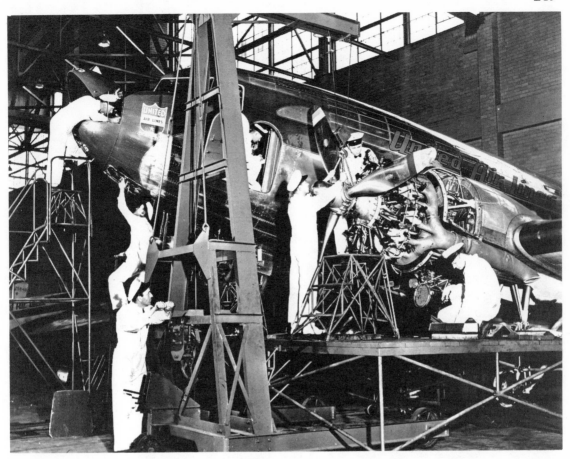

Crews giving "Sleeper" its periodic once-over.

Upper berths could be folded up into the ceiling when not in use, and lower berths were converted into 36" wide overstuffed reclining chairs. The cabin portion was 6'5" high by 7'8" wide by some 27' long. A hot food dispensing buffet was up front with mail-cargo compartments forward of that; a baggage compartment of 110 cu. ft. capacity was to the rear of cabin area with access from inside or out. In the rear portion men and women had separate lavatories and dressing rooms to offer comfort and privacy. The cabin was heavily sound-proofed and insulated; steam-heat and ventilation was also provided to keep cabin at comfortable levels. The pilot's compartment was entered through the main cabin area, or through a side door up forward; an emergency exit for the pilots was provided in the ceiling. The 4 fuel tanks with 822 gal. capacity in total were in the wing's center section, 2 on each side; front tanks were of 210 gal. cap. and rear tanks were of 201 gal. cap. The DST was normally equipped with a full complement of night flying equipment, and the very latest in radio gear; some airplanes were also equipped with de-icing systems and automatic pilot. The next Douglas Transport development was the unusual, high-winged DC-5 as described in the chapter for ATC # 727.

Listed below are DSTA-S1CG entries as gleaned from registration records: for # 671:

NC-18145;	DSTA-S1CG	(# 1977)	GR-1830-S1CG.
-18146;	"	(# 1978)	"
-25682;	"	(# 2222)	"
-25683;	"	(# 2223)	"
-25619;	"	(# 3263)	"
-25620;	"	(# 3264)	"
-33640;	"	(# 3265)	"
-33641;	"	(# 4113)	"
-33642;	"	(# 4114)	"

This approval also for airplanes listed in ATC # 647—all (ser. # 1951-60) eligible when modified to conform; all airplanes on ATC # 647 and # 671 also eligible as DC-3A when modified to conform; 16 of the Twin-Wasp-powered DST-A in service with USAAF in WW2 as C-48B.

ATC # 672
(10-30-37)
HOWARD, MODEL DGA-11

"Buffs" claim DGA-11 was best "Howard" ever built.

Among "Howard" enthusiasts of the past, and even those of the present, the model DGA-11 was perhaps the ultimate in a high performance cabin monoplane for private, or business use. The basic "Howard" design was replete with all kinds of potential, and all of this came thundering to the fore when combined with the gutsy Pratt & Whitney "Wasp Jr." SB engine of some 400-450 h.p. Oftentimes an airplane will not surrender its full capability unless prodded with extra horsepower, and in this case the DGA-11 happily released absolutely all that it had in it. Almost immediately the saucy DGA-11 took on a reputation, as is most often the case with a high performance airplane, as a cranky and vicious machine. But, that certainly was not true. The "Howard" in general, and the DGA-11 in particular, was for long a much-maligned airplane; it surely was not the monster that many hangar fliers portrayed. True, it was quite a handful, and it required something close to complete devotion, but the effort was more than well repaid. As once put by an admiring pilot, "you get goose-pimples just being around this airplane!" There were not many like it. Being fairly expensive, and perhaps just too sporty for most, the DGA-11 remained in very small number, but the roster of owners was very impressive. David S. Ingalls had been a long-time aviation enthusiast, and he always owned good

airplanes, so it is logical he would be drawn to the DGA-11. Wallace Beery, the big, likeable movie actor, also had an eye for good airplanes; he heaped praise on his DGA-11 quite often. Jose Iturbi, famous musician and conductor, seems like an unlikely candidate for an airplane such as the DGA-11, but they say he enjoyed it immensely and admired it greatly. Yes, the Howard model DGA-11 was an overwhelming airplane; it had lovely form, a stunning beauty, and breath-taking performance. Perhaps most flying people found this all too much to cope with.

The "Howard" model DGA-11 can be described as a high-winged cabin monoplane with seating arranged for 5, but people who know good airplanes would hardly consider this as adequate. As an airplane that was closely related to the famous "Mr. Mulligan" it has to be said that this was an exciting machine. Its composure and haughty stance almost demanded admiration, and a walk-around treated one to its many outstanding features; this was no ho-hum airplane. You were gripped by it, and from then on you found yourself somewhat luke-warm in enthusiasm for other airplanes of this type. Benny Howard was particularly proud of this combination and on this he rest his laurels, because he had soon after detached himself from the company. There would be other airplanes

Former DGA-8 shown here as DGA-11.

built by Howard Aircraft, but they would be overshadowed by the DGA-11 and the "waves" it left behind. As powered with the 400 h.p. "Wasp Jr." SB engine the model DGA-11 had the low power-loading to deliver a sensational performance for this type of airplane. There is still talk of its unbelievable cruising speeds, its terrific climb out, and its ability to operate efficiently at levels where many airplanes feared to tread. But, any pilot that sat behind the wheel of this one had better pay attention, because the DGA-11 tempered all that good with just a little bad. She was solid, a little heavy, but very responsive; the airplane was quite "clean" so build-up of excessive speed came almost without warning. "Red-line" speeds were a thing to watch. She "stalled" easily, but a tail buffet gave plenty of warning so there was time to decide. As with any high performance airplane, she would impose some moments of stress on a pilot, but as pilot and airplane got better acquainted the relationship became friendly and finally a pleasure for both. Some say the DGA-11 was forgiving, but to qualify the statement, she was forgiving to determined and heavy-handed manipulation, but not to meekness nor ignorance. The high wing-loading had many advantages, and among these was a super smooth ride in rough air at high speeds. The DGA-11 was a pretty terrific airplane, so when the news got around it is not surprising that some owners of the DGA-8 began inquiring about a conversion to the DGA-11; any "Howard" was eligible when modified to conform. The type certificate for the model DGA-11 was issued early in 1938, but made retroactive to 10-30-37. Manufactured by the Howard Aircraft Corp, in Chicago, Ill. Ben O. Howard was pres.; B. D. DeWeese (formerly of Stinson) was V.P. & gen. mgr.; Carl W. Freitag (also of Stinson) was sales mgr.; and W. T. Brownell was chf. engr. When Benny Howard left the company DeWeese became pres. & gen. mgr. and Gordon Israel became

V.P. & chf. engr. When asked why DGA-13 was not used as a model designation, Howard said "I'm not really superstitious, but why push your luck!"

Listed below are specifications and performance data for the Howard model DGA-11 as powered with "Wasp Jr." SB engine rated 400 h.p. at 2200 r.p.m. at 9600 ft. (450 h.p. available for take-off); length overall 25'5"; height overall 8'5"; wingspan 38'0"; wing chord at root 72"; total wing area (including fuselage section) 210 sq. ft.; airfoil NACA-2R12; wt. empty 2450 lbs.; useful load 1650 lbs.; payload with 97 gal. fuel 845 lbs. (4 pass. & 165 lbs. bag. & extras); payload with 127 gal. fuel 658 lbs. (3 pass., 148 lbs. bag. & extras); gross wt. 4100 lbs.; max. speed 196 at sea level; cruising speed (.65 power) 203 at 10,000 ft.; landing speed (with flaps) 55; landing speed (no flaps) 65; climb 2200 ft. first min. at sea level; ser. ceiling 26,000 ft.; gas cap. normal 97 gal.; gas cap. max. 127 gal.; oil cap. 7-8 gal.; cruising range (2000 r.p.m. at 9600 ft.) at 23 gal. per hour was 800-1040 miles; price $17,685 at factory. The DGA-11 was normally equipped with Hamilton-Standard controllable prop.

The fuselage framework of the DGA-11 was more or less similar to the DGA-8, but there were some modifications and minor structural changes. There was ample room for 5 with deep, soft comfort and welcome quiet; fresh air vents and cabin heat were also provided. A large baggage compartment behind the rear seat had allowance for 120 lbs. with a hat shelf across the top for personal items. Because of its custom-built nature the DGA-11 was generally fitted with very plush decor and all the latest in operating equipment. The cabin section (exterior) of the fuselage was covered with dural metal panels, and fabric covered to the tail. The robust wing panels were first covered with plywood sheet, then also covered with fabric to take a high-gloss finish. Three fuel tanks, easily filled from the

Jose Iturbi, noted composer and conductor, was owner of this beautiful DGA-11.

ground, were fitted into the belly; a main tank of 60 gal. and a rear tank of 37 gal. was the normal capacity, but a forward tank of 30 gal. was available for a 127 gal. capacity. The tall landing gear of 90 in. tread was fitted with Howard made oil-spring shock struts; 7.50x10 wheels with Goodyear hydraulic disc-brakes were fitted with 8.50x10 (6 ply) tires. Wheels were normally encased in streamlined metal wheel pants. The toe-operated wheel brakes were also fitted with a parking lock. The 10.5 in. tail wheel was steerable and fitted with a fore-and-aft lock. A Hamilton-Standard controllable prop, electric engine starter, battery, generator, fuel pumps fuel gauges, compass, clock, wheel brakes, parking brake, dual control wheels, oil cooler, Cuno oil filter, carburetor heater, cabin heater, wheel streamlines, fire extinguisher, ash trays, map pockets, assist ropes, safety belts, and first-aid kit were standard equipment. A constant-speed prop, extra instruments, pressure-type fire ex-

tinguisher, 3 fuel tanks to 127 gal. cap., landing lights, paraflares, bonding & shielding, radio gear, parachute-type seats by Irvin or Switlik, and custom colors were optional. The next Howard Development was the DGA-15 series as described in the chapter for ATC # 717.

Listed below are DGA-11 entries as gleaned from registration records:

NC-14871;	DGA-11	(# 72)	SB-400.
-14875;	''	(# 78	
-18208;	''	(# 300)	''
-18210;	''	(# 301)	''
-18211;	''	(# 302)	''
-22402;	''	(# 303)	''

This approval for ser. # 71 and up when modified to conform; this approval still in force during 1940; ser. # 300 to David S. Ingalls; ser. # 301 to Wallace Beery; ser. # 303 to Jose Iturbi; NC-22404 may also have been a DGA-11.

Wallace Beery, noted movie-star and lover of fine airplanes, owned this highly-polished DGA-11.

ATC # 673
(10-30-37)
LOCKHEED, 14-WG3B

Lockheed 14-G3B as built for Japan.

Although anyone would hardly know the difference, the only time the Lockheed model 14-WG3B was ever seen in this country was when they were being delivered to ports of export for shipment abroad. The 14-WG3B, a particular model of the "Super Electra" with Wright "Cyclone" engines, was also offered in this country, but no orders were placed here and all were exported overseas; of the 34 that were built, Lockheed delivered 4 to Roumania for the LARES airline system, and 30 to Japan. This along with an agreement to allow Japan to build copies of this celebrated "Super Electra" for their proposed airline system. Japan is such a small country that there was very little reason to support a commercial aircraft industry; what machines were needed were easily bought from abroad under most advantageous conditions. The few aircraft plants they did have were building only military machines, and most of these were copies of airplanes produced by other countries. Japan began stocking up on aviation supplies about 1937, and they also planned to implement an extensive airline network. The 30 examples of the "Lockheed 14" shipped to Japan were mustered into this new airline system thereby linking most of Japan's larger cities, and also routes to Chosen, Taiwan, and Manchuria. It was then reported that Kawasaki, one of the largest manufacturers in Japan, began building the "Fourteen" under license as the "Toby" in a commercial version, and as the "Thelma" in a modified military version. It is quite likely that very soon after this all of the "Super Electra" type, including the 30 shipped over by Lockheed, were modified into machines to be used for varied military use. At the time it was wagered

here that this activity was taking place under the guise of preparation for defense, but military historians now have mixed opinions. In retrospect, it is ironic that Lockheed Aircraft would be supplying a nation with potential military vehicles, only 3 or 4 years prior to their invasion on us, but Lockheed was not alone in this, there were many others in this nation that did likewise. Business and the profits of war

The Lockheed model 14-WG3B was an all metal, twin-engined, low-winged, transport monoplane with features that made it just about the fastest transport airplane in the world. Normally, the "14" was arranged to carry 10 or 11 passengers and a crew of 3, but the versatile interior was adapted quickly to other uses. The removal of all seating provided an ample amount of floor space for cargo hauling, and it was no particular problem to modify the "14" for various military uses; the belly compts. which normally carried the baggage were easily converted into bomb bays, and gun turrets could be located easily in several positions. The 14-WG3B were sold to Japan as commercial airliners, but it is not out of place to imagine that all were eventually put into service as bombers, or at least in some military capacity. The 4 airplanes sold to Roumania were oufitted for airline use, but it is conceivable that even they in time were adapted to military uses. As powered with 2 of the big Wright "Cyclone" GR-1820-G3B engines of 840 h.p. each this version of the "Super Electra" had terrific performance throughout the entire range of flight, and was particularly suited for frequent hops of short duration; it is easy to see why Japan and Roumania would be particularly interested in an

254

Lockheed 14 became basis for several Japanese designs.

airplane of this type. Blessed with a hefty power reserve the 14-WG3B offered peace of mind in the tough places, and its one-engine performance in emergency was outstanding. The Lockheed 14 was designed as a working airplane, and pilots had to work at it to fly it properly, but it was rewarding duty and most pilots enjoyed it. The buxom and robust "Super Electra" had built-in muscle, remarkable stamina, and unusual reliability, but she was always a lady and never got easily riled. Usually asked to work among natural hazards that tore the heart out of an ordinary airplane, the "14" had fantastic ability to adapt and it fairly reveled in its ability. The type certificate for the model 14-WG3B was issued 10-30-37 and some 34 examples of this model were manufactured by the Lockheed Aircraft Corp. at Burbank, Calif.

Listed below are specifications and performance data for the Lockheed model 14-WG3B as powered with 2 Wright "Cyclone" GR-1820-G3B engines rated 840 h.p. at 2100 r.p.m. at 8000 ft. (900 h.p. at 2350 r.p.m. available for takeoff); length overall 44'4"; height overall 11'10"; wingspan 65'6"; wing chord at root 153"; wing chord at tip 48"; total wing area (incl. fuselage section) 551 sq. ft.; airfoil NACA-23000 series; wt. empty 11,025 lbs.; useful load 6475 lbs.; payload with 644 gal. fuel 1821 lbs. (10 pass. & 121 lbs. baggage); payload with 400 gal. fuel 3285 lbs. (11 pass. & 1415 lbs. baggage-cargo); gross wt. 17,500 lbs. (normal gross wt. was 15,650 lbs., but provisional gross wt. of 17,-500 lbs. was allowed for airline use); max. speed 248 at 8000 ft.; cruising speed (using 600 h.p. from each engine) 240 at 13,000 ft.; landing speed (with flaps) 65; climb 1580 ft. first min. at sea level; ser. ceiling 24,700 ft.; max. of 11,000 ft. on one engine; gas cap. max. 644 gal.; oil cap. max. 44 gal.; cruising range (.75 power) at 88 gal. per hour 1600 miles; price not announced.

The construction details and general arrangement of the Lockheed model 14-WG3B was typical to that of the models 14-H2 and 14-WF62 except for minor modifications to suit this combination. The most significant difference in the model 14-WG3B was installation of the geared GR-1820-G3B engines which were more highly supercharged for operation at higher altitudes. The cabin interior was over 6 ft. high, nearly 66 in. wide, and easily adaptable for many uses; for cargo hauling the nose compt. was allowed up to 1500 lbs., forward belly compt. was allowed up to 800 lbs.; middle belly compt. was allowed up to 400 lbs.; and rear belly compt. was allowed up to 700 lbs. This amount of payload would only allow about 380 gal. of fuel, and even less if the cabin area was loaded. The max. of 644 gal. of fuel was carried in center portion of the wing, and divided among 4 tanks; 2 front tanks at 150 gal. each and 2 rear tanks at 172 gal. each. The retractable landing gear of 15'6" tread used heavy-duty "Aerol" shock struts and 15.00x16 Goodyear "airwheels" with hydraulic brakes. A pressure-type fire extinguisher was mounted in each engine nacelle, and fire bottles were mounted in the cabin. The cabin was provided with a heating-ventilating system and a lavatory was optional. The huge "Fowler Flaps" decreased landing speeds by nearly 20% and shortened takeoff runs considerably; these variable-area flaps were primarily high-lift devices, but also contributed as drag-brakes. The ailerons, rudder, and elevators were fitted with adj. trim tab. Hamilton-Standard controllable (constant speed) props, electric engine starters, battery, generator, fuel pumps, oil coolers, wheel brakes, exhaust collector-rings, fire extinguisher, dual controls, airline seating, cabin upholstery, cabin heat & ventilation, cabin lights, airline type instrument group, and first-aid kit were standard equipment. Navigation lights, landing lights, paraflares, lavatory, bonding & shielding, radio gear, auto-pilot, spl. interior, and de-icing equipment were optional. The next "Super Electra" development was the model 14-N as described here in the chapter for ATC # 683.

Listed below are 14-WG3B entries as gleaned from various records:

;	14-WG3B	(# 1426)	GR-1820-G3B.		;	"	(# 1459)	"
;	"	(# 1427)	"		;	"	(# 1460)	"
;	"	(# 1428)	"		;	"	(# 1461)	"
;	"	(# 1433)	"		;	"	(# 1462)	"
;	"	(# 1434)	"		YR-LIB;	"	(# 1463)	"
;	"	(# 1435)	"		YR-LIC;	"	(# 1464)	"
;	"	(# 1436)	"		YR-LIR;	"	(# 1465)	"
;	"	(# 1437)	"		YR-LIS;	"	(# 1466)	"
;	"	(# 1438)	"		;	"	(# 1477)	"
;	"	(# 1445)	"		;	"	(# 1478)	"
;	"	(# 1446)	"		;	"	(# 1479)	"
;	"	(# 1447)	"		;	"	(# 1480)	"
;	"	(# 1448)	"		;	"	(# 1481)	"
;	"	(# 1449)	"					
;	"	(# 1452)	"					
;	"	(# 1453)	"					
;	"	(# 1454)	"					
;	"	(# 1455)	"					
;	"	(# 1456)	"					
;	"	(# 1457)	"					
;	"	(# 1458)	"					

This approval for ser. # 1426 and up; ser. # 1463-1466 del. to LARES of Roumania—all the rest del. to Japan; this batch of 34 airplanes was del. from 3-12-38 through 9-17-38; this approval expired 1-24-41.

Fowler variable-area wing as first tested on a Pitcairn fuselage.

Dart GK with "Ken-Royce" engine.

The stubby "Dart" had spent several years of its life looking for a formal identity. It certainly had the lineage that any airplane would be proud of, but it came from a family of airplanes that strived valiantly for prominence and failed. The design for what finally became the "Dart" was originated by Al W. Mooney who had previously designed the Alexander "Bullet," and a very similar "Mooney" design that had failed to develop; traces of both these designs were subtly present in the "Dart." Before it finally became the "Dart" this little airplane was conceived and built by Al Mooney while working for "Monocoupe" (Lambert Aircraft); it was an open-seated craft temporarily called the "Monoprep G." A conversion of this ship into a coupe-type airplane (the "Monosport G") lessened the overall drag and it became quite an interesting machine; it was approved on a Group 2 memo numbered 2-541 and Clare Bunch announced production for Oct. of 1935. The company did have some trouble in staying solvent at this particular time, so the model was not seriously considered for production. When Mooney left Lambert Aircraft he teamed with K. K. Culver and together they formed the Dart Aircraft Co., buying the design and manufacturing rights, some 3 or 4 uncompleted airplanes, and fashioned these into an improved version that would now be formally known as the "Dart." This chubby airplane was designed on the principal of exploiting the advantages of the "low aspect ratio," a ratio of deep chord or width in relation to the span or length. This theory produced an airplane that had eager spirit and exceptional maneuverability; a rather sensitive machine that responded quickly to the flex of a pilot's finger. Not particularly blessed with power, the normal "Dart" couldn't show its full potential, but some conversions with more than double the power, later confirmed that the "Dart" certainly had scads of latent ability. First introduced as the "Dart G" this airplane was powered with the 5 cyl. Lambert R-266 engine of 90 h.p., but Lambert engines were getting hard to come by, so other powerplants had to be considered. As powered with the 90 h.p. "Ken-Royce" engine (formerly LeBlond) it became the model GK, and as powered with the 90 h.p. "Scarab Jr." engine by Warner it became the model GW. The "Dart" was a pretty good airplane with any of the 3 engines, but the Warner-powered version was no doubt the most popular. Acceptance of the "Dart" was rather heartening, but production remained very modest. In 1939 the company was reorganized into the Culver Aircraft Co. and the airplanes being rolled out were now known as the Culver "Dart," a proper and fitting name for an airplane that almost became an orphan. Nearly 50 of the assorted "Dart" were built in Ohio, and then K. K. Culver decided to move to Wichita. It was here that Mooney and Culver rolled out a terrific little airplane called the Culver "Cadet." Manufacture of the "Dart" was discontinued, but the story doesn't end there. In 1946 the firm

Monosport G that fostered the "Dart" line.

of Applegate & Weyant acquired all rights to the airplane, and came out with a modified version called the "Dart GC." The engines formerly used in the "Dart" were now unavailable, so Applegate installed a 6 cyl. (opposed) Continental engine of 100 h.p.; other useful changes were made also and the "Dart" was being promised a new lease on life. The new firm made its home in Quincy, Mich. and for a time in Elkhart, Ind., but assembly of the airplane actually took place in the plant shared by Al Meyers, the Meyers Aircraft Co. of Tecumseh, Mich. This new "Dart GC" failed to cope with the terrific post-war competition and it sort of died on the vine, but even yet the sassy "Dart" is an airplane well remembered.

Dart G was a sassy little sport.

Listed below are specifications and performance data for the "Dart G" as powered with Lambert R-266 engine rated 90 h.p. at 2375 r.p.m. at sea level; length overall 18'7"; height overall 6'0"; wingspan 29'6"; max. wing chord 75"; total wing area 146 sq. ft.; airfoil NACA-2315; wt. empty 922 lbs.; useful load 595 lbs.; payload with 25 gal. fuel 252 lbs. (1 pass. & 82 lbs. bag. & extras); gross wt. 1517 lbs.; max

speed (with wheel pants) 135; cruising speed (.75 power) 118; landing (stall) speed 45; climb 950 ft. first min. at sea level; ser. ceiling 16,000 ft.; gas cap. 25 gal.; oil cap. 2 gal.; cruising range (.75 power) at 5 gal. per hour 500 miles; price $3460 at the factory. This model was originally offered as open-cockpit monoplane for $2995.

Specifications and data for "Dart GK" as powered with Ken-Royce 5-F engine rated 90 h.p. at 2250 r.p.m. at sea level, same as above except as follows; total wing area (incl. fuselage section) 176 sq. ft.; wt. empty 950 lbs.; useful load 590 lbs.; payload with 25 gal. fuel 247 lbs. (1 pass. & 77 lbs. baggage); gross wt. 1540 lbs.; max. speed (no wheel pants) 130; cruising speed (.75 power) 115; landing (stall) speed 46; climb 800 ft. first min. at sea level; ser. ceiling 16,000 ft.; gas cap. 25 gal.; oil cap. 2.5 gal.; cruising range (.75 power) at 5.2 gal. per hour 490 miles; price $3500 at the factory.

Specifications and data for "Dart GW" as powered with Warner "Scarab Jr." engine rated 90 h.p. at 2025 r.p.m. at sea level, same as above except as follows; length overall 18'8"; height overall 6'1"; wt. empty 940 lbs.; useful load 600 lbs.; payload with 25 gal. fuel 257 lbs. (1 pass. & 87 lbs. for baggage & extras); gross wt. 1540 lbs.; max. speed (no wheel pants) 131; cruising speed (.75 power) 118; landing (stall) speed 46; climb 810 ft. first min. at sea level; ser. ceiling 16,000 ft.; gas cap. 25 gal.; oil cap. 2.5 gal.; cruising range (.75 power) at 5.2 gal. per hour 495 miles; price $3900 at factory. The "Dart GW" was also tested with Warner 125-145 h.p. engines; the performance increase was quite substantial.

Specifications and data for "Dart GC" as powered with 6 cyl. Continental A-100 engine rated 100 h.p. at 2500 r.p.m. at sea level, same as above except as follows; length overall 19'6";

Post-war "Dart" had 6 cyl. engine.

height overall 6'2"; wt. empty 960 lbs.; useful load 590 lbs.; payload with 25 gal. fuel 247 lbs.; gross wt. 1550 lbs.; max. speed 137; cruising speed (.75 power) 120; landing (stall) speed 48; climb 900 ft. first min. at sea level; ser. ceiling 16,500 ft.; gas cap. 25 gal.; oil cap. 3 gal.; cruising range (.75 power) 500 miles; price not announced. The "Dart GC" was also offered in kit form for home assembly at $1250 (less engine & propeller), but this combination was never approved.

The chubby "Dart" was a low-winged coupe-type monoplane with side by side seating for two. The most unusual features of the compact "Dart" were its extremely short coupling and its wide, elliptical cantilever wing; features that together spelled rigidity, exceptional strength and neck-jerking maneuverability. The "low aspect ratio" principle avoided much of the useless weight and overall bulk, a configuration that some designers used occasionally to trim and condense an airframe so there was nothing superfluous; a claim that every pound of its overall makeup would be a useful contribution. This was all well and good, but a design of this type also imposed certain characteristics that had to be accepted; it was certainly not for the ham-handed pilot because things happened too quickly. In no sense could the twittery "Dart" be considered a working airplane; it was meant to be a fun-loving sport coupe and so it lived, a strictly-for-fun airplane. As powered with any of the three 90 h.p. engines the little "Dart" had a bubbly performance and a gay personality, traits that worried some pilots at first, but it just took a little understanding. The "Dart" had much latent ability that was brought out further and further as the power was increased. As the "Dart G" this airplane was powered with the 5 cyl. Lambert R-266 engine, as the "Dart GK" it was powered with the 5 cyl. Ken-Royce 5-F engine,

and as the "Dart GW" it was powered with the 5 cyl. "Scarab Jr." engine by Warner; the "Dart" was a good combination with any of these 90 h.p. engines. The post-war "Dart GC" by Applegate & Weyant was powered with the 6 cyl. Continental A-100 engine rated 100 h.p.; performance of the "GC" was somewhat better, but this combination was not all that successful in the face of overwhelming competition. The type certificate for the "Dart G" was issued 10-30-37 and amended 4-19-38 to include the models GK and GW; the post-war GC was also on this approval. Some 50 of the "Dart" were manufactured by the Dart Manufacturing Corp. at Port Columbus, O. In April of 1938 the Port Columbus Airport unveiled its extensive improvements by having an air show, and the "Dart" factory was just about ready for production. During the air show a "Dart" demonstrator was busy stirring up local interest. Later reorganized as the Culver Aircraft Corp. it was K. K. Culver, Jr. as pres. & gen. mgr.; K. K. Culver, Sr. was V.P. & treas.; Albert W. Mooney was V.P. & chf. engr.; and V. L. Wikoff was sales mgr.

The fuselage framework was built up of welded 4130 steel tubing, heavily faired with wooden formers and fairing strips, then fabric covered. Seating was side by side and occupants were protected by a large windshield and a sliding Pyralin canopy; dual controls were of the "stick" type. A baggage compartment with allowance for 40 lbs. was behind the seat back; no baggage was allowed when parachutes were carried. The "GW" was allowed no baggage when fitted with a metal prop. The engine, in each case, was tightly encased in an NACA-type (low-drag) engine cowl; the early "G" cowling had "humps" over the cylinders, but the GK and GW cowling was smooth. The elliptical cantilever wing was built up of laminated spruce spar beams with spruce and plywood truss-type wing ribs; double drag bracing, above and below the spar, provided unusual torsional stiffness. The leading edges were covered with dural metal sheet and the completed framework was covered in fabric. A 12.5 gal. fuel tank was mounted in the wing flanking each side of the fuselage; a fuel pump provided fuel flow to the engine. The fuselage-to-wing juncture was finished off with a large metal fillet; a wing walk was provided on each side. The gangly looking tripod landing gear of 78 in. tread used oil-draulic shock struts made by Dart Manufacturing.; 18x8-3 Goodyear airwheels were fitted with brakes. Streamlined metal wheel pants were optional with 6.00x6 wheels and tires. The spring leaf tail skid was fitted with a tail wheel assembly. There had been plans for a retractable landing gear on the "Dart"; it was developed and tested, but not used. The fabric covered tail group was a cantilever structure built up of welded steel tubes and sheet steel formers; a bungee-cord device on the "stick" was used to adjust "trim." A Hartzell wooden prop, engine cowl, exhaust collector-ring, fuel pump, wobble pump, fuel gauges, dual controls, tail wheel, safety belts, and first-aid kit were standard equipment. A metal prop (GW only), electric engine starter, battery, wind-driven generator, compass, clock, cabin heater, carburetor heat-box, dual brake pedals, wheel pants, navigation lights, and fire extinguisher were optional. The next Culver development was the little "Cadet" as described in the chapter for ATC # 730.

Listed below are "Dart" entries as gleaned from registration records:

Applegate and the new "Dart."

NC-11791;	Dart G	(# G-1)	Lambert 90.
-18064;	''	(# G-2)	''
-18065;	''	(# G-3)	''
-18066;	''	(# G-4)	''
-20401;	Dart G	(# G-5)	Lambert 90.
-18443;	''	(# G-6)	''
-18449;	''	(# G-7)	''
-20990;	Dart GK	(# GK-8)	Ken-Royce 90.
-20991;	Dart G	(# G-9)	Lambert 90.
-20992;	''	(# G-10)	''
-20993;	''	(# G-11)	''
-20994;	''	(# G-12)	''
'	''	(# G-13)	
-20996;	Dart G	(# G-14)	Lambert 90.
-20995;	Dart GK	(# GK-15	Ken-Royce 90.
-20997;	Dart G	(# G-16)	Lambert 90.
-20998;	Dart GK	(# GK-17)	Ken-Royce 90.
-20999;	''	(# GK-18)	''
-20910;	''	(# GK-19)	''
-20911;	Dart GW	(# GW-20)	Warner 90.

-20913;	''	(# GW-21)	''
-20914;	Dart G	(# G-22)	Lambert 90.
NX-20912;	GW-Spl.	(# GW-23)	Warner 145.
-20915	Dart GK	(# GK-24)	Ken-Royce 90.
-20916;	Dart GW	(# GW-25)	Warner 90.
-20917;	Dart G	(# G-26)	Lambert 90.
-20918;	Dart GW	(# GW-27)	Warner 90.
-20919;	''	(# GW-28)	''
-20920;	Dart GK	(# GK-29)	Ken-Royce 90.
:	''	(# GK-30)	''
-20922;	''	(# GK-31)	''
-20923;	''	(# GK-32)	''
-20924;	''	(# GK-33)	''
-20930;	''	(# GK-34)	''
-20931;	Dart GW	(# GW-35)	Warner 90.
-20932;	Dart GK	(# GK-36)	Ken-Royce 90.
-20933;	''	(# GK-37)	''
-20934;	''	(# GK-38)	''
-20935;	''	(# GK-39)	''
-20936;	''	(# GK-40)	''
NX-20937;	GW-125	(# GW-41)	Warner 125.
-20938;	Dart GK	(# GK-42)	Ken-Royce 90.
-20939;	''	(# GK-43)	''
-20940;	Dart GW	(# GW-44)	Warner 90.
-20941;	Dart GK	(# GK-45)	Ken-Royce 90.
-20942;	''	(# GK-46)	''
:	''	(# GK-47)	''
-20944;	''	(# GK-48)	''

This approval for ser. # G-2 and up as Dart G; ser. # G-1 (Monosport G) also eligible when modified to conform; for ser. # GK-8 and up as Dart GK; for ser. # GW-20 and up as Dart GW; ser. # G-3, GW-21, GW-25, GW-28, and GW-35 del. to Parks Air College; ser. # GW-23 tested with Warner "Super Scarab" (145 h.p.) engine; ser. # GW-41 tested with Warner "Scarab" (125 h.p.) engine; ser. # GW-44 first as Dart GK; ser. # G-13 apparently not used; this approval also for Dart GC, of which about 10 were built.

ATC # 675
(4-26-38)
AERONCA "CHIEF," KCA (50-C)

Aeronca KCA still shows K-type lines.

Continental Motors had their new 50 h.p. (A-50) flat-four engine under development for over a year; nearly all of the lightplane manufacturers were waiting patiently for its government approval and its eventual release to the industry. They at Aeronca already had a completed airplane waiting for delivery of the engine; it was sitting there on the assembly floor ready to go, and just waiting for the powerplant that would bring it to life. The new engine was finally released and "Aeronca" got the jump on the other lightplane builders; they rolled out their airplane as the first to be powered with the Continental A-50 engine. This new airplane by Aeronca was the model KCA; the KCA was actually little more than a redesigned model KC, but its eventual improvements came along as it was being built. By the time the slightly larger and heavier model 50-C came around the changes and improvements in this series were becoming very obvious. We have to note that the A-50 engine was a milestone in lightplane engine development; it was this engine that sparked a revolution in the airplane engine business, convincing other powerplant manufacturers that the future lay with this type of engine. After some 65 of the model KCA were built, Aeronca introduced the improved model 50-C "Chief" which incorporated a wider fuselage, a bigger wing, and other useful improvements. The popular Aeronca "K" was still being built, at least 350 of these were built in all, and perhaps 200 or more of the

50-C were rolled out for delivery. By 1939 the rugged Continental A-50 engine was redesigned a little and rerated to deliver 65 h.p.; with it Aeronca proudly introduced the model 65-C. Spurred by the increase in performance they again looked around for records to smash. Equipped with "Edo" floats, Henry Chapman flew a brand new 65-C on a non-stop record flight from New York to New Orleans, a 1180 mile over-water hop on which he averaged 88 m.p.h. for a total flight time of 13.5 hours. Taking off at gross weight of 1593 lbs. the 65-C had 81 gals. of fuel aboard, and 20 gals. of it were still left at the finish. Aeronca reminded all that this beat a "Taylorcraft" record of 902 miles. Without a doubt, the Aeronca "Chief" was getting to be quite an airplane by now. The Aeronca 65-C and the improved 65-CA were basically the same airplane as the earlier "Chief," but of course, they were heavier, much improved, and packed the extra horsepower. These were the "Super Chief."

In some people the new "Aeronca" inspired adventure, and so it happened to Johnnie Jones, a DC-3 pilot for American Airlines. Can you imagine a non-stop flight from Los Angeles to New York in a 50 h.p. lightplane? This unbelievable plan was instigated by Wooten and Friedlander of "Aeronca," and Jones practically begged to be the pilot for this jaunt. A Continental-powered model 50-C was picked to do the job, and Jones spent all his free time in seeing it

Aeronca 50-C showed many improvements.

prepared for the flight. After flight testing, Jones and the 50-C left the Aeronca factory for the west coast where the proposed record hop would begin. Literally surrounded by 146 gals. of fuel, and tipping the scales at 1925 lbs., nearly 800 lbs. over-weight, Jones "gunned" the wobbly 50-C (at 6:30 A.M. on 29 Nov. 1938) and was airborne in less than 3000 ft. Climb was sluggish and response to controls was slower, but Jones had "Lady Luck" riding with him, so he eased through the treacherous San Gorgonio Pass without a jolt. With some apprehension behind him, Jones settled down and relaxed to save energy for the job ahead. After being jostled about by the hot desert below, Jones finally arrived over El Paso, Texas in exactly 12 hours flying time. The quiet night fell clear with up to 60 miles of visibility at times, so Jones followed the flashing beacons to Texarkana which was about midway to New York. Shortly after daybreak he flew over the "Aeronca" factory where hundreds of people were waving and cheering him on. By "buzzing the field" he acknowledged their good luck wishes and pressed on; he was in the home stretch now. The murky cloud ahead was "Smoky City" (Pittsburgh) and beyond that the many oil-rigs of Pennsylvania. A blizzard over the Alleghennies put a stop to the sight-seeing for a while, and Jones had to "go on instruments." Breaking out into the clear over Teterboro, N.J., Jones was met by another "Aeronca" and the two flew in formation to Roosevelt Field. Signalling thanks to his new found friend, Jones slanted down to land and his wheels touched the runway at 4:18 P.M. He had been in the air for 30 hrs. and 47 min., covering 2785 miles at an average speed of 90 m.p.h.!!Planned by Aeronca to promote their new line of airplanes, this flight

left no doubt that the current lightplane was no longer "a flivver," and could really perform a useful service. Because of this flight and other developments in 1938 the aviation industry as a whole was taking a good look at the Aeronca, Piper, and Taylorcraft with better appreciation of their capabilities.

All of the airplanes in this particular "Aeronca" series were light cabin monoplanes with side by side seating for two. This prolific series was kicked off with the model "KCA" which was basically an improved "KC" airframe fortified with the power of a Continental A-50 (50 h.p.) engine. When the "Model 50" series was introduced it was first powered also with the A-50 engine, and was labeled the 50-C. This airplane, somewhat bigger and a little heavier, was of the type made famous by a non-stop flight across the nation; a towering example of "Aeronca" dependability. In 1939 when the 4 cyl. Continental engine was improved, run at a higher r.p.m., and rerated to 65 h.p., Aeronca had modified their basic airplane into a model 65-C; an airplane which was again a bit heavier and also a better airplane. Yearly improvement was inevitable and the final improvement in this popular series was the model 65-CA (1941) which had all the room, convenience, and performance that one could rightfully expect in a light airplane. As powered with the 50 h.p. Continental A-50 engine the models KCA and 50-C (Chief) were both respectable lightplanes that had worked their way out of the "flivver" class, and proved that a lightplane of this day need not be restricted to aimless circles within sight of an airstrip. As powered with the 65 h.p. Continental A-65 engine the 65-C and the 65-CA (Super Chief) were good examples of the strides taken in light airplane development; their popularity

262

Army tested 50-C, but disapproved of side-by-side seating.

50-C with 50 h.p. Continental engine was big seller.

was proof that "Aeronca" was giving the airplane-buyer a lot for his money. Flying schools, both large and small, were especially fond of the rugged "Aeronca" as were flying clubs, weekend sportsmen, and an increasing number of small business houses. As war clouds drew ever nearer "Aeronca" suspended civilian production, and became totally involved in the war-time effort. The type certificate for the models KCA and 50-C was issued 4-26-38 and later amended to include the models 65-C and 65-CA. The Aeronautical Corp. of America in Cincinnati, Ohio had produced about 65 of the KCA, nearly 200 of the 50-C, and literally hundreds of the models 65-C and 65-CA.

Listed below are specifications and performance data for the "Aeronca" model KCA as powered with Continental A-50-1 engine rated 50 h.p. at 1900 r.p.m. at sea level; length overall 20'7"; height overall 6'6"; wingspan 36'0"; wing chord 50"; total wing area 146.35 sq. ft.; airfoil Clark Y; wt. empty 630 lbs.; useful load 450 lbs.; payload with 10 gal. fuel 210 lbs. (1 pass., 20 lbs.

bag., 20 lbs. extras); gross wt. 1080 lbs.; max. speed 100; cruising speed (.85 power) 90; landing (stall) speed 35; climb 550 ft. first min. at sea level; ser. ceiling 14,000 ft.; gas cap. 10 gal. oil cap. 4 qts.; cruising range (.85 power) at 3.75 gal. per hour 250 miles; price $1695 at factory. Gross wt. later amended to 1130 lbs. to allow heavier empty weight.

Specifications and performance data for the "Aeronca" model 50-C as powered with Continental A-50-1 engine rated 50 h.p. at 1900 r.p.m. at sea level; length overall 21'1"; height overall 6'3"; wingspan 36'0"; wing chord 58"; total wing area 169 sq. ft.; airfoil Clark Y; wt. empty 670 (690) lbs.; useful load 460 lbs.; payload with 12 gal. fuel 210 lbs. (1 pass. & 40 lbs. baggage); gross wt. 1130 (1150) lbs.; figures in parentheses as later amended; max. speed 100; cruising speed (.85 power) 90; landing (stall) speed 36; climb 500 ft. first min. at sea level; ser. ceiling 13,000 ft.; gas cap. 12 gal.; oil cap. 4 qts.; cruising range (.85 power) at 3.75 gal. per hour 270 miles; price $1795 at factory, lowered to

$1695 in 1939. Also eligible as sea plane on Edo 60-1320 twin-float gear at 1253 lbs. gross wt.

Specifications and performance data for the "Aeronca" model 65-C as powered with Continental A-65 engine rated 65 h.p. at 2350 r.p.m. at sea level; length overall 21'0"; height overall 6'3"; wingspan 36'0"; wing chord 58"; total wing area 169 sq. ft.; airfoil Clark Y; wt. empty 675 lbs.; useful load 480 lbs.; payload with 12 gal. fuel 230 lbs. (1 pass., 40 lbs. bag., 20 lbs. extras); gross wt. 1155 lbs.; max. speed 105; cruising speed (.85 power) 95; landing (stall) speed 37; climb 600 ft. first min. at sea level; ser. ceiling 14,000 ft.; gas cap. 12 gal.; oil cap. 4 qts.; cruising range (.85 power) at 4.5 gal. per hour 260 miles; price $1795 at factory.

Specifications and performance data for the "Aeronca" model 65-CA as powered with Continental A-65 engine rated 65 h.p. at 2350 r.p.m. at sea level; length overall 20'10"; height overall 6'3"; wingspan 36'0"; wing chord 58"; total wing area 169 sq. ft.; airfoil Clark Y; wt. empty 744 lbs.; useful load 506 lbs.; payload with 17 gal. fuel 226 lbs. (1 pass., 40 lbs. bag., 16 lbs. extras); gross wt. 1250 lbs.; max speed 105; cruising speed (.85 power) 95; landing (stall) speed 39; climb 550 ft. first min. at sea level; ser ceiling 14,000 ft.; gas cap. 17 gal.; oil cap. 4 qts.; cruising range (.85 power) at 4.5 gal. per hour 260 miles; price $1895 at factory. Also available for $598 down and balance in 12 months.

The fuselage framework was built up of welded 4130 and 1025 steel tubing, heavily faired to shape with wooden formers and fairing strips, then fabric covered. The 65-CA had an entry door on each side; other models had one door on the right; an extra door for the others was optional. Dual wheel-type controls were standard, but stick-type controls were optional in all models. The baggage compartment was behind the seat. The Continental engine was fully cowled-in on all models; the 50-C, by the way, was first of the lightplanes to have a fully cowled engine. Other manufacturers followed suit as

time went by. The 10-12-17 gal. fuel tanks were mounted high in the fuselage behind the firewall; an 8 gal. aux. tank could be mounted in the baggage area. The wing framework, in 2 halves, was built up of solid spruce spar beams with spruce and plywood truss-type wing ribs; the leading edges were covered with dural metal sheet and the completed framework was covered in fabric. Freise-type ailerons were a dural metal frame covered with fabric. The vee-type wing bracing struts were of streamlined dural tubing. The split-type landing gear of 2 "faired vees" used oleo-spring shock struts; 6.00x6 wheels with mechanical brakes were standard, but 16x7-3 Goodyear "airwheels" with disc brakes were optional. A leaf-spring tail skid was standard, but a tail wheel assembly was available. The fabric covered tail group was built up of welded steel tubing; the left elevator was fitted with adjustable trim tab. A Flottorp wooden prop, dual control wheels, basic engine & flight instruments, safety belts, wiring for navigation lights, carburetor heat-box, upholstery of imitation leather, sliding windows, seat cushions, and first-aid kit were standard equipment. Navigation lights, cabin heater, carpet, battery, wind-driven generator, landing lights, extra cabin door, parking brake, tail wheel assy., wheel pants, Goodyear airwheels, fire extinguisher, skis, Edo pontoons, and radio gear were optional. The next Aeronca development was the models KM and 50-M as described here in the chapter for ATC # 676.

Listed below is partial listing of KCA entries as gleaned from registration records:

NC-19785;	KCA	(# 1)	Cont. A-50.
-21016;	"	(# 2)	"
-21017;	"	(# 3)	"
-21018;	"	(# 4)	"
-21019;	"	(# 5)	"
-21021;	"	(# 6)	"
-21022;	"	(# 7)	"

65-CA showed many refinements and more power.

-21023;	"	(# 8)	"
-21024;	"	(# 9	"
-21025;	"	(# 10)	"
;	"	(# 11)	"
-21029;	"	(# 12)	"
-21030;	"	(# 13)	"
-21032;	"	(# 14)	"
-21034;	"	(# 15)	"
-21036;	"	(# 16)	"
-21037;	"	(# 17)	"
-21038;	"	(# 18)	"
-21041;	"	(# 19)	"
-21042;	"	(# 20)	"
;	"	(# 21)	"
-21043;	"	(# 22)	"
-21044;	"	(# 23)	"
-21062;	"	(# 24)	"
-21048;	"	(# 25)	"
-21049;	"	(# 26)	"
-21051;	"	(# 27)	"
-21047;	"	(# 28)	"
-21054;	"	(# 29)	"
-21057;	"	(# 30)	"
-21055;	"	(# 31)	"
-21056;	"	(# 32)	"
-21058;	"	(# 33)	"
-21059;	"	(# 34)	"
-21014;	"	(# 35)	"

Listed below is partial listing of 50-C entries as gleaned from regstration records:

NC-21070;	50-C	(# C-1018)	Cont. A-50.
-21098;	"	(# C-1048)	"
-21301;	"	(# C-1058)	"
-21091;	"	(# C-1068)	"
-21302;	"	(# C-1078)	"
-21303;	"	(# C-1088)	"
-21304;	"	(# C-1098)	"
-21305;	"	(# C-1118)	"
-21306;	"	(# C-1128)	"
-21307;	"	(# C-1138)	"
-21309;	"	(# C-1148)	"
-21310;	"	(# C-1158)	"
-21312;	"	(# C-1178)	"
-21313;	"	(# C-1188)	"
-21314;	"	(# C-1198)	"
-21315;	"	(# C-1208)	"
-21317;	"	(# C-1228)	"
-21318;	"	(# C-1238)	"
NC-330;	"	(# C-1268)	"
-21323;	"	(# C-1288)	"
-21324;	"	(# c-1298)	"
-21325;	"	(# C-1308)	"
-21326;	"	(# C-1318)	"
-21327;	"	(# C-1328)	"
-21328;	"	(# C-1338)	"
-21329;	"	(# C-1358)	"
-21330;	"	(# C-1368)	"
-21331;	"	(# C-1378)	"
-21332;	"	(# C-1388)	"
-21333;	"	(# C-1398)	"
-21334;	"	(# C-1408)	"

-21336;	"	(# C-1428)	"
-21337;	"	(# C-1438)	"
-21339;	"	(# C-1458)	"
-21340;	"	(# C-1468)	"
-21341;	"	(# C-1478)	"
-21344;	"	(# C-1498)	"
-21345;	"	(# C-1508)	"

Listed below is partial listing of 65-C entries as gleaned from registration records:

NC-22100;	65-C	(# C-3029)	Cont. A-65.
-22332;	"	(# C-3399)	"
-22378;	"	(# C-3509)	"
-22352;	"	(# C-3539)	"
-22366;	"	(# C-3659)	"
-22367;	"	(# C-3719)	"
-22374;	"	(# C-3759)	"
-22380;	"	(# C-3799)	"
-22382;	"	(# C-3809)	"
-22377;	"	(# C-3819)	"
-22381;	"	(# C-3829)	"
-22383;	"	(# C-3839)	"
-22384;	"	(# C-3849)	"
-22386;	"	(# C-3859)	"
-22387;	"	(# C-3869)	"
-22388;	"	(# C-3879)	"
-22392;	"	(# C-3909)	"
-22393;	"	(# C-3919)	"
-22385;	"	(# C-3929)	"
-22394;	"	(# C-3939)	"
-22395;	"	(# C-3949)	"
-22396;	"	(# C-3959)	"
-22451;	"	(# C-3999)	"
-22452;	"	(# C-4009)	"
-22453;	"	(# C-4019)	"
-22457;	"	(# C-4049)	"
-22458;	"	(# C-4059)	"
-22459;	"	(# C-4069)	"
-22460;	"	(# C-4079)	"
-22455;	"	(# C-4089)	"
-22463;	"	(# C-4109)	"
-22465;	"	(# C-4139)	"
-22466;	"	(# C-4149)	"
-22467;	"	(# C-4159)	"
-22470;	"	(# C-4169)	"
-22462;	"	(# C-4179)	"
-22468;	"	(# C-4189)	"
-22473;	"	(# C-4199)	"

This approval for models KCA, 50-C (S-50-C seaplane), 65-C (S-65-C seaplane), 65-CA (S-65-CA seaplane; the model KCA was numbered # KCA-1, KCA-2, etc.; the prefix C in model 50-C numbering denoted Continental engine; "Chief" numbering advanced 10 for each airplane and last number denoted year of manufacture; we had no listing available for (1940) model 65-CA; one 65-CA in USAAF as L-3F.

Aeronca KM with rare Menasco M-50 engine.

The development of a new generation of lightplane engines had become quite an absorbing pastime during 1937; at least a half-dozen manufacturers were toiling and burning the midnight oil to have them ready for the lightplane industry during the early months of 1938. This was no secret to anyone, and everybody was quite excited. Engine-maestro Al Menasco was one of these aspirants also. Of course, he was busy enough tending to his marvelous racing engines, but he did find time to develop the little M-50 "Pirate," a 4 cyl. flat-four engine of 50 h.p. quite similar to the already-popular "Continental" A-40. Apparently they at "Aeronca" were receptive to his overtures, so Al Menasco packed up an engine and hied himself quickly to the Aeronca factory. With a K-type airplane already available he supervised the initial installation, he witnessed the maiden flight of the prototype in Dec. of 1937, then he even helped to get the first 10 Menasco-powered airplanes rolled out of final assembly. These airplanes, despite the change in engines, were more or less directly related to the earlier model KC (ATC # 655). There were no problems to speak of, and everyone seemed happy with this new airplane, so it was added to the swelling Aeronca lineup as the Model KM. About this time the improved "Model 50" was in testing with the Continental A-50 engine, and soon after this the same airplane was going through the paces with a Menasco M-50 on its nose; as such it was labeled the Model 50-M. There is no doubt that the "Aeronca" with a Menasco M-50 engine in it flew well and was a

pretty good combination; in all the enthusiasm someone gave Al Menasco an order for 500 of these engines! This order must have been more enthusiasm than promise, because no other Menasco-powered "Aeronca" were built after this initial batch. This engine (M-50) was also offered to C. G. Taylor and Wm. T. Piper, but they apparently declined the offer.

Al Menasco organized the Menasco Motors Co. in Los Angeles during 1926; he had found a way to convert the 9 cyl. war-time Salmson Z-9, a (French) water-cooled "radial" engine into an air-cooled radial engine of some 200-300 h.p. — it was actually rated 250 h.p. at 1500 r.p.m., or a maximum of 290 h.p. at 1750 r.p.m. This engine was mounted in several airplanes on the west coast during the "twenties," and it seemed to perform very well, but its potential was never fully developed. Al Menasco's 4 cyl. air-cooled inverted inline "Pirate" engine was introduced in 1930 and it became the basis for several outstanding racing engines. The 4 cyl. "Pirate" was also used in many civil airplanes that were quite successful, and it performed very well in these combinations. After the A.C.E. "Cirrus" engine and the "Wright-Gipsy" engine were discontinued, Menasco bought up all that was left from both operations to provide parts and service to the many operators who still used these engines. Meanwhile, Menasco developed the 6 cyl. "Buccaneer" and other famous racing engines, but this business was actually more headache than profit. Menasco then turned his efforts to the light opposed-type engine because it looked like a great future was developing for this powerplant concept. The little M-50 "Pirate," a 4 cyl. opposed engine of the type made famous by Continental, was a flat-head (L-head) design that seemed to have good possibilities, but its future was strangled by developments of Continental, Lycoming, and Franklin.

The Aeronca model KM was a light high-winged cabin monoplane with side by side seating for two; the improved model 50-M was similar, but had a little more room in the cockpit. The model KM was practically identical to the earlier "KC", but the 50-M was a slightly larger airplane with more wing area to better handle the 50 h.p. engine. There was a terrific scramble among lightplane manufacturers to keep up with engine developments, and Aeronca rose to the task with a prolific line of models, offering a larger selection than anyone in the lightplane business. In fact, Aeronca was the only major manufacturer that offered an airplane with the new 4 cyl. "Menasco" M-50 engine. As powered with the Menasco M-50 engine rated 50 h.p. the models KM and 50-M offered the performance increases that buyers were coming to expect, and both were good examples of "Aeronca" dependability. The various other "Menasco" engines had a good reputation in air-racing circles, and it was hoped the little "M-50" would tickle the fancy of the average lightplane buyer, but Aeronca had similar models powered with 3 of the more famous engines (Continental-Lycoming-Franklin) and it was these the people were buying. The models KM and 50-M were actually pretty good airplanes, and there's no reason to doubt this, but sales were skimpy, so these particular models were eventually strangled by other developments. The type certificate for the models KM and 50-M was issued 4-26-38 and only 10 examples in all were manufactured by the Aeronautical Corp. of America on Lunken Airport in the outskirts of Cincinnati, Ohio. Walter J. Friedlander was pres.; Carl Friedlander was V.P. & gen. mgr.; Carl B. Wooten was sales mgr.; and James A. Weagle was chf. engr.

Listed below are specifications and performance data for the Aeronca model KM as powered with Menasco M-50 engine rated 50 h.p. at 2500 r.p.m. at sea level; length overall 20'7"; height overall 6'7"; wingspan 36'0"; wing chord 50"; total wing area 146.35 sq. ft.; airfoil Clark Y; wt. empty 628 lbs.; useful load 452 lbs.; payload with 10 gal. fuel 214 lbs. (1 pass., 20 lbs. bag., 24 lbs. extras); gross wt. 1080 lbs.; max. speed 100; cruising speed (.85 power) 90; landing (stall) speed 35; climb 550 ft. first min. at sea level; ser. ceiling 14,000 ft.; gas cap. 10 gal.; oil cap. (in sump) 4 qts.; cruising range (.85 power) at 4 gal. per hour 225 miles; price approx. $1590 at factory field.

Listed below are specifications and performance data for the Aeronca model 50-M as powered with Menasco M-50 engine rated 50 h.p. at 2500 r.p.m. at sea level; length overall 21'0"; height overall 6'3"; wingspan 36'0"; wing chord 58"; total wing area 169 sq. ft.; airfoil Clark Y; wt. empty 690 lbs.; useful load 460 lbs.; payload with 12 gal. fuel 210 lbs. (1 pass. & 40 lbs. baggage); gross wt. 1150 lbs.; max. speed 100; cruising speed (.85 power) 90; landing (stall) speed 36; climb 500 ft. first min. at sea level; ser. ceiling 13,000 ft.; gas cap. 12 gal.; oil cap. 4 qts.; cruising range (.85 power) at 4 gal. per hour 270 miles; price approx. $1695 at factory field.

The Aeronca model KM was built up around the newer K-type airframe as used in the earlier "Model KC." The fuselage was fitted with the simpler tripod-type landing gear of 70 in. tread instead of the two stiff cantilever legs as used on the earlier Model K. The only significant difference in the "KM" was installation of the 4 cyl. Menasco M-50 "Pirate" engine, and some small modifications necessary to this combination. The wings for the KM were the same high aspect-ratio panels (50 in. chord) as used on the earlier Model K. The new 50-M was more or less the same without any major structural changes except that the fuselage was widened for more elbow room, and a redesigned wing had 8 ins. more chord for more area. Dual control wheels were normally provided, but dual stick-type controls were optional. Fuel capacity for the KM was 10 gal. while the 50-M was allowed 12 gal, The landing gear was fitted with 6.00x6 wheels and tires with no brakes; 16x7-3 or 18x8-3 Goodyear "airwheels" with brakes were optional. A spring-leaf tail skid was normally installed, but a tail wheel assembly was available. A baggage compartment with allowance for 20 lbs. (KM) or 40 lbs. (50-M) was behind the rear seat. The models KM or 50-M were not lavishly equipped, but quite a few options were available at extra cost. A Flottorp wooden prop, dual control wheels, safety belts, engine & flight instruments, carburetor heat-box, wiring for navigation lights, and first-aid kit were standard equipment. A cabin heater, battery, navigation lights, left-hand door, tail wheel assy., wheel brakes; wheel pants, stick-type controls, parking brake, wind-driven generator, fire extinguisher, landing lights, skis, and radio gear were optional. The next "Aeronca" development was the model KF and 50-F as described here in the chapter ATC # 688.

Listed below are KM and 50-M entries as gleaned from registration records:

NC-19792;	KM	(# KM-1)	Menasco M-50
-21026;	"	(# KM-2)	"
-21031;	"	(# KM-3)	"
-21039;	"	(# KM-4)	"
-21040;	"	(# KM-5)	"
-21045;	"	(# KM-6)	"
-21050;	"	(# KM-7)	"
-21052;	"	(# KM-8)	"
-21307;	"	(# KM-9)	"
-21070;	50-M	(# M-1018)	"

This approval for ser. # KM-1 and up, and for ser. # M-1018 and up; after test ser. # KM-1 was del. to flying-club in Iowa; apparently there was only one example of the 50-M; ser. # M-1018 first used for prototype testing of 50-C, then also for 50-F and 50-L; ser. # KM-6 was del. to (Maui) Hawaii; this approval expired 12-11-42.

ATC # 677
(4-29-38)
WACO, MODEL AVN-8.

Civil Aeronautics Authority operated this AVN-8.

In the "Model N" series Waco Aircraft had taken an unusual step to offer a "Custom Cabin" biplane that would be easy enough to handle and simple enough to fly well by even the average private-owner pilot. The secret to all of this was to be mainly the 3-wheeled landing gear; a system that offered taxiing with good visibility over the nose, takeoff would be merely driving the "Model N" down the runway, because it tracked straight ahead so beautifully, and letting it practically lift off by itself when it was ready. Landings were also more simple because flare-out was more or less on an even keel, and once down, any tendency to waver was more easily controlled. Takeoffs and landings were still the most difficult stages of flying a normal airplane, and Waco Aircraft felt sure the "tricycle" landing gear would eventually prove its merit. Outside of the unusual undercarriage the "Model N" was basically a "Custom Cabin" design with all the room, comfort, and style that had become the trade-mark of this airplane series built by "Waco". After nearly 3 years of experimentation with the 3-wheeled "Model N" it made its formal debut at the National Air Races for 1937 where it "wowed" everybody; it was the most radical airplane that Waco had built since the famous "Taperwing." They say demonstrations were watched with extreme interest as the "N" showed everyone that it was practically fool-proof; it showed them how it would eliminate many of the intricate techniques necessary in the handling of a normal airplane. Definitely leveled at a certain non-professional clientele the hand-some three-wheeler was offered as the model ZVN-8 with a 285 h.p. Jacobs L-5 engine, and as the model AVN-8 with a 300 h.p. Jacobs L-6 engine; performance was more or less comparable to the current "Custom Cabin" (Model C) that were being built, but its ground and air characteristics were unique unto itself. Earlier studies of the market pointed to a definite need for an airplane of this type, but as it turned out, the customers that could afford an airplane in this price range usually engaged a professional pilot to do the flying, and customers that would benefit the most in having this type of airplane couldn't afford to buy it! It is ironies such as this that affect the future of an airplane; although production of the N-series never reached any great number, it is still remembered as one of the more outstanding "Waco" airplanes.

The Waco models AVN-8 and ZVN-8 were "Custom Cabin" biplanes with seating arranged loosely for 4 or tightly for five. Primarily, the unusual "Model N" was designed as a family-type airplane, or for use by the average businessman who would venture to do his own piloting. Aimed specifically at the older person who found it more difficult, or even exasperating, to learn techniques necessary to fly a normal airplane, especially a high-performance airplane, the "Model N" stressed simplicity and more safety in the portion of flying that was the most critical—takeoffs and landings. The three-wheeled landing gear was to make all this so much easier, and the extra wing-flap area induced the extra drag to forestall the building up of excessive speeds.

Ground-looping was practically impossible, and crosswind landings were managed easily. In fairly good hands the "Model N" was so adept at getting into short airfields that it could actually get into a place it couldn't take off from! Some have said this actually happened. As powered with the popular Jacobs L-5 engine of 285 h.p. the model ZVN-8 had performance comparable to any of the "Custom Cabin" line with like power; the 3-wheeled undercarriage, although heavier, was not that much of a hindrance. As powered with the Jacobs L-6 engine of 300-330 h.p. the model AVN-8 was a somewhat better airplane and it did offer some power reserve; this model was clearly the favorite of the two. Both of the "Model N" had good flight characteristics and promised "to let the young fly sooner, and the old fly longer." The type certificate for the models ZVN-8 and AVN-8 were issued 4-29-38 and in total about 20 were manufactured by the Waco Aircraft Co. at Troy, Ohio.

Listed below are specifications and performance data for the Waco model ZVN-8 as powered with Jacobs L-5 engine rated 285 h.p. at 2000 r.p.m. at sea level; length overall 27'7"; height overall 8'6"; wing span upper 34'9"; wing span lower 24'6"; wing chord upper 72"; wing chord lower 48"; wing area upper 168 sq. ft.; wing area lower 78 sq. ft.; total wing area 246 sq. ft.; airfoil Clark Y; wt. empty 2447 lbs.; useful load 1203 lbs.; payload with 45 gal. fuel 725 lbs. (4 pass. & 45 lbs. baggage); payload with 70 gal. fuel 575 lbs. (3 pass. & 65 lbs. bag.); gross wt. 3650 lbs.; max. speed 156 at sea level; cruising speed (.75 power) 137 at sea level; cruising speed (.75 power) 148 at 6000 ft.; landing speed (with flaps) 56; climb 775 ft. first min. at sea level; ser. ceiling 13,000 ft.; gas cap. normal 70 gal.; gas cap. max. 95 gal.; oil cap. 5-6 gal.; cruising range (.75 power) at 17 gal. per hour (70 gal.) was 600 miles; price $10,695 at factory field. Perfor-

mance figures given here are with Hamilton-Standard controll. propeller. Gross weight allowance with controllable prop later raised to 3800 lbs.

Specifications and data for model AVN-8 as powered with Jacobs L-6 engine rated 300 h.p. at 2100 r.p.m. at 3700 ft. (330 h.p. at 2200 r.p.m. for takeoff), same as above except as follows: wt. empty 2493 (2564) lbs.; useful load 1307 (1236) lbs.; payload with 70 gal. fuel 679 (608) lbs. (3 pass. & 169-98 lbs. baggage); gross wt. 3800 lbs.; wts. in parentheses as later amended; max. speed 161 at sea level; cruising speed (.75 power) 139 at sea level; cruising speed (.75 power) 151 at 6000 ft.; landing speed (with flaps) 60; climb 900 ft. first min. at sea level; ser. ceiling 14,200 ft.; gas cap. normal 70 gal.; gas cap. max. 95 gal.; oil cap. 5-6 gal.; cruising range (.75 power) at 19.5 gal. per hour (70 gal.) was 550 miles; price $11,375 at factory field, later raised to $12,800. Performance figures given here are with Hamilton-Standard controll. propeller; empty wt. later increased to accommodate radio gear & extra equipment.

The construction details and general arrangement of the "Model N" were typical to that of other models in the "Custom Cabin" line, including the following. The interior was rather spacious and upholstered in fine Laidlaw fabrics; cabin vents and a cabin heater kept the interior at a comfortable level. A large baggage compartment behind the rear seat, with access from inside and outside, had allowance to 100 lbs.; the top of this compartment was a hat-shelf for personal items. A throw-over control wheel was normally installed, but a Y-type column with dual wheels was optional. A convenient step was provided to get up on the wing-walk, and the door was large enough for easy entry. An extra door on the right side was optional, and also a cargo-type interior. Vacuum-operated trailing edge wing flaps were mounted on all 4 panels,

ZVN-8 shows off tricycle landing gear.

and the extra area produced considerable drag for steeper approaches and slower landings; flaps not to be lowered above 100 m.p.h. A 35-gal. fuel tank was mounted in each upper wing root for a normal 70 gal. cap.; 47.5 gal. tanks were optional. The tricycle landing gear of 99 in. tread was fitted with long-stroke oil-spring shock struts; the free-castering nosewheel had 7.50x10 wheel and tire, and main wheels had 8.50x10 tires. The main wheels were encased in streamlined metal wheel pants, and the nosewheel was encased in a streamlined metal cuff. The main wheels (in back) had pedal-operated hydraulic brakes. The tail group was similar in construction, but differed slightly in area and shape. Part of the fin and rudder was below the fuselage lines like a sub-dorsal fin; a tail-skid protected the lower end from scrapes. The wing roots, strut stations, and landing gear components were all streamlined with metal fairings or cuffs. A Curtiss-Reed metal prop, electric engine starter, battery, generator, oil cooler, hydraulic wheel brakes, parking brake, wheel streamlines, carburetor heater, navigation lights, landing lights, throw-over control wheel, assist ropes, ash trays, fire extinguisher, and first-aid kit were standard equipment. A Hamilton-Standard controllable prop, Y-type control column, bonding & shielding, radio gear, paraflares, leather upholstery, cabin heater, extra fuel cap. to 120 gal.; extra door & wing-walk, cargo-type interior, and pressure-type fire extinguisher were optional. Interiors and color schemes were fashioned to order. For the earlier prototype development of the "Model N" (ZVN-7) see the chapter for ATC # 686.

Listed below are AVN-8 and ZVN-8 entries as gleaned from company records:

NC-19356;	AVN-8	(# 5018)	Jacobs L-6.
-19372;	ZVN-8	(# 5019)	Jacobs L-5.
VT-AKI;	"	(# 5026)	"
-19399;	"	(# 5100)	"
19361;	AVN-8	(# 5102)	Jacobs L-6.
-19362;	ZVN-8	(# 5103)	Jacobs L-5.
NC-2273;	AVN-8	(# 5104)	Jacobs L-6.
-19370;	"	(# 5105)	"
-19368;	"	(# 5106)	"
19374;	ZVN-8	(# 5107)	Jacobs L-5.
-19367;	AVN-8	(# 5108)	Jacobs L-6.
-19369;	"	(# 5109)	"
NC-2276;	"	(# 5110)	"
-19378;	"	(# 5111)	"
-19377;	"	(# 5112)	"
NC-2278;	"	(# 5113)	"
-19387;	"	(# 5114)	"
NC-17;	"	(# 5115)	"
-20904;	"	(# 5116)	"
-19385;	"	(# 5117)	"

This approval for ser. # 5018 and up; ser. # 5026 del. to Bombay, India; ser. # 5110 del. to TWA as trainer at the Kansas City terminal; ser. # 5113 del. to State of Penna.; ser. # 5115 del. to CAA at Wash., D.C.; ser. # 5116 del. to Brewster Aircraft Corp.; one of these "Model N" was owned by an older woman, and she flew it herself for business & pleasure; 3 of the AVN-8 were in USAAF as UC-72J, and one ZVN-8 was in USAAF as UC-72L; this approval expired 4-13-43.

AVN-8 slated for service in India.

ATC # 678
(4-29-38)
STINSON "RELIANT", SR-10C.

An SR-10C with Lycoming engine.

The Stinson "Reliant" had always been a masterpiece of classic styling and it is remarkable that it could be steadily improved just about every model year. For 1939, once again the "Reliant" was improved in the new SR-10 series, and this time there were some 25 structural and aerodynamic changes. It is nigh onto impossible to make something that's already good, any better, but Stinson design-engineers met this same challenge just about every model change, and proved again in the SR-10 they were quite equal to the task. The new SR-10 was a big, beautiful airplane and it is easy to see where the designers had done their work. The formerly rigid cabin entrance steps were now retracted out of sight, cabin doors were flush-mounted to reduce surface drag, all junctures were smoothed out, the whole inside was completely restyled, and pilots were treated to finger-tip control. The redesigned engine cowl was very snug for reduced drag, and the exhaust system was greatly improved. There was much more than this, of course, but it had to be seen and felt to be fully appreciated. Each year the "Reliant" was getting a little heavier, and sometimes a little bigger, but it remained always a marvelously graceful airplane. The SR-10 series more or less fell into 3 different groups, and the group under consideration here were all powered with various "Lycoming" engines. The SR-10B (economy model) was powered with the 9 cyl. R-680-D6 engine of 245 h.p., the SR-10C (standard model) was powered with the R-680-D5 engine of 260

h.p., the SR-10G was powered with the R-680-E1 engine of 290 h.p., the SR-10H was powered with the R-680-E2 engine of 280 h.p., and the SR-10J was powered with the R-680-E3 engine of 300 h.p. Here indeed was a selection of air-planes that would suit just about any need and preference. Of the 5 models offered with power by "Lycoming," the SR-10C seemed to have the edge and became the most popular version. Prices for the new "Reliant" ranged at or above $12,000, so not too many were bought by private-owners; just about all of the new "Reliant" went to corporations, and the larger commercial operators. Each of these new "Reliant" were as versatile as any that were ever built, and operated on wheels, skis, or floats. Some were even drafted by the USAAF for war-time service.

The Stinson "Reliant" in the SR-10 series was a high-winged cabin monoplane of imposing proportions with seating arranged for four or five. Because of the ominous shaping of world events, Stinson designers and engineers sensed that perhaps this would be the last of the "Reliant" series; because of this they channeled their efforts into making this series the finest that was ever put together. An airplane of this type could not be built cheaply, so the price tag was relatively high; this narrowed down the circle of potential customers, and drew the "Reliant" into competition with other airplanes that promised just as much for about the same price. Still, the "Reliant's" reputation was known far and wide,

A later SR-10C shows changes in engine cowl.

so it did not suffer too badly in the competition. The most prolific group in the SR-10 series were all powered with the 9 cyl. "Lycoming" engine, and with 5 of these models to choose from a customer was bound to better fit his particular needs. In this group there were the SR-10B, SR-10C, SR-10G, SR-10H, and SR-10J; an SR-10G3 and SR-10J3 were also available. Only 2 of the SR-10B were built, and the SR-10H was offered, but apparently not produced. The power spread in this group was from 245 h.p. to 300 h.p., and it stands to reason that the "Reliant" itself was much happier with the more powerful engines. As powered with the Lycoming R-680-D5 engine of 260 h.p. the model SR-10C was the happy medium in price and in performance, so it became more or less the favorite. The SR-10C had a marvelous performance and a very deliberate character. Reaction was generally a little bit slower than what "Reliant" pilots were used to, but very precise, and there was no need for all that hurry — she did everything best in her own time. This is not to say she couldn't be "spurred," she could indeed, but she was happier having her own way. The (245 h.p.) SR-10B was on the low end of the scale, and the (300 h.p.) SR-10J was on the high end of the scale; so then, performance and character would vary accordingly. The type certificate for the SR-10 as powered with various Lycoming engines was issued 4-29-38 and some 45 to 50 examples were built in all. Manufactured by the Stinson Aircraft Corp. at Wayne, Mich.

Listed below are specifications and performance data for the "Reliant" model SR-10C as powered with Lycoming R-680-D5 engine rated 245 h.p. at 2100 r.p.m. at sea level (260 h.p. at 2300 r.p.m. for takeoff); length overall 27'8"; height overall 8'7"; wingspan 41'11"; max. wing chord 96"; total wing area 258.5 sq. ft.; airfoil Mod. Clark Y; wt. empty 2530 lbs.; useful load 1345 lbs.; payload with 76 gal. fuel 682 lbs. (3 pass. & 171 lbs. baggage, or 4 pass. & no bag.); gross wt. 3875 lbs. (later raised to 3900 lbs.); max. speed 150 at sea level; cruising speed (.75 power) 147 at 7000 ft.; landing speed (with flaps) 57; climb 880 ft. first min. at sea level; ser. ceiling 13,500 ft.; gas cap. 76 gal.; oil cap. 5 gal.; cruising range (.75 power at 4600 ft.) at 16 gal. per hour 660 miles; price $10,995 at factory. The SR-10B had Lycoming R-680-D6 engine rated 225 h.p. at 2100 r.p.m. at sea level (245 h.p. for takeoff) and all specifications were identical, except for slightly lower performance. The SR-10C was eligible as seaplane on Edo 39-4000 twin-float gear at 4210 lbs. gross wt.

Listed below are specifications and performance data for the SR-10G and SR-10J in that order. The SR-10G was powered with Lycoming R-680-E1 engine rated 275 h.p. at 2200 r.p.m. at sea level (290 h.p. at 2300 r.p.m. for takeoff), and SR-10J was powered with R-680-E3 engine rated 285 h.p. at 2200 r.p.m. at sea level (300 h.p. at 2300 r.p.m. for takeoff); length overall 27'10"; height overall 8'7"; wingspan 41'11"; max. wing chord 96"; total wing area 258.5 sq. ft.; airfoil Mod. Clark Y; wt. empty 2605 (2610) lbs.; useful load 1395 (1390) lbs.; payload with 76 gal. fuel 730 lbs.; payload with 100 gal. fuel 573 lbs.; gross wt. 4000 lbs. with 6-ply tires, otherwise at 3900 lbs.; max. speed 160 at sea level; cruising speed (.75 power) 150-152 at optimum altitude; landing speed (with flaps) 59; climb 920-930 ft. first min. at sea level; ser. ceiling 15,000 ft.; gas cap. 76-100 gal.; oil cap. 5-7 gal.; cruising range (.75 power at 7000 ft.) at 18 gal. per hour 600-800 miles; price approximately $12,585 at factory. The SR-10H was offered with R-680-E2 engine rated 265 h.p. at 2200 r.p.m. at sea level (280 h.p. at 2300 r.p.m. for takeoff); all specs were the same and performance was only slightly less. The latest offerings were the SR-10G3 and SR-10J3.

The construction details and general arrangement of the "Reliant" had been more or less the

The SR-10 was ultimate in "Reliant" development.

same for several years now, and the SR-10 series varied only in basic detail. Interiors progressively got bigger and a little finer, the entry doors were getting bigger and getting in was easier, vision was constantly being increased or improved, extra fuel capacity was allowed for greater range, and in-the-air or on-the-ground operation was enhanced by electric or hydraulic aids; outside of this the "Reliant" were still pretty much alike. The most significant difference in the new SR-10 series was particular attention to reducing drag, the addition of little niceties that would appeal to prospective buyers, and enhance their desire for comfort. Standard equipment that was normally installed left very little to be desired, but many useful options were still available. Some customers opted for just bare minimums, but others insisted on all that was available; this usually amounted to several thousands of dollars extra. Like its earlier counterparts the SR-10 was also a very versatile machine; it was just as happy in being a well-kept "executive transport" for some corporation, or hauling supplies to some wilderness camp. The SR-10 had room enough for 5, but fuel load had to be reduced if any amount of baggage was carried; with normal fuel load, 3 passengers and a pilot, the baggage allowance was 150 lbs. The cabin was tight, quiet, stylish, and could be very plush; a far cry from the Stinson of 10 years previous. All control surfaces were aerodynamically balanced for fingertip control, and the pilot had everything he needed within easy reach. A Lycoming-Smith controllable prop, electric engine starter, battery, generator, fuel gauges, carburetor heater, compass, clock, dual control wheels, navigation lights, hydraulic wheel brakes, 7.50x10 wheels

with 8.50x10 tires, parking brake, cabin heater, cabin vents, vacuum-operated wing flaps, bonding & shielding, full-swivel tail wheel, map pockets, ash trays, nickeled hardware, assist ropes, and first-aid kit were standard equipment. A Hamilton-Standard controllable prop, wheel pants, landing lights, paraflares, pressure-type fire extinguisher, extra fuel tanks, radio gear, Edo pontoons, custom interiors, and custom colors were optional. The next "Reliant" development was the Wright-powered SR-10D and SR-10E as described here in the chapter for ATC # 679.

Listed below are Lycoming-powered SR-10 entries as gleaned from registration records:

NC-18477;	SR-10C	(# 3-5801)	Lyc. 260.
-18481;	"	(# 3-5803)	"
-18480;	SR-10B	(# 3-5804)	Lyc. 245.
-18487;	SR-10C	(# 3-5805)	Lyc. 260.
-18484;	"	(# 3-5806)	"
NC-2285;	"	(# 3-5807)	"
-18499;	"	(# 3-5808)	"
-18490;	"	(# 3-5810)	"
-18482;	"	(# 3-5811)	"
-18485;	"	(# 3-5813)	"
-18493;	"	(# 3-5814)	"
-18489;	"	(# 3-5816)	"
-18488;	"	(# 3-5817)	"
-18492;	"	(# 3-5818)	"
G-AFHB;	SR-10B	(# 3-5819)	Lyc. 245.
NC-2430;	SR-10C	(# 3-5821)	Lyc. 260.
-18497;	"	(# 3-5822)	"
-21100;	"	(# 3-5823)	"
-18498;	"	(# 3-5824)	"
-21103;	"	(# 3-5825)	"

-21124;	"	(# 3-5827)	"
-21107;	"	(# 3-5828)	"
-18496;	"	(# 3-5829)	"
-21104;	"	(# 3-5830)	"
NC-2330;	"	(# 3-5838)	"
-21105;	"	(# 3-5839)	"
-21106;	"	(# 3-5840)	"
-21118;	"	(# 3-5842)	"
-21109;	"	(# 3-5844)	"
-21129;	"	(# 3-5854)	"
-21130;	"	(# 3-5855)	"
-21131;	"	(# 3-5856)	"
-21132;	"	(# 5901)	"
-21133;	"	(# 5902)	"
-21135;	SR-10G	(# 5903)	Lyc. 290.
-21174;	SR-10C	(# 5907)	Lyc. 260.
-21182;	"	(# 5908)	"
-22528;	SR-10G	(# 5909)	Lyc. 290.
-22540;	SR-10C	(# 5913)	Lyc. 260.
-22529;	"	(# 5915)	"
-22555;	"	(# 5916)	"
-22580;	"	(# 5919)	"
-22583;	"	(# 5920)	"

-23722; SR-10G (#5927) Lyc. 290.

This approval for ser. # 3-5801, 5901 and up; 5800 series were manufactured in 1938, and 5900 series were manufactured in 1939 and beyond; only 2 of SR-10B were built; records note that 46 of SR-10C were built, 12 of the SR-10G, none of the SR-10H, and 11 of the SR-10J, this includes SR-10G3 and SR-10J3 versions; OK-ATZ was SR-10C in Holland, and G-AFVT was SR-10J in England (ser. nos. unknown); ser. # 3-5813 del. to Scintilla Magneto Co.; ser. # 3-5824 del. to Dept. of Aero., State of Mich.; ser. # 3-5830 del. to Shell Aviation of St. Louis—later modified to SR-10G; ser. # 3-5838 del. to Penna. State Police—later modified to SR-10G; ser. # 3-5842 del. to Florida State Road Dept.; ser. # 3-5828, 3-5844, 3-5854-55-56 del. to All-American Aviation (2 or 3 pl.) for experiments in airmail pick-up; ser. # 5919 del. to Maine Dept. of Fisheries; 5 of SR-10C in USAAF as UC-81K and 2 of SR-10G as UC-81A; this approval expired 2-28-41.

SR-10C was most popular Lycoming-powered version

ATC # 679
(5-12-38)
STINSON "RELIANT," SR-10E.

An SR-10E in service with American Airlines.

The Wright-powered "Reliant" was always more expensive than the normal "Stinson" line, so it was generally put together with the best of finery for that small circle of well-heeled customers. It stands to reason that if customers were willing to pay that much more for these models they would also expect the best in all that was available. For the 1938-39 season Stinson offered the SR-10D with 285 h.p. and the SR-10E with 320 h.p.; both models were powered with the famous 7 cyl. R-760-E series engine. Owning a Wright-powered "Reliant" had developed into a prestige symbol, so they were seen only at the better places, and the airplanes always glowed with signs of care and attention. The roster of owners was rather small, but a very impressive group. As nearly always, there were those that yearned for still more power, and tantalized Stinson Aircraft with the idea, so such an airplane was developed in 1939. This was the thundering and stomping SR-10K that bellowed out with defiance to make sure everyone realized what a special airplane it really was; it growled and it snarled, but it had no bite, because after all, it was only a more powerful high performance "Reliant." This was to be the end of the line for the civil "Reliant" because of wartime

commitments, and the last was built in 1941. They all stayed in service for many years to come, and stories of their exploits grew richer as the years went by. In fact, the "Stinson" saga is so replete with special sanctity that if you ever got caught in the telling of a really tall airplane tale, you need but to say that you were flying a Stinson SR-something-or-other, and your reputation was saved, no questions asked. There were 3 versions of the Wright-powered (SR-10 series) "Reliant" and every one was the finest airplane that Stinson craftsmen could put together; they were always rolled out with pride and the customer, or the customer and his hired pilot, were usually waiting at the door.

The Wright-powered "Reliant" (SR-10D, SR-10E, SR-10K) were high-winged cabin monoplanes with seating normally arranged for 4 or five; they were big, impressive airplanes and some say you could almost detect their air of self-importance. Whether this be true or not, we have to concede that the Wright-powered "Reliant" has always been a rather special airplane. In years previous the "Reliant" (Wright-powered) series always catered to people with position and lots of money, but this final offering of the series was practically involved in nothing

New York City picks SR-10K for harbor patrol.

but big business. Names like Gulf Oil, Texaco, etc. were not new on Stinson rolls, and once again they were on the roster. As powered with the 7 cyl. Wright R-760-E1 engine of 285 h.p. the SR-10D was built in only 3 examples and these were shipped off to Brazil as utility airplanes; the Latin Americans had a high regard for Wright-powered airplanes. As powered with the R-760-E2 engine of 320 h.p. the SR-10E was the most popular and thereby the most prolific; its every-day performance was more than upholding the sanctity of "Reliant" tradition. As powered with the 9 cyl. Wright R-975-E3 engine of 420 h.p. the SR-10K was a special high performance airplane designed for the requirements of the New York Police Dept.; it was not exactly a chase-plane, but it had abilities that qualified it for all kinds of police work. This model was offered to others, but only 2 were built. The SR-10 series was first rolled out in 1938 and they continued in occasional production into 1941; Stinson Aircraft like other airplane manufacturers was phasing into wartime production and this would keep them very busy for the next 5 years. The civilian "Reliant" was finished, it had its day in the limelight, but it did contribute further by being a pattern for design of the famous V-77 and AT-19 of which at least 500 were built. The type certificate for the (Wright-powered) "Reliant" SR-10 series was issued 5-12-38 and some 21 examples were built in all. Manufactured by the Stinson Aircraft Corp. at Wayne, Mich. The talented Gordon Israel, co-designer of the famous "Howard" monoplanes, was now proj. engr. at Stinson; his influence was clearly showing in the SR-10.

Listed below are specifications and performance data for the "Reliant" model SR-10D as powered with Wright R-760-E1 engine rated 285 h.p. at 2100 r.p.m. at sea level (300 h.p. at 2250 r.p.m. for takeoff); length overall 27'9"; height overall 8'7"; wingspan 41'11"; max. wing chord 96"; total wing area 258.5 sq. ft.; airfoil Mod. Clark Y; wt. empty 2725 lbs.; useful load 1425 lbs.; payload with 76 gal. fuel 761 lbs. (4 pass. & 81 lbs. baggage); payload with 100 gal. fuel 606 lbs. (3 pass. & 96 lbs. baggage); gross wt. 4150 lbs.; max. speed 160 at sea level; cruising speed (.75 power) 150 at 5500 ft.; landing speed (with flaps) 60; climb 920 ft. first min. at sea level; ser. ceiling 15,000 ft.; gas cap. normal 76 gal.; gas cap. max. 100 gal.; oil cap. 5-6.5 gal.; cruising range (2000 r.p.m. at 5500 ft.) at 18 gal. per hour 650-780 miles; price approximately $14,000 at factory field.

Specifications and data for the model SR-10E as powered with Wright R-760-E2 engine rated 320 h.p. at 2200 r.p.m. at sea level (350 h.p. at 2400 r.p.m. for takeoff) same as above except as follows; length overall 27'10"; wt. empty 2730 lbs.; useful load 1420 lbs.; payload with 76 gal. fuel 756 lbs. (4 pass. & 76 lbs. baggage); payload with 100 gal. fuel 601 lbs. (3 pass. & 91 lbs. baggage); gross wt. 4150 lbs.; max. speed 163 at sea level; cruising speed (.75 power) 155 at 6300 ft.; landing speed (with flaps) 60; climb 970 ft. first min. at sea level; ser. ceiling 17,000 ft.; gas cap. normal 76 gal.; gas cap. max. 100 gal.; oil cap. 5 to 6.5 gal.; cruising range (2000 r.p.m. at 6300 ft.) at 19 gal. per hour 620-750 miles; price $14,350 and up at the factory field. All options were extra.

Specifications and data for the model SR-10K as powered with Wright R-975-E3 engine rated 420 h.p. at 2200 r.p.m. at 1400 ft. (450 h.p. at 2250 r.p.m. for takeoff) same as above except as follows; length overall 28'0''; wt. empty 3045 lbs.; useful load 1605 lbs.; payload with 100 gal. fuel 786 lbs. (4 pass. & 106 lbs. bag.); gross wt. 4650 lbs.; max. speed 175 at 1400 ft.; cruising speed (.75 power) 168 at 7000 ft.; landing speed (with flaps) 65; climb 1250 ft. first min. at sea level; service ceiling 19,400 ft.; gas cap. 100 gal.; oil cap. 6.5 gal.; cruising range (.75 power at 7000 ft.) at 25 gal. per hour 670 miles; price approximately $19,000 at factory. The SR-10K was also eligible as seaplane on Edo 59-5250 twin-float gear at 5200 lbs. gross wt.

The construction details and general arrangement of the "Reliant" models SR-10D, SR-10E, SR-10K were typical to those as described here in the chapter for ATC # 678, including the following. The basic airframe was similar in all models except for the SR-10K which was strengthened in various portions to withstand the stresses of extra horsepower. The "Reliant" was getting quite big and rather heavy, but the thick, massive wing still generated more than enough lift to do the job. Baggage allowance in this series was 150 lbs. for all models; 50 lbs. under the rear seat and 100 lbs. in the baggage compartment. Like other airplanes in this "Reliant" series the SR-10D, SR-10E, SR-10K were restyled with more than 25 improvements, both structural and aerodynamic. It is doubtful if the "Reliant" could have been improved much more. The models SR-10D and SR-10E were normally equipped with a Lycoming-Smith controllable propeller, but the SR-10K was equipped with a Hamilton-Standard "constant speed" prop to better handle the extra power; the SR-10K was also eligible as a seaplane on Edo twin-float gear. For all models, 7.50x10 wheels were fitted with 8.50x10 tires; the SR-10K required 6-ply tires on the main wheels and the tail wheel also. The 5900 series of the SR-10 were same as the 5800 series except for vertical tail surfaces, battery installa-

tion, fuel system layout, exhaust collector-ring, engine cowling, control wheels, and configuration of the pilot's seat. An electric engine starter, battery, generator, carburetor heater, oil cooler, fuel gauges, compass, clock, dual control wheels, navigation lights, hydraulic wheel brakes, parking brake, cabin heater, vacuum-operated wing flaps, bonding & shielding, full-swivel tail wheel, map pockets, assist ropes, ash trays, nickeled hardware, and first-aid kit were standard equipment. Wheel pants, landing lights, paraflares, pressure-type fire extinguisher, extra fuel tanks, custom interiors, custom colors and finishes were optional. The next "Reliant" development was the SR-10F as described here in the chapter for ATC # 685.

Listed below are SR-10D and SR-10E entries: -19368;

NC-18478;	SR-10E	(# 5-5802)	Wright 320.
-18486;	''	(# 5-5809)	''
-18491;	''	(# 5-5812)	''
-21101;	''	(# 5-5820)''	
;	SR-10D	(# 5-5843)	Wright 285.
-21120;	SR-10E	(# 5-5851)	Wright 320.
-21127;	''	(# 5-5852)	''
-21128;	''	(# 5-5853)	''
-21147;	SR-10K	(# 5905)	Wright 420.
-21148;	''	(# 5906)	''
-22526;	SR-10E	(# 5914)	Wright 320.
;	SR-10D	(# 5917)	Wright 285.
-23787;	SR-10E	(# 5925)	Wright 320.
;	SR-10D	(# 5959)	Wright 285.

This approval for ser. # 5-5802 and up; # 5-5802 del. to Texaco, Inc.; ser. # 5-5809 del. to Gulf Oil Co.; ser. # 5-5812 del. to Holland Furnace Co.; ser. # 5-5851-52-53, 5914 and 5925 del. to American Airlines; ser. # 5905-5906 del. to New York Police Dept.; ser. # 5-5843, 5917, 5959 del. to Brazil; one SR-10E to USAAF as UC-81H; this approval expired 2-28-41.

SR-10E shows familiar "Reliant" form.

ATC # 680
(10-30-37)
FLEETWINGS "SEABIRD," F-5.

Fleetwings "Sea Bird" was at home on land or water.

The silver "Seabird" by Fleetwings was pretty much an unusual airplane, but unique mainly because it was built of "shot-welded" (spot-welded) stainless steel construction. It was not the first airplane to be built up in this manner, but it was the first airplane of "stainless" to be awarded an ATC approval, and the first airplane of this type to be built in any number. The Budd "Pioneer" seaplane, identical to the Savoia-Marchetti SM-56, was the first to be built of stainless steel in 1931; it was actually lighter and stronger than the airplane it duplicated. Years of severe testing proved it to be practically ageless. The initiative for this departure from normally used materials came from the steel industry. Much development money was gambled in hopes that more steel could be used in airplane structures, thereby developing a new market for steel sheet. Intrigued with the possibility of building a strong, efficient airplane of stainless steel, Fleetwings experimented for several years to perfect fabrication methods, and the design of structural members best suited for the unusual properties of stainless steel sheet. No doubt, Fleetwings, Inc. picked the "amphibian" as their first airplane to produce because a water-going airplane would certainly be the test for this type of construction, and the many innovations it promised. Jim Reddig, who had long been associated with plane builder Grover Loening, was picked to design the airplane, an airplane which

was based on lines quite similar to one of the last of the "Loening" amphibians. The former "Keystone" plant in Bristol, Pa. and right on the shore of the Delaware River, was acquired for the production of these airplanes which was planned in the hundreds. That they picked a somewhat flimsy-looking, wire-braced monoplane seems a little odd, but all in all, it proved to be a tough airplane and a rather serviceable configuration. It is remarkable to note that of the six airplanes that were finally built, there are two that are flying yet.

The problem of designing airplanes in stainless steel was much more complex than a mere changing over, section for section, from other more commonly used materials; a totally new design concept was required. "Fleetwings" craftsmen headed by Cecil DeGanahl, had been studying the application of electrically-welded stainless steel to aircraft construction for over 10 years, and came to understand the capabilities of this material. But, it certainly taxed a designer's ingenuity. One of the principal advantages of stainless steel in airplanes is that it may be used in closed sections without fear of corrosion. As no heat-treat, anodizing, or protective coating is necessary, the cost of fabrication and maintenance can be greatly reduced. "Shot-welding" eliminates rivets, screws, or other fasteners and it's an easier fabrication procedure; spot-welds weigh nothing so they may be placed

"Sea Bird" shown taxiing out of water onto ramp.

very close together if need be. Because thinner gauges are used in stainless steel sheet there is some problem with local stiffness, so the "skin" is reinforced with stringers and not called upon to carry heavy skin stresses. But, because of the novel fabrication procedure the stainless steel airplane literally becomes one strong all-metal unit. "Stainless" is also excellent material for fuel and oil tanks; beside the saving in weight, another advantage is that small leaks may be repaired in place with a hot iron and soft solder. Commercial grade stainless steel as used for aircraft was coded 18-8.

The burnished Fleetwings "Seabird" model F-5 was a wire-braced, high-winged cabin monoplane of the flying-boat type with seating arranged for 4 or 5. A novel retracting landing gear allowed it to operate as an "amphibian" off land or water. With design goals set to overcome some of the compromises inherent in an airplane that operates both from land and water, the "Seabird" got around most of these handicaps nicely, and was rolled out as quite an airplane. The obvious utility of a capable amphibian was a versatile tool for business, and a convenience for sport, so all of the "Seabird" were working in the pursuit of business, or gadding about the more famous waterholes with some wealthy sportsman. The "Seabird" amphibian practically had the market for this type of airplane all to iself, but oddly enough, "amphibians" were not selling all that well, so Fleetwings had very few names on the order-books. But, because it was an oddity and a very unusual airplane at that, its press coverage and its exposure to the trade was far beyond what it had actually earned. For Fleetwings it was nice to have all that publicity, but it did very little good. As powered with the Jacobs L-5 engine of 285 h.p. the "Seabird"

turned in a whopping good performance despite the handicaps present in a design of this type; it was capable, fast, and economical. Its water behavior was excellent, but the high-mounted engine made land operations a little touchy; it was top-heavy. The airplane was docile in the air having pleasant characteristics, it was comfortably stable yet quite maneuverable. The "Seabird" did require a little special care in its handling, but it was practically ageless, and maintenance was minimal during normal operation. Two of the "Seabird" that are still flying are nearly 40 years old, and practically as good as new. The type certificate for the "Seabird" model F-5 was issued retroactive to 10-30-37 and only 5 examples of this model were manufactured by Fleetwings, Inc. on the banks of the Delaware River in Bristol, Pa. Carl DeGanahl was pres. & gen. mgr.; Wilson L. Sutton was V.P. & chf. engr.; and Kenneth B. Walton was V.P. in charge of sales. It is interesting to note that Carl, Chas. F., Chloe, Jos., and Frank DeGanahl were on the board of directors. Fleetwings, Inc. later continued in the design, engineering, and fabrication of stainless steel assemblies for other manufacturers. They later were busy in wartime production.

Listed below are specifications and performance data for the Fleetwings "Seabird" model F-5 as powered with Jacobs L-5 engine rated 285 h.p. at 2000 r.p.m. at sea level (300 h.p. at 2125 r.p.m. for takeoff); length overall 32'0"; height overall (on wheels) 12'6"; wingspan 40'6"; wing chord 72"; total wing area 235 sq. ft.; airfoil NACA-2412; wt. empty 2500 (2550) lbs.; useful load 1300 lbs.; payload with 70 gal. fuel 672 lbs. (4 pass. & no baggage, or 3 pass. & 162 lbs. baggage); gross wt. 3800 (3850) lbs.; figures in parentheses as allowed with controllable

High mounting of Jacobs engine produced top-heavy moments.

A "Sea Bird" operated by mining company in Canada.

"Sea Bird" skims over water on take-off.

propeller; max. speed 150 at sea level; cruising speed (.75 power) 139 at 3000 ft.; landing speed (with flaps) 58; landing speed (no flaps) 64; takeoff run (fully loaded) off water 25 sec.; climb 900 (1080) ft. first min. at sea level (the higher figure with controllable prop); ser. ceiling 14,500 ft.; gas cap. 70 gal.; oil cap. 5 gal.; cruising range (.75 power) at 3000 ft. using 17.5 gal. per hour was 520 miles; price $22,500 at the factory slip.

The two-step, semi-monocoque hull was a stainless steel (18-8) framework covered with .010 in. thick stainless steel sheet; everything was fastened together by spot-welding. The hull was divided into 5 watertight compartments; the bow housed the anchor, mooring gear, tool kit, engine cover, plus baggage to an allowance of 76 lbs. The second compartment was the pilot's station which was just ahead of the wing, the third compartment was the cabin area for 2 or 3 passengers, and the fourth compartment was the baggage hold with a hatch overhead for access to the cabin. The fifth compartment formed the tail end for mounting the tail wheel, water rudder, and the empennage. A large bubble-type windshield of formed Pyralin protected the pilot's station and provided excellent visibility; a large rounded window each side provided excellent visibility for the passengers, and these windows doubled as escape hatches also. The main baggage hold with allowance for 65-150 lbs. was behind the cabin area which also contained steps to enter the cabin from the top; the main entry hatch was topside just behind the wing, and steps to this entry were in the side of the hull. A hatch in the bow opened up topside for anchoring and mooring; there was a gangway in the pilot's station for entry into the bow from within. The main cabin was soundproofed, well upholstered, the seats were comfortable, and noise was at a fairly low level. The 7 cyl. radial engine, mounted in a streamlined nacelle and encased in a NACA low-drag engine cowl, was perched high atop a steel-tube pylon mount to keep the whirling prop out of damaging water spray; the nacelle was rigged with up-thrust to overcome the nose-down tendency during bursts of power. The semi-cantilever wing framework, in 2 panels, was built up with stainless steel box-girder spar beams with built-up stainless steel wing ribs; the completed framework was covered

with fabric. The wing was braced from top and bottom with heavy-gauge streamlined stainless steel wires; this was an archaic method of bracing, but it held up fairly well in service. Balanced ailerons were of the slotted Friese type, and split-type drag flaps of 15.1 sq. ft. area were hydraulically operated; a manual hand lever was provided for emergency. A 35 gal. fuel tank was mounted in the root end of each wing half; fuel flow was provided by an engine-driven fuel pump or hand operated wobble pump. A 5 gal. oil tank was in the engine nacelle. The retractable landing gear of 94 in. tread was a novel mechanism that folded flush into the hull sides with only the "panted" wheel projecting into the airstream; 7.50x10 wheels fastened to oleo-spring shock struts were fitted with hydraulic brakes. The 13 in. steerable tail wheel also retracted; both landing gear and tail wheel were extended or retracted hydraulically, or manually in emergency. A water rudder improved handling in close quarters, and tip floats kept the wing from heeling in. The tail group was a spot-welded stainless steel structure and all surfaces were fabric covered; elevators and rudder were fitted with adjustable trimming tabs. A Curtiss-Reed metal prop, electric engine starter, generator, battery, fuel pump, fuel gauges, engine & flight instruments, throw-over control wheel, exhaust collector-ring, carburetor heater, cabin heater, compass, clock, navigation lights, fire extinguisher, anchor & mooring gear, engine cover, tool kit, life belts, and first-aid kit were standard equipment. A controllable prop, bonding & shielding, landing lights, paraflares, and radio gear were optional.

Listed below are "Seabird" entries as gleaned from registration records:

NC-16793;	F-4	(# F-401)	Jacobs L-5.
-16918;	F-5	(# F-501)	"
-19191;	"	(# F-502)	"
-19192;	"	(# F-503)	"
-19193;	"	(# F-504)	"
-19194;	"	(# F-505)	"

This approval for ser. # F-501 and up; ser. # F-401 was on Group 2 approval # 2-540; ser. # F-401 later in Canada as CF-BGZ; this approval expired 2-19-41.

Cockpit view shows passageway to bow, and the swing-over wheel.

The "STA Special" had advantage of more power.

The "Ryan ST" was hardly 5 years old, but already it was a classic airplane of considerable accomplishment; not everyone yearned to own it, but they surely flocked around to see it. The gleaming "ST" and its later variants all had a particular charm that quickly drew a crowd; those operators that had them to rent out reported doing a brisk business, especially the ten hour acrobatic course for one hundred dollars. As a new entry in the Ryan sport-trainer line-up the "STA Special" with its supercharged Menasco engine was introduced orginally for the sportsmen who wanted yet more dazzling performance, especially over the high ground of our western regions. The heart of the "STA Special" was the new 4 cyl. supercharged Menasco C4S engine; with a "blower ratio" of nearly 10 to 1 the C4S delivered 150 h.p. at 3000 ft. and at least 159 h.p. was available for takeoff. It was planned too that the "Special" would be ideal for the high altitudes of Mexico and Central America, so the "STM" (military version) was groomed for export. A team from Ryan was sent south of the border to work some of the Latin American countries and they came home with a pocketful of orders. Not many will disagree that the civilian "Special" and the military "STM" were lovely airplanes, and they had performance to match; it was relatively easy to sell the export

version (STM) to military people of our neighboring countries. They admired the sleek, racy lines, and they loved the dash and spirit. Six of the 150 h.p. model STM were sold to the Mexican Air Force, 3 were sold to Honduras, and 12 were delivered to Guatemala; most of these were used as trainers, but a few were fitted with guns and bombs as standby for tactical missions. Ryan sales to the Spanish speaking nations had increased to the point now where it was necessary to prepare manuals and catalogs in the Spanish language. A few civil versions of the supercharged "Special" had been sold to prominent sportsmen, but the grumblings of an impending war had slowed civil sales considerably; as a consequence, Ryan Aero looked more to military markets for sustenance. The coupe-type "Ryan SC" was being produced at this time also, and much of Ryan's metal-working machinery was kept busy making stainless steel exhaust collector-rings, exhaust muffler systems, carburetor heat-boxes, and heater muffs. Much of this activity was but a prelude to the hundreds of airplanes that would be rolling out the doors very soon.

The silvery-shiny Ryan "STA Special" was a low-winged open cockpit monoplane with seating arranged for 2 in tandem; the interior could be best described as intimate. This airplane was

STA Spl. as Air Corps trainer was also a show-off.

specially custom-crafted for high performance at the higher altitudes; it was still going strong at altitudes where other airplanes had run out of steam. With concern for the beauty of lines, and for the perfection of detail, this airplane was also one of the handsomest in the sky. As a sport-plane it was designed for the lighthearted pilot who flew with dash, and who would enjoy what this airplane had to give; slender and trim of figure with tantalizing curves in all the right places, the "Special" had a definite feminine personality that was fun to woo and easy to adore. She was lovely, vivacious, and very capable; and, she didn't like to be ignored. As the model STM, an export version for the military, it was delivered to several Latin American countries where it served on training and tactical missions. As powered with the supercharged air-cooled inverted inline Menasco C4S engine of 150 h.p. the "STA Special" (STM) was blessed with a good measure of high performance, that got better as it went higher; it was "supercharging" that made the difference. The "Special" was an all-around dazzler, and a first flight in this airplane was guaranteed to flush your cheeks. As one enthusiastic pilot put it, "it's a real kick in the pants flying this ship." With the lore it left behind there's no doubt the "Special" had a vibrant, energetic personality that was satisfaction for the demanding sportsman, and a useful attribute for military activities. Otherwise, the airplane was tough, predictable, and quite easy to get along with; maintenance was minimal, easy when required, and operating costs were relatively low. The "Special" (STM) was designed for a purpose and it handled its chores very well; it is remarkable to realize the many

variants that were yet to evolve from this basic design. The type certificate for the "Special" (STM) was issued retroactively to 10-30-37 and some 34 or more examples were manufactured by the Ryan Aeronautical Co. on Lindbergh Field in San Diego, Calif.

Listed below are specifications and performance data for the Ryan "STA Special" (STM) as powered with Menasco C4S engine rated 150 h.p. at 2260 r.p.m. at 3000 ft. (159 h.p. for takeoff); length overall 21'6"; height overall 6'11"; wingspan 29'11"; wing chord 56"; total wing area 124 sq. ft.; airfoil NACA-2412; wt. empty 1046 (1058) lbs.; useful load 529 (542) lbs.; payload with 24 gal. fuel 192 (210) lbs.; gross wt. 1575 (1600) lbs.; figures in parentheses for STM; max. speed 160 at 3000 ft.; cruising speed (.75 power) 135 at 3000 ft.; landing speed (with flaps) 45; landing (stall) speed (no flaps) 55; takeoff run 600 ft., or 435 ft. with 15 deg. of flap; climb 1300 ft. first min. at sea level; ser. ceiling 21,000 ft.; gas cap. 24 gal.; oil cap. 2.5 gal.; cruising range (.75 power) at 3000 ft. using 8.6 gal. per hour 340 miles; basic price was $5185 at the factory. The "STA Special" was later also allowed a 1600 lb. gross wt.

The construction details and general arrangement of the Ryan "STA Special" (STM) were typical to that of the models "ST" and "STA" as described in the chapters for ATC # 541 and # 571, including the following. It is natural that changes and some improvements to the basic design were occasionally made as production continued. The supercharged Menasco C4S engine was mounted completely in rubber, baffled for efficient cylinder cooling, and cowled tightly to eliminate undue drag. The improved

D4S engine, with down-draft carburetion, was also eligible on later installation. The "Special was also eligible to operate as a single-place airplane carrying extra fuel; in this case an 18 gal. fuel tank was mounted in the front cockpit, and the cockpit was then closed over with a detachable metal cover. When not carrying extra fuel the front cockpit could also be used for extra strapped down baggage; a canopy enclosure was also available for the rear cockpit. The military-type STM was quite similar to the civil "Special" except for provisions to mount duplicate instruments and controls in the front cockpit, plus appropriate brackets and racks to mount machine guns and small bombs. The treadle-type landing gear of 66 in. tread used long-stroke "Aerol" (air-oil) shock struts and Goodyear 18x8-3 airwheels were fitted with brakes; the locking device formerly used was eliminated and the tail wheel was now steerable. The elevators were now rigged for 29 deg. up travel and 26 deg. down travel; this a scheme to eliminate excessively violent maneuvers. A Hartzell or Fahlin wooden prop, wheel and landing gear fairings, wiring for navigation lights, dual stick-type controls, removable seat cushions, safety belts, 8 in. steerable tail wheel, manually operated wing flaps, adj. elevator trim tab. oil cooler, fire extinguisher bottle, first-aid kit, tool kit, and log books were standard equipment. A metal prop, electric engine starter, battery, wobble pump, extra fuel cap., bonding & shielding, navigation lights, cockpit covers, a cockpit enclosure, compass, clock, extra instruments, and radio gear were optional. The next Ryan development was the model ST3-KR as described in the chapter for ATC # 749.

Listed below are "STA Special" entries as confirmed by company records:

STA Spl.	(# 121)	Menasco C4S.	NR-16032;
"	(# 141)	"	NC-17307;
"	(# 156)	"	-17352;
"	(# 164)	"	-17359;
"	(# 173)	"	-17368;
"	(# 174)	"	-17369;
"	(# 180)	"	NACA-96;
"	(# 181)	"	-18903;
"	(# 188)	"	-18904;
"	(# 198)	"	-18902;
"	(# 199)	"	-18905;
"	(# 200)	"	-18906;
"	(# 339)	"	-18921;

This approval for ser. # 121, 141 and up; ser. # 121 as single-place airplane; ser. # 141 later delivered to Nicaragua; ser. # 156, 164 first as (125 h.p.) model STA; ser. # 180 to NACA for test; ser. # 182-187 to Mexican Air Force as STM; ser. # 189-190 to Honduras Air Force as STM; ser. # 192-197 to Guatemala Air Force as STM; ser. # 300-305 also to Guatemala Air Force as STM; ser. # 339 manufactured in 1940; ser. # 184, 192, 193, 195, 302, 304 some time later returned and registered in U.S.A. as civilian airplanes; 108 of the STM-S2 that were operated by the Dutch Navy out of Java during 1941-42 were also manufactured under this approval; this approval expired 7-24-41.

An "STM" slated for Mexico.

ATC # 682
(5-27-38)
GWINN "AIRCAR," MODEL 1.

Gwinn "Aircar" shows its unusual profile.

Of the many so-called foolproof airplanes that were designed for the man in the street, the Gwinn "Aircar" seemed to be the most likely to succeed. It was thoroughly captivating to watch it operate, and everyone thought it was some "gee whiz" airplane even though it had all the grace and beauty of a bullfrog. It is hard to imagine what this airplane was inspired by, but nonetheless it was one of the most unusual machines of this time. It was already being put together in late 1935, but there were many problems to solve, both mechanical and monetary, so the airplane didn't fly until early 1937. Designed primarily as a "safety plane" it looked very much like an automobile inside, and was very simple to fly; in fact, they say anybody could fly it. It was basically a two-control airplane, there being no rudder, and it was almost impossible to make it "stall," or fall off into what people called "the dreaded spin." There had been much interest in the so-called "foolproof airplane" since the Bureau of Air Commerce launched its competition a few years back, so the "Aircar" was being studied and watched carefully by all in the industry. The "Aircar" soon demonstrated that it really was

quite a machine with hint of a promise that it could possibly revolutionize private flying. It was an airplane that just anybody could learn to fly safely in just a few hours; if you could drive an automobile you could surely fly an "Aircar." Its potential soon caught the eye of Frank Hawks, famous racing pilot and record setter, who was captivated by the "Aircar's" ability; after a few flights in the machine he was hooked completely. Hawks signed up to demonstrate the ship across the country, and Nancy Love, another famous pilot, was to assist in the demonstrations by lending the ladies' touch. Nancy Love officiated over the exhibit of an "Aircar" at the Chicago Air Show early in 1938, promoting the merits of this odd little craft to thousands of onlookers, many of them women. A west coast showing was also planned. Speed-loving Frank Hawks was having fun demonstrating the "Aircar;" he convinced a lot of people that it was just about the safest airplane that could be built. The irony of it all was that Frank Hawks was killed in the "Aircar" on Aug. 23 of 1938; he failed to clear some high-tension wires on takeoff. The fatal air crash was such a blow to Joe Gwinn personally that he suspended all plans for production and closed down the plant. It is interesting to speculate what would have become of the "Aircar" had this not happened.

The plump Gwinn "Aircar" was an unusual cabin biplane with side by side seating for two. Because of its odd configuration, its slow-turning 4-bladed propeller, its oversized tricycle landing gear, and its auto-like interior, it attracted crowds of the curious wherever it went. As designed by Joseph Gwinn, formerly chief engineer of Consolidated Aircraft, the "Aircar" was of unusual construction and its unconventional arrangement, though seemingly complicated, was quite functional. The bugaboo of learning to fly a conventional airplane was the necessity of coordinating the use of three controls; by eliminating the rudder, a control that most people had trouble with, the "Aircar" became a simple two-control airplane that just about anybody could master. An auto-type "steering wheel" was used for turns in the air and it also steered the nose-wheel when on the ground; a fore-and-aft movement of the steering column controlled the up and down. A floor-mounted accelerator pedal on the far right operated the engine's throttle for takeoff and landing; a dash-mounted throttle control was used in the air. A floor-mounted pedal on the left operated the air-brakes (wing flaps) and another pedal to the right operated the wheel brakes. Because of these controls it was said that a good auto driver could quickly become a good Aircar driver. As powered with the 7 cyl. geared Pobjoy "Niagara" engine of 90 h.p. the "Aircar" delivered a fair performance, but in some instances it appeared to be underpowered. It was designed to be a go-anywhere airplane, but in this it was hampered by the low power. A proposed "Aircar" with the 130 h.p. Pobjoy engine was calculated to do much better. The patented "Air-

car" was a noble experiment in putting the average man in the air — it's a pity the project ended in tragedy. The type certificate for the Gwinn "Aircar" (Model 1) was issued 5-27-38 and only a prototype and one production model were manufactured by the Gwinn Aircar Co., Inc. of Buffalo, N.Y. Joseph Marr Gwinn, Jr. was pres. & chf. engr.; Frank M. Hawks was V.P. in charge of sales; Nancy Love was a special sales rep.; and Richard K. Bennett (or Benson) conducted all initial testing — he gave Frank Hawks his first ride in the "Aircar."

Listed below are specifications and performance data for the Gwinn "Aircar" (Model 1) as powered with 7 cyl. Pobjoy "Niagara" engine (geared) rated 90 h.p. at 3500 r.p.m. at sea level; length overall 16'3"; height overall 6'10"; wingspan upper and lower 24'0"; wing chord upper & lower 43.5"; total wing area 169.4 sq. ft.; airfoil NACA-4418; wt. empty 1095 lbs.; useful load 437 lbs.; payload with 12 gal. fuel 180 lbs. (1 pass. & 10 lbs. baggage); gross wt. 1532 lbs.; max. speed 120 at sea level; cruising speed (3200 r.p.m. at 1000 ft.) 108; takeoff run (with partial flap) over 50 ft. barrier was 730 ft.; landing speed (with flaps) 49; landing speed (no flaps) 55; minimum speed under power 41 m.p.h.; climb 450 ft. first min. at sea level; ser. ceiling 10,000 ft.; gas cap. max. 25 gal.; oil cap. 2 gal.; cruising range on 12 gal. at 5 gal. per hour 225 miles; price was not announced. An "Aircar" (Model 2) was proposed with 130 h.p. "Niagara" engine; carrying capacity & performance was to be considerably better.

The guppy-like fuselage was an all metal monocoque structure of 17ST rings covered with heavy-gauge 52S alloy metal sheet; 7 sub-assemblies were bolted together to make up the completed framework. A convenient step and a large door on each side provided easy entry to the

"Aircar" over Buffalo, N.Y.

"Aircar" was designed to be nearly fool-proof.

auto-like interior which seated 2 across on a wide seat; the cabin was enclosed with Pyralin panels. Sound proofing and a well-muffled engine provided unusual quiet in the cabin allowing conversation in a normal tone. A baggage compartment with allowance for 40 lbs. was behind the seat, with access through a hinged hat shelf. The rubber mounted Pobjoy (British) engine was completely enclosed with an NACA-type low-drag cowl; the reduction-gear housing was offset upward putting the prop high off the center line. The engine was geared down to a ratio of .47 to 1 so normal r.p.m. of the big prop was about 1600 revs. The thick wing framework, in 4 panels, was built up of solid spruce spar beams with stamped out aluminum alloy wing ribs; the leading edges were covered with dural metal sheet and the completed framework was covered in fabric. The wings were braced together with an N-type strut on each side, and interplane bracing was of the (Waco-type) tension-compression strut that eliminated the normal criss-cross wires. The tricycle landing gear of 70 in. tread was of 3 streamlined legs using oil-spring shock struts; 6.00x6 wheels and tires were fitted with mechanical brakes and encased in streamlined metal wheel pants. The nose-wheel was steerable

and not fitted with a brake. The large vertical fin was actually part of the fuselage and a rudder was not used; the fin was fitted with an adjustable tab for directional trim. The horizontal stabilizer (17ST) and elevators (welded steel tube) were all metal structures covered with fabric. A Fahlin wooden prop, electric engine starter, battery, generator, oil cooler, navigation lights, landing lights, compass, clock, fire extinguisher, wheel pants, wheel brakes, cabin vents & heater, glove compartment, ashtrays, sun visors, tool compartment, and first-aid kit were standard equipment. Bonding & shielding, paraflares, and radio gear were optional. We note that the lower wing was staggered back excessively to permit entry to the cabin right from the ground, thus avoiding getting up on the wing.

Listed below are "Aircar" entries as gleaned from registration records:

NX-1271; Aircar Model 1; (# 501)   Pobjoy 90.
NC-16921;   ”   (#   )   ”

This approval for ser. # 501 and up; NC-16921 was most likely ser. # 502; ser. # 502 and up eligible when inspected prior to each approval.

ATC # 683
(10-30-37)
LOCKHEED, MODEL 14-N2

Lockheed 14-N shows off its huge "Fowler Flaps."

The Lockheed model 14-N was a little-known version in the "Super Electra" series, but it was perhaps the foremost "star" of the whole lineup. It was the fastest, the most aggressive, and it literally clamored noisily for attention; in this way it caught the attention of a young man that was to make it famous. Howard Hughes, dapper millionaire businessman and flying enthusiast, was thoroughly involved with aviation and especially bent on setting records; he already set a few and was thinking of a few more. When Hughes first considered the around-the-world flight he thought he might use the revolutionary Douglas DC-1, and then he was attracted to a special Sikorsky S-43-W amphibian which he began preparing for the flight, but finally decided on the faster "Lockheed 14," actually a model 14-N2. This was the airplane he knew could make the dash, such as he planned, in record time. On 10 July 1939 the modified 14-N2 carrying a full crew, and loaded to an unbelievable gross weight of over 25,000 lbs., lifted neatly from Floyd Bennett Field in New York and headed east across the Atlantic Ocean. The first stop was in Paris, France, then on to Moscow in Russia; from there he made his way across Siberia. Roaring across Russia's vast frozen wilderness, as if to tarry would be suicidal, they were finally back on American soil in Fairbanks, Alaska. Pushing on, they made their way across Canada to Minneapolis, a short stop for fuel, and then on to New York City. Landing there amid crowds and turmoil on July 14, the ship had flown 14,824 miles in the elapsed time of 3 days and 8 minutes; it was a tough and treacherous flight, but the big Wright "Cyclone" engines hadn't missed a beat. Think of it — they had left New York City on a Sunday, went clear around the world, and were back in New York on a Thursday afternoon! The world certainly took note of this, and the capabilities of such an airplane were cause for some reflection. Then too, Lockheed was openly promoting their "fast all-metal twin" as a utility-bomber, a warplane that could be quickly converted from the basic civil arrangement, and put "on the front" in the least amount of time. It was these circumstances and the urgency of war in Europe that gave birth to one of the most famous "bombers" of all time, the Lockheed "Hudson." The fabulous "Hudson" warrants much more than we could say here, because its history in action was so exciting, but one thing stands out above all. They called her "Old Boomerang"—she almost always came back.

The Lockheed model 14-N was also an all-metal, twin-engined, low-winged cabin monoplane that was offered normally as an "executive model" for the businessman or the wealthy sportsman. There was no standard interior arrangement because the airplanes were custom-fitted to order; overstuffed reclining chairs, a sofa, a bar, a table, pantry, and complete lavatory were among the appointments available. Interior decor was also custom tailored to the customer's order with a large choice of fabrics and trim combinations. Of the 4 airplanes built in the 14-N version all were plush private transports except the one used by Howard Hughes for his globe-girdling flight. This was a specially fitted airplane that contained all the instruments, navigational aids, and long range fuel capacity necessary for a flight of this kind. As powered with the various Wright "Cyclone G" engines rated from 900 h.p. to 1100 h.p., the 14-N was a combination of exceptional ability and very high performance. Its aggressiveness was brought about by a very low power loading, and this also translated into a sizeable power reserve under normal operating conditions; the 14-N could fly easily on only one engine, even at .65 power. The model 14-N was also offered as a 14-N2 and a 14-N3; the only difference in these 3 models were the "Cyclone" engines that varied in power ratings at different altitudes under different operating conditions. Ratings were governed by compression ratio, octane rating of the fuel, and the amount of supercharging applied; this then tailored an engine to specific modes of operation. Takeoff power was limited to one minute. The type certificate for the model 14-N series was issued retroactive to 10-30-37 and only 4 examples were manufactured by the Lockheed Aircraft Corp. at Burbank, Calif.

Listed below are specifications and performance data for the Lockheed model 14-N as powered with 2 Wright "Cyclone" GR-1820-G105 engines rated 900 h.p. at 2200 r.p.m. at 6000 ft. (1100 h.p. at 2350 r.p.m. for takeoff); length overall 44'4"; height overall 11'5"; wingspan 65'6"; wing chord at root 153"; wing chord at tip 48"; total wing area 551 sq. ft.; airfoil 23000 series; wt. empty 11,000 lbs.; useful load 4650 lbs.; payload with 400 gal. fuel 1685 lbs. (6 pass. & 665 lbs. baggage); standard gross wt. was 15,650 lbs. — provisional gross wt. was 17,500 lbs.; max. speed 260 at 6000 ft.; cruising speed (.75 power) 235 at 6000 ft.; landing speed (with flaps) 65; climb (at 15,650 lbs. gross) 1800 ft. first min. at sea level; ser. ceiling 26,000 ft.; gas cap. max. 644 gal.; oil cap. max. 44 gal.; cruising range (.75 power) using 400 gal. at 90 gal. per hour was 950 miles; price not announced.

Hughes ship being prepared for record flight.

Hughes pauses in Paris during around-the-world flight.

The 14-N2 was powered with 2 "Cyclone" GR-1820-G102 engines rated 900 h.p. at 2200 r.p.m. at 6000 ft. (1100 h.p. at 2350 r.p.m. for takeoff); the 14-N3 was powered with 2 "Cyclone" GR-1820-G105A engines rated 900 h.p. at 2300 r.p.m. at 6700 ft. (1100 h.p. at 2350 r.p.m. for takeoff); all engines used 90-95 octane fuel.

The construction details and general arrangement of the Lockheed model 14-N were typical to that of the 14-H as described here in the chapter for ATC # 657. The basic difference in the model 14-N, and its variants the 14-N2 and 14-N3, was installation of the more powerful "Cyclone G" engines and any modifications necessary to these combinations. The 14-N series were fitted with custom-crafted interiors to do a specific job; two were fitted as business planes, one was a plush private air-yacht, and one was specially fitted for the record breaking around the world flight. Standard gross weight of the "14" was 15,650 lbs., but a provisional gross wt. of 17,500 lbs. was allowed when the airplanes were equipped with de-icing equipment and fuel dump valves. Landings at 17,500 lbs. weight were not permitted; hence, the fuel dumping valves. The robust landing gear of 15 ft. 6 in. tread was fitted with 15.00x16 (8 ply) tires when operating at the provisional gross wt. Controllable metal (constant speed) props, electric engine starters, generator, battery, oil coolers, dual controls, complete set of airline-type engine & flight instruments, fuel pumps, vacuum pumps, hydraulic pumps, cabin vents, cabin heater, cabin lights, navigation lights, cabin carpet, lavatory, pantry, landing lights, paraflares, pressure-type fire extinguisher, fire extinguisher bottles, bonding & shielding, 3 belly compartments and a nose compartment for baggage, ashtrays, and first-aid station were standard equipment. Custom-tailored interiors, auto-pilot, de-icing equipment, radio gear, fuel dumping valves, plexiglass nose-piece for directional loop, fixed wing-slots, oxygen installation, & interphone were optional. The next Lockheed development was the Model 18 "Lodestar" as described in the chapter for ATC # 723.

Listed below are 14-N versions as gleaned from registration records:

NC-18138;	14-N	(# 1416) GR-1820-G105.
NC-2333;	"	(# 1417) "
NX-18973;	14-N2	(# 1419) GR-1820-G102.
NC-17398;	14-N3	(# 1496) GR-1820-G105A.

This approval for ser. # 1416 and up; ser. # 1416 to Mesta Machine Co. of Pa.; ser. # 1417 del. to Harold S. Vanderbilt with Russell Thaw as pilot; ser. # 1419 del. to Howard Hughes; ser. # 1496 del. to Superior Oil Co.; ser. # 1416-17, 1419 del. in 1938 and # 1496 del. in 1939; this approval expired 1-24-41.

ATC # 684
(6-15-38)
BEECH, MODEL 18-D (A-18-D).

An 18-D with Prairie Airways in Canada.

The relative success of the 18-B instigated development of the model 18-D, which was more or less the same airplane, but it was to take advantage of the new L-6 engines. The Jacobs L-6 series engines were just a little bit bigger (in displacement) and developed 300-330 h.p. The added power boosted performance by a noticeable margin at altitude, yet economy of operation was not affected in the same proportion. The model 18-D was not an instant success, to be sure, but Walter Beech believed in it and was willing to wait a while. By now the "Beech 18" had been service tested from the frozen north to the sweltering tropics, on either wheels, skis, or floats; only 8 or so of the "Twin Beech" had been delivered by 1939, but that caused a glimmer of hope and it was some sign of success. Becoming somewhat impatient in time, Beech began hammering at resistance, complacency, and what he called downright ignorance until he finally lowered the barriers and convinced the people he was right all along. As a consequence, 34 of the "Twins" were sold in 1940. By then an improved version of the 18-D was offered as the A-18-D and it became the SA-18-D when fitted with floats as a seaplane. As more and more of the "Twin Beech" began to operate they began to attract notice and close attention; the military services of this country were especially inquisitive and submitted several orders. Of course, the military required an airplane with special characteristics, but this was no problem because the "Model 18" was a very versatile design which lent itself quite well to increases in power and to allocation of duties. A less determined man perhaps would have given up in the face of the resistance, worry, and financial threat caused by the "Model 18," but Walter Beech hung on to his dream in spite of adversity, and made it pay off!!

The Beech model 18-D was also an all-metal, twin-engined, low-winged cabin monoplane with seating normally arranged for 6 to 9 passengers and a crew of two. Because the airplane was actually designed for a great variety of services the interior could be arranged and fitted for just about any purpose; the ship was actually tailor-made at the factory to fit the job it would be doing, and was always tested to customer's satisfaction before it left the factory. Beech was not delivering very many of the "Model 18" yet, but those that were delivered were certainly operated by satisfied customers. Several engine combinations had been tried by now on the "18"; the 18-A with its Wright engines was so far the most powerful, the 18-B was the economy model, and the 18-D was introduced as sort of a happy medium. Of course, the "Model 18" was fitted with a lot more power later on, as we shall see, but the 300 h.p. range was deemed sufficient for now. The model 18-D was a compatible combination with its improved Jacobs engines, and it began to create considerable interest in the "Twin Beech" in general. As powered with 2 Jacobs L-6 engines of 300-330 h.p. each the 18-D

Beech offered 18-D as a business-plane or a small airliner.

still operated very economicaly, yet delivered a respectable increase in all around performance. It did very well on the smaller airports, and was versatile enough to operate also on skis and floats. It proved rugged under most primitive conditions, flew well on one engine after it reached a safe altitude, and generally had the stability of a doting grandmother. Pilots had to pay attention to bring out the best in the 18-D, but it seems that most were quite comfortable with it. The L-6 powered model 18-D was offered through 1939, and in 1940 an improved version was offered as the A-18-D. There is some speculation that the Wright-powered model A-18-A of 1940 was also on this approval, but no confirmation was evident. The type certificate for the model 18-D was issued 6-15-38 and an amendment was issued 5-7-40 for the A-18-D. Manufactured by the Beech Aircraft Corp. at Wichita, Kan. It is appropriate to note here that by 15 May of 1938 some 66 new airplane designs had been submitted to CAA and were awaiting approval. The fruitful minds of America's aeronautical engineers were constantly at work, and that is why we led the world in commercial aviation.

Listed below are specifications and performance data for the Beech model 18-D as powered with 2 Jacobs L-6C engines rated 300 h.p. at 2100 r.p.m. at 3700 ft. (330 h.p. at 2200 r.p.m. for takeoff); length overall 31'11"; height overall 9'5"; wingspan 47'8"; wing chord at root 126"; wing chord at tip 42"; total wing area 347.5 sq. ft.; airfoil NACA-230 series; wt. empty 4336 lbs.; useful load 2864 lbs.; payload with 100 gal. fuel & 2 crew 1849 lbs. (9 pass. & 319 lbs. baggage); payload with 160 gal. fuel & 2 crew 1444 lbs. (7 pass. & 254 lbs. baggage); gross wt. 7200 lbs.; max. speed 205 at 1500 ft.; cruising speed (using 210 h.p. each engine at 10,000 ft.)

195; takeoff run approx. 10 secs.; landing speed (with flaps) 59; landing speed (no flaps) 65; climb 1200 ft. first min. at sea level; ser. ceiling 20,000 ft.; gas cap. normal 160 gal.; gas cap. max. 210 gal.; oil cap. 10-16 gal.; cruising range (2000 r.p.m. at 10,000 ft.) using 35 gal. per hour 800 miles; price approx. $37,000 at factory. Single-engine ceiling was 4000 ft. Gross wt. for A-18-D was raised to 7500 lbs.

All the "Model 18" were of a kind, more or less, except for the powerplants installed. The most significant difference in the model 18-D was installation of the new Jacobs L-6 engines, and any modifications necessary to this combination. The Jacobs L-6, L-6M, or L-6MB were all eligible; a battery and a generator were required for each engine when operated on battery ignition. The interior could be fitted for as many as 9 passengers, or custom arrangements with couch and reclining chairs were also available; when cleared of all seating the interior could be fitted for cargo hauling. Normal fuel capacity was 160 gal. (two 80 gal. tanks in C/S), but an extra 50 gal. tank could be mounted in forward baggage compartment. Other features at random include; wing flaps of 14 sq. ft. area, landing gear of 12 ft. 11 in. tread using 29x13-5 Goodyear airwheels with hydraulic brakes, "Aerol" shock struts were of the easy-riding long-stroke type, full swivel tail wheel was also retractable, trim tabs were fitted to elevators, rudder and one aileron, control wheels were dual, engines and instrument panels were fastened to "Lord" rubber mounts, and a whole big list of useful options were available. Controllable props, electric engine starters, 2 batteries, generators, complete set of engine & flight instruments, wheel brakes, parking brake, wheel fenders, cabin vents, cabin heaters, cabin lights, compass, clock, dual controls, fuel pumps, fuel gauges, wobble pump, carburetor heaters, navigation lights, exhaust collector-rings, fire extinguisher bottles, assist ropes, and first-aid kit were standard equipment. Curtiss-Reed metal props, oil coolers, dual brake pedals, landing lights, paraflares, cargo-type interior, executive-type interior, bonding and shielding, radio gear, pressure-type fire extinguisher, extra fuel tank, lavatory, pantry, skis, and pontoons were optional. The next "Twin Beech" development was the famous 18-S as described in the chapter for ATC # 710.

Listed below are 18-D entries as gleaned from registration records:

NC-18578;	18-D	(# 169)	2 Jacobs L-6
-18571;	"	(# 175)	"
-18572;	"	(# 176)	"
-20775;	"	(# 221)	"
CF-BKO;	"	(#)	"
NC-1284;	"	(#)	"
NC-3250;	"	(#265)	"

This approval for ser. # 62 and up when modified to conform; ser. # 175 as 8 pl. del. to Puerto Rico; CF-BKO (ser. no. unknown) del. to to Canada; ser. no. unknown for NC-1284; ser. # 265 del. as 7 pl. custom.

18-D was powered with new Jacobs L-6 (330 h.p.) engines.

ATC # 685
(6-22-38)
STINSON "RELIANT," SR-10F.

SR-10F proves that "Reliant" grew more handsome year after year.

The big and bold Stinson "Reliant" model SR-10F was perhaps the absolute pinnacle of achievement in this long-running series of airplanes, and as Stinson put it, "This is no doubt our last and our very best." Stinson had a prolific line of models to choose from in this last series of "Reliant" airplanes, but the SR-10F, as powered with the 450 h.p. "Wasp Jr." engine had special appeal to the monied customers. Be they private, corporate, or governmental, they were willing to pay well to enjoy all the extras their money could buy. Of certain models in years previous Stinson Aircraft had said "This is the greatest airplane we have ever built," but that was then, and now they would have to say it again! There's no doubt about it, the SR-10F was truly a superb airplane; it had good looks, it had "class," it had unusual ability, and altogether it was a special kind of airplane. The circle of owners was fairly small, but were a proud group and they never failed to exhibit that pride in their choice wherever they went. The fancied-up SR-10F, because of its characteristics, was used mostly as a "limousine" for private-owner transport, but an airplane with so much ability was bound to be considered as a working airplane where its talents would also be of great value. At least one of the SR-10F went to Alaska to work "in the bush," and the U.S. Dept. of Agriculture used their SR-10F for urgent jobs not many other airplanes could do as well. Routinely it would drop in supplies to inaccessible firefighters, and oc-

casionally to a stranded prospector, or a trapper; it was able in all emergencies and no job was apparently too difficult. During the early part of World War II some 8 of the SR-10F were impressed in USAAF service as the UC-81F; there was also one experimental model (XC-81D) to be used in testing procedures of glider pick-up. Of course, most of the SR-10F survived the war period and served on faithfully in many capacities for years to come.

The Stinson "Reliant" model SR-10F was a big looking, high-winged cabin monoplane with seating arranged for 5 in ample comfort. This airplane was truly elegant, very plush in the expensive "Deluxe" version, and usually adorned with all the extras that one could possibly buy for an airplane of this type. As generally used in the pursuit of business matters, as an executive transport, or the exploiter of a product, the very capable SR-10F offered speed and utility with an intimate type comfort. Like some of the other "Reliant" before it this was an impressive airplane, and it had the knack of making its presence felt; this was good for business. The SR-10F was rather big and heavy, but the massive wing created plenty of lift, and this translated into surprising short-field performance with a sizeable payload. It is logical too that the SR-10F, with all its muscle and ability, would be offered as a multi-purpose airplane (SR-10FM) for freight, charter, or what-have-you. In this version the interior was metal-clad

SR-10F was terrific as a seaplane.

and larger doors allowed the loading of boxes, bundles, barrels, or whatever. This airplane was also available as a seaplane on Edo twin-float gear. The "Reliant" was an airplane with a many-faceted personality—it could put-on-the-dog with the best of them, but it really didn't mind getting its face and hands dirty, either. As powered with the 9 cyl. "Wasp Jr." SB or TB engine of 400-450 h.p. the SR-10F was a lively brute that reveled noisily in its unusual abilities and its high performance. It got off the ground very quickly, had a terrific climb-out, and when leveled off in proper trim it was also hard to catch. Pilots have said that with all this power surging through its frame it was inclined to be a brute at times, but it was inherently amiable and responded well to firm handling. The type certificate for the model SR-10F was issued 6-22-38 and some 18 examples of this model were manufactured by the Stinson Aircraft Corp. at Wayne, Mich. The factory airport was a dinky little field, and Stinson often pointed out that if an airplane could operate out of here, it could operate just about anywhere. W. H. Beal was now pres.; Wm. A. Mara was V.P. in charge of sales; Lew Reisner was gen. mgr.; and R. W. Middlewood was chf. engr. We note in passing that responsibilities of the former Bureau of Air Commerece (BAC) were taken over by the new Civil Aeronautics Authority (CAA) on 23 June of 1938.

Listed below are specifications and performance data for the "Reliant" model SR-10F as powered with "Wasp Jr." SB engine rated 400 h.p. at 2200 r.p.m. at 5000 ft. (450 h.p. at 2300 r.p.m. for takeoff); length overall 27'11"; height overall 8'7"; wingspan 41'11"; max. wing chord 96"; total wing area 258.5 sq. ft.; airfoil Mod. Clark Y; wt. empty 3045 lbs.; useful load 1605 lbs.; payload with 60 gal. fuel 1026 lbs.; payload with 100 gal. fuel 786 lbs. (4 pass. & 106 lbs. baggage); gross wt. 4650 lbs.; max. speed 170 at sea level; cruising speed (.75 power) 177 at 9600 ft.; landing speed (with flaps) 63; climb 1330 ft. first min. at sea level; ser. ceiling 21,000 ft.; gas cap. normal 100 gal.; gas cap. max. 124 gal.; oil cap. 6.5-8 gal.; cruising range (.75 power at 9600 ft.) using 25 gal. per hour was 680-850 miles; price not announced because of the variables in the way it was equipped. Also available with "Wasp Jr." TB engine of 420-440 h.p., or the SB2 or SB3 series.

The construction details and general arrangement of the model SR-10F were quite typical to that of the previous SR-9F except for the following modifications and improvements. The fuselage framework was also beefed up in places to handle the stresses of 450 h.p.; the windshield was now again built up of flat panels because the panoramic "formed" windshield had proven somewhat unsatisfactory during production and it presented some areas of distortion. The engine's exhaust system was improved, and the entire engine cowling with improved baffling, was redesigned for better cooling and less drag. The spacious, plush cabin was an eye-opener, and the soft rear seat accommodated 3 across with surprising comfort. Baggage allowance was 150 lbs. with 50 lbs. of it under the rear seat, and 100 lbs. in the compartment behind the rear seat; a hat shelf was also provided. The big, unusual wing was pretty much the same, but there was improvement in some detail. Three fuel tanks (38-38-24 gal.) in the wing comprised the normal fuel supply, but an extra 24 gal. tank was available for a total of 124 gal. Because of high operating weights the 7.50x10 wheels were fitted with (6-ply) 8.50x10 tires; streamlined metal wheel pants were optional. The "multi-purpose" (SR-10FM) equipment included a metal-lined

SR-10F as used by Forestry Div.

cabin interior, extra door, and cargo tie-downs; the baggage compartment was eliminated to lengthen floor space. The SR-10F and SR-10FM were also eligible as seaplanes on Edo 59-5250 twin-float gear at 5200 lbs. gross wt. In the later "5900 series" the SR-10F was more or less the same, but differed slightly in the fuel system, battery locations, engine exhaust system, engine cowling, pilot's seat, the control wheels, and vertical tail surfaces. A controllable "constant-speed" prop, electric engine starter, generator, battery, oil cooler, carburetor heat-box, wheel brakes, parking brake, dual controls, cabin vents & heater, roll-down windows, fire extinguisher, navigation lights, clock, compass, map pockets, 10 in. tail wheel, bonding & shielding, safety belts, assist ropes, and first-aid kit were standard equipment. An extra battery, extra fuel tank, extra instruments, radio gear, multi-purpose equipment, wheel pants, cactus-proof tires, pressure-type fire extinguisher, freight pickup equipment, landing lights, fog lights, paraflares, parachute-type seats, vacuum pump, corrosive protection for seaplane, and a 16-coat hand rubbed finish in custom colors was optional. The next Stinson

development was the little "Model 10" as described in the chapter for ATC # 709.

Listed below are SR-10F entries as gleaned from registration records:

NC-18479;	SR-10F	(# 7-5815)	Wasp Jr. 400.
-18494;	"	(# 7-5826)	"
-18495;	"	(# 7-5832)	"
-21108;	"	(# 7-5833)	"
-21112;	"	(# 7-5834)	"
NC-2428;	"	(# 7-5835)	"
-21116;	"	(# 7-5836)	"
NC-2429;	"	(# 7-5837)	"
NC-2166;	SR-10FM	(# 7-5845)	"
-21111;	"	(#)	"
NC-2311;	SR-10F	(# 5910)	"

Ser. # 7-5815 del. to Gulf Oil Co. in Pa.; two SR-10F del. to Texas, 2 del. to Florida, and one each to No. Dakota, Illinois, New Jersey, Oregon, and Delaware; NC-21111 (ser. no. unknown) was del. to Alaska; there is record that 18 of the SR-10F were built, but no complete listing was available; this approval expired 2-28-41.

SR-10F as outfitted for summer service in Alaska.

ATC # 686
(10-30-37)
WACO, MODEL ZVN-7.

ZVN-7 poses on factory field.

Shown here are views of the model ZVN-7, Waco's first three-wheeler. It is hard to imagine how Waco Aircraft could have kept this airplane "under wraps" for as long as it did; whatever went on at the "Waco" plant was always good scuttlebutt and worth discussion, but news of this development didn't get out very far. So then, after some 3 years of experimentation and development the unusual three-wheeler was considered ready and prepared for its showing. What better place than the National Air Races for 1937 held at Cleveland to show off a new airplane. It was here that the "Model N" had its formal debut where it strutted before thousands of people and created some lively discussion. The "tricycle" landing gear was not an innovation, of course, because plane builders had used it as much as 30 years earlier, but it certainly was a new idea on an airplane such as the "Cabin Waco," and they were anxious to justify its use. They also say that demonstrations were watched with great interest while the "Model N" showed all that it was practically foolproof, and how it would eliminate many of the intricate techniques necessary in the handling of a normal "tail dragger" airplane. There had always been speculation that many people shied away from flying and owning an airplane simply because it was so relatively difficult to learn to handle a normal airplane well, and there was very little room allowed for error; error in pilotage near the ground was usually costly and quite often fatal. And, because the most critical times of flying an airplane were takeoffs and landings the 3-wheeled undercarriage was designed to eliminate all this necessary finesse. Sitting in practically a level position it would be easy to see out of when

on the ground, it tracked straight ahead for landings and takeoffs, and there was no danger of nose-over when braking hard. Wing flap area was also increased to produce more drag, and to steepen the glide-path, thus eliminating many of the precise calculations normally necessary. While Waco Aircraft was sampling reaction to this airplane they called the "Model N" (prototype) the ZVN-7, and began making plans for production. The production models were introduced in 1938, and built in 2 versions under ATC # 677.

The Waco model ZVN-7 was an experimental "Custom Cabin" biplane with seating arranged for 4 people. Primarily, this craft was designed as a family-type airplane, or for use by the average businessman who would do his own piloting. Aimed more specifically at the older person who found it more difficult, or exasperating, to learn the techniques necessary to fly a normal high performance airplane, the "Model N" stressed simplicity and safety in that portion of flying that was the most critical—namely, takeoffs and landings. Many tests had already proven that the three-wheeled landing gear was to make all this so much easier to accomplish, and the extra wing-flap area induced the extra drag to forestall the build-up of excessive speeds. It has been said that in fairly good hands the "Model N" was so adept at getting into ridiculously small airfields that it could actually get into a place that it couldn't take off from! As powered with the popular Jacobs L-5 engine of 285 h.p. the ZVN-7 had performance more or less comparable to any of the (1937) "Custom Cabin" line of like power; the 3-wheeled landing gear, though somewhat heavier, was well streamlined and it wasn't that much of a hindrance. As reported from many sources the ZVN-7 had pleasant flight characteristics, needed less precise attention, and promised "to let the young fly sooner, and the old fly longer!" After a thorough round of testing and evaluation the ZVN-7 was retired and production was started on a slightly revised version in 1938. The type certificate for the model ZVN-7 was issued rather late so it was dated retroactive to 10-30-37; only one example was manufactured by the Waco Aircraft Co. at Troy, Ohio.

Listed below are specifications and performance data for the Waco model ZVN-7 as powered with Jacobs L-5 engine rated 285 h.p. at 2000 r.p.m. at sea level; length overall 26'8"; height overall 8'6"; wingspan upper 34'9"; wingspan lower 24'6"; wing chord upper 72'; wing chord lower 48"; wing area upper 168 sq. ft.; wing area lower 78 sq. ft.; total wing area 246 sq. ft.; airfoil Clark Y; wt. empty 2401 lbs.; useful load 1249 lbs.; payload with 70 gal. fuel 621 lbs. (3 pass. & 100 lbs. baggage); gross wt. 3650 lbs.; max. speed 157 at sea level; cruising speed (.75 power) 140 at sea level; cruising speed (.75 power) 148 at 6000 ft.; landing (stall) speed (with flaps) 55; climb 775 ft. first min. at sea level; ser. ceiling 13,000 ft.; gas cap. 70 gal.; oil cap. 6 gal.; cruising range (.75 power at 6000 ft.) using 17 gal. per hour was 600 miles; price was tentatively set at $9985 with standard equipment.

The construction details and general arrangement of the Waco "Model N," in this case the ZVN-7 (prototype), were typical to that of other models in the 1937 "Custom Cabin" line, including the following. The interior was quite roomy for four, and neatly upholstered in fine Laidlaw fabrics; cabin vents and a cabin heater kept the interior at a comfortable level. The front side-windows could be cranked down. A large baggage compartment was behind the rear seat with allowance for up to 100 lbs.; there was access from inside or out. A throw-over control wheel was standard, but dual control wheels were available. A step was provided to get up on the wing walk, and the door was large for easy entry. A door on the right side was to be optional. The vacuum-operated trailing edge wing flaps were mounted on all 4 panels and the extra area produced considerable drag; flaps not to be lowered above 100 m.p.h. If the throttle was opened for a "go-around" the flaps would automatically "bleed" closed. A 35 gal. fuel tank mounted in each upper wing root provided the normal 70 gal. cap.; 47.5 gal. tanks were optional. The tricycle landing gear of 99 in. tread was fitted with oil-spring shock struts; the nose-wheel had 6.50x10 wheel fitted with a 7.50x10 tire. The main wheels were 7.50x10 fitted with 8.50x10 tires, and all 3 wheels were encased in steamlined metal wheel pants; main wheels were fitted with pedal operated hydraulic brakes. The tail group was similar to previous Waco construction, but differed in area and shape. Part of the fin and rudder was below the fuselage line acting as a sub-dorsal fin; a small skid protected this assembly from scrapes. The wing roots, strut stations, attachments, and landing gear components were all neatly streamlined with metal fairings and cuffs. A Curtiss-Reed metal prop, electric engine starter, battery, generator, carburetor heater, oil cooler, navigation lights, wheel streamlines, landing lights, hydraulic wheel brakes, parking brake, throw-over control wheel, assist ropes, safety belts, and first-aid kit were standard equipment. This approval was for one airplane only. Airplane serial # 4675 was completed 9-2-37 and used by Waco Aircraft for test purposes only; it was finished in Cadmium Cream with Havana Brown trim and Berry Red edging. The airplane was permanently dismantled on 7-24-39; production models were manufactured under ATC # 677. The next Waco development was the famous "Model E" as described in the chapter for ATC # 714.

NC-17731;   ZVN-7   (#4675)   Jacobs L-5.

This airplane approved as 4 pl. only; this approval expired 9-30-39.

The 3-wheeled ZVN-7 was a most unusual "Waco."

ATC # 687
(6-25-38)
LUSCOMBE, MODEL 90.

The Luscombe 90 with 5 cyl. "Scarab Jr." engine.

The beautiful Luscombe "Phantom" was a love affair designed for the accomplished pilot, and priced for the wealthy sportsman. Unfortunately, the accomplished pilot was not always wealthy, and the wealthy sportsman was not always an accomplished pilot. Somewhere in between there lay a happy medium, and the "Luscombe 4" (Model 90) was groomed to be it. The basic design of the lovely "Phantom" was still the actual inspiration for the new Model 90, but there was no intricate metal work to run up the price, and the overall configuration was simplified. It was, of course, to bear heavily on all-metal construction for strength and durability —no wood, no nails, no glue. During 1937 the Luscombe plant was a mecca for rumor hunters; most of the outlandish rumors were discounted by Don Luscombe, but he did confirm the "Model 4" and also the up-coming "Luscombe 50" which he promised would revolutionize the thinking in lightplane design. As it rolled out one day the sparkling "Luscombe 90" was posing this way and that as a very lovely airplane; they at Luscombe Aircraft were rightfully proud of it. Still it was plain to see that just about everyone was enamored with the talked-about coming of the little "Luscombe 50"; as a consequence, the Model 90 was not "pushed" all that hard for the industry's acceptance or recognition. Dapper "Don" A. Luscombe, known for years as a doer and a go-getter, had a trade school going too (Luscombe School of Aeronautics) where stu-

dents were learning the art of airplane manufacture while building and assembling "Luscombe" airplanes. The plant was busy enough with one thing and another, and a handful of the Model 90 did get built and sold, but the rosy glow of the "Luscombe 8" on the horizon was taking up most of everyone's attention. The Luscombe "Model 90" was quite rare, but it too was one of a very remarkable family. It should be appropriate to mention here that the BAC (Bureau of Air Commerce) was initiated by the government in July of 1934; some 4 years later in June of 1938 the BAC was reorganized into the CAA (Civil Aeronautics Authority) an agency that was to preside over civil aviation for many, many years.

The Luscombe "Model 90" (or Model 4) was a light all-metal, high-winged cabin monoplane with side by side seating for two. This airplane was certainly no "Phantom," but it borrowed conspicuously from the previous Luscombe design. To make its way in a lower price bracket the new design dictated less power, simpler lines for easier manufacture, and less attention to fancy drag reducing embellishments. In spite of the simplified structure and the rather plain configuration the Model 90 was very efficient, and milked each horsepower to the last drop. Overall, it was actually a more realistic airplane that could sell for far less money, and still give you features not found elsewhere at this time. The trim "Model 90" was a good airplane, there's no doubt about that, but the looming boom in the lightplane field was holding back its prospects to nothing but a doubtful and limited future. As powered with the 5 cyl. Warner "Scarab Jr." engine of 90 h.p. the Model 90 scampered around with eagerness, and its overall performance was about the best available for an airplane of this type. The "Luscombe 90" was a strong airplane, and somewhere the news got around that it was "acrobatic"; of course it was not in the true sense, but it was strong enough to hold together while pilots cavorted around dangerously in their ignorance. Normally the Model 90 was fun to fly, and she had good manners, but you had better listen to what she was saying, or end up embarrassed. An airplane of this type and class, no matter how good, had a slim future at this particular time so the "90" was quite rare; it was rare in number perhaps, but it was very well known among aviation people. The type certificate for the "Luscombe 4" (Model 90) was issued 6-25-38 and some 7 or more examples were manufactured by the Luscombe Airplane Development Corp. on Mercer Airport in West Trenton, N.J. Don A. Luscombe was pres. & sales mgr.; Fred G. Knack was V.P. & chf. engr.; Roger Johnson was sec-treas.; and Ben Melcher was plant manager.

Listed below are specifications and performance data for the Luscombe "Model 90" as powered with Warner "Scarab Jr." engine rated 90 h.p. at 2025 r.p.m. at sea level; length overall 20'11"; height overall 6'6"; wingspan 32'1"; wing chord 62"; total wing area 140 sq. ft.; airfoil NACA-2412; wt. empty 1103 lbs.; useful load 622 lbs.; payload with 30 gal. fuel 258 lbs. (1 pass., 60 lbs. baggage, & 28 lbs. extras); gross wt. 1725 lbs.; max. speed 136 at sea level; cruising speed (.85 power) 120 at sea level; landing speed (with flaps) 40; landing (stall) speed (no flaps) 47; climb 750 ft. first min. at sea level; ser. ceiling 15,000 ft.; gas cap. 30 gal.; oil cap. 2 gal.; cruising range (.85 power) at 6 gal. per hour 580 miles; price less than $4000 at factory. Wts. given above are for fully equipped airplane with metal propeller.

The rounded monocoque fuselage structure was built up of 17ST metal rings covered with heavy-gauge 17ST "Alclad" metal sheet. There was a large entry door either side with side by side seating for 2 on a 40 in. wide seat. Baggage compartment with normal allowance for 60 lbs. was behind the seat back; dual stick-type controls were provided. A Shakespeare throttle control was in center of dash panel. The windshield and cabin windows were of Pyralin, and a skylight was provided overhead. The tightly cowled engine was mounted in "Lord" rubber bushings. The wing framework, in 2 halves, was built up with extruded (17ST) I-beam spars with stamped out 17ST metal wing ribs; the leading edges were covered with dural metal sheet and the completed framework was covered in fabric. Vee-type struts braced the wing to lower fuselage. Metal-framed ailerons were of the (balanced-hinge) Freise type, and trailing edge wing flaps of 7 sq. ft. area were manually operated. A 15.5 gal. fuel tank was mounted in root end of each wing half; fuel gauges were visible from the cockpit. The cantilever landing gear of 92 in. tread was fitted with "Luscombe" oleo shock struts; 6.50x10 wheels were fitted with low pressure tires and mechanical wheel brakes. The tail skid was fitted with a small swiveling rubber wheel. The cantilever tail group was an all-metal structure of 17ST spars and former ribs; fixed surfaces were covered with (17ST) "Alclad" metal sheet and movable surfaces were covered in fabric. A bungee mechanism on the stick was adjusted for "trim." A Sensenich wooden prop, NACA-type engine cowl, a normal set of engine & flight instruments, carburetor heater, navigation lights, fuel gauges, dual controls, and first-aid kit were standard equipment. A metal prop, electric engine starter, battery, wind-driven generator, bonding & shielding, radio gear, fire extinguisher, and 18x8-3 Goodyear airwheels with brakes were optional. The next Luscombe development was the popular "Model 8" as described here in the chapter for ATC # 694.

Listed below are Model 90 entries as gleaned

Luscombe 90 lines reminiscent of earlier "Phantom."

"Ninety" shows wide stance and good proportion.

from registration records:

NX-1017;	Model 90	(# 100)	Warner 90.
NC-1253;	"	(# 400)	"
-1325;	"	(#)	"
-1337;	"	(# 403)	"
-1344;	"	(# 404)	"

NC-22026;   "   (# 405)   "

Ser. # 100 was experimental prototype; this approval for ser. # 400 and up; no listing available for ser. # 401-402; this approval expired 7-16-41.

ATC # 688
(6-28-38)
AERONCA "CHIEF", KF (50-F)

The rare Aeronca KF with 50 h.p. Franklin engine.

They at "Aeronca" already had some experience with the "Franklin" engine when they built and tested a rare combination called "CF"; for this version (ATC # 655) they used a de-tuned 4AC-150 powerplant that was rated 40 h.p. But normally, this engine was easily capable of 50 h.p., so the re-rated engine was installed in the new K-type airframe and tested as the Model KF. Only 5 or so of these (KF) were built because by then "Aeronca" had already developed a better airplane they called the "Model 50." One particular airplane had been used as the prototype in these various tests, and with it they had already developed the models 50-C and 50-M; by installing the "Franklin" engine they tested further and so developed the model 50-F. The "Model 50" was a slightly larger airplane than the earlier "K-type," it had much more room in the cockpit, and the wing was redesigned with more chord to increase the area. The "Fifty" was a good little airplane and was now offered with 50 h.p. engines by Continental, Menasco, and Franklin; the new "Lycoming" engine of 50 h.p. was tested some time later and this combination then became the Model 50-L. The 4 cyl. Franklin 4AC engine was later increased to 171 cu. in. and rated conservatively at 60 h.p.; this engine was also eligible in the "Aeronca 50" and "the extra horses" were a boon to all-around performance. Fired up by the relative popularity of the 1938-39 "Aeronca," the front office introduced a gimmick that sold even more airplanes — "buy an Aeronca and

we'll teach you to fly it, free!" However, most of the Aeronca customers were already licensed pilots, and many of them came to the factory to make their choice and fly it home. Aeronca had labeled their 40 h.p. airplanes as the "Scout," but the monicker was used very little; the 50 h.p. models were named the "Chief" and later models were daringly called the "Super Chief." In time these names became very popular, and became a household word, around the airport at least.

The "Aeronca" models KF and 50-F were both light high-winged cabin monoplanes with side by side seating for two. The model KF was slightly improved over the earlier "Model K" and was the best version in this particular line of airplanes; this "Chief" series was also available as the models KCA, CF, and KM. As the "KF" this airplane was powered with the 50 h.p. Franklin 4AC-150 engine and was very much like others in this particular design series. Aeronca was the first builder to use the new "Franklin" engine; the engine showed promise early of becoming a very popular powerplant for the lightplane. In a complete redesign (of configuration but not structure) the Franklin-powered "Aeronca" became the model 50-F, and the name "Chief" was now stressed a little more in company ads and other promotion. The "Model 50" series was a somewhat bigger airplane offering more room inside, it had more wing area, and it was substantially heavier. Nevertheless, it was judged a much better airplane because lightplane pilots had been complaining of the tight squeeze in most side by side airplanes, and in the "Aeronca 50" they could spread out a little. Most pilots were also happy with the measurable boost in power which was responsible in bringing the average lightplane out of the "flivver-plane" class. As powered with the 4 cyl. Franklin 4AC-150 engine rated 50 h.p. the model "KF" was said to be a spritely little airplane, and handled itself well, but it came out on the tail end of this particular K-series line, and was overshadowed by newer developments. The model 50-F as also powered with the 50 h.p. Franklin engine was a bigger, more comfortable airplane and surprisingly, gave up only very little in overall performance; some say hardly noticeable. The 50-F was a pleasant little airplane, but it was relatively rare because "Aeronca" concentrated more of their output on other versions of the "Fifty." the type certificate for the models KF and 50-F was issued 6-28-38 and a total of some 36 or so examples were manufactured by the Aeronautical Corp. of America on Lunken Airport in the outskirts of Cincinnati, Ohio. Jim Welch was doing sales promotion on the road, introducing many people to the new "Aeronca 50."

Listed below are specifications and performance data for the Aeronca model KF as powered with Franklin 4AC-150 engine rated 50 h.p. at 2300 r.p.m. at sea level; length overall 20'7"; height overall 6'7"; wingspan 36'0"; wing chord 50"; total wing area 146 sq. ft.; airfoil Clark Y; wt. empty 628 lbs.; useful load 452 lbs.; payload with 10 gal. fuel 214 lbs. (1 pass., 20 lbs. baggage, 24 lbs. extras); gross wt. 1080 lbs.; max. speed 100; cruising speed (.85 power) 90; landing (stall) speed 35; climb 550 ft. first min. at sea level; ser. ceiling 14,000 ft.; gas cap. 10 gal.; oil cap. 4 qts.; cruising range (.85 power) at 4 gal. per hour 225 miles; price $1565 at factory. The gross wt. was later amended to 1150 lbs. to permit heavier empty wt. without losing normal payload.

Listed below are specifications and performance data for the Aeronca model 50-F as powered with Franklin 4AC-150 engine rated 50 h.p. at 2300 r.p.m. at sea level; length overall 21'1"; height overall 6'3"; wingspan 36'0"; wing chord 58"; total wing area 169 sq. ft.; airfoil Clark Y; wt. empty 670 (690) lbs.; useful load 460 lbs.; payload with 12 gal. fuel 210 lbs. (1 pass. & 40 lbs. baggage); gross wt. 1130 (1150) lbs.; figures in parentheses as later amended; max. speed 100; cruising speed (.85 power) 90; landing (stall speed) 35; climb 500 ft. first min. at sea level; ser. ceiling 13,000 ft.; gas cap. 12 gal.; oil cap. 4 qts.; cruising range (.85 power) using 4 gal. per hour was 270 miles; price $1695 at factory. Model 50-F also eligible as seaplane on Edo 60-1320 twin-float gear at 1253 lbs. gross wt. This airplane also eligible with 60 h.p. Franklin 4AC-171 engine.

Both the model KF and the 50-F were typical of then-current Aeronca-type construction and only differed in size and configuration. Dual controls were normally of the wheel type, but stick-type controls were optional. Baggage compartment was behind the seat back; the KF was allowed 20 lbs. and 50-F was allowed 40 lbs. The gross wt. was later amended to 1150 lbs. for both models, and both models were then allowed 40 lbs. baggage. The KF was allowed 10 gal. of fuel, and the 50-F was allowed 12 gal.; fuel tanks were high in the fuselage just behind the firewall. The wing panels were of similar construction, but the 50-F had a deeper chord for more area. Warner 6.00x6 wheels with mechanical brakes were standard, but 16x7-3 Goodyear "airwheels" with multiple-disc brakes were optional. Landing gear modifications for skis were optional for both models, as was Edo 60-1320 twin-float gear. The Franklin 4AC-150 engine normally operated with single-magneto ignition, but dual magnetos were optional. A tail wheel assembly was available as a clamp-on for the standard leaf-spring tail skid. A Flottorp wooden prop, the necessary engine and flight instruments, dual wheel controls, carburetor air heater, wiring for navigation lights, safety belts, fuel gauge, and first-aid kit were standard equipment. A cabin heater, carpet, battery, wind-driven generator, right hand door, navigation lights, landing lights, wheel pants, parking brake, dual brake pedals, 5 gal. aux. fuel, fire extinguisher bottle, and radio gear were optional. The next "Aeronca" development was the model 50-L and subsequent variants as described in the chapter for ATC # 702.

Listed below are KF and 50-F entries as gleaned from registration records:

NC-21027;	KF	(# KF-1)	Franklin 50.
-21063;	"	(# KF-2)	"
;	"	(# KF-3)	"
;	"	(# KF-4)	"
-21092;	"	(# KF-5)	"
-21070;	50-F	(# F-1018)	"
-21093;	"	(# F-1038)	"
-21316;	"	(# F-1218)	"
-21319;	"	(# F-1248)	"
-21320;	"	(# F-1258)	"
-21385;	"	(# F-1958)	"
-21386;	"	(# F-1978)	"
-21391;	"	(# F-2028)	"
-22107;	"	(# F-2138)	"
-22115;	"	(# F-2198)	"
-22133;	"	(# F-2349)	"
-22137;	"	(# F-2389)	"
-22155;	"	(# F-2539)	"
-22159;	"	(# F-2549)	"
-22179;	"	(# F-2839)	"
-22180;	"	(# F-2849)	"
-22188;	"	(# F-2929)	"
-22328;	"	(# F-3309)	"
-22311;	"	(# F-3139)	"
-22348;	"	(# F-3469)	"
-22358;	"	(# F-3589)	"
-22373;	"	(# F-3749)	"
-22474;	"	(# F-4209)	"
-23561;	"	(# F-5179)	"
-23582;	"	(# F-5429)	"
-23902;	"	(# F-5619)	"

-23984;	"	(# F-5819)	"
-23951;	"	(# F-6099)	"
-23954;	--	(# F-6189)	"
-23969;	"	(# F-6279)	"
-24265;	"	(# F-7009)	"

This approval for ser. # KF-1 and up as model KF; this approval also for model 50-F ser. # F-1018 and up; ser. # F-1018 also used as prototype for models 50-C, 50-M, 50-L; model 50-F also eligible as (S-50-F) seaplane; ser. # F-1038 was on floats in W. Va.; ser. # F-3139 (like several others) was owned and flown by a lady pilot; ser. # F-6279 used in promotion by Franklin Motors; ser. # F-7009 del. to Puerto Rico; note that last digit in ser. no. was year of manufacture—# F-1018 was built in 1938 and # F-2349 was built in 1939; this approval expired for both models on 12-11-42.

ATC # 689
(8-26-38)
BEECH, MODEL F-17-D

The handsome F-17-D with 330 h.p. Jacobs L-6 engine.

The decidedly trim Beech model F-17-D was a happy medium sort of airplane; it was powered enough to be quite frisky, but yet economical enough for most normal uses. Actually, the lowest-powered "Beech" biplane did not exploit the design's full potential, and the high-powered models were just too much for the average owner. That's why the F-17-D (powered by a 300-330 h.p. Jacobs engine) was considered by a lot more people, and the roster of owners would tell us who they were. Several of the (deluxe-equipped) F-17-D went to oil companies who were always in the market for a good airplane, some went to mining companies, one to a milk processing company, some went to sportsman-pilots such as Col. Elliott White Springs, and the dapper gentleman known to all as "Pop" Cleveland; others went to commercial operators who always picked an airplane carefully, and some went overseas where "Beech" already had an enviable reputation. The well-planned F-17-D was a versatile machine which could be fitted for extra long cruising range, it was a spectacular actor in short-field operations, and took to water operations (on floats) like the proverbial duck. A dressed up F-17-D wore a rather hefty price tag for the times, but the value was there to soften sales resistance. A few of the F-17-D were built in the latter part of 1938, but the most were built in 1939; only a few were built in 1940-41 and the last example rolled off the line in 1942. Beech Aircraft was by then thoroughly committed to war work, and the F-17-D was not on the government's procurement list, but at least 38 of the privately owned F-17-D were impressed into USAAF service as the UC-43C; they looked somewhat drab, meek, and shabby in their dull war paint, but as always they did their job well.

The Beech model F-17-D was a distinctive cabin biplane with seating arranged for 4 or 5; there was surely enough room for 5, but that extra passenger usually called for some trade-off in fuel or baggage. The beautifully rounded contours and the sweeping curves were patiently achieved by extensive "fairing," the reckless use of plywood formers and a jillion spruce stringers; although an odd mixture of materials the Model 17 we feature here was beautifully built. Any "Stagger-Wing," and the F-17-D included, was sleek as a greyhound and strong as an ox. It has been written perhaps more than a thousand times that the two-winged "Beechcraft" was a remarkable airplane, and that's as it should be; without detracting an iota from the capabilities of previous models, it is quite appropriate to say that the F-17-D was also a remarkable airplane and one that made ordinary out of the sometimes spectacular. As powered with the 7 cyl. Jacobs L-6 engine of 300-330 h.p. the F-17-D was perhaps modestly powered, but it still had that breathtaking performance that has been associated with the "Stagger-Wing." The F-17-D was not really all that spectacular because it went about its duties in a rather modest way, but a concerted measure of its real performance potential brought surprising reactions. They have said it was a "honey" in the air, and from what they say, it could seduce a pilot in no time at all. Some

F-17-D was at its best when up high and going fast.

outlandish stories have been told about this airplane, and it is quite likely that nearly all are true! The type certificate for the model F-17-D was issued 8-26-38 and some 59 examples of this model were manufactured by the Beech Aircraft Corp. at Wichita, Kan. Walter H. Beech was pres. and gen. mgr.; R. K. Beech was V.P.; John P. Gaty was V.P. in charge of sales; Ted A. Wells was V.P. in charge of engrg.; Olive Ann Beech was sec-treas.; and C. W. Drake was plant mgr.

Listed below are specifications and performance data for the Beech model F-17-D as powered with Jacobs L-6 engine rated 300 h.p. at 2100 r.p.m. at 3700 ft. (330 h.p. at 2200 r.p.m. for takeoff); length overall 25'11"; height overall 8'0"; wingspan upper and lower 32'0"; wing chord upper & lower 60"; total wing area (including fuselage section) 296.4 sq. ft.; airfoil NACA-23012; wt. empty 2155 (2255) lbs.; useful load 1395 (1335) lbs.; payload with 77 gal. fuel 725 lbs. (4 pass. & 45 lbs. baggage); gross wt. 3550 (3590) lbs.; figures in parentheses as later amended; max. speed 185 at 3700 ft.; cruising speed (.75 power) 180 at 10,000 ft.; landing speed (with flaps) 50; climb 1300 ft. first min. at sea level; ser. ceiling 18,000 ft.; gas cap. 77 gal.; oil cap. 5 gal.; cruising range (.75 power) at 17 gal. per hour 750 miles; price $13,980 at factory. F-17-D also eligible with skis or floats; seaplane empty wt. approx. 2650 lbs. with gross wt. allowed to 3940 lbs.; seaplane cost nearly $4000 more. Eligible with two-position controllable, or a constant-speed propeller. The controllable props allowed more "service ceiling" altitude.

The Beech model F-17-D had the long fuselage of the D-series, but still retained the braced empennage of the low-power group. The wingtips were reinforced with plywood sheet to avoid tip deflection, and wing-rib spacing was 8 in.; ailerons in the upper wings were "slotted" and "balanced." Plain (aileron-type) wing flaps were in the lower wings; the flaps had an area of 17.8 sq. ft. and were not to be lowered above 110 m.p.h. Overall, the F-17-D was a strong airplane; the structure was stressed for 6-G positive and 4-G negative. The cabin was insulated with "Seapak," and upholstered in leather trimmed Laidlaw fabrics; custom interiors were optional. The baggage compartment with allowance for 125 lbs. was behind the rear seat; baggage was accessible from inside or out. A 29 gal. fuel tank was in forward fuselage under cabin floor, and a 24 gal. tank was mounted in each lower wing root; 24 gal. tanks in each upper wing root were optional. The standard Jacobs L-6 engine was normally installed, but the L-6M or the L-6MB were optional. The retractable landing gear of 86 in. tread used oil-spring shock struts; 7.50x10 wheels were fitted with Goodyear hydraulic brakes. Also eligible on skis, or Edo pontoons. The tail-group was a composite structure of wood and steel; fixed surfaces were of spruce spars and ribs with plywood sheet cover. The movable surfaces were of welded steel tubing covered in fabric; the elevators had adjustable trim tabs. A Curtiss-Reed (fixed-pitch) metal prop, electric engine starter, battery, generator, fuel pump, fuel gauges, compass, clock, wobble-pump, dual controls, navigation lights, carburetor heater, cabin heater, ashtrays, assist ropes, and first-aid kit were standard equipment. A Hamilton-Standard controllable prop, oil cooler, pressure-type fire extinguisher, bonding & shielding, landing lights, paraflares, parachute-type seats by Irvin or Switlik, extra fuel cap. to 124 gal., dual brake pedals, radio gear, and custom interiors were optional. The next "Stagger-Wing" development was the model D-17-A as described in the chapter for ATC # 713.

Listed below are F-17-D entries as gleaned from registration records:

NC-18786;	F-17-D	(# 211)	Jacobs L-6.
NC-285Y;	"	(# 225)	"
NC-2099;	"	(# 226)	"
CF-BKQ;	"	(# 227)	"
PP-FAA;	"	(# 229)	"
-19466;	"	(# 230)	"

-18782;	"	(# 240)	"
-18783;	"	(# 241)	"
-19454;	"	(# 242)	"
-19471;	"	(# 243)	"
-19472;	"	(# 244)	"
-19473;	"	(# 245)	"
-19474;	"	(# 246)	"
-19475;	"	(# 247)	"
VH-ACU;	"	(# 248)	"
-19477;	"	(# 249)	"
NC-2595;	"	(# 250)	"
-19480;	"	(# 252)	"
-18568;	"	(# 255)	"
-18573;	"	(# 256)	"
-18574;	"	(# 257)	"
NC-290Y;	"	(# 258)	"
NC-289Y;	"	(# 259)	"
NC-291Y;	"	(# 261)	"
-19492;	"	(# 262)	"
-20787;	"	(# 270)	"
-20785;	"	(# 271)	"
NC-238Y;	"	(# 272)	"
NC-292Y;	"	(# 273)	"
-20789;	"	(# 275)	"
-20790;	"	(# 276)	"
-20791;	"	(# 277)	"
NC-2627;	"	(# 281)	"
-18792;	"	(# 282)	"
-NC-2626;	"	(# 283)	"
-20769;	"	(# 307)	"
-20770;	"	(# 308)	"
-20772;	"	(# 310)	"
-20773;	"	(# 311)	"
-20774;	"	(# 312)	"

NC-2663;	"	(# 330)	"
-19451;	"	(# 331)	"
-46296;	"	(# 332)	"
-20798;	"	(# 333)	"
XB-AGO;	"	(# 334)	"
-48968;	"	(# 335)	"
-20771;	"	(# 337)	"
20780;	"	(# 339)	"
-47571;	"	(# 389)	"
21921;	"	(# 391)	"
NC-2801;	"	(# 392)	"
-21922;	"	(# 393)	"
-20786;	"	(# 394)	"
-21932;	"	(# 412)	"
-21935;	"	(# 413)	"
-21931;	"	(# 414)	"

This approval for ser. # 211 and up; ser. # 225 del. to Col. Elliott White Springs; ser. # 227 del. to Canada; ser. # 229 del. to Brazil; ser. # 230 del. to "Pop" Cleveland as "Miss Aerol # 5"; ser. # 248 del. to Australia; ser. # 255 and # 414 operated as seaplanes; ser. # 259 to Standard Oil Co. of N.J.; ser. # 272 del. to Williams Gold Rfg. Co.; ser. # 275 to Mosser Oil Co. of Texas; ser. # 281, # 283 to Socony-Vacuum Oil Co.; ser. # 334 del. to Mexican mining company; ser. # 211 thru # 255 mfgd. 1938; ser. # 256 thru # 339 mfgd. 1939; ser. # 389 thru # 410 mfgd. 1940; ser. # 412 mfgd. 1941; ser. # 413-14 mfgd. 1942; 38 of F-17-D impressed into USAAF service as UC-43C.

An F-17-D slated for Brazil.

Porterfield CP-50 with 50 h.p. Continental engine.

The perky-looking model CP-50 fairly radiated with "Porterfield" heritage, and it had much to draw from, so the new lines were tempered slightly with some of the past. Standing wide-eyed and taut, as if eager to get going, it had unmistakable character, and was perhaps the best looking of the current crop of low-powered lightplanes. With the country mobilizing, sometimes feverishly in preparation for threats of war, it was estimated that we would need many thousands of pilots, so the CP-50 "Collegiate" was offered primarily as a trainer; basically, as a trainer for the CPTP program to teach our young men the basic rudiments of piloting an airplane. Porterfield aircraft had long been known as good training airplanes and the new CP-50, they say, was designed to be one of their best. The basic design emerged first in 1936 as the 40 h.p. "Zephyr" and later remodeled into the CP-40. When the 50 h.p. engines of Continental, Franklin, and Lycoming were put on the market the design was modified again into the CP-50 and aptly called the "Collegiate"; of course, it was now slightly bigger and a little heavier, but it was better suited for teaching and training the so-called average student-pilot. All other lightplane manufacturers were also going into 50 h.p. engines, so it was a natural trend that all would follow. During development of the CP-40 and the CP-50, Ed Porterfield had taken on a famous partner, the illustrious Col. Roscoe Turner; Turner was surely known the country

over, and was calculated to be an asset to the company as sales manager and director of national advertising. It was good publicity, but it had very little effect on sales because "Porterfield" airplanes stood on their own merits; they hardly needed endorsement from a racing pilot. In the "Standard" version the CP-50 was offered as a training airplane with durable interior and no frills, nor extras; as the "Deluxe" version the CP-50 was loaded with conveniences and all kinds of extras to entice and please the sportsman-pilot. Joe Plosser, noted fixed-base-operator in California had 4 different "makes" of trainers in his busy flying school during 1940; because of students jumping from one airplane to another he saw need to standardize and the unanimous choice was his CP-50. So, he bought 7 more, and sold his other trainers.

The Porterfield "Collegiate" model CP-50 was a light high-winged cabin monoplane with seating arranged for two in tandem. Although definitely in the lightplane category the frisky "Collegiate" seemed like a larger airplane than the better known Aeronca-Taylor-Piper types; more than likely it was the configuration that suggested more airplane than was actually there. The CP-50 provided ample room inside, but in width it still retained that obvious Porterfield characteristic of being "slim as an arrow." The basic CP-50 was primarily offered as a trainer, but optional dress and appointments were available for the sportsman who desired more

CP-50 prototype on early flight; note different rudder shape.

comfort, convenience, and a little bit to show off to bolster his pride. As powered with the Continental A-50 engine of 50 h.p. the model CP-50 had adequate performance as a primary trainer with surprising economy for profitable operation; the sportsman on a low budget also found the performance quite satisfying, and the economy of operation allowed many more hours of enjoyable flying on his nominal budget. The "Collegiate" (CP-50) was rather easy to fly, had amiable characteristics that allowed relaxed enjoyment, and was tough enough to allow a little manhandling or unintentional abuse. Of course, the Porterfield CP-50 was not as numerous nor as popular as "the big three" in lightplane manufacture (Aeronca-Taylor-Piper), but CP-50 popularity came from many directions, so they were seen quite often, and were most often busy flying. The type certificate for the model CP-50 was issued finally on 10-7-39 and some 50 or more examples of this model were manufactured by the Porterfield Aircraft Corp. at Kansas City, Mo. Ed E. Porterfield was pres. & gen. mgr.; Col. Roscoe Turner was V.P. in charge of sales; C. W. Frey was sec-treas.; and Frank Johnson was chief engineer during this period. Waine Archer had been the previous chief engineer, being replaced by Johnson, who in turn was shortly replaced by H. S. Stillweld; it is most likely that varying and differing opinions in aircraft design caused this unusual turnover in the engineering staff. Louise Thaden, for a time, was Porterfield's traveling sales lady.

Listed below are specifications and performance data for the Porterfield model CP-50 as powered with Continental A-50-4 engine rated 50 h.p. at 1900 r.p.m. at sea level; length overall 22'6"; height overall 7'0"; wingspan 34'9"; wing chord 60"; total wing area 168.8 sq. ft.; airfoil Mod. Munk M-6; wt. empty 659 lbs.; useful load 449 lbs.; payload with 11 gal. fuel 205 lbs. (1 pass. & 30 lbs. baggage); gross wt. 1108 lbs.; max. speed 102; cruising speed (.80 power) 90; landing (stall) speed 40; climb 460 ft. first min. at sea level; ser. ceiling 12,000 ft.; gas cap. 11 gal.; oil cap. 4 qts.; cruising range (.80 power) at 3.8 gal. per hour 270 miles; price $1495 at factory. Available as "Standard" model for training, or as "Deluxe" model for sport. Deluxe version was $200 more.

The fuselage framework was built up of welded 4130 and 1025 steel tubing in a Warren truss, lightly faired to shape with wooden fairing strips, then fabric covered. A large rectangular entry door was on the right side. The seats were arranged in tandem, and dual stick-type controls were provided. Normally, the interior was upholstered in leatherette, or plain durable fabrics, but Spanish leather was optional. A baggage compartment with allowance for 30 lbs. was behind the rear seat; "solo" flying was from the front seat only. The windshield and cabin windows were of Pyralin; side windows could be slid open for ventilation. A skylight in cabin roof was optional; the trainer could also be equipped with drop-away door for emergency. The 4 cyl. engine was completely enclosed in a pressure-type cowling to provide positive cooling. The wing framework, in 2 halves, was built up of solid spruce spar beams with spruce and plywood truss-type wing ribs; the leading edges were covered with dural metal sheet and the completed framework was covered in fabric. Wing bracing struts, parallel to each other, were fastened to lower longerons. The split-axle landing gear of 69 in. tread used "Rusco" (rubber) shock absorbing rings; 6.00x6 wheels were fitted with low-pressure tires, and mechanical brakes were optional. Goodyear 16x7-3 airwheels with brakes were also optional. A leaf-spring tail skid

CP-50 shows its perky profile.

was standard, but a tail wheel assembly, either full-swivel or steerable, was available. The 10 or 11 gal. fuel tank was mounted high in the fuselage just behind the firewall; the firewall was of terne-plate, but stainless steel was available. No airplane of this model was eligible with single ignition engines after 8-1-41. The fabric covered tail group was built up of welded steel tubing; a bungee device was fastened to stick controls for adjustment of trim. A Fahlin wooden prop, dual controls, carburetor heater, standard group of engine and flight instruments, fuel gauge, fire extinguisher bottle, safety belts, and first-aid kit were standard equipment. Dual ignition, ball bearing controls, battery, navigation lights, wheel brakes, compass, cabin heater, carpet, custom upholstery, overhead skylight, prop spinner, tail wheel assy., wheel pants, and hand rubbed finish were as "Deluxe" equipment, or optional. Standard colors were Porterfield Red with Insignia Blue trim, or colors could be reversed; White or Cream with matching trim was available on order. The next Porterfield development was the model CP-55 and CP-65 as described in the chapter for ATC # 720.

Listed below are CP-50 entries as gleaned from registration records:

NC-21953;	CP-50	(# 550)	Continental 50.
-21954;	"	(# 551)	"
-21955;	"	(# 552)	"
-21967;	"	(# 553)	"
-21968;	"	(# 554)	"
-21969;	"	(# 555)	"
-21970;	"	(# 556)	"
-21971;	"	(# 557)	"
-21972;	"	(# 558)	"
-21973;	"	(# 559)	"
-21974;	"	(# 560)	"
-21975;	"	(# 561)	"
-21976;	"	(# 562)	"
-21980;	"	(# 563)	"
-21981;	"	(# 564)	"
-21982;	"	(# 565)	"
-21983;	"	(# 566)	"
-21984;	"	(# 567)	"
-21985;	"	(# 568)	"
-21986;	"	(# 569)	"
-21987;	"	(# 570)	"
-21988;	"	(# 571)	"
-21989;	"	(# 572)	"
-21993;	"	(# 573)	"
-21999;	"	(# 579)	"
-21997;	"	(# 580)	"
-21992;	"	(# 582)	"
-25408;	"	(# 583)	"
-25409;	"	(# 584)	"
-25410;	"	(# 585)	"
-25411;	"	(# 586)	"
-25412;	"	(# 587)	"
-25413;	"	(# 588)	"
-25414;	"	(# 589)	"
-25415;	"	(# 590)	"
-25416;	"	(# 591)	"
-25417;	"	(# 592)	"
-25419;	"	(# 593)	"
-25420;	"	(# 594)	"
-25421;	"	(# 595)	"
-25422;	"	(# 596)	"

This approval for ser. # 550 and up; records show that ATC was pending since mid-1938 then finally approved on "Type Certificate" on 10-7-39; all of the aircraft listed here were manufactured in 1939; no listing available for ser. # 574-78, and 581; ser. # 562, 568, 570, 580, 585, 594, 595 unverified as to correct reg. no.; no listing available beyond ser. # 596; ser. # 592 delivered to Hawaii; this approval expired 4-20-42.

ATC # 691
(7-14-38)
PIPER "CUB," J3C-50 (J3C-65).

J3C-50 in west-coast markings during 1942.

Piper Aircraft was doing extremely well with the (J-3) "40 Horse Cub," but they too were eyeing development of the 50 h.p. Continental engine very closely; they were anxious also to get one of these new long-awaited powerplants into one of their "Cub" airplanes. Ten horsepower may not seem like all that much to get excited about, but to pilots tutored in the navigation of an airplane on 40 h.p. it was to be quite a pleasant surprise. As it finally rolled out for its maiden flight the "Cub" as powered with the new Continental A-50 engine was labeled the J3C-50, and it too was offered in a "Trainer" version and a fancy "Cub Sport." As soon as the J3C-50 began rolling off the assembly line it just about stopped production of the 40 h.p. model J-3, but the lovable J-3 hung on in token production into 1939. Meanwhile, orders poured in for the J3C-50 by the hundreds; many dealers were receiving them by the boxcar load, and mass delivery flights left the factory nearly every day. As flying-schools were updating their equipment to the new "50 Horse Cub" there happened to be many used 40 h.p. "Cub" out on the market, but prices were good and they sold off fast. Fifty horsepower engines were soon introduced also by Franklin and Lycoming; Piper was obligated to offer these powerplants in their "Cub" line also, but the J3C-50 with its popular Continental

engine remained the overall favorite for some time. By design and intention the Continental A-50 engine was under-stressed, and as soon as it had proven that it indeed was to be a reliable engine, it was modified only slightly and rerated to deliver 65 h.p. at a higher r.p.m.; basically it was still the same engine. Because other lightplane manufacturers, namely Aeronca and Taylorcraft, had already gone to 65 h.p. in 1939 it was imperative that Piper follow suit in 1940. A slight redesign and a little strengthening of the "Cub" was just about all that was necessary to come up with a model J3C-65. Of course, the J3C-65 with its Continental A-65 engine was again quite an improvement over the J3C-50, but the gains now were not seemingly all that significant. Nevertheless, this is the Piper "Cub" that the multitudes will remember most because it was built in the thousands, and enlisted into duties never before thought possible with an airplane. After World War 2 Piper went on to build all sorts of different airplanes, but they never did discontinue "the dear old Cub" until 1950. We still know it nowadays as the "Super Cub," and it is still quite a special airplane.

The new Piper Cub model J3C-50 and its subsequent variants were light high-winged cabin monoplanes with seating arranged for 2 in tandem. Word about this new, more powerful

J3C-65 on Edo floats.

"Cub" traveled fast and soon they were dotting the countryside like spring flowers; the price was certainly right and some operators were buying them by the half-dozen. The "Yellow Cub" was certainly a strange phenomenon; there were other types of lightplanes that were as good or better than the "Cub," but for many there seemed to be something like a magnetic force that drew them to its side. Many have tried to explain it, but can't find the words. Needless to say, the J3C-50 was soon selling in the hundreds, and the improved J3C-65 was selling just as well, or better. To stay ahead of the projected demand they at Piper were building a "Cub" every 70 minutes, but salesmen were finding it hard to sell all of these, and they were beginning to pile up. There were some grumbles about this, but it all leveled out. Because of our preparation for war, production of the J-3 series for civil use was ended in 1942 with nearly 300 airplanes delivered to flying schools in that year alone; military deliveries continued. The part that the "Cub" played in World War 2 is a book-length story in itself, so suffice it to say that it was one of the most versatile pieces of equipment that we had

in this war. Civil production of the J-3 series resumed again in 1945, and over 900 were built and delivered; they were nearly the same as prewar models. Expecting a great boom in private flying, Piper built 1320 of the J-3 type in 1946 and kept rolling them out as fast as they could be made; by 1947 the unsold "Cub" were stored in hangars all over the country and dealers were crying out frantically to stop the unending flow from the factory. Still, 720 were built in 1947 and this brought the "Cub" population to over 14,000! In late 1947 the (PA-11) "Cub Special" (65 to 90 h.p.) was introduced and manufactured on this same ATC; about 1400 were built by the time it was phased out in 1950. In 1949 the (PA-18) "Super Cub" was introduced, and the story goes on and on from there! As powered with the Continental A-50 engine of 50 h.p. the model J3C-50 was quite an improvement over earlier "Cub," and the J3C-65 with its Continental A-65 engine of 65 h.p. was even better. The airplanes were more capable, they flew a little better, and finally got out of the flivver class. The new Continental engines were an instant hit, and became favorites

"Cub" called "Flitfire" in RAF colors.

of nearly all lightplane pilots; they were dependable. The type certificate for the model J3C-50 was issued 7-14-38 and amended occasionally to include all the variants of this original design. Literally thousands were manufactured by the Piper Aircraft Corp. at Lock Haven, Pa.

Listed below are specifications and performance data for the Piper "Cub" model J3C-50 as powered with Continental A-50 engine rated 50 h.p. at 1900 r.p.m. at sea level; length overall 22'3"; height overall 6'8"; wingspan 35'3"; wing chord 63"; total wing area 178 sq. ft.; airfoil USA-35B; wt. empty 635 lbs.; useful load 465 lbs.; payload with 12 gal. fuel 215 lbs.; baggage allowance was 20 lbs.; gross wt. 1100 lbs.; max. speed 90; cruising speed (.85 power) 80; landing (stall) speed 35; takeoff run less than 700 ft.; climb 500 ft. first min. at sea level; ser. ceiling 10,000 ft.; gas cap. 12 gal.; oil cap. (in sump) 4 qts.; cruising range (.85 power) at 3.5 gal. per hour 250 miles; price $1499 at factory, lowered to $1368 in 1940. J3C-50 also eligible as seaplane on Edo 54-1140 twin-float gear.

Specifications and data for Piper "Cub" model J3C-65 as powered with Continental A-65 engine rated 65 h.p. at 2350 r.p.m. at sea level, same as above except as follows; wt. empty 640 lbs.; useful load 460 lbs.; payload with 12 gal. fuel 210 lbs.; baggage allowance was 20 lbs.; gross wt. 1100 lbs.; max. speed 92; cruising speed (.80 power) 82; landing (stall) speed 35; takeoff run less than 600 ft.; climb 575 ft. first min. at sea level; ser. ceiling 12,000 ft.; gas cap. 12 gal.; oil cap. 4 qts.; cruising range (.80 power) at 4 gal. per hour 250 miles; price $1598 at factory. J3C-65 also eligible on skis, or Edo twin-float gear.

The construction details and general arrangement of the model J3C-50 and its subsequent variants were typical to that of the original J-3 as described here in the chapter for ATC # 660. There were changes and improvements from time to time, but none were of the nature to change the basic design. Occasionally the hardware was improved and relocated, seats and belts were improved, and everything took on a

J3C-65 on skis in Canada.

In Canada, as in America, the Piper "Cub" was popular with flying clubs.

more careful finish, but otherwise the "Cub" remained more or less the same, and looked the same for some 10 years. In later postwar versions the wing was fitted with extruded aluminum alloy spar beams, wing-bracing struts were strengthened, the brakes were improved, and the engine cowling was redesigned for better airflow. The interior of the "Cub" was always rather bare, but there was no reason to include much finery, so whatever was included was adequate. Thousands of the "Cub" never saw the inside of a hangar being staked outdoors in all kinds of weather; they got a little shabby at times, but held up well and that is tribute to Piper manufacture. The standard finish was now "Cub Yellow" with Black trim, and it was recognizable from miles away. The "Cub" was easy to maintain; everything was easily replaced, or easy to fix. A Sensenich wooden prop, dual stick-type controls, wiring for navigation lights, fuel gauge, seat cushions, safety belts, and first-aid kit were standard equipment. A battery, navigation lights, carburetor heater, cabin heater, 18x8-3 Goodyear airwheels with brakes, wheel pants, prop spinner, tail wheel assy., a fire extinguisher bottle, skis, and Edo pontoons were optional. The next Piper development was the Franklin-powered model J3F-50 as described here in the chapter for ATC # 692.

NC-21480;	J3C-50	(# 2327)	Continental 50.
-21490;	"	(# 2339)	"
-21489;	"	(# 2340)	"
-21486;	"	(# 2342)	"
-21482;	"	(# 2344)	"
-21499;	"	(# 2345)	"
-21518;	"	(#2347)	"
-21516;	"	(# 2349)	"
-21519;	"	(# 2350)	"
-21515;	"	(# 2351)	"
-18988;	"	(# 2355)	"
-21520;	"	(# 2356)	"
-21502;	"	(# 2357)	"
-21503;	"	(#2358)	"
-21524;	"	(#2359)	"
-21504;	"	(# 2360)	"
-21523;	"	(# 2361)	"
-21500;	"	(# 2362)	"
-21501;	"	(# 2363)	"
-21505;	"	(# 2366)	"
-21525;	"	(#2373)	"
-21526;	"	(# 2374)	"
-21536;	"	(# 2379)	"
-21528;	"	(# 2380)	"
-21529;	"	(# 2381)	"
-21532;	"	(# 2382)	"
-21531;	"	(# 2383)	"
-21509;	"	(# 2384)	"
-21539;	"	(# 2385)	"
-21538;	"	(# 2386)	"
-21534;	"	(# 2387)	"
-21537;	"	(# 2388)	"
-21543;	"	(# 2391)	"
-21547;	"	(# 2392)	"
-21544;	"	(# 2395)	"
-21542;	"	(# 2396)	"
-21554;	"	(# 2400)	"
-21553;	"	(# 2405)	"
-21559;	"	(# 2407)	"
-21558;	"	(# 2409)	"
-21564;	"	(# 2412)	"
-21570;	"	(# 2413)	"
-21567;	"	(# 2414)	"
-21568;	"	(# 2415)	"
-21566;	"	(# 2419)	"
-21565;	"	(# 2426)	"
-21596;	"	(# 2427)	"
-21582;	"	(#2430)	"
-21590;	"	(# 2442)	"
-21595;	"	(# 2443)	"
-21594;	"	(# 2445)	"
-21603;	"	(# 2448)	"
-21605;	"	(# 2449)	"
-21604;	"	(# 2450)	"
-21811;	J3C-40	(# 2587)	Continental 40.
-22899;	"	(# 2804)	"
-22942;	"	(#2835)	"
-26044;	J3C-65	(# 3995)	Continental 65.
-26073;	"	(# 4017)	"

The 40 h.p. J-3 was being built during this time also; a complete listing of all the J3C-50 and J3C-65 versions would be pages no end, so we present only a partial list of early production; many of the J3C-50 and J3C-65 near suitable waterways were operated as seaplanes; there were "Cub" delivered to every state of the union, plus Alaska, Canada, and Hawaii, but the largest concentration seemed to be in the southwest; this approval also included a few J3C-40 which were manufactured into 1939; the USAAF versions of the J3C-65 were 0-59, L-4, L-4A, L-4B and were also eligible on this approval.

ATC # 692
(7-14-38)
PIPER "CUB," J3F-50 (J3F-65)

Piper J3F-60 with Franklin engine.

When builders of the elegant "Franklin" air-cooled automobile decided to enter the aircraft engine field they wisely considered the small opposed-type engine, an engine that was becoming such a smashing success in the low-powered lightplane. Having considerable knowledge and experience already in the building of reliable air-cooled engines it was almost certain that the new "Franklin" airplane engine would be a worthy addition to the lineup available to lightplane manufacturers. For an engine that had been not too long on the market the 4 cyl. "Franklin 50" was almost an immediate success; news gets around fast in aviation circles, and apparently the "Franklin" engine was getting some good support. As other lightplane manufacturers were altering designs slightly to incorporate the new Franklin 4AC-150 engine of 50 h.p., so it behooved Piper to do likewise; it was no problem to mount this engine and the "Cub" actually approved of it. It was a good combination. Almost obligated to do so, we might say, Piper offered the new "Cub" with this engine as the J3F-50 and it became an early hit; operators were buying them a half-dozen or more at a time! Some operators bought 2 or 3 at first, and as they needed additional airplanes, these too were the J3F-50. The "Cub" was easy to buy at $433.00 down, and most paid for themselves in no time at all. The J3F-50 was built through 1939 and it sold in the hundreds; they were literally all over the place, as one traveling pilot put it. Later into 1939 as Continental and Lycoming started to manufacture 65 h.p. engines, so did Franklin Motors. They added a few cu. ins. to the basic

4AC engine and came up with the 4AC-171 which developed 60 to 65 h.p. The Franklin 4AC-171 was then mounted in the improved "Cub" for 1940, and it too sold in the hundreds. It was a popular version and it was labeled the J3F-65. General consensus was that the "Cub" powered by Continental was the most popular, but if Piper had not offered a Franklin-powered "Cub" it is almost certain they would have lost many sales to other lightplane builders that did offer the "Franklin" engine; such is the whimsy of the flying public.

The Piper "Cub" model J3F-50 was a light high-winged cabin monoplane with seating arranged for 2 in tandem. Along with the increase in power came more room in the cabin, and many other little improvements that made for a better and a better-looking airplane. Born into a world of small sod 'fields and seat-of-the-pants flying, the "Cub" harbored very few frills, and promised only full enjoyment under best possible economy. It was a chilly airplane in blustery weather because the cold air found its way through, but it was great fun in the summer, especially with the doors swung open to let the mild breezes in. As the J3F-50 powered with the 50 h.p. Franklin 4AC-150 engine the 1938 "Cub" was a great improvement over earlier "40 horse" models; ten horsepower was quite a kick in the pants for a light airplane that learned to do fairly well on less. In less than a year's time the "Cub" by Piper was already one of the all-time great airplanes, and there was very little one could actually improve on, so the only way to go now was more power. Engine manufacturers anticipated this and began developing more powerful engines. As soon as the "Franklin 60" became available it was put into the (J3F-60) "Cub," and as soon as the "Franklin 65" was available it went into the "Cub" also. As powered with the Franklin 4AC-176 engine of 65 h.p., the model J3F-65 was a terrific little airplane, and it astounded everyone with its quicker takeoff, its better climb-out, and improved all-around ability. Even as the J3F-65 was being built, the 40-horse "Cub" and the 50-horse "Cub" were still available, but buyers were spoiled by the promise of more performance and many shunned the lower-powered airplanes; Piper's low-powered versions were eventually phased out as new models took up the slack. The J3F-65 found its greatest popularity in flying schools around the country, but its appeal to private owners and weekend fliers was also a big factor. The extra power now enhanced the "Cub's" utility by a big margin, so it was also a useful airplane in combination with skis and floats. In 1942 the J3F-65 was put into military dress as the L-4D and served the Army well in various capacities. With the war eventually over, the "Cub" picked up its former popularity, and continued to offer civilians the best in flying fun for the lowest investment. The type certificate for the Franklin-powered "Cub" was first issued on 7-14-38 and it can only be estimated that hundreds of these airplanes were manufactured by the Piper Aircraft Corp. at Lock Haven, Pa.

Listed below are specifications and performance data for the Piper "Cub" model J3F-50 as powered with Franklin 4AC-150 (Series 50) engine rated 50 h.p. at 2300 r.p.m. at sea level; length overall 22'4"; height overall 6'8"; wingspan 35'3"; wing chord 63"; total wing area 178 sq. ft.; airfoil USA-35B; wt. empty 635 lbs.; useful load 465 lbs.; payload with 12 gal. fuel 215 lbs.; baggage allowance 20 lbs.; gross wt. 1100 lbs.; max. speed 90; cruising speed (.85 power) 80; landing (stall) speed 35; takeoff run less than 700 ft.; climb 500 ft. first min. at sea level; ser. ceiling 10,000 ft.; gas cap. 12 gal.; oil

cap. (in sump) 4 qts.; cruising range (.85 power) at 3.5 gal. per hour 250 miles; price $1499 at factory, lowered to $1298 with Franklin 60 in 1940.

Specifications and data for "Cub" model J3F-65 as powered with Franklin 4AC-176 engine rated 65 h.p. at 2200 r.p.m. at sea level, same as above except as follows; wt. empty 640 lbs.; useful load 460 lbs.; payload with 12 gal. fuel 210 lbs.; gross wt. 1100 lbs.; max. speed 92; cruising speed (.80 power) 82; landing (stall) speed 35; takeoff run less than 600 ft.; climb 575 ft. first min. at sea level; ser. ceiling 12,000 ft.; gas cap. 12 gal.; oil cap. 4 qts.; cruising range (.80 power) at 4 gal. per hour 250 miles; price $1548 at factory.

Everything about the J3F-50 "Cub" was more or less the same as the J3C-50 except installation of the 4 cyl. Franklin engine, and any modifications necessary to this combination. For easy entry there were 2 big barn-doors, split horizontally, with a handy step on the right side. If you like the open cockpit feel you could fly with the doors open and become part of the sky. Nearly all of the "Cub" were used as trainers; the great majority (nearly 70% they say) of planes used in the CPTP program were the Piper "Cub." These were almost evenly represented by the 3 different "Cub" versions prevalent at this time; the most popular engines were the Continental, the Franklin, and Lycoming—the "Cub" used all three. A somewhat disconcerting fact to some was that the "Cub" must be flown "solo" from the rear seat only; those that elected to fly from the front seat had to sandbag the rear seat. The baggage compartment in back was little more than a clothes hamper for 20 lbs.; a couple of rags, some tools, tiedown ropes, a can of oil, and perhaps a picnic lunch was all that it would carry. Later models sported a small skylight overhead, and sometimes a fire extinguisher bottle. The landing gear with spools of shock-cord encased in muffs to keep the rubber clean had 8.00x4 wheels with brakes; the clamp-on tail wheel assy. was later steerable. Big, roly-poly 18x8-3 Goodyear airwheels were optional. Dual stick-type controls were standard, and the

J3F-50 as seaplane on Edo floats.

horizontal stabilizer was adjustable in flight. The "Cub" was not fast, it wasn't "acrobatic" by any means, nor was it terribly efficient, but it was cheap and over 5500 of them were built in the period of 1938-40. A Sensenich wooden prop, dual controls, a standard (lightplane group) of engine & flight instruments, wiring for navigation lights, fuel level gauge, seat cushions, safety belts, and first-aid kit were standard equipment. A battery, cabin heater, navigation lights, carburetor heater, wheel pants, prop spinner, steerable tail wheel assy., fire extinguisher bottle, skis, and Edo pontoons were optional. The next Piper development was the Lenape-powered model J3P-50 as described here in the chapter for ATC # 695.

Listed below are J3F-50 entries as gleaned from registration records:

NC-21506;	J3F-50	(# 2364)	Franklin 50.
-21522;	"	(# 2365)	"
-21521;	"	(# 2367)	"
-21507;	"	(# 2368)	"
-21508;	"	(# 2369)	"
-21535;	"	(# 2377)	"
-21533;	"	(# 2378)	"
-21541;	"	(# 2389)	"
-21530;	"	(# 2390)	"
-21548;	"	(# 2394)	"
-21556;	"	(# 2398)	"
-21551;	"	(# 2399)	"
-21552;	"	(# 2401)	"
-21557;	"	(# 2402)	"
-21563;	"	(# 2406)	"
-21555;	"	(#2408)	"
-21562;	"	(# 2411)	"
-21572;	"	(# 2417)	"
-21569;	"	(# 2418)	"
-21573;	"	(#2420)	"
-21579;	"	(# 2423)	"
-21581;	"	(# 2432)	"
-21577;	"	(# 2433)	"
-21583;	"	(# 2436)	"
-21585;	"	(# 2439)	"
-21591;	"	(# 2441)	"
-21597;	"	(# 2446)	"
-21607;	"	(# 2451)	"
-21589;	"	(# 2453)	"
-21602;	"	(# 2454)	"
-21606;	"	(# 2455)	"
-21618;	"	(# 2462)	"
-21623;	"	(# 2463)	"
-21622;	"	(# 2464)	"
-21477;	"	(# 2465)	"
-21627;	"	(# 2466)	"
-21574;	"	(# 2487)	"
-20149;	"	(#2488)	"
-20151;	"	(# 2489)	"
-20878;	"	(# 2508)	"
-20859;	"	(# 2509)	"
-21629;	"	(# 2510)	"
-21630;	"	(#2511)	"
-21633;	"	(# 2512)	"
-21636;	"	(# 2514)	"
-21635;	"	(# 2515)	"
-21641;	"	(# 2522)	"
-21642;	"	(# 2523)	"
-21648;	"	(# 2527)	"
-21645;	"	(# 2530)	"

A complete listing of all J3F-50, J3F-60, and J3F-65 versions would be pages no end, so we present only a partial listing of early production; many of the Franklin-powered "Cub" that were adjacent to waterways operated as seaplanes; ser. #2439 delivered to Alaska; ser. # 2487 flown by Howard Piper, son of Wm. T. Piper; 5 of the J3F-65 were in USAAF as the L-4D.

A J3F-60 in Canada.

ATC # 693
(10-31-37)
PHILLIPS "AERONEER," 1-B.

"Aeroneer" 1-B shows its advanced technology.

The "Aeroneer" model 1-B was an all-metal sport-trainer monoplane that was conceived and built by a group of pilots in Long Beach, Calif. in 1936. Built by the Aero Engineering Co. reportedly, the "Aeroneer" was being put through various flight tests in the last 4 months of 1936 by Albert C. Reid, but it was nearly another year before it was finally approved for manufacture. With James A. Phillips presiding, the prototype airplane was shown at the Los Angeles Air Show in March of 1937, and Paul Lansing then later continued the static tests and other development tests necessary for its approval. The Aero Engrg. Co., designers of the "Aeroneer," had planned to set up for a production run of 25 airplanes, but lack of finances for tools and material soon aborted the project. A reorganization of the company in October of 1937 prompted a move to Van Nuys, Calif. on the Metropolitan Airport, and shop was set up in Hangar #2. James A. Phillips of the Phillips Aviation Co. had financed the reorganization and the plant was moved into one of his hangars; Phillips owned half of the Metropolitan Airport. Sixteen various craftsmen were on the payroll and everyone was anxious to get into production, but altogether it was nearly 2 years (in June of 1938) before the "Aeroneer" was finally approved and cleared for manufacture. By that

time the flush of interest in this type of sport-trainer had fizzled, so Phillips made plans to interest foreign countries in a redesigned "Aeroneer"; it would be a utility-type trainer that could handle both primary and advanced training methods. The shiny "Aeroneer" was a good-looking airplane, and was frequently seen about the Los Angeles area when on test or local promotion; it also appeared in several movies. In late 1938 the "Aeroneer" was fitted with a 6 cyl. inline "Ranger" engine and offered as the military-type "XPT" (registered to Florence R. Phillips), but even in this combination it failed to attract any military orders. The "Aeroneer" was certainly a very attractive airplane, and its performance was surely among the best for this type, but it failed for whatever reason, and was built only in the prototype example. The road to progress in aviation was a rough road indeed, and it was strewn with wreckage along the wayside of those that didn't make it.

The Phillips "Aeroneer" model 1-B was a light all-metal, low-winged coupe-type monoplane with side by side seating for two. The "Aeroneer" was offered as a better sport-trainer, and in general looked very much like the "Ryan SC." Sliding Pyralin panels formed the cabin, and it could be flown with the canopy open or closed. The prototype "Aeroneer" was

Aeroneer shown here in movie role.

well over 2 years in development, so what was at first an interesting offering turned out to be an airplane that couldn't find a place for itself on the prevailing market. The airplane market of 1937-39 was generally fickle and changes were often swift, so many good airplanes were now and then stranded because of lack of interest. In desperation, after deciding there was perhaps no U.S. market, the "Aeroneer" was redesigned as a military-type trainer, but its side by side seating would not be accepted by the Air Corps, and those hoped-for foreign orders never came either. As powered with the 4 cyl. inverted inline Menasco C-4 engine of 125 h.p. the "Aeroneer" 1-B was quite capable and performed in a rather exciting manner. The ship was "loose" and quite maneuverable, did extremely well in short-field operations, and was strong enough to absorb a lot of abuse; these were valuable assets for a good trainer. Not much lore exists about the "Aeroneer," but it has been said that it was a

very good airplane, and very enjoyable to fly. There is perhaps a lot more story to this that was never told, but that is not so unusual in aviation because advancements were so swift there was hardly time to tarry, or to look back. The type certificate for the "Aeroneer" 1-B was actually issued in June of 1938, but awarded retroactive to 10-31-37; the purpose for this we cannot guess. It is apparent that only one airplane of this type was built by the Aero Engineering Co. of Los Angeles, Calif. James A. Phillips was pres. & gen. mgr.; R. M. Scott was V.P.; Ben Williams was sales mgr.; and Carlos C. Wood was chf. engr. Later reorganized as the Phillips Aviation Co. of Van Nuys, Calif. with James A. Phillips still as pres. & gen. mgr.; A. J. Cornelson as V.P.; R. E. Browning (formerly with Glenn L. Martin) as chf. engr.; Paul Lansing was plant mgr.; and Herb White was chf. pilot.

Listed below are specifications and perfor-

Aeroneer canopy slid back for easy entry.

mance data for the "Aeroneer" model 1-B as powered with Menasco C-4 engine rated 125 h.p. at 2175 r.p.m. at sea level; length overall 24'0"; height overall 7'8"; wingspan 32'6"; wing chord at root 84"; wing chord at tip 35.5"; total wing area 168 sq. ft.; airfoil NACA-2212; wt. empty 1444 (1505) lbs.; useful load 716 (695) lbs.; payload with 40 gal. fuel 276 (255) lbs.; gross wt. 2160 (2200) lbs.; figures in parentheses as later amended; max. speed 140 at sea level; cruising speed (.75 power) 130 at 8000 ft.; landing speed (with flaps) 49; landing (stall) speed (no flaps) 57; takeoff run (no wind) 755 ft.; climb 750 ft. first min. at sea level; climb to 8000 ft. in 16 mins.; ser. ceiling 15,000 ft.; gas cap. 43 gal.; oil cap. 4 gal.; cruising range (.75 power) at 7.8 gal. per hour 600 miles; price originally posted as $4950 at factory, no other price announced. This airplance also available with Menasco B4-95 or C4S-150 engines.

The semi-monocoque fuselage was an all-metal framework of 24ST rings and stringers covered with 24ST heavy-gauge "Alclad" metal sheet. The sport-type canopy was divided using 2 sliding Plasticelle panels; a panel was fitted to each side. The wide seat accommodated 2 across and dual stick-type controls were provided. The cabin was upholstered in leatherette; a baggage compartment with allowance for up to 80 lbs. was behind the seat back. The engine was mounted in rubber on a steel-tube frame, was fully enclosed and baffled for positive cooling. The all-metal cantilever wing framework, a center-section and 2 outer panels, was a single main dural (24ST) spar beam, auxiliary spars, 24ST metal wing ribs, and covered with 24ST "Alclad" metal sheet; manually-operated split-type trailing edge wing flaps (26 sq. ft.) covered 66% of the wingspan. Right and left fuel tanks were in the center section panel; a fuel pump and wobble-pump provided fuel flow. The streamlined cantilever landing gear of 80 in. tread was 2 individual assemblies using air-oil shock struts of 7 in. travel; 6.50x10 wheels were fitted with hydraulic brakes, and encased in streamlined metal wheel pants. The full-swivel tail wheel had fore-and-aft lock for takeoffs and landings; all controls were mounted in ball bearings. The cantilever tail group was an all-metal structure using 24ST spars, and ribs; fixed surfaces were covered in "Alclad" metal sheet, and movable surfaces were covered with fabric. All movable surfaces were aerodynamically balanced for ease of control. Elevators were fitted with adjustable trim tabs, and the rudder tab was ground-adjustable. The tail cone was removable for maintenance to tail wheel assy., and workings of the tail group. It is easy to see that this airplane was designed by pilots. A wooden prop, battery, wheel brakes, parking brake, dual controls, fuel pump, wobble-pump, fire extinguisher bottle, normal set of engine and flight instruments, seat cushions, tool kit, and first-aid kit were standard equipment. A Hamilton-Standard metal prop, electric engine starter, navigation lights, bonding and shielding, and radio gear were optional. The next Phillips development was the model CT-1 training biplane as described in the chapter for ATC #731.

NC-16075; Aeroneer 1-B (# 1) Menasco C-4, register to Aero Engineering Co.

Also as X-16075 when modified to XPT with 6 cyl. Ranger engine.

Wing flaps show large braking area.

ATC # 694
(8-11-38)
LUSCOMBE, MODEL 8.

"Luscomee 50" on an early flight.

During most of 1937 the Luscombe plant was a mecca for curious visitors and rumor-hunters; most of the outlandish rumors were discounted by Don Luscombe, but he did confirm the upcoming "Luscombe 50" (Model 8) which he promised would revolutionize the thinking in lightplane design. In early 1938, Luscombe already had this little beauty sitting on the assembly floor just waiting for the new 50 h.p. Continental engine. Finally airborne after much excitement, the "Luscombe 50" filled everyone with enthusiasm because it was bound to promise a whole new idea in lightplane construction, and gosh, wasn't she pretty. The airplane was approved in August of 1938 and production had already begun on a few units. The "Luscombe 8" was going to cost more than other lightplanes, but it only took a flight or two to discover that here indeed was no ordinary lightplane—it was a harbinger of the lightplane's future! Of course, the "Luscombe 50" was an immediate hit and dealers were lining up anxiously to get at least one airplane; before long, Don Luscombe had nearly 100 dealers across the country, and the "Model 8" was being sold as fast as it could be built. Quite a few were sold to private owners, but most went to flying schools which advertised, "We really teach you to fly." The "Model 8" was an excellent trainer; a little more difficult to master perhaps, but it kept student-pilots on their toes, and they learned to love the challenge. About 100 of the "Luscombe 50" were built going into 1939 and production was phased out because Continental had released their new 65 h.p. engine; this powerplant

was going into the "Model 8-A." There were hardly any changes otherwise in this new model, but it turned out to be quite an airplane.

The "Luscombe 50" was a good airplane and people were happy with it, but the more powerful "Luscombe 65" was even better; an added 15 h.p. doesn't seem like all that much, but in the sensitive "Luscombe" it translated into a whole new set of traits and capabilities. In fact, it was such an inspiring airplane that daring pilots all over the country were vying with each other to see how fast they could go, how high they could go, or how far they could fly. Several of these accomplishments became national records. Private-owners were tickled pink with the "Luscombe 8-A," and some were used for business, but most of the 8-A were busy on the flight-line of the nation's flying schools; the CPTP Program was gaining momentum and schools were popping up all over the country. The "Model 8-A" was, of course, being outsold by the Aeronca, Piper and Taylorcraft models, but everyone showed the "Luscombe" admiration and unusual respect. Lycoming Motors introduced their new 65 h.p. engine shortly after the Continental A-65 made its debut, and Luscombe mounted the new "Lyc" in the model 8-B; it was offered first as a rather stark "Trainer" for a reduced price, but it was also available in Standard and Deluxe models. By 1941 Luscombe had introduced the snappy "Silvaire," a beautiful little charger that was powered with Continental's new 75 h.p. engine; this combination was offered as the standard 8-C, or the deluxe model 8-D. By this time several

The 8-A was fitted with Continental engine of 65 h.p.

hundred of the "Luscombe" were built, mostly in the 8-A version; in 1942 after about 1200 airplanes were built, Don Luscombe was asked to halt all production because of our involvement in World War 2. Shortly after the war began, Don Luscombe disposed of his holdings (about 65%) in the company to Leopold Klotz; Klotz converted the factory into building components for military aircraft.

During contract investigations it was discovered that Leopold Klotz was not a U.S. citizen, so the Luscombe factory became a government-operated facility. Klotz, a citizen of Austria, became a naturalized citizen of the U.S.A. and his holdings were then returned. After hostilities ceased in 1945, Klotz built a new, larger plant near Dallas, Tex. and hired Eugene W. Norris as his chief engineer. It was Norris who designed the new all-metal wing supported by a hefty single strut. From mid-1946 all "Luscombe" models had this new wing; the 85 h.p. model 8-E was making quite a showing; in 1948 the 90 h.p. model 8-F was introduced and it

offered all the luxury that a buyer could afford. In the spring of 1949 the Luscombe Co. was finding itself in dire straits for money, and finally went into bankruptcy; the big postwar boom that everyone predicted became a bust instead. Temco Engineering, who was already building the Globe "Swift," and had manufacturing rights for the "Fairchild 24," also took over the remnants of "Luscombe." After building a few airplanes, they ceased all production in 1950; the last airplane out of "Temco" was an 8-F with serial # 6775. In 1955 production was again resumed by a group in Colorado, but financial difficulties were a plague that seemed to follow the lovely "Silvaire" wherever it went; by 1960 the doors were closed again and that was that. It has been many years since the last "Luscombe" was built, but the airplane still abounds by the hundreds in the skies of today, and it will never be forgotten. It was that kind of airplane.

The pert Luscombe "Model 8" was a light, high-winged cabin monoplane with side by side seating for two. By anyone's criteria there's no

8-C was a "Silvaire" with 75 h.p.

The trim 8-D was popular with sportsmen.

doubt that the "Luscombe" was a pretty little airplane, one of the prettiest little airplanes ever built. Fashioned in gleaming metal of rounded contours the fuselage was borne on strong little legs, and the slender wing gave it the look of a sailplane. Being of slight build she didn't provide all that much room, and it could get crowded inside, but smaller folks found it adequate. The "Luscombe," whether on the ground or in the air, looked dainty and very feminine, but she was strong as an ox and sly as a fox. There was no in-between with the "Luscombe 8," you were either smitten by its charms and adored her, or you would have nothing to do with her. People reacted strongly to this airplane; she was either an adorable companion or a miserable wench. The "Luscombe" was not exactly controversial, but it was the subject of many, many stories; most of them were untrue and told by folks who no doubt had very little experience with the airplane. The fact is that the "Luscombe," especially in the higher-powered models, was such an eager, sensitive, and responsive airplane that you had to, and were expected to "be the pilot" at all times; never turn your back or ignore this lady—she didn't like that. As powered with the 50 h.p. Continental A-50 engine the "Model 8" (Luscombe 50) was a spritely airplane in spite of its nominal power, and surely outclassed anything in the lightplane field; it was almost unfair to compare the "Luscombe 50" with any other lightplane of the times. The "Fifty" sold fairly well, but Continental Motors soon introduced their A-65 engine of 65 h.p. and this fired everyone's enthusiasm—a "Luscombe 8" with 65 h.p. should be something else! And it was. As powered with the 65 h.p. Continental A-65 engine the "Model 8-A" was quite a surprise; it was short of remarkable the amount of performance that was gained by just adding 15 h.p. The 8-A at first was still quite typical of the 8, but it did everything much better and quicker. Several flying schools were now using the "Luscombe," and they were openly boasting that they were producing "real pilots."

When Lycoming Motors introduced their 65

This was author's pride and joy in 1946-48.

Post-war 8-A shows single strut and metal wing.

h.p. engine, Luscombe proposed a "Trainer" version called the model 8-B. As powered with the 65 h.p. Lycoming 0-145-B engine the model 8-B was quite typical of the 8-A, and designed to operate more cheaply in student-pilot training. It was every bit a good airplane, but stripped of all the so-called finery that was unnecessary in a trainer. Don Luscombe, who had strong likes and dislikes, favored the reliable Continental engine and this reflects in the fact that every model of the "Luscombe," except the 8-B, was powered by Continental engines. The sassy and sporty "Silvaire" was introduced in 1941 with the 75 h.p. fuel-injected Continental engine as the model 8-C in a deluxe private-owner type, and as the 8-D in a version designed to be suitable as an advanced trainer. Needless to say, both of these were high-performance airplanes and had limited appeal. The spiffy model 8-E with 85 h.p. up front was introduced in the foreboding atmosphere of impending war, and had very little

hope for its proper development. As powered with the Continental C-85 engine of 85 h.p. the model 8-E was an airplane strictly for sport; it had tremendous capabilities and many judge it to be the finest airplane that Luscombe ever built. The Luscombe company was asked to suspend production early in 1942, and shortly after the plant was busy making components for various military airplanes. The type certificate for the "Model 8" was issued 8-11-38 and this same approval was amended at different times to include all of the "Model 8" series. It is estimated that some 1200 airplanes were built into 1942 by the Luscombe Airplane Development Corp. on Mercer Airport in West Trenton, N.J. Don A. Luscombe was pres. & sales mgr.; Roger Johnson was sec-treas.; Frederick J. Knack was V.P. & chf. engr.; and Ben Melcher was plant manager.

After World War 2 in 1946 the "Luscombe 8" series took on a little different character with its

An 8-E over San Francisco—a beautiful shot.

all-metal wing, its single strut bracing, and other pertinent improvements. The model 8-A with an improved Continental engine of 65 h.p. was again the most in demand, but other models such as the 8-E were built also. Performance of all models was a bit better in this new combination, with more strength and more durability. When first introduced the model 8-F with 90 h.p. was the ultimate in a light sporting airplane, but competition among lightplane manufacturers was rather fierce by now, and the 8-F only had limited appeal. The basic 8-F was then modified into a tandem-seated version that had very unusual possibilities; this was the "Observer" (T8F) that was slanted towards possible military use, but its time was spent mostly in aerial photography, or looking for schools of fish. That lovely postwar boom that everyone had predicted had fizzled into a big bust instead; Luscombe Aircraft suffered along with the many other manufacturers that couldn't stay above water, so to speak. Reflecting back on the many different models that Luscombe had produced it is safe to say that the "Model 8" series were the best airplanes of their type, here or anywhere; the pilots who knew and respected these airplanes still get very enthusiastic when memories are brought forth to savor. The "Luscombe" had many virtues, and some faults too, but it certainly wasn't a ho-hum airplane; because of its spirited nature it is still the favorite of many old-timers. When the young pilots of today find it out they can't help but love it too. When Don A. Luscombe divested himself of his holdings in the company it became the Luscombe Airplane Corp. of which J. H. Torrens was pres.; Leopold Klotz was V.P. & gen. mgr.; R. H. Washburn was sales mgr.; J. G. Rising was chf. engr.; and C. Holloway was their chf. pilot. After the war Klotz engaged Eugene W. Norris as his chief engineer and from then on personnel changes were quite frequent. The "Luscombe" didn't exactly suffer in its casting about from one hand to another, but that's because the original design was so excellent. Don Luscombe was no engineer, but he had uncanny insight into what it takes to make an outstanding airplane. If ever a lightplane of the past were to be singled out for special accolades, the "Luscombe 8" would have to be it.

Listed below are specifications and performance data for the "Luscombe 50" (Model 8) as powered with Continental A-50 engine rated 50 h.p. at 1900 r.p.m. at sea level; length overall 20'0"; height overall 5'10"; wingspan 35'0"; wing chord 50"; total wing area 140 sq. ft.; airfoil NACA-4412; wt. empty 630 (650) lbs.; useful load 500 (550) lbs.; payload with 14 gal. fuel 238 (288) lbs.; gross wt. 1130 (1200) lbs.; figures in parentheses as later amended; max. speed 107; cruising speed (1800 r.p.m.) 94; landing (stall) speed 37; climb 500 ft. first min. at sea level; ser. ceiling 13,000 ft.; gas cap. 14 gal.; oil cap. 4 qts.; cruising range (1800 r.p.m.) at 3.5 gal. per hour 360 miles; price to $1895 early in 1939.

Specifications and data for model 8-A

(Master) as powered with Continental A-65 engine rated 65 h.p. at 2350 r.p.m. at sea level, same as above except as follows; wt. empty 665 lbs.; useful load 535 lbs.; payload with 14 gal. fuel 273 lbs.; gross wt. 1200 lbs.; max. speed 115; cruising speed (.75 power) 102; landing (stall) speed 38; climb 650 ft. first min. at sea level; ser. ceiling 15,000 ft.; gas cap. 15 gal.; oil cap. 4 qts.; cruising range (.75 power) at 4.2 gal. per hour 370 miles; price $1975 early in 1939. Also eligible as seaplane on Edo floats for $3170. Price for landplane was $2195 in 1941, lowered to $1975 in 1948. Standard equipment on 8-A was dual ignition, wheel brakes, swivel tail wheel, cabin heater, cabin vents, and compass. Model 8-A2 (Deluxe Master) was fitted with deluxe interior and extra equipment (baggage allowed to 55 lbs.) at $2495 with $629 down and balance in 12 months.

Specifications and data for model 8-B (Trainer) as powered with Lycoming O-145-B engine rated 65 h.p. at 2550 r.p.m. at sea level, same as "Model 8" above except as follows; wt. empty 663 lbs.; useful load 537 lbs.; payload with 15 gal. fuel 269 lbs. (2 parachutes at 20 lbs. each as part of payload); gross wt. 1200 lbs.; max. speed 112; cruising speed (.80 power) 102; landing (stall) speed 38; climb 650 ft. first min. at sea level; ser. ceiling 15,000 ft.; gas cap. 15 gal.; oil cap. 4 qts.; cruising range (.80 power) at 4.3 gal. per hour 360 miles; price was $1785 to $1885 in 1940-41. The model 8-B2 had deluxe equipment.

Specifications and data for model 8-C (Silvaire Deluxe) as powered with the fuel-injected Continental A-75 engine rated 75 h.p. at 2600 r.p.m. at sea level, same as above except as follows; wt. empty 700 (720) lbs.; useful load 560 (540) lbs.; payload with 15 gal. fuel 292 (272) lbs.; gross wt. 1260 lbs.; max. speed 118; cruising speed (.80 power) 107; landing (stall) speed 40; climb 800 ft. first min. at sea level; ser. ceiling 15,500 ft.; gas cap. 15 gal.; oil cap. 4 qts.; cruising range (.80 power) at 4.5 gal. per hour 340 miles; price $2795. Model 8-C1 had engine starter, wheel pants, and other refinements. Baggage allowance was 45 lbs.

Specifications and data for model 8-D (Silvaire Trainer) as powered with the fuel-injected Continental A-75 engine rated 75 h.p. at 2600 r.p.m. at sea level, same as above except as follows; wt. empty 710 lbs.; useful load 600 lbs.; payload with 24 gal. fuel 278 lbs. (2 parachutes at 20 lbs. each as part of payload); gross wt. 1310 lbs.; max. speed 118; cruising speed (.80 power) 107; landing (stall) speed 42; climb 780 ft. first min. at sea level; ser. ceiling 15,000 ft.; gas cap. 24 gal.; oil cap. 4 qts.; cruising range (.80 power) at 4.5 gal. per hour 540 miles; price $2795 and up. Standard equipment includes fuel injection system. steerable tail wheel, wheel brakes, dual ignition, and engine starter. Baggage allowance was 45 lbs.

Specifications and data for model 8-E (Silvaire Deluxe) as powered with Continental C-85 engine rated 85 h.p. at 2575 r.p.m. at sea level, same as above except as follows; height overall 6'3"; wt. empty 810 lbs.; useful load 590 lbs.; payload with 24 gal. fuel 267 lbs.; gross wt. 1400 lbs.; max. speed 122; cruising speed (.75 power) 112; landing (stall) speed 48; climb 850 ft. first min. at sea level; ser. ceiling 16,000 ft.; gas cap. 25 gal.; oil cap. 5 qts.; cruising range (.75 power) at 5 gal. per hour 510 miles; price $2995. Baggage allowance to 75 lbs.

Specifications and data for model 8-F (Silvaire 90) as powered with Continental C-90 engine rated 90 h.p. at 2475 r.p.m. at sea level, same as above except as follows; max. speed 125 cruising speed (.75 power) 115; landing speed (with flaps) 40; climb 900 ft. first min. at sea level; ser. ceiling 17,000 ft.; gas cap. 25 gal.; oil cap. 5 qts.; cruising range (.75 power) at 5.5 gal. per hour 490 miles; price not announced. Baggage allowance to 75 lbs.

The all-metal monocoque fuselage structure was built up of 17ST dural oval bulkheads covered with formed heavy-gauge 17ST "Alclad" metal sheet; wing struts and the under-carriage were attached to dural forgings in the forward section. The engine mount was of welded 4130 steel tubing, and the engine was mounted in rubber bushings. A cushioned bench-type seat accommodated 2 across with entry through a large door on each side. Seat-back folded forward for access to baggage compartment of 5 cu. ft. capacity. A fuel tank of 14 or 15 gal. capacity was high in the fuselage just above the baggage compartment; the fuel gauge was about at eye level. Windshield and the side windows were of Pyralin; left hand window opened out for ventilation. The cabin was neatly up-holstered, and there was a skylight in the cabin roof. Dual controls were stick-type, the throttle was in center of dash-panel, and a bungee-mechanism was used for "trim." The semi-cantilever wing framework was built up of extruded dural (17ST) I-beam spars and built-up 17ST dural wing ribs; the leading edges were covered with dural metal sheet and the completed framework was covered in fabric. The slender wing was braced by vee-type struts of streamlined steel tubing; ailerons were metal-framed and metal covered. The wing on postwar models was a single box-spar all-metal structure covered with "Alclad" metal sheet, and braced by a single, hefty strut on each side. The model 8-D and subsequent models in production had a 12 gal. fuel tank mounted in each wing root. The semi-cantilever landing gear of 76 in. tread was of 2 streamlined vee-type legs and heavy steel wire attached to an oil-spring shock strut that was buried in the fuselage; wheels were 6.00x6 and mechanical brakes were standard or optional. The spring-leaf tail skid was fitted with a swiveling, or steerable tail wheel assembly. Metal wheel pants were standard on models 8-C and 8-D, and optional on others. The cantilever tail group was built up of 17ST dural spars and ribs covered with coarsely-corrugated 17ST "Alclad" metal sheet. A Sensenich wooden prop, dual controls, fuel gauge, carburetor

heater, wiring for navigation lights, and a normal set of engine and flight instruments were standard equipment. A metal prop, Pyrene fire extinguisher, navigation lights, cabin heater, wheel brakes, wheel pants, and Edo 1320 twin-float gear were optional. Postwar models were better equipped even in standard versions, and offered several more options such as electric engine starter, landing lights, trim tab on elevator, extra instruments, gas tanks in the wings, and radio gear. The next "Luscombe" development was the four place "Sedan" as described in the chapter for ATC # 804.

Listed below are "Luscombe 50" (Model 8) entries as gleaned from registration records:

NC-1304;	Model 8	(# 800)	Continental 50.
-1327;	"	(# 801)	"
-2590;	"	(# 803)	"
-2591;	"	(# 804)	"
-2592;	"	(# 805)	"
-2355;	"	(# 807)	"
-2390;	"	(# 808)	"
-2391;	"	(# 809)	"
-2193;	"	(# 810)	"
-2289;	"	(# 811)	"
-2336;	"	(# 812)	"
-2381;	"	(# 814)	"
-2386;	"	(# 815)	"
-2417;	"	(# 816)	"
NC-20654;	"	(# 817)	"
-20655;	"	(# 818)	"
-20656;	"	(# 819)	"
-20657;	"	(# 820)	"
-20658;	"	(# 821)	"
-20659;	"	(# 822)	"
-20660;	"	(# 823)	"
-20661;	"	(# 824)	"
-20662;	"	(# 825)	"

NC-20663 was ser. # 826 and numbers ran consecutively to NC-20669 which was ser. # 832; NC-20679 was ser. # 833 and numbers ran consecutively to NC-20696 which was ser. # 850; NC-22001 was ser. # 851 and numbers ran consecutively to NC-22025 which was ser. # 875; NC-22050 was ser. #876 and numbers ran consecutively to NC-22066 which was ser. # 892; it is likely that NC-22067 (ser. # 893) was the last of the Model 8; this approval for ser. # 800 and up; no listing available for ser. # 802, 806, 813; ser. # 804 del. to Hawaii; ser. # 811 delivered to Continental Motors; most of the "Luscombe 50" were delivered to western parts of U.S.A.

Listed below are Model 8-A entries as gleaned from registration records:

NC-22068;	Model 8-A	(# 894)	Continental 65.
-22069;	"	(# 895)	"
-22070;	"	(# 896)	"
-22071;	"	(# 897)	"
-22072;	"	(# 898)	"
-22073;	"	(# 899)	"
-22074;	"	(# 900)	"

The 8-E was finest in the lightplane field.

NC-22079 was ser. # 901 and numbers ran consecutively to NC-22092 which was ser. # 914; no listing for ser. # 915-16-17; NC-22096 was ser. # 918 and numbers ran consecutively to NC-22099 which was ser. # 921; NC-22093 was ser. # 922; no listing for ser. # 923; NC-23000 was ser. # 924; no listing for # 925; NC-23003 was ser. # 926 and numbers ran consecutively to NC-23005 which was ser. # 928; NC-23002 was # 929; NC-23007 was ser. # 930 and numbers ran consecutively to NC-23022 which was ser. # 945; no listing for #946; NC-23024 was # 947 and NC-23025 was # 948; NC-23006 was #949; NC-23027 was ser. #950 and numbers ran consecutively to NC-23041 which was ser. # 964; no listing for # 965; NC-23043 was ser. # 966 and numbers ran consecutively to NC-23054 which was ser. # 977; NC-23023 was #978; NC-23055 was ser. # 979 and numbers ran consecutively to NC-23057 which was ser. # 981; NC-23062 was # 982; NC-23059 was # 983; NC-23060 was # 984; NC-23061 was # 985 and NC-23058 was # 986; NC-23063 was ser. # 987 and numbers ran consecutively to NC-23099 which was ser. # 1023; NC-25100 was ser. # 1024 and numbers ran consecutively to NC-25170 which was ser. # 1094 and so on; we had no listing for models beyond the 8-A.

J3P with 3 cyl. Lenape engine was an oddity, but an excellent combination.

More or less reminiscent of the earlier Taylor "Cub" model F-2 (ATC #525) the new "Piper" model J3P-50 was also a rather odd-looking airplane in the popular "Cub" lineup. But then, it was odd only because the "Cub" was more or less associated with the 4 cyl. opposed (flat-four) engine, and many argued the 3 cyl. radial-type engine just looked somewhat out of place. Actually, the J3P-50 didn't look all that odd with the 3 cyl. Lenape "Papoose" engine on its nose; in fact, you might say it had quite a bit of character. The engine was not exactly an unknown either, because it actually was the former "Aeromarine" AR-3 engine under a new name. In spite of its 50 h.p. rating the twin-ignition Lenape "Papoose" seemed like a much stronger engine, and it seemed to give the J3P a stronger will and a rather lively nature. Actual performance figures do not bear this out, but the three-cylindered J3P could actually out-fly every other 50 h.p. "Cub" in Piper's 1938-39 lineup. For instance, the Miami Air Races in the winter of 1938 featured a "Cub Race" open to all comers; Cub-pilot Ellis Eno squared off with all of the other entries in a new J3P-50, and whipped the whole field by a wide margin. The race was actually a closed-course record for "Cub" airplanes at 86.175 m.p.h. This engine, the former "Aeromarine" AR-3, became known as the Lenape "Papoose" LM-3 early in 1938 when all assets of the former manufacturer were acquired by Lenape Aircraft & Motors, Inc. of Matawan,

N.J. They also built 5 cyl. and 7 cyl. versions of this engine, but were favored with only moderate success. The model J3P-50 with its 3 cyl. engine up front was not a normal "Cub" we must agree, and not nearly as prolific as other "Cub" models in Piper's abundant lineup. Of the 3 other "Cub" models available at this time, all were powered with 4 cyl. opposed engines by either Continental, Franklin, or Lycoming; this was the wave of the future, and there was no way to ignore it. Yet, the saucy J3P had its staunch band of followers who probably praised it beyond reason, and it was still a force to be reckoned with in 1938-39.

The new Piper "Cub" model J3P-50 was a light high-winged cabin monoplane with seating arranged for 2 in tandem. As it poses here for us to judge the J3P was not exactly a normal every-day "Cub" because of its 3 cyl. Lenape engine, but as dolled up in optional "Sport" livery it did attract a good number of sporting pilots, pilots that enjoyed its special nature. All in all the model J3P-50 was a good airplane, a very capable airplane, but its talents were overshadowed by other "Cub" models; but, overshadowed by sheer number only. A small number of the J3P-50 were employed by flying schools for normal primary pilot-training, but most operators tended to favor other "Cub" models in the interests of economy. Generally costing more, and usually fitted with optional extras the J3P therefore was leveled at the so-called sportsman-pilot, pilots who would be more appreciative of an airplane of this type. As powered with the 3 cyl. Lenape "Papoose" LM-3 engine of 50 h.p., the J3P-50 was a relatively strong performer in spite of its modest horsepower, and has been described frequently as the best of the 50 h.p. "Cub" lineup. In the strictest sense the average "Cub" was not all that great in diverse utility, but the J3P was strong enough to operate quite successfully on wheels, skis, or floats. There was no great to-do about the Lenape-powered J3P-50, not even by Piper Aircraft, but those who did fly it enough to get to know it well have naught but pleasant memories of it. The type certificate for the "Cub" model J3P-50 was issued 8-23-38 and some 30 or more examples were manufactured by the Piper Aircraft Corp. at Lock Haven, Pa. The "Papoose" engine was manufactured by the Lenape Aircraft & Motors, Inc. at Matawan, N.J. with J. B. Helme as pres.; M. A. Cooper as V.P. & gen mgr.; J. J. Boland was chf. engr.; and G. W. Fritz was plant mgr.

Listed below are specifications and performance data for the "Cub" model J3P-50 as powered with 3 cyl. Lenape "Papoose" LM-3 engine rated 50 h.p. at 2200 r.p.m. at sea level; length overall 22'4"; height overall 6'8"; wingspan 35'3"; wing chord 63"; total wing area 178 sq. ft.; airfoil USA-35B; wt. empty 630 lbs.; useful load 470 lbs.; payload with 9 gal. fuel 238 lbs.; payload with 12 gal. fuel 214 lbs.; baggage allowance 20 lbs.; gross wt. 1100 lbs.; max. speed 92; cruising speed (.75 power) 81; landing (stall) speed 35; climb 500 ft. first min. at sea level; ser. ceiling 12,000 ft.; gas cap. 12 gal.; oil cap. 4 qts.; cruising range (.75 power) at 3.5 gal. per hour 270 miles; price approx. $1495 at factory. Also available as seaplane on Edo D-1140 or 54-1140 twin-float gear. Piper tested one airplane in late 1939 with the 3 cyl. Lenape LM3-65 engine rated 65 h.p. at 2350 r.p.m. as the model J3R-65, but apparently no production of this model was intended.

The fuselage framework was built up into a Warren truss of welded 4130 and 1025 steel tubing, faired to shape and fabric covered. The interior of the J3P, and other 1938-39 "Cub" models was a little longer for leg room, and seats were a bit wider and a bit deeper. The most significant difference in the J3P was installation of the 3 cyl. Lenape engine which required a different engine mount, and engine cowling. The wing halves were built up of solid spruce spar beams, and stamped out "Nicral" metal-alloy wing ribs; the leading edges were covered with dural metal sheet and the completed framework was covered in fabric. Ailerons were normally of the plain-hinge type, but Friese-type "balanced-hinge" ailerons were optional. The 12 gal. fuel tank was mounted high in the fuselage just behind the firewall; a bobber-type fuel gauge protruded from the cap. A 9 gal. tank was optional replacement. The split-axle landing gear of 71 in. tread used "Rusco" rubber shock-rings; 8.00x4 wheels were fitted with low-pressure tires and no wheel brakes. The big and fat Goodyear 18x8-3 airwheels with disc-type brakes were optional. The fabric-covered tail group was built up of welded steel tubing and steel channel ribs; the rudder had aerodynamic balance and the horizontal stabilizer was adjustable for trim in flight. A Sensenich wooden prop, dual stick-type controls, wiring for navigation lights, carburetor heater, spring-leaf tail skid, seat cushions, safety belts, and first-aid kit were standard equipment. A steerable tail wheel assy., battery, navigation lights, dual brake pedals, fire extinguisher bottle. prop spinner, and wheel pants were optional. The next Piper "Cub" development was the model J3L-50 as described here in the chapter for ATC # 698.

Listed below are J3P-50 entries as gleaned from registration records:

NX-20280;	J3P-50	(# 2080) Lenape 50.
;	"	(# 2325) "
NC-21480;	"	(# 2327) "
-21490;	"	(# 2339) "
-21489;	"	(#2340) "
-21486;	"	(# 2342) "
-21499;	"	(# 2345) "
-21518;	"	(# 2347) "
-21516;	"	(# 2349) "

This J3P was flown for fun and evaluation by Piper employees.

-18988;	"	(# 2355)	"
-21527;	"	(# 2375)	"
-21588;	"	(# 2440)	"
-21621;	"	(# 2471)	"
-21620;	"	(# 2473)	"
-21561;	"	(# 2474)	"
-21634;	"	(# 2521)	"
NX-21662;	"	(# 2548)	"
-21682;	"	(# 2567)	"
-21695;	"	(# 2575)	"
NX-21806;	"	(# 2595)	"
-21822;	"	(# 2604)	"
-22821;	"	(# 2746)	"
-22905;	"	(# 2816)	"
-22979;	"	(# 2875)	"
-23298;	"	(# 3051)	"

-24567;	"	(# 3255)	"
-24666;	"	(# 3337)	"

This approval for ser. # 2325 and up; ser. # 2080 used in prototype tests by Lenape Motors; ser. # 2440 delivered to Alaska; ser. # 2548 and 2567 used in Piper tests; ser. # 2595 later tested by Piper as J3R-65; ser. # 2875 delivered to Dept. of Agriculture; ser. # 4373, 4419, 4435, 4438, 4445-46-47, 4449-50-51-52, 4457-58-59-60, 4464, 4466-67, 4469, 4471, 4473-74-75, 4477-78, 4495, and 4502 also eligible when modified to conform; the "Cub" (1940) J-3 series available with 40-50-60-65 h.p. engines; this approval expired 1-10-42.

In this view J3P could be mistaken for any "Cub."

ATC #696
(8-24-38)
TAYLORCRAFT, BC (BC-65).

Natty model BC with 50 h.p. Continental engine.

Maestro C. G. Taylor of Taylor-Young had also anticipated using the 50 h.p. Continental engine, an engine that everyone was waiting for eagerly, but he was rather late with his offering because the (40 h.p.) "Model A" was doing so well. Everyone was so pleased with the Model A the company was almost reluctant to discontinue its production. However, the 50 h.p. engine was bound to make a good airplane even better, so Taylor introduced the new combination as the "Model BC," that is, it was a Model B with "Continental" power. The "Taylorcraft" enthusiasts were a happy lot, and busy enjoying their Model A in their various pursuits, so there was no great clamor for the "BC" at first, but as the good word got around the inquiries came fast and furious. It is true that extra horsepower can make a good airplane better, so with the advantage of 10 h.p. the model BC was certainly a lot better. After several hundred of the Continental-powered Model BC were built and sold Taylor was trying out the new 65 h.p. engine by Continental that had just been released; this new version was offered as the model BC-65 in 1939 and they were soon being sold as fast as they could be made. The BC-65 was touted as an affordable high-performance airplane for the private-owner, but its utility was broad enough to handle many, many jobs. The CPTP pilot-training program was just getting some momentum, and the BC-65 being also an excellent training airplane was used by many schools that participated in the nationwide program. A few of the "Taylorcraft" were used in the U.S. Army maneuvers of 1941 as the 0-57, and these later became the L-2 series which were part of the

celebrated "Grasshopper" fleet. The model BC-65 that came on the scene late in 1939 was proof enough indeed that each succeeding version of the "Taylorcraft" was getting better and better. Again slightly improved, the BC-12-65 was the version introduced for 1941, and by now the "Taylorcraft" was getting to be one fine airplane. As the war clouds were gathering, and as our participation in this holocaust was assured, Taylor Aviation was asked to suspend all civil production and gear itself to war work. After World War 2 the "Taylorcraft" production was resumed with the models BC-12-65 and the BC-12-D, both of which became one of the most popular lightplanes in the U. S. A. After all these years, it is still fact that "Taylorcraft" enthusiasts are the most staunch and faithful supporters of any in the country.

The "Taylorcraft" model BC-50 and subsequent models labeled BC-65 and BC-12-65 were all light high-winged cabin monoplanes with side by side seating for two. The new BC, sometimes also as BC-50, was a little slow in catching on at first, but soon sales actually outnumbered the production available. The BC-65 followed shortly, riding on the momentum that was created and enjoyed the same nationwide acceptance; by this time the "Taylorcraft" had been restyled a little and looked especially trim in its full-cowled engine. The ship was quite handsome, but looked more attractive in the lighter colors. The BC-12-65 for 1941 was again spruced up a little and now sported a good looking two-toned paint scheme. The model BC-50 had been a considerable jump ahead of the earlier "40 horse" Model A, and the BC-65 again improved all the good characteristics, but the BC-12-65 and versions beyond that were mostly improved in detail, and better performance was more implied than real. That is to say, that the biggest surprises were in the earlier models and after that the gains were only slight, but still the overall was comparable to the best. Postwar models were the "Ace," the "Twosome," and the "Sportsman"; they resumed their taking ways, sold very well for several years, and continued their popularity long after they had been discontinued. The BC-50 with its (50 h.p.) Continental A-50 engine was a gutsy little airplane in spite of its modest power; the BC-65 and the BC-12-65, both mounting the (65 h.p.) Continental A-65 engine, were proof enough that the design improved as power was added. The "Flat-four" Continental engines had built up a good reputation with pilots; the engines were now quite snappy, economical, and fairly tolerant of extremes in operating temperatures. It has to be said that the "Taylorcraft" was a fine primary trainer; "feel" of the controls was good, they were nimble with relatively high performance, and too, they were stable and very tolerant. Most pilots were elated over the fine flight characteristics and especially "the nice clean spin," this meaning that "spins" were very clean with good recovery. The capable "Taylorcraft" was popular all over the country, there was one just about everywhere, but it was liked especially in the high country of our west; a BC-50 pilot stated with pride that quite often his was the only lightplane flying out of the high-altitude 'port in Albuquerque, N. Mex. Incidentally, the largest fly-away delivery of lightplanes at this time (1940) was the convoy of 20 "Taylorcraft" that were flown to California for various schools that were participating in the CPTP Program. The type certificate for the Continental-powered BC series was issued 8-24-38 and several hundred of each were manufactured by the Taylor-Young Airplane Co. at Alliance, O. In 1939 the firm was reorganized as the Taylorcraft Aviation Corp. with a slight reshuffle of managing personnel.

Listed below are specifications and performance data for the Taylorcraft model BC (sometimes as BC-50) as powered with Continental A-50-1 engine rated 50 h.p. at 1900 r.p.m. at sea level; length overall 22'0"; height overall 6'8"; wingspan 36'0"; wing chord 63"; total wing area (including fuselage section) 168 sq. ft.; airfoil NACA-23012; wt. empty 632 lbs.; useful load 468 lbs.; payload with 12 gal. fuel 218 lbs.; baggage allowance 30 lbs.; gross wt. 1100 lbs.; max. speed 101; cruising speed (.80 power) 91; landing (stall) speed 35; climb 450 ft. first min. at sea level; ser. ceiling 14,000 ft.; gas cap. 12 gal.; oil cap. 4 qts.; cruising range (.80 power) at 3.7 gal. per hour 270 miles; cruising range at .90 power was 230 miles; price $1495 at factory. Also eligible as seaplane on Edo 54-1130 or 60-1320 twin-float gear with A-50-2 or A-50-3 engines. Two parachutes, when carried, were part of the payload.

Listed below are specifications and performance data for the model BC-65 as powered with Continental A-65 engine rated 65 h.p. at 2300 r.p.m. at sea level; length overall 22'0"; height overall 6'8"; wingspan 36'0"; wing chord 63"; total wing area 168 sq. ft.; airfoil NACA-23012; wt. empty 640 lbs.; useful load 510 lbs.; payload with 12 gal. fuel 260 lbs. (1 pass., 2 parachutes, 30 lbs. baggage., and 20 lbs. extras); gross wt. 1150 lbs.; max. speed 105; cruising speed (.80 power) 95; landing (stall) speed 38; climb 640 ft. first min. at sea level; ser. ceiling 15,000 ft.; gas cap. 12 gal.; oil cap. 4 qts.; cruising range (.80 power) at 4 gal. per hour 250 miles; price $1495 and up at the factory. Eligible also as seaplane on Edo 60-1320 twin-float gear.

Specifications and data for the model BC-12-65 (1941) as powered with Continental A-65 engine rated 65 h.p. at 2300 r.p.m. at sea level, same as above except as follows; length overall 21'10"; wt. empty 730 lbs.; useful load 470 lbs.; payload with 12 gal. fuel 220 lbs. (1 pass., 30 lbs. baggage, and 20 lbs. extras); gross wt. 1200 lbs.; max. speed 105; cruising speed (.80 power) 95; landing (stall) speed 40; climb 600 ft. first min. at sea level; ser. ceiling 14,500 ft.; gas cap. nor-

BC-12-65 seaplane struts over Seattle area.

BC-12-65 trainer was stripped of extras.

BC-65 skims along on Edo floats.

mal 12 gal.; gas cap. max. 18 gal.; oil cap. 4 qts.; cruising range (.80 power) at 4 gal. per hour 250-390 miles; prices varied with options installed. Aux. fuel of 6 gal. was eligible. Also eligible as seaplane on Edo 60-1320 twin-float gear.

The fuselage framework in a Warren truss was built up of welded 4130 and 1025 steel tubing, faired to shape and fabric covered. The entry door with convenient step was on the right side, and the horsehair filled seat was a snug fit for two. A door and handy step on the left side was standard for the seaplane and optional for the landplane; later models were standard with 2 doors. A baggage compartment with allowance for 30 lbs. was behind the seat. The "Model B" wing framework, in 2 halves was built up of heavy solid spruce spar beams and metal wing ribs; the leading edges were covered with dural metal sheet and the completed framework was covered in fabric. Vee-type bracing struts were

of streamlined steel tubing. A 12 gal. fuel tank was high in the fuselage just behind the firewall; an aux. fuel tank of 6 gal. was optional. Engine cylinders on the BC-50 and some of the BC-65 were exposed to the windstream, but on later models the engine was fully cowled-in for less drag and better cooling. The tripod landing gear of 72 in. tread was snubbed with rubber shock-cord; the spool of shock-cord was buried in underside of the fuselage to lessen drag. Wheels were 6.00x6 and fitted with mechanical brakes; streamlined wheel pants were optional. The fabric-covered tail group was built up of welded steel tubing; the stabilizer was fixed and a pair of "trimming tabs" were mounted on the fuselage just below stabilizer. The spring-leaf tail skid was fitted with a full-swivel tail wheel assy.; a steerable unit was optional. The 1941 (B-12) "Taylorcraft" introduced a two-tone paint scheme, and several options were now included

BC-65 shows that seaplane required two doors.

BC-12-65 "Deluxe" introduced two-tone paint and other deluxe features.

as standard. A Sensenich or Flottorp wooden prop, dual control wheels, wheel brakes, carburetor heater, wiring for navigation lights, seat cushions, safety belts, and first-aid kit were standard equipment. A prop spinner, compass, wheel pants, cabin vents, cabin heater, L.H. door, Fyr-Fyter bottle, parking brake, dual brake pedals, battery, radio gear, skis, and Edo twin-float gear were optional. The next Taylorcraft development was the model "BF" as described here in the chapter for ATC # 699.

Listed below are Taylorcraft model BC entries as gleaned from registration records:

Reg.	Model	Serial	Engine
NC-21210;	BC	(# 1002)	Continental A-50.
-21231;	"	(# 1003)	"
-21214;	"	(# 1004)	"
-21215;	"	(# 1005)	"
-21217;	"	(# 1007)	"
-21219;	"	(# 1009)	"
-21220;	"	(# 1010)	"
-21221;	"	(# 1011)	"
-21223;	"	(# 1013)	"
-21225;	"	(# 1015)	"
-21226;	"	(# 1016)	"
-21227;	"	(# 1017)	"
-21228;	"	(# 1018)	"

-21229;	”	(# 1019)	”
-21230;	”	(# 1020)	”
-21233;	”	(# 1023)	”
-21234;	”	(# 1024)	”
-21237;	”	(# 1027)	”
-21239;	”	(# 1029)	”
-21240;	”	(# 1031)	”
-21241;	”	(# 1032)	”
-21243;	”	(# 1034)	”
-21244;	”	(# 1035)	”
-21245;	”	(# 1036)	”
-21246;	”	(# 1037)	”
-21249;	”	(# 1042)	”
-21252;	”	(# 1044)	”
-21253;	”	(# 1045)	”
-21251;	”	(# 1046)	”
-21254;	”	(# 1048)	”
-21258;	”	(# 1051)	”
-21260;	”	(# 1053)	”
-21261;	”	(# 1054)	”
-21262;	”	(# 1055)	”
-21268;	”	(# 1061)	”
-21269;	”	(# 1062)	”
-21270;	”	(# 1063)	”
-21277;	”	(# 1070)	”
-21280;	”	(# 1073)	”
-21294;	”	(# 1088)	”
-21295;	”	(# 1092)	”
-20409;	”	(# 1097)	”
-20410;	”	(# 1098)	”
-20416;	”	(# 1104)	”
-20417;	”	(# 1105)	”
-20418;	”	(# 1106)	”
-20419;	”	(# 1107)	”
-20421;	”	(# 1109)	”
-20422;	”	(# 1110)	”
NC-23611;	BC-65	(# 1335)	Continental A-65.
-23625;	”	(# 1350)	”
-23634;	”	(# 1364)	”
-23635;	”	(# 1365)	”
-23638;	”	(# 1368)	”
-23641;	”	(# 1371)	”
-23645;	”	(# 1376)	”
-23646;	”	(# 1377)	”
-23674;	”	(# 1378)	”
-23648;	”	(# 1379)	”
-23649;	”	(# 1380)	”
-23657;	”	(# 1388)	”
-23659;	”	(# 1390)	”
-23660;	”	(# 1391)	”
-23662;	”	(# 1393)	”
-23664;	”	(# 1395)	”
-23668;	”	(# 1399)	”
-23647;	”	(# 1407)	”
-23675;	”	(# 1408)	”
-23676;	”	(# 1410)	”
-23677;	”	(# 1411)	”
-23678;	”	(# 1412)	”
-23681;	”	(# 1415)	”
-23684;	”	(# 1418)	”
-23688;	”	(# 1422)	”
-23697;	”	(# 1431)	”
-23699;	”	(# 1433)	”
-23802;	”	(# 1436)	”
-23806;	”	(# 1440)	”
-23810;	”	(# 1444)	”
-23813;	”	(# 1447)	”
-23819;	”	(# 1453)	”
-23829;	”	(# 1465)	”
-23835;	”	(# 1471)	”
-23845;	”	(# 1481)	”
23848;	”	(# 1484)	”
-23860;	”	(# 1496)	?”
-23895;	”	(# 1530)	”
-24008	”	(# 1543)	”
-24018;	”	(# 1553)	”

All ser. numbers to # 1129 were manufactured in 1938; ser. # 1141 and up were manufactured in 1939; ser. # 1016 operated on floats as BCS; ser. # 1017 delivered to Alaska; ser. # 1031 operated with single-bladed "Everel" prop; ser. # 1073 delivered to Continental Motors; 3 airplanes shipped to Palestine in 1938; ser. numbers shown are only partial listing; no listing available for BC-12-65 and subsequent models.

ATC # 697
(9-7-38)
MARTIN "CLIPPER," 156-C.

Martin 156 being towed to water.

The apparent success of the Martin M-130 "Clipper" ships as operated by Pan American Airways prompted Martin to design a similar ship that would be bigger, and could actually be classed as an "ocean-going" airplane. At first glance there is considerable similarity in the two designs, but the 156-C (as compared to the 130) was some 2 ft. longer, sat about 3 ft. higher on its beaching gear, and the wingspan was 27 ft. greater with approximately the same area. The most significant difference was in the weights; the 156-C tipped the scales at nearly 7000 lbs. heavier when empty, carried 2½ tons more of useful load, some 600 gal. more of fuel, and weighed a whopping 6 tons more when fully loaded. The huge 156-C was powered with 4 Wright "Cyclone" engines that delivered a total of 4000 h.p. on takeoff, but the big craft could not actually boast of better performance; the only gain to speak of was more payload and some increase in cruising range. After successful tests by Ken Ebel, tests that were actually monitored by Glenn L. Martin via two-way radio, the craft was finally approved and preparations were being studied for its manufacture. Because of circumstance, there was no great surge of interest in this airplane. The approved prototype meanwhile, was flown to New York City where it was carefully dismantled and boxed in 3 huge cases for shipment to Russia, apparently the only customer for this airplane. The airplane's story after this is a mystery. This craft was a milestone in the development of big ocean-crossing flying-boats, and it did prove also that the necessary range needed to safely reach the European continent from our shores would cut deeply into the payload; some 30 passengers seemed to be the practical limit, and this promised to be unprofitable. Larger flying-

boats of this type, "boats" that would carry twice the load, and assure more range, were already on the drawing boards at Martin, but impending war stifled any more research. The eventual operation of landplanes to other continents during wartime service discounted the absolute necessity of using huge flying-boats for over-ocean travel, and the idea was no longer pursued. The romance of the "flying-boat" had its day, and shall be remembered fondly.

The Martin 156-C was a huge multi-engined monoplane of the flying-boat type with sufficient range to make an Atlantic Ocean crossing. It had capacity for various seating arrangements dictated by actual length of the trip; in short haul configuration the "liner" could seat 46 to 53 passengers in good comfort, and on long flights the interior was arranged for 33 passengers in a lounge-type atmosphere, or as a "sleeper" with 26 berths. The ship actually carried more useful load than its own empty weight. It was a grandiose airplane that was purported to pave the way for scheduled across-the-ocean travel. The design of the model 156-C was not actually a breakthrough in technique because it followed the proven concepts closely as introduced in the earlier "China Clipper" (M-130) type, but there were some innovations that allowed it to operate with much greater loads. The versatile "sea wings," somewhat like a lower stub-wing, were primarily used to provide stability in the water; they also added to the overall lift and provided space for most of the fuel. The only visible features that set the M-156 apart from the M-130 was the longer, more tapered wing, and the twin-tailed steering system. As it broke water from Chesapeake Bay in Nov. of 1937 the thundering Martin 156 was the largest airplane in the world. After 25 hours of rigorous testing

336

Martin 156 flies gracefully over Maryland.

Beaching "156" required many men and hard work.

for approval the big boat was flown ceremoniously up the coast to New York City and boxed for shipment to Russia. As powered with 4 Wright "Cyclone" GR-1820-G2 engines rated 850 h.p. each, the M-156 was an impressive mass of machinery and people came from miles around just to watch it fly. In fact, the newsmen were always alerted when the "156" would fly, so it was covered thoroughly by newsreel men from the ground and from the air. The largest airplane in the world was "good copy" at that time. When loaded to its maximum capacity the "big boat" was not exactly spritely, but it handled well and conducted itself

in a majestic fashion. The rosy promises for this airplane were more implied than real, but it was another good example of innovative engineering that paved the way to bigger and better airplanes. A Group 2 approval numbered 2-537 was issued for the prototype on 10-30-37 and a type certificate for the 156-C was issued 9-7-38. Apparently only one example of this airplane was built by the Glenn L. Martin Co. at Baltimore, Md. Glenn L. Martin was pres. & gen. mgr.; G. T. Hartson was exec. V.P.; B. C. Boulton was V.P. of engrg.; and Wm. "Ken" Ebel was chf. engr. & chf. pilot.

Listed below are specifications and performance data for the Martin 156-C flying-boat as powered with 4 Wright "Cyclone" GR-1820-G2 engines rated 850 h.p. at 2100 r.p.m. at 5800 ft. (1000 h.p. at 2200 r.p.m. for takeoff); length overall 92'3"; height overall (on beaching gear) 27'2"; wingspan 157'0"; total wing area 2300 sq. ft.; airfoil NACA-23000 series; wt. empty 31,292 lbs.; useful load 31,708 lbs.; payload with 3800 gal. fuel and 5 crew was 6438 lbs. (30 pass. and 1338 lbs. baggage); gross wt. 63,000 lbs.; max. speed 182 at 5800 ft.; cruising speed (.65 power) 140 at 5800 ft.; landing speed (with flaps) 70; climb 500 ft. first min. at sea level; ser. ceiling 12,000 ft.; gas cap. normal 3800 gal.; gas cap. max. 4460 gal.; oil cap. 216 gal.; cruising range (.65 power at 5800 ft.) using 180 gal. per hour was 23.5 hours or 3290 miles; price was not announced. Operable altitude with any 3 of its engines was 8000 ft. or less.

The huge two-step hull was an all-metal (24ST) semi-monocoque structure covered in a combination of corrugated and smooth "Alclad" (24ST) metal sheet. The huge cabin interior was divided into 5 water-tight compartments. There were 4 soundproofed sleeping compartments, and the berths were convertible into comfortable settees for day-flight use. An informal day-lounge was used as a dressing room at night; lavatories with hot and cold water were in the aft section. The bow of the hull had an anchor compartment, space for all sea gear, and a bin for 2000 lbs. of mail-cargo. The so-called "bridge" had seating for a crew of 4; the "steward" who ranged the length of the ship had a place in the bridge, or aft of the cabin area. Passengers were allowed to have 30 lbs. of luggage under their seats, and 2 compartments in the rear had space for 2500 lbs.; this could be a mix of baggage, mail, or cargo. Large windows on each side were of shatterproof glass; certain windows could be used for emergency escape. For long-range flights the interior was very plush, arrangements were planned to be mixed, and the atmosphere was informal; seating

allowance was governed by the cruising range required. The huge all-metal (24ST), highly tapered, semi-cantilever wing was perched atop a streamlined pylon, and braced to the hull with heavy struts; the sea-wings stabilized the large boat as it maneuvered in the water, and provided space for most of the fuel. A max. fuel capacity of 4460 gal. was stored in 6 tanks; 2 in the sea-wings (outboard) at 870 gal. each, 2 in the sea-wings (inboard) at 1260 gal. each, and two 100 gal. tanks up in the main wing; fuel transfer was provided by a system of pumps. The 4 engine nacelles were built into the wing's leading edge; fold out portions in the wing provided a work stand on each side of each engine for servicing and maintenance. The huge (twin-tailed) tail group was all-metal (24ST) structure perched on a pylon that was integral to the hull. Fixed surfaces were covered with "Alclad" (24ST) metal sheet, and all movable surfaces, including ailerons and wing flaps, were covered in fabric. The ailerons, elevators, and rudders were fitted with pilot-adjustable trim tabs. Hamilton-Standard controllable props, hand-electric engine starters, batteries, generators, fuel pumps, fuel gauges, fire extinguishing system, dual controls, navigation lights, landing lights, paraflares, bonding and shielding, a first-aid station, complete set of airline-type engine and flight instruments, lavatories, hot food galley, radio gear, de-icing equipment, survival gear, and automatic-pilot were to be standard equipment in the 156-C as a commercial carrier. The next Martin development was the "202" airliner series as described in the chapter for ATC # 795.

NX-19167;   156-C   (# 714) 4 Wright 850.

Serial # 714 was delivered 1-20-38; this approval for ser. # 715 and up; ser. # 714 (on Grp. 2-537) was eligible when modified to conform; this approval expired 4-2-41 and any airplanes of this type built after this date must be inspected and approved on an individual basis.

In its time, Martin 156 was largest seaplane in the world.

J3L-65 as L-4C with "observation" windows.

Lycoming Motors worked feverishly to introduce their new 50 h.p. powerplant when they realized what a boon this type of engine would be to the lightplane industry, an industry that was now expanding to unprecedented proportion by leaps and bounds. Just as soon as the 4 cyl. Lycoming 0-145 was approved, 3 of these engines were loaded into a company Stinson "Reliant" and flown hurriedly to Piper, Aeronca, and Taylorcraft on the same day. All 3 of the manufacturers were waiting for this new engine. Piper Aircraft was planning to do extremely well with the new Continental A-50 engine in the J3C-50, but they knew very well there were hundreds out there that would favor the new "Lycoming" powerplant; this because of the motor company's long success in engine building. The "Cub" with the Lycoming 0-145 engine was rolled out as the J3L, or J3L-50, and it almost immediately picked up a substantial following. Offhand it would be rational to say

that the new J3L-50 was comparable to the Continental-powered J3C-50, or the Franklin-powered J3F-50, but there were those that argued for the Lycoming setup. The new J3L was not built in such large amounts at first, but it was a very capable combination and was built in much larger numbers as time went on. It was inevitable too that the Lycoming 50 would soon be rerated to 65 h.p., because once a trend is started by one manufacturer, in this case it was Continental, the others must follow suit. As powered with the 65 h.p. Lycoming 0-145-B the "Cub" in this combination was labeled the J3L-65. A large portion of the J3L version was bought up by weekend fliers who were gaining force by the hundreds, but the building up of our defenses in 1940-41 diverted most all of the J-3 type to CPTP flying schools, and also into military service. It is estimated that nearly 75% of the fliers serving in World War 2 received their first training in the Piper "Cub"; in war-

The J3L-50 was popular everywhere.

time the "Cub" also served in various frontline capacities overseas. Civil production was suspended early in 1942, but Piper went on to deliver over 5600 of the "Cub" to the U. S. Armed Forces between 1941-45.

The Piper "Cub" model J3L-50 and subsequent models labeled J3L-55 and J3L-65 were all light high-winged cabin monoplanes with seating arranged for 2 in tandem. By the time the J3L was introduced the models J3C and J3F had already been built in the hundreds, but the J3L was catching on fast and it too was being built in the hundreds. Many of the contracted flying schools were buying them by the dozen or half-dozen for the expanded CPTP program. Private owners were buying the J3L also because it was such a good bargain, but they were soon cut short by the wartime curtailment of civilian flying. Outside of the J3P, which had a 3 cyl. engine, one would think that all these other "Cub" would be more or less alike, but that was not necessarily so. If one paid attention closely it was noticeable they responded just a little differently, the sounds and noises varied, and even the smells were different. That's why pilots had their preferences. As powered with the 50 h.p. Lycoming 0-145-A engine the "Cub" was a busy-body, and a pleasant little machine—with the 65 h.p. 0-145-B engine it was almost feisty. The 65 h.p. version was not that much faster, but the added power improved its whole flight range. The argument about which airplane was "the best trainer in the lightplane field" will no doubt be rehashed till doomsday, but the "Cub" had the edge by sheer numbers at least. Nearly 650 of the Piper "Cub" were built in 1938, nearly 1400 in 1939, and nearly 2000 in 1940; production was cut back to 1850 in 1941 and production was halted at 296 units in 1942. After the war (1945) Piper introduced the same familiar airplane as the "Cub Special," selling nearly 8000 of them in 3 years; after that the "Cub" was formally called the PA-11 and it sold into 1950 when the celebrated "Super Cub" had

taken over. The type certificate for the J3L-50 was issued 9-17-38 and amended at different times to include the J3L-55 and J3L-65. Hundreds of these were manufactured by the Piper Aircraft Corp. at Lock Haven, Pa. Wm. T. Piper was pres., treas., and gen. mgr.; son Wm. T. Piper, Jr. was sec. and asst. to the pres.; Ted V. Weld was V.P.; Walter C. Jamouneau was chf. engr.; W. B. St. John was sales mgr.; and C. Wetzel was chf. pilot. Wm. T. Piper, Sr. was thoroughly airminded; he learned to fly at age 50, there were 5 pilots in the Piper family, and more than one third of the factory people were pilots. Factory personnel could learn to fly in a "Cub" for $1.00 per hour!

Listed below are specifications and performance data for the "Cub" model J3L-50 as powered with Lycoming 0-145-A1 engine rated 50 h.p. at 2300 r.p.m. at sea level; length overall 22'4"; height overall 6'8"; wingspan 35'3"; wing chord 63"; total wing area 178 sq. ft.; airfoil USA-35B; wt. empty 635 lbs.; useful load 465 lbs.; payload with 12 gal. fuel 215 lbs.; baggage allowance 20 lbs.; gross wt. 1100 lbs.; max. speed 90; cruising speed (.85 power) 80; landing (stall) speed 35; takeoff run approx. 700 ft. with full load and no wind; climb 500 ft. first min. at sea level; ser. ceiling 10,000 ft.; gas cap. 12 gal.; oil cap. 4 qts.; cruising range (.85 power) at 3.5 gal. per hour 250 miles; price $1298 to $1499 at factory. The J3L-50 also eligible as seaplane on Edo 54-1140 twin-float gear; J3L also eligible with 0-145-A2 or -A3 engines rated 55 h.p. as J3L-55.

Specifications and data for the "Cub" model J3L-65 as powered with Lycoming 0-145-B engine rated 65 h.p. at 2550 r.p.m. at sea level, same as above except as follows; wt. empty 640 lbs.; useful load 460 lbs.; payload with 12 gal. fuel 210 lbs. (no baggage allowed when parachutes are carried); gross wt. 1100 lbs.; max. speed 92; cruising speed (.80 power) 82; landing (stall) speed 35; takeoff run approx. 600 ft. with full load and no wind; climb 575 ft. first min. at sea level; ser. ceiling 12,000 ft.; gas cap. 12 gal.; oil cap. 4 qts.; cruising range (.80 power) at 4 gal. per hour 250 miles; price $1598 at factory. The J3L-65 was also eligible as seaplane on Edo 54-1140 or 60-1320 twin-float gear.

The most distinctive feature on the Piper "Cub" would have to be the entry door, a large barn-door type of portal that was split horizontally; the upper half swung up to fasten in a clip anchored in the wing, and the lower half dropped down alongside the fuselage. On fair days it was not unusual to see a "Cub" flying along with the upper door swung open, and sometimes even the lower door was dropped down; this promoted an outdoorsy feeling that many enjoyed. Some pilots soon found too that the lower door was a good "stall warning" device; at high angles and at low speeds the door would lift up to warn the pilot of changes in airflow and diminishing airspeeds. A bit of annoyance to some was the fact that the "Cub" had to be flown "solo" from the rear seat only; this was a rather lonely feeling with the empty seat and the panel so far up ahead, but the inconvenience was generally overcome. The distinct advantage of flying cross-country in a "Cub" was the unhurried pace you had to maintain; consequently, you didn't miss much of anything as you made your way. Flying along slow and usually low it was easy to see the unfolding panorama as it slowly drifted by; a farmer plowing a pattern in his field, groups of automobiles threading their way into town, children playing in a schoolyard, a lazy river meandering through the countryside as if picking places of least resistance, or the smoky haze of some big town up ahead. It was these things that

were savored, enjoyed, and they all helped to pass the time as an hour went by. There may be disagreement, but this was flying at its best. A Sensenich wooden prop, dual stick-type controls, fuel gauge, carburetor heater, wiring for navigation lights, spring-leaf tail skid, basic group of engine and flight instruments, seat cushions, safety belts, and first-aid kit were standard equipment. A steerable tail wheel, battery, navigation lights, dual brake pedals, Goodyear "airwheels," fire extinguisher bottle, prop spinner, wheel pants, skis, and Edo pontoons were optional. The next Piper development was the model J-4 series "Cub Coupe" as described in the chapter for ATC # 703.

Listed below are J3L series entries as gleaned from registration records:

NC-21678;	J3L	(# 2490) Lycoming 50.
-21631;	"	(#2513) "
-21815;	"	(# 2598)
-21816;	"	(# 2599) "
-22715;	"	(# 2689) "
-22759;	"	(# 2706) "
-22744;	"	(# 2716) "
-22782;	"	(# 2725) "
-22823;	"	(# 2747) "
-22879;	"	(# 2793) "
-22895;	"	(# 2811) "
22903;	"	(# 2813) "
-22911;	"	(# 2817) "
-22924;	"	(# 2823) "
-22938;	"	(# 2838) "
-22940;	"	(# 2843) "
-22955;	"	(# 2851) "
-22958;	"	(# 2855) "

J3L-65 as seaplane at Cabrillo Beach.

-22985;	"	(# 2874)	"
-22990;	"	(# 2876)	"
-22991;	"	(# 2878)	"
-22994;	"	(# 2880)	"
-22986;	"	(# 2887)	"
-23112;	"	(# 2892)	"
-22996;	"	(# 2893)	"
-23110;	"	(# 2895)	"
-23123;	"	(# 2901)	"
-23121;	"	(# 2903)	"
-23120;	"	(# 2904)	"
-23132;	"	(# 2906)	"

-23139;	"	(# 2919)	"
-23140;	"	(# 2926)	"
-23125;	"	(# 2929)	"
-23148;	"	(# 2930)	"
-23150;	"	(# 2931)	"
-23151;	"	(# 2932)	"
-23149;	"	(# 2933)	"
-23155;	"	(# 2934)	"
-23154;	"	(# 2935)	"
-23152;	"	(# 2936)	"
-23153;	"	(# 2937)	"
-23157;	"	(# 2938)	"

J3L-65 of 1941 in RAF markings.

NX-23117;	"	(# 2908)	"
NX-23118;	"	(# 2909)	"
-23119;	"	(# 2911)	"
-23127;	"	(# 2912)	"
-23130;	"	(# 2913)	"
-23126;	"	(# 2914)	"
-23124;	"	(# 2916)	"
-23135;	"	(# 2918)	"

-23156; " (# 2939) "

Serial # 2490 used in Piper test; Ser. # 2513 delivered to Lycoming Motors; ser. # 2598 operated by Tom Piper; ser. # 2706, 2823 operated on floats; ser. # 2908-09 operated as one-place specials; this is only a partial listing; no listings available for models J3L-55 or J3L-65.

ATC # 699
(9-19-38)
TAYLORCRAFT, BF (BF-65)

Model BF was delightful combination with 50 h.p. Franklin engine.

The new 4 cyl. "Franklin 50" engine was receiving some very good reports; both Aeronca and Piper had models out and selling with this engine, so it behooved Taylor to develop a Franklin-powered version also. With years of experience already in the building of aircooled engines, Franklin Motors was almost expected to produce a fine engine, and so they did. Because of its careful design the "Franklin 50" was a very good powerplant; it was light, economical, smooth-running, and dependable. Some say it was a little cranky in summer's heat, but most all engines get cranky at one time or another. The Franklin-powered "Taylorcraft" was first introduced as the model BF with the 4AC-150 engine of 50 h.p.; nearly 100 of these were built and sold. In 1939 the Franklin engine was increased in size by 21 cu. in. to deliver 60 h.p. as the 4AC-171; this was then mounted in a Taylor version called the model BF-60. In the meantime both Continental and Lycoming had jumped to 65 h.p. engines, so it seems that the BF-60 was either shunned at the marketplace, or Taylor was holding out for a 65 h.p. engine by Franklin. The 65 h.p. Franklin engine did come out shortly after as the 4AC-176; enlarged ever so slightly and now producing 65 h.p. with very little effort, the engine was still light, economical, smooth-running, and dependable. The Taylorcraft mounted this more powerful engine as the model BF-65 in 1940 and as the

BF-12-65 in 1941. The Franklin-powered "Taylorcraft" was a rather fine combination, perhaps as good as any, but it didn't seem to go over as well as the other 2 combinations offered by Taylor. It is quite likely that Taylor favored the other engines, and promoted their use instead. Piper also had a Franklin-powered "Cub" in their lineup, and it was selling faster than any of their other versions, so we can't assume the "Franklin" engine was at fault at Taylorcraft. Needless to say, the Franklin-powered BF series of the "Taylorcraft" remained quite popular in certain areas, and built up a rather good reputation for performance and dependability.

The Taylorcraft model BF (sometimes as BF-50) and subsequent models labeled BF-60, BF-65, and BF-12-65 were all light high-winged cabin monoplanes with side by side seating for two. The model BF-50 started off well and sold in good number, but the model BF-60 was practically shunned; later models with Franklin power fared a bit better. The "Franklin" engine was snappy and smooth-running but reports circulated that they were cranky at times, and such talk was mostly unfair. All airplane engines have their characteristics, likewise, all engines have their supporters and their critics. However, the BF series of the Taylorcraft did please many people and did well to promote the airplane's overall popularity. Most of the BF type were operated on the east coast and the midwest, but

BF-65 with fully cowled engine on skis in Canada.

a few did get out to the far west. As powered with the 4AC-150 engine of 50 h.p. the "BF" was a lively sort; the airplane also compared favorably with the best of others in versions powered with the (60 h.p.) 4AC-171 and the (65 h.p.) 4AC-176 engines. Many small flying clubs were started around the BF, and it seemed to be very popular as a trainer. Embryo pilots enjoyed the nice feel, the smoothness in all maneuvers, and appreciated the stability in normal flight. In spite of this, though, the "Taylorcraft" was not all that easy to fly; it couldn't stand timidity, nor ham-handed manipulation, so pilots felt a certain pride when they learned to master this airplane, and exploit its full potential. The Taylorcraft was the type of airplane that only released its full capability under proper handling. There are many that still sing praises to the early "Taylorcraft," and of these there are many that remember the Franklin-powered series with fond memories, in particular. The type certificate for the model BF was issued 9-19-38 and amended at various times to include subsequent models. Altogether, several hundred of these were manufactured by the Taylor-Young Airplane Co. at Alliance, Ohio. The firm was later reorganized as the Taylorcraft Aviation Corp. Boss-man C. G. Taylor was still pres.; Richard H. "Dick" Depew was now V.P., gen. mgr., & treas.; Carl Elkins was sales mgr.; & Raymond V. Carlson was chf. engr.

Listed below are specifications and performance data for the Taylorcraft model BF as powered with Franklin 4AC-150 (Series 50) engine rated 50 h.p. at 2300 r.p.m. at sea level; length overall 22'0"; height overall 6'8"; wingspan 36'0"; wing chord 63"; total wing area (including fuselage section) 168 sq. ft.; airfoil NACA-23012; wt. empty 632 lbs.; useful load 468 lbs.; payload with 12 gal. fuel 218 lbs.; baggage allowance 30 lbs.; gross wt. 1100 lbs.; max. speed 101; cruising speed (.80 power) 91;

landing (stall) speed 35; climb 450 ft. first min. at sea level; ser. ceiling 14,000 ft.; gas cap. 12 gal.; oil cap. 4 qts.; cruising range (.80 power) at 3.5 gal. per hour 275 miles; price approx. $1495 at factory. Also eligible as seaplane on Edo 54-1140 twin-float gear.

Listed below are specifications and performance data for the model BF-60 as powered with Franklin 4AC-171 engine rated 60 h.p. at 2350 r.p.m. at sea level; length overall 22'0"; height overall 6'8"; wingspan 36'0"; wing chord 63"; total wing area 168 sq. ft.; airfoil NACA-23012; wt. empty 638 lbs.; useful load 512 lbs.; payload with 12 gal. fuel 262 lbs. (1 pass., 2 parachutes, 30 lbs. bag., & 22 lbs. extras); gross wt. 1150 lbs.; max. speed 103; cruising speed (.80 power) 93; landing (stall) speed 38; climb 620 ft. first min. at sea level; ser. ceiling 14,800 ft.; gas cap. 12 gal.; oil cap. 4 qts.; cruising range (.80 power) at 3.9 gal. per hour 255 miles; price $1549 and up at the factory. BF-60 was eligible as seaplane on Edo 60-1320 pontoons. This airplane also eligible as model BF-65 with Franklin 4AC-176 engine rated 65 h.p at 2200 r.p.m. at sea level; performance throughout was comparable to that of model BC-65.

Specifications and data for the model BF-12-65 as powered with Franklin 4AC-176 engine rated 65 h.p. at 2200 r.p.m. at sea level, same as above except as follows; length overall 21'9"; wt. empty 738 lbs.; useful load 462 lbs.; payload with 12 gal. fuel 212 lbs. (1 passenger, 30 lbs. baggage, 12 lbs. extras); gross wt. 1200 lbs.; max. speed 105, cruising speed (.80 power) 95; landing (stall) speed 40; climb 600 ft. first min. at sea level; ser. ceiling 14,500 ft.; gas cap. normal 12 gal.; gas cap. max. 18 gal.; oil cap. 4 qts.; cruising range (.80 power) at 4 gal. per hour 250-390 miles; price not announced. Aux. fuel of 6 gal. was eligible provided payload was reduced by 40 lbs. Also eligible as seaplane on Edo 60-1320 twin-float gear.

The Franklin-powered "Taylorcraft" model

BF and subsequent versions in the BF series were typical to that of the BC series as described here in the chapter for ATC # 696, except for the engine installation. Early installations of the Franklin engine had exposed cylinder heads, but later versions had a fully cowled engine that lessened the drag and promoted better cooling during normal flight. Dual control wheels were the standard installation, but dual stick-type controls were available as option. Early models had only one door on the right side, a door on the left was optional, but later models offered a door on each side. Taylorcraft introduced a two-tone paint scheme in 1941, and this was available to the BC, BF, and BL versions. According to registered numbers the BF series were not as popular as either the BC or the BL series, but they (the BF series) did pile up a good service record and a staunch group of followers. A Sensenich or Flottorp wooden prop, dual control wheels, wheel brakes, carburetor heater, wiring for navigation lights, seat cushions, safety belts, fuel gauge, and first-aid kit were standard equipment. A prop spinner, compass, wheel pants, steerable tail wheel, cabin vents, cabin heater, R.H. door, Fyr-Fyter bottle, parking brake, dual brake pedals, 6 gal. aux. fuel, radio gear, skis, and Edo 54-1140 or 60-1320 twin-float gear were optional. The next Taylorcraft development was the Lycoming-powered model BL as described here in the chapter for ATC # 700.

Listed below are Taylorcraft model BF entries as gleaned from registration records.

NC-21212;	BF	(# 1001) Franklin 50.	
NX-21216;	"	(# 1006)	"
NC-21222;	"	(# 1012)	"
-21224;	"	(# 1014)	"
-21232;	"	(# 1021)	"
-21235;	"	(# 1025)	"
-21236;	"	(# 1026)	"
-21238;	"	(# 1028)	"
-21242;	"	(# 1033)	"
-21247;	"	(# 1038)	"
-21250;	"	(# 1043)	"
-21256;	"	(# 1049)	"
-21257;	"	(# 1050)	"
-21259;	"	(# 1052)	"
-21266;	"	(# 1056)	"
-21264;	"	(# 1058)	"
-21265;	"	(# 1059)	"
-21267;	"	(# 1060)	"
-21271;	"	(# 1064)	"
-21272;	"	(# 1065)	"
-21273;	"	(# 1066)	"
-21276;	"	(# 1069)	"
-21281;	"	(# 1074)	"
-21282;	"	(# 1075)	"
-21283;	"	(# 1076)	"
-21284;	"	(# 1077)	"
-21285;	"	(# 1078)	"
-21287;	"	(# 1081)	"
-21288;	"	(# 1082)	"
-21289;	"	(# 1083)	"
-21290;	"	(# 1084)	"
-21291;	"	(# 1085)	"
-21292;	"	(# 1086)	"
-20406;	"	(# 1094)	"
-20407;	"	(# 1095)	"
-20412;	"	(# 1100)	"
-20413;	"	(# 1101)	"
-20414;	"	(# 1102)	"
-20415;	"	(# 1103)	"
-20426;	"	(# 1113)	"
-20431;	"	(# 1119)	"
-20435;	"	(# 1120)	"
-20432;	"	(# 1121)	"
-20437;	"	(# 1125)	"
-20440;	"	(# 1128)	"
-20445;	"	(# 1133)	"
-20446;	"	(# 1134)	"
-20447;	"	(# 1135)	"
-20448;	"	(# 1136)	"
-22200;	"	(# 1138)	"
-22201;	"	(# 1139)	"
-22206;	"	(# 1144)	"
-22207;	"	(# 1145)	"
-22214;	"	(# 1152)	"
-22215;	"	(# 1153)	"
-22665;	BF-60	(# 1312) Franklin 60.	
-23622;	"	(# 1347)	"
-23667;	"	(# 1398)	"
-23673;	"	(# 1406)	"

The first model BF was delivered to a flying club in Indiana; ser. # 1006 was operated by Franklin Motors; all airplanes to ser. # 1134 were manufactured in 1938—ser. # 1135 and up were manufactured in 1939; Joan Heinz of "57 varieties" fame was owner and pilot of ser. # 1145; ser. # 1347 also operated by Franklin Motors; several of the BF-60 were unlisted; no listing was available for BF-65 or BF-12-65 versions; we show only a partial BF (BF-50) listing.

ATC # 700
(9-22-38)
TAYLORCRAFT, BL (BL-65).

The handsome model BL with 50 h.p. Lycoming engine.

The Lycoming 0-145, a 4 cyl. opposed engine, finally elbowed its way into the lightplane market, and soon became a power package to be reckoned with. As soon as the powerplant was okayed for release, 3 of the brand new 50 h.p. engines were loaded into a Stinson "Reliant" and whisked off to Aeronca, Piper, and Taylorcraft on the same day. It took Taylor nearly 3 months to develop a "Taylorcraft" with this engine and he finally offered this combination as the "Model BL." Taylor now had 3 versions of the popular "Taylorcraft" in this power range, but it seemed the "BL" was getting special attention. As soon as a seaplane version was approved, big and jolly Dewitt Eldred took off from New York and flew nonstop to Daytona Beach, Florida, a record distance of 975 miles. This was quite an achievement in a 50 h.p. airplane because Eldred weighed 215 lbs. and he took on 66 gals. of fuel; this amounted to a considerable overload, yet he still averaged some 71 m.p.h. In late 1939 the Lycoming 0-145 engine, slightly modified, was rerated to 65 h.p. and Taylor then offered the spritely BL-65. The "BL" had literally sold like hotcakes, and sales of the BL-65 were taking off like a house afire. A BL-65 was delivered to Hawaii early in 1940 and it later became the first civil airplane casualty at "Pearl Harbor" when trying to make a getaway. Because of its suitability as a primary trainer, many of the various "Taylorcraft" were used by contract flying schools in the CPTP pilot training program. The BL-65 as a trainer was dependable and became quite popular, so early in 1941 Taylor ordered 200 "Lycoming" engines; this happened to be the first boxcar-load delivery to any airplane manufacturer. Expansion of facilities was inevitable because of the tremendous increase in business, so a new factory was dedicated in Feb. of 1941. The year 1941 was good times for Taylorcraft Aviation, and many of the owners and dealers were helping out with the airplane's promotion. As an example, a BL-65 on "floats" was flown across country from New York to Seattle to prove that a good seaplane could find plenty of places to land on a journey of this type; this was no record flight, but did prove it was possible. The natty, two-toned BL-12-65 was the "Deluxe" offering for 1941, and soon after Taylor was asked to discontinue civil production and commit the plant to warwork. The postwar "Taylorcraft" was offered in the hustle-bustle of 1946 and rode along with the "aviation boom" for a while, but the so-called boom peaked early and turned into a fizzle.

The Taylorcraft model BL (sometimes as BL-50) and subsequent models labeled BL-55, BL-65, and BL-12-65 were all light high-winged cabin monoplanes with side by side seating for two. The "Lycoming" engine was a good combination with the "T-Craft" and was perhaps the best dollar-for-dollar value in the lightplane field. Lycoming Motors was prone to say that their new engine was quiet as a mouse and quick as a cat; admittedly, it was a nice smooth engine with strength, but not quite as snappy as other comparable engines. Roscoe Turner, famed racing-pilot, had been studying the lightplane field and with enthusiasm elected to become a Taylorcraft dealer in 1940. At this time the "Taylorcraft" was touted as an excellent training airplane, the BL series in particular, and schools nationwide were turning out thousands of pilots. The weekend sportsmen were also taking to this

"BL" shows form that became very familiar in America.

airplane, it was enjoyed by novice and expert alike, but the impending ban on civilian flying was putting a crimp into private-owner sales. As powered with the 50 h.p. Lycoming 0-145-A engine the model BL was a lively sort, and quite a surprise to those that had been tutored to get by on less power. The models BL-65 and BL-12-65 as powered with the modified 0-145-B engine of 65 h.p. were again a noticeable improvement, and opened up a whole new batch of capabilities. Of course, like most any airplane the "Taylorcraft" did get noticeably better as power was added, but it didn't lose any of its delightful characteristics, and it sponsored a large and happy following over the years. C. G. Taylor didn't have any trouble selling his airplanes, but finances for expansion continued to be his everlasting problem. In a move to get some money quick, Fairchild Aviation was used as a go-between to rustle up a $25,000 loan; consequently, this caused a reshuffle of Taylor personnel. Taylor was now surrounded by Fairchild people in a so-called move to protect their interests; this came to be his undoing. The type certificate for the model BL was issued 9-22-38 and amended at various times to include subsequent models as they came out. The firm was now billed as the Taylorcraft Aviation Corp. at Alliance, O. and company officers were as noted in the previous chapter. Among added personnel, Dale Ludwig was appointed chief inspector and also as chief pilot.

Listed below are specifications and performance data for the Taylorcraft model BL as powered with Lycoming 0-145-A1 engine rated 50 h.p. at 2300 r.p.m. at sea level; length overall 22'0"; height overall 6'8"; wingspan 36'0"; wing chord 63"; total wing area 168 sq. ft.; airfoil NACA-23012; wt. empty 630 lbs.; useful load 470 lbs.; payload with 12 gal. fuel 220 lbs. (1 passenger, 2 parachutes, 10 lbs. baggage); gross wt. 1100 lbs.; max. speed 101; cruising speed (.80 power) 91; landing (stall) speed 35; climb 450 ft. first min. at sea level; ser. ceiling 14,000 ft.; gas cap. 12 gal.; oil cap. 4 qts.; cruising range (.80 power) at 3.5 gal. per hour 275 miles; price $1495 and up at factory. Also eligible as seaplane on Edo 54-1130 or 60-1320 twin-float gear. This airplane also eligible as model BL-55 as powered with Lycoming 0-145-A2 engine rated 55 h.p. at 2300 r.p.m. at sea level; performance was slightly improved.

Specifications and data for the model BL-65 as powered with Lycoming 0-145-B1 engine rated 65 h.p. at 2550 r.p.m. at sea level, same as above except as follows; wt. empty 640 lbs.; useful load 510 lbs.; payload with 12 gal. fuel 260 lbs. (1 passenger, 30 lbs. baggage, 2 parachutes, 20 lbs. extras); gross wt. 1150 lbs.; max. speed 105; cruising speed (.80 power) 95; landing (stall) speed 38; climb 640 ft. first min. at sea level; ser. ceiling 15,000 ft.; gas cap. 12 gal.; oil cap. 4 qts.; cruising range (.80 power) at 4 gal. per hour 255 miles; price $1549 and up at factory. Eligible also as seaplane on Edo 60-1320 twin-float gear, and with 0-145-B2 or -B3 engines.

Specifications and data for the model BL-12-65 as powered with Lycoming 0-145-B2 engine

The BL was also eligible with 55 h.p. Lycoming engine.

rated 65 h.p. at 2550 r.p.m. at sea level, same as above except as follows; length overall 21'9"; wt. empty 738 lbs.; useful load 462 lbs.; payload with 12 gal. fuel 212 lbs. (1 passenger, 30 lbs. baggage, 12 lbs. extras); gross wt. 1200 lbs.; max. speed 105; cruising speed (.80 power) 95; landing (stall) speed 40; climb 600 ft. first min. at sea level; ser. ceiling 14,500 ft.; gas cap. normal 12 gal.; gas cap. max. 18 gal.; oil cap. 4 qts.; cruising range (.80 power) at 4 gal. per hour 250-390 miles; price not announced. Aux. fuel of 6 gal. was eligible provided payload was reduced by 40 lbs. Also eligible as seaplane on Edo 60-1320 twin-float gear, and with 0-145-B3 engine.

The B-series of the "Taylorcraft", as offered at various times, were all alike except for the installation of different powerplants; Continental, Franklin, and Lycoming were the engines used. Early attempts at "cowling in" the engine were little more than sheet-metal hoods over the exposed cylinders, but a more efficient "full cowl" was soon adopted. The trainer-version was usually left uncowled for quicker servicing. Dual control wheels were standard, but stick-type dual controls were available for the trainer; one airplane as a "transition trainer" had a control wheel on the left, and a control "stick" on the right. The deluxe model of 1941, leveled at the private-owner, had a door on each side, wheel pants, parking brake, cabin heater, the engine was fully cowled, and a two-toned paint scheme. The Lycoming-powered BL series were available with 50-55-65 h.p. engines into 1941. The postwar versions had 65 h.p. in this series. A Sensenich or Flottorp wooden prop, dual controls, wheel brakes, carburetor heater, wiring for navigation lights, fuel gauge, basic group of engine and flight instruments, seat cushions, safety belts, and first-aid kit were standard equipment. A prop spinner, compass, wheel pants, cabin vents, cabin heater, steerable tail wheel, L.H. door, Fyr-Fyter bottle, dual brake pedals, parking brake, 6 gal. aux. fuel, radio gear, skis, and Edo 54-1140 or 60-1320 twin-float gear were optional. The next Taylorcraft development was the tandem-seated "Model D" series as described in the chapter for ATC # 746.

Listed below are Taylorcraft model BL entries as gleaned from registration records:

BL as seaplane in Seattle area.

348

Reg.	Model	Ser.	Engine
NX-20576;	BL	(# 1000)	Lycoming 50.
NC-21218;	"	(# 1008)	"
-21248;	"	(# 1039)	"
NX-21255;	"	(# 1047)	"
NC-21263;	"	(# 1057)	"
-21274;	"	(# 1067)	"
-21275;	"	(# 1068)	"
-21278;	"	(# 1071)	"
-21279;	"	(# 1072)	"
-21286;	"	(# 1079)	"
-21293;	"	(# 1087)	"
-21296;	"	(# 1093)	"
-20408;	"	(# 1096)	"
-20411;	"	(# 1099)	"
-20420;	"	(# 1108)	"
-20423;	"	(# 1111)	"
-20427;	"	(# 1114)	"
-20424;	"	(# 1115)	"
-20429;	"	(# 1117)	"
-20430;	"	(# 1118)	"
-20433;	"	(# 1122)	"
-20434;	"	(# 1123)	"
-20436;	"	(# 1124)	"
-20438;	"	(# 1126)	"
-20439;	"	(# 1127)	"
-20442;	"	(# 1130)	"
-20443;	"	(# 1131)	"
-20444;	"	(# 1132)	"
-20450;	"	(# 1137)	"
-22202;	"	(# 1140)	"
-22205;	"	(# 1143)	"
-22209;	"	(# 1147)	"
-22211;	"	(# 1149)	"
-22213;	"	(# 1151)	"
-22222;	"	(# 1160)	"
-22220;	"	(# 1162)	"
-22223;	"	(# 1163)	"
-22226;	"	(# 1172)	"
-22227;	"	(# 1173)	"
-22229;	"	(# 1175)	"
-22233;	"	(# 1179)	"
-22244;	"	(# 1182)	"
-22235;	"	(# 1183)	"
-22237;	"	(# 1185)	"
-22240;	"	(# 1188)	"
-22242;	"	(# 1190)	"
-22243;	"	(# 1191)	"
-22245;	"	(# 1192)	"
-22247;	"	(# 1194)	"
-22249;	"	(# 1197)	"
-22251;	"	(# 1199)	"
-22253;	"	(# 1201)	"
-22256;	"	(# 1204)	"
-22257;	"	(# 1205)	"
-22258;	"	(# 1206)	"

Listed below are BL-65 entries as gleaned from registration records:

Reg.	Model	Ser.	Engine
NC-23613;	BL-65	(# 1337)	Lycoming 65.
-23619;	"	(# 1344)	"
-23621;	"	(# 1346)	"
-23624;	"	(# 1349)	"
-23626;	"	(# 1351)	"
-23629;	"	(# 1360)	"
-23630;	"	(# 1361)	"
-23631;	"	(# 1362)	"
-23636;	"	(# 1366)	"
-23637;	"	(# 1367)	"
-23639;	"	(# 1369)	"
-23640;	"	(# 1370)	"
-23642;	"	(# 1372)	"
-23643;	"	(# 1373)	"
-23644;	"	(# 1375)	"
-23650;	"	(# 1381)	"
-23651;	"	(# 1382)	"
-23652;	"	(# 1383)	"
-23654;	"	(# 1385)	"
-23656;	"	(# 1387)	"
-23658;	"	(# 1389)	"
-23663;	"	(# 1394)	"
-23665;	"	(# 1396)	"
-23669;	"	(# 1400)	"
-23670;	"	(# 1403)	"
-23671;	"	(# 1404)	"
-23679;	"	(# 1413)	"
-23680;	"	(# 1414)	"
-23686;	"	(# 1420)	"
-23689;	"	(# 1423)	"
-23692;	"	(# 1426)	"
-23693;	"	(# 1427)	"
-23694;	"	(# 1428)	"
-23698;	"	(# 1432)	"
-23800;	"	(# 1434)	"
-23801;	"	(# 1435)	"
-23805;	"	(# 1439)	"
-23807;	"	(# 1441)	"
-23808;	"	(# 1442)	"
23809;	"	(# 1443)	"
-23811;	"	(# 1445)	"
-23812;	"	(# 1446)	"
-23815;	"	(# 1449)	"
-23817;	"	(# 1451)	"
-23821;	"	(# 1455)	"
-23831;	"	(# 1467)	"
-23834;	"	(# 1470)	"
-23836;	"	(# 1472)	"
-23837;	"	(# 1473)	"

This approval for ser. # 1000 and up; ser. # 1000 was in Taylor test as prototype; ser. # 1008 del. to Lycoming Motors for test; ser. # 1047 operated as seaplane; ser. # 1123 was Taylor demonstrator; ser. # 1000 thru # 1134 mfgd. 1938—ser. # 1137 and up mfgd. 1939; this is only a partial listing of BL and BL-65 entries; no listings available for BL-12-65 and subsequent models.

BL-65 introduced fully cowled engine.

APPENDICES

BIBLIOGRAPHY

BOOKS:

The Stinsons: John W. Underwood
The Plane that Changed the World: Douglas J. Ingells
Staggerwing!: Robert T. Smith
Ryan, The Aviator: William Wagner
Legacy of Leadership: Trans-World Airlines
Ryan Guidebook: Dorr Carpenter & Mitch Mayborn
Yesterday, Today, Tomorrow: Fairchild-Hiller Corp.
Vintage & Veteran Aircraft Guide: John W. Underwood
Cessna Guidebook: Mitch Mayborn & Bob Pickett
U. S. Army Aircraft: James C. Fahey

PERIODICALS:

Flying
Aviation
The Pilot
Sport Aviation
Antique Airplane News
Air Trails
Plane & Pilot
Airways
Aero Album
Sport Flying
Aero Digest
Western Flying
AOPA Pilot
Journal of AAHS
Popular Aviation
Air Progress
Waco Pilot
Air Classics
Historical Aviation Album
Armchair Aviator

SPECIAL MATERIAL:

Brochures & Factory Literature

PHOTO CREDITS

Photo Credits are listed by page number.

American Airlines: 29, 69, 274

Balzar, Gerald H.: 43, 58, 123, 131, 132, 134, 178, 179, 193, 221, 257 (top), 258, 262 (top and bottom), 263, 271, 301
Barnes Aerial Survey: 137, 305
Barnes Flying Service: 13, 20, 22
Beech Aircraft Co.: 138, 175 (bottom), 176, 177, 197, 290
Besecker, Roger: 35, 42, 51, 151
Bowers, Peter M.: 27, 28, 49, 50, 55, 57, 62, 64 (top), 65, 80, 112, 120, 124 (bottom), 125, 135, 150, 190 (bottom), 191, 192 (top), 207 (bottom), 214, 227, 228, 229, 231, 253, 254, 265, 287, 292, 310, 311 (top and bottom), 312 (top), 315, 316, 321 (bottom), 323 (top), 326, 331, 332 (top and bottom), 333 (bottom), 339, 340, 341, 343, 348
Breyette, John W.: 338
Businger, Ted: 87

Cessna Aircraft Co.: 84, 85, 86, 236, 237, 238
Christy, Joe: 14, 56, 175 (top), 262 (top)
Convair: 284, 285
Cresswell Photo: 46, 48, 307, 308
Cull, Geo. E.: 159
Curtiss Wright: 108, 110

Dart Mfg. Corp.: 256
Douglas Aircraft Co.: 31, 240, 241 (bottom)

Eastern Air Lines: 70
Edwards, Jerry L., Collection: 295 (top)
Erickson Photo: 181, 182

Fairchild-Hiller: 17, 18 (top and bottom), 19 (top and bottom), 24, 25 (top and bottom), 26, 44, 45, 116, 117, 118 (top), 119, 121 (top and bottom), 122, 220, 222, 232, 233, 234, 235, 255
Fleetwings, Inc.: 277, 279 (top)

Glenn Rider Photo: 90
Goodrich, B. F., Co.: 288 (bottom)

Havelaar, Marion, Collection: 105, 143, 172
Hirsch, Robt. S.: 67, 93, 149 (bottom), 207 (top), 215, 252 (bottom)
Hudek Aeronautical Collection: 53

Jefferies, Walter M.: 245 (bottom)
Juptner, Jos.: 322 (bottom)

Kapec Photos: 318 (top)
Kupka, Wm. P.: 54

Larkins, Wm. T.: 38, 41, 142, 321 (top), 323 (bottom)
Longley, Charles: 261
Lowry, Louis M.: 183

Macdonald Photo: 9
Mayborn, Mitch, Collection: 63, 157, 201, 202 (bottom), 230, 243, 245 (top), 278, 279 (bottom), 280, 288 (top), 319, 336 (top),
McDonnell Douglas: 30, 128, 247 (top)
Molson, Ken: 23, 34, 36, 39, 64 (bottom), 81 (bottom), 95 (bottom), 98, 100, 124 (top), 144, 155, 217 (bottom), 218, 279 (center), 312 (bottom)
Morrison, R. C.: 286

Nortell, Ralph: 113 (top), 211
Northwest Airlines: 199

Oelke, Merle: 101, 102, 103
Olmstead, Merle C.: 99, 140, 192 (bottom)
Ortho of K.C.: 186

Pan American World Airways: 72, 239
Payette Collection: 259
Peck, Ed, Collection: 127
Pentecost, Walter: 210, 226
Pratt & Whitney Aircraft: 202 (top)

Rearwin Airplanes, Inc.187
Reed, Earl C.: 257 (bottom)
Ryan Aero Co.: 203, 204 (bottom), 205, (top and bottom), 205, 281, 282, 283

Shipp, Warren D.: 52, 88, 94, 106, 107 (top), 109, 160, 163 (bottom), 198 (bottom), 208, 276, 322 (top)
Spartan School of Aeronautics: 104
Speed's Photos: 318 (bottom)
Smith, Edgar B.: 15, 136, 145, 146, 147, 304, 306
Smithsonian Institution: 161, 163 (top)
Strasser, Emil: 16, 40, 114, 314, 327, 328, 329
Steele, Bob, Collection: 164, 291
Stinson Aircraft Corp. 33, 81 (top), 82

Trans World Airlines: 71, 129, 130 (top and bottom)

Underwood, John W., Collection: 10, 11, 12, 47, 89, 91 (top), 95 (top), 133, 153, 154 (top and bottom), 156, 162, 206, 213, 216, 217 (top), 250, 251, 252 (top), 289, 299, 300, 320, 330, 342, 345, 346, 347 (top)
United Airlines: 74, 75 (top and bottom), 76, 77, 167 (left and right), 168 (top and bottom), 169, 241 (top), 242 (top), 246, 247 (bottom), 248, 249
United Technologies Archives: 107 (bottom), 200, 260, 293, 294

Waco Photo: 97, 139, 148, 149 (top), 170, 171, 223, 244, 267, 269, 296, 297

Watson Air Fotos: 317
Williams, Gordon S.: 59, 66, 78, 91 (bottom), 111, 113 (bottom), 118 (bottom), 166, 184, 185, 189, 190 (top), 194, 195, 196, 198 (top), 224, 242 (bottom), 268, 270, 272, 273, 275, 295 (bottom), 309, 333 (top), 335, 336 (bottom), 337, 347 (bottom)

Wilson, Kenneth D.: 21, 60, 158, 174

INDEX

Joseph P. Juptner saw his very first airplane, a decrepit OX-5 Standard, in 1925 at the age of 12. Childlike, he enjoyed listening to pilots' wild stories about flying, and he washed down many oil-soaked airplanes in exchange for rides. Soon he graduated to "throttle-watcher," he studied to be a mechanic, amateur airplane designer and builder, a private pilot, and became crew-chief in an Air Force Fighter Group. After the war he became partner in a flying school operation, hobby shop operator, wind tunnel model builder, and experimental machinist.

Always interested in airplane manufacture and aviation history, he amassed a valuable collection of historical data, books, magazines, and photos on civil aircraft. His study of airplane history indicated the dire need for a factual record, in numerical order, of certificated aircraft in the U.S.A. Thus, Juptner compiled what can be called the "Family Tree of the ATC." In semi-retirement on his farm in Tennessee, Juptner continued his study of airplane manufacture in America.

Returning to California, he wrote several more volumes of the set that will be the most complete record of civil aircraft manufacture in the U.S.A. since 1925. Retiring in 1976, he has devoted full time to completing this series of books, an incomparable undertaking authenticated by years of research and personal experience. Historians, and antique airplane buffs have lauded this work as the most ambitious venture in aeronautical book publishing.